CANADIAN INDUSTRIAL RELATIONS

Second Edition

Jon Peirce

Prentice Hall

Toronto

National Library of Canada Cataloguing in Publication Data

Peirce, Jon
    Canadian industrial relations / Jon Peirce. – 2nd ed.

Includes biographical references and index.
ISBN 0-13-094581-1

    1. Industrial relations – Canada. I. Title.

HD8106.5.P45 2003   331'.0971   C2002-901274-0

ISBN 0-13-094581-1

Vice President, Editorial Director: Michael J. Young
Acquisitions Editor: James Bosma
Executive Marketing Manager: Cas Shields
Developmental Editor: Meaghan Eley
Production Editor: Judith Scott
Copy Editor: Gail Marsden
Production Coordinator: Janette Lush
Photo Research: Lisa Brant
Page Layout: Anne MacInnis
Art Director: Mary Opper
Interior Design: Julia Hall
Cover Design: Michelle Bellemare
Cover Image: Getty Images

For Alex, Lauren, and Elizabeth,
and to John Fryer with gratitude, for taking a chance,
and in the hope that his collaborative vision of
public sector labour–management relations,
which I share, will be realized.

CONTENTS

CHAPTER 6: UNION ACTIONS AND IMPACTS   158

CHAPTER 7: EMPLOYMENT LEGISLATION   185

PREFACE

The field of IR has indeed been through "interesting times" since the publication of the first edition of this book. The economy has moved from its longest period of sustained growth since the 1970s into at least a mini-recession, and federal spending priorities would appear to have been significantly reordered by the tragic and horrific events of September 11, 2001. In the public sector, as the readers of Chapter 9 will quickly see, the past three years have been marked by an escalation of the labour–management tension already very much apparent at the time of the first edition. Among the most serious manifestations of this conflict (though far from the only ones) have been a nation-wide wave of strikes in the health care sector, and several serious and quite lengthy public transit strikes. As this book was going to press, Ontario government employees were entering the second week of a full-scale strike against the provincial government. It was during this period as well that the Advisory Committee on Labour–Management Relations in the Federal Public Service, with which I had the good fortune to be connected, was doing its research and issuing its reports, culminating in a series of recommendations that if enacted would help bring about a more collaborative approach to public service labour–management relations.

On the international scene, the ongoing wave of globalization and trade liberalization has focussed increased attention on the plight of the world's poorest countries. Less noticed, perhaps, but of no less importance, Europe took a major step toward full integration with the adoption of a common currency, the euro. In a not unrelated and highly symbolic acknowledgment of that growing integration, a Swiss referendum to bring that country into the United Nations was approved, albeit narrowly, just as the new edition of this book was being completed.

FEATURES

The second edition of *Canadian Industrial Relations* has retained the informal language, readability, and use of concrete practical examples that were the hallmark of the first edition. The second edition's special features include:

- The addition of a new chapter on international and comparative IR;
- An expanded discussion of the public sector, in light of the recommendations for a collaborative model of public sector labour–management relations put forward by the Advisory Committee on Labour–Management Relations in the Federal Public Service;
- New cases on contemporary issues such as the use of volunteers as drivers for non-profit organizations and the dismissal of restaurant workers for pregnancy-related reasons;

- The combination of the previous edition's chapters on the negotiation process and the collective agreement into a single chapter;

- An annotated list of some of the most important labour- and IR-related Web sites, in both Canada and the U.S; and

- A glossary of some of the terms most commonly used in IR.

Like the first edition, the second edition contains a conclusion with key themes that tie the course together. And like its predecessor, the strike chapter looks at four recent Canadian strikes.

CASE APPENDIX AND VIDEO CASES   As was the case in the first edition, case materials have been prepared with an eye to emerging trends. Health and safety and human rights cases have been included, and labour board and arbitration cases address such topics of current interest as certification procedures for bargaining units composed mainly of part-time workers and (as noted previously) the use of volunteers as drivers by non-profit organizations. Where appropriate, the cases have been linked to specific chapters of the text. The brief video cases at the end of the book shed additional light on contemporary developments by examining such issues as absenteeism and the recent strike at the *Calgary Herald*.

WHAT THE BOOK COVERS

Chapter 1 (introduction) discusses the importance of the world of work, defines the term "industrial relations," considers some of the most important IR theories, and looks at five different perspectives on the field.

Because the state of the economy is critical to the functioning of the IR system, we consider this next, in Chapter 2. As was indicated earlier, some key issues here are the recent growth of contingent or "atypical" employment, and the recent phenomenon of extensive overtime existing alongside continuing high unemployment.

The next four chapters focus on the roles of management and labour, the two major actors in the IR system. Chapter 3 deals with management, arguably the system's single most important actor. Special emphasis is placed on the evolution of Canadian management practice and on the extent to which management organizations today are making use of innovative or "progressive" approaches to human resource management. The three subsequent chapters deal with labour's role, starting in Chapter 4, which looks at that role from an historical perspective. Chapters 5 and 6 focus more specifically on the role and activities of unions. Chapter 5 examines union membership, growth, and structure and also considers the vexed question of union democracy. Chapter 6 deals with union actions (among them the publicity campaigns mentioned earlier) and impacts, including both economic and non-economic ones.

The following group of chapters is devoted to the IR system's legal aspects. Chapter 7's focus is on employment legislation affecting all workers, but of particular importance to those who don't belong to unions. Special emphasis is placed on new and emerging areas of legislative protection, and on the extent to which legislation is enforced by provincial and federal governments. Chapter 8 deals with private sector labour relations legislation. A major concern here is provincial variations in labour relations legislation. The chapter also discusses the administration of labour relations law, and the extent to which the duty to accommodate workers with disabilities or members of ethnic and religious minority groups in the workplace is likely to affect the drafting and interpretation of collective agreements. Chapter 9 considers collective bargaining and labour legislation in the public sector. A major focus here is the current state of public sector collective bargaining, which many have argued is in a state of profound crisis.

From here, it's a fairly natural progression to our next group of chapters, which deal with the bargaining process supported by public and private sector labour legislation, with the results of that process, and with the conflict that often arises during collective bargaining. Chapter 10 looks at the negotiation process in some detail. It also examines bargaining structures, which make up an important element of the environment in which bargaining takes place, and concludes with an examination of collective agreements—the documents that serve as a record of the negotiation process.

No IR text would be complete without a discussion of strikes—the most talked-about but perhaps least understood aspect of the IR system. In addition to discussing changing the patterns of strike incidence in Canada and looking at a variety of possible causes for strikes, Chapter 11 features brief descriptions of four recent Canadian strikes. Chapter 12 considers grievances and features a detailed examination of an actual grievance case. A key element of this chapter is its discussion of major criticisms of the conventional grievance process and of alternatives to conventional arbitration, including expedited arbitration, grievance mediation, and preventive mediation.

Chapter 13, the international chapter, is new to this edition. With an eye to seeing Canadian IR developments in comparative perspective, it features an examination of IR systems in both developed and developing countries, and pays special attention to the changes these systems have been undergoing in recent years.

Chapter 14, the book's conclusion, is an attempt to "pull the pieces together." This chapter looks at the Canadian IR system as a whole in the light of recent developments such as globalization, trade liberalization, and the growth of a contingent work force. This examination focuses on five key themes and some of the most important findings and policy suggestions related to those themes.

Although the book does not contain a separate chapter on Quebec, a discussion of key features of that province's quite distinctive IR system, such as the extension of collective agreements to non-unionized firms through the decree system, has been incorporated into the text where appropriate, including the new comparative chapter. Other comparative elements have also been incorporated into chapters where appropriate.

SUPPLEMENTS

Canadian Industrial Relations is accompanied by a comprehensive supplements package.

INSTRUCTOR'S RESOURCE MANUAL WITH VIDEO GUIDE (0-13-039445-9) This comprehensive guide contains a detailed lecture outline of each chapter, suggested answers to discussion questions, and helpful case and video case notes.

TEST ITEM FILE (0-13-039446-7) The test item file contains over 1000 multiple-choice, true/false, and short essay questions. Answers, with page references, are given for all objective questions and suggested answers are provided for essay questions. All questions are rated by level of difficulty (easy, moderate, challenging). The Test Item File is available in an electronic format.

PEARSON EDUCATION CANADA TESTGEN (0-13-094583-8) Utilizing our new Test Management program, the computerized test bank for *Canadian Industrial Relations,* Second Edition offers a comprehensive suite of tools for testing and assessment. Test Manager allows educators to easily create and distribute tests for their courses, either by printing and distributing through traditional methods or by on-line delivery via a Local Area Network (LAN) server. Once you have opened Test Manager, you'll advance effortlessly through a series of folders allowing you to quickly access all available areas of the program. Test Manager has removed the guesswork from your next move by incorporating Screen Wizards that assist you with such tasks as managing question content, managing a portfolio of tests, testing students, and analyzing test results. In addition, this all-new testing package is backed with full technical support, telephone "request a test" service, comprehensive on-line help files, a guided tour, and complete written documentation. Available as a CD-ROM.

PEARSON EDUCATION CANADA/CBC VIDEO LIBRARY Pearson Education Canada and the CBC have worked together to bring you two segments from the CBC series *The National.* Designed specifically to complement the text, this case collection is an excellent tool for bringing students in contact with the world outside the classroom. These programs have extremely high production quality and have been chosen to relate directly to chapter content. Teaching notes are provided in the Instructor's Resource Manual with Video Guide. Please contact your Pearson Education Canada sales representative for details.

Acknowledgments

As was the case with the first edition, Pearson staff have been extremely helpful throughout the long and sometimes difficult process of preparing this second edition. Acquisitions Editor James Bosma has offered solid support throughout. Developmental Editor Pam Voves provided invaluable advice and encouragement and much useful editorial guidance during the project's early stages. When Pam was sidelined due to an accident, Meaghan Eley stepped in and carried the ball with nary a hitch. Production Editor Judith Scott has shown the right mix of patience and firmness in dealing with an author who is seriously absent-minded. Copy Editor Gail Marsden has made the task of reviewing the book's editorial content *almost* a pleasant one.

I have been blessed with a stimulating work environment throughout the preparation of the second edition. Colleagues, first at the Fryer Committee and Public Service Staff Relations Board (where the Fryer Committee had its offices) and more recently at the Professional Institute, have given me much food for thought over the past two years. Special thanks are due to Maureen King, the Institute's data analyst and guardian of its library, for bringing my attention to a great many new articles, studies, and reference works that I might well otherwise have missed. I'm also most grateful to Sally Diehl, my section head at the Institute, for her understanding in allowing me to arrange my work schedule to facilitate completion of the new edition.

Once again, I'd like to acknowledge the contribution made by my intellectual development in IR by Bernie Adell, who taught me at Queen's University, and Roy Adams, who taught me at the University of Toronto. It was largely as a result of their influence that I developed the interest in international and comparative IR that ultimately led to the inclusion of the comparative chapter in this edition of *Canadian Industrial Relations*.

To Rick Harkin, long-time librarian at the Public Service Staff Relations Board, I owe a huge, huge debt. Not only did Rick put his dazzling array of research skills at my service, allowing me to locate materials I otherwise never would have known about; he also served as colleague, friend, debate-partner, and much more throughout the long process of revision. Thanks are also due to Rick's colleagues at the PSSRB Library and to the staff of the Canada Industrial Relations Board and Industry Canada libraries for their assistance in obtaining material used in this book.

Reviewer Acknowledgments

I would like to thank the following reviewers for their feedback: Allan C. Fraser, University College of Cape Breton; Andy Andiappan, University of Windsor; Fiona

McQuarrie, University College of the Fraser Valley; Ian Sakinofsky, Ryerson Polytechnic University; Claude Dupuis, The University of Calgary; Susan Thompson-Graham, Nova Scotia Community College; G. Ross Playter, Brandon University; Joseph B. Rose, McMaster University; Robert A. Grant, Queen's University; Basu Sharma, University of New Brunswick; Robert Hebdon, McGill University; John Fakouri, Algonquin College; Jerome J. Collins, St. Clair College of Applied Arts and Technology; and Thomas R. Knight, University of British Columbia. These reviewers' comments, some of which were so helpful as to amount to something close to intellectual midwifery, have done much to strengthen this book. Naturally, I assume sole responsibility for any errors that remain.

J.P.
Ottawa, March 2002

CHAPTER 1

INTRODUCTION TO
INDUSTRIAL RELATIONS

Today's Canadian work force includes a large number of women and members of ethnic minority groups.

The first part of this chapter considers the significance of work in most Canadians' lives. After a brief discussion of the inter-disciplinary nature of our field of study, some definitions for the term "industrial relations"(IR) are offered. A discussion of some of the best-known theories of industrial relations, including the systems framework and the strategic choice theory, follows. Five perspectives for the study of IR are examined, and the chapter concludes with a brief outline of what the rest of the book will cover.

THE SIGNIFICANCE OF WORK

Welcome to the study of industrial relations!

Industrial relations is about the world of work: its joys and sorrows, its satisfactions and frustrations. The importance of work in the lives of most Canadians is immense. Most of us spend about one-quarter of our time working, which is more than we spend doing anything else, except sleeping. Through work, we seek to live our dreams and realize our ambitions. To a large extent, our adult identity is shaped by the work we do and the jobs we hold. We meet many of our friends at work; a good many of us meet our life partners there. A fulfilling job, working among congenial people in pleasant surroundings, can be the source of immense satisfaction. By the same token, unfulfilling work performed in the company of people one finds indifferent or hostile can be the source of such intense frustration that it can affect one's mental health. As we see in Chapter 7, work can also pose physical risks.

Landing a job is often an occasion for celebration. Losing one can lead to feelings of inadequacy, guilt, or anger that can last for months or even years. Those people who don't have jobs—for whatever reason—often feel like second-class citizens who aren't contributing to society. Work is addictive to some, so much so that they feel more comfortable at the plant or the office than at home. Even when they're supposed to be on vacation, such people try to maintain constant connection with their work through faxes, long-distance phone calls, or e-mail. Others develop such strong attachment to their work and to their places of work that when they retire (especially if the retirement has been abrupt or involuntary), they find themselves unable to cope with the separation. It isn't uncommon for these retirees to suffer heart attacks or develop severe depression.

Work's economic impact is equally important. The majority of Canadians—except for those lucky few who inherit fortunes or draw winning lottery tickets—derive almost all their income from work-based earnings. Those who lose their jobs generally suffer severely reduced buying power, despite the existence of social support programs like Employment Insurance (EI). When a large number of people in the same community lose their jobs, as when a plant closes or relocates, that community's very existence may be imperilled.

At an even more basic level, work is essential to produce goods and services, like food, housing, telephone service, and electric power, on which we all depend. If people didn't work, or hadn't worked in the past, such goods and services wouldn't be available for our use. When work is interrupted, whether because of a labour dispute or because of a natural disaster like a fire or an ice storm, the disruption of people's daily lives can be severe.

The Changing World of Work

Of late, the world of work has been changing quite dramatically. Until quite recently, most jobs in Canada were full-time and full-year. Most people worked on a regular schedule—typically from 9 to 5, Monday through Friday. Once you found a job, you could generally expect to keep it for a while, assuming that your performance and attendance remained satisfactory. Many people stayed with one employer, or at most two or three, throughout their entire working lives. While changes in occupation weren't unknown, they were the exception rather than the rule.

Over the past two decades, the incidence of "atypical" forms of employment has increased dramatically. These include regular part-time work; casual work; work done on a short-term contractual basis; work performed at home rather than on the employer's premises; and self-employment.

These atypical employment patterns have increased so much that, according to the most recent Statistics Canada data, barely a majority of Canadian workers work under "standard" arrangements. Such dramatically shifting work patterns pose a major challenge for individual workers, for the unions that represent or seek to represent their interests, and for public policy-makers responsible for regulating working conditions. As we'll discuss more fully in Chapter 2, the Canadian work force has been changing no less dramatically. Once predominantly male and almost all white, our work force now reflects the diversity of a country with a multicultural population. About 46 percent of all Canadian workers are women, and the country's work force includes people from many different ethnic and religious backgrounds.

Our work force also includes people with varying types and degrees of physical and mental disabilities. This new, more diverse work force has also brought new challenges to unions and policy-makers, but especially to employers. For a variety of reasons (some

Today, far too many people are working part-time, often in coffee shops like this one, because it is the only work they can find.

An increasing number of women are balancing work and family responsibilities. Between 1978 and 2001, the proportion of women participating in the labour force increased from 45 percent to just under 60 percent.

of which are the result of recent legislation), employers are under increasing pressure to provide various physical facilities, like wheelchair-accessible entrances, to meet the needs of workers with physical disabilities; to provide same-sex medical benefits to meet the needs of gay and lesbian couples; or to provide flexible work schedules to meet the needs of single parents or members of religious minorities.

Few young people entering today's work world can realistically expect to stay with one employer, or even one occupation, throughout their entire careers, as many of their parents and grandparents did. This has its advantages and disadvantages. On the one hand, people who frequently change employers or occupations may be less apt to become bored and may achieve more job satisfaction than people who stay in the same place for many years. On the other hand, there is no question that today's increasingly fluid arrangements breed considerable insecurity.[1] As well, generating loyalty and commitment from workers becomes extremely difficult when few of these workers have any assurance that they will still be on the payroll in six months' time. We'll revisit these issues in Chapter 3.

WHAT IS INDUSTRIAL RELATIONS?

Industrial relations is an interdisciplinary subject. It draws on fields as diverse as economics, law, history, business management, political science, psychology, and sociology in analyzing, and proposing solutions for, workplace problems (Dunlop, 1958).

A simple example may help illustrate why many different academic disciplines are necessary to study problems arising out of the world of work. Let's suppose we're trying to explain why union membership rates are higher in Canada than in the United States. (This isn't simply a hypothetical exercise. Union-growth analysts have been trying to get at this question for many years.) What "tools" would we need to answer this question?

Union growth is clearly related to broad trends in the economy, like unemployment and inflation. Obviously, anyone looking at the question would need to have some understanding of economics. But this only gets us part of the way. In recent years, union membership rates in Canada and the United States have diverged quite sharply, despite generally similar economic conditions. Clearly, we need more than economics to answer the question fully.

Legislation regarding how unions are certified and who is allowed to join unions can have an important effect on membership rates. If, for example, one government allows unions to become certified through a simple count of signed membership cards while another requires a formal vote, membership rates will likely be higher under the first government, because it's more difficult for a union to become certified where there is a formal election process. Since the United States (where private sector labour legislation is under federal jurisdiction) requires a vote and many Canadian jurisdictions allow certification through signed membership cards, membership rates will likely be higher in Canada, other things being equal (see Figure 1.1). In addition, some governments allow most workers, other than managers, to join unions; while other governments may exclude members of specific groups, like professionals, domestics, and agricultural workers. Other things being equal, the jurisdiction that allows a greater number of occupational groups of workers to belong to unions is likely to have significantly higher union-membership rates (Peirce, 1989). Since American law, as currently interpreted, excludes more potential union members than Canadian law, our country's membership rates again should be higher.

In addition, different political arrangements may be more or less conducive to union growth. Union-growth analysts have generally found that rates go up when a labour or social democratic government is in power and down when a conservative government holds sway (Maki, 1982; Bruce, 1989). Indeed, a labour-oriented party can influence union membership growth even from a balance-of-power or strong opposition position. In Canada, threat of defeat by the CCF party, which was the forerunner to the NDP, was a primary factor inducing Prime Minister Mackenzie King to introduce *PC 1003*, the bill first granting collective bargaining rights to Canadian workers (Morton, 1995). Without such a political party, the possibility of using the political arena to enhance union growth is significantly diminished. The fact that Canada does have such a party (the NDP), while the United States doesn't, arguably contributes to higher membership rates here (Meltz, 1985; Bruce, 1989). So does Canada's multiparty parliamentary system, which has made it much easier for a party like the NDP to get started here than it would be in the United States (Bruce, 1989).

History also plays a role, as well as law and political science. In cities where there is a history of strong, positive labour organizations, unions are likely to have an easier time recruiting new members than in cities lacking such a history, or (perhaps worse still) where unions have made a practice of exploiting their members or becoming involved with organized crime. Since union membership involves a group dynamic, the values attached by a given community to union membership may also play a role. Those communities in which union membership is looked on favourably will likely see better

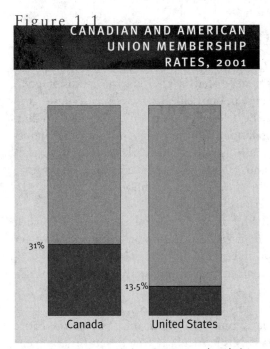

Figure 1.1

CANADIAN AND AMERICAN UNION MEMBERSHIP RATES, 2001

31%

13.5%

Canada   United States

Source: for Canada, *Workplace Gazette*, 4:3 (2001); for U.S., drawn from the Web site of Department of Labor's Bureau of Workplace Statistics.

success in organizing drives than those where a more individualistic ethic prevails, like high-tech communities. Here, the study of sociology will prove helpful, and psychology is useful in determining what motivates some individuals to join unions, but not others (Kervin, 1988).

Depending on the industrial relations issue we're looking at, many other academic disciplines could come into play. For example, a knowledge of literature would be helpful in analyzing the writings of working people (often an important source of IR knowledge). A knowledge of music and folklore could be very useful in studying work songs, which in turn may offer some important clues to the work process in a given occupation or community (Seeger, 1972). Today, a knowledge of ergonomics could prove extremely useful in understanding contemporary health and safety issues, like the growing incidence of carpal tunnel syndrome among grocery cashiers and secretaries.

Industrial relations is obviously a subject requiring many different kinds of knowledge. To many (including the author), this is one of the field's enduring fascinations. To others (Laffer, 1974), it is a source of frustration, as is the apparent lack of a single, overarching theory (Heneman, 1969), comparable to, for example, the law of supply and demand in economics. The debate over what the field of industrial relations should include has been raging for some time and seems unlikely to end soon. Suffice to say that, for now, experience suggests the world of work isn't always a neat and tidy place, and that attempts to analyze it as if it were are probably doomed to fail.

Defining Industrial Relations

How should we define "industrial relations"? A possible starting point might be, "the relations between unions and management." That is all right, as far as it goes. Union–management relations are at the core of our field. But as we will soon see, and as some of you may have sensed already, the field takes in a good deal more than that.

To begin with, union–management relations in Canada, as in most other industrialized countries, are conducted within a legislative framework devised by government—in this case, both provincial and federal governments, since both have jurisdiction over various aspects of the IR system. Any definition of IR that fails to take governments' role into account is seriously deficient.

It's also inaccurate to confine any definition to the unionized part of the work force. Fewer than one-third of all Canadian workers are union members. We can't simply fail to consider the remaining two-thirds.

In a broader sense, the IR system affects the lives of almost all Canadians, including those who aren't themselves workers, such as children or retired people. If a private-sector firm undergoes a **strike**, not only are its employees, managers, and their families affected, so are its customers, its suppliers, and not infrequently the entire community in which the firm is located. This is particularly true if that firm happens to be the community's only employer or one of its major ones. In the case of a public sector dispute involving groups like transit workers or sanitation workers, the entire community may feel the effects very quickly, particularly if the service that the striking workers normally provide is one for which there is no readily available substitute. In the case of a big-city transit strike, even people who normally drive to work will be affected because many of those who can't take the subway will also be driving, making traffic heavier and progress slower.

Clearly, then, a broad definition is needed if we are to take into account all the ways in which the IR system affects people: as workers or managers, as taxpayers, and as consumers. I have not seen a better definition of IR than the one put forward by Thomas Kochan (1980:1): "All aspects of the employment relationship."[2] Almost every other definition—and there are a good many—leaves out one or more important aspects.

To be sure, other disciplines also deal with the world of work. These disciplines include, among others, organizational behaviour (OB), human resource management (HRM), sociology, labour economics, and labour studies. Where industrial relations differs from other disciplines is in what Noah Meltz (1989a) describes as its concern for balancing efficiency and equity, the interests of management and those of workers, as well as its interdisciplinary approach. Thus, while OB and HRM courses tend to take a pro-management approach, and labour studies courses take a pro-labour and often pro-union approach, IR courses seek to make students aware of the needs and interests of both workers and management. While labour economics courses focus on the economic aspects of work, and sociology courses focus on the behavioural and psychic aspects, IR courses treat the different aspects of work as interrelated. In these ways, industrial relations has a valuable, perhaps even unique contribution to make to the study of work-related issues.[3]

THEORIES OF INDUSTRIAL RELATIONS

Dunlop's Systems Theory

As noted previously, few industrial relations experts would maintain that the field possesses a single, strong, explanatory theory. Nonetheless, there have been several attempts at developing such a theory. The most important of these theories is that of John Dunlop (1958). Dunlop (1958:5) defines an **industrial relations system** as "an analytical subsystem of an industrial society." In his view, the IR system is equally as important as the economic subsystem, but not a part of it. This will be an important point to remember throughout this book, especially when we begin to consider elements of behaviour, like certain types of strikes, that appear to be economically irrational. As we shall soon see, actors in the IR system may and often do have concerns beyond purely economic ones. Economic theory (Dunlop, 1958:5) can't be expected to explain all aspects of these concerns, though it can explain some of them. While there are areas of overlap between the economic and IR subsystems, there are some aspects of the IR system (such as elements of workplace rule making) that fall outside the scope of the economic subsystem.

At any one time, says Dunlop (1958:7), an IR system comprises certain actors, certain contexts, a body or web of rules governing the actors' workplace behaviour, and a common ideology binding the system together. The actors include managers, workers and their representatives, and government or specialized private agencies (i.e., arbitration panels) appointed by workers and management to handle certain aspects of their relationship. The workers may be unionized or not. It is their job to do the work, following instructions given to them by management, whose job is to provide such instructions (Dunlop, 1958). Government's primary interest is as a peacekeeper and rule maker, though within the public sector government also wears a second hat as employer. The complications resulting from government's dual role here will be discussed in more detail in the public sector chapter (Chapter 9).

The contexts within which the actors operate include market (economic), technical, and power (political) ones. To a considerable extent, these contexts determine the balance of power between the two most important actors (workers and management). Changes in these contexts are likely to produce shifts in that balance of power. Each of the contexts has its greatest impact on a subset of the rules. For example, the market context affects pay and benefit levels, while the power context affects legislation governing union **certification** and strike procedures (Anderson and Gunderson, 1982).

The web of rules includes substantive rules regarding system outcomes such as pay, benefits, hours of work, and workplace safety, and procedural rules on such matters as collective bargaining, grievance procedures, and transfer or promotion procedures (Dunlop, 1958; Anderson and Gunderson, 1982). For the most part, labour relations legislation (discussed in Chapter 8), or the web of rules established to govern behaviour in unionized workplaces, is of a procedural nature. On the one hand, the assumption here is that as long as the parties are placed on a relatively level playing field through the establishment of appropriate procedures for collective bargaining, the handling of impasses, and the like, they'll negotiate better outcomes than the government could. On the other hand, employment standards legislation (discussed in Chapter 7), or the web of rules applied to all workers but of particular importance in non-unionized establishments), does prescribe certain outcomes. These include minimum wages, maximum hours of work, minimum vacation entitlements, and safety regulations governing the maximum permissible level of discharge of certain substances into the air or water.

It's customary to speak of these two sets of rules as separate entities, and to a large extent they are indeed distinct from one another. At the same time, the two complement each other in some important ways. To begin with, employment standards legislation applies to all workplaces (unionized as well as non-unionized). It is, therefore, illegal for a union and an employer to negotiate any terms and conditions poorer than those provided in employment standards legislation (i.e., a wage below the provincial minimum). Employment standards legislation thus serves as the floor on which collective bargaining can begin. Unions also have an important role to play in enforcing employment legislation in the workplace, in educating workers about their rights under this legislation, and in enhancing minimum legislated standards through the collective bargaining process. Again, these points are discussed in more detail in Chapter 7.

The notion of a common ideology between the actors in the IR system has led to some confusion and a fair amount of debate. By "ideology" Dunlop (1958:16–17) means "a body of common ideas that defines the role and place of each actor and that defines the ideas which each actor holds toward the place and function of the others in the system." He further suggests (1958:17) that "[t]he ideology or philosophy of a stable system involves a congruence or compatibility among these views and the rest of the system." What has never been clear is just how far the idea of a "common ideology" should be taken. It would probably be fair to say that most North American employers and workers share a common preference for a democratic, capitalist system of government, rather than a totalitarian one like Communism or fascism. This assumption doesn't, however, take us very far towards understanding the extent to which workplace conflict would be restrained or modified as a result of that common ideology. Confusion about this point and various others has led to a number of criticisms of the systems framework over the years.

Criticisms of the Systems Framework

Dunlop's systems framework offers useful insights into the interdisciplinary nature of industrial relations. It also offers a convenient introductory approach to the study of foreign IR systems with which a researcher is unfamiliar. By looking at the actors, the contexts in which they operate, and the web of rules governing the actors' behaviour, one can learn a good deal about such systems.

In many other ways, however, the systems framework has proved disappointing. Dunlop (1958:6) had anticipated that his approach would provide IR with a theoretical core and turn it into "a genuine discipline." While most industrial relationists today would probably agree that IR is a genuine discipline, few would agree that the systems framework has provided a theoretical core that can generate testable research hypotheses. As Anderson and Gunderson (1982:5) note, the most common criticism has been that it is "only a taxonomy which has resulted in descriptive rather than explanatory research."

Another problem is that, by viewing the IR subsystem in at least relative isolation (1958:2), Dunlop tends to minimize the importance of various environmental inputs beyond the three contexts he identifies. But the most serious problem with the systems framework has to do with the role of conflict. Granted, Dunlop doesn't ignore the role of conflict; indeed, he suggests that at times, when the actors don't share a common ideology (1958:17), the system will lack stability and may require major changes. He doesn't, however, distinguish between relatively positive or "cathartic" conflict, of the type that can be worked out through collective bargaining and other activities, and destructive or dysfunctional conflict, which could impair or even permanently destroy the actors' relationship. Dunlop also doesn't indicate to what extent conflict is inherent within the employment relationship—or, for that matter, if any kind of conflict at all is inherent. This seems a serious omission, particularly given that his view of the employment relationship is an extremely traditional one in which managers give orders and workers execute them. More generally, Dunlop seems to assume that IR systems possess a greater degree of stability than most actually do. His inadequate treatment of conflict has been criticized by earlier writers like Singh (1976) and by more recent ones like Kochan, McKersie, and Cappelli (1984).

Some of the problems just noted were solved when Alton Craig (1967, 1983) put Dunlop's model into more conventional systems form with the use of an input-output framework and a feedback loop (Anderson and Gunderson, 1982:6). Among other things, the input-output framework allows for the use of a broader range of inputs. It also provides a fuller representation of the inputs' role in shaping the IR system's outputs, through various conversion processes, and helps to show the system's connection to and interdependence with other systems instead of representing it in isolation as Dunlop does. Finally, on the important question of conflict, Craig is somewhat more explicit than Dunlop. By identifying the **grievance** process, strikes, and **lockouts** as conversion processes, and the latter as system outputs, Craig (1983) implies that some degree of conflict is inherent to the IR system, but that much of it can be worked out through the system's normal operations.

While in many ways an improvement on Dunlop's original framework, Craig's model isn't without its own problems. First, as we'll discuss in more detail in Chapter 3, Craig pays little attention to the role of management. Profit, market share, and the good or service being produced aren't even listed as outputs. The only "organizational" outputs listed are collective agreement provisions. Second, although Craig doesn't explicitly limit his model to unionized workplaces, almost all his conversion processes and system outputs presuppose a collective bargaining process, severely limiting the model's applicability in non-unionized settings. Implicitly at least, the model appears to presuppose a strategy of union acceptance on the part of management. Third, although again Craig isn't explicit on this point, the model appears to assume that most workplace conflict can be contained within, if not worked out through, the IR system. Developments in the past two decades have cast increasing doubt on such an assumption.

The Strategic Choice Model

Concerned that much of the IR literature paid insufficient attention to management's role as a key actor in the system, Thomas Kochan and his associates (Kochan et al., 1984) sought to develop a new theory that would give appropriate emphasis to that role. Kochan et al. were also troubled by Dunlop's notion of shared ideology, which they believe focusses too much on events at the bargaining table and not enough on events at other levels of the organization, where such shared understandings don't necessarily exist (Kochan et al., 1984:20). Still another concern was that industrial relations developments had, in the past, generally been considered in isolation from other developments within unions, governments, and especially within firms.

As Kochan et al. see it, to fully understand IR and human resources (HR) strategies, one needs to see how these strategies are linked to firms' larger global strategies and to their strategies at the workplace or shop-floor level. Beyond that, Kochan and his associates believed conflict had been inadequately handled in much of the IR literature. In their view, one shouldn't necessarily assume that conflict can be worked out within the IR system. The level of conflict is now a question to be measured empirically rather than taken as a given (Verma, 1992).

A prime example is a firm's attitude and behaviour towards its unions. In the past, management and unions might have battled vigorously at the bargaining table or in the political arena, but rarely with the idea that the other party shouldn't have the right to exist. By the early 1980s, with anti-union ideology and behaviour becoming more respectable again, especially in the United States, many unionized firms were beginning to give serious thought to removing their unions, while non-unionized firms were hiring consultants or intimidating and harassing suspected union activists in a bid to remain union-free (Anderson, 1989a). Clearly, such attitudes and behaviour would be likely to give rise to a more serious kind of conflict than a bargaining-table dispute over wages.[4] No longer could anyone assume that the IR system would be able to resolve conflict. Collective bargaining is the IR system's main mechanism for resolving conflict. By their actions, the management of the organizations in question would have indicated their unwillingness, if not outright refusal, to engage in the process. In such circumstances, it would also be extremely difficult to speak of any sort of "shared ideology" between management and unions. How much ideology can management realistically be said to share with unions, when they aren't even willing to sit down at a table and negotiate with them?

While the systems framework continues to have some applicability within a comparative context, as noted above, overall the **strategic choice framework** seems to offer a fuller and more accurate explanation of recent North American IR developments. Although the actors have used different strategies in Canada than in the United States, the strategic choice framework is nonetheless applicable here, as well as in the United States. While the framework can apply to unions and governments as well as management, it is of particular importance in explaining management behaviour. Accordingly, a full discussion has been left to Chapter 3.

PERSPECTIVES ON INDUSTRIAL RELATIONS

Another reason to question Dunlop's notion of a shared ideology within the IR system is the existence of a number of different perspectives among industrial relationists (Anderson, Gunderson, and Ponak, 1989; Godard, 1994). Even within unions or management organizations, different individuals may hold different views on key issues. The five perspectives we'll be discussing apply to such things as the individual's primary research focus, the importance individuals attach to unions, the extent to which a person believes conflict is inherent in the IR system, and the individual's location on the political spectrum (right to left). While, as Godard notes (1994:26), not all industrial relationists can be consistently identified with one of the five perspectives, these perspectives nonetheless help to highlight differing opinions within the field on such issues as the role of unions or the appropriate managerial policies to follow to maximize efficiency and productivity. They will thus be useful throughout the book.

Neoclassical Perspective

Strictly speaking, the right-wing neoclassical perspective is more of a pure economics perspective than an IR perspective. Indeed, the discipline of industrial relations really began in North America as a result of the University of Wisconsin's John R. Commons' recognition that neoclassical economics was inadequate in explaining real-life problems such as poverty and unemployment, and in providing practical solutions to those problems. This recognition permeates such works as his *History of Labor in the United States* (1918), as well as the works of a number of other early twentieth-century writers whom Commons influenced. Throughout the postwar period, few if any leading Canadian industrial relationists adopted the neoclassical perspective, though with the return of competitive labour markets and the ascendancy of the political right in recent years, there have been an increasing number of attempts to apply elements of that perspective to the IR system (Peirce, 1996). Generally, a desire to increase competitiveness has been the rationale behind such attempts. The neoclassical approach has perhaps been more popular in the United States, where, in recent years, it has been adopted by such prominent writers as Troy (1992).

Neoclassicists believe, above all else, in the free and unfettered operation of markets, especially labour markets (Ehrenberg and Smith, 1985). In their view, the labour–management relationship is, in the words of John Godard (1994:27), "a free and equal exchange between two parties with different yet compatible interests." Neoclassicists also believe that managers should have unfettered authority to run their enterprises as they see fit. If workers don't like the way management is running the enterprise, they are always free to quit and find a job more to their liking. Members of this school have little or no use for unions, which they view as organizations that can only increase inefficiency and unemployment by raising wages above the "equilibrium point"at which labour markets clear and there is full employment. Those adopting the **"coercive drive"** approach to management, discussed in more detail in Chapter 3, are generally of a neoclassical persuasion and tend to take what Adell (1988a) has described as a "unitary" or "unchained entrepreneurship" perspective on labour law.

Within IR, neoclassicists' primary research focus is on labour markets. Logically enough, since they believe that unions and the government agencies that regulate them shouldn't exist in the first place, they tend to have little or no interest in the practical workings of these organizations. Their research tends to be highly quantitative and statistical, to make heavy use of large databases, and to focus on such issues as unions' impact on wages (Anderson et al., 1989). For the most part, members of this school tend not to concern themselves with questions of conflict, since they believe all such questions can be resolved through the operation of market forces (Godard, 1994:27).

Managerial Perspective

While the neoclassical perspective is closely linked to the discipline of economics, the managerial one is related to organizational behaviour. It arose out of the work of such varied people as F.W. Taylor and Elton Mayo (Gunderson and Ponak, 1995). Many working in personnel and human resource departments take this perspective.

Managerialists' main concern is the motivation of workers, both individually and in small groups. They believe that properly motivated workers will be more productive. Unlike the neoclassicists, they seek to motivate through positive incentives rather than through fear. They also tend to be, at best, ambivalent towards unions. Where unions exist already, they'll often seek to establish a cooperative relationship (Gunderson and Ponak, 1995). For the most part, however, they believe that if intelligent and progressive human resource management policies are followed, unions should be unnecessary, and that while the interests of workers and managers may diverge in the short term, over the longer term they'll converge, again assuming appropriate management techniques are used to link the company's interests to individual workers' needs (Gunderson and Ponak, 1995). Managerialists tend to be particularly interested in employee involvement and other quality of worklife programs, as well as in a variety of incentive-based compensation schemes. Much research conducted from this perspective has focussed on such issues as why some employees are more likely than others to go on strike or take industrial action, and what management techniques and organizational structures will reduce an individual's propensity to engage in industrial conflict (Kervin, 1988:219). While much of this research has been valuable, in general it has paid little attention to the role of unions (Kervin, 1984, 1988; Gunderson and Ponak, 1995). The omission seems somewhat surprising, given that, in Canada at least, only a duly certified union can legally call a strike.

Institutional Perspective

The institutional perspective has generally been the one adopted by most mainstream industrial relationists. Arising out of the work of people like John R. Commons, this perspective holds that in a competitive marketplace, individual workers are unable to resist the demands of powerful employers. Unions and collective bargaining are, therefore, needed to balance what would otherwise be a seriously uneven playing field (Barbash, 1984). This perspective entails more government intervention than the two perspectives already discussed, since government is needed to establish and administer labour relations legislation, without which most unions would be unable to function (see Chapter 8). In the view of institutionalists, there's no denying that workplace conflict exists. However, much if not all of it can be dissipated through collective bargaining and other activities of the IR system.

As their name suggests, institutionalists have a strong interest in real-world IR institutions—unions, management organizations, and the government agencies that regulate the IR system. Much of their research tends to be of a practical nature, and many institutionalists have a keen interest in public labour policy issues. While members of this school don't confine themselves to a single research approach, in general (Anderson et al., 1989) institutionalists tend to rely more heavily on interviews and case studies and less heavily on statistical analysis than do neoclassicists. Noted Canadian institutionalists have included H.D. Woods, chairman of a well-known federal task force on labour relations, and the Abbé Gérard Dion, founder of the industrial relations program at Laval University and long-time editor of the Canadian journal *Relations Industrielles*.

Reformist Perspective

Members of this school think that collective bargaining and labour relations legislation *could* work, under the right circumstances, but that as things stand, the odds are weighted too heavily in favour of employers, and the rich and powerful in general. While they are supportive of unions in principle (Godard, 1994), they are critical of a system that, all too often, doesn't allow unions to offer workers any real protection, especially in small organizations. Accordingly, reformists seek major economic redistribution, such as changes in the tax system, as well as pay and employment equity and other employment law reforms designed to correct what many of them view as widespread structural and political inequality (Godard, 1994).

One group of reformists, represented most notably by David Beatty (1983, 1987; Adell, 1988a), takes what Adell describes as an "egalitarian individualist" approach to issues of labour law and social justice more generally. In Adell's words, Beatty believes "that the justice of social institutions should be appraised on the basis of their effects on the worst-off members of society" (1988a:116). Beatty would use the *Charter of Rights and Freedoms* to bring about fairer labour relations legislation. For example, he would use it to remove existing exclusions from this legislation (such as those of management personnel, agricultural workers, and domestics), on the grounds that all workers should have the right to join a union, whether or not they choose to exercise that right (Beatty, 1987; Adell, 1988a).[5] More generally, Beatty views the Charter as providing a constitutional guarantee of the right to join a union and to strike (Beatty and Kennett, 1988).[6] But his program for labour law reform doesn't stop with the Charter. While this would guarantee fair procedures, workers also need substantive legislative protection of the type provided by human rights and employment standards legislation (Beatty, 1987; Adell, 1988a).

A second group comprises mainly academics in such disciplines as history, sociology, and political science, as well as a few industrial relationists of progressive bent (Haiven, McBride, and Shields, 1990). This group's work focusses quite strongly on issues of power in the workplace and in Canadian society at large. Often they have been critical of the role of the state in maintaining or even fostering existing power imbalances (Haiven et al., 1990). Others have focussed on such issues as discrimination, unsafe working conditions, **layoffs** and plant closures, and wage inequities (Godard, 1994:31). For example, Canadian legal scholar Harry Glassbeek has long been interested in the issue of corporations' legal liability for workplace injuries and illnesses (Glassbeek and Rowland, 1979).

Radical/Political Economy Perspective

Those holding this perspective, unlike those holding the previous four, believe that widespread inequality is an integral part of capitalist society and can't be overcome under existing economic and political arrangements. In the past, most radicals were of a Marxist or quasi-Marxist bent.[7] They believed that all members of society are divided into two classes: the working class, or proletariat, and the capitalist class, or bourgeoisie. The bourgeoisie, in this view, own the means of production, while members of the working class don't, and are thus forced to sell their labour to those who do. Most workers produce goods or services of far greater value than their wages and the costs of production put together. The difference between the value of the goods or services produced and the total costs of production (including wages) is kept by the capitalists as profits, and is referred to by Marxists as "surplus value."

To the Marxist, trade unions are at best a Band-Aid solution, at worst a distraction from what should be the working class's main mission: to overthrow capitalist society.[8] Classical Marxists thought this would happen through a combination of political means and direct action. Syndicalists (represented in North America mainly by the Industrial Workers of the World) had little use for politics, believing that a giant general strike would eventually bring the capitalist class to its knees. The failure of the Winnipeg General Strike (described in Chapter 4) meant the end of serious syndicalism in Canada. Classical Marxism hung on somewhat longer, as Communists continued to play a significant role in the Canadian labour movement through the early fifties (Morton, 1995). Marxist scholarship, however, has played far less of a role in North American than in European industrial relations (Hyman, 1975). One notable exception is the work of Harry Braverman (1974). Taking a Marxist perspective on technological change, Braverman argues that the major effect of such change is to "deskill" workers, thus further increasing managers' and employers' control over the labour process.

Over the past few years, a new political economy school has arisen in North American industrial relations.[9] Members of this school agree with traditional Marxists as to the centrality of power issues and the importance of relating IR to larger developments in the economy and society (Godard, 1994; Lipsig-Mumme, 1995). Their prescriptions for change are, however, generally quite different. In place of traditional Marxist calls for the violent overthrow of capitalist society, one hears calls for employee ownership and management of business enterprises (Godard, 1994). In place of calls for unions to serve as foot soldiers in the giant revolution, one hears calls for them to reach out to the communities in which their members live (Lipsig-Mumme, 1995:216) and, at the same time, to operate in a more genuinely international fashion (Lipsig-Mumme, 1995:218), to better serve the workers of transnational enterprises affected by recent North American trade agreements.

Most industrial relationists who take a political economy perspective would agree that there are serious problems with the Canadian IR system as presently constituted. Particular difficulties include the inadequate representation of women (Forrest, 1997) and of workers in small firms and peripheral areas of the economy (Lipsig-Mumme, 1995). Few, however, have gone so far as to call for the outright dismantling of the present Canadian IR system. Most appear to believe that, imperfect though that system may be, workers are still better served with it than they would be without it.

WHAT THE BOOK WILL COVER

This chapter has offered a very basic introduction to industrial relations: what it is, what some leading theories say, and what some different perspectives on the field have to say about such issues as the role of unions and the importance of power and conflict in the workplace.

Since the state of the economy is crucial in determining who will hold the balance of workplace power, or even who will hold a job, we consider the economy first in Chapter 2. A central issue here is the recent growth of contingent or "atypical" work, and the effect this has had on the actions of management and unions.

The next group of chapters is devoted to studying the roles of management and labour, the two major actors in the IR system. We start, in Chapter 3, with management, which most industrial relations experts agree is now the IR system's single most important actor. A key element of this chapter is its discussion of the historical evolution of Canadian management practice. The following three chapters consider the role of labour. Chapter 4 looks at labour's role from an historical perspective, while Chapters 5 and 6 focus specifically on the role and activities of unions. The former looks at union membership, growth, and structure, while the latter deals with union actions and impacts, including both economic and non-economic ones.

We then move on to the legal aspects of the IR system. Chapter 7 discusses employment legislation affecting all workers, but focusses on that of particular relevance to non-unionized ones. Among the topics we consider here are work standards legislation affecting such things as minimum wages and maximum allowable hours of work, health and safety legislation, human rights legislation, and workers' compensation legislation. We also consider what redress a non-unionized individual has against a dismissal he or she considers to have been arbitrary.

In Chapter 8, we consider private sector labour relations legislation. In addition to enumerating both historical and recent developments in the field, the chapter demonstrates the rationale for such legislation and discusses some of the variations in provincial labour legislation. Chapter 9 focusses on collective bargaining and labour legislation in the public sector, with special emphasis on the federal public service. This sector is of particular interest, both because of the crucial nature of the services it provides and because it has recently been the setting for many of our country's most bitter labour disputes.

The next group of chapters is primarily concerned with the bargaining process and with the conflict that often arises during that process. In Chapter 10, we look at the negotiation process in some detail. We also consider bargaining structures, since they comprise a key element of the environment in which bargaining is conducted. The chapter concludes with a discussion of collective agreements, in which we discuss the evolution and philosophy of Canadian collective agreements and look at various types of agreement provisions.

Strikes are the aspect of the IR system most familiar to the average reader because of the prominence they receive in the media. After clarifying what a strike is in Chapter 11, we consider the changing patterns of strike incidence in Canada, including changing patterns in different industries and provinces. We then go on to look at a variety of possible causes for strikes. We close the chapter with a look at some of the dispute resolution methods used to prevent strikes, or at least reduce their adverse effect on innocent parties. A highlight of this chapter is its description of four recent major Canadian strikes.

Chapter 12 focusses on grievances and the grievance process. Part of the chapter is devoted to an examination of an actual grievance case. In addition, we consider what a grievance is, how a typical grievance process works, and some of the most important criticisms of the grievance process. We close by relating grievances to other forms of industrial conflict, like strikes, and by proposing alternatives to conventional grievance processes.

Chapter 13, on comparative industrial relations, is new to this edition. We start with a brief look at some broad international IR models, before taking a closer look at some countries of special interest to Canada, including Germany, Japan, and the U.S. The chapter closes with a consideration of how recent developments such as globalization and liberalized trade have affected labour movements internationally.

In the final chapter, Chapter 14, we revisit the Canadian IR system as a whole in light of important recent developments like globalization, liberalized trade, increased work hours, and the growth of a **contingent work force**. To this end, we examine five key themes and discuss some of the most important findings related to those themes.

Although we have added a chapter on comparative IR to this edition, we have also continued our earlier practice of using evidence from foreign IR systems to show the Canadian system in a comparative perspective. Likewise, a discussion of key features of Quebec's quite distinctive IR system has been incorporated into the chapters where appropriate.

QUESTIONS FOR DISCUSSION

1) What has your experience of work been, to this point? What have you liked best (and least) about it?

2) How has your experience of work compared with that of your parents, or with that of people of your parents' generation?

3) What are some of the major strengths of the systems framework? What are some of its major weaknesses?

4) How have Thomas Kochan and his associates sought to address the systems framework's perceived problems through their strategic choice theory?

5) What are the key features of each of the five major perspectives on IR? Which do you find most convincing, and why?

6) How does IR differ from other disciplines that deal with the world of work, such as labour history or organizational behaviour? What has been IR's distinctive contribution to the study of work?

SUGGESTIONS FOR FURTHER READING

Adams, Roy. (1995a). "Canadian industrial relations in comparative perspective." Morley Gunderson and Allen Ponak (Eds.), *Union-Management Relations in Canada*, 3rd edition (chap. 17). Don Mills ON: Addison-Wesley. For those interested in learning more about how other countries' IR systems operate, this is a first-rate introduction.

Adams, Scott. Dilbert cartoons (in most newspapers, particularly on Saturdays). The Dilbert strip offers a funny and often extremely penetrating look at the follies and foibles of North American workplaces. It's particularly good on management practice. In addition, Adams has written a number of "Dilbert" books.

Godard, John. (2000). *Industrial relations: The economy and society*. Toronto: Captus. 2nd edition of an excellent and very readable textbook written from a political economy perspective.

Terkel, Studs. (c.1975 [1972]). *Working*. New York: Avon. Though possibly a bit dated by now, this series of interviews with more than 100 Americans about their jobs (from business executives to hookers) remains a classic.

CHAPTER 2

THE ECONOMY
AND ITS IMPACTS

Conditions in the kitchen shown here look good compared to those in kitchens Montreal *Star* journalist Sheila Arnopoulos visited during the 1970s, in which large numbers of mainly immigrant workers were putting in long hours.

The state of the economy is critical to the functioning of the industrial relations system, since the economy is largely responsible for determining the relative balance of power between employers and workers. In this chapter, we start by looking at some broad relationships between the economy and the IR system and at the current state of the Canadian economy. Next, we consider how the country's labour force has changed in recent years, with particular emphasis on the growth of contingent and part-time work. We then seek to determine the impact of globalization and trade liberalization on the Canadian IR system. The rest of the chapter is devoted to unemployment, which has begun to climb again after falling steadily for a number of years.

SOME BASIC DYNAMICS

In the previous chapter, we pointed out that industrial relations is about a good deal more than just money. Nonetheless, at the most basic level, the economy is critical to the functioning of the IR system. When inflation is high, workers may want to join unions to help protect their real wage levels. Since the demand for goods and labour is also generally high in times of high inflation, workers already in unions are more likely to strike in support of wage demands. Knowing that their employers want to get them back to work as soon as possible to avoid losing business, workers also know that their employers are more likely to meet their wage demands. Moreover, even if some unionized workers are laid off because employers believe they can't meet the union's wage demands without **layoffs**, when the demand for goods and labour is high (the 'high' end of the business cycle, as it is sometimes called), it is usually relatively easy for them to find new jobs.

By the same token, when inflation is low, workers are less apt to seek to join unions to protect their real wages. (They may want to join for other reasons, such as to protest against what they see as arbitrary management practices, but that is another matter.) As well, those already in unions are less apt to go on strike over wages. Normally when inflation is low, the general demand for goods and labour is also low (the 'low' end of the business cycle). At such times, it may not be that important for employers to get their workers back on the job, as they may not have a backlog of unfilled orders. Indeed, they sometimes have large unsold inventories and may even welcome a strike as a way of reducing their wage bill. Unions are less likely to press wage demands in bad times for two reasons. First, any strike that does occur may last longer, since employers have less incentive to settle than they would in good times. This means that the strike's cost to the workers will be higher than in good times. Second, if workers get laid off because the employer can't meet the union's wage demands without cutting jobs, it may be difficult if not impossible for them to find other jobs when unemployment is already high. Again, this doesn't mean that strikes don't take place in bad times. What it does mean is that strikes are less likely to be over wages and more likely to be over other issues.

Granted, the preceding picture has been painted with an extremely broad brush. In the last analysis, each workplace is unique, with its own history, politics, and cast of characters. Still, though such broad economic indicators as the national unemployment and inflation rates don't explain everything about the IR system, they do explain quite a bit, especially at the national level. Table 2.1 offers some sense of these broad relationships from the end of World War II to the present. You can see from the table that periods of high inflation have generally featured increases in union membership and strike activity, while periods of high unemployment and low inflation have usually seen lower union membership rates and strike activity.

Table 2.1

RATE OF CHANGE IN CONSUMER PRICE INDEX, UNEMPLOYMENT RATE, UNION DENSITY RATES, NUMBER OF STRIKES, AND STRIKES AS A PERCENTAGE OF WORKING TIME LOST, CANADA, 1946–2001

Year	CPI Change (%)	Unempl. (%)	Un. Dens. (%)	Strikes	Strikes as % of Lost Worktime
1946	2.8	3.4	27.9	226	0.54
1947	9.8	2.2	29.1	234	0.27
1948	13.8	2.3	30.3	154	0.10
1949	3.6	2.8	29.5	135	0.11
1950	2.8	3.6	†	160	0.15
1951	10.1	2.4	28.4	258	0.09
1952	3.0	2.9	30.2	219	0.29
1953	-1.2	3.0	33.0	173	0.14
1954	0.6	4.6	33.8	173	0.15
1955	0.0	4.4	33.7	159	0.19
1956	1.8	3.4	33.3	229	0.11
1957	2.9	4.6	32.4	245	0.13
1958	2.3	7.0	34.2	259	0.25
1959	1.7	6.0	33.3	216	0.19
1960	1.1	7.0	32.3	274	0.06
1961	1.1	7.1	31.6	287	0.11
1962	1.1	5.9	30.2	311	0.11
1963	1.6	5.5	29.8	332	0.07
1964	2.1	4.7	29.4	343	0.11
1965	2.0	3.9	29.7	501	0.17
1966	4.0	3.4	30.7	617	0.34
1967	3.4	3.8	32.3	522	0.25
1968	4.2	4.5	33.1	582	0.32
1969	4.5	4.4	32.5	595	0.46
1970	3.4	5.7	33.6	542	0.39
1971	2.8	6.2	32.4	569	0.16
1972	4.8	6.2	33.9	578	0.43
1973	7.7	5.5	35.4	724	0.30
1974	10.7	5.3	35.2	1218	0.46
1975	10.9	6.9	35.6	1171	0.53
1976	7.5	7.2	36.9	1040	0.53
1977	7.8	8.1	36.3	806	0.15
1978	9.0	8.4	37.1	1057	0.32
1979	9.2	7.5	−†	1049	0.33
1980	10.1	7.5	35.7	1028	0.37
1981	12.4	7.6	35.4	1049	0.35
1982	10.9	11.0	35.7	679	0.23
1983	5.8	11.9	36.4	645	0.18
1984	4.3	11.3	37.2	717	0.15
1985	4.0	10.5	36.4	825	0.12

Table 2.1
(continued)

Year	CPI Change (%)	Unempl. (%)	Un. Dens. (%)	Strikes	Strikes as % of Lost Worktime
1986	4.1	9.6	36.0	748	0.27
1987	4.4	8.9	35.2	668	0.14
1988	4.0	7.8	34.8	548	0.17
1989	5.0	7.5	34.5	627	0.13
1990	4.8	8.1	34.5	579	0.17
1991	5.6	10.4	34.7	463	0.09
1992	1.5	11.3	35.7	404	0.07
1993	1.8	11.2	35.8	382	0.05
1994	0.2	10.4	35.6	374	0.06
1995	2.2	9.5	34.3	328	0.05
1996	1.6	9.7	33.9	328	0.11
1997	1.6	9.2	34.1	279	0.12
1998	1.6	8.3	32.7	381	0.08
1999	1.7	7.6	32.6	413	0.08
2000	2.7	6.8	31.9	319	0.05
2001	2.6	7.2	31.3	N/A	N/A

* Union density is defined as the percentage of non-agricultural paid workers belonging to unions. Union density figures are lower than in previous HRDC charts (i.e., the 1993 *Directory of Paid Labour Organizations*) because the number of non-agricultural paid workers used in the calculation for 1996 is higher than that used in previous calculations.

† Data were not collected for these years.

Sources: CPI data to 1997, Statistics Canada Cat. No. 62-001-XPB, page i, Table A. Unemployment data to 1997, Statistics Canada Cat. No. 71-201-XPB. CPI and unemployment data, 1998–2001, Statistics Canada Web site. Union membership data 1946–1970, Eaton, 1975. For 1971–1976, Labour Canada, 1992. For 1977, Workplace Information Directorate (WID), Human Resources Development Canada (HRDC), 1996, *Directory of Labour Organizations in Canada.* For 1978–1997, WID, HRDC, 1997, *Directory of Labour Organizations in Canada.* For 1998–2001, *Workplace Gazette*, winter 2001. Strike data, 1946–1975, Labour Canada, Strikes and Lockouts in Canada, various issues. For 1976–1997, data provided by the Work Stoppage Bureau, WID, HRDC. For 1998–2000, HRDC Web site.

TODAY'S ECONOMY

Table 2.1 also reveals that today's economy has quite high unemployment (by historical standards) and low inflation. As we pointed out earlier, high unemployment and low inflation are characteristic of periods at the low end of business cycles and suggest an environment in which employers have a good deal more power than workers and their unions. But there is growing reason to believe that the changes we are seeing in today's economy aren't simply the result of a cyclical downturn in the economy.

Rather, the economic changes appear to be the result of more fundamental changes, like trade liberalization and deindustrialization. It should also be noted that after years of improvement, the Canadian economy started to take a nosedive late in 2001, showing significant increases in such key indicators of poor performance as unemployment and part-time work as a percentage of total employment.[1] It's important to recognize that while the events of September 11, 2001 definitely took their toll on the Canadian economy, particularly in industries such as the airlines, one of which (Canada 3000) declared bankruptcy while another (Air Canada) was forced to lay off large numbers of employees due to a sharp drop in air travel, the downward trends so much in evidence at the end of the year had already begun to emerge before the terrorist attacks on the U.S. (See *Economist*, August 2001.) For instance, the high-tech sector, a major engine of growth in previous years, saw share prices tumble, which led to the layoff of thousands of workers in that industry. Most of these lay-offs had already taken place before September 11. In B.C., the loss of 60 000 jobs in 2001 was spearheaded by major job losses in the forestry and wood products industries throughout the year.

Through the early 1970s (Chaykowski and Verma, 1992), relatively high tariffs protected most Canadian businesses from serious foreign competition. Increasingly, this protection is being removed. In the wake of a series of free trade agreements (discussed in more detail later in the chapter), Canadian firms have been forced to compete not just with each other, but with firms in the United States and Mexico, where production costs are generally a good deal lower. They have responded with massive restructuring and downsizing, causing many thousands of workers to lose their jobs, while others have been forced to accept lower pay, fewer benefits, and poorer working conditions.

As we'll discuss in more detail later, many of the jobs that were lost during the nineties, particularly manufacturing jobs, aren't expected to come back. While some jobs have been created over the past decade, most of them are in the private-service sector rather than in manufacturing. They typically pay a good deal less than the manufacturing jobs they are "replacing" and they are often part-time. Even if they are full-time, they generally offer employees poorer benefits and less job security than the manufacturing positions did.

The 1990s was a decade of massive job losses. (See among many others Donner, 1994:4). In previous recessions, those laid off were often younger workers with little experience, or older workers with little education and few marketable skills. That is no longer true. The past decade's layoffs have spared no one. Younger workers have been hard hit once again, but so have older workers (Foot, 1997). Public-sector workers, who were once comparatively well protected in times of economic downturn, are little more immune from layoffs this time around than their private-sector counterparts (Rose, 1995; Swimmer, 2000). Most recently, this has been illustrated by the actions of the British Columbia provincial government, which has announced it will be reducing the size of its public service by about one-third over the next three years. Nor are education or experience any guarantee of job security. People with graduate and professional degrees have been laid off, as have growing numbers of managers (see Payne, 1998). And, as just noted, in the year 2001, the once glamorous high-tech sector shed many thousands of jobs as stock prices plummeted.

With even prosperous firms that have posted large profits going in for large-scale layoffs, few people feel their jobs are really secure. Those who do manage to keep their jobs often find themselves working longer and harder than ever before. In recent years, there has been an epidemic of overtime—much of it unpaid. The result is a society in which many people are working far more hours than they want to, while others (the unemployed or partially employed) are working far fewer. For example, many university graduates are working part-time in fast-food establishments and convenience stores because that is the only work they can find.

Another important change has been in the scheduling of work. Until very recently, the majority of working Canadians were full-time employees working on a regular schedule—typically seven to eight hours of work per day, five days a week. The past few years have seen huge growth in a wide range of so-called "atypical" work arrangements, including part-time work, self-employment, home-based work, shift work, work done at irregular hours, and short-term, temporary, and contractual work. Unable to find full-time positions, a growing number of Canadians are piecing together a living out of two or more of these part-time or short-term jobs.

Taken together, these changes have bred considerable economic insecurity and frustration. People in large organizations undergoing restructuring are fearful that they may be the next to go. Working parents forced to put in long overtime hours are resentful that they can't spend more time with their families, and the added stress of long hours has begun to take its toll on people's health, as well (Shields, 2000), as those shifting to longer hours tended to eat more, smoke and drink more, and experience a greater number of depressive episodes. And young university graduates who can do no better than flipping hamburgers or pouring coffee are bitter over the waste of their talents and creative energies.

While the economic environment has been changing rapidly, so has the Canadian labour force. Once mainly male and predominantly white, it is now nearly half female and includes growing numbers of ethnic and religious minorities. It is to this changing labour force that we now turn.

THE CHANGING CANADIAN LABOUR FORCE

The **labour force** includes all employed workers and all unemployed ones who are looking for work. Today's Canadian labour force differs in some important ways from the labour force of a generation or two ago. By comparison, it is older, includes more women and members of ethnic minorities, and contains more part-time workers, more self-employed individuals, and more people doing all or part of their work at home. Over the years, the proportion of Canadians working in primary industries like agriculture, forestry, and fishing has declined substantially. Throughout most of the postwar period (Craig and Solomon, 1996:51), the proportion working in secondary industries like manufacturing has also been declining. In contrast, the proportion working in tertiary or service industries like utilities, trade, finance, education, and public administration has risen steadily. These changes, some of which have occurred fairly recently, have important implications for Canadian workers and their unions, employers, and governments.

An Older Labour Force

Canada's labour force is aging along with its population. Indeed, it may be aging even more rapidly than the population as a whole, owing to the recent sharp decline in younger workers. In 1978, the labour force contained 3.05 million workers aged 15 to 24; this group comprised 27 percent of the total labour force. By December 2000, there were only 2.68 million younger workers in the labour force, comprising just 16.6 percent of the total (Stat Can, Cat. 75-001-XPE: 2001). Because youth unemployment remains very high (12.5% in December 2000, or nearly twice the overall level), a major concern is young people's growing lack of work experience. Between 1989 and 1996, the proportion of people aged 15 to 24 with no work experience doubled from 10 to 20 percent (Statistics Canada, 1997). For those aged 15 to 19, the rate increased from 18 to 34 percent (Statistics Canada, 1997). One result of high youth unemployment is that an increasing number of young people are electing to remain in school—in many cases not because that is what they really want to do, but

With youth unemployment still very high, a growing number of young Canadians are reaching their 20s with no work experience at all.

because they believe it is better for their future prospects to be in school doing something than unemployed doing nothing (O'Hara, 1993:37).[2] Though the rate of full-time school attendance did drop slightly, to 56%, in 2000 (Bowlby, 2001), this figure is far above the 40–45% levels that were the norm during the early 1980s.

The aging of the labour force has other important implications for employers, unions, and governments. Motivating older workers can be extremely difficult in organizations with few opportunities for advancement (Reid and Meltz, 1995:34). In such situations, the challenge for HR managers is to make the work itself more interesting, or to find non-monetary ways of honouring older workers for their special skills and knowledge.[3] In the absence of imaginative HR practices, employee burnout can be a serious problem in organizations with a high proportion of older workers—a problem with potentially serious economic consequences for organizations (Minnehan and Paine, 1982) and for individual workers.

Understandably, older workers often place a high premium on job security (Reid and Meltz, 1995:34), since a job loss can be extremely costly. Older workers may have invested many years in an organization and may find it very difficult to obtain a new position. In collective bargaining, they are apt to put relatively greater emphasis on benefits, such as health plans and pensions, and less on up-front wages (Reid and Meltz, 1995). Within unions, they tend to be strong defenders of seniority and are often opposed to new workplace practices that go against traditional, seniority-based approaches. But because older workers generally have less need for up-front wages and a greater preference for additional free time (Gunderson and Riddell, 1993), they may be quite open to reducing overtime hours or even entering into job-sharing arrangements that create or preserve jobs for younger workers (CLMPC, 1997:47–48).

As more and more people born during the postwar "baby boom" enter middle age, **mandatory retirement** has become an issue of increasing concern for workers, employers, and governments alike. All provinces ban workplace discrimination on the grounds of age; however, all but two (Quebec and Manitoba) apply the anti-discrimination provisions only to those aged 64 and under, in effect allowing firms to force workers 65 and over to retire. Proponents say that mandatory retirement at age 65 creates jobs for younger workers and allows older workers to retire with dignity (Gunderson and Riddell, 1993:601). Another argument in favour of mandatory retirement is that most older workers have pensions that will provide them with adequate post-retirement income. Thus they will be in a better economic position than unemployed young people, who don't have pensions to fall back on.

Opponents argue that forced retirement is simply discriminatory and no more justifiable than discrimination on the basis of sex, race, or religion (Gunderson and Riddell, 1993). They also argue that at a time when increasingly few workers stay with one employer or even a single occupation, and when many parents have interrupted their careers to raise children, it is no longer safe to assume that a worker of 65 will have an adequate pension to fall back on. Others say that with growing

Mandatory retirement? It may create jobs, but for many older people, their work is their life.

pressure on public pension funds (Gunderson and Riddell, 1993), it is counterproductive to increase the pressure on those funds further by forcing people who would rather be working to retire, thus turning them from contributors to the funds into beneficiaries. It has also been suggested that where hiring freezes are in place, the forced retirement of older workers may not create any additional jobs, but will simply leave "survivors" with heavier workloads.

With human rights issues becoming ever more prominent, and as more aging baby-boomers retire over the next decade, the pressure to do away with mandatory retirement is likely to increase. But even if mandatory retirement is eliminated, most workers will likely still choose to retire at 65 or even earlier, thus leading to growing pressure on pension funds, which will have fewer younger workers paying into them and more retirees drawing benefits from them (see Sunter, 2001). The large number of retirements may well create skill shortages, especially in certain highly skilled occupations (Schetagne, 2001; Dohm, 2000), some of which are already facing such shortages (Galt, 2000). The aging of the work force and of the population is also likely to increase the already severe pressures on the health care system and other social programs (Sunter, 2001), which in turn is likely to increase pressures on families, who will have more responsibilities for care of elderly and infirm relatives downloaded to them due to government cutbacks (see Maxwell, 2001).

More Women At Work

Perhaps the most important recent change in the Canadian labour force has been the increase in the number of women working or seeking work. In 1978, just under 45 percent of all women 25 and over [4] were classified as active labour force participants. By the end of 2000, that figure had risen to 59.7 percent (see Figure 2.1B), and the number of women participating in the labour force had doubled, from 2.98 million to just under 6.0 million (Sunter, 2000). During this same period, the female share of the labour force grew from 36 percent to 46 percent (see Figure 2.1A). The growing presence of women in Canadian workplaces has forced employers and employees alike to become more aware of sexual harassment issues. Since many working women have family responsibilities, employers have also had to start paying more attention to work–family issues, like demands for workplace day-care centres, or for more flexible schedules or personal leave time to enable workers to attend to family emergencies.[5]

The increase in the number of working women has had major implications for unions as well. Women now comprise 47 percent of all Canadian union members (Akyeampong, 2001), and their presence has put issues like paid maternity leave, demands for flexible scheduling, child care, pay equity, sexual harassment, and affirmative action onto bargaining agendas all across the country, in addition to increasing women's profile within the Canadian labour movement as a whole.

For governments, increased female labour force participation means more demand for a broad range of anti-discrimination legislation, on subjects ranging from sexual harassment to equal pay and employment equity. (Bear in mind that women continue to earn substantially less than men, despite years of pressure from women's

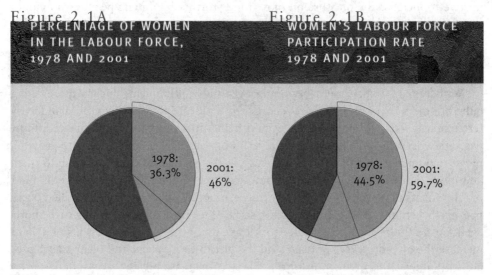

Figure 2.1A
PERCENTAGE OF WOMEN IN THE LABOUR FORCE, 1978 AND 2001

1978: 36.3% 2001: 46%

Figure 2.1B
WOMEN'S LABOUR FORCE PARTICIPATION RATE 1978 AND 2001

1978: 44.5% 2001: 59.7%

Sources: 1978: calculated from Statistics Canada, Cat. No. 71-201-XPB, page 17. 2001: Statistics Canada, CANSIM II, tables 279-0003, 279-0010, 279-0014, 279-0018, 279-0020, and 279-0023, as found on Statistics Canada Web site.

groups, unions, and others. In many cases, they also still face discrimination in hiring and promotion opportunities.) As the negative effects on health and family life of increased overtime become clearer (see Shields, 2000; Hudson, 2000), women both within the labour movement and outside of it may spur demands for changes to employment standards legislation governing overtime.

A More Diverse Work Force

In recent years, ethnic and religious minorities have entered the labour force in growing numbers, due to increased immigration. Employers must ensure that the work environment is free from discrimination against those of different ethnic origins or religions. As a result of the "duty to accommodate," which will be discussed in more detail in the employment law and labour relations law chapters (Chapters 7 and 8), employers may be obliged to draw up special schedules to allow for time off on religious holidays and for celebrations. They may also need to provide language training for workers for whom English or French is a second language.

Unions, which until comparatively recently were dominated by white males, also need to address the concerns of today's increasingly diverse labour force. As Galt (1994) notes, this may mean using immigrants to organize other immigrants, and being sure that issues of concern to immigrants, such as literacy training and anti-discrimination protection, are on bargaining agendas.

A growing number of workers with physical and mental disabilities have also been entering the labour force in recent years. Again, employers may have a duty to accommodate such employees' special needs by making their premises wheelchair-accessible, providing special equipment, modifying the workers' duties, or altering their schedules so they can keep medical appointments (see Carter, 1997). And as in the case of ethnic minorities, employers must ensure that workers with disabilities aren't harassed by fellow workers or supervisors.

More Part-Time Workers

Since 1976, the proportion of workers employed only part-time has increased substantially, from just under 11 to about 18 percent of total employment in 1999 (see Table 2.2). Of particular importance is the increase in **involuntary part-time work,** or part-time work done by people who would rather be working full-time, but can't find a full-time job. This rate has increased significantly faster than either the part-time rate or the unemployment rate. In 1976, 12 percent of all part-time workers would rather have been working full-time. By 1993, the proportion of part-time work that was involuntary had tripled to 36 percent, though it has since dropped back to 27 percent in 1999 (Marshall, 2001). The rate of involuntary part-time work has been particularly high among prime-age workers; in 1994, 45 percent of all part-timers aged 25 to 44 would have preferred full-time work (CLMPC, 1997, Table A2), while in 1999 (see Marshall, 2001), over half of all male part-timers between 25 and 54 were involuntary.

Table 2.2

PART-TIME AND INVOLUNTARY PART-TIME EMPLOYMENT COMPARATIVE PERCENTAGES, AGE 15 AND OVER, CANADA, 1976 TO 1996 AND 1999–2000

Year	Part-Time as % of Employment	Involuntary P/T as % of P/T	Involuntary P/T as % of Employment
1976	10.9	12.0	1.3
1977	11.6	15.0	1.7
1978	13.3	17.0	2.3
1979	13.8	17.0	2.3
1980	14.4	18.0	2.6
1981	14.9	18.0	2.7
1982	15.9	25.0	4.0
1983	16.8	29.0	4.9
1984	16.8	30.0	5.0
1985	17.0	30.0	5.1
1986	16.9	28.0	4.7
1987	16.6	27.0	4.5
1988	16.8	24.0	4.3
1989	16.6	22.0	3.7
1990	17.0	22.0	3.7
1991	18.1	28.0	5.1
1992	18.5	33.0	6.1
1993	19.1	36.0	6.9
1994	18.8	35.0	6.6
1995	18.6	35.0	6.5
1996	18.9	29.0	5.5
1999	18.5	27.0	5.0
2000	18.1	25.3	4.6

Sources: Part-Time Employment, CLMPC, Table A1 (1976 and 1977); Statistics Canada, Cat. No. 71-201-XPB, p. 5 (1978 through 1996). Involuntary part-time, (1976 through 1994) CLMPC, Table A2; Statistics Canada Cat. No. 71-001-XPB, page B-34 (1995 and 1996). Involuntary part-time as percentage of employment was derived by multiplying part-time as a percentage of employment by involuntary part-time as a percentage of part-time. For 1999, Marshall (2001). For 2000, Statistics Canada Web site. Note: involuntary part-time data not available for 1997–8. For 1997, the part-time rate was 19.1%; by 1998 it had dropped to 18.9%.

Part-time work isn't always a bad thing. In many cases, part-time work arrangements can benefit both employers and workers (CLMPC, 1997:43), particularly workers with family responsibilities and students attending high school or university. There is even reason to believe that working part-time rather than full-time may lower a person's stress level in some cases (see Marshall, 2001:24). Nonetheless, the growing incidence of part-time work, and especially of involuntary part-time work, raises a number of serious concerns. To begin with, part-timers' wages are generally a good deal lower than those of full-time workers—usually from 15 to 35 percent lower, depending on the industry (CLMPC, 1997:Chart 8). Given that part-time workers already work fewer hours than full-timers, the lower wage rates increase the often already serious economic stress on these workers and their families. This is especially true in occupations, like retail trade, that feature a good deal of shift work, and where the availability and predictability of hours is thus a serious concern for workers (CLMPC, 1997:46). Moreover, far fewer part-timers than full-timers enjoy benefits like occupational pensions, paid health and dental plans, and sick leave (CLMPC, 1997:44). In addition, from a national macroeconomic perspective, lower wages and benefits paid to a sizeable number of workers means lower tax revenues and fewer dollars flowing through the economy, which in turn means slower rates of job creation and investment.

Many employers like to use part-time workers because it costs them less. Nonetheless, the growing incidence of part-time work is far from being an unmixed blessing for managers. Part-time workers are frequently less committed to their jobs than are full-timers and may be more likely to quit if something better comes along. Low wages, lack of benefits, and frequent lack of job security may lead to lower morale and productivity among part-timers. Scheduling can also become more difficult when there are large numbers of part-timers, particularly in situations where there is also shift work.

For unions, the growing trend to part-time work represents a major challenge. Not surprisingly, a significantly higher proportion of full-timers than part-timers belong to unions (Murray, 2001).[6] Part-timers tend to be relatively less attached to their jobs and more apt to quit rather than to stay and try to improve conditions where they are. Many are also concentrated in the private-service sector, where employer opposition to unions has been particularly strong. The fact that part-timers often work in smaller organizations makes them more expensive for unions to organize, and some jurisdictions have also put legislative barriers in the way, such as the requirement that part-timers have separate **bargaining units** (LLCG, 1984:3–151).[7] While including part-timers in regular bargaining units is probably a more equitable solution, it can also pose problems for unions, since the interests of part-time and full-time workers may diverge significantly (England, 1987:10–13).

Polarization of Work Hours

Related to the trend towards part-time work is a growing polarization of work hours and a decline in the number of people working a "standard" work week of 35 to 40 hours. In 1999, only 59 percent of all workers put in "standard" hours, as compared to 65 percent in 1976. The decrease is the result of increases in the proportion of people putting in both short and long hours—increases which have been striking enough that at least one group (32 Hours, Budgetary Submission, 1998) has described Canada as "being stuck in a paradox of overwork and unemployment." Between 1976 and 1995, the proportion of people working fewer than 35 hours per week increased from 16 to 24 percent, while the proportion working 41 or more hours a week grew from 19 percent to 22 percent (Sheridan, Sunter, and Diverty, 1996:C-5).

The implications of this broad trend toward polarization of work hours are discussed in some detail below, in the section on overtime and unemployment. One such implication may be the growing earnings gap between the richest and poorest Canadians. In 1996, the bottom fifth of the Canadian population received only 6.1% of the country's total income—its smallest share at any time in the previous two decades. In contrast, the top fifth received over 40% of the country's total income (Adams, 1997).

More Self-Employed People

The proportion of Canadian workers described as self-employed increased by over one-third, from 13.2 percent in 1978 to 17.8 percent in 1997 (see Figure 2.2), much of this increase occurring between 1995 and 1997, before declining somewhat to 16.2% in 2000 (see Figure 2.2). The rise during the mid 1990s may have been a response to tighter EI eligibility rules that took effect in early 1997. It may also in part have been a response to the 15 percent decline in public administration employment that occurred between 1993 and 1997 (CANSIM, 1998), as laid-off public service workers set up shop as consultants. The importance of self-employment is underscored by the fact that between 1989 and 1997, virtually all employment growth in the Canadian economy took this form (Sunter, 2001). With the improvement in the economy since 1997, self-employment (along with part-time work) has leveled off somewhat, but the rates of both remain significantly higher than they were during the 1970s and early '80s.

Figure 2.2

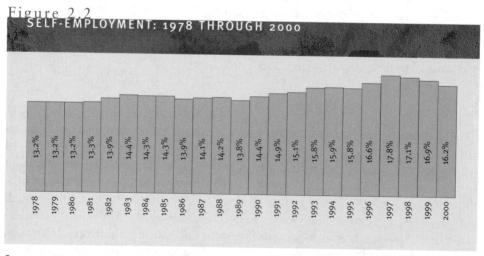

SELF-EMPLOYMENT: 1978 THROUGH 2000

1978	1979	1980	1981	1982	1983	1984	1985	1986	1987	1988	1989	1990	1991	1992	1993	1994	1995	1996	1997	1998	1999	2000
13.2%	13.2%	13.2%	13.3%	13.9%	14.4%	14.3%	14.3%	13.9%	14.1%	14.2%	13.8%	14.4%	14.9%	15.1%	15.8%	15.9%	15.8%	16.6%	17.8%	17.1%	16.9%	16.2%

Sources: 1978 to 1997: Calculated from Statistics Canada, Cat No. 71-201-XPB, page 23. 1998 to 2000, calculated from Statistics Canada, Cat. No. 89F0133XIE, as drawn from the Statistics Canada Web site.

The most serious implications of self-employment are probably for unions since, with fewer people in employee status, they must work harder to maintain their membership levels. There is also evidence to suggest that self-employed workers tend to keep working longer than those working for others (Sunter, 2001).

Other Recent Trends

Home-Based Work

Home-based work isn't new in Canada (see England, 1987), but its incidence has been increasing significantly in recent years, thanks to communications and computer technologies that make it easier for work to be done outside central offices. Between 1991 and 1995 (CLMPC, 1997:35), the proportion of paid employees doing all or part of their paid work at home increased from about 6 to about 9 percent. Home-based work was slightly more common among women than among men, and most prevalent in service industries like health care, community services, wholesale trade, and finance/insurance/real estate. In 1995, nearly half of all home-based workers worked at home because the job required them to do so. Those who chose to work at home most often did so because of better working conditions, other work-related reasons, or savings in time and money (CLMPC, 1997:36).

For individual workers, concerns include isolation and lack of interaction with other people, and the possibility of work intensification or overload. Employers often like having people work at home because building overhead and supervision costs are lower; however, there may be problems in controlling the quality of work done in this way (CLMPC, 1997).[8] For unions, home-based work poses severe challenges both in organizing workers and in monitoring working conditions. The challenges may be equally severe for government agencies, like labour ministries, that are charged with regulating employment standards legislation. How, for example, can anyone monitor health and safety standards (CLMPC, 1997) in a multitude of home-based workplaces, where workers frequently provide their own equipment and furniture?

Flexible Work Schedules

With the recent increase in the number of working women and dual-income families, **flexible work schedules** can be useful in helping people meet both work responsibilities and family commitments. In 1991, some 16 percent of employed Canadians had the freedom to choose their hours, within certain limits. By 1995 (CLMPC, 1997:32–4), this figure had increased to 24 percent. While there was little difference between men and women, married workers were a good deal more likely to have flexible schedules, as were non-unionized workers (CLMPC, 1997:34). **Flextime** was much more common in professional, white-collar, and service industries and occupations than in blue-collar or goods-producing ones. Nearly half those in management and administrative occupations had flexible schedules in 1995, compared to only 10 percent in processing and machining occupations. Flextime was most common in public administration and the finance/insurance/real estate industries.

Flextime is generally popular with workers. While many employers also find it of benefit since it can improve morale and productivity by reducing work–family stress on employees, some dislike it because it complicates scheduling decisions (CLMPC, 1997:31).

Temporary, Casual, and Contractual Work

In addition to the growth in part-time work, another important trend is the growth in temporary or contractual work, where a worker is hired for a short term or for a specific job or project on a contractual basis. In the year 2000, about 12 percent of all employees, but nearly 30 percent of those aged 15–24, worked on a temporary basis (Bowlby, 2001:82). Term and casual employment has become particularly prominent in the federal public service. By March 1999, over 18 percent of all federal public service employees were on a term or casual basis. For younger employees, this figure was much higher. Terms and casuals comprised about 40 percent of all federal government employees under 35, half of those between 25 and 30, and 80 percent of those between 21 and 25 (Fryer, 2000:10).

There is a great deal of variation in the sorts of contractual arrangements under which people work. Contracts for professionals like computer programmers or researchers may offer high pay and reasonable working conditions. On the other hand, contracts for garment workers assembling goods at home may constitute severe exploitation (see Lipsig-Mumme, 1995:208–209). What is common to almost all temporary and short-term contracts is that they provide little security and few if any benefits like sick leave or a pension plan.[9] These arrangements are popular with employers, since they allow them to avoid the costs of benefits and payroll taxes they would have to pay regular employees (Lipsig-Mumme, 1995:209). Many employers have also found that hiring people only for peak periods allows them to reduce their wage bills considerably. Still another advantage for employers is that temporary or contractual positions tend to be difficult if not impossible to unionize. In the federal public service, for example, those on terms of less than six months are not eligible to join a union.

Moonlighting

The incidence of **moonlighting,** or holding more than one job, has remained relatively steady, at just under 5 percent, since about 1990 (Sheridan et al., 1996:C-7; Bowlby, 2001:82), after increasing from a rate of 2 percent during the 1970s (Sheridan et al., 1996). However, the pattern of moonlighting appears to have changed somewhat. In the past, most moonlighters were people already employed full-time holding down a second job. Today's moonlighter is more likely to be a younger person, attempting to piece together a living with a series of part-time jobs that among them still may not provide the same number of hours as a single full-time job (Sheridan et al., 1996).

Implications of Recent Trends

Taken together, the labour market trends we have explored suggest that far fewer Canadians today have steady, relatively well-paying jobs with regular work hours and decent benefits than in the past. So many people now work under "atypical" employment arrangements that these arrangements have become all but the norm. A growing number of Canadians work for themselves, and even those working for others are more apt to be employed on a temporary, contractual, or part-time basis. While not all such jobs pay less per hour or day than comparable full-time ones, few provide workers with any real job security or offer much in the way of benefits. When added to the growing number of layoffs resulting from ongoing mergers and restructuring activities, the trend towards atypical employment arrangements has added to Canadians' growing economic insecurity. The trend towards atypical employment arrangements is likewise of concern to unions, since people working under such arrangements are extremely difficult to organize.

EMPLOYMENT IN DIFFERENT INDUSTRIES

In addition to working different hours, Canadians are also working in different industries than they were 100, 50, or even 20 years ago. In 2001, just over one-quarter (26 percent) of all Canadians worked in goods-producing industries in the primary and secondary sectors (see Figure 2.3). About 4 percent worked in primary industries like agriculture, mining, and fishing, while the rest worked in secondary industries like manufacturing and construction, the former accounting for about 15 percent of total employment. The service sector provided work for the remaining 74 percent of employed Canadians. About 16 percent worked in trade, 10 percent in health and social services, and 6 percent in educational services. Trade, information, culture and recreation, professional, scientific and technical services, and manufacturing experienced the largest employment growth during the year 2000. In contrast, employment levels actually declined in public administration, "other" services, educational services, and agriculture (Bowlby, 2001:69).

Since 1900, the changes in the distribution of employment by industry have been profound. As we note in the labour history chapter (Chapter 4), Canada was slow to industrialize. In 1911, just before the First World War, just less than 40 percent of all Canadians still worked in primary industries (Ostry and Zaidi, 1979). Of these, the vast majority (34 percent) were in agriculture. Manufacturing and construction employed 17.4 percent of the work force, while another quarter were in the service sector, including government, trade, and finance (Ostry and Zaidi, 1979).

Figure 2.3

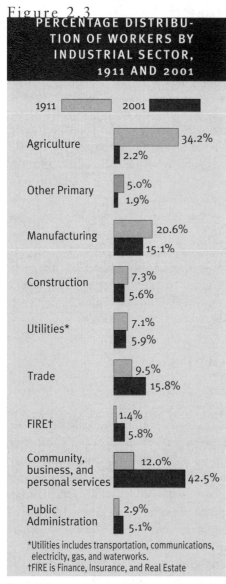

PERCENTAGE DISTRIBU-
TION OF WORKERS BY
INDUSTRIAL SECTOR,
1911 AND 2001

1911 [ ]   2001 [ ]

	1911	2001
Agriculture	34.2%	2.2%
Other Primary	5.0%	1.9%
Manufacturing	20.6%	15.1%
Construction	7.3%	5.6%
Utilities*	7.1%	5.9%
Trade	9.5%	15.8%
FIRE†	1.4%	5.8%
Community, business, and personal services	12.0%	42.5%
Public Administration	2.9%	5.1%

*Utilities includes transportation, communications, electricity, gas, and waterworks.
†FIRE is Finance, Insurance, and Real Estate

Source: For 1911, Ostry and Zaidi, 1979; for 2001 Statistics Canada CANSIM II, tables 279-0003, 279-0010, 279-0014, 279-0018, 279-0020 and 279-0023 and Catalogue 71F0004XCB, as drawn from the Statistics Canada Web site.

Between 1911 and 1951 (Ostry and Zaidi, 1979), both the secondary and service sectors grew substantially, at the expense of the primary sector. By 1951, the secondary sector accounted for more than 40 percent of total employment (26 percent in manufacturing), while another 35 percent were working in the service sector. The primary sector had shrunk to just over 21 percent, 16 percent being in agriculture (Ostry and Zaidi, 1979).

Since 1951, there has been a continuing decline in agriculture and other primary industries like mining. Much of this decline can be attributed to mechanization. But in addition to the long-term decline in primary employment, the postwar period has seen a significant decline in secondary industries like manufacturing and construction. Here, too, mechanization has made production more efficient, with the result that factories now require fewer workers to produce the same quantity of goods. Another important cause is deindustrialization (discussed later in the chapter), particularly since the implementation of the Canada–U.S. Free Trade Agreement. As Figure 2.3 indicates, trade, public administration, and above all the various service industries have come to account for a far larger share of Canadian employment than they did in the past.

The shift in the distribution of employment by industry has significant implications for unions. During the postwar period, employment has declined in manufacturing, mining, and construction—all occupations that tend to be relatively heavily unionized. More recently, employment has also declined in public administration and educational services, where unionization rates are extremely high. Most recent increases have been in private service industries like trade and business and personal services, where unionization rates are low and where organizing tends to be difficult. Unions are also concerned that the new private-service sector jobs tend to be poorly paid, are often part-time, and frequently involve home-based work (as in the case of insurance company employees processing claims from home computers). As we noted already, these are all factors that make service sector organizing even more difficult than it would otherwise be.

EFFECTS OF GLOBALIZATION AND TRADE LIBERALIZATION

One of the main reasons for the more uncertain economic conditions described in the previous paragraph is the globalization of the world economy. Throughout the world, over the past two decades, there has been a growing emphasis on international trade. Instead of simply producing to meet domestic markets, as many did in the past, businesses must now operate with a continental or even global market in mind. In Chapter 13 (comparative IR), we look more fully at the effects that globalization has had on the world's workers, especially those in the developing world.

Among other things, this trend has driven a return to more competitive labour markets, particularly in industries like the garment industry which, when they haven't shifted production offshore, have reverted to the use of contractors and homeworkers (Lipsig-Mumme, 1995:208). Exempt from labour legislation and virtually impossible to regulate in any event, such industries may indeed represent a return to the fully competitive labour markets of the nineteenth century (described in more detail in the management and labour history chapters). Now as then, such markets have featured extremely long hours, wretched and often unsafe working conditions, and abysmally low pay. Even so, as a number of commentators have indicated, competition from Third World countries where workers are paid but a tiny fraction of Canadian wages may still make these industries "too expensive" to retain in Canada.

This trend towards globalization has had important consequences for both businesses and workers. As Anthony Giles (1996:4) notes, world merchandise trade alone increased ten-fold between 1950 and 1992. National borders mean far less to business now than they once did, since it is increasingly easy for capital, labour, knowledge, information, and images, as well as goods to flow across those borders (Giles, 1996). The growth in world trade and decline in protective tariffs has clearly meant a greater emphasis on controlling labour costs (Gunderson and Riddell, 1993:215), since domestic producers can no longer rely, as they once did, on those tariffs to shield them from the competition of low-cost foreign producers.

Globalization has not been confined to markets. It has also had profound effects on the way in which goods are produced. For example, as Giles points out, quoting Robert Reich, precision hockey equipment is now:

...designed in Sweden, financed in Canada, and assembled in Cleveland and Denmark for distribution in North America and Europe, respectively, out of alloys whose molecular structure was researched and patented in Delaware and fabricated in Japan. (1996:5)

With modular production processes of this sort becoming increasingly common, it is now much easier for multinational corporations in particular to shift all or part of their production to countries where labour costs are lower (Giles, 1996). The multinationals' growing clout is one reason for the increasing internationalization of production. According to one estimate Giles quotes (Giles, 1996:6), multinationals now account for about 25 percent of total world production and more than 40 percent of world trade, even though they employ just 3 percent of the world's labour force.

Globalization has also had important political impacts, as the growing dominance of the multinationals, ultimately answerable to no national government at all, weakens the governments' ability to regulate their domestic economies and IR systems. Thus far, to be sure, globalization doesn't seem to have had the effect of doing away with distinctive national systems of IR regulation. However, in the longer term, there is a serious danger that governments will pay more heed to the multinationals' demands than to those of their own citizens, for example by weakening environmental regulations, reducing taxation, or cutting domestic social welfare programs to attract or retain transnational investment (Giles, 1996:10). Of particular concern to industrial relationists is the possibility that growing multinational domination of national political agendas will lead to a situation where, even in prosperous Western countries, fundamental workers' rights[10] are subordinated to economic development imperatives, as has long been the case in many Asian countries (Deery and Mitchell, 1993; Verma, Kochan, and Lansbury, 1995).

The Free Trade Agreements

An important element of globalization has been the formation of regional trading blocs in North America, Europe, and Asia (Giles, 1996:5). Major trade agreements have been implemented within each of these blocs.

In North America, a Canada–U.S. agreement (FTA) phasing out both tariff and nontariff barriers over a 10-year period went into effect in 1989. In 1994, the agreement was extended to Mexico in a new North American Free Trade Agreement (NAFTA). Since then, Chile has been invited to join, and there are plans to create a comprehensive free trade zone throughout the Americas (Craig and Solomon, 1996:49).

The rationale for establishing agreements like FTA and NAFTA goes back to the classical economists and their theory of comparative advantage, which you may recall from earlier economics courses. According to this theory (see Reynolds, 1982:90; Reid and Meltz, 1995:47), world output increases and, in the long run, everyone benefits if countries specialize in producing those goods in which they are most efficient. By helping to relocate production to countries where it is more efficient, free trade agreements, in theory, reduce costs and increase the real incomes of citizens in all countries signing those agreements (Reid and Meltz, 1995:47).

Proponents of free trade, such as the MacDonald Royal Commission on the Economic Union, predicted that it would bring a 3 to 5 percent increase in national income over a 10-year period, and that Canada would also benefit from changes in inefficient regulatory regimes, market structures, and work practices that would come into effect as a result of freer trade (Reid and Meltz, 1995:47–48). Opponents (Laxer, 1986; Cohen, 1987) saw major economic dislocation, like layoffs and even plant closings, as well as reduced income even for those workers who kept their jobs. An even more fundamental criticism (see Laxer, 1986) was that the free trade agreement would put Canada's sovereignty at risk by forcing it to harmonize its taxation, social, economic, and labour standards with those of the United States to remain competitive. By the time FTA had been in effect for a few years, others (i.e., Drache and Glassbeek, 1992; Robinson, 1994) were suggesting that it had helped lead to major deindustrialization and loss of manufacturing jobs. These critics also suggested that free trade had weakened the Canadian labour movement severely, both by reducing unions' ability to resist employer demands in the face of widespread layoffs and by increasing employers' ability to resist new union organizing drives.

Disentangling the trade agreements' specific effects on the Canadian economy is extremely difficult, because they didn't occur in isolation from other important developments in the Canadian economy, like growing competition from outside North America, widespread technological change, major labour force changes, and the severe recession of the early 1990s (Reid and Meltz, 2001). It is also extremely difficult to say how the United States would have responded had Canada not implemented the FTA, as might have been the case had the Conservatives been defeated in the 1988 federal election. Would the United States have retaliated with a series of non-tariff barriers, whose effect would have been to shut many Canadian businesses out of the U.S. market? Lacking a retrospective crystal ball, one can only speculate.

What can be said is that, whatever the causes may be, times are much tougher for many Canadians since the first free trade agreement went into effect. Unemployment has generally been higher since 1990 than it was during most of the eighties. As we noted earlier, hundreds of thousands of well-paid, relatively secure manufacturing jobs have been lost (Drache and Glassbeek, 1992; Godard, 1994). While new jobs have been created, most of them have been lower paying and far less secure; many have been temporary or part-time and a fair number have entailed self-employment. As well, the country's social safety net is much weaker than it was 10 years ago. EI benefits are provided to fewer people and run for a shorter period of time, and there have also been major cuts to health care, social assistance, and other social programs. While it is true that such developments might have taken place had the free trade agreements never been signed, at best they hardly suggest that the free trade agreements have benefitted most Canadians. Not surprisingly, the prospect of further extension of the trade agreements to all of North America is one which most Canadian unionists view with alarm.

Meanwhile, whatever the trade agreements' specific impacts may have been, the new economic environment brought about by globalization and trade liberalization has created significant challenges for Canadian businesses. Almost 80 percent of the establishments in the Human Resource Practices Survey conducted by Betcherman, McMullen, Caron, and Leckie (1994:11) report a significant increase in the degree of competition in the five years prior to the survey. Keeping costs down has been a major concern: about 65 percent of the responding firms identify reducing labour costs as a significant element of their business strategies, while an even larger number are concerned with reducing non-labour costs (Betcherman et al., 1994:21). Canadian firms have also been making much more extensive use of computer-based technologies (Betcherman et al., 1994), which certainly could reduce their future demand for labour, although this isn't necessarily the case. Similar results were obtained by Reitsma (1993), whose respondents identify automation, reduction of both staff and management, and product specialization as strategies most often used to promote international competitiveness. More recently, similar findings have been reported by Betcherman (1999) and Verma and Chaykowski (1999). Even given overall improvements in the Canadian economy since the mid 1990s, controlling labour costs to increase global competitiveness appears to be a primary concern for large numbers of Canadian employers and managers.

One manifestation of this concern for controlling labour costs has been a high (by historical standards) level of unemployment in Canada throughout most of the past decade. It is to this phenomenon that we now turn.

UNEMPLOYMENT

What Is Unemployment?

According to Statistics Canada, which conducts a monthly Labour Force survey, an individual is unemployed if he or she doesn't have a job during any given week, but has looked for work at some point during the four weeks preceding the survey.

It's important to remember that unemployment is not measured by the number of people drawing EI benefits. Some EI recipients are in fact employed, albeit only part-time.[11] Moreover, many unemployed individuals aren't eligible for EI benefits, most notably those who have just entered the labour force and those who have exhausted their benefits.

Different Types of Unemployment

It is useful to distinguish between different types of unemployment, since solving them requires different types of government policy. The three types of unemployment to which we'll refer are frictional, structural, and demand-deficient.

Frictional unemployment affects those who are changing jobs and have a certain period of time between their departure from the first job and arrival at the second. A certain amount of this type of unemployment (probably around 2 percent) is normal in dynamic labour markets. Indeed, its incidence may be higher in a strong economy than in a weak one, since people are more willing to leave jobs they do not really like in good times than in bad. Most economists agree that no special government policies are needed to deal with this type of unemployment, which is usually quite brief, often voluntary, and almost certainly represents a small portion of the total amount of unemployment in Canada today.

Structural unemployment refers to a situation in which there is a mismatch of available jobs and skills, or in which unemployed workers live in different locations from the places where jobs are available. For example, there may be a shortage of skilled computer technicians in Ottawa, while at the same time there is extremely high unemployment among fishers in B.C. It would seem that the logical solution here would be to retrain the unemployed fishers as computer technicians and then help them move to Ottawa, but as noted earlier, this is often more easily said than done. The unemployed fishers may lack the aptitude, the desire, or the education needed to become computer programmers, and in any case, family considerations and the expenses and trauma involved with moving may make this an impractical idea for many of them. To the extent that moving is a practical and economically rational solution, education and training, along with relocation assistance, are the government policies that best address structural unemployment. But it is important to recognize that in a country as large and geographically and culturally diverse as Canada, structural unemployment will never be easy to overcome. There is reason to believe that over the past year, the combination of high unemployment in some sectors (such as the high-tech and forestry sectors) with continuing shortages in certain professional fields represents an increase in the level of structural unemployment.

Demand-deficient unemployment refers to an overall lack of jobs, especially at provincial and national levels. It is this type of unemployment that is most prevalent during depressions like that of the 1930s, or major recessions like those of the early 1980s and early 1990s. In dealing with this type of unemployment, governments find that education and training by themselves aren't enough, though general training in basic literacy and numeracy can certainly help unemployed workers take advantage of what vacancies there are. Governments have two options available to them here. The first is broad, macroeconomic stimulation to increase demand. This is typically achieved through major changes in monetary, fiscal, and taxation policies or major public works spending, and was the approach taken in the United States and, to a much lesser degree, in Canada during the depression of the 1930s. The second option is reducing work hours to spread the available work around more evenly (Donner, 1994; O'Hara, 1993). Both are discussed in more detail in the chapter's concluding section.

Different Ways of Measuring Unemployment

There has been widespread debate over how accurately the official unemployment rate measures the true level of joblessness in Canada. Some (i.e., O'Hara, 1993) have argued that as high as the official rates are, they severely understate the real unemployment level.

Many economists are prepared to agree that in addition to those officially classified as unemployed, governments should also take into account those known as **discouraged workers**. Such individuals are unemployed, but have stopped looking for work because they believe there are no jobs available for them. Economists do not agree about how many people should be classified as discouraged workers. O'Hara (1993:35) suggests that if only those who have given up looking for work during the past six months are counted, the national unemployment rate will increase by about 1 percent.

There is also the issue of whether involuntary part-time workers should be counted as employed or unemployed. Earlier (see Figure 2.2), we pointed out that involuntary part-time work as a proportion of employment rose from 1.3 to 4.6 percent between 1976 and 2000. If each involuntary part-timer had been counted as half-employed, the unemployment rate for the years from 1993 through 1995 would have risen by more than 3 percent, since the involuntary part-time rate was more than 6 percent in each of those years. Even allowing for the reduced incidence of involuntary part-time work in 2000, the unemployment rate would still have risen by 2.3 percent for that year.

Recently, Statistics Canada, recognizing the complexity of the measurement problems around unemployment, has begun publishing eight different measures of unemployment, using alternative measures of the term. The most restrictive of these measures (R1) enumerates only those unemployed for one year or more. The most comprehensive (R8) includes discouraged workers, those awaiting recall, and involuntary part-timers. In 1999 (Stat Can, 2000), the 'official' unemployment rate (R4) stood at 7.6%. The rates for those unemployed three months or more and 12 months or more were far lower (2.8 and 0.8 percent, respectively). But adding discouraged workers (R5) increased the rate to 8.0 percent. And when discouraged workers, those waiting for recall, and the underutilized portion of involuntary part-timers were added (R8), the rate rose to 10.9 percent, or nearly half again the official rate.

Finally, we must note that the above rates are *averages* of the number of *individuals* likely to be affected *at any given time*. The average number of people belonging to a family affected by unemployment will always be higher than the average number of affected individuals. In 1998, an average of 14 percent of people were in a family affected by unemployment at any given time; for 1999, that figure was 13 percent (Sussman, 2000:10). Moreover, a far larger number of people are affected by unemployment during the course of any given year (see Sussman, 2000) than during the one-week reference period used to calculate standard unemployment rates. For example, during 1997, over 19 percent of individuals were unemployed at some point, and about 38 percent of all Canadians belonged to a family in which at least one person was unemployed. Newfoundland had by far the highest rates for both measures, with 39 percent of individuals employed at some point during the year and 58 percent belonging to a family affected by employment. The rates for the three Prairie provinces were much lower for both measures, but even there, between 13 and 15 percent of individuals experienced unemployment at some point during the year (Sussman, 2000:14).

Statistics Canada's use of these different measures of unemployment has done much to add to our understanding of this unfortunate phenomenon. While there continues to be much debate over the 'appropriate' level of Canadian unemployment,[12] the rates obtained by using the various alternate measures just described suggest that the unemployment problem is likely far more severe than most people realize, even in years in which the economy seems to be performing relatively well.

Changing National Unemployment Patterns

Overall, Canadian unemployment levels have risen substantially since the end of the Second World War. Despite the generally improved economic conditions of recent years, the 2001 rate of 7.2 percent was more than double the 1946 rate of 3.4 percent (see Table 2.1). The sharp increase posted in the rate during the last month of 2001, from 7.5 to 8.0 percent (Labour Force Survey, Dec. 2001), certainly does not augur well for 2002. For most of the first quarter-century after the war, the unemployment rate[13] didn't rise above 5 percent, as governments generally practised full employment policies (Morton, 1982:106). Since 1970, it has never fallen *below* 5 percent, and except for the years from 1999 through 2001 has been above 7.5 throughout the past two decades. Were the rate to take into account involuntary part-time workers and discouraged workers, as suggested above, it would have ranged from 13 to 15 percent or even higher during the 1990s. The effects of increased unemployment have been particularly severe for many because of the cutbacks in EI benefits and other government-supported social programs that have been occurring throughout the past 15 years or so.

One reason for the rise in unemployment has been governments' abandonment of full employment policies in favour of a concern with deficit and debt levels. Another reason may well be the recent wave of deindustrialization and restructuring discussed earlier in the chapter. Though the manufacturing sector has recovered somewhat during the past five years, it is unlikely to get back anything like the huge number of jobs it lost during the late 1980s and early 1990s (see Godard, 1994:421). Whether the service sector can make up for the loss of so many well-paying manufacturing jobs is at best problematic.

In addition to the number of people unemployed, it is important to consider the duration of unemployment, or the length of time people are unemployed. This statistic is of particular significance because those who have been unemployed for a long time often find it very difficult to land another job. In 1980, the average duration for all age groups was about 10 weeks (Gunderson and Riddell, 1993:625). In general, older workers stayed unemployed for longer than younger ones. By 1991 (Gunderson and Riddell, 1993:629), the average duration had increased to more than 18 weeks, and the proportion unemployed for six months or longer had increased from 15 percent to 21 percent. An ominous sign was that even in the good economic years of 1988 and 1989, the average duration of unemployment was significantly higher than it had been before the recession of the early 1980s (Gunderson and Riddell, 1993:628).

Youth Unemployment

While no group has escaped the effects of Canada's rising unemployment rate, the country's young people have been particularly hard hit. The official unemployment rate among workers aged 15 to 24 has been in double digits throughout the past two decades (see Table 2.3). Typically, it has been at least 50 percent higher than the overall rate (Gunderson and Riddell, 1993). At the trough of the 1982 to 1983 recession, it was more than 20 percent. While it has dropped somewhat since the mid 1990s, it hasn't dropped as rapidly as has overall unemployment; thus the youth rate is now over 80 percent higher than the overall rate, as compared to a 50–60 percent differential during the 1980s and early '90s (see Table 2.3). Again, it is important to bear in mind that as high as the official youth unemployment rates are, they would be higher yet were it not for the large numbers of young people attending school and university because they really have nothing better to do.

There are many reasons why continuing high youth unemployment should be of concern. First (Craig and Solomon, 1996:57), it's expensive to provide welfare or EI to unemployed young people, or to keep them in school when they don't really want to be there. (Though tuition fees have risen in recent years, they still cover only a small portion of universities' costs.) Second, unemployed young people are more likely than employed ones to turn to drink, drugs, or crime.[14] The cost of keeping someone in a prison cell or a drug rehabilitation program is far greater than that of providing that person with a full-time job. Third, as noted earlier in the chapter, there is an increasing number of young people with no formal work experience at all. The longer it takes someone to find a job, the more difficult the adjustment to the working world when she does find a job. To put it mildly, a situation in which large numbers of young people reach their twenties without obtaining any work experience can hardly be said to augur well for Canada's future economic growth or international competitiveness.

Unemployment Rates in Different Industries

National unemployment rates can only provide part of the unemployment picture. To gain a fuller understanding of that picture, it is also necessary to consider unemployment levels in different industries and parts of the country.

As Figure 2.4 shows, there is wide divergence in different industries' unemployment rates. For 2001 these rates ranged from highs of just under 11 percent in forestry, fishing, mining, oil and gas and just over 9 percent in construction to lows of 2 percent in finance/insurance/real estate, utilities and health care and social assistance and just over 3 percent in public administration and educational services.

Table 2.3

UNEMPLOYMENT, AGE 15 TO 24, CANADA, 1978 TO 2000, SELECTED MEASURES

Year	(2) Unemp., 15-24	(3) Unemp., All Ages	(2) as % of (3)
1978	14.6	8.4	174
1979	12.8	7.5	171
1980	13.1	7.5	175
1981	13.1	7.6	172
1982	18.6	11.0	169
1983	19.7	11.9	166
1984	17.2	11.3	152
1985	16.3	10.5	155
1986	15.0	9.6	156
1987	13.5	8.9	152
1988	11.9	7.8	153
1989	11.2	7.5	149
1990	12.7	8.1	157
1991	16.2	10.4	156
1992	17.8	11.3	158
1993	17.7	11.2	159
1994	16.5	10.4	160
1995	15.6	9.5	164
1996	16.1	9.7	166
1997	16.7	9.2	182
1998	14.7	8.3	177
1999	13.0	7.6	171
2000	12.5	6.8	184

Source: Statistics Canada, Cat. No. 71-201-XPB (1997 edition), pages 4 & 8, 1998–2000, Statistics Canada, Cat. No. 71-201-XPB (2000 edition), pp. 4, 8.

Reflecting the shift to increased service sector employment, unemployment was about 50 percent lower in the service sector than in the goods-producing sector. The comparatively high unemployment rates in most goods-producing industries pose a challenge to unions, since they have far more of a presence there than in the private-service industries where unemployment is generally lower.

Unemployment by Province

Provincial unemployment rates vary almost as much as do those of different industries. In 2001, when the national rate was 7.2 percent, provincial rates ranged from lows of 4.6 percent in Alberta and 5 percent in Manitoba to a high of over 16 percent in Newfoundland. Despite the variation in individual provinces' rates, throughout the past 20 years the provincial pattern has been fairly consistent. Newfoundland has normally had at least twice the national rate and the other Atlantic provinces are also well above it. Quebec's rate has usually been slightly above the national one, while

British Columbia's has on average been quite near it. Ontario and the remaining western provinces have generally had rates well below the national one (see Table 2.4). However, even in these comparatively fortunate provinces, the rate has almost never been below 5 percent since before the 1982 to 1983 recession. In the five eastern provinces, the rate has almost always been at double-digit levels throughout the past 20 years. West of Quebec, unemployment has almost always stayed in single digits, except in British Columbia.[15]

One reason for the disparity in provincial unemployment rates may be a high concentration of layoff-prone and sometimes seasonal resource industries in Atlantic Canada and B.C. (see Heron, 1989:xii). Another reason is the general state of underdevelopment in Atlantic Canada, where wage levels also tend to be a good deal lower than in the rest of the country (Craig and Solomon, 1996:56) and where small businesses have historically had a great deal of difficulty obtaining capital (Jackson and Peirce, 1990; ECNL, 1989).

Figure 2.4

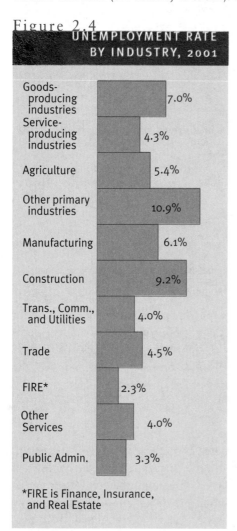

Source: Statistics Canada, Labour Force Survey, Table 279-0009, from Statistics Canada Web site.

PUTTING THE PIECES TOGETHER

As this chapter was being written, there were ominous signs that the economy was beginning to return to the high unemployment levels that plagued it throughout most of the 1990s, after a brief period of improvement late in the decade and at the beginning of the new millennium (see *Economist*, Aug. 2000). That economy was arguably the most difficult one facing workers and their unions at any time since the end of the Second World War. The wave of mergers, restructurings, and layoffs that has taken place over the past 10 to 15 years has left few unaffected. The turmoil has hit public as well as private sector organizations and shows little sign of abating as the decade closes. Many high-paying jobs have been lost in the manufacturing sector, possibly forever. To the extent that these jobs have been replaced, it has been by lower-paying jobs in the private-service sector.

Table 2.4

	UNEMPLOYMENT RATE (IN PERCENTAGE), CANADA AND PROVINCES, 1977 TO 2001										
Year	NF	PEI	NS	NB	QU	ON	MB	SK	AB	BC	CAN
1977	15.7	9.7	10.5	13.2	10.3	7.0	5.9	4.4	4.6	8.5	8.1
1978	16.1	9.7	10.5	12.5	10.9	7.2	6.5	4.9	4.8	8.4	8.4
1979	14.9	11.0	10.2	11.1	9.7	6.5	5.4	4.2	3.9	7.7	7.5
1980	13.2	10.8	9.7	11.1	9.9	6.9	5.5	4.4	3.8	6.8	7.5
1981	13.9	11.2	10.1	11.6	10.4	6.6	5.9	4.6	3.9	6.7	7.6
1982	16.7	12.9	13.1	14.1	13.9	9.7	8.5	6.2	7.7	12.2	11.0
1983	18.8	12.4	13.1	14.8	14.0	10.4	9.5	7.4	10.7	13.9	11.9
1984	20.4	12.9	13.0	14.9	12.9	9.0	8.4	7.9	11.1	14.8	11.3
1985	20.8	13.4	13.6	15.2	11.9	8.1	8.2	8.1	10.1	14.2	10.5
1986	19.2	13.5	13.1	14.3	11.0	7.0	7.7	7.7	9.9	12.5	9.6
1987	18.0	13.1	12.4	13.1	10.3	6.1	7.4	7.4	9.7	12.0	8.9
1988	16.4	12.8	10.2	12.0	9.4	5.0	7.9	7.5	8.1	10.3	7.8
1989	15.7	14.0	9.9	12.4	9.3	5.1	7.6	7.5	7.3	9.1	7.5
1990	17.0	14.9	10.6	12.1	10.2	6.3	7.3	7.0	7.0	8.4	8.1
1991	18.3	17.0	12.0	12.8	12.0	9.6	8.9	7.3	8.3	10.0	10.4
1992	20.2	17.9	13.1	12.8	12.8	10.9	9.7	8.2	9.5	10.5	11.3
1993	20.1	18.1	14.6	12.5	13.2	10.6	9.3	8.0	9.7	9.7	11.2
1994	20.4	17.2	13.3	12.5	12.2	9.6	9.2	7.0	8.6	9.4	10.4
1995	18.3	14.7	12.1	11.5	11.3	8.7	7.5	6.9	7.8	9.0	9.5
1996	19.4	14.5	12.6	11.7	11.8	9.1	7.5	6.6	7.0	8.9	9.7
1997	18.8	14.9	12.2	12.8	11.4	8.5	6.6	6.0	6.0	8.7	9.2
1998	18.0	13.8	10.5	12.2	10.3	7.2	5.5	5.7	5.6	8.8	8.3
1999	16.9	14.4	9.6	10.2	9.3	6.3	5.6	6.1	5.7	8.3	7.6
2000	16.7	12.0	9.1	10.0	8.4	5.7	4.9	5.2	5.0	7.2	6.8
2001	16.1	11.9	9.7	11.2	8.7	6.3	5.0	5.8	4.6	7.7	7.2

Sources: Statistics Canada Cat. No. 71-201-XPB (through 1997); Statistics Canada Web site (since 1997).

This structural shift has posed major challenges for unions, since private-service establishments are generally more difficult to organize than manufacturing firms. At the bargaining table, the tough economic conditions have left most unions fighting to hold on to existing wage and benefit levels, rather than seeking improvements as they generally did in the past.

Throughout most of this period, unemployment has remained stubbornly high. The Atlantic provinces, where the official rate has sometimes approached 20 percent, have been particularly hard hit, as have younger workers. Moreover, even those who have continued to be employed have had to adjust to profound changes in the way work is organized and scheduled. Far fewer workers than in the past enjoy any real job security, and there have been large increases in the rates of part-time, temporary, and contractual work, home-based work, and self-employment. These developments have contributed to a general feeling of economic insecurity and frustration among

Rural parts of Atlantic Canada, like the Newfoundland outport shown above, have unemployment rates far higher than the national average.

Canadian workers and may be a source of the renewed industrial conflict discussed in Chapter 11. The impending retirement of large numbers of "Baby Boomer" workers may help matters, particularly for managers, professionals, and others with scarce skills. But there is little evidence that these retirements will be of much benefit to the country's less educated and less highly skilled workers.

Of particular concern is the existence of such continuing high unemployment alongside a high rate of overtime work. On average in 1999 (Statistics Canada, 2000:35), over 18 percent of all workers—some 2.06 million Canadians in all, worked overtime. More than 52 percent of those working overtime weren't paid for their efforts. Over the first four months of 1997, the average overtime worker was putting in nine extra hours per week (*Better Times*, 9/97). Had Canadian firms hired additional workers instead of working existing ones longer and harder, the unemployment rate would have dropped substantially.

In addition to being a major drain on the national economy, continuing high unemployment rates are emotionally and even physically unhealthy for unemployed workers themselves, and for their family members (see Brenner, 1973; Carrothers, 1979). This suggests that reducing unemployment *should* be a major concern of governments. Regrettably, there is little evidence that any Canadian government, with the possible and partial exception of that of Quebec, which has for some years been actively encouraging reduced work hours as a way of creating jobs, has the political will to implement the sort of policies that could make a real dent in the unemployment rate. The question is, what in fact can be done?

Traditionally, economic theory has prescribed stimulation of the economy, through public works programs or changes in taxation and spending policies, as the best solution for demand-deficient unemployment (see Meltz and Reid, 1989). In the past, governments have used this approach with some success. Through the 1990s, this approach was essentially ruled out, owing to governments' continuing concern with debt and deficit levels. Though most Canadian governments now have their deficit situation in order, few show any enthusiasm for a return to the kind of counter-cyclical job creation policies commonly used during the early postwar period. Another concern is that major stimulation of the economy could damage our already fragile environment. Because of these concerns, many economists like Donner (1994) don't believe that stimulation alone can produce significant and lasting reductions in the unemployment rate. Nor is stimulation alone likely to be the best approach to structural unemployment, of which there appears to have been a resurgence of late.

Given the existence of large amounts of overtime alongside continuing high unemployment, a more appropriate solution might be to spread the available jobs around more evenly by reducing work hours. This solution, the one historically favoured by the labour movement (see Heron, 1996 and Hunnicutt, 1988), seems particularly attractive in view of the growing number of working women and two-earner families in the Canadian labour force. Reducing work hours would provide people with more time to attend to family as well as work responsibilities and might well make them more productive at work (CLMPC, 1997:26). In addition, it could conceivably provide jobs for hundreds of thousands of unemployed Canadians.

One option discussed by Reid and Meltz (1995:46) is the use of EI funds to provide short-term compensation for employees on reduced work weeks. This program has been in effect since early 1982 and appears to have functioned quite effectively during the recession of the early 1980s (see Meltz and Reid, 1989). Under the most commonly used version of this program, employees receive their regular wages for the four days a week they work, and an amount equal to the EI benefit for the fifth day on which they don't work. At current EI benefit rates, this would amount to 91 percent of regular wages for a four-day week.[16] The program has long been popular with employees and would appear to be far more equitable than laying off 20 percent of the work force during a recession (Reid and Meltz, 1995:46). While the policy is still in effect today (Reid, 2001), it has been given little publicity and appears to be far less widely used than it was during the recession of the 1980s.

In addition to the short-term compensation program already in existence, there are many other possible ways to cut overtime hours. They include increases in the overtime premium to discourage the use of regularly scheduled overtime; a reduction in the standard hours of work, after which overtime must be paid; and amending employment standards legislation to allow workers to choose to work shorter hours, at a corresponding reduction in pay (Reid, 1997). Another possibility would be to reduce payroll taxes for employers reducing work hours to create or maintain jobs. A number of European countries like France and Italy have gone even farther, legislating major reductions in standard work weeks, typically to 35 hours (Hayden, 1998). In Canada, some important initiatives have been taken by the province of Quebec, which has for some years been providing financial assistance to firms willing to reduce hours to create or retain jobs (Donner, 1994:42). While none of these options would be completely trouble-free, all seem preferable to the current situation, in which many workers are working far more hours than they would like to be, while many others are working far fewer or even none at all, in both cases often at considerable cost to their physical and mental well-being.

It isn't clear which of the above approaches would be most effective at creating additional jobs. At the end of the day, what may be more important than the particular approach taken may be the demonstration that Canadian governments actually possess the political will to mount a sustained attack on the unemployment problem. As indicated earlier, such political will has for the most part been singularly lacking.

QUESTIONS FOR FURTHER DISCUSSION

1) Compare the number of jobs you have held with the number your parents (or children, if you are an older student) have held. Also compare the length of time you have held each job.

2) If you have ever been unemployed for a fairly lengthy period (say, more than three months), what was that experience like? If you have ever been overworked for a fairly lengthy period, what was that experience like? Were there similarities between the two experiences?

3) Explain why, in general, unions fare better at high points of the business cycle and worse at low points.

4) What have been some of the most important changes in the economy over the past 15 to 20 years?

5) Why do many people argue that the changes we are seeing in today's economy are not simply the result of a cyclical downturn?

6) What are some of the major implications of Canada's aging labour force for governments? For employers? For unions?

7) What are some of the key implications of increased female labour force participation for employers? For governments? For unions?

8) Why are more people working part-time these days? What are some of the implications of increased part-time work for workers, unions, and employers?

9) Distinguish between frictional, structural, and demand-deficient unemployment, and discuss some policy solutions appropriate for each.

10) In his book *Working Harder Isn't Working*, Bruce O'Hara proposes a legislated four-day week at a little over 90 percent of the worker's previous salary as the solution for continuing high unemployment. Discuss the pros and cons of O'Hara's suggestion. If you agree that shorter hours are needed in Canada, but don't think legislation will work, how do you think shorter hours could best be achieved?

SUGGESTIONS FOR FURTHER READING

Betcherman, Gordon, Kathryn McMullen, Christina Caron, and Norm Leckie. (1994). *The Canadian workplace in transition*. Kingston: Queen's IRC Press. This study offers detailed evidence about how globalization and foreign competition are changing Canadian workplaces.

Giles, Anthony. (1996). "Globalization and industrial relations." In *The globalization of the economy and the worker:* Selected papers presented at the 32nd annual Canadian industrial relations conference held in Montreal, June, 1995. Quebec City: CIRA. Still the best brief discussion I have seen on globalization and its impact on the IR system. For a more detailed treatment, see Loxley (1998), discussed more fully in Chapter 13.

O'Hara, Bruce. (1993). *Working harder isn't working*. Vancouver: New Star Books. Yes— O'Hara is evangelical at times. But the case he makes for a shorter work week is compelling, and the discussion of how to bring it about offers a wealth of practical suggestions. A must read for anyone seriously interested in the work hours issue.

CHAPTER 3

MANAGEMENT AND
INDUSTRIAL RELATIONS

In today's climate, no group is immune from layoffs–including high-tech workers like the ones shown here. In 2001, the high-tech industry lost about 15 000 jobs in the Ottawa area alone.

More than at any other time in the postwar period, management has become the key actor in the industrial relations system. This chapter seeks to explain why this is so, while also outlining some of the new challenges management faces in an era of globalization, trade liberalization, and rapidly changing technology. We begin by outlining some of these challenges, then go on to examine the evolution of management practice from the early industrial period to the present. Special emphasis is placed on those factors that have led the balance of workplace power to shift in management's direction in recent years. Next, we discuss the strategic choice theory, along with some of its implications for the management of industrial relations. The chapter concludes by examining new directions in management practice.

MANAGEMENT'S GROWING ROLE IN IR

The growing recognition of management's crucial role in the industrial relations system represents perhaps the greatest single change in the field over the past two decades. Many earlier textbooks (i.e., L. Reynolds, 1982), and indeed even some recent ones (i.e., Craig and Solomon, 1996), do not contain a chapter on management. The assumption here appears to have been that industrial relations is primarily about unions and the government agencies that regulate them; to learn about management, one should take a course in that area.[1] Even when management *was* considered, its role in the IR system tended to be treated as separate from its other activities.

It is impossible to see how anyone can obtain an accurate understanding of the IR system without considering the role played by one of its key actors. As for the separation of management IR activities from other management activities, this may not have been a totally inaccurate reflection of the world of the 1950s and 1960s, when IR functions often appear to have been carried out in isolation from the rest of the firm's activities. Since then, an increasing number of firms have sought to link their IR and HR strategies to their overall objectives. Most recent Canadian IR textbooks' treatment of management (i.e., Anderson, 1989a; Godard, 2000; Thompson, 2001) has reflected this more sophisticated and integrated understanding of management's IR role.

At a more practical level, the increasing emphasis on management's role reflects a long-term shift in workplace power away from workers and unions and towards management. This shift has been more pronounced in the United States than in Canada, due mainly to a weaker American labour movement and less strictly enforced labour legislation. Nonetheless, it would be a mistake to conclude that such a shift had not occurred here as well as in the United States. Arguably, the shift *has* taken a different form in Canada; this point will be discussed in more detail later in the chapter.

Continuing high unemployment has probably been the most important factor driving the shift in the balance of workplace power over the past two decades. Other important factors include the privatization of many formerly government-owned enterprises, the deregulation of many previously highly regulated ones, trade liberalization, growing foreign competition, and technological change. Taken together, these forces have led to the emergence of an increasingly market-oriented economy. At the same time, provincial and federal governments, under growing pressure to attack deficit and debt levels, have weakened the social safety net. For example, EI benefits have declined over time as a percentage of the unemployed worker's weekly salary. At the same time, eligibility rules have tightened so that many unemployed part-time workers who would formerly have qualified for EI now do not. These changes in the macroeconomic environment have clearly altered the context within which collective bargaining takes place. As will be noted in this chapter and in Chapter 5, they have significant implications for the strategies of both management and unions.

Obviously, today's economic environment has made life more difficult for workers and their unions. But in many respects it has also complicated managers' lives. To begin with, managers have been no less immune from the effects of downsizing and restructuring than the workers reporting to them. Beginning with the recession of the 1980s, and continuing through to the present, many organizations began flattening their management structures. While this may have improved internal communication and productivity, it also meant that many middle managers lost their jobs (Osterman, 1988), while others found their responsibilities significantly changed. Again, like the workers under them, surviving managers have had to "do more with less"; a recent Statistics Canada survey (*Better Times*, 9/97) found that 31 percent of the country's managers had put in significant unpaid overtime hours during the first four months of 1997. Not surprisingly, in such circumstances, stress-management workshops appear to have become an almost routine feature of corporate life.[2]

There's reason to believe that IR and HR managers may have been particularly hard hit by corporate downsizing and restructuring. Often, the unspoken if not explicit assumption is that "people managers" are more dispensable than others. In times of crisis, they may well be among the first to be let go. Indeed, evidence we'll be discussing later in the chapter suggests that the thinning of IR and HR management personnel has been going on for some time. As well, many find that the nature of their work has changed—often in a way they don't like. In place of the proactive training and development activities that took up much of their time in the past, many are now chiefly occupied in terminating their fellow employees (Berridge, 1995), a situation few can find pleasant.

Nor are these the only pressures facing managers in the first decade of the new millennium. Globalization, combined with the almost instantaneous availability of information and the free movement of capital from country to country, means that the pace of decision making has stepped up considerably. Changes in technology have meant that competitive advantages, which once could be counted on to last years, may now last only a few months, or even weeks. And growing foreign competition, resulting in large measure from recent trade agreements, has put even more pressure on management to contain labour costs without compromising product quality.

Driving the wave of downsizing and restructuring have been stockholder demands for immediate, short-term profits. According to Kochan and Osterman (1994:113–114), these demands, sometimes reinforced by pressures from finance-oriented managers also of a short-term bent, tend to discourage managers from making long-term investments in human resources. Instead, they are all often encouraged to use the axe to boost their firms' current balance sheets. Whatever its other virtues, such an approach is almost certain to increase labour–management friction, adding further to the stresses on already beleaguered IR and HR managers.

Over the past three decades, there appears to have been at least a partial reversion from accommodationist postwar management practice to the more hard-line approach typical of the twentieth century's first decades. This same period has seen major reductions in the number of IR and HR management staff, and a diminution in their relative authority and influence within firms. These trends have come on the heels of a much longer (75-year) period generally marked by a progressive liberalization of management practice and a greater emphasis on IR and HR functions within firms. While it may still be too early to say whether the recent trends represent a fundamental change in direction or a pause within the longer trend, they are certainly disquieting to many industrial relationists and will bear close examination in coming years.

We can better understand recent management trends if we view them in the broader context of the historical evolution of management IR practice in Canada. Accordingly, it is to this evolution that we now turn.

The Evolution of Management IR Practice

Management's major aims are to make a profit and to maintain control of the enterprise. The development of management IR practice reflects management's attempt to achieve these objectives in the face of varying degrees of resistance by workers (and sometimes unions) seeking to maximize their wages and maintain or increase job security—objectives that most managers, most of the time, have seen as largely incompatible with their agendas. As well, particularly since the Second World War, management has had to operate within the constraints of a broad range of provincial and federal government labour relations and employment standards legislation. This legislation, often passed as a direct result of the labour movement's pressure on governments, applies to matters as varied as wages and work hours, the handling of health and safety issues and the accommodation of people with disabilities in the workplace (Carter, 1997).

When worker/union resistance has been relatively effective, management has had to compromise on one or both of its main objectives. In addition, there have always been some organizations that have largely succeeded at reconciling their objectives with those of their employees, and some industries where a cooperative approach is more common than in others. There have also, as we'll see, been periods when worker–management cooperation was easier to achieve and was thus more widely practised than at other times.

Charting the development of management practice isn't an easy task. As Claude George (1968:vii) notes, though there have long been managers, it wasn't until comparatively recently that people began thinking or writing about management in a systematic fashion. And where contemporary developments are concerned (Thompson, 1995a:106), accessibility often becomes an issue. Many firms don't want their management practices made known, for fear of divulging valuable information to competitors. Others want those practices kept secret because they don't want the public made aware of their ethically, or possibly even legally, dubious nature.

Despite these problems, it is possible to trace the broad outlines of management IR practice. While there have been variations, most of that practice has taken four basic forms: **paternalistic, coercive drive, welfare capitalist,** and bureaucratic.

Paternalistic Management

In Canada, prior to the country's first industrial revolution, relatively few people worked for others, at least on a permanent basis. Most Canadians were self-employed farmers, fishers, or artisans. Manufacturing establishments were extremely small by today's standards, with an average of only five employees per firm (Godard, 1994). Those who did work for someone else generally worked for a family member, friend, or neighbour; apprentices might well live in the master's house. The mode of control most employers exercised over their employees in this period is best described as paternalistic. In most cases, the owner of a business was also its manager and personally oversaw all work done on its premises.

Legally, workers had virtually no rights; servants who left their masters' employ without permission could be imprisoned (Morton, 1995:133). Still, while working for a relative or neighbour was no guarantee against arbitrary or even abusive treatment, craft traditions, community norms, and peer pressure probably provided some check on at least the more extreme forms of abuse and exploitation that characterized work in the early industrial period in Canada, in Britain, and in the United States. More important, most firms used limited technology and few sought to serve markets beyond their immediate local areas (see Commons, 1909). Indeed, most probably did not seek to compete on the basis of price, relying more on reputation and quality. For these reasons, the profit motive as such did not play the same role in pre-industrial business that it was to play starting in the industrial period (Godard, 1994), and thus it was not necessary for managers to seek to extract the maximum possible "value" from workers—the critical assumption of the "coercive drive" system.

Coercive Drive System

With the growth of factories during the early industrial period, many more people entered into employee status, and many began working for people they had not previously known. The early factory system also saw the growth of a new management class between owners and workers (Yoder, 1962) as factories grew large enough that in most cases owners could no longer personally oversee all their workers. The result was the rise of a new supervisory class (foremen or supervisors) between owners and workers, whose sole raison d'être was to extract the maximum possible production from the workers under them (George, 1968). A plentiful supply of labour and an almost total absence of protective government intervention (Yoder, 1962) made it possible for employers and managers to exercise virtually unfettered sway. The one partial exception here was skilled tradespeople, like printers and coopers, who might not always be easy to replace and who, in good times, could often set their own rates (Morton, 1995). However, women and children were often preferred to experienced adult male workers (Yoder, 1962), because their wages were lower and because they were generally considered more tractable.

Fear was what motivated workers, in a system where work was irregular and there was no employment security (Yoder, 1962), where most were paid barely enough to keep body and soul together (Morton, 1984), and where the six-day week and ten-hour or even twelve-hour day were the norm. Managerial control was exercised through ever-stricter monitoring of output and enforced through fines and even, on occasion, beatings (Heron, 1989). Not surprisingly, perhaps, such management practices and working conditions led to increased labour–management conflict, as workers sought to beat a system that appeared bent on extracting the last possible ounce of effort from them (George, 1968). With the formation of some of the craft unions described in Chapter 4, and with the Canadian government's growing if grudging recognition of working-class political power, some of this conflict began to be carried out in more organized fashion than had typically been the case in the pre-industrial period.

Scientific Management

The **scientific management** approach (**Taylorism**) pioneered by F.W. Taylor is commonly treated in industrial relations courses and texts as part of, or indeed the culmination of, the coercive drive system. Further examination of scientific management, carried out as part of the research for this book, has convinced this author that, when viewed as a whole, the system is both more comprehensive and more complex than it generally has been perceived to be. Viewed from this broader perspective, Taylorism does indeed contain some elements consistent with the coercive drive system. But it also contains other elements much more consistent with the welfare capitalism approach of the early twentieth century, which in many ways it undergirded (Anderson et al., 1989:6–7).

Taylor's aim was nothing short of a rationalization of the entire work process. Through detailed time-motion studies, he sought to break individual jobs down into their smallest and simplest components, simplifying each worker's task to allow each worker to achieve the maximum possible output from any given amount of effort. An appropriate quota, based on the results of those time-motion studies, would be set for each job. Those who exceeded it would be rewarded through incentive pay; those who did not meet it would be penalized (George, 1968). Nor was the scientific approach to be confined to job processes; it was also to be applied to such matters as worker selection, job determination, and the creation of a proper working environment. Only if workers and management cooperated in applying this scientific approach to all aspects of work, Taylor believed, could society reap the maximum benefits.

A crucial if highly controversial element of Taylor's program was his rigid separation of managerial work from that performed by ordinary workers. As he saw it, both inefficiency and frustration resulted when labour was asked to take on tasks properly within management's domain, such as "planning, organizing, controlling, methods determination, and the like" (George, 1968:90). Everyone would be happier and things would get done far more efficiently if management took care of all planning and control functions and workers simply executed the orders given to them by management—a situation referred to by Godard (1994:112) as the "think-do" dichotomy.

Like managers under coercive drive, Taylor sought to maximize worker output, and his system provided managers with the means to do so to a far greater degree than had previously been possible. The deskilling of workers associated with his "think-do" dichotomy was also consistent with earlier deskilling brought about, less systematically, during the early industrial period. Beyond that, Taylorism provided a basis for industrial innovations, like the moving automobile assembly line (Godard, 1994; Radforth, 1991), which essentially forced human workers to adapt their pace to that of machines.

In other ways, Taylorism differed significantly from coercive drive management. Appalled at the conflict he saw in late-nineteenth-century factories, Taylor sought to achieve worker–management cooperation—mostly through the substitution of objective quotas for standards arbitrarily determined by foremen. Granted, it was true that such a quota might still, in effect, be unilaterally determined by management, since management would be hiring the experts whose time-motion studies were determining the quotas. This problem could never be fully addressed without a worker representation mechanism legally guaranteeing workers some say in determining their terms and conditions of employment. Still, it can at least be said that Taylor's aim was a harmonious workplace and also one in which workers would be rewarded for superior effort and would share in their firms' gains. In these respects, his system represented a significant advance over conventional nineteenth-century management practice.

Particularly notable was scientific management's concern for the total workplace environment—psychological as well as physical. Such concern was especially true among one group of scientific managers initially known as the behavioural school. This school arose out of early efforts to, in George's words, "recognize the centrality of the individual in any cooperative endeavor" (1968:141–142). This school of thought became much more prominent as a result of the now-famous experiments conducted by Elton Mayo and his Harvard colleagues at the Western Electric Company's Hawthorne plant. These experiments had interesting and somewhat surprising results. They revealed that workers' productivity went up not only when lighting was increased, but also when it was *decreased*. Mayo's conclusion was that if firms wished to increase productivity, they should pay more attention to their workers' needs (Anderson et al., 1989). Accordingly, the behaviourists, now known as the human relations school, started to do just that, focussing much of their attention on such things as individual motivation, group dynamics, and social support for employees (George, 1968; Anderson et al., 1989). Their work eventually led to the development of organizational behaviour as an independent field of study (Anderson et al., 1989).

Welfare Capitalist Management

The link between worker morale and efficiency established by scientific management, broadly applied, provided the rationale for many of the far-reaching changes in management philosophy and practice that occurred between 1900 and 1930.

These changes ranged from the provision of employment security and company-paid benefits like pensions, to the establishment of various types of worker-representation systems and company athletic teams and recreational facilities.

A key development was the launching of large numbers of personnel departments in American and Canadian firms. Initially, these departments performed mainly employee welfare functions, as they had in Britain as early as the 1890s (Niven, 1967; George, 1968). Over time, they came to play a larger and more proactive role within organizations. As early as 1903 some writers were suggesting that, in the interest of maintaining labour peace, personnel (or labour) departments should address any worker complaints that could not be resolved between workers and their foremen—in effect serving as informal arbitrators (Carpenter, 1903). Spurred on by the example of innovators like National Cash Register's John Patterson, a number of firms set up departments to do just that. In addition to handling employee welfare issues and resolving disputes, some of the new departments were also used to administer suggestion box systems—another turn-of-the-century innovation (Holman, 1904; Patterson, 1901).

During and after the First World War, many firms transferred all or at least a great deal of hiring and firing authority away from line supervisors to the new personnel departments (Slichter, 1929). The move corresponded with a growing shift away from the old temporary employment system to one of relatively permanent job tenure—something that the more enlightened sort of manager had been advocating for some time (Fitch, 1917; Erskine and Cleveland, 1917). If a firm was going to make the substantial investment in workers implied by the provision of job security, it would make sense to use professionally trained people to screen and select those workers.

Personnel departments grew in size and sophistication during the 1920s. A survey conducted in 1930 (Mathewson, 1931–1932) showed that more than 80 percent of all firms were keeping labour turnover records by the end of the decade, and about 40 percent were conducting regular job analyses. In addition, personnel departments were responsible for administering a broad range of employee benefits, including paid vacations, pensions, life and accident insurance plans, stock purchase plans, employee savings plans, low-cost loans, and home-ownership assistance plans. On the development front, personnel departments provided or arranged for on-the-job training for new hires and Americanization courses for new arrivals, helped set up sports teams and other recreational organizations, and arranged night school or correspondence courses for those in need of them (Mathewson, 1931–1932; Slichter, 1929). As if all that were not enough, these departments were also responsible for keeping abreast of the growing body of employment-related legislation.

A number of First World War-era scientific management experiments had found little or no drop in productivity resulting from shorter hours (Nyland, 1989). Supported by those experiments, most major American employers brought in the eight-hour day during the 1920s (Hunnicutt, 1988). Canadian workers also saw their hours shortened, though not to the same extent (Malles, 1976). At the same time, many firms established "works councils" or other worker representation bodies, while others established internal promotion ladders based on merit or converted wage-earning positions to salaried status (Slichter, 1929). Like the benefit plans, the reductions in hours, works councils, and internal promotion ladders were designed to increase workers' loyalty and reduce costly turnover. Another equally important objective was becoming (or remaining) union-free. To this end, many firms used hard tactics to drive out unions, but then adopted softer paternalistic welfare capitalist practices to keep them out later on (Slichter, 1929:349).

The evidence suggests that welfare capitalist firms in the 1920s were generally successful in achieving their two major objectives. The decade was marked by a large increase in productivity and substantial declines in union membership rates, strikes, and turnover (Slichter, 1929).[3] Some contemporary observers (i.e., Slichter) feared that company benefits had become so pervasive as to sap workers' individual initiative and their drive towards cooperative self-help. Whether or not this was the case, few employers made any bones about the anti-union animus underlying their welfare capitalist practices. This animus, too, troubled thoughtful contemporary observers like Slichter, but by and large those working under welfare capitalist systems in the 1920s appear to have been happy enough to accept an "implicit contract" providing them with job security and relatively good pay and benefits in return for loyalty, commitment, and union-free status.

What is not clear is how many, even among male workers, were in fact working under such systems. Observers like Epstein (1932) have suggested that the proportion was small— perhaps 10 to 15 percent. Undoubtedly many workers, especially in peripheral regions like the American South (Hunnicutt, 1988) or Canada's Maritimes, continued to work under authoritarian coercive

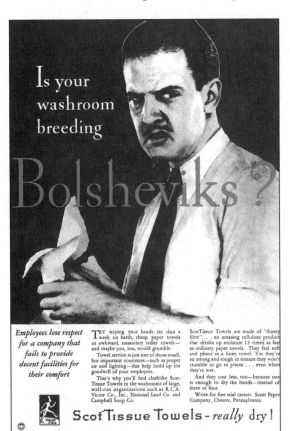

During the 1920s, the Scott Paper Company took advantage of employers' fear of militant employee action to sell its then-new disposable paper towels.

drive conditions.[4] There is also little evidence to suggest that welfare capitalist provisions were ever applied to any significant number of women. Nonetheless, welfare capitalism did have a lasting impact, as evidenced by the degree of conflict that ensued when firms started to abandon it during the 1930s.

With the advent of the Great Depression, many firms, unable to maintain their welfare capitalist practices, reverted to the hard-line coercive drive approach (Osterman, 1988). No better example of the change in thinking can be found than Henry Ford. Ford, known in the 1920s as the pioneer of the eight-hour day and $5 minimum daily wage, and as an employer willing to hire workers with partial disabilities, during the 1930s became notorious for hiring avowed criminals to beat up United Auto Workers organizers seeking to unionize his plant (Gannon, 1972; Lacey, 1986).

In the short term, reversion to coercive drive management led to increased workplace conflict. In the longer term, the result was large-scale unionization (see Osterman, 1988), which in turn led to yet another transformation of management practice, as management organizations were forced to adapt their practices to conform to the new labour relations legislation and the collective agreements made possible by that legislation.

Bureaucratic Management Practice

There is some disagreement in the literature about the extent of change in personnel practice during the early Depression years, prior to the legalization of collective bargaining in the United States. Some (Epstein, 1932) see abandonment of welfare capitalism as total; others (Balderston, 1933; Brown, 1934–1935) indicate that a significant number of welfare capitalist personnel practices remained in place.

In any event, by the mid 1930s collective bargaining had become a major concern of personnel departments (Cowdrick, 1934). In a parallel development, renewed emphasis was placed on supervisor training, since they would have to be the ones to administer the new collective agreements on a day-to-day basis (Cowdrick, 1934). With the legalization of collective bargaining and the signing of large numbers of collective agreements, many firms set up industrial relations departments to carry out collective bargaining and related activities, like grievance-handling. The growth of such departments in turn spurred the growth of large numbers of academic industrial relations departments in the early postwar years.

Under collective bargaining, management practice was based on having workers adhere to two sets of formal, codified rules: those contained in company personnel manuals, administered by management, and those contained in collective agreements, administered jointly by management and unions. Of necessity, personnel practice in unionized firms became quite legalistic, since collective bargaining is a process tightly regulated by legislation. Already quite bureaucratic in large firms—it would have been impossible to run a large, complex organization without clear rules and procedures governing production and personnel policy—non-union personnel policy also became more legalistic during the 1930s and 1940s, as firms were expected to adhere to a growing body of employment standards legislation covering such diverse issues as wages, hours of work, overtime policies, and health and safety procedures. Some unionized practices, like seniority-based promotion, spilled over into the non-unionized sector, as non-unionized firms sometimes found these practices convenient. In other cases, like that of Dofasco Steel, some of those practices, along with high wage levels, might be adopted as part of a broader union-avoidance strategy (Storey, 1983).

Collective bargaining certainly did not do away with worker–management conflict. The very early postwar period in particular saw a huge wave of strikes in Canada and in the United States (see Chapter 11 for details). However, with workers now able to strike legally and union recognition no longer at issue, these strikes were generally conducted in a more civilized fashion than pre-war strikes had been (see Heron, 1989), and seldom resulted in bloodshed. Meanwhile, industrial relations departments grew significantly during the postwar period as more firms were unionized and as collective bargaining was conducted over a broader range of issues, making both bargaining and contract administration more complex. A similar pattern of growth occurred in personnel departments, charged with administering an increasingly broad range of benefits, from pensions to insurance plans. Such developments were part of a broader pattern of growth of specialized management staff that was, perhaps, inevitable given many firms increasing size and complexity during this period. By the 1960s, Yoder (1962:47) was suggesting a ratio of one specialized professional and technical IR staff member per 133 employees as a minimum acceptable standard. A later survey discussed by Ash (1967) found a ratio of one IR staffer to every 115 employees. Where the IR function had been decentralized, this ratio was even higher.

While burgeoning benefit plans gave personnel departments plenty to do, there was growing concern that, stripped of their earlier conflict-resolution roles, which had generally been taken over by IR departments, personnel staff were becoming "managers of records" rather than of people (Owen, 1940–1941; Worthy, 1948). Such concerns continued into the 1960s (Heneman, 1960; Dunnette and Bass, 1963; Sokolik, 1969). By this time, however, others (Fischer, 1968) were predicting a more creative and proactive role for personnel departments. Anticipating to some extent the approach taken in the 1980s by Thomas Kochan and his associates, Fischer suggested that, in the future, the personnel function would assume a more strategic role in the overall management of the enterprise; that it would be responsible for furthering the organization, not just maintaining it; and that top management would become directly involved in the development and deployment of human resources.

A series of economic, social, and political developments beginning around 1970 was to create a quite different IR environment and lead to yet another transformation of management practice. The economic environment had become increasingly difficult as a result of inflation arising out of the Vietnam War and the energy shock of 1973. These new economic pressures meant that management could no longer "buy off" union discontent with large wage and benefit packages, as it often had during the early

postwar period (MacDonald, 1967). In any case, a new, more highly educated generation of workers had also come to look for more from their jobs than a paycheque.
Riots at General Motors' Lordstown, Ohio, plant in 1970 demonstrated the need for
management to attend to workers' intrinsic as well as extrinsic motivation. In the wake
of Lordstown and a broad wave of both active and passive rebellion by discontented
younger workers (Murray, 1971), many firms began instituting various **quality of
worklife (QWL)** schemes aimed at addressing their workers' intrinsic needs. Some
unions signed on. Others resisted, feeling that the QWL programs intruded on their
authority to represent workers' interests in the workplace. That debate continues
today. In the meantime, complicating matters for suddenly extremely busy IR and HR
staff was a new wave of litigation, arising from the broad range of civil rights and
employment-related legislation passed during the 1960s and early 1970s. Such legislation, in the view of Arnold Deutsch (1979), amounted to nothing less than a human
resources revolution, and meant that human resources would now affect every aspect
of the organization, from hiring to marketing to investor attitudes. The legislation
would also lead to the increased application of strategic planning and analysis to
human resource management (Kochan and Barocci, 1985).

While all this was going on, the American labour movement was running out of
steam. Largely as a result of the American Federation of Labour and Congress of
Industrial Organizations (AFL-CIO) president George Meany's lack of interest in
organizing the unorganized (Goulden, 1972; Winpisinger, 1989), the American
labour movement was, by the 1970s, representing an ever-declining share of that
country's workers. Politically, it had lost considerable clout as well, chiefly because of
the AFL-CIO's willing collaboration with the Central Intelligence Agency (CIA) in
overseas cloak-and-dagger work, Meany's support of the Vietnam war and major
weapons systems, and his attacks on anti-war protesters, whom he had accused of
being Communist-inspired (Goulden, 1972; Robinson, 1990). This reactionary political stance effectively severed the AFL-CIO's long-standing ties to Congressional liberals, costing it much-needed political support (Robinson, 1990).

Taken together, these developments would, at least in the United States, lead to a
much more management-oriented type of IR. This move to a "new industrial relations" was less widely adopted in Canada than in the United States. More broadly,
though, in both countries, some of the limitations of the bureaucratic approach to
management were becoming apparent. While many firms continue to use the older
approach, in whole or in part, many others have spent much of the intervening period
searching for alternatives.

THE SEARCH FOR ALTERNATIVES

It would appear that, in recent years, no single type of management practice has pre-
dominated as bureaucratic management did during the first quarter century after the
First World War. Writing in 1971, Marvin Dunnette confessed to being unsure about

the future direction of industrial psychology and personnel practice. Later, Paul Osterman (1988) would arrive at a similar conclusion. Noting the emergence of a broad range of diverse, even contradictory, human resource policies during the previous decade, Osterman said that while the human resource management system of many firms was clearly being transformed, the overall direction of that transformation was difficult to determine. After extensive study and observation, he could do no better than conclude that "something is happening and that the 'something' is extensive" (1988:61–62).

The quest to cut labour costs led many employers to go in for tough **concession bargaining**, resulting in some cases in two-tier wage systems. Other employers engaged in even more hard-line practices such as layoffs of previously secure employees, shifts of employment outside the firm (often to non-unionized establishments), increased use of temporary and casual workers, the substitution of machinery for human labour, or the relocation of plants to "union-free" areas like the American South (Osterman, 1988; Kochan, McKersie, and Cappelli, 1984). Other employers took an approach focussing on increasing employees' productivity by increasing their loyalty and commitment to the firm. Such employers might adopt employee-involvement or participation schemes, sometimes in connection with new job-security commitments. They also tended to go in for a variety of joint labour–management training programs. Other employers eliminated or reduced traditional distinctions between white-collar and blue-collar work (Kochan et al., 1984). In certain cases, firms simultaneously adopted hard-line practices (concession bargaining or the use of layoffs and the threat of relocation) together with more participative shop-floor practices (Kochan et al., 1984), thus adding to the apparent confusion as to the overall direction of IR and HR practice.

The Strategic Choice Theory

The "strategic choice" perspective on IR arose out of concerns of Thomas Kochan and his associates[5] that the then-dominant systems framework gave inadequate attention to the role of management, which in their view had become the dominant actor. While British IR literature (i.e., Gospel and Littler, 1982) had begun to pay more attention to management, the American literature to date had not done so. It was important, said Kochan et al., to appreciate that management now played a proactive role in IR, not the reactive role with which it had generally contented itself during the early postwar period. Most recent changes in IR, they argued, were the result of management initiatives. Kochan et al. were also critical of the notion, central to Dunlop's view of the systems framework, that the actors in the IR system shared a common ideology as a result of their experience working together to establish rules. While this may have been true with respect to management IR personnel and union officials working at the collective bargaining level, Kochan et al. suggest it doesn't take into account important decisions affecting IR strategy made at other levels, where there may be no common ideology or shared experience. The systems framework thus overemphasizes the importance of the collective bargaining level and underestimates the importance of other levels. It also tends to underestimate the potential extent of workplace conflict, not all of which can be contained or worked out through collective bargaining.

A key element of the strategic choice theory is that IR and HR policies and strategies are not made in isolation from firms' overall competitive strategies. The human resource strategies a firm follows or the type of stance it takes towards unions are directly related to such "big-picture" decisions as what product line it will enter or remain in, where it will establish new plants, and what type of new technology it will buy. To help readers visualize such linkages, Kochan et al. propose a three-level industrial relations strategy matrix (23) comprising a macro or global level, an employment relationship or collective bargaining level, and a workplace or shop-floor level. The matrix outlines the nature of the IR-related decisions to be made by all three main actors (employers, unions, and government). The authors hypothesize (36) that more effective and lasting changes will occur when there is consistency in strategies across the three levels and a match between the strategies of different actors. Instability is more likely to occur when strategies at different levels are inconsistent.

To see how IR strategies might be integrated with overall firm strategies, let's take a look at some possible employer decisions at all three levels of the strategy matrix. At the macro or global level, a firm that had both unionized and non-unionized plants might decide to invest in new technology for the latter but not the former as a way of putting added pressure on its union and possibly inducing workers to reconsider the value of union membership. Or the firm could also invest heavily in new technology at its unionized sites simply as a way of cutting labour costs, by substituting the new machines for human labour. If the firm were an American one, it could place new plants in a Southern "union-free" zone, both as a way of cutting its labour costs and to put added competitive pressure on existing unionized plants. While such an option is not possible in this country, a Canadian firm can seek to achieve more or less similar objectives by opening its new plants in remote rural areas where workers may be less likely to unionize. In certain extreme cases (i.e., that of the Michelin Tire Company in Nova Scotia), it may also put pressure on government to change the bargaining structure, to make it next to impossible for a union to succeed in any organizing drive.[6]

Overall, a key assumption behind macro-level management decisions under strategic choice is that **union acceptance** is no longer a given as it is in the systems framework. As just noted, such decisions may be designed, quite deliberately, to weaken the union's influence or even drive it out altogether (the union-replacement approach). Clearly, the possibility of operating union-free opens up to management a broader range of possible decisions than it would have if it assumed it would have to remain unionized. The same is true for firms not currently unionized. Under strategic choice, they can decide whether to accept unionization, should it occur, or to establish policies and strategies aimed at preventing it (the **union-avoidance** approach). Firms that have decided to try to remain union-free have the further choice of whether to use a hard-line approach based on fear, or a softer approach based on removing workers' incentive to join unions by providing union-style benefits themselves. Both types of union-avoidance approach have been used in Canada. Service industries like the chartered banks and Eaton's Department Stores have typically resorted to the stick (Lowe, 1980; Morton, 1995). While Eaton's refused to sign a first collective agreement, the banks used such tactics as the transfer of union activists, direct managerial statements to employees expressing disapproval of unions, and the sending of employer memos to employees in branches the union was seeking to organize (Lowe, 1980). In both cases, the basic aim was the same: winning through intimidation. In contrast, the Dofasco Steel Company of Hamilton, Ontario, has remained union-free in an otherwise heavily unionized industry by matching union wage rates, giving employees a profit-sharing plan, and sponsoring large numbers of social and recreational events (Storey, 1983; Thompson, 1995a). Very much in the spirit of the 1920s' welfare capitalism discussed previously, Dofasco has convinced the majority of its employees that, with the firm providing all these benefits, a union isn't needed.

A broad range of factors may underlie a firm's choice of hard or soft union-avoidance tactics. These include the degree of unionization in the industry, worker and community characteristics, managerial values, and many others (Anderson, 1989a). For example, Dofasco management, operating in an industry where unionization is the norm and in a community with a strong labour tradition, undoubtedly know they would face militant opposition were they to use hard tactics to keep their firm union-free. For the banks' management, the situation was quite different. To begin with, the industry had almost no tradition of unionization; thus there was no requirement to meet union wage norms to keep the banks union-free. Coming from an industry with little history of unionization, bank managers perhaps felt freer than would steel plant managers to engage in overtly anti-union behaviour. In addition, bank managers might well have seen the heavily female and part-time work force as easier to intimidate than would steel managers dealing with full-time predominantly male workers; while, for their part, the white-collar bank workers may have felt more ambivalent towards unions than would blue-collar workers. Finally, community characteristics would have played little role in the case of the banks, since the bank branches were scattered all across the various provinces instead of being concentrated in one location, as the steel plant is. The small number of employees in each branch may have been a further impetus to hard-line employer tactics, since workers in larger groups tend to be harder to intimidate than workers in small groups.

At the collective bargaining level, most ordinary management activities are not very different than they would be under the systems framework. Collective bargaining, contract administration, and the establishment and administration of personnel policies continue to be management's major preoccupations at this level. Even here, however, strategic choice opens up some additional options. Particularly in the

United States, the threat of relocation to a union-free zone makes it easier for management to wring concessions out of its union (even if it actually has no intention of relocating). More generally, with removal of the union now a serious option, "investment" approaches to collective bargaining (e.g., Fisher and Williams, 1989:187) aimed at building relationships and maintaining long-term industrial peace may assume lower priority (although this will not necessarily be the case).[7] Indeed, management may even seek to provoke a strike it knows the union can't win, with an eye specifically to weakening or even destroying it.

At the workplace or shop-floor level, the strategic choice theory points towards a significant increase in worker-participation schemes, some aimed at individuals, others at small groups. Within the bureaucratic management paradigm, motivational issues were typically handled indirectly, through collective bargaining or in some cases joint union–management committees. Strategic choice suggests a more direct approach to these issues.

With an eye to increasing both motivation and productivity, employers might introduce quality circles or other types of employee-involvement schemes. They might bring in suggestion boxes or introduce some other mechanism for obtaining employee input. More fundamentally, they could move to self-directed work teams responsible for handling many decisions, including personnel-related ones like hiring, disciplining, and firing normally handled exclusively by management. Work schedules might be changed to allow employers greater production flexibility. With respect to compensation, possible innovations could include profit sharing, gain sharing, employee stock purchases, and pay-for-knowledge, pay-for-performance, and incentive-based bonus plans.

There are a number of ways in which a firm's shop-floor objectives might be related to its objectives at the collective bargaining level. First, increasing employees' job satisfaction through encouraging their participation might allow a firm to get by with smaller pay increases than would otherwise be necessary. Second, if the joint participation programs succeeded and if the union were involved, they could help bring about an improvement in the long-term union–management relationship. Such programs could, unfortunately, also be used to circumvent the collective bargaining process, which is one reason why such programs are often problematic for unions.

Workplace objectives may be even more closely linked to a firm's macro-level ones. This is perhaps most obviously the case when employee participation programs are introduced as part of a union-replacement strategy (another reason why unions must be cautious about endorsing such programs), or in connection with massive layoffs, as in the horrifying but instructive Eastern Airlines case (Woodworth and Meek, 1995). In non-union firms, employee participation schemes may be linked to the firms' desire to remain union-free. Even when such schemes are not part of a broader anti-union strategy, they may well serve to reduce the extent to which the union functions primarily as an advocate for workers by, in effect, making the union co-manager of the enterprise. Some (Halpern, 1984; Verma, 1995) suggest that such a change in the union's role may be best for all concerned. Others (Godard, 1991) are more skeptical, and some (Wells, 1993) are totally opposed to such a change, believing strong unions to be incompatible with employee participation schemes and other elements of what is now known as the progressive human resource management paradigm.

Strategic Choice in Canada

It is possible to argue, as Thompson (1995a) and others have, that the strategic choice theory has not thus far applied to Canada. Certainly no one could deny that Canadian union rates have not gone down as they have in the United States, or that a great many Canadian employers have been reluctant to use the sort of hard-line union-replacement and union-avoidance approaches taken by many of their American counterparts over the past two decades.[8] In addition, much of the descriptive evidence cited by Kochan et al. in support of the strategic choice theory is highly U.S.-specific. Nonetheless, there are reasons to believe that the strategic choice theory may be applicable to the Canadian situation. We would argue that the different results observed in Canada may have come about not because the theory itself does not apply, but because it has been operating in a different environment, one that has often dictated different choices regarding such issues as a firm's strategy towards unions.

The most important environmental difference is the existence, in the United States, of virtual "union-free" zones, particularly in the South and West. These zones were created as a result of the "right-to-work" provisions of the 1947 *Taft-Hartley* amendments to the *National Labour Relations Act*, which allowed any state that so wished to opt out of union security provisions. From a strategic perspective the existence of **"right-to-work"** states has made union-replacement strategies a viable option for U.S. employers. In addition, even employers not immediately seeking to drive their unions out can always use the threat of relocation to extract greater concessions at the bargaining table. Lacking the equivalent of a "right-to-work" zone, Canadian employers have historically found it far more difficult to use union-replacement strategies. The generally stricter Canadian labour board enforcement of unfair labour practice legislation (Bruce, 1990) also makes such strategies more problematic for Canadian employers.

Another important difference is the existence in Canada—in large measure as the result of past efforts of the labour movement and its political allies—of publicly funded medical care and various social programs, including a more generous unemployment insurance program (even after recent cuts).[9] Canada's more generous social safety net has arguably allowed Canadian unions to resist employer demands for concessions more firmly than their American counterparts realistically can, thereby making concession bargaining likelier in the United States than here.

In the U.S. environment, then, marked by a large "union-free" zone and generally lax enforcement of labour legislation, hard-line anti-union approaches are easy and relatively "cheap" for employers. Up until now at least, such strategies have been harder to pursue here, and also relatively "costly" if pursued. The result has been that employers have tended to pursue other strategies, among them mergers, reorganizations, large-scale layoffs, changes in product line, plant closings, and technological changes (Godard, 1995). In addition, the move from full-time to part-time work has been far more pronounced in Canada than in the U.S. (see Marshall, 2001). While such strategies may not lead to a labour board complaint, it would be a mistake to think of them as relatively benign just because most have not entailed a frontal attack on a union. All that these strategies suggest is that given the different Canadian political environment, management here has chosen different ways to cut labour costs than those often used in the United States. The fundamental direction and effect of these changes have remained the same.

CURRENT MANAGEMENT PRACTICE: REALLY NEW OR MORE OF THE SAME?

In the previous edition of this book we suggested that the overall direction of Canadian management practice appeared to be unclear. In our view, this is still the case. It still seems that no single model of management practice prevails throughout the economy.

As is noted in more detail below, a relatively small number of firms appear to have comprehensively adopted the principles of **progressive human resource management** (defined in the next section). A larger number of firms have adopted certain progressive HRM elements, combining them with elements of traditional management practice. And in many firms, particularly smaller ones in the private service sector, traditional management practice (including many elements of the coercive drive approach discussed earlier in this chapter) continues to hold sway.

Although the overall direction of management practice remains unclear, there are now somewhat clearer indications as to the conditions under which progressive HRM practices are likely to be adopted, and the impact that these practices have on such measures of firm performance as productivity and profitability. In the next section, after examining some key trends in current management practice, we consider these issues in detail.

Some Key Trends

Downsizing and Restructuring

In the previous edition (see especially Chapters 2, 4, and 9), we noted that downsizing and restructuring became facts of Canadian economic life during the 1990s. The decade saw manufacturing firms and public sector organizations alike shed hundreds of thousands of jobs across the country.

More recently, there have been signs that the decline in manufacturing employment has started to level off. Also, many (though not all) governments find themselves in a hiring mode after years and years of cutbacks. But this doesn't mean that downsizing and restructuring activities have ended. They have merely been shifted—to a degree—to different sectors of the economy. Today the high-tech sector, recently so strongly touted as the growth engine for the entire economy, has fallen on hard times. High-tech giants like Nortel have shed large portions of their work force as their share prices have tumbled. In the wake of the September 11, 2001 terrorist attacks, the airline industry has undergone a similar contraction.

Even in many parts of the old economy, as Betcherman (1999:34) has pointed out, "ongoing rationalization and short-term performance appear to be at a premium." The result is that a fair amount of downsizing has continued, even in profitable and well-performing organizations in industries that are not contracting. Forced to respond to continuing competitive pressures, the organizations studied by Verma and Chaykowski (1999b) did so in part by shedding older, lower-value-added operations, especially those falling outside core business areas. Operations that were retained were often restructured through such means as geographic consolidation, removal of layers of management, and the introduction of new technology.

Overall, a key lesson arising from the recent literature on Canadian management is that, despite all the publicity progressive HRM has received in recent years, much Canadian management practice remains surprisingly traditional (Downie & Coates, 1993; Betcherman, 1999). In traditionally-managed firms, cost reduction continues to be an important, even key element of management strategy. Often, such cost reduction is still achieved through what Downie and Coates (1993:v) describe as the "blunt instrument of downsizing,"even in the face of growing evidence that downsizing may not be at all compatible with effective human resource utilization and quality improvement (Wagar, 1999; Betcherman, 1999; Lam and Reshef, 2000).

"I am afraid this is not a propitious time for a raise, Adams. Or, as my father would have said, why the devil should I give you a raise? Or, as my grandfather would have said, GET THE HELL OUT OF HERE!"

Decline in Number of IR/HR Staff and Change in Their Work

Over the years, the relative numbers of IR and HR staff have been declining, and the focus of their activities has been changing.

During the 1960s, as noted earlier, an IR staff to total staff ratio of about 1:125 appears to have been the norm. In contrast, a survey conducted by Thompson (1995 and 2001) found a ratio of 1:497. Only 22 percent of the firms surveyed had a ratio greater than 1:200, and 37 percent had more than 600 employees per IR staff member. In addition to increasing the stress on IR managers, the shrinking of IR departments has weakened the position of the management group most strongly committed to union acceptance and collective bargaining (see Kochan et al., 1984; Osterman, 1988). It may also have led to increased union–management friction, as manifested in such ways as increased grievance activity, as a result of the unions' frustration at their poorer 'servicing' by management (Downie & Coates, 1993:32).

Particularly for IR managers, preparation for bargaining, the conduct of negotiations, and contract administration continue to be core activities (Thompson, 2001). Nonetheless, both in Britain and North America, IR and HR staff are spending an increasing share of their time on activities associated with firms in decline (Berridge, 1995; Koch and Barocci, 1985), like downsizing employees or arranging for retraining and career or outplacement counselling.

Strategic Role for IR/HR Departments

In the past, IR and HR departments have sometimes operated in relative isolation from the rest of the organization. Increasingly, this is no longer the case (Kochan, et al., 1984; Downie & Coates, 1993). The role of these departments has become more strategic and business-driven, and they are expected to contribute to the organization's bottom line (Betcherman, 1999; Downie & Coates, 1993). A related trend is the integration of IR and HR departments. Taken together with the downsizing noted above, these trends have led management to become less concerned with union–management issues, which in turn has made it more difficult to build cooperative relationships with unions (Downie & Coates, 1993).

More Line-driven Type of IR/HR

Much responsibility for IR and other 'people' issues is now devolved to line managers. This has led to a shift in the role of IR/HR managers. Instead of directing line managers, they have to come to play more of a facilitative or advisory role (Downie & Coates, 1993; Fryer, 2001:47). While the new partnerships between IR/HR managers may have yielded many benefits, there have also been difficulties. Not all line managers are temperamentally suited to their new roles as people managers, while others lack the requisite interpersonal or communications skills or knowledge of labour relations and human resource management (see Fryer, 2001:47 and Macleod, 2000). Resenting the new roles they're expected to play, some have become "roadblocks to change." Likewise, some IR/HR managers have had difficulty adjusting to their new roles (Downie & Coates, 1993:vi).

Limited Change to Collective Bargaining

It would appear that changes to the collective bargaining process have been relatively limited over the past decade (Downie & Coates, 1993; Verma & Chaykowski,
1999b). In particular, there appears to have been only a marginal trend toward the
formation of joint union–management alliances (Verma & Chaykowski, 1999b;
Chaykowski and Verma, 1992). While there *has* been some movement toward a more
cooperative approach to bargaining, this movement has been gradual and incremental (Verma & Chaykowski, 1999a). In general, both parties have, with some modest
exceptions, remained wedded to traditional, adversarial approaches to collective
bargaining (Kumar, Murray & Schetagne, 1998; Downie & Coates, 1993).

TWO TYPES OF HRM

While this is admittedly an oversimplification, one can identify two broad patterns of
human resource management arising out of the strategic choice theory and the work
of other writers such as Pfeffer (1994) and Verma & Chaykowski (1999a). The first,
referred to by Verma and Chaykowski as the "low road" approach and by Godard
(2001) as the "disposable workplace" approach, entails obtaining competitive advantage primarily by minimizing labour costs. In theory, Canadian firms wishing to take
this approach might cut wages to levels prevailing in the countries with which we're
competing. For a variety of reasons, including the big disparities between Canadian
wages and those in many competitor countries, the existence here of minimum wage
and other protective employment standards legislation, and the likelihood of severe
labour–management conflict or even social chaos if such cuts were made, severe wage
cuts are generally not feasible, particularly in unionized establishments (see Verma &
Chaykowski, 1999a:11).[10] Instead, Canadian employers have generally relied on
other cost-cutting methods such as layoffs, the substitution of new technology for
human labour, relocation, outsourcing, or in some cases **two-tier wage systems**
whereby new hires earn substantially lower wages than existing workers. But whatever the method, employee involvement and other methods of building trust and
commitment are generally of little interest or relevance to such employers. As is the
case under the coercive drive approach to management discussed earlier in the chapter, fear of job loss is usually enough to induce employees to work longer and harder (see Godard, 2001:42).

Verma and Chaykowski's "high-road" approach involves competing on the basis
of a differentiation strategy emphasizing the development of particular niche markets,
high product quality, and the ability to develop new products and fill specialized
orders quickly. Far from adopting a low-wage strategy, firms taking this approach
may even need to raise wages to attract and maintain the highly-skilled, dedicated
people they'll need if the approach is to succeed. Such organizations also tend to put
heavy emphasis on training, to go in for increased employee involvement and flexible

forms of work organization such as team-based work, and to adopt incentive-based pay schemes that support their overall objectives (see Verma & Chaykowski, 1999a:12). Overall, these organizations seek to provide employees with positive motivation to keep learning and to improve their performance.

Employee involvement schemes, improved workplace design and job enrichment which result in a richer work experience for employees, and certain types of enlightened personnel policies such as internal justice systems and employee stock ownership plans, have all been characterized by John Godard (1994:146–7) as part of the progressive human resource management paradigm. The idea here is that if workers are able to achieve their individual potential and find greater satisfaction on the job, the firm will benefit through increased productivity and, eventually, higher profits as well.

Like the welfare capitalism programs of the 1920s, today's progressive HRM regimes provide generous benefits as a way of building employees' loyalty to the organization. But many go far beyond welfare capitalism, as for example by eliminating most layers of management and redesigning work so that most of it is done in autonomous or semi-autonomous work teams (Godard, 1994). Generally this kind of redesign entails a fundamental change in the role of management, particularly lower- and middle-level managers, who in traditional organizations were expected to provide close oversight of workers' performance (the "guard dog" function). With the emphasis on trust and many fewer managers on payroll, such close oversight is no longer possible or even desirable (Halpern, 1984 and 1992). Now the manager's role is much more of a facilitative one. He or she is there to help team members solve their own problems, rather than to keep tabs on them. In some cases (Halpern, 1984), the work teams not only control the pace of work and assignment of particular tasks, but have considerable say over the hiring of new team members and the disciplining of poorly performing ones. However, it should be noted that organizations adopting such sweeping job redesign remain a very small minority within the broader Canadian context.

A Closer Look at Progressive HRM

How Widely Has Progressive HRM Been Adopted?

In the first edition of this book, we noted that while a fair number of firms have adopted various progressive HRM practices, this adoption has generally been more or less piecemeal. Since the mid 1990s, there appears to have been somewhat broader adoption of these practices. But again, the organizations that have adopted progressive HRM in any comprehensive fashion remain a distinct minority.

Downie and Coates (1993) suggest that, overall, Canadian employers' response to change has been relatively conservative, featuring mainly downsizing and adoption of new technology, and that the rhetoric around workplace change has been somewhat inflated. Nonetheless, they see some real change in management style, particularly with respect to information-sharing.

In a 1996 study, Terry Wagar found that there continues to be substantial variation among Canadian employers with respect to the adoption of progressive HRM practices and employee involvement schemes. A majority of the firms he surveyed had brought in problem-solving groups, joint employee involvement programs, and total quality management (TQM). About 40 percent of the sample had gone in for autonomous work teams, job-sharing, and job enlargement/enrichment. A smaller proportion had gone in for quality circles, quality of worklife (QWL) programs, or incentive-based compensation schemes such as profit-sharing or employee stock ownership plans.

Gordon Betcherman (1999) found that while many of the firms in the Workplace Training Survey had brought in various HRM innovations, a majority continued to practice 'traditional' HRM overall.[11] Formal communications and team-based systems were adopted by a majority of the sample, and formal training and employee involvement by slightly less than half. Like Wagar, Betcherman found variable compensation schemes the least common type of innovation, adopted by only slightly over a quarter of the sample. His work appears to confirm patterns of piecemeal adoption found in earlier studies such as those of Smith (1993) and Godard (1995).

Where Is Progressive HRM More Likely To Be Adopted?

Both Human Resource Practices Survey data and Workplace Training Survey (WTS) data discussed by Betcherman (1999:34–5) indicate that progressive HRM practices are more likely to be adopted in larger, more established firms. The WTS found that formal communications and information-sharing, team-based work systems, formal employee involvement programs, formal training, and variable compensation schemes were all more likely to occur in organizations with 100 or more employees than in those with fewer than 20. In the case of training, the difference between large and small organizations was more than 2:1. Betcherman (1999:36) suggests that one reason for the strong correlation between establishment size and HRM innovation is that larger organizations may get a greater return for adopting progressive practices. Another is that human resource management tends to be less formal and hence more difficult to identify in smaller organizations. Betcherman (1999:30) also observes that firms seeing themselves as facing a turbulent environment were more likely to adopt progressive HRM innovation than those seeing their environment as more stable. Godard (2001:33) arrives at a similar conclusion, noting in particular that international competitive pressures appear to increase the likelihood of adoption. As well, since at least some measure of job security has long been viewed as essential if employees are to trust management's motives for introducing employee involvement and other change programs, it has been argued that adoption, or at least successful adoption, is more likely in profitable firms (see Godard, 2001:13).

Given the ongoing debate over whether progressive HRM programs such as employee involvement schemes help or hurt unions, it's interesting to note that at least one important study (Wagar, 1994) has found that firms' union status appears to have had little effect on the likelihood of progressive HRM adoption, with the exception of profit-sharing and other variable compensation schemes. Indeed, it has even been suggested that progressive HRM innovations may be *more* effective in unionized establishments because the union can help reduce "trust problems" often associated with these innovations (see Godard, 2001). However, the extent to which this will actually be the case depends on a variety of factors, among them management's reasons for introducing the innovations, the union's response to the specific program or programs in question, and the history of union–management relations in the organization in question (see among others Downie, 1989).

What Are the Benefits of Progressive HRM?

Overall, as Kochan and Osterman have suggested (1994:56), progressive HRM policies together with a reasonable degree of job security help firms maintain a core of loyal and committed employees—something that takes on added relevance at a time of growing skill shortages in professional and managerial occupations (see Pfeffer, 1994; CLBC, 2000). More specifically, "high-performance" organizations in which progressive HRM has been adopted have achieved significantly better financial results than more 'traditional' organizations (Betcherman, 1999:32–3; Betcherman, Leckie, & McMullen, 1997). Among other things, firms adopting participative management practices had lower unit costs, higher profits and market share, and lower quit, grievance, and customer complaint rates than traditionally managed firms. An important finding from Betcherman's 1999 study is that positive outcomes increase when progressive practices are adopted as a package rather than piecemeal. Another important finding is that the overall labour–management climate and a supportive work system appear to be more important to organizational performance than the specific type of progressive HRM innovation adopted (Wagar, 1994).

On the other side of the ledger, Lam and Reshef (2000) found that downsizing undertaken during quality improvement initiatives eroded trust and leadership and led to a deterioration in service quality. As the downsizing progressed, rivalry between workers increased and the union became more adamantly opposed to the exercise. Lam and Reshef's conclusion was that employers should be extremely cautious about using downsizing and quality improvement initiatives simultaneously, since doing so not only reduces support for the quality improvement initiative, but tends to demoralize employees and reduce their overall productivity and commitment to the organization.

Barriers to Adoption of Progressive HRM

It seems fair to ask why progressive HRM hasn't been more fully adopted if it has all the advantages its proponents claim for it. There are, in fact, a number of barriers to its adoption. One is the direct cost to employers, which may be more than that of alternative, control-based methods of improving performance (Godard, 1991, 1994, 2001; Kochan and Osterman, 1994). A related obstacle is that such programs, which assume that workers are worth investing in, seem to fly in the face of a North American corporate culture still extremely short-term in its overall orientation and still strongly devoted to cutting labour costs, even in the face of growing evidence of skill shortages (see Downie & Coates, 1993; Donner, 1994; Betcherman, 1999). Third, progressive HRM presupposes a certain sophistication and willingness to change on the part of both managers and employees. By no means all managers and employees, particularly in small firms, possess the necessary sophistication and willingness to change.

Beyond that, it's important to recognize that progressive HRM necessitates a certain degree of power-sharing. Some managers may simply not be prepared to share their power. On the union side, some unionists are opposed in principle to any joint participation schemes, believing it isn't the union's role to co-manage the organization and "help management clean up its messes" (see Wells, 1993; CAW, no date). Others fear, sometimes with good reason, that the programs may be used to weaken the union or that they may lead to large-scale layoffs. To be sure, there are also those unionists who believe it is in their organizations' best interest to participate in the programs, but even those unions that are most strongly supportive, such as the CEP and Steelworkers, generally insist on a major role before agreeing to participate (see Verma, 1995). On occasion, unions may also insist on a no-layoff clause.

While the barriers to progressive HRM remain formidable, there are other reasons to believe it will become increasingly common in the years ahead. As Verma and Chaykowski (1999a:11) have noted, it's extremely difficult for Canada to compete with less-developed economies on a basis of lower labour costs alone. As a result, Canada is likely to have difficulty retaining low labour cost industries (i.e., the garment industry), which in turn will mean that more and more of its competition will be on the basis of product quality rather than cost. As we have already seen, progressive HRM practices are extremely useful if one wishes to recruit and retain a loyal and skilled work force to enable the firm to compete on the basis of product quality.

Moreover, the young people entering the Canadian work force today have, on average, more education than any previous generation of Canadian workers. Some recent studies on the difficulties of recruiting young people into the federal public service suggest that these young workers have little tolerance for the bureaucracy and hierarchy that have traditionally characterized public service work (see Luce, 2000; Smith and Snider, 1998). Over time, young people's higher education levels are also likely to make them intolerant of authoritarian management styles. But their desire for challenging and varied work that makes a difference and uses their skills, while allowing them to work in collaboration with others, makes progressive HRM seem particularly suited to these younger workers (Lowe, 2001; Bernard, Cosgrave & Welsh, 1998). Managers have also become more educated, with more of them likely to have acquired the skills needed to maintain a progressive HRM policy.

NEW CHALLENGES FOR TODAY'S MANAGERS

At the beginning of this chapter, we listed a number of challenges facing managers, especially IR and HR managers. These include a much more rapid pace of decision-making, equally rapid technological change, and severe cutbacks in the number of IR and HR managers. (While the economy has improved in recent years, there is little evidence to suggest that firms have been hiring back many of the people they let go during the downsizings of the 1980s and '90s).

In addition to these 'old' challenges, a number of new ones have arisen. These include: 1) the need to increase employee training; 2) the need for managers to develop cross-cultural communications and negotiation skills; 3) recruitment and retention; and 4) a new role for IR and HR departments.

TRAINING It appears that, by and large, workplace training has not kept pace with increased globalization and technological change. Though Canadian firms may talk a lot about training, their rhetoric doesn't seem to have been matched with increased financial commitment, despite improved economic conditions. A recent Conference Board survey of 175 large and medium-sized organizations found that on average, these organizations were spending only about $10 per employee more on training in the year 2000 than they had in 1993 (Gordon, 2001). Moreover, as noted earlier, the work done by Betcherman found that many organizations haven't adopted *any* kind of formal training program. The Conference Board study concluded that Canadian firms will have to increase their training efforts significantly if they are to compete internationally (Gordon, 2001).

CROSS-CULTURAL SKILLS As Canadian firms do more and more international business and compete ever more intensively in international markets, it will be necessary for them to provide their employees and, especially, their management with specific training in communications and negotiation skills appropriate for the countries in which they're doing business. Most of us have probably heard of situations in which a seemingly innocuous remark or gesture from our culture gave great offence in another. What's perhaps less well-known is that the entire pace and timing of negotiations can differ between countries, or even within different regions of the same country (see Lewicki, et al., 1997). It behooves Canadian firms to ensure that their staff and management know these things before going to another country to conduct negotiations. Clearly, too, foreign language training, which in recent years has been given short shrift at certain Canadian schools and universities (see among others Peirce, 2000:97), takes on added importance in international settings. An added benefit of cross-cultural skills and foreign language training is that they can help managers deal more effectively with increasingly diverse multicultural work forces here at home.

RECRUITMENT AND RETENTION   After years in which they did little hiring, many organizations in both the private and public sectors are now finding that they have to hire large numbers of new employees to replace those who have already retired or are nearing retirement age (CLBC, 2001). Driving the demographic crunch is a declining number of Canadians aged 20 to 44. This number has been declining since 1996 and will continue to decline, by another 5%, for at least the next decade (Fryer, 2001:11). While the demographic challenge is one that faces almost all organizations, it seems particularly acute in the public sector, whose work force is generally older than the Canadian average (see Fryer, 2001; Lowe, 2001).

In addition to finding new employees, many organizations are faced with the challenge of keeping those they already have, many of whom have been profoundly demoralized by years of cutbacks, the loss of friends and colleagues, and the intensification of their jobs (see among others Fryer, 2000). In many cases, retention of older employees is necessary to avoid loss of institutional memory. But it may be extremely difficult to motivate someone whose sole reason for continuing to work is to avoid the loss of pension benefits that would result if he or she were to retire.

NEW IR/HR ROLE   Earlier in the chapter, we referred to the new and, to some degree, reduced role played by IR and HR departments, as many of their responsibilities have been devolved to line managers. Within organizations, IR and HR managers often receive lower salaries than marketing, finance, or R&D managers and may find their work valued less highly than that of colleagues engaged in large-scale capital spending or downsizing activities (Peirce, 2000; Kochan and Osterman, 1994).

There are certainly benefits to be achieved from integrating IR/HR functions into line management, particularly if line managers start achieving appropriate training in labour relations and conflict resolution (Macleod, 2000; Fryer, 2001). But this alone may not be enough. If organizations are to live up to their frequently-heard claim, "People are our greatest resource," they will need to start giving their people managers the same status they now give their money managers. Significant increases in workplace training could indirectly benefit the people managers who are generally charged with administering training programs. So, too could holding line managers accountable for the labour relations performance of their units, as measured by such indicators as grievance, absenteeism, and quit rates (Macleod, 2000; Fryer, 2001).

QUESTIONS FOR DISCUSSION

1) If you work for someone else, describe your manager's style in terms of the various approaches to management discussed in this chapter. Does the style seem to you to be effective?

2) If you are a manager yourself, what approaches do you use to try to motivate your subordinates?

3) Describe the main stages in the development of management thought, and give some reasons for changes in management approach between one stage and another.

4) How does the strategic choice framework integrate IR strategies with firms' overall strategies?

5) What have been some major innovations in management practice during the past two decades?

6) Why do you think these innovations haven't been more widely adopted?

7) Discuss the evolution of personnel and IR departments, and relate it to the evolution of management practice traced in the chapter.

8) Does the organization you work for proclaim "People are our greatest resource"? If so, does it "walk its talk"? Why, or why not?

9) To what extent has the organization for which you work adopted progressive HRM practices? Which of these practices has it adopted? How well have they worked? What have been some of the barriers to successful adoption?

10) How do you think the entry of more highly-educated young people into the labour force and the current recruitment and retention crunch will affect management philosophy and practice in Canada?

SUGGESTIONS FOR FURTHER READING

Betcherman, Gordon (1999). "Workplace Change in Canada: the broad context." In A. Verma and R. Chaykowsi (eds.), *Contract and Commitment: Employment Relations in the New Economy*. Kingston: Queen's IRC Press. A thorough and very thoughtful overview of recent management trends in Canada.

Godard, John. (1991). "The progressive HRM paradigm: A theoretical and empirical re-examination." In *Relations Industrielles*, 46. Offers a balanced if skeptical appraisal of the progressive HRM paradigm, including barriers to its adoption.

Kochan, Thomas, Robert McKersie, and Peter Cappelli. (1984). "Strategic choice and industrial relations theory." In *Industrial Relations*, 23(1). Perhaps the single most important article on management and IR to have appeared in the past twenty years.

CHAPTER 4

THE HISTORY OF THE
CANADIAN LABOUR MOVEMENT

Canadian labour has come a long way since 1900, when many people were still self-employed farmers working their land with horses or mules and simple hand tools.

Like unions in all countries, the Canadian unions we know today are the product of economic, social, and political circumstances, as well as (at least in part) the shapers of their own destinies. In this chapter, we trace Canadian unions through three stages of development—from craft through industrial to public service unionism. Along the way, we also consider the role of government in the development of Canada's labour movement, the nature of political involvement entered into by Canadian unions, and the role played by international unions, or unions headquartered in the United States but with branches in this country. The chapter ends with a discussion of the challenges facing the Canadian labour movement at the start of the new millennium.

THE DEVELOPMENT OF CANADIAN UNIONS: A BRIEF OVERVIEW

Very broadly, today's Canadian labour movement can be described as one that seeks to strike a balance between the pragmatic, economically-oriented approach characteristic of American unions and the more politically and socially conscious approach generally taken by European unions. Numerically, too, Canada's union movement, with membership rates of about one-third of the country's work force, holds an intermediate position between heavily unionized countries such as Sweden and Denmark, and those with low membership rates such as the United States and Japan (Bamber and Lansbury, 1993; Adams, 1995a).

That movement has come a long way from the small, locally-based movement of the early-to-mid nineteenth century. But the evolution has been a difficult and often tortuous one. In addition to overcoming obstacles common to most Western labour movements, such as employer and government opposition (Adams, 1995a), the Canadian movement has had to contend with problems peculiar to this country, such as sparse population, a high degree of outside control over the Canadian economy, general economic underdevelopment (Lipton, 1973), and severe regional imbalances (Heron, 1989). These factors tended to retard the development of an independent Canadian labour movement, as did heavy waves of out-migration of Canadian workers to the United States (Drache, 1984) and the fragmentation of Canadian labour into separate English-Canadian and French-Canadian movements (Drache, 1984; Lipsig-Mumme, 1995).

An even greater obstacle was the tendency of many Canadian workers to affiliate with the U.S.-based **international unions** (Heron, 1989). There were good reasons why Canadian workers often found the internationals attractive. For one thing, American unions were generally bigger, stronger, and wealthier, with larger strike funds and more experienced organizers (Logan, 1948). For another, an American union card was a valuable possession for a Canadian worker who, due to the seasonal nature of work in much of the country, might well find himself forced to move to Massachusetts or Ohio for at least part of the year (Lipton, 1973; McKay, 1983:137). Still, there were inherent problems with a situation in which Canada's labour movement did not really control its own affairs. After surfacing periodically throughout much of the nineteenth century, these problems would come to a head just after the turn of the century, just before the First World War, and then again during the 1960s and 1970s.

Despite these and other obstacles, the Canadian labour movement has, over time, managed to achieve impressive gains, both for its members and for society at large. Unionized workers have benefitted greatly from the higher wages and benefits, safer workplaces, and generally improved working conditions that have resulted from collective bargaining. Almost all Canadians have benefitted from the minimum wage and other employment standards legislation and from the social programs and universal health-care insurance achieved largely through the labour movement's work in the political arena (Richardson, 1985). Canadian unions continue to fight to maintain these social programs today, even as the wave of globalization, trade liberalization, economic restructuring, and deindustrialization described in Chapter 2 has made it increasingly difficult for them to maintain their members' jobs and incomes.

Heron (1989:xvi) identifies four key periods for the Canadian labour movement when it expanded its membership and goals. These four periods were the 1880s, the end of each world war, and the decade after 1965. Each of the four saw an upsurge of labour revolt during a time of economic transformation; in each, workers were able to "coalesce into a united force capable of articulating and pursuing common goals" (Heron, 1989). In three (all but the 1880s), the role of government was also important. During the First World War, the government used the *Industrial Disputes Investigation Act* to prevent employers from discharging workers for union activity—thereby hindering the war effort. This encouraged union organization (Morton, 1995), though workers in war industries were still barred from striking. Later, Canada's first general collective bargaining legislation (*PC 1003*) spurred post-Second World War union growth, while the growth of the 1960s and 1970s was mainly the result of public sector legislation such as the *Public Service Staff Relations Act*. In all three cases, the passage or extension of the legislation in question was a direct government response to labour militancy, albeit one designed to channel if not blunt that militancy (see Godard, 1994: 260–261).

The Pre-Industrial Period (to 1850)

The earliest recorded strikes in Canada appear to have taken place in the eighteenth century at the royal shipyard in Quebec City (Moogk, 1976:33) and in the fur trade at Lac la Pluie (Lipton, 1973:1). But such disputes were rare in the early pre-industrial period. Most Canadians were self-employed farmers, fishers, or artisans. Those who did work for hire generally did so on a seasonal basis or for a relatively short period of time; few expected to remain employees indefinitely. Employees worked under a paternalistic system (often one of formal apprenticeship). They would normally work side-by-side with their employers and eat with the family (Heron, 1989:2–3).

As we noted in the management chapter, the term "paternalism" does not mean that all employees were well-treated. Employers' treatment of their employees could be arbitrary or even brutal (Heron, 1989:3; Godard, 1994:101–102). At the same time, it's important to remember that work was generally organized in a very different way under pre-industrial craft production than it would have been in any factory. With most transactions being between members of the same community, the quality and dependability of goods mattered as much as, if not more than, their price, and the pace at which work was done was based on the amount of work at hand rather than the clock (Godard, 1994:101–102).

The first significant wave of worker organization appears to have taken place shortly after the War of 1812. By the 1830s, there was significant organization in a number of towns, including Halifax, Quebec City, Montreal, Toronto, Hamilton, and

Saint John (Forsey, 1982:9–18). To avoid harsh anti-conspiracy legislation, such as Nova Scotia's 1816 law that provided three-month jail terms for those entering into union contracts (Morton and Copp, 1980; Forsey, 1982; Heron, 1989),[1] unions generally operated as "friendly societies" providing members with a degree of mutual insurance against death, accidents, sickness, or unemployment (Forsey, 1982; Heron, 1989). Most early unions were purely local organizations involving skilled craftspeople such as tailors, shoemakers, carpenters, printers, bricklayers, and masons (Forsey, 1982:30–31). Few were confrontational. Shared craft traditions tended to blur the distinctions between masters and journeymen and apprentices (Heron, 1989:7).

Beginning in the 1830s, with the arrival of large numbers of unskilled Irish, Scottish, and English immigrants, "crowd" behaviour became a factor during times of labour strife (Heron, 1989:5). Such behaviour typically involved direct action against the perpetrator of the alleged wrong, such as the burning of effigies or attacks on owners' or managers' homes. Violence would often ensue, especially if police or troops were called in (Heron, 1989).

"Crowd" behaviour evolved into a more organized form of labour strife with the arrival, in the 1840s, of even larger numbers of Irish immigrants, many of whom found work as canal labourers. These labourers were incensed at the conditions they were expected to endure, including 14-hour days, payment in goods rather than money, grossly inadequate wages, and long waits between paydays (Bleasdale, 1981:124). In response, they took desperate measures. Their tactics ranged from more or less conventional work stoppages to patrolling the canals driving off other potential job hunters and halting navigation on the Welland Canal, or even attacking vessels and their passengers (Bleasdale, 1981:130–136). Although these tactics led to harsh reprisals from both employers and the government, they did often result in higher wages.

Early Labour Organization in Quebec

Effective labour organization was generally slower to develop in Quebec than in the rest of British North America. Like their English-Canadian counterparts, French-Canadian workers did not relish employee status. Most sought to become self-employed and economically independent (Moogk, 1976:15) and would remain employees only until they had saved enough money to achieve that end. Like the Nova Scotia and Canada West legislatures, the royal administration in Quebec had banned workers' associations for fear they would restrain competition in commerce and force up prices (Moogk, 1976:5). Both the courts and public officials persistently rebuffed workers' associations in their quest for economic protection and sought to limit their powers (Moogk, 1976:5).

But the Quebec authorities' suppression of collective activity went well beyond English Canada's criminal conspiracy laws against unions. Public protests over high prices and shortages were treated as sedition (Moogk, 1976). While expressions of craft fellowship were tolerated, they were channelled into the harmless (from the administration's perspective) form of religious confraternities whose activities were limited to devotions and banquets. The confraternities were subordinated to the Roman Catholic Church (Moogk, 1976:7). Later, their powers were further limited by a French parliamentary decree that denied them the powers of discipline and compulsion over their members. Without any meaningful economic or political role, the confraternities did not provide Quebec workers with the sort of training in collective organization that English Canada's friendly societies did. The result was that, in the industrial era, Quebec workers lacked such training and were far slower to unionize than workers in the rest of Canada (Moogk, 1976:34–35).

In addition, French-Canadian workers often faced discrimination when they sought work elsewhere in British North America. Often passed over in favour of Irish labourers for canal work, in part because of the Lower Canada Legislative Assembly's desire to "anglicize Quebec by means of immigration" (Drache, 1984:20), they responded by migrating in droves to New England. When they were hired in English Canada, they were often given low-end jobs, which again led many to seek their fortune in New England rather than in English Canada (Drache, 1984:21). Quebec workers' tendency to try to improve their lot through emigration proved to be yet another obstacle to union growth in that province.

Labour in the First Industrial Revolution

What is known as Canada's "First Industrial Revolution" began shortly after 1850. Craft shops expanded into sizeable factories, and employers built lumber mills, canneries, and large coal mines. (Heron, 1989:8). Instead of the handful of people employed by traditional craft establishments, these new enterprises often employed hundreds. They also needed to draw on wider markets beyond strictly local areas to stay in business.

With factories selling to expanded markets, profits became all-important. As manufacturers began to sell their goods to people they had never met, they could often compete only on the basis of cost (Commons, 1918). Profits were also necessary to enable employers to pay for all the costly new machinery they had just installed.

To make profits, employers had to control their costs. Since they could generally do little about the costs of raw materials, land, or capital equipment, they focussed their attention on controlling the cost of labour, which they could do something about. To this end, they brought in strict time-scheduling and monitoring of workers' output. Bells and clocks became common in factories, and the new, stricter schedules were enforced through fines and even beatings (Heron, 1989; Trofimenkoff, 1977:213). Work was sped up, mechanized, and simplified as much as possible so that more could be produced in less time with fewer people. With an eye to saving on wages, employers relied less on skilled artisans, flooding the market with cheaper, less skilled workers, including boys and women, (Heron, 1989:8–9) and replacing skilled workers with machines where possible (Morton and Copp, 1980:22; Bercuson and Bright, 1994:78). Many employers were especially partial to female employees because, in addition to commanding lower wages than men, they were seen as docile, clean, quick, and sober (Trofimenkoff, 1977:220).

In reaction to harsher workplace conditions and employers' frequent attempts to deskill their jobs and cut their wages, workers began increasingly to form **craft unions**, some of which began to affiliate with American internationals (Heron, 1989:10–11). Cigar makers, coopers, molders, machinists, iron-puddlers, and loco-motive engineers were among the groups that began to form unions after 1850. By the 1870s, coal miners were also starting to organize (Heron, 1989:10). Inspired by British "New Model" unionism, the new Canadian craft unions sought to formalize their relations with employers and to put themselves on a more secure footing through high dues and strong, centralized leadership (Heron, 1989; Morton and Copp, 1980). A union's bargaining strategy typically consisted of posting its wage demands on the factory or shop doors. If times were good and demand for the prod-uct high, the employer might well meet the demands. Otherwise, he would generally refuse the demands, and a strike or lockout might then ensue. Often such a dispute would result in the workers' dismissal; sometimes it would even lead to the union's dissolution. As Morton and Copp (1980:10) note, nineteenth century unions could generally succeed only when there were lasting labour shortages. Still, though strikes remained a very risky business at a time when merely belonging to a union could leave a worker open to criminal conspiracy charges, they became more and more fre-quent as industrialization progressed, (Heron, 1989:12).

Beyond the Workplace: Making Common Cause

Confederation, increased industrialization, the growth of central labour organizations in Ontario and Quebec, and growing international awareness of the industrial system's abuses led Canadian workers in the 1870s to mobilize around issues of broad interest to all workers, such as shorter working hours and improved workplace safety (Godard, 1994; Morton, 1995). Nine-hour Leagues in Hamilton and Montreal marked the beginning of broader workers' solidarity in Canada (Heron, 1989:14–15), with their strategy based on a series of strikes to support the demand for shorter hours (Godard, 1994:105). In the short run, the strategy failed, as Toronto printers struck George Brown's *Globe* ahead of schedule in 1872, causing Brown to charge the strik-ers with conspiracy and preventing the achievement of the nine-hour day for the time being (Morton, 1995:134). But the incident did provide politicians with some evidence of working people's potential political power and may well have been responsible, at least in part, for the Macdonald government's enactment, later in 1872, of a *Trade Union Act* removing peaceful picketing from criminal prosecution (Heron, 1989:17). While this law gave unions little in the way of substantive protection, since employers still had recourse to civil conspiracy actions (Heron, 1989:18) and could still use any number of union-busting techniques (Lipton, 1973:65), it did provide unions with some measure of political legitimacy (Godard, 1994:106). In the years to come, the *Trade Union Act* was followed by more substantive legislation, such as the repeal (sub-ject to certain limitations)[2] of the harsh *Masters and Servants Act* prohibitions on strikes (Morton and Copp, 1980; Godard, 1994) and the passage of various provin-cial *Factory Acts*, applied mainly to women and children (Morton and Copp,

1980:84). Another, though short-lived, legacy of the period was the Canadian Labour Union, formed in Toronto in 1873 to address larger political issues and, in effect, serve as a kind of national labour federation (Morton, 1995:134).

The Knights of Labor

Expanded industrialization and strong manufacturing sector growth led to a new wave of unionization in the 1880s. The decade saw a revival of the craft unions and the formation of the Provincial Workmen's Association, a Nova Scotia miners' union (Heron, 1989:20). Antagonism between workers and employers became more pronounced during this period, as employers sped up assembly lines and sought to impose even stricter controls on workers in an attempt to extract still more production from them (Kealey and Palmer, 1981:240–241).

At this juncture, with the social costs of industrialization becoming ever more apparent (Kealey and Palmer, 1981:241), the **Knights of Labor** appeared on the Canadian scene, starting their first Canadian local assembly in Hamilton in 1875 (Craig and Solomon, 1996:115). This organization, which had been founded in Philadelphia in 1869 (Godard, 1994:107), was quite unlike any previous labour organization. As their leaders often said (Kealey and Palmer, 1982), they did not seek to make richer people; they sought to make better people. While conventional craft unions sought to improve the terms and conditions of employment at individual workplaces, the Knights aimed at nothing less than a moral and social transformation of industrial society (Godard, 1994; Kealey and Palmer, 1982).

In pursuit of such transformation, the Knights relied mainly on education and politics. During their brief time in Canada, they opened reading rooms and libraries and supported weekly newspapers, as well as developing producer and consumer co-operatives (Heron, 1989:25–27; Kealey and Palmer, 1981:250). Unlike most other labour organizations of their day (McKay, 1983:125), the Knights admitted women as well as men and unskilled as well as skilled workers, excluding only the Chinese (Kealey and Palmer, 1981; 1982). So broad and so persuasive was their appeal that in Ontario alone they organized at least 21 800 members over their history, according to Kealey and Palmer (1981:245).

Politically, they achieved their greatest gains at the municipal level, including earlier closing hours, union wages for municipal workers, and improved public transit (Kealey and Palmer, 1981:256). At provincial and national levels, while unable to achieve their goal of creating an independent working-class party (Kealey and Palmer, 1981), they did succeed in getting labour's voice heard by the politicians. During the 1890s, both the federal and the Ontario provincial governments implemented many of the Knights' recommendations, including factory acts, bureaus of labour statistics, arbitration measures, extension of the suffrage, and employers' liability acts (Kealey and Palmer, 1981:265). Perhaps most noteworthy of all, the first Monday in September was established as a holiday in 1894 in recognition of the dignity of labour (Morton, 1995:135).

The Knights' role in strikes has generated considerable controversy (Morton, 1995;

Kealey and Palmer, 1981;1982). Undeniably they were less enthusiastic about strikes than were most conventional craft unions, generally preferring to resolve disputes through conciliation or arbitration instead. At the same time, the record shows that they took part in and even led a good many strikes in Ontario during the 1880s (Kealey and Palmer, 1981:258). It also shows that after a downturn in the economy in the late 1880s, the Knights became more cautious about striking, and that during a London cigar makers' strike, they signed up scab cigar makers and allowed them to use the Knights' label in competition with the cigar makers' union (Heron, 1989:26–27). This action outraged international unionists and caused many to leave the order (Heron, 1989:28). Essentially, it was the beginning of the end for the Knights, though they were to linger on in Canada until the Berlin Convention of 1902. But whether or not the Knights' conception of broad-based industrial unionism was wildly ahead of its time, as Morton (1995:135) suggests, their vision of a genuine alternative culture would inspire former members until well into the twentieth century (Kealey and Palmer, 1981:229–230).

Trades and Labour Congress

The rise and fall of the Knights of Labor were far from the only significant developments on the Canadian labour scene during the 1880s. A more lasting development was the formation, in 1886, of the Trades and Labour Congress of Canada (TLC). This organization, which would remain Canada's major labour confederation until its 1956 merger with the Canadian Congress of Labour, would meet annually to address such labour-related issues as immigration policy, enforcement of factory acts, free education for children, and shorter work hours (Forsey, 1982; Morton and Copp, 1980). Like Samuel Gompers' American Federation of Labor, it did not affiliate itself with any political party, instead lobbying governments on an issue-by-issue basis.

Labour in the Second Industrial Revolution

American Federation of Labor

A second industrial revolution began in Canada during the 1890s. Factories became larger and more capital-intensive (Heron, 1989:30–31; Kealey and Palmer, 1981:235), and supervision grew even stricter under the coercive drive system (discussed in detail in Chapter 3). Not surprisingly, worker–management struggles for workplace control intensified (Heron, 1989; Kealey, 1976). Meanwhile, wages for most workers remained low despite the period's vast accumulation of capital. As late as 1890, Toronto printers were earning $12 for a 54-hour week (Lipton, 1973:79)— and they were among the period's more privileged workers. Less-skilled adult male workers, let alone women and children, generally earned far less (Morton and Copp, 1980; Lipton, 1973; Bullen, 1986; McIntosh, 1987).

Conditions were clearly ripe for a new wave of union organizing. As in the past,

Canadian workers found help south of the border. In the middle of his own organizing drive, **American Federation of Labor** (**AFL**) president Samuel Gompers realized that if Canada were not organized, all the AFL's efforts might be futile since American employers could procure cheaper Canadian labour (Morton, 1995:136). To prevent this from happening, Gompers enlisted the services of John Flett, a Hamilton carpenter and one-time socialist. Flett's turn-of-the-century campaign proved astoundingly successful. He was responsible for 57 new AFL locals in Canada in 1901 and for most of the 50 new locals added the following year (Morton and Copp, 1980:70). This wave of AFL organizing transformed the Canadian labour movement, firmly setting it on an international path. By 1902, fully 95 percent of all Canadian unionists belonged to international unions. The international direction of the Canadian labour movement was confirmed by Flett's election to the TLC presidency at the organization's 1902 convention, held in Berlin, Ontario (Morton and Copp, 1980).[3]

The Berlin Convention

Up until the **Berlin Convention**, the TLC had been less doctrinally rigid about its unionism than had the AFL. It had included local assemblies of the Knights of Labor alongside traditional craft unions—a practice that the AFL, and Gompers in particular, loathed.[4] Berlin changed all that. After the convention, no national union would be recognized by the TLC when an international union existed, and in no case would more than one central body be chartered in any city or town (Morton and Copp, 1980:74). This prohibition of "dual" unionism led the TLC to expel its remaining Knights assemblies, as well as other national unions organizing the same industries as AFL unions. The 33 expelled unions comprised about one-fifth of the TLC's total membership (Drache, 1984:27).

Historians and industrial relations experts differ on the significance of the Berlin Convention. To some (Morton, 1995:137), the linkage between American and Canadian labour movements established at Berlin was only common sense, since Canadian unionists "wanted to share a North American standard of living." To others (Drache, 1984:26–28), the move effectively split the Canadian labour movement by tying it to an American federation actively seeking to hinder its development as an independent, nationalist, and progressive force. Most likely, the truth lies somewhere in the middle. While Berlin did, to a degree, split the Canadian movement (especially insofar as it maintained TLC control in central Canada, leaving eastern and western unions out in the cold), it did not and could not destroy a persistent nationalist spirit within that movement. That spirit would find expression in a series of nationally oriented union federations, from the National Trades and Labour Congress (later known as the Canadian Federation of Labour) in the first quarter of the twentieth century through the **All-Canadian Congress of Labour** (**ACCL**) (1927–1940) to the **Canadian Congress of Labour** (**CCL**) (1940–1956). Unlike the TLC, the ACCL and CCL would both seek to organize workers on an industry-wide rather than craft basis and would place considerable emphasis on political action (Craig and Solomon, 1996:120–123).

Radical Unionism

While the Berlin Convention appeared to set the Canadian labour movement on a moderate as well as international course, there were a good many radical unions operating in Canada during the first two decades of this century. Berlin may even have heightened some unions' radicalism, by confirming that there was no place for them within the mainstream labour movement.

The century's first decade saw a series of increasingly violent strikes, often involving the use of police and volunteer militia to suppress them. Many of these disputes involved street-railway workers. Indeed, it seems that almost every Ontario city of any size had at least one major street-railway strike between 1895 and 1910 (Morton and Copp, 1980:77). These strikes helped develop strong public support for the labour movement (Heron, 1989:34–36), particularly since both workers and railway-riding members of the general public were seeking to have the monopolies placed under public ownership, as most eventually were.

Many other strikes occurred in the coal mines of Nova Scotia (McKay, 1983; Frank, 1983; McIntosh, 1987) and in the mines, logging camps, and railway gangs of British Columbia (McCormack, 1975; Mouat, 1990). On the railway gangs, for instance, a 12-hour day and seven-day week were standard. The work was back-breaking, and accidents, including fatal ones, were far from uncommon. Foremen often drove the men with their fists, and in some cases workers were watched by armed guards (McCormack, 1975:327). Given such conditions, it is hardly surprising that the largely unskilled and immigrant workers should have turned to a radical union like the **Industrial Workers of the World (IWW)** for help. Like some other unions of its day, the IWW had a syndicalist philosophy. This meant that it placed little faith in either collective bargaining or political action, believing instead in a huge general strike that would destroy capitalism (McCormack, 1975:329–330). A belief in direct industrial action made a good deal of sense to the IWW's members, few of whom could vote. Meanwhile, the "Wobblies" were able to provide their members with a good deal of practical help in the here and now. Their organizing was done in at least 10 different languages, and their union halls served as mail drops and dormitories, as employment agencies, infirmaries, and classrooms (McCormack, 1975:328).

IDI Act (1907)

It was a coal strike that led Parliament to pass, in 1907, the *Industrial Disputes Investigation Act*, arguably the most significant piece of labour legislation Canada had yet seen. A nine-month strike of coal miners in the Lethbridge district in 1906 had come close to leaving residents facing a prairie winter without heat (Baker, 1983; Morton and Copp, 1980). Appalled by the near miss in Lethbridge, and by the increasing violence of other disputes, such as a strike in a suburban Ottawa lumber yard that left three dead that same year (Morton and Copp, 1980:88), the public demanded government action to help stem the increasing labour bloodshed.

The *IDI Act* was based primarily on Prime Minister King's belief that public exposure would moderate the behaviour of unreasonable parties. The Act required all
workers and employers in transportation, resources, and utilities industries to submit
their disputes to a three-person conciliation board before starting a strike or lockout.
Even after the board had issued its report, a further "cooling-off" period was
required before any strike or lockout could become legal (Heron, 1989:47). As will
be seen in more detail in Chapter 8, *IDI's* basic principles have remained central features of most Canadian labour legislation to this day.

The TLC initially gave the act cautious approval, but quickly changed its mind
(Morton and Copp, 1980:89–90). Not only did *IDI* not require collective bargaining; it did nothing to prevent employers from using the "cooling-off" periods to
stockpile goods to prepare for strikes, or from imposing yellow-dog contracts barring employees from union membership, recruiting strike-breakers, hiring private
police, or firing and blacklisting union activists (Morton and Copp, 1980:89;
Heron, 1989:47; MacDowell, 1978:660). In the view of industrial relations author
Stuart Jamieson, the act delayed the evolution of mature collective bargaining in
Canada (see Morton and Copp, 1980:90).[5]

Even in the short term, *IDI* probably did little to improve labour–management
relations. The period just before the First World War continued to be marked by bitter workplace struggles, as managers schooled in the newly fashionable scientific
management (discussed in detail in Chapter 3) sought to speed up production lines
and extract still more effort from their workers. Socially and politically, as well, the
period was one of great ferment and rapid change. In Europe, most mainstream
labour movements had by this time adopted some form of socialism (Adams,
1995a:497). While the TLC didn't do this, many workers and union leaders did, moving well beyond the cautious "labourism" that had been Canadian working people's
primary political creed for the previous half-century (Heron, 1989:49–51; 1984).
None of this was likely to be changed by the requirements for a conciliation board
report and cooling-off period before a legal strike could take place.

The First World War and Its Aftermath

The First World War saw a rapid increase in union membership, an increase spurred
both by rising prices and by wartime labour shortages. Between 1914 and 1919,
Canadian union membership more than doubled (Godard, 1994:95) as the wartime
organizational surge brought unskilled workers, municipal government employees, and
even teachers and other white-collar workers into the labour movement for the first
time (Heron, 1989:53–54). These new unionists had grievances that went beyond soar-
ing wartime prices. Unlike the British, French, and American governments, the
Canadian government made no attempt to consult with union leaders or socialist politicians during the war, even though the TLC had obediently endorsed the war effort in
1914 (Heron, 1989:53; Morton and Copp, 1980:103). Further frustrated by their
inability to elect members to Parliament on a labour ticket (Heron, 1989:56), Canadian

unionists turned to radical protest and direct action. The period from 1917 to 1920 saw a wave of strike activity across Canada, inspired at least in part by a worldwide workers' revolt set in motion by the Russian Revolution of 1917 (Heron, 1989:55).

After the largely western-based radicals lost out to the conservative craft unionists at the 1918 TLC convention, they launched a new industrial union known as the **"One Big Union" (OBU)** with socialist leadership. Their aim was to create a broad-based union free of traditional craft jurisdictional barriers. A key demand was for a six-hour day to reduce unemployment (Heron, 1989:57–58). The launching of the new union was, however, quickly overshadowed by some dramatic events taking place in Winnipeg and a number of other Canadian cities during the spring of 1919.

The Winnipeg General Strike

In April 1918, Winnipeg's workers had successfully staged a general strike over city workers' right to strike (Morton and Copp, 1980:115). Just over a year later, on May 15, 1919, they tried the same tactic to show sympathy with the building and metal trades unions, which had been denied collective bargaining rights (Heron, 1989:59). On that day, more than 25 000 workers walked off their jobs, launching a six-week strike (Morton and Copp, 1980:119). Though the Winnipeg strike would spark a wave of 30 sympathy strikes extending eastward to Amherst, Nova Scotia, and westward to Vancouver (Kealey, 1984:203–206), it proved a colossal failure in the end, as all three levels of government combined to crush the strike (Heron, 1989:60–61), continuing a pattern of government repression that had begun during the war with the banning of socialist and radical organizations and the closure of foreign-language newspapers (Morton and Copp, 1980:113). Strike leaders were arrested and threatened with deportation (Morton and Copp, 1980), and the city's police force was dismissed for its pro-strike leanings and replaced by untrained special constables. Most important of all, on "Bloody Saturday" (June 21), the RCMP charged a crowd of strikers, using bullets as well as their horses to suppress the crowd in the most authoritative way possible. Four days later, the strike was over (Morton and Copp, 1980:122).

To all intents and purposes, the collapse of the Winnipeg General Strike marked the end of the radical labour movement in Canada (Morton and Copp, 1980:122–123). Even as many of the Winnipeg strike leaders went off to prison, the OBU was being reduced to insignificance, weakened both by employers who refused to have anything to do with it and by craft unionists who collaborated in undermining its strikes (Heron, 1989:59).

The Postwar Retreat

Ushered in by a severe depression that led to massive layoffs and hopeless strikes against draconian wage cuts (Heron, 1989:60), the 1920s were to prove extraordinarily difficult years for the Canadian labour movement. Continuing government repression, a renewed employer offensive against labour, and deep schisms within the movement itself combined to weaken labour's position dramatically and to bring "fearfulness, fatalism and cynicism" back into the working-class consciousness (Heron, 1989). Throughout most of the decade, union membership fell sharply. So did wage rates, at least during the early part of the decade (Morton and Copp, 1980:125–126). Ongoing waves of immigration throughout the decade helped ensure that unemployment levels remained relatively high and that unskilled and semi-skilled workers would continue to be easy to replace (Godard, 1994:117).

Having failed at radical industrial action, the labour movement returned to more conventional electoral politics at the start of the decade. In Ontario and Alberta, labour parties elected enough members to form coalitions with farmers' parties. These were not, however, political marriages made in heaven. Some modest reforms ensued, but basic disagreements over such issues as work hours, prohibition, free trade, and taxation levels prevented the alliances from lasting very long (Heron, 1989:61–62). By the end of the decade, most mainstream TLC unionists had reverted to the old Sam Gompers method of lobbying individual politicians on single issues of direct concern to unions (Morton, 1995:140).

With wages falling, unemployment rising, and working people generally on the defensive, many early postwar employers found it easy to simply crush unions by intimidating and harassing any workers known or suspected to have had anything to do with them. For those who disliked such heavy-handed tactics, there was the new paternalistic management, or "American Plan" as it was often called.[6] The main idea here was to reduce workers' desire to join unions by providing company-dominated unions, or industrial councils, as channels through which workers could voice their concerns without posing any fundamental challenge to management's authority (Godard, 1994:113–115; Heron, 1989:59–60; Morton and Copp, 1980:130–131; Slichter, 1929). It isn't clear just how widely paternalistic management practices were adopted in Canada. But where they were adopted, they appear to have been fairly successful at keeping unions out (Godard, 1994:117; Slichter, 1929).

Catholic and Communist Unionism

As if the challenges from without were not difficult enough, the 1920s saw the Canadian labour movement split in several different directions. We have already discussed the emergence of a number of different nationalist labour federations unhappy with the TLC's strong ties to the AFL. More serious, perhaps, because it pointed to new schisms within the labour movement, was the emergence of Catholic confessional and Communist union federations. The former had its roots in traditional Quebec nationalism, heightened by the First World War conscription crisis, and in a long-standing tradition of Church involvement in settling labour disputes in the province (Morton and Copp, 1980:131). Since early in the century, Quebec's Catholic hierarchy had been working for a distinctly Catholic unionism that would promote Catholic and francophone values, rather than the secular and socialistic values they saw arising out of the then-dominant international unions (Heron, 1989:60; Boivin, 1982:426–427).

Their efforts bore fruit in 1921 with the establishment of the **Confédération des travailleurs catholique du Canada (CTCC)**, which claimed to represent some 26 000 members (Boivin, 1982:427). A key aspect of confessional unionism was the attachment of a priest to each local, ostensibly as an adviser, but more often than not as its de facto president. The CTCC also stressed the common interests of workers and employers, shunning strikes in favour of less confrontational approaches such as conciliation and arbitration.[7] The new Catholic unions clearly represented a serious challenge to the internationals and the TLC (Morton and Copp, 1980:131), since in many cases they were competing for members with the older federations.

The challenge posed by the Communists, who launched their new party in Ontario in 1921, was equally severe. Since the Canadian party took its orders from Moscow, its labour strategies underwent a number of bizarre, even embarrassing, shifts resulting from Soviet policy changes (Morton and Copp, 1980:133–134). Early in the decade, the orders were to "bore from within," taking over the conservative AFL and TLC and transforming them into radical bodies. Unsuccessful in this attempt, the Communists in 1927 turned their attention to the new, more progressive ACCL and sought to bring in a number of like-minded unions in a bid to wrest control of the federation from its founder, Aaron Mosher. All this did was to earn the Communists the enmity of the non-Communist nationalist unions (Heron, 1989:70) and get them expelled from the ACCL (Morton and Copp, 1980:134). In 1930, the Communists formed their own labour federation, the **Workers' Unity League (WUL)**, dedicated to "militant industrial unionism and socialist revolution" (Heron, 1989:70). Finally, in 1935, still under orders from Moscow, the Communists changed their strategy yet again, disbanded the WUL, and rejoined the mainstream labour movement with an eye to forming broad-based anti-fascist alliances.

Clearly, the WUL did much useful work within the Canadian labour movement, particularly by assuming leadership of the great majority of Canadian strikes carried out during the early 1930s (Heron, 1989:70–71). But by fragmenting the already small left-wing opposition to the American-dominated TLC within Canada's labour movement, the Communists also helped delay the emergence of strong, progressive national unionism.

Judicial Fragmentation

The final cause of fragmentation within the Canadian labour movement was neither a union nor a political party, but the British Privy Council, which in the Snider case of 1925 overruled a solid majority of Canadian judges to declare the *IDI Act* unconstitutional because it applied to municipal institutions (Craig and Solomon, 1996:206). Since then, labour law, except in the case of undertakings clearly of a federal nature, has been held to be under provincial jurisdiction. In addition to making life more complicated for all actors in the IR system by in effect establishing 11 IR jurisdictions instead of one,[8] provincial jurisdiction has arguably promoted a decentralized union structure (Murray, 1995) that has made it that much more difficult for the Canadian labour movement to pursue coordinated national economic and political strategies.

Labour During the Depression

The Great Depression of the 1930s offered conclusive evidence of the failure of conventional approaches to economic and political problems. Like many other groups, the Canadian labour movement began to try out a variety of new approaches both in workplaces and in the political arena. It was helped greatly by the American movement, which used a politically sympathetic government to achieve gains it had previously only dreamed of, including the granting of collective bargaining rights.

By 1933, one worker in four was unemployed, an increase of more than 300 percent in the national unemployment rate since 1929, and 15 percent of the population was on relief (Morton and Copp, 1980:139–140). For those leaving school, job prospects were poor to non-existent. Many would be condemned to a life of "riding the rods" in search of any work they could get, or an even harder life in the government-sponsored relief camps established in 1932, which provided their inmates with room and board and 20 cents a day in return for six days a week of hard labour (Morton and Copp, 1980; Brown, 1970).

Few had really secure jobs. Both in the resource industries and in manufacturing, massive layoffs were the order of the day. At Ford Motor Company, employment fell from 7100 to 2174 between 1929 and 1932. Workers often had to bribe their way into even low-paying menial jobs (Manley, 1986:556).

WUL Activity

Under such conditions, most conventional union organizing and strike activity was out of the question, as the major federations hunkered down to protect existing members (Morton and Copp, 1980:142; Manley, 1986:557). The one big exception was the Communists' Worker Unity League, for whom the Depression was tailor-made, since it seemed to confirm the Communists' thesis of the need for broader class struggle (Morton and Copp, 1980:142). In Flin Flon, Manitoba, and Estevan, Saskatchewan, the WUL led bitter and ultimately unsuccessful mining strikes. Though the strikes failed, the courage shown by the workers would inspire many others over the years. The WUL's efforts were more successful in Ontario, where it managed to organize a fair number of furniture, textile, and garment workers despite ferocious redbaiting and frequent repression by provincial police and troops (Morton and Copp, 1980; Heron, 1989).

Government Repression

Government repression was by no means confined to strikers. A common enough feature of 1930s' life generally, it was applied most often and most brutally to the hordes of single, unemployed men who were the Depression's worst victims, and from whom the government seemed to feel it had most to fear (Morton and Copp, 1980:145–146). While the relief camp inmates did not wear uniforms (Morton and Copp, 1980:147), in most other ways they lived and worked under military-style discipline. Inmates were barred from filing group petitions to seek improvement of their wretched conditions, or from making speeches, writing letters to newspapers, or doing anything else "to bring accusations before the tribunal of public opinion" (Brown, 1970:606–607). In 1933, authorities banned May Day parades in Regina and Saskatoon and had the RCMP raid a union hall in Moose Jaw and seize a list of names of "troublemakers" who had refused to work in the relief camps (Brown, 1970:600). Two years later, when unemployed workers made an "On-to-Ottawa" trek to press such radical demands as relief camp workers' right to vote and the removal of the camps from Defence Department control, they were met with RCMP billy clubs in a bloody July 1 riot in Regina (Brown, 1970:610–611; Morton and Copp, 1980; Scott, 1945).

Though anti-Communist laws were not new to Canada (Scott, 1932), the Conservative government of R.B. Bennett applied them with particular rigour, as did Bennett's provincial allies such as Ontario Premier Howard Ferguson. In 1931, the Communists' Toronto office was raided and eight of its leaders arrested; seven were later imprisoned (Morton and Copp, 1980:145). Other Communist leaders were deported (Morton and Copp, 1980), a phenomenon that had become increasingly common since the First World War (White, 1932).[9] As the decade wore on, similar or even harsher treatment would be meted out to Communists, social democrats, and unionists by the authoritarian governments of Quebec Premier Maurice Duplessis and Ontario Premier Mitch Hepburn, who replaced Ferguson later in the decade (Morton and Copp, 1980:158–160, 163, 191).

Hopeful American Developments

South of the border, however, things were beginning to look more hopeful, particularly after 1933 when Franklin D. Roosevelt took office as President. Roosevelt's "New Deal" launched large public works projects and, in general, stimulated the U.S. economy greatly, leading to a substantial reduction in unemployment rates by the mid 1930s.

Influenced by business lobbying and by conservatives within his administration, Roosevelt didn't give the labour movement the legislated six-hour day and 30-hour week it had been seeking as a means of reducing unemployment (Hunnicutt, 1988). But he saw that he would have to give the labour movement a good deal to make up for the loss of the six-hour law. His broad package of reforms eventually included a social security plan generous enough to allow older workers to retire with dignity, and employment standards legislation providing for an eight-hour day and 40-hour week—still far shorter than that worked by most workers in industrialized countries (Hunnicutt, 1988). The centrepiece was the 1935 *National Labor Relations Act (NLRA)*, or *"Wagner Act,"* as it is more commonly known. This bill allowed most American private-sector workers[10] to bargain collectively and to strike without fear of employer intimidation, harassment, or reprisal. Standards for employer unfair labour practice were defined and a National Labor Relations Board established to administer and enforce the act. Free of the fear that hostile employers could fire union organizers and members, American unions signed up hundreds of thousands of new members in the years immediately following passage of the *Wagner Act*.

Industrial Unionism

A particularly important consequence of the *Wagner Act* was that it facilitated unionization of unskilled and semi-skilled workers who would otherwise have had difficulty forming unions, since they lacked the scarce skills needed to withstand employer anti-union initiatives. Many of the country's more farsighted union leaders, such as John L. Lewis of the United Mine Workers, were quick to recognize the huge growth the labour movement might achieve by organizing unskilled and semi-skilled workers in mass-production industries. Unlike traditional craft unionism, the **industrial unionism** envisaged by Lewis and his allies would seek to organize all workers in an industry and would use political action and mass worker mobilization, as well as collective bargaining, in an attempt to achieve its objectives.

Disgusted with what they saw as the AFL craft unions' conservative, elitist, and defeatist strategy, Lewis and other industrial unionists launched a Committee for Industrial Organization within the AFL (Abella, 1975). When its members were expelled from that federation two years later (Morton and Copp, 1980:153), the Committee became the **Congress of Industrial Organizations**, or **CIO** (Heron, 1989:73). The CIO's efforts would quickly bear fruit, with the organization of such mass-production industries as autos, steel, rubber, and meatpacking.

Industrial unionism was slower to take hold in Canada, in large measure because Canadian workers still didn't enjoy basic bargaining rights. But CIO organizers nonetheless began working in Ontario, and in February 1937, a proposed 20 percent speed-up of the General Motors Oshawa plant assembly line led to a plant-wide strike that in turn led to a compromise settlement whereby the union won most of its substantive demands without gaining formal recognition (Morton and Copp, 1980; Abella, 1975). With this victory, the Canadian industrial union movement was launched, though it would continue to find the going tough in the absence of legislation protecting basic union organizing rights (Morton and Copp, 1980; Abella, 1975). Over the next few years, CIO unions would be established in Kitchener's rubber plants, Sault Ste. Marie's steel mills, and Montreal's dress factories (Morton and Copp, 1980:160–163). In 1939, the TLC would follow the AFL's lead and expel its CIO unions (Heron, 1989:73), which then merged with Aaron Mosher's ACCL to form the Canadian Congress of Labour, or CCL (Morton, 1995:143).

The Founding of the CCF

Desperate for solutions to the Depression, Canadians tried out a broad range of schemes ranging from social credit and religious fundamentalism to varying degrees of socialism (Morton, 1995, 141; Ferguson, 1935). The period's most important political development was arguably the founding of the **Co-Operative Commonwealth Federation,** or **CCF,** launched in Calgary and Regina in 1932–1933 under the leadership of J.S. Woodsworth. The party was made up of socialists, progressive farmers, old-style labourites, and a number of urban intellectuals (Morton, 1995; Underhill, 1932). Its eight-point program included a planned system of social economy, socialization of the banking sector, public ownership of the natural resource sector, socialized medical care, and adequate work or unemployment insurance for the unemployed under federal government auspices (Underhill, 1932).

Though many in the labour movement were initially cool to the new party (Morton, 1995:141), it gained increasing union support over time, earning, for example, the endorsement of Aaron Mosher's CCL. During its first five years, it won only scattered seats, but by the late 1930s it was winning large numbers of seats in B.C. and Saskatchewan. In 1944, it formed the government in the latter province (King, 1944). By this time, it was so strong both federally and in Ontario that it posed a serious threat to both governments. Canada's labour movement finally had an effective political party of its own.

Labour During the War Years

If the Depression's dominant themes had been industrial unionism and political mobilization, that of the war years was legislative enactment of fundamental union bargaining rights. For labour, this period's pivotal event was undoubtedly the enactment, in 1944, of *PC 1003*, the bill granting Canadian workers such basic rights as the right to join a union, bargain collectively, and strike.

The achievement of basic bargaining rights didn't come easily. Though wartime labour shortages and government orders-in-council curbing employers' right to fire workers again spurred union organization, Prime Minister King remained convinced of the perfection of the *IDI Act* and unwilling to move beyond it. In a bid to maintain labour peace, the government did, in 1940, put forward an order-in-council urging employers to recognize unions voluntarily. But as L.S. MacDowell notes, this policy was "ignored by employers and never followed by the government itself in the industries under its own control" (1978:662). In the absence of any legislation compelling them to deal with unions, many employers continued to refuse to do so. In a situation of wartime labour shortage, where wages were strictly controlled but prices generally were not (MacDowell, 1978), serious labour strife was virtually guaranteed. A bitter gold mining strike at Kirkland Lake, Ontario, in 1942 and an equally bitter steel strike the following year united the formerly divided labour movement against the government. Both major labour federations demanded that workers be given the same basic bargaining rights American workers had long enjoyed under the *Wagner Act* (MacDowell, 1978:669). A similar conclusion was reached by the National War Labour Board in 1943, in a report prepared by Mr. Justice C.P. McTague, who had been the conciliator in the Kirkland Lake dispute. Still King did not act (Morton and Copp, 1980:183).

What the McTague report could not do, the growing threat from the left could. In August 1943, the Liberals lost four federal by-elections, two to the CCF (Morton and Copp, 1980). The defeats and the CCF's high poll standings elsewhere appear to have convinced King that if he didn't move the Liberals to the left, he might well lose the next election. Accordingly, he established a system of family allowances and promised full postwar employment and universal medical care (Morton, 1995:143). Most important of all, he finally granted Canadian workers their long-awaited collective bargaining rights.

Collective Bargaining Legislation: *PC 1003*

The legislation providing for those rights, Order-in-Council *PC 1003*, was proclaimed in February 1944, by which time similar legislation had already been put into effect in Ontario and B.C. (Heron, 1989:80). Now, employers could not refuse to bargain with unions that had proved to the new labour relations board that they had the majority support of workers in any given workplace. This meant that strikes for union recognition would no longer be necessary; in fact they would be illegal. Otherwise, the right to strike, within limits, was now protected, but *IDI's* conciliation process (including the "cooling-off" period) would still have to be observed before any strike or lockout would be legal (Heron, 1989:80–81). Strikes were not legal during the life of a contract. Instead, every collective agreement was assumed to contain a grievance procedure, culminating in binding arbitration, for the handling of disputes over contract interpretation (Craig and Solomon, 1996:207). The new board, to be known as the Canada Labour Relations Board, was charged with overseeing certifications and ruling on unfair labour practices (Heron, 1989:80).

Thanks to favourable wartime conditions, union membership rates had already risen dramatically. Between 1939 and 1945, the number of Canadian union members doubled, while union density increased from 17 to 24 percent of paid non-agricultural workers (Godard, 1994:96). Now, thanks to *PC 1003*, the unions would be able to maintain those gains during the postwar period. Indeed, membership rates continued to rise during the late 1940s, aided both by the legislation and by a booming postwar economy that proved conducive to union growth.

Maintaining Union Security: The *"Rand Formula"*

Another piece of legislation that may have contributed to postwar union growth by enhancing unions' security was the so-called *"Rand Formula,"* introduced in 1945. The formula, devised by Justice Ivan Rand to help settle a Ford Motor Company dispute he was arbitrating, did not require employees to join unions that had been certified for their bargaining units, but did require them to pay union dues, since all bargaining-unit employees, whether union members or not, benefitted from the union's efforts on their behalf. Free of the threat of compulsory union membership, which they bitterly opposed, most employers adopted the dues **"checkoff"** whereby employees' union dues were deducted at the source. This gave unions a solid financial basis of support and helped ensure their survival (Heron, 1989:85).

With the war over, the federal government could no longer maintain its jurisdiction over labour legislation. But in 1948, it enacted a slightly modified version of the wartime order, the *Industrial Relations and Disputes Investigation Act of 1948* (Morton and Copp, 1980:198). The new law was intended to serve as a model for the provinces and to provide some degree of uniformity for labour law across the country (Carter, 1995:62). To a degree, it did. Within two years, every province had adopted some version of the federal legislation. Many provincial acts, however, particularly those of the Atlantic provinces and Alberta, were significantly more restrictive than the federal one.[11] The one area of uniformity was the compulsory conciliation provision, a holdover from the old *IDI Act*, which was adopted in every province except Saskatchewan.

Postwar Strikes

The Ford strike just mentioned was but one of a huge wave sweeping across Canada during the early postwar years. Workers needed substantial wage increases to keep pace with postwar inflation. And thanks to the new labour legislation, even the unskilled could now strike to support wage demands without risking dismissal or harassment from their employers. In 1946 alone, a year that saw the highest level of Canadian strike activity since 1919, strikes shut down the entire B.C. logging industry, the Ontario rubber industry, the entire steel industry, the Southam newspaper chain, and central Canadian ports (Heron, 1989:84). Though often long and sometimes bitter, these strikes were of a different character than the ones that had swept Canada after the First World War. With union recognition as such no longer at issue, the primary aim now was not mass mobilization, but the winning of specific contract demands. While picket lines continued to be tense places, bloodshed and loss of life were far rarer than in pre-war strikes. Thanks again to the new legislation, the strike had become less of a political weapon and more of an economic one (see Heron, 1989:85 and Morton, 1995:145).

Women: The Forgotten 50 Percent

While *PC 1003* and the *Rand Formula* were certainly of great benefit to male workers, especially blue-collar workers in industries important to the war effort, it is doubtful whether this legislation was of much immediate benefit to female workers. The legislation didn't apply to public sector workers (except in Saskatchewan); by and large these workers continued to be legally barred from joining unions. In the private-service sector, where many other women worked, any significant degree of unionization would simply not be in the cards for the foreseeable future.[12]

Since most heavy industries had been unionized, the new labour legislation might have benefitted the sizeable contingent of women who had left their homes to take wartime defence plant jobs—except for one minor detail. With the end of the war,

As this photo suggests, logging could be an extremely dangerous business.

An illustration from Dante's *Inferno*? Actually, it's a rather typical scene from a 19th century factory.

Brutal suppression of strike activity, as in the case of the Winnipeg General Strike, was more the rule than the exception before Canadian workers received official bargaining rights.

Quebec workers take to the streets in a demonstration against the authoritarian regime of Premier Maurice Duplessis.

Even before World War II was over, advertisers were campaigning hard to ensure that "Rosie the Rivetter" would turn back into "Henrietta the Homemaker" as soon as possible after the end of hostilities.

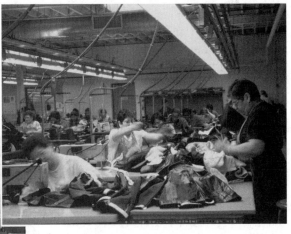

Like many generations of garment workers before them, these garment workers, many of whom are recent immigrants to Canada, must work long hours at very low wages.

United Food and Commercial Workers urge a boycott of Gainer's meats during their now-famous 1986 strike in Edmonton.

women were leaving those plants in droves. To help ensure that the exodus continued, governments closed workplace day-care centres and cancelled wartime tax concessions (Roberts and Bullen, 1985:387). Not surprisingly, the female proportion of the labour force dropped from 31 to 23 percent between 1945 and 1946 (Bland, 1983:681), while marriage and birth rates soared. After the war, the country's advertisers did their part to complete the metamorphosis of "Rosie the Rivetter" into "Henrietta the Homemaker" by painting bright pictures of an appliance-filled future in which women were portrayed primarily as consumers (Bland, 1983:707). At home with her washer and dryer and high-gloss paste wax, a woman would have little reason to concern herself with such things as unions and labour legislation.

Labour During the 1950s

After the radicalism of the 1930s and rapid expansion of the 1940s, the 1950s was a decade of consolidation and stabilization, if not stagnation, for the labour movement. Overall, it was an era of economic and political conservatism. Few people, within the labour movement or outside of it, cared to rock the boat. While unions were generally accepted throughout most of Canada, they had to operate within fairly narrow bounds. In return for this acceptance, they were expected to concentrate on wages and benefits and not concern themselves with more fundamental questions of control or management of the enterprise (Heron, 1989:86–87). In addition, they also lost the mid-term strike and other traditional tools of direct action (Heron, 1989:91–92). With the mid-term strike barred in favour of the grievance procedure, many believed union leaders were increasingly being made to function as the managers of discontent. Whether or not this was the case, it was definitely true that they now had to function in an increasingly bureaucratic and legalistic workplace environment, one in which administrative and negotiating skills were more important than the ability to mobilize workers or move a crowd (Heron, 1989:86–89).

At the bargaining table, unions racked up impressive gains for their members. Wages increased dramatically, and the eight-hour day and five-day week became the norm. Paid vacations, pensions, and medical plans were all brought in (Roberts and Bullen, 1985:393–394). For the first time, ordinary workers were able to buy cars, appliances, TV sets, and other items of which they had previously only dreamed (Heron, 1989:99). At the same time, more and more union members tended to view their unions instrumentally, as essentially their business agents. Attendance at union meetings dwindled, except at negotiation time (Heron, 1989).

Union membership rates edged up to 34 percent in 1958, then started a slow drop towards the trough of 28 percent they would reach six years later. There were a number of possible explanations: public perception that union leaders had become "fat cats" and that unions had lost touch with "the little guy"; negative fallout from disclosures of union corruption and violence in the United States;[13] the apparent saturation of unions' traditional power bases in manufacturing, mining, construction, and transportation; and an unsympathetic Conservative government headed by John Diefenbaker.

With the onset of the Cold War, Communists had gradually been pushed to the sidelines. By 1950, CCFers and others had rid the CCL of any remaining Communist influence (Morton, 1995:145). The TLC had been slower to get in on the Cold War hysteria, but in 1949 it suspended its largest Communist organization, the Canadian Seamen's Union (Heron, 1989:90); five years later it also got rid of the west coast fishermen's union (Heron, 1989). In hindsight, the TLC may have come to regret expelling the Seamen's Union, which was replaced with the gangster-ridden Seafarers' International Union (SIU), leading to one of the sorriest chapters in Canadian labour history (Heron, 1989). Using intimidation, beatings, and sweetheart deals with companies to defeat other unions, SIU leader Hal Banks would leave a black mark on the Canadian labour movement for years to come. Only after six years and 75 proven instances of violence would the **Canadian Labour Congress** (successor to the TLC) expel the SIU (Morton and Copp, 1980:233–236).

The Communist purges definitely ended that party's influence within the Canadian labour movement. Surprisingly, they didn't seem to benefit the social democratic CCF, now the only remaining labour-oriented party on the left. Far from growing as a result of its old rival's demise, it fared poorly in most federal and provincial elections through the 1950s (Morton and Copp, 1980:227). Only after the party modernized itself, diluting its socialist agenda and broadening its appeal to middle-class voters after the fashion of the British Labour Party (Heron, 1989:110), would it do better at the polls. This new, more centrist party, known after 1961 as the New Democratic Party (NDP), would play a critical role in the expansion of collective bargaining to the public service and liberalization of federal labour legislation by virtue of the balance-of-power position it held in several Liberal minority governments (Heron, 1989:110–112). Provincially, its impact would be even greater, as NDP governments elected in three Western provinces between 1969 and 1972 would introduce a broad range of progressive labour legislation on issues ranging from occupational health and safety to technological change (Heron, 1989:112).

Federation Mergers

The decade's major event, in terms of labour politics, was the merger of the two great federations, the TLC and CCL, which took place in 1956, just a year after the American AFL and CIO had merged under the presidency of George Meany. The two longstanding rivals formed a new organization, under the presidency of Montrealer Claude Jodoin, known as the Canadian Labour Congress. The merger appeared to make a good deal of sense, since it would end the union raiding that had become common during the postwar period and would also allow for the pooling of scarce organizational resources (Morton and Copp, 1980:216–220).

Amid the labour movement's growing bureaucratization, there were a few reminders of its stormier past. In 1957, Quebec Premier Maurice Duplessis crushed an illegal strike at Murdochville, Quebec, that resulted when the Gaspé Copper Company refused to recognize a duly certified Steelworkers' local. Provincial police stood by as **strikebreakers** stoned picketers and hoodlums ransacked the union office. Eventually, two-thirds of the strikers lost their jobs and the union was sued for nearly $3 million (Morton and Copp, 1980:228). In 1959, Newfoundland Premier Joey Smallwood, himself a former socialist and union organizer, decertified the International Woodworkers of America (IWA) during a bitter, but legal, loggers' strike in Badger. A few days later, after vigilantes had smashed the IWA headquarters in Grand Falls, employers signed agreements with a new local union created by Smallwood himself (Morton and Copp, 1980:230–231).

Automation

Fears that technological change, or automation as it was then known, would displace and deskill large numbers of workers resurfaced at the end of the 1950s. The switch from steam to diesel locomotives threatened the jobs of thousands of railroad firemen. The switch to computerized typesetting was an even greater threat to printers' jobs. In numerous other occupations, from mining and logging to banking and postal work, rapidly emerging new technologies transformed the way work was done, in the process putting thousands of workers' jobs and skills at risk.

In a few cases, such as longshoring in Montreal, comprehensive modernization agreements were worked out. Like a similar agreement on the Pacific Coast, the Montreal agreement allowed employers to proceed with mechanization and automation of longshoring work in return for job protection for those working full time on the docks (Picard, 1967). Others were not so lucky. Many Toronto printers lost "their jobs, their savings, and ... their craft" (Morton and Copp, 1980:240) in a lengthy, bitter, and ultimately hopeless strike against computerized typesetting at the city's daily newspapers. During the early 1970s, both the federal government and the three Western provinces with NDP governments wrote modest protection against the effects of technological change into their labour acts. But the legislation proved largely ineffectual, mainly because labour boards were extremely reluctant to intervene, even in cases where the legislation had clearly been violated (Peirce, 1987).[14]

The Canadian Labour Movement's New Face

The 1960s was a decade of renewed radicalism and questioning of conventional wisdom and received authority in most areas of Canadian life, from economics and politics to music and personal morality. The labour movement was no exception. By the end of the decade, it wore a very different face, mainly as a result of something previously considered unthinkable—full-scale unionization of the public sector, including federal and provincial public servants.

Unlike private sector unionization, which had evolved gradually, public sector unionization came very quickly to Canada once the forces leading to it had been set in motion. Through the 1950s and into the 1960s, the notion of parliamentary sovereignty had been used to deny public sector workers collective bargaining rights. As the sovereignty argument eroded and public sector workers became more militant, there were growing demands that they be allowed to join unions.

By the end of 1964, full collective bargaining rights, including the right to strike, had been granted to most of Quebec's public sector workers (Hébert, 1995:202). Meanwhile, federal government employees, frustrated with years of lagging pay, the transformation of their workplaces into large impersonal bureaucracies (Heron, 1989:106), and an unsympathetic Conservative federal government, were demanding similar rights. Elected in 1963, Lester Pearson's Liberal government initially promised to grant its employees collective bargaining rights with binding arbitration (Swimmer, 1995:369). A nation-wide postal strike in 1965 and the Liberals' tenuous minority position, in which the pro-labour NDP held the balance of power, pushed them to go further than that. The result was a piece of comprehensive collective bargaining legislation, the *Public Service Staff Relations Act (PSSRA)*, which broke new ground in a number of different ways. Most notably, the bill gave the union the right to choose between binding arbitration and the conventional conciliation-strike route of resolving disputes (Swimmer, 1995). A Public Service Staff Relations Board was set up to administer the act and determine appropriate bargaining units (Swimmer, 1995:370). To safeguard the public health and welfare during public service strikes, the bill also established a procedure for designating employees whose services were deemed essential (Swimmer, 1995:377).

The *PSSRA* had a number of significant impacts on the labour movement all across the country. To begin with, a number of provinces (including Newfoundland and New Brunswick) soon followed the federal government's lead, passing their own "mini-*PSSRA*" bills legalizing full public sector collective bargaining, including the right to strike. Other provinces (including Ontario and Alberta) granted public employees bargaining rights, but substituted binding arbitration for the right to strike. By the early 1970s, some form of collective bargaining covered every provincial government worker in Canada (Fryer, 1995:343–346). By decade's end, collective bargaining rights had likewise been extended to all the country's teachers and health care workers. The *PSSRA* and its provincial counterparts also facilitated unionization of professionals and other private sector white-collar workers. Once they saw their public sector colleagues benefitting from unionization, they came to realize that they could, as well. By the 1970s, an increasing number of private sector professionals had taken out union membership (Thompson, 1982).

Even more important, the *PSSRA* and the various provincial laws brought large numbers of women into the Canadian labour movement for the first time, since women made up a large proportion of the public sector work force. Among other things, this development would have a significant impact on the public sector unions' bargaining agendas. Unions with large female memberships soon began to demand improved maternity leave provisions, provisions allowing for more flexible working hours, and other benefits reflecting the reality of women's dual roles as workers and homemakers. The relatively greater concentration of professionals in public sector unions led to a greater emphasis on intrinsic working conditions than one would find in most blue-collar unions, and bargaining table demands for in-service training and joint labour–management committees (Ponak: 1982, 351–353).

Private Sector Militancy

The 1960s also saw increased militancy in Canada's private sector unions. In 1966, strikes had reached their highest level in 20 years (Godard, 1994:96), spurred by rising inflation. The middle of the decade saw the previously mentioned postal strike, the country's first national railway strike, a strike along the St. Lawrence Seaway, and disputes at Heinz Foods, Canada Packers, International Nickel, and in B.C.'s logging industry (Morton and Copp, 1980:248–251). Across the country there was a wave of wildcat strikes (in 1966 these amounted to one-third the total number of strikes) and increasing **rank-and-file** rejection of contracts negotiated by union leaders (Heron, 1989:104; Morton, 1995:109). Alarmed at the growing turbulence in the country's industrial relations system, Prime Minister Pearson struck a Royal Commission under the direction of Dean H.D. (Buzz) Woods of McGill University to see what could be done (Morton and Copp, 1980:253–254). The Woods Task Force report, released in early 1969, recommended relatively minor changes such as the formation of employer associations to balance unions and the creation of a public interest disputes commission to deal with strikes in essential industries—a recommendation repeated in the recently-released Fyrer Committee Report on the federal public service (discussed in more detail in Chapter 9). Overall, its message was that the Canadian IR system was, if not perfect, probably among the least of possible evils and that industrial conflict was an inevitable price to be paid for living in a democratic society (Morton and Copp, 1980:262–264).[15]

Changes in Quebec

Nowhere did the Canadian labour movement change more quickly during the 1960s than in the province of Quebec. The changes were greatest of all within the former confessional union movement, which by this time had gone through a number of different metamorphoses to emerge as the leading exponent of radicalism in the province.

Forced to become more militant to compete with other federations that were actively organizing in the province, the CTCC had, during the Second World War, dropped its "Catholic-only" clause and opposition to strikes and started operating more like a conventional trade union (Boivin, 1982:427). Later, under the leadership of Jean Marchand, it played a leading role in the Asbestos strike of 1949 and the opposition to the Duplessis regime during the 1950s. In 1960, it severed its remaining ties with the Catholic Church and renamed itself the **Confédération des syndicats nationaux (CSN)**. Buoyed by Duplessis's replacement by Liberal premier Jean Lesage, the CSN grew rapidly in both size and influence during the 1960s. A key player during the "Quiet Revolution," the federation benefitted particularly from the unionization of public sector workers mentioned previously (Boivin, 1982:429–430).

After Marchand's departure in 1965, the federation took an increasingly radical and separatist course under Marcel Pépin, losing much of its mainstream public support as the result of a major hospital strike in 1966 and a Montreal Transit strike during Expo 1967 (Boivin, 1982). By 1968, the CSN had expanded its efforts to the quest for a "Second Front" outside collective bargaining, which sought alliances between the labour movement and other progressive organizations such as tenants' groups and credit unions in local "political action committees" (Heron, 1989:117). With other provincial labour organizations, such as the **Quebec Federation of Labour (QFL)** and teachers' union **(CEQ)** also taking an increasingly radical stance (Heron, 1989), the CSN in 1971 published two radical manifestos that made the case for an independent and socialist Quebec (Boivin, 1982:430).

Brought together, at least for the time being, by their radicalism, the three major federations in 1972 established a "Common Front" for public sector negotiations with the provincial government involving some 250 000 workers (Boivin, 1982). The failure of those negotiations led to a massive public sector strike, the largest in Canadian history, which would eventually result in the jailing of the leaders of all three federations for defying back-to-work orders (Heron, 1989:118). Though the strike spread to the private sector, becoming a general strike in some parts of the province, it ended about a week later (Heron, 1989). The "Common Front" days were to be the high-water mark for both labour radicalism and labour unity in the province. Within two years of the great strike, dislike of the CSN's radicalism had prompted three large groups to break away from the federation and adopt a much more moderate political course (Déom and Boivin, 1995). Moreover, the QFL and CSN were back at loggerheads over the organization of construction workers on the James Bay construction site (Boivin, 1982:431). The election of a separatist and pro-labour Parti Québécois (PQ) government in 1976 arguably helped reduce Quebec labour radicalism, although there would be resurgences, especially in the PQ's second term, when it froze the right to strike and rolled back public sector salaries by almost 20 percent (Heron, 1989:128).

A New Breed of Worker

The young people entering the work force for the first time during the 1960s posed problems both for employers and for the unions seeking to represent their interests. More highly educated than their parents had been, these young people had been raised in a culture of permissiveness and brought up to believe there should be a good deal more to a job than a paycheque. With their disdain for dress codes and traditional social mores generally, they found it hard to adjust to life in mainstream organizations with conventional top-down management practices.[16]

Often they gave their union leaders nearly as hard a time as their employers. Many were impatient with unions' often bureaucratic ways of doing things and with seniority-based systems that left them at the bottom of the ladder. Also, their bargaining agenda often conflicted with that of older, more established workers. Many of the older workers had bought into the postwar compromise whereby unions negotiated for wages and benefits and intrinsic concerns were, in effect, left outside the factory gate or office door. For young people raised with such high expectations of work and life, and who had seldom known real, grinding poverty, the old compromise simply wasn't good enough. It wasn't enough that a job be secure and pay a decent wage, it had to be interesting and socially worthwhile as well.

Younger workers' unhappiness with established ways of doing things was probably a factor in the high rate of wildcats and contract rejections during the 1960s.
Later (as we noted in Chapter 3), it would prove a stimulus to the broad range of
quality of worklife initiatives introduced during that decade—often in the face of
union leaders' indifference or outright hostility.

Those Left Behind

Again, many didn't share in the general prosperity of the 1960s and early 1970s. In big
cities like Montreal, immigrant workers, mainly women, continued to toil 50 to 60 hours
a week or even longer, exposing themselves to heat, cold, toxic chemicals, and grossly
inadequate sanitation in abattoirs, factories, hotels, and restaurants. If they were lucky,
they would receive the minimum wage. Many did not. Fearing deportation or dismissal,
most of those who didn't were afraid to complain. Even the few who did had no guarantee of success, given the lack of inspectors and of political will to enforce minimum
wage and health and safety legislation (Arnopoulos, 1974). For Ontario's farm workers,
conditions were little better. At a time when the average industrial wage was $3.17 an
hour and the Ontario minimum wage $1.60, the top 54 percent of farm workers were
averaging $1.71 an hour; fully 94 percent of all fruit and vegetable workers were getting
less than the provincial minimum (Ward, 1974:302). Despite such pathetically low wages
and primitive working conditions, the provincial government did not extend the
minimum wage or other basic employment standards to farm workers (Ward, 1974).

A New Era of Restraint

Despite a number of differences with the federal government, the Canadian labour movement was, in 1974, in the strongest position it had been in since the end of the Second
World War. The wave of public sector legislation that followed the *PSSRA* had brought
hundreds of thousands of new members into the Canadian labour movement for the first
time. Union membership rates had risen from 29 percent of the country's labour force in
1964, to 35 percent in 1974 (Godard, 1994:96–97). Across the country, labour relations
acts had been liberalized. Politically, as well, the labour movement was in a strong position in 1974, thanks to the growing popularity of its ally, the New Democratic Party.
Federally, the NDP held the balance of a power in a minority Liberal government;
provincially, it formed the government in three of four Western provinces (Manitoba,
Saskatchewan, and British Columbia) and was also a significant player in Ontario.

Starting in 1974, all this changed. With the 1973–1974 energy crisis and subsequent wave of inflation and unemployment, the country's economic and political climate turned notably more conservative. The 1974 federal election was an omen of
hard times to come. In that election, the NDP lost half its seats (including that of its
leader, David Lewis) and its balance-of-power position as Pierre Trudeau's Liberals
swept to a strong majority. The next year, B.C.'s NDP government was defeated, and
in 1977, the party lost power in Manitoba.

Though he'd ridiculed wage-price controls during his 1974 election campaign,

Trudeau introduced a comprehensive three-year program on Thanksgiving Day, 1975 (Reid, 1982). The labour movement was outraged. In protest, it withdrew labour representatives from most tripartite government bodies, such as the Economic Council of Canada, and staged a one-day general strike against the controls and the government's Anti-Inflation Board in 1976. To some (i.e., Panitch and Swartz, 1988), the controls mark the beginning of the end of free collective bargaining in Canada. Even those (i.e., Reid, 1982:501) who felt the controls had been on balance effective and believed the labour movement's fear about them had been largely unfounded admitted that the program "had imposed severe strains on both the social fabric and the industrial-relations system."

When "normal" collective bargaining resumed in 1978, it was in an environment increasingly hostile to workers and their unions, particularly the public sector unions. A wave of public sector strikes, particularly a series of lengthy disputes involving Canada Post (Swimmer, 1995:385–386) and the Montreal Transit system, had soured many Canadians on the whole idea of free collective bargaining in the public sector. By the late 1970s, there were numerous calls for the federal government to abolish its workers' right to strike. Despite strong public pressure, it did not do that. But it did severely restrict its workers' right to strike in two other ways: by increasing the proportion of workers designated as "essential" and thus compelled to work during a strike (Swimmer, 1995; Panitch and Swartz, 1988), and through an increased use of back-to-work legislation (Panitch and Swartz, 1988:31), a device also used by provincial governments.

A second energy crisis, starting in 1979, launched the country into a new inflationary spiral as serious as the 1973–1974 one had been. Federal and provincial governments responded, once again, with wage control legislation—legislation this time aimed exclusively at the public sector. Federal wage restraint legislation limited increases to 6 percent in the first year and 5 percent in the second (Swimmer, 1995). Some provinces' legislation was even more restrictive. This was especially true in Quebec, where the PQ government in 1982 imposed a 20 percent reduction on public sector workers' salaries (Hébert, 1995:222–223), and in B.C., where wage restraint legislation was accompanied by legislation effectively giving the provincial cabinet the authority to terminate any public sector worker unilaterally, under the guise of restraint (Panitch and Swartz, 1988:41).

The 1980s Recession and Its Aftermath

Beginning in 1981, Canada plunged into its most serious recession since the Second World War. In 1983, some 1.3 million Canadians (or more than 12 percent of the country's work force) were officially unemployed (Heron, 1989:125; Morton, 1995:151). In some parts of the country, such as Newfoundland, the official unemployment rate was more than 20 percent.[17] Food banks, which had not been seen since the Great Depression, began to appear in major Canadian cities as unemployment increased and more and more people exhausted their unemployment benefits (Heron, 1989:125–127).

Though the economy started to recover in the mid 1980s in central Canada, many of the high-paying jobs lost in manufacturing and resources never came back. Thereafter, high unemployment would be a more or less permanent feature of the Canadian labour market (Heron, 1989:125; Morton, 1995:151–152). The new jobs that replaced those well-paying jobs were mainly in the low-paying, hard-to-organize private-service sector. Knowing they had few other options if they wanted to replace the thousands of members lost in manufacturing and resources during the recession, the unions made a valiant effort to organize the service industries, focussing their attention on the chartered banks and on retail giants like Eaton's. But Eaton's refused to sign a first collective agreement (Morton, 1995:152), and the bid to unionize the banks proved largely unsuccessful due to determined employer resistance marked by the frequent intimidation, harassment, and transfer of union activists (Lowe, 1980).

A Harder Management Line

In such a difficult economic environment, workers and unions were reluctant to press demands too hard, while management felt it could safely take a much tougher stance in dealing with unions. By the early 1980s, management was starting to bring its own list of demands to the bargaining table. These demands often included outright wage freezes or even rollbacks, reductions in paid holiday time, and cuts in employer-paid benefit plans (Heron, 1989:136–137). By the mid 1980s, some employers were demanding that unions accept **two-tier wage schemes**, whereby new hires were paid far less than experienced workers. To back up their demands for concessions, employers often forced a strike or locked out their workers. Increasingly, they used the threat of closing down or relocating the plant to achieve concessions (Heron, 1989). Given the tough economic environment and increasingly unsympathetic political climate, such threats seemed all too real to most workers. The new employer militancy approach (discussed in some detail in Chapter 3) was used most often in historically anti-union Alberta. There, construction employers virtually destroyed the building trade unions in 1984 by means of a lockout that enabled them to break an expired collective agreement legally (Heron, 1989:136), while Peter Pocklington tried and failed to break the United Food and Commercial Workers (UFCW) union at his Gainer's meat-packing plant in Edmonton during a bitter strike that attracted nation-wide attention (Godard, 1994:380–381).

The Mulroney Years

Life became even more difficult for the Canadian labour movement following the 1984 landslide election of a Conservative federal government under Brian Mulroney. Sharing much of U.S. President Ronald Reagan's political ideology, if not his personal dislike of unions, Mulroney pushed an agenda featuring large-scale privatization of public enterprises, deregulation of regulated ones, free trade with the United States, and relaxation of foreign investment controls. The effect of this agenda was to greatly increase foreign competition for Canadian businesses, thereby putting even more pressure on employers to cut labour costs. This in turn led to even more plant closures, a proliferation of mergers and acquisitions, large-scale layoffs, the substitution of technology for human labour, and harder work and longer hours for those who remained—all in the name of "rationalization" (Heron, 1989:134).

Schisms and Breakaways

As if it didn't face difficult enough challenges in its battles with employers and governments, the Canadian labour movement during this period was becoming increasingly divided against itself. The period was marked by major schisms within labour federations, a growing number of breakaways of Canadian branches from U.S.-based international unions, and a number of serious incidents of union raiding, or attempts by one union to sign up members of another (Godard, 1994:244).

THE CANADIAN FEDERATION OF LABOUR (CFL) Traditionally more conservative than most other unions, the building trade unions had long been unhappy with the Canadian Labour Congress (CLC). Major irritants included the CLC's support for the NDP and its refusal to move to a block voting pattern, similar to that of the AFL-CIO, that would give union leaders more power (Heron, 1989:151; Morton, 1995:151). But nothing upset these labour traditionalists more than the CLC's granting of partial autonomy to its Quebec arm, the Quebec Federation of Labour, which allowed construction unions that had broken away from the internationals to remain affiliated. CLC leaders, reluctant to aggravate an already difficult situation in Quebec, did not act despite the building trades' protests that the dual unions violated the CLC's constitution, whereupon 12 of the construction unions, representing about 350 000 workers, withheld their congress dues in 1980 (Heron, 1989; Morton, 1995). A year later, the CLC suspended the building trades unions; in 1982, most of them formed their own federation, a new Canadian Federation of Labour based on internationalism and the apolitical, bread-and-butter approach of Samuel Gompers (see McCambly, 1990). The CFL operated quite successfully for 15 years. But in 1997, crippled by the loss of 40 percent of its members after the International Brotherhood of Electrical Workers returned to the CLC, it ceased to operate as a central labour body, leaving its long-time rival as English Canada's only umbrella labour organization (McKinley, 1997).

BREAKAWAYS FROM U.S. INTERNATIONALS The secession of the Canadian branches of U.S. international unions from their parent organizations was not new in the 1980s; however, the trend towards Canadianization of the labour movement gained a higher public profile as the result of several widely publicized breakaways, including most notably that of the **Canadian Auto Workers (CAW)** from the United Auto Workers (UAW) in 1985.

By the late 1960s and early 1970s, the Canadian branches of U.S.-based international unions had begun breaking away from their parent unions and forming independent unions. The reasons ranged from dislike of U.S. control over the Canadian labour movement and resentment at the poor servicing of Canadian branches, to more specific disagreements over bargaining strategy and political issues such as Canadian unionists' support for the NDP or the Americans' support for the Vietnam War (Heron, 1989:149).

The growing number of secessions from the internationals led the CLC to establish a number of autonomy guidelines for the Canadian branches of U.S. internationals in 1970 and 1974 (discussed in more detail in Chapter 5). By 1980, the CLC reported that the guidelines were providing more freedom for the Canadian branches of internationals (Heron, 1989:150–151). Still, the wave of secessions continued apace. The communications workers left their American parent in 1972, the paper workers in 1974, and energy and chemical workers in 1980 (Heron, 1989:152).

The Canadian Auto Workers' 1985 secession from the United Auto Workers was based to a large extent on bargaining strategy. The Canadian division had refused to go along with the international's concession bargaining approach in the previous round of negotiations and eventually reached a settlement differing significantly from the American one. The bitter dispute that resulted eventually became a major factor in the CAW's departure from the UAW (Craig and Solomon, 1996:186–18; Godard, 1994: 248–249).

UNION MERGERS AND RAIDING   To make up for the membership lost through economic restructuring and deindustrialization, many of the big industrial unions, such as the steelworkers and autoworkers, were forced to look farther afield, to workers in totally unrelated industries. Often they turned to the unorganized. Occasionally, however, they turned to workers already represented by a union, as in the now-celebrated dispute between the CAW and the **United Food and Commercial Workers (UFCW)** over the right to represent fisheries workers in Atlantic Canada.

In 1987, the 23 000-member Newfoundland branch of the UFCW announced its decision to affiliate with the CAW. The ensuing battle between the two unions, eventually won by the CAW, went before the courts as well as the labour boards and proved a major embarrassment to the labour movement (Craig and Solomon, 1996:170; Heron, 1989:152). The brouhaha did lead to a major change in the way the CLC handles jurisdictional disputes. Until 1988, it had employed a permanent umpire to rule on such disputes. After the CAW-UFCW episode, it brought in tough new anti-raiding rules and gave its executive committee the responsibility of settling jurisdictional disputes itself. But while both these changes probably made sense, they didn't put a stop to raiding. In 1992, the CLC's executive committee imposed heavy sanctions on the International Woodworkers of America's Canadian division for raiding the Canadian Paperworkers Union (Craig and Solomon, 1996:170–171). More recently, a bitter dispute between the CAW and the Service Employees' International

Union over the former's alleged raiding of the latter prompted the CLC to impose sanctions on the CAW. The dispute continued until sanctions were lifted in May 2001 (CNW, 2001).

Canadian Labour in the 1990s

As we noted in the first edition of this book(see especially Chapter 2), the 1990s was a decade of fundamental change in the economic and political environment. These changes led to equally major changes in the way work is organized and scheduled, in unions' strategies, and in national governments' willingness and ability to regulate economic and IR-related issues. For the most part, these changes left the Canadian labour movement in an even weaker position than it had been in at the start of the decade. Among the most crucial developments of the period were the implementation of comprehensive free trade agreements, a squeeze on public sector workers, a wave of union consolidation and mergers, and a questioning of labour's traditional links with its longstanding political partner, the NDP.

Free Trade and Its Implications

The period's single most important development was arguably the formation of a North American trading bloc (Lipsig-Mumme, 1995), following the implementation of Canada-U.S. and North American free trade agreements in 1989 and 1994, respectively. In a related move (Reid and Meltz, 1995:47), Canada in 1994 signed on to a broad range of worldwide tariff reductions resulting from a new round of negotiations under the General Agreement on Trade and Tariffs (GATT). Over the past five years, Canada has been a party to further moves to liberalize trade throughout the western hemisphere. The wave of globalization and trade liberalization had the effect of intensifying the wave of restructuring begun during the late 1980s, leading to heavy job losses in the manufacturing sector and, starting near the end of the decade, the financial sector as well. By the late 1990s, there were signs that the free trade agreements had had an effect on collective bargaining settlements. In early 1998, for example, workers at Maple Leaf Foods Company in Brampton, Ontario, narrowly approved a deal that saw average wages reduced by more than 40 percent. The deal, which seemed to refute the conventional industrial relations wisdom that Canadian workers would never go in for concession bargaining, was attributed almost entirely to the free trade agreements. Quite simply, without a drastic reduction in labour costs, it appeared that Canadian meat producers could no longer compete with lower-cost producers in the United States and Mexico.

Workers' job security was a major casualty of economic restructuring, as many firms adopted a "lean production" mode whereby they retain only a small core of permanent workers, using short-term, temporary, or contractual workers to meet peak-period demands. Those few who remain more or less steadily employed must often work longer and harder than in the past, since there are now so many fewer regular

Figure 4.1

A SCHEMATIC OUTLINE OF EVENTS IN THE HISTORY OF TRADE UNION MOVEMENTS IN THE UNITED STATES AND CANADA

The United States

1869 *Knights of Labor*
— uplift unionism
— membership not restricted
— craft and mixed locals

1886–1955 *American Federation of Labor (AFL)*
— a loose federation of craft-oriented unions
— excluded Knights of Labor because of dual unionism
— little activity in politics
— each affiliate was autonomous
— preferred little government intervention

1938–1955 *Congress of Industrial Organizations (CIO)*
— unions expelled from AFL
— wanted to unionize unskilled labourers
— wanted industrial unions
— more active in politics than AFL
— organized mass production workers

1955 *AFL-CIO*
— merger of AFL and CIO affiliated unions
— no-raiding pacts between unions affiliated with each federation
— craft and industrial unions
— conservative philosophy
— supports Democratic party
— code of ethical practices
— little control over affiliates

Canada

1875–1910 *Knights of Labor*
— active in Que., Ont., and N.S.
— uplift unionism
— membership not restricted
— craft and mixed locals
— problems with R.C. Church in Que.

1908–1927 *Trades and Labour Congress (TLC)*
— included Knights of Labor, N.S. Provincial Workman's Assoc. and other Canadian unions
— nationalistic in orientation
— dominated by regional interests
— wanted more Canadian control

1919–1956 *One Big Union (OBU)*
— mainly in western Canada
— dissatisfaction with TLC
— opposed to craft unions
— felt TLC structure not suited to western Canada
— influenced by radical IWW
— played an active role in Winnipeg General Strike of 1919
— became part of CLC in 1956

1927–1940 *All-Canadian Congress of Labour (ACCL)*
— remnants of CFL of 1908, OBU, and CBRE
— wanted industrial unions
— critical of American control
— critical of conservative philosophy of TLC

1940–1956 *Canadian Congress of Labour (CCL)*
— Canadian branches of CIO unions
— remnants of ACCL
— wanted to unionize unskilled labourers
— wanted industrial unions
— active in politics
— organized mass production workers
— wanted less control from U.S.
— wanted more government action than TLC

1956 *Canadian Labour Congress (CLC)*
— merger of TLC and CCL affiliated unions
— no-raiding pacts between unions affiliated with each federation
— craft and industrial unions
— less conservative philosophy than AFL-CIO
— has supported NDP, but link now being revisited
— code of ethics
— little control over affiliates
— standards of self-government to apply mostly to Canadian districts of international unions

1982–1997 *Canadian Federation of Labour (CFL)*
— formed by construction unions, but others also affiliated
— wanted more voting power in CLC

Figure 4.1
(continued)

- non-partisan political stance and closer ties with government than CLC
- folded in 1997

1991 *Federal Public Service Strike*
- sign of increasing public sector militancy
- result of government imposition of wage freeze
- PSSRB found Treasury Board guilty of bargaining in bad faith with PSAC

2001 *Nation-wide health care strikes*
- result of years of salary freezes, cutbacks to health system
- also result from restriction of health care workers' bargaining rights
- N.S. premier threatened end to arbitration, backed off and sent dispute to final offer
- contract imposed in B.C. dispute (Aug., 2001)

2001 *Public Service Strikes*
- National Gallery strike featured colourful protest methods
- one-day strikes (Aug., 2001) to back demands for higher wages
- public service irate at 2% offer when MPs, PS executives received much bigger pay increases.

Union Developments in Quebec

1900 *Major strike in Quebec City, arbitrated by Archbishop of Quebec*
- confessional unions formed across the province
- meetings dominated largely by clergy
- influenced by Papal encyclicals

1921–1960 *Canadian and Catholic Confederation of Labour (CCCL)*
- founding convention in Hull, Quebec, in 1921
- brought workers together into a confederation
- wanted to keep workers Catholic and French-speaking
- dominated largely by clergy until 1940s
- adhered largely to teachings of Papal encyclicals

1947 *Asbestos strike*
- a turning point in Quebec's economic and social history
- broke ties between government and church
- lay leaders began to play major role in unions after mid-1940s

1960 *Confederation of National Trade Unions (change of name to CNTU)*
- dropped Catholic from name
- has about ten sectors
- became radical during the 1970s, but more pragmatic during the 1990s
- smaller than Quebec Federation of Labour (provincial arm of CLC)
- part of "Common Front" in 1972 and 1982
- QFL and CNTU cooperate and raid

1991 *Social Contracts*
- response to recession of early 1990s
- signed by both CNTU and QFL unions
- mainly in metal and pulp and paper industries
- guarantee long-term labour peace in return for employment stability, joint union-management administration of the agreement

1998 *Politcal Protests*
- major demonstrations and protest against P.Q. government cuts to health, education

Source: Adapted from Craig and Solomon, 1996.

employees. The result is a situation where many workers are putting in long overtime hours while others remain unemployed or underemployed (O'Hara, 1993). As we noted in Chapter 2, "atypical" work arrangements, with workers provided little if any job security and few benefits, have become much more common now than they were in the past. The growth of such atypical work arrangements poses major organizing challenges for unions, since part-time and temporary workers are normally a good deal more difficult to organize than full-timers.

The Public Sector Squeeze

The 1990s were particularly hard on public sector workers. In 1991, the federal government's imposition of a wage freeze caused the Public Service Alliance of Canada to launch its first-ever full-scale national public service strike (Swimmer, 1995). The strike was followed by a five-year suspension of collective bargaining, and even when bargaining resumed in 1996, salary arbitration remained suspended for five more years (Fryer, 2001). At provincial levels as well, most public sector workers had to endure wage freezes if not outright rollbacks, and suspension of normal collective bargaining procedures (Fryer, 1995). Downsizing and program cuts meant that, as in the private sector, there have been fewer people to do the work needing to be done, which in turn led to increased overtime—much of it involuntary and unpaid. (See, among others, PSES, 1999). Beyond that, large-scale health-care and education restructuring initiatives in Alberta and Ontario led to massive layoffs. While different provinces took different approaches to the question of public sector restructuring, few public sector workers escaped unscathed. Governments' tough stance toward their own employees was undoubtedly a crucial factor in the wave of public sector strikes, particularly in health care, that has been taking place during the preparation of the second edition of this book.

Union Consolidation

The 1990s also saw the consolidation of Canada's previously highly fragmented union movement, mainly through a variety of mergers (Heron, 1989; Murray, 1995). The most notable of these involved the Communications Workers of Canada, Energy and Chemical Workers Union, and Canadian Paperworkers Union, which in 1992 joined forces as the **Communications, Energy and Paperworkers Union of Canada,** or **CEP.** The Canadian Auto Workers and Steelworkers were also heavily involved in merger activity during the decade (Murray, 1995:178; Craig and Solomon, 1996:190–193). The rationale behind many of these mergers was that the new, larger unions are likely to be in a better position to carry out intensive organizing and otherwise provide a broad range of services to their members than the smaller ones they replaced.

Closely related to the merger trend, in fact a direct result of it, was the evolution of a number of industrial unions, including the Auto Workers and Steelworkers, into general or conglomerate unions claiming to represent all workers, not just those in a particular industry. Though the trend led to a number of jurisdictional disputes, it also increased representational possibilities for previously hard-to-organize private

service sector workers. For example, the Steelworkers, who had already been organizing groups as diverse as zoo and security guards, hotel and restaurant workers,
and Montessori teachers, increased their private service sector organizing following
their 1993 merger with the Canadian section of the Retail, Wholesale and
Department Store union (Murray, 1995:178). For its part, the CAW organized at least
two British Columbia branches of the Starbucks coffee chain (Murdock, 1997).

Revisiting the NDP Link

Earlier, we indicated that the English-Canadian labour movement has generally relied
on the New Democratic Party to help it achieve its political objectives, such as labour
law reform or improved health and safety legislation. Union support was critical to
the election of NDP provincial governments in Ontario, Saskatchewan, and British
Columbia early in the 1990s. As in the past (Heron, 1989), these governments often
proved disappointing to their labour supporters once in office (Lipsig-Mumme,
1995:207). This was especially true in Ontario, where, in 1993, the NDP government
imposed a "social contract" suspending free public sector collective bargaining and
forcing workers to take unpaid days off (Murray, 1995:189). Loss of labour support,
especially from the public sector unions, was clearly a factor in the NDP's disastrous
1993 federal election showing and in its defeat in the 1995 Ontario election. Though
the party rebounded somewhat in the 1997 federal election, doing particularly well
in the Atlantic region, its failure to win a single Ontario seat as well as its wretched
showing in the 1999 Ontario election[18] suggested that the tensions resulting from the
"social contract" had not yet been resolved. Similar tensions surfaced in Quebec
regarding the labour movement's link to the Parti Québécois, as a result of provincial
government cutbacks to health care and education. As we will see in the next section,
these tensions have remained unresolved into the new millennium.

Labour Strategy in Quebec

In Quebec, the labour movement responded quite differently to the economic crisis of the
1990s than it did in the rest of Canada. During the 1970s, the Quebec labour movement
was by far the most radical in the country. During the '90s, supported by a succession of
provincial governments that took a far more active role in socio-economic planning than
even most NDP governments in English Canada, its strategy became one of tripartite
cooperation with employers and government in the interest of creating and maintaining
jobs (Lipsig-Mumme, 1995; Boivin and Déom, 1995). The decade saw both the Quebec
Federation of Labour (QFL) and Confederation of National Trade Unions (CSN) sign on
to long-term peace agreements, agreements that, unlike the botched Ontario experiment,
can legitimately be called social contracts, since the unions were full partners in negotiating and implementing them (Boivin and Déom, 1995:461). The most widely publicized
examples have been in the steel industry (Verma and Warrian, 1992:128–129); others
have been negotiated in the pulp and paper and garment industries (Boivin and Déom,

1995:461). In return for a long-term guarantee of labour peace (generally for five years or more), the union receives employment security for its members and is given joint administration of the agreement. In addition, employees are provided with full information about the firm's financial situation. To help compensate the union for giving up its right to strike for five years or longer, most agreements allow for arbitration of monetary clauses after three years (Boivin and Déom, 1995). While it is not clear just how widely the Quebec social contracts have been adopted, they do appear to have had a positive effect on labour–management relations in the province. Among other things, they may well have been a factor in the province's substantial reduction in strike activity since the mid 1980s (see Chapter 11 for more details).

CANADIAN LABOUR AT THE DAWN OF THE NEW MILLENNIUM

The changes to the economic and political environment of the IR system over the past 15 years or so have not been merely cyclical ones. Rather, they represent a fundamental "sea change" in the way work is organized and scheduled, in employers' and unions' strategies, and in national governments' willingness and ability to regulate economic and IR-related issues.

As we noted in Chapter 2, on the economy, many workers don't even have a regular workplace any more. A growing number work out of their homes or on short-term contracts—a situation that is likely to prevent them from forming relationships with fellow workers and makes it more likely that their response to what they perceive to be poor working conditions will be to quit rather than to stay and try to improve conditions where they are. Even those with more or less regular jobs often have little job security; many, particularly in the private service sector, work such irregular shifts that they may know few if any of their workmates by name. The loyalty and sense of mutual obligation that were once not uncommon features of labour–management relationships are now extremely rare. In the high-tech sector, a sudden downturn in 2001 has cost many thousands of Canadian workers their jobs; in other industries, even profitable firms have laid off large numbers of employees, not because they were performing badly but in order to pay higher dividends to shareholders (see Peirce, 2000:89).

With the formation of broader regional trading blocs, not just in North America but also in Europe and Asia, it's no longer possible for Canadian employers, workers, or unions even to pretend Canada can insulate itself from larger world economic developments. As Richard Marsden (2001:76) has noted, unionized garment workers in Montreal now find themselves competing with workers in Romania and the Ivory Coast. As we noted in Chapter 2 and will note again in Chapter 11, in connection with the Falconbridge Mine strike, entire chains of production have become globalized, making it more difficult for unions to mount effective strikes against manufacturers. As if all this were not enough, there is reason to believe that a growing number of young workers have highly individualistic values, values of the kind that leave little room for unions and collective workplace action (see Barnard, Cosgrave and Welsh, 1996). Worse still, the labour movement has again been fighting against itself, as evidenced by the SEIU-CAW dispute which led the CLC to impose sanctions on the CAW from 2000 through May 2001 (CNW, 2001), as well as by the CSN's successful raid, in 2001, of correctional officers formerly represented by the Public Service Alliance (PSSRB, 2000 and 2001).

Marsden sums up the current situation well when he notes (2001:76): "The foundation upon which the post-World War II industrial relations system was based—long-term employment expectations that provided incentive for employee voice and a degree of protection from the full forces of the marketplace—has proved ephemeral." Taken together, the economic, political, and social changes just described have arguably left the Canadian labour movement in its weakest position since the Great Depression. While Canadian unions have maintained their membership levels surprisingly well so far, particularly in comparison with their counterparts in the U.S. (see Murray, 1995 and 2001), they will be increasingly hard-pressed to do so in the 21st century. Among their most serious challenges will be:

- That of providing representation to an increasingly diverse and geographically dispersed work force—many of whom do not even have a regular workplace, and others who would appear to have little use for unions as such;

- That of countering increasingly fierce employer opposition to unions, in both the private and public sectors—an opposition that has manifested itself in a growing willingness to use replacement workers, resort to injunctions and other legal tactics during strikes, and even (as in the case of the Falconbridge strike discussed in Chapter 11) resort to violence against strikers;

- That of countering growing schisms within the labour movement and of making the movement appear attractive to young people; and

- That of finding an effective political partner to help with legislation and political advocacy, whether that partner be a renewed NDP or some other party.[19]

The Canadian labour movement's ability to maintain relatively steady membership rates, in the face of an increasingly difficult economic and political environment, suggests that it possesses considerable resiliency. It will need all that resiliency and more if it is to meet the challenges it is likely to face in the decades to come.

QUESTIONS FOR DISCUSSION

1) What did you know about unions and Canadian labour history at the start of this course? What was your impression of unions and what they do?

2) What were some of the barriers to unions found in most industrialized countries? What were some barriers unique to Canada?

3) How did the Quebec labour movement develop differently from the English-Canadian one?

4) Why was the Canadian labour movement closely tied to the American one for many years? What factors contributed to the loosening or severing of many of those ties?

5) What was the significance of the Berlin Convention of 1902 to the development of the Canadian labour movement?

6) Why did the Canadian labour movement become more militant during the two world wars?

7) How did the industrial unionism introduced during the 1930s and 1940s differ from traditional craft unionism? Did it succeed in bringing unionization to all Canadian workers who wished to join? Why, or why not?

8) Do you think Mackenzie King helped or hindered the development of the Canadian labour movement?

9) How has the Canadian labour movement benefitted from its affiliation with political parties such as the NDP? Why are many in the labour movement now reviewing the linkages between it and the NDP (and the Parti Québécois in Quebec)?

10) Who are some of the groups Canadian unions must reach if they wish to retain their existing membership levels in the decades ahead? What are some strategies that might help them achieve this objective?

SUGGESTIONS FOR FURTHER READING

Heron, Craig. (1996). *The Canadian labour movement: A short history*. Toronto: Lorimer. First published in 1989, this has become a classic thanks to its readable style and the vivid picture it portrays of the lives of Canadian working people. The introductory section provides an extremely useful discussion of the barriers to the formation of an independent Canadian labour movement.

MacDowell, Laurel Sefton, and Ian Radforth (Eds.). (1991). *Canadian working class history*. Toronto: Canadian Scholars' Press. An extremely useful collection of articles covering many different aspects of Canadian labour history, from pre-Confederation days right through to modern times. Contains a number of articles on the role of women and immigrants—information that is often hard to obtain elsewhere.

Morton, Desmond. (1990). *Working people: An illustrated history of the Canadian labour movement*. Toronto: Summerhill. Another very readable history of the Canadian labour movement that has gone through several editions. Excellent illustrations. Those with a real taste for history may wish to compare Morton's institutionalist perspective with Heron's political economy one. Both books are well worth reading.

CHAPTER 5

UNION MEMBERSHIP
AND STRUCTURE

Volunteer union officials, like the steward shown here talking to a member about her grievance, put in hundreds of thousands of unpaid hours each year and are really what keep the organizations going in many cases.

Unions are the organizations most directly responsible for representing the interests of Canada's working people. We begin this chapter with a brief look at what unions are and at the functions they serve. Next we look at changing patterns of union membership, both for Canada as a whole and within different industries and provinces. Among the issues considered here is the divergence between Canadian and American union membership rates. The chapter then considers the structure of the Canadian labour movement, looking at activities carried out at the local, provincial, and national level, and at the role played by international unions based outside Canada—a distinctive feature of the Canadian labour movement. We conclude with a discussion of union democracy, or the extent to which unions are responsive to their members' wishes.

UNIONS: A BRIEF OVERVIEW

Unions have been defined as workers' associations formed to enhance their power in dealings with employers (Craig and Solomon, 1996:9), particularly in negotiating the terms and conditions under which work is performed and in handling workers' grievances. But while collective bargaining and grievance-handling are their core functions, unions do many other things as well. In Canada, as in most other countries, many unions are heavily involved in political action aimed at passing legislation that will advance the interests of working people. Beyond that, union political activities may include joining coalitions with other organizations such as anti-poverty groups, and serving on joint union–employer industry panels aimed at advancing the interests of a particular industry. In recent years, unions have also become increasingly involved in publicity campaigns of various kinds: some rather specifically focussed on mobilizing support for specific bargaining items, others designed to call public attention to problems of a more general nature, such as ongoing cutbacks in the federal and provincial governments. We'll be looking at the various types of union activity in more detail in the next chapter.

Before we get to that, it's important to look at the changing patterns of union membership in Canada, and at the structure of the country's labour movement, to get a better sense of how unions operate and why they operate as they do. As we'll soon see, while overall union membership rates have remained quite stable, there has been considerable change in the composition of the labour movement. In particular, the movement includes many more women, professionals, and white-collar workers than it did just a generation ago. As well, the movement's structure has changed significantly, with new labour federations springing up both at the national level and in Quebec, some secession from the country's largest labour federation, and many traditional industrial unions expanding their organizing efforts in an attempt to attract workers from the private-service sector or even on occasion the federal public service. It is to these questions of union membership and structure that we now turn.

UNION MEMBERSHIP

National Membership Trends

Except for brief periods of decline during the early 1920s, 1930s, and 1960s, Canadian union membership grew steadily throughout most of the twentieth century. In 1911 (Eaton, 1975, not shown in table), there were about 130 000 union members in Canada. By 1945, that number had grown to just over 700 000. As of 2001 (see Table 5.1), there were just over 4.1 million Canadian union members. Through the past decade, union membership has not declined, but it also hasn't increased. This stagnation of union membership growth is in sharp contrast to the roughly 400 000 member increase posted between 1980 and 1987 and the nearly 1 million member increase posted between 1970 and 1977.

Table 5.1

	UNION MEMBERSHIP AND UNION DENSITY, CANADA AND THE UNITED STATES, 1945–2001			
Year	Union Membership Canada (thousands)	Union Membership U.S. (thousands)	Union Density Canada (%)	Union Density U.S. (%)
1945	711	12 254	24.2	30.4
1946	832	12 936	27.9	31.1
1947	912	14 067	29.1	32.1
1948	978	14 272	30.3	31.8
1949	1 006	13 936	29.5	31.9
1950	—	14 294	—	31.6
1951	1 029	15 139	28.4	31.7
1952	1 146	15 632	30.2	32.0
1953	1 220	16 310	33.0	32.5
1954	1 268	15 809	33.8	32.3
1955	1 268	16 217	33.7	31.8
1956	1 352	16 446	33.3	31.4
1957	1 386	16 498	32.4	31.2
1958	1 454	15 571	34.2	30.3
1959	1 459	15 438	33.3	29.0
1960	1 459	15 516	32.3	28.6
1961	1 447	15 401	31.6	28.5
1962	1 423	16 894	30.2	30.4
1963	1 449	17 133	29.8	30.2
1964	1 493	17 597	29.4	30.2
1965	1 589	18 269	29.7	30.1
1966	1 736	18 922	30.7	29.6
1967	1 921	19 668	32.3	29.9
1968	2 010	20 017	33.1	29.5
1969	2 075	20 186	32.5	28.7
1970	2 173	20 990	33.6	29.6
1971	2 231	20 711	32.4	29.1
1972	2 388	21 206	33.9	28.8
1973	2 591	21 881	35.4	28.5
1974	2 732	22 165	35.2	28.3
1975	2 884	22 207	35.6	28.9
1976	3 042	22 153	36.9	27.9
1977	3 149	21 632	36.3	26.2
1978	3 278	21 757	37.1	25.1
1979	—	22 025	—	24.5
1980	3 397	20 968	35.7	23.2
1981	3 487	20 647	35.4	22.6
1982	3 617	19 571	35.7	21.9
1983	3 563	18 634	36.4	20.7
1984	3 651	17 340	37.2	18.3

Table 5.1
(continued)

Year	Union Membership Canada (thousands)	Union Membership U.S. (thousands)	Union Density Canada (%)	Union Density U.S. (%)
1985	3 666	16 996	36.4	18.3
1986	3 730	16 975	36.0	17.4
1987	3 782	16 913	35.2	16.5
1988	3 841	17 002	35.0	16.1
1989	3 944	16 960	34.8	15.7
1990	4 031	16 740	34.8	15.2
1991	4 068	16 568	34.8	15.3
1992	4 089	16 390	35.8	15.1
1993	4 071	16 598	36.0	15.8
1994	4 078	16 748	36.1	15.5
1995	4 003	16 360	34.7	14.9
1996	4 033	16 269	34.3	14.5
1997	4 074	16 110	34.5	14.1
1998	3 938	16 211	32.7	13.9
1999	4 010	16 447	32.6	13.9
2000	4 058	16 257	31.9	13.5
2001	4 111	16 275	31.3	13.5

Notes: Union density is defined as the percentage of non-agricultural paid workers belonging to unions. No figure is reported for 1950 because the reference date of Labour Canada's survey was changed from Dec. 31 to Jan. 1 in that year. No survey was conducted in 1979. Data for Canada are not strictly comparable before and after 1978 because the number of paid non-agricultural workers was adjusted upwards after that year. Data for the United States are not strictly comparable before and after 1983 because of the different sources used by Kumar for U.S. union membership figures. Figures for 1998–2001 are based on new series of non-agricultural paid workers, and hence differ slightly for years before 1988 and from those for later years appearing in the first edition of this book.

Sources: For Canada, 1946–1970, Eaton, 1975. For 1971–1976, Labour Canada, 1993, *Directory of Labour Organizations in Canada*, p. xvi, Table 1. For 1977–1987, HRDC, 1996 and 1997, *Directory of Labour Organizations in Canada*. For 1988–2001, *Workplace Gazette*, Vol. 4, No. 3, p. 36, Table 1. For the U.S., 1945–1992, Kumar, 1993. For 1993–2001, Bureau of Labor Statistics, U.S. Dept. of Labor. The Dept. of Labor statistics are not entirely consistent with those used by Kumar; however, the differences are not great. (U.S., 1997-01)

Union density, or the percentage of organizable workers belonging to unions,[1] has also generally increased throughout most of the century, again excepting brief periods of decline during the early 1920s and 1960s. It should be noted, however, that union density has not increased over the past two decades and that it has been declining slowly but fairly steadily since 1984. In 1921, the first year for which we have density data, Canadian union density stood at 16 percent (Eaton, 1975). This figure dropped to 12 percent through most of the 1920s, but rose steadily during the 1930s and soared during the Second World War, reaching a level of just over 24 percent by 1945 (see Table 5.1). From 1945 through 1958, union density rose steadily to just over 34 percent. The next six years saw a decline, to just over 29 percent in 1964, but then membership rates started rising again, peaking at 37.1 percent in 1978. Between 1978 and 1984, union density hovered between 35.4 and 37.2 percent; since 1984, it has been slowly declining to its current level of 31 percent.

Why have union membership and density rates risen and fallen as they have? As we pointed out in the previous chapter, labour shortages during both world wars increased workers' power relative to that of employers and made it easier for them to join unions. In addition, the extension of the *IDI Act* to all war industries encouraged union organization, especially during the First World War (Morton, 1995:139). The declines in membership and density levels during the 1920s were due largely to a determined employer anti-union offensive, facilitated by a postwar depression and by the government's dropping of wartime *IDI* restrictions against intimidation and harassment of union activists. The two major periods of growth during the post-Second World War period, those from 1945 to 1958 and 1965 through 1977, can be closely linked to legislative changes making it easier for workers to join unions. As we also noted in the previous chapter, *PC 1003*, passed in 1944, extended unionization rights to most blue-collar workers. The decade or so following passage of this legislation saw the organization of large numbers of semi-skilled workers in heavy industries such as autos, steel, rubber, and meatpacking. Similarly, large numbers of government workers and other public sector workers such as teachers and nurses entered the labour movement during the decade or so after the passage of major public sector legislation across Canada.

The lack of any major new legislative initiatives comparable to *PC 1003* or the more recent *Public Service Staff Relations Act* may be one reason why union growth has slowed over the past two decades. As for the recent stagnation in growth and decline in density, the major reason is probably the loss of hundreds of thousands of manufacturing jobs, most in heavily unionized sectors (Morton, 1995:153; Godard, 1994:421). Another reason is a more conservative political climate and increasingly restrictive certification procedures in many jurisdictions (see Chapter 8 for more details). Yet despite severe losses in traditional manufacturing strongholds, the Canadian labour movement as a whole has fared significantly better than those of many other industrialized countries, such as Britain, Japan, Australia, and the United States (Bamber and Whitehouse, 1993:310), all of which have experienced significant declines in union density since 1980.

Changing Union Membership Components[2]

Growing Unionization of Women

While overall Canadian union density rates have remained fairly steady, this apparent stability masks many changes in the composition of the Canadian labour movement. Forty years ago, the typical Canadian union member was white, male, and employed full-time at a blue-collar job. Today, nearly half the country's union members are women (see Figure 5.1), and people from many different religious and ethnic minorities have joined the labour movement. As we will see later on, sizeable numbers of part-timers have become union members, and white-collar workers are now nearly as likely to be members as blue-collar workers. But the single greatest change has been the growing number of women in the labour movement. As late as 1967, fewer than 20 percent of the country's union members were women, and the male union density rate (41 percent) was well over twice the female density rate of 16 percent. The two major reasons for this large increase in female union membership are women's growing participation in the labour force (discussed in detail in Chapter 2) and the extension of unionization to the public sector, where large numbers of women work. By 1991 (Swimmer and Thompson, 1995:4), some 60 percent of all public sector union members were women; in the private sector, the figure was only 22 percent. Virtually all of the 100 percent increase in overall Canadian union membership since 1967 has come from women (Akyeampong, 1997). As a result, women now make up 47 percent of the country's union members, and their density rate of 29 percent is nearly that of men at 30.7 percent.

It's somewhat harder to pinpoint the reasons for the corresponding decline in male union density. However, one reason may well have been the recent wave of deindustrialization (also discussed in Chapter 2), which has resulted in the loss of hundreds of thousands of manufacturing jobs, many in traditionally heavily unionized sectors.[3]

Figure 5.1

WOMEN AS A PERCENTAGE OF UNION MEMBERS, 1967 AND 2000

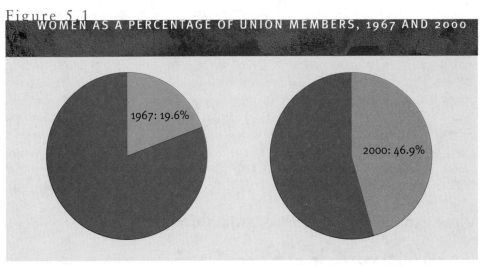

1967: 19.6%

2000: 46.9%

Source: For 1967, CALURA (1967); for 2000 (January to September average), Statistics Canada Labour Force Survey, as quoted in Akyeampong (2001), p. 51, Table 2.

Figure 5.2

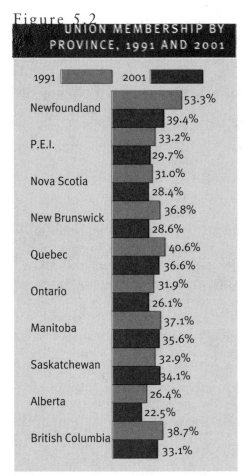

UNION MEMBERSHIP BY PROVINCE, 1991 AND 2001

1991 ■ 2001 ■

Newfoundland	53.3%
	39.4%
P.E.I.	33.2%
	29.7%
Nova Scotia	31.0%
	28.4%
New Brunswick	36.8%
	28.6%
Quebec	40.6%
	36.6%
Ontario	31.9%
	26.1%
Manitoba	37.1%
	35.6%
Saskatchewan	32.9%
	34.1%
Alberta	26.4%
	22.5%
British Columbia	38.7%
	33.1%

Sources: Sources: for 2001: Labour Force Survey as quoted in Akyeampong (2001), p. 49, Table 1; for 1991, CALURA, 1993:25.

Union Membership by Province

For some time, there has been a good deal of variation in provincial union membership rates. In 2001, provincial union density rates ranged from a low of 22.5 percent in Alberta to a high of more than 39 percent in Newfoundland (see Figure 5.2). In 1991, the range was even greater: from 26 percent in Alberta to 53 percent in Newfoundland.[4] By and large, provincial rankings stayed pretty much the same. Quebec, British Columbia, and Manitoba ranked above the national average both times, while Ontario, Nova Scotia, and Prince Edward Island were well below it.

What accounts for differing provincial union membership rates? The subject is one of increasing interest within the Canadian IR profession. Over the past two decades, there have been a number of studies that have shed light on various aspects of the question (see, for example, Maki, 1982; Meltz, 1989b; Ng, 1992; Martinello, 1996). To date, however, the definitive study on this important issue has yet to appear. Among the determinants most often identified are industrial structure, the type of labour legislation in place, and the presence (or absence) of pro-labour governments.

Certain industries, such as forestry and transportation, have traditionally been heavily unionized. Certain others, such as agriculture and finance, have traditionally had few unions. It follows that provinces with large numbers of heavily unionized industries should, other things being equal, have higher union membership rates than provinces with few such industries. The existence of strong forestry, pulp and paper, and (until recently) fishing sectors in Newfoundland and British Columbia is likely one reason for these provinces' relatively high density rates. Conversely, Prince Edward Island's focus on agriculture and lack of a strong industrial base may be one reason why that province has generally had union density rates well below the national average.

An equally if not more important factor is the type of labour legislation a province has in place. Clearly, certain types of provisions can help union growth, while other types are more likely to retard it.[5] For example (Peirce, 1989), some provinces have relatively liberal exclusion policies governing who can and cannot join unions, barring only management and confidential labour relations personnel. Others have more restrictive policies that serve to prevent people such as professionals, domestics, and farm workers from joining unions in addition to the groups already mentioned. Not surprisingly, membership rates are generally higher in the provinces with liberal exclusion policies than in those with restrictive ones, since they have a larger pool of potential members to choose from.

Another relevant factor is the presence of a pro-labour (NDP or Parti Québécois) government that can help the labour movement advance its cause in the political arena. As Maki (1982) has suggested, such governments can help increase union membership both directly, by passing legislation designed to make it easier for unions to attract new members, and indirectly, by improving labour's public profile (as when unionists are appointed to cabinet positions), thus making union membership seem a more attractive proposition. Maki's study has directly linked the presence of NDP governments to higher union membership rates. In connection with this point, it is worth noting that except for Newfoundland, all of the provinces whose union membership rates are above the national average have at some point had NDP or PQ governments. In contrast, only one of the provinces (Ontario) with below-average density rates has ever had an NDP or PQ government, and in that case the government served just one term, which may not have been long enough to have made a lasting difference.[6] Similar comparative studies (see Freeman, 1989; Bean, 1994) have linked support for labour or social democratic parties to increased union membership rates in various countries that are members of the Organisation for Economic Co-operation and Development (OECD).

Unionization Rates by Industry

Union membership rates vary even more by industry than they do by province. In 2000 (see Akyeampong, 2001) rates ranged from a low of less than 3 percent in agriculture to 68 percent in education and 66 percent in public utilities (see Table 5.2).[7] Other heavily unionized industries included public administration and transportation/communication/storage, the latter, like utilities, being "quasi-public" in that it is marked by a high degree of public ownership and regulation (see Murray, 1995). Manufacturing and construction had density rates near the national average, while trade and finance/insurance/real estate were both well below it.

Over the years there have been major shifts in the composition of Canadian union membership by industry. While the public sector has been making up an increasingly large share of the labour movement, the proportion contributed by traditionally heavily unionized private-sector industries such as manufacturing and construction has been steadily declining. In 1966 (Murray, 1995:167), manufacturing accounted for 39 percent of the country's union members. By 1977 (Chaison, 1982:151), its share had dropped to 28 percent; by 2000 (see Akyeampong, 2001), that figure was just

Table 5.2

	UNION MEMBERSHIP AND DENSITY BY WORK STATUS AND INDUSTRY, 2000	
Work Status	Membership (thousands)	Density (%)
Full-time	3 251	31.6
Part-time	490	22.2
Industry		
Goods-producing industries	999	31.2
Agriculture	3	2.7
Other primary	66	28.0
Manufacturing	688	31.5
Construction	165	30.6
Utilities	77	65.9
Service-producing industries	2 742	29.5
Trans. and warehousing	266	41.6
Trade	265	13.2
FIRE*	67	9.0
Public Administration	497	65.2
Education	632	68.0
Health and Soc. Assistance	695	52.4

* FIRE = Finance, Insurance and Real Estate
Sources: Labour Force Survey (2001), as quoted in Akyeampong (2001).

over 18 percent. As Murray (1995:167) notes, this shift has been the result both of declining density rates and of an absolute decline in the numbers of union members employed in the manufacturing sector. Between 1966 and 2000, the manufacturing density rate dropped from 44 percent (Murray, 1995) to 31.5 percent (Table 5.2). Moreover, between 1977 and 2000 alone, the number of union members employed in manufacturing dropped by nearly one-quarter, from 869 000 (Chaison, 1982:151) to 688 000 (Akyeampong, 2001). Similarly, in construction, the industry's share of the country's union members dropped from 10 percent in 1977 (Chaison, 1982:151) to 8 percent through the 1980s (Rose, 1992; WID, 1997) and 4.5 percent in 2000 (Table 5.2). The decline in this industry's density rate was even greater than the corresponding decline in manufacturing. In 1977 (Rose, 1982:400), about two-thirds of all construction workers were union members. By 2000 (Table 5.2), the rate had dropped to 30.6 percent.

In contrast, membership rates have been rising for such private-service industries as trade and finance/insurance/real estate. For example, in 1977 (Chaison, 1982:151), fewer than 8000 union members were employed in finance, insurance, and real estate. This figure represented only about 0.2 percent of the country's total union membership. By 2000, there were about 67 000 union members from this sector, or just under 2 percent of the national total (Akyeampong, 2001). Similarly, in trade, the number of union members doubled from 132 000 to 265 000 between 1977 and 2000, while the industry's share of total Canadian union membership increased from 4 percent to 7.5 percent. While such increases are certainly encouraging to the labour movement, it is doubtful whether the private-service sector, which in much of the Western industrialized world has typically had lower membership rates than either the public sector or private goods-producing sector (see Clegg, 1976), can make up for the heavy membership losses that have already occurred in such traditional strongholds as manufacturing and construction, and that could well occur in the public sector as cash-strapped governments follow the lead of Ontario, Alberta, and B.C. and downsize and restructure public services such as health care and education.

Other Union Membership Components

PUBLIC VERSUS PRIVATE SECTOR STATUS As has been the case for some time (see Rose, 1995), the public sector continues to be far more heavily unionized than the private sector. In 2001 (Akyeampong, 2001), more than 71 percent of Canadian public sector workers were unionized, as opposed to just over 18 percent of the country's private sector workers. The extremely high unionization rates in such sectors as education (68 percent), public administration (66 percent), and health care explains why over half (52 percent) of the country's union members come from the public sector, even though fewer than one-quarter of all Canadians are employed there.

FULL VERSUS PART-TIME STATUS As has also been the case for some time (see England, 1987), part-time workers are significantly less likely to be union members than full-timers. In 2001 (Akyeampong, 2001), the density rate for full-timers was 31.5 percent, compared to a rate of just over 23 percent for part-timers. The lower unionization rate for part-timers may reflect, among other things, the greater difficulty and expense of organizing these workers, many of whom work in the traditionally non-union private-service sector.

AGE AND EDUCATIONAL ATTAINMENT Generally, union membership rates do not appear to be very strongly affected by individuals' age or educational attainment, except that very young workers (those aged 15 to 24) are far less likely than others to be union members. For workers aged 15 to 24, the 2001 density rate was just under 13 percent. For other age groups, the range was from 30 to 42 percent, the latter being the rate for workers aged 45 to 54. The likeliest explanations for the extremely low density rate among young workers are the high proportion of young workers who work part-time (see Chapter 2 for more details) and the frequency with which young people tend to change jobs. As is noted in more detail in the section on job tenure, those who don't keep their jobs for very long are extremely unlikely to become union members.

Educational attainment appears to be of even less importance than age in determining a worker's union membership status. The likeliest to join unions were people with university degrees (34 percent), possibly reflecting a high concentration of educated individuals in the heavily unionized public sector, which more than balanced out the large number of excluded managers and administrators with university degrees. Next likeliest to join were those with a postsecondary certificate or diploma (34 percent) and those with Grade 9 or less (30 percent). Those least likely to join were individuals with some postsecondary education, whose 2001 density rate was 23 percent.

FIRM SIZE Those working in large establishments are far more likely to be union members than those working in small ones. While only 13 percent of those in firms with fewer than 20 employees were union members, the ratio rose to 30 percent in firms of 20 to 99 employees, 42.5 percent in firms of 100 to 500 employees, and 54 percent in firms of more than 500 employees. Given these figures, the fact that most recent job growth has been in small or medium-sized businesses does not augur well for the Canadian labour movement.

JOB TENURE As with firm size, union density rates rise with increased job tenure. Only 14.5 percent of all workers with a year or less on the job belong to a union, and the density rate is still low (just under 22 percent) for those with one to five years' service. After five years, the likelihood of union membership is greatly increased. For those with five to nine years' tenure, the density rate is 32 percent, and for those with more than 14 years, it rises to 54.5 percent. Although this last group of experienced workers makes up less than 20 percent of the country's employed labour force, it accounts for well over a third of all Canadian union members (see Akyeampong, 2001).

Canadian Versus American Union Membership Rates

Many of the same factors that explain differing union membership rates in different Canadian provinces may also help explain differing Canadian and American union membership rates. While a number of studies of both Canadian and American union membership growth have found economic factors to be of great significance (Ashenfelter and Pencavel, 1969; Bain and Elsheikh, 1976; Eastman, 1983), economic factors arguably do little to explain the growing divergence in Canadian and American union membership rates over the past 40 years, a period when Canada and the United States have had roughly similar economic experiences and when their economies have become increasingly integrated.

In 1965, as Table 5.1 shows, American union density was just slightly higher than that of Canada, both being around 30 percent. By 1980, the Canadian rate had risen to almost 36 percent, or more than half again greater than the U.S. rate of just over 23 percent. Since 1986, the Canadian rate has invariably been more than twice that of the United States.

Industrial relations scholars have put forward a variety of explanations for the growing divergence in the two countries' membership rates. One is differing public labour policy. In Canada, such policy has generally been more supportive of unions than it has in the United States.

First, union security is more carefully guarded in Canada than in the United States. Every Canadian jurisdiction has in place some version of the *Rand Formula* (discussed in detail in the labour history chapter) providing for dues checkoff deductions at the source. In contrast, many U.S. states (the so-called "right-to-work" states) have no union security protection in place. The existence of this sizeable "right-to-work" zone may be the single most important difference in the Canadian and American labour policy environments. As Noah Meltz (1989b) points out, union density rates in the "right-to-work" states are generally extremely low, sometimes even in single digits (i.e., 3.2 percent in North Carolina and 3.5 percent in South Carolina in 1999 (BLS, 2001)). In general, the difference in density rates between the right-to-work states and those with union security provisions in place (i.e., New York, 25.3%) is far greater than that between any two Canadian provinces (Meltz, 1989b).

Second, at least until recently, the process by which a union becomes certified has been quite different in Canada and the United States. Though this has changed significantly over the past decade (see Chapter 8 for details), in most Canadian jurisdictions certification has traditionally been through a count of signed membership cards. As a result of the 1947 *Taft-Hartley Act*, which was designed specifically to curb unions' powers, any American union wishing to gain certification since then has had to go through a formal election. This is a process that many have argued gives employers the opportunity to intimidate and harass union activists and influence employees' opinion (Weiler, 1980 and 1983a; Mills, 1989). Such arguments are supported by studies showing increasingly low union success rates in elections held since 1950 (Weiler, 1983a).

Third, collective bargaining rights for public sector workers are generally a good deal stronger in Canada. In the United States, these rights were provided at the federal level through a 1961 executive order by President John F. Kennedy (Mills, 1989:536–537). They have generally not included the right to strike, and in the case of the federal public service, do not include the right to bargain over salaries. At the state level, nearly two-fifths of all states, as of 1985, did not permit their employees to engage in collective bargaining as such, while only 11 states permitted employees to strike at all, and then usually under very limited circumstances (Mills, 1989:530). As we will see in more detail in the public sector chapter, most Canadian public sector workers do enjoy the right to strike and, in general, possess more collective bargaining rights than their U.S. counterparts (Mills, 1989:412). These greater rights appear to have made union membership a more attractive proposition for Canadian than for American public sector workers.

Finally, labour relations legislation appears to be more strictly enforced in Canada than in the United States. A study by Peter Bruce (1990) of the handling of employer unfair labour practice cases in the United States[8] and in Ontario finds that cases in Ontario were dealt with more quickly, were more likely to result in a conviction, and were far less likely to be appealed to the courts. Bruce's conclusion is that, in Ontario, employers contemplating engaging in unfair labour practice would likely be deterred, knowing that they would have a high probability of being convicted, whereas in the United States, they would be much more likely to proceed, given the low probability of a timely conviction there. Given that employer opposition has been shown to be a significant factor in explaining union growth and decline (see Kochan, McKersie, and Cappelli, 1984; Freeman, 1989), Canada's generally stricter enforcement of labour legislation is probably at least in part responsible for this country's higher union membership rates.

The political environment is also significantly different in the two countries. For the past 60-odd years, Canada has had a social democratic party (known first as the CCF and now as the NDP) dedicated to advancing unions' interests in the political arena. While not strong by European standards, the NDP has often held power provincially in Canada and on a number of occasions has held the balance of power federally. In all of these situations, it has been in a position either to pass union-friendly labour legislation directly (as it has done in B.C., Saskatchewan, Manitoba, and Ontario when it formed the government there) or to demand that its coalition partner pass such legislation as the price of continued NDP support (as it appears to have done in the case of the *PSSRA*). In Quebec, the Parti Québécois has generally played a similar role. Lacking a political ally, the American labour movement has often had considerable difficulty advancing its legislative agenda, as its failure to win passage of President Jimmy Carter's labour law reform bill during the late 1970s illustrates. Overall, the evidence suggests that the NDP and PQ have helped increase or at least maintain union membership rates in Canada, while conversely, the lack of a labour or social democratic party may help explain the recent decline in union density in the United States (see Bruce, 1989; Meltz, 1989b; Rose and Chaison, 2001).

Yet another difference is the extent of union organizing efforts in the two countries. As Ian Robinson (1990) notes, Canadian unions have generally made far more effort to organize unskilled workers than have their American counterparts. The difference between Canadian and American organizing efforts was particularly great during the last years of George Meany's presidency of the AFL-CIO. Like many conservative craft unionists before him, Meany cared little about the fate of unskilled workers and generally gave organizing a low priority. Indeed, he was quoted in a national news magazine as saying that the size of the American labour movement made no difference to him (Goulden, 1972; I. Robinson, 1990)! Canadian unionists never shared this lackadaisical attitude towards organizing; not surprisingly, this country's unions greatly out-organized those of the United States, to the degree that in some years, despite the two countries' difference in size, Canadian unions actually signed up more new members than American unions did (Rose and Chaison, 1990)![9]

Despite the apparently strong evidence of growing divergence of Canadian and American union density rates, some (including most notably Troy [1992]),[10] have argued that this divergence is no more than a short- to medium-term trend and that in the longer run, economic factors such as globalization and trade liberalization will lead to a new convergence of those rates at a level much lower than the current Canadian one. Moreover, even those who have thus far emphasized the divergent nature of the Canadian and American labour movements (e.g., Robinson, 1994) have admitted that major economic changes such as those brought about as a result of the North American Free Trade Agreement (NAFTA) could lead to a convergence of labour legislation, which in turn could lead to major reductions in Canadian union membership rates. Recent changes to labour legislation in such jurisdictions as Ontario and B.C. (discussed in more detail in Chapter 8) suggest there is probably some basis for these concerns. Still, provincial jurisdiction over labour legislation means that such a process of convergence is less likely to come about than it would otherwise be, or will at least take longer than it might otherwise, given that changes must be made to not one but many sets of labour legislation.

UNION STRUCTURE

Canadian labour organizations conduct their business at local, provincial, national, and in some cases international levels. In general, the Canadian labour movement operates in a quite decentralized fashion, at least by international standards (see Rogow, 1989a:158–161 and Chaykowski, 1995:231). The **Canadian Labour Congress**, Canada's largest and most important central labour body, has little power over the unions affiliated with it, other than the power to expel, suspend, or reprimand them for offences such as raiding other unions. By international standards, as well, Canadian unions carry out a great deal of their bargaining at the local union-local plant level, a situation in sharp contrast to that prevailing in many European countries such as Germany and Sweden, where bargaining has normally been conducted at industry or even national levels (Fuerstenberg, 1993; Hammarstrom, 1993).[11] Canada's decentralized bargaining structure has sometimes been identified as a possible cause of its relatively high strike incidence (see Chapter 11 for more detail on this point).

Canada's union structure is also generally considered quite **fragmented**. This means that by international standards, Canada has a large number of small unions. While Table 5.3 shows that some Canadian unions are quite large, representing upwards of 100 000 workers, many of these big unions are in the public sector. In the private sector, there is still a good deal of fragmentation, despite recent mergers such as that of the Communications, Energy, and Paperworkers unions and a fair amount of diversification and expansion on the part of traditional industrial unions like the Autoworkers and Steelworkers (see Murray, 1995). One result of such fragmentation can be **dual unionism,** or competition between two or more unions to represent workers in the same sector. Such competition can lead to friction or even, sometimes, violence, as the case of competition within Quebec's construction industry, discussed

Table 5.3

TEN UNIONS WITH LARGEST MEMBERSHIP, 2001 (1997)		
Union (federation)	**Membership (thousands)**	
Canadian Union of Public Employees (CLC)	505.0	451.5
National Union of Public and General Employees (CLC)	325.0	309.0
National Automobile, Aerospace, Transportation and General Workers Union of Canada (CLC)	220.0	205.0
United Food and Commercial Workers International Union (AFL-CIO/CLC)	220.0	197.0
United Steelworkers of America (AFL-CIO/CLC)	190.0	200.0
Communications, Energy and Paperworkers Union of Canada (CLC)	149.0	167.5
Public Service Alliance of Canada (CLC)	148.7	167.8
International Brotherhood of Teamsters (AFL-CIO/CLC)	102.0	95.0
Fédération de la santé et des services sociaux (CSN)	100.2	97.0
Service Employees International Union (AFL-CIO/CLC)	85.0	80.0

Sources: Workplace Information Directorate, Human Resources Development Canada, Directory of Labour Organizations in Canada, 1997, p. xix (1997): *Workplace Gazette*, Vol. 4, No. 3, Table 2, p. 37 (2001).

later in this section, will illustrate. As recent observers like Lipsig-Mumme (1995:218) suggest, it could also hinder the Canadian labour movement's attempts to form effective international sectoral alliances. Finally, smaller unions simply cannot offer the same range of services that larger ones can. While size isn't everything, it can make a good deal of difference when it comes to issues such as organizing, research, publicity, and legislative lobbying. By and large, bigger unions have the funds to pay for more of these kinds of services, which (as we point out in the next chapter) are becoming increasingly important elements of unions' day-to-day activity.[12]

Union Locals

A union local (sometimes referred to as a local union) organizes workers within a given geographic area (most commonly a city). In some cases, it will represent all workers in its area; in other cases, it represents only workers at a particular work site. Public sector locals may represent all workers throughout a municipal region or even an entire province (Godard, 1994:226).

In some cases, a union local will remain unaffiliated with any labour federation. In this case, the union is known as an **independent local** and the local is the union. More often, however, a union will affiliate with a provincial and federal federation (most often the Canadian Labour Congress, described in detail below). In this case, the local is the union's basic building block (see Figure 5.3).

Locals in different types of unions tend to operate somewhat differently from each other. For example, in craft unions (those representing workers from a single occupation, such as carpenters or bricklayers) and professional-employee unions, bargaining is often conducted at the local level (Chaison and Rose, 1989). In addition, in craft unions in particular, the membership may be widely dispersed over a large geographical area, making it difficult for part-time volunteers to provide effective service (Godard, 1994). In such cases, the local will sometimes employ an individual known as a **business agent** to serve as chief spokesperson at negotiations, handle grievances, deal with members' problems, and liaise with other unions. In addition, business agents can often serve as trustees for the locals' health, welfare, and pension funds (Godard, 1994). Industrial and public service unions, where bargaining is often conducted at the industry, provincial, or even national level (as in the case of the federal public service) don't normally employ business agents, though these unions do often use provincial and national representatives to provide some of the same services a business agent might otherwise perform. In these cases, the local officers with whom members have most contact are **shop stewards**. Generally unpaid, shop stewards work for the union on a part-time basis. Their major responsibility is usually investigating grievances and representing members at grievance hearings; however, they may also be involved in such activities as recruiting new members or encouraging participation at meetings (Godard, 1994).

Whichever type of union a worker belongs to, the local is the level of the union with which he or she is generally most familiar. It is at the local's meetings, normally held monthly, where officers are elected, policies established, the broad outlines of bargaining strategy set,[13] and strike votes taken. Though attendance at monthly meetings is generally extremely low, for reasons to be discussed shortly, meetings involving the election of officers or discussion of possible strike action will normally see a far better turnout.

As is the case with many other organizations, much of the local's work is done by a variety of committees. Typically a union will use both standing, or permanent, committees to deal with ongoing issues such as bargaining, grievances, pensions, and finances, and ad hoc committees created for a particular purpose, such as job action committees to plan strike strategy, or strike committees to coordinate strike activities. Many of these committees entail a heavy time commitment on the part of participating members. Grievance committees, for example, often meet weekly, and individual committee members may spend additional time discussing the details of grievors' cases with them individually. Job action committees may meet weekly or even more often during the lead-up to a possible strike, and of course being part of a bargaining

Figure 5.3

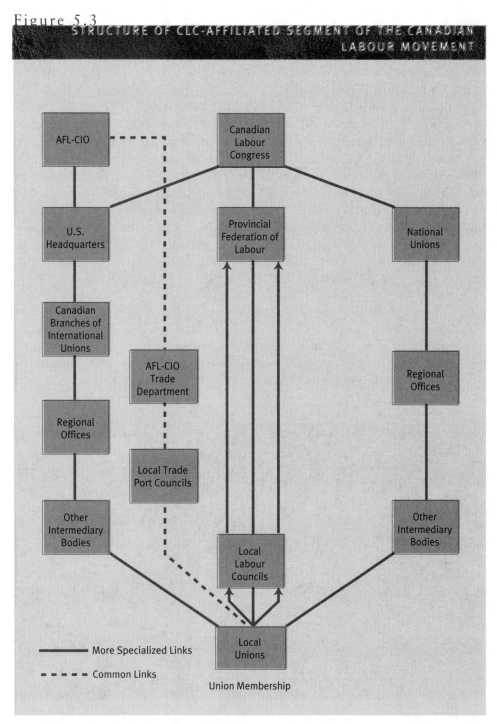

STRUCTURE OF CLC-AFFILIATED SEGMENT OF THE CANADIAN
LABOUR MOVEMENT

Source: Craig and Solomon, 1996.

committee may entail several hours of work a day, or perhaps even some all-night sessions during negotiations. While many union leaders are concerned, and rightly so, about the low attendance figures for most monthly meetings, these figures must be balanced against the hundreds of volunteer hours put in each month by the members of a typical union's many committees.

In addition to their provincial and federal affiliations (discussed in detail in the next section), most locals are affiliated with one of Canada's 120-odd **district labour councils**. These councils, funded by a per capita tax on the locals (Craig and Solomon, 1996:156), are designed to advance the labour movement's interests at the local and municipal levels. In practice, this could mean anything from running an information booth at a Labour Day fair to providing a union perspective to the media on contemporary economic and political developments or lending support to a striking union in the area (Craig and Solomon, 1996). In larger centres, in particular, district labour councils can be a potent force. For example, the Toronto and District Labour Council was heavily involved in organizing protest actions against the Ontario provincial government in 1997 and 1998.

National and Provincial Labour Federations

Some unions, most typically those representing professionals such as nurses (Boivin and Déom, 1995) or university professors, choose to remain completely independent of affiliations with other unions.[14] Most unions, however, see distinct advantages in

Municipal and district labour councils such as this one help raise the profile of unions and the labour movement in communities all across Canada.

joining forces with other unions at national and provincial levels. Unions working together through a labour federation, or association of unions, often find they can accomplish many things that they could not have achieved on their own.

By far the most important labour federation in Canada is the Canadian Labour Congress (CLC), which represents about two-thirds of the country's union members (see Murray, 2001). The organization's policies are established and constitution amended at its biennial conventions, attended by thousands of delegates from affiliates. It is also at these conventions that the CLC elects its officers and decides whether to admit, suspend, or expel individual unions (Godard, 1994:245). In between conventions, an executive council made up of the CLC's president, vice presidents, and secretary-treasurer is responsible for policy decisions (Godard, 1994).

The CLC does not normally engage in collective bargaining with employers. Its major functions are: (1) representing the Canadian labour movement politically, (2) providing services, such as research and organizing assistance, to its affiliated unions, (3) managing relations between its affiliated unions, (4) enforcing its ethical code, and (5) representing the Canadian labour movement internationally.

Political Representation

As we point out in the union action section of the next chapter, unions need to become involved politically to influence the passage of the legislation affecting workers and their unions. Over time, the Canadian labour movement has found that it makes sense to coordinate much of its political activity in Ottawa, the seat of Parliament.[15]

The CLC's political representation takes a variety of forms. Among the most important of these is liaison with the labour movement's political partner, the NDP. In addition, the CLC uses various other means in seeking to influence government legislation and policy. These include lobbying of Cabinet members and government officials, the issuing of press releases in response to economic developments, and the preparation of briefs or research studies on issues it considers of major importance, such as unemployment (Craig and Solomon, 1996:164). On issues it considers critical, the CLC will play a more active role in public debate; for example, in the case of the Canada-U.S. Free Trade Agreement, it issued numerous public statements and campaigned against the deal during the 1988 federal election campaign (Craig and Solomon, 1996). When it feels its advice isn't being heeded, it will go even further, organizing demonstrations and publicity campaigns in the hope of spurring the government into action. This was the case in 1993, when the CLC organized a massive Parliament Hill demonstration to protest what it saw as the job-killing effects of the free trade agreements (Craig and Solomon, 1996:165).

Assistance to Affiliated Unions

The CLC provides a broad range of services for its members, many of which (particularly smaller unions) lack the money or expertise to carry out for themselves. Such services can include labour education (discussed in more detail in the union action section of the next chapter), research for collective bargaining, and organizing assistance (Godard, 1994:244–245).

Maintaining Relations Between Affiliates

Next to its political work, the CLC's most important activity is maintaining (or trying to maintain) harmonious relations between its affiliated unions. Of particular concern here are jurisdictional disputes, or battles over which union will represent a given group of workers. Such disputes have become increasingly common in recent years as the big industrial unions, seeking to make up for the membership lost through dein- dustrialization and economic restructuring, have been forced to look farther afield for new members. In most cases, these unions have focussed on organizing the unorga- nized, but on occasion they have attempted to sign up workers already belonging to another union—an action known as **union raiding**. Raiding is a serious concern to the CLC, since it not only saps the morale of many of those involved and wastes valuable money and human resources that should be directed elsewhere (Godard, 1994:244), but can also cause the entire labour movement major public embarrassment.

In 1987, there was a serious incident of this kind involving the Canadian Auto Workers (CAW) and United Food and Commercial Workers (UFCW). That year, the CAW began to sign up Atlantic fishery workers already represented by the UFCW. After a battle that ended up being heard by both labour boards and courts, the CAW won the right to represent the 23 000 fishery workers (Craig and Solomon, 1996:170). The dispute led the CLC to change the way it handles jurisdictional disputes, from referral to a standing umpire to handling by its own executive committee. It also adopted tough new anti-raiding rules (Craig and Solomon, 1996:170–171). While these changes probably made sense, they have not been enough to prevent other instances of raiding, such as the International Woodworkers of America's 1992 raid of the Canadian Paperworkers' Union (see Craig and Solomon, 1993:111).

Another serious case of raiding, also involving the CAW, took place in 2000. This time, the international union the CAW was accused of raiding was the Service Employees International Union (SEIU), and this time, the CLC did not side with the Auto Workers, imposing sanctions which remained in effect until the parties resolved their dispute in May 2001 (CNW, 2001). Raids and attempted raids have also become more common in the public sector. For example, in 1999, the Teamsters' Union narrowly missed becoming the bargaining agent for a group of Canadian Food Inspection Agency veterinarians represented by the Professional Institute. In 2001, federal correctional officers shifted their allegiance from the Public Service Alliance to the CSN, after a lengthy battle between the two unions (PSSRB, 2000 and 2001).

Though regrettable, union raiding is probably inevitable in the current environ- ment of constant economic restructuring, one in which unions must compete increas- ingly fiercely for members. One change that could help would be to grant the CLC additional disciplinary powers, such as the ability to levy fines. To date, however, there have been few signs that any affiliates would be willing to grant the Congress such expanded powers.

Maintaining the Code of Ethics

To help ensure that its affiliates behave honourably, the CLC has written into its constitution a code of ethics. This code prohibits corrupt leadership practices and specifically guarantees union members the right to have honest and democratic elections, to run for union office, and to get fair treatment from their union's officials. The CLC's executive is charged with enforcing this code, although here, as in the case of union raiding, its powers are quite limited (Godard, 1994:244). In 1956, the CLC did expel the Teamsters union for gross corruption, following a U.S. Congressional investigation that found widespread corruption among the union's leaders (Craig and Solomon, 1996:171).

International Representation

Canada is active in a number of international labour organizations, including most notably the International Labour Organization (ILO) and International Confederation of Free Trade Unions (ICFTU). The ILO is a United Nations agency that investigates workers' rights and working conditions all around the world and sets international standards, or conventions, that apply to all member countries. These conventions have been established for issues such as freedom of association, the right to strike, hours of work, and the abolition of forced labour (LaBerge, 1976). Its powers are mainly limited to those of persuasion since, like the CLC, it lacks any real power to enforce its rulings (Godard, 1994; Craig and Solomon, 1996). The ICFTU is heavily involved in training unionists and in establishing and maintaining workers' rights in developing countries, where such rights are often far from a given (Craig and Solomon, 1996; Fashoyin, 1991). As the body representing the majority of Canada's unionists, the CLC represents the Canadian labour movement in these organizations, often playing a key leadership role. For example, former CLC president Shirley Carr was vice president of the ICFTU, while she and another former CLC president, Joe Morris, have both served as head of the ILO workers' group (Craig and Solomon, 1996:172).

Provincial Labour Federations

Provincial labour federations play an extremely important role in Canada, since most labour legislation is under provincial jurisdiction; hence the importance of maintaining a strong political presence at the provincial as well as federal level. The CLC has 12 provincial and territorial labour federations affiliated with it. Like the national federation, the provincial ones generally carry out activities that most unions lack the resources to carry out for themselves, such as political and legislative lobbying, research, and labour education. Their range of activities is often extremely broad. For instance, in one recent year (OFL, 1994), the Ontario Federation of Labour (OFL) submitted briefs on subjects ranging from workers' compensation and unemployment insurance to the possible incorporation of physicians and sustainable economic development. The Federation also carried out a substantial research program on health-related issues, successfully lobbied the provincial government to stop the introduction of user fees for drugs for seniors, organized an international symposium on the arts and labour, and held seminars on homeworking and teleworking, in addition to making plans for a joint conference with the Ontario Environment Network and helping to develop a dispute resolution process to deal with forest land-use claims.[16]

Quebec's Special Situation: Multiple Federations

Every province and territory except Quebec has a single provincial labour federation affiliated with the CLC. Like the other provinces, Quebec has its CLC affiliate, the Quebec Federation of Labour. There are, however, two important ways in which Quebec's union structure is different from that in other provinces. First, unlike any other province, Quebec has several different labour federations, as well as a sizeable number of **independent unions** not affiliated with any federation. The most important of the federations is the Confédération des syndicats nationaux (CSN), the former Catholic confessional federation that, as we pointed out in the labour history chapter, has undergone many metamorphoses since its formation just after the First World War. With about 250 000 members, or just over 6 percent of Canada's total union membership, the CSN is now heavily involved in promoting joint labour–management ventures (see Lipsig-Mumme, 1995:214)—a major change from its hard-line militancy of the 1960s and early 1970s. Other Quebec-wide federations include the education federation, the Centrale de l'enseignement du Québec (CEQ), and the **Centrale des syndicats démocratiques (CSD)**, a small group of mainly private sector unions that left the CSN during the 1970s in protest over that federation's radicalism. The CEQ, formerly a confessional federation like the CSN with membership restricted to elementary and secondary schoolteachers, has evolved into a broad-based secular industrial union representing all workers in education, including caretakers and maintenance staff as well as teachers (Boivin and Déom, 1995:467). Like the CSN, it has a history of militancy and continues to practise a strongly politically conscious brand of social unionism. In contrast, the CSD, most of whose members work in the clothing, chemical, and metal industries, operates according to business union principles and has taken a militantly apolitical stance (Boivin and Déom, 1995). The independent unions, which represent about one-quarter of the province's union members, have been most active in the public and parapublic sector, the two most important independent organizations being those representing provincial government employees.

Unlike any other Canadian province, then, but like many European countries, Quebec has a situation where a number of different labour federations are actively competing for new members, both with each other and with the independent unions.

As in the case of many European countries, such as Germany and the Netherlands (Bean, 1994:27), Catholic opposition to the secular and (so the church hierarchy maintained) radical orientation of the dominant mainstream secular federation was a big reason for the establishment of a separate Catholic federation. Even after the secularization of the major confessional federations (the CSN and CEQ), politics has played a role in the further fragmentation of the Quebec labour movement, most notably in the departure of the conservative CSD unions from the CSN. The existence of multiple labour federations in Quebec has always been a source of friction and on occasion has resulted in violence, as in the case of the QFL's and CSN's pitched battles over the organization of James Bay construction workers during the 1970s (Boivin, 1982:431). At the same time, it can't be denied that when the federations have pulled together, as they did during the 1972 Common Front strike, the result has been a provincial labour movement of unusual cohesiveness and strength. Thus the jury must remain out on the question of whether Quebec's multiple federations have strengthened or weakened the province's labour movement overall.

The second distinctive feature of Quebec's union structure is the unusual degree of freedom granted the CLC's Quebec affiliate, the QFL. Unlike other provincial CLC affiliates, the QFL has always been in the position of having to compete for members, which almost by definition makes its situation a special one. When the debate over Quebec independence began to heat up, it was able to make the case that it would need special powers and more money than other provincial labour federations if it was to continue to attract new members. The CLC responded in 1974 by granting the QFL what amounted to partial autonomy, yielding its usual jurisdiction over labour education and local labour councils, and allowing the provincial federation to recoup funds for national services that provided Quebec members no tangible benefit, such as unilingual English newspapers (Boivin, 1982:433). Twenty years later, the CLC went even further, granting its Quebec affiliate what some have referred to as "sovereignty-association" status within the national federation. A 1994 agreement worked out at the Congress's convention in Toronto gave the QFL powers that would normally be granted only to a national labour organization, such as the right to designate its own representatives to activities held by international labour groups like the ILO and ICFTU. In addition, the QFL president was automatically made a voting member of the Congress's executive, and the QFL was given the right to observe its own protocols on matters such as internal jurisdictional disputes and labour education, as well as control over the money that the CLC would normally have allocated for these activities (Boivin and Déom, 1995:465).

Quebec's "special status" within the CLC has often been a source of friction and resentment, especially for conservative international unions like those representing the building trades. As we noted earlier, this special status was a major reason why the building trade unions left the CLC in 1982 to form the now-defunct Canadian Federation of Labour (CFL). Undoubtedly there are others within the CLC who resent the QFL's special status. But given Quebec's always-delicate political situation and the realities of operating in an environment where the QFL must compete for members with strongly and avowedly nationalist federations, "sovereignty-association" status may represent the only feasible way for the CLC to keep its Quebec affiliate from leaving altogether.

National and International Unions

Canada is among the few industrialized countries to have a sizeable number of union members represented by unions headquartered outside the country. Generally known as **"international" unions**, these organizations are in reality American unions with Canadian branches. Their role in the Canadian labour movement has been controversial throughout the past century. It continues to generate controversy even at a time when some observers (i.e., Lipsig-Mumme, 1995) have begun to argue for closer links between unions in Canada, the United States, and Mexico in response to the continental integration resulting from the Canada-U.S. and North American Free Trade Agreements.

In the labour history chapter, we pointed out that there were good reasons for Canadian unionists in the late nineteenth and early twentieth centuries to choose to be represented by American unions. Bigger, more experienced, and stronger American unions could provide money and logistical and organizing support that simply weren't available in this country. Moreover, at a time when many jobs were still seasonal, an American union card served almost as a meal ticket for many Canadian workers forced to seek employment in the United States (see Lipton, 1973 and McKay, 1983).

But if there were good reasons for the "internationalization" of the Canadian labour movement in the late nineteenth and early twentieth centuries, there have been equally good reasons for its more recent Canadianization, which has taken place mainly over the past 35 years. Numerically, as Table 5.1 shows, the American labour movement is far weaker than it was during the early postwar period. Union density in the United States is now less than half what it was in 1947; indeed, the actual number of union members in that country has dropped by more than one-third since 1976 despite a sizeable increase in its labour force. As a number of observers have pointed out, the decline in the size of the American labour movement has been mirrored by a decline in its political clout (see Lipsig-Mumme, 1989; Robinson, 1990 and 1994).

Far from being stronger than the Canadian labour movement, as it was through the early years of this century, the American labour movement is now considerably weaker than its northern counterpart. This growing weakness has led many Canadian unionists to question the value of continued affiliation. After all, if American unions lacked the money and human resources to conduct organizing campaigns at home (see Chaison and Rose, 1991:28–29; Rose and Chaison, 2001), how much help could they realistically be to their Canadian affiliates? In these circumstances, many Canadian unionists have suggested that Canadian members are paying more in international dues than they're getting back in benefits, making continued international affiliation a losing proposition.

Nor are these the only forces that have led to the nationalization of the Canadian labour movement. An equally important development has been the growth of public sector unionism in Canada. Excluded from unionization in most jurisdictions, public sector workers were an insignificant part of the Canadian labour movement through the early postwar period.[17] Once federal and provincial government employees and other public sector workers were granted the right to bargain collectively, they joined the labour movement in huge numbers (Rose, 1995). It was estimated that by the beginning of the 1980s, nearly half the country's union members worked in the public sector (Ponak, 1982:345; Rose, 1995:22). Today (see Chapter 9), the figure is more than half.

Almost by definition, public sector unions are **national unions**. It is difficult to imagine how a union based in another country could provide effective representation to Canadian government employees, schoolteachers, or health-care workers. Indeed, any serious attempt by an American union to organize Canadian public sector workers, particularly federal or provincial government employees, would likely raise major concerns around issues of national sovereignty. Moreover, Canadian public sector workers would generally have little if anything to gain from affiliation with an American union, given the far less liberal public sector bargaining legislation in the United States (see Craig and Solomon, 1996:183).

In the private sector, issues leading many Canadian unions to break away from their American internationals have included disputes over strike funding, bargaining strategy, and political disagreements. As we noted earlier, some international head offices strongly disapproved of their Canadian branches' support for the social democratic NDP; for their part, many Canadian unionists were strongly opposed to their internationals' support for the Vietnam War. More generally, the 1960s and 1970s were a time of growing nationalism and questioning of authority across Canada, a time when many Canadians were becoming increasingly displeased with the degree of American ownership of and control over this country's economy. In such a volatile political climate, (see Ponak, 1982:349), the labour movement could not expect to escape unscathed. To many Canadian unionists, a situation in which their unions were controlled outside the country had become unacceptable as such, beyond specific disagreements over bargaining strategies or political affiliation.

Taken together, the developments just described have transformed the Canadian labour movement from a primarily U.S.-based one to a primarily national one. In 1920 (Chaison, 1982:152), Canadian national unions represented just over 5 percent of the country's union members. As recently as 1962 (see Table 5.4), more than 70 percent of all Canadian union members still belonged to internationals. By 1980, half the country's union members were in Canadian-based national unions; as of 2001, that figure stood at more than 65 percent (Table 5.4). As Table 5.3 indicates, the country's three largest unions, and six of its ten largest, are now Canadian-based.

The best-known secession of a Canadian union from its American international parent was undoubtedly that of the Canadian Auto Workers from the United Auto

Table 5.4

	NATIONAL VERSUS INTERNATIONAL COMPOSITION OF UNIONS AND UNION MEMBERS, SELECTED YEARS, 1962-2001					
	Number of Unions			**Number of Members (thousands)**		
	National	**International**	**Other***	**National**	**International**	**Other**
Year	N (%)	N (%)	N (%)	N (%)	N (%)	N (%)
1962	51 (11.5)	108 (24.3)	285 (64.2)	335 (23.5)	1 025 (72.0)	63 (4.4)
1978	88 (16.6)	121 (22.8)	321 (60.6)	1 553 (47.4)	1 638 (50.0)	87 (2.6)
1990	234 (23.0)	61 (6.0)	721 (71.0)	2 563 (63.6)	1 283 (31.8)	184 (4.6)
1997	233 (23.0)	51 (5.0)	727 (71.9)	2 663 (65.4)	1 217 (29.9)	195 (4.8)
2001	219 (22.2)	47 (4.8)	720 (73.0)	2 694 (65.5)	1 198 (29.5)	204 (5.0)

Source: Workplace Information Directorate, HRDC, Directory of Labour Organizations in Canada, 1997, p. xii. (1962-1997); *Workplace Gazette*, Vol. 4, No. 3, p. 41, Table 6 (2001).

*Other refers to directly chartered unions *and* independent local organizations.

Workers, in 1985. Here, the major issue was the Canadian branch's refusal to accept the international's concession bargaining strategy. But the CAW's breakaway from the UAW was just one of a number taking place through the 1970s and 1980s and into the 1990s. Unions such as the Communication Workers and Paperworkers broke completely away from their American "parents," while others, such as the National Association of Broadcast Employees and Technicians and Brotherhood of Railway, Airline, and Steamship Clerks, drafted their own constitutions and elected their own officers while maintaining a loose affiliation with their parent unions (Craig and Solomon, 1996:187).

Even Canadian unions remaining within their internationals have often been able to achieve a significantly higher degree of autonomy and self-sufficiency than they previously enjoyed (Godard, 1994:250). In large measure, this appears to have been the result of the CLC's autonomy guidelines, passed in 1970 and again in 1974. These guidelines include: the election of Canadian officers by Canadians; the right of Canadian officers and members to determine union policies dealing with national affairs; the authority for Canadian officers to speak for their union in Canada; separate affiliation for Canadian sections in international labour bodies; and assurance from the internationals that Canadian members could take full part in their country's social, economic, cultural, and political life (Heron, 1989; Craig and Solomon, 1996).

Whether the guidelines have succeeded in reducing the number of secessions is an interesting question, but one that is very difficult to answer, given the available evidence (see Chaison and Rose, 1989). What can be said is that the pace of secession has slowed considerably, if not halted altogether, in recent years. In 2001, the proportion of union members belonging to international unions (Table 5.4) was virtually unchanged from what it had been in 1994 (Murray, 1995:177). As was noted earlier in the chapter, if anything the trend now may be back in the direction of some kind of internationalism, given the increasing global and continental economic integration described in detail in Chapter 2.

UNION DEMOCRACY

Union democracy is important to the labour movement for many reasons, not least because actual or even perceived lapses in democracy can hurt the movement's public image, causing it to lose much-needed support. Cynics sometimes say that the very notion of union democracy is an oxymoron. Others (i.e., Craig and Solomon, 1996:173) suggest that, given the serious constraints under which unions often operate, their achievements in the area of democracy are admirable. The issue has been of increasing interest both to unionists and to the general public since the 1950s, when widespread corruption was revealed in such American unions as the Teamsters and the Longshoremen's. These revelations were followed by a number of congressional investigations of labour racketeering, and eventually by the passage, in 1959, of the *Landrum-Griffin Act*, which imposed strict controls on the internal operations of American unions, including the possibility of an appeal to the Secretary of Labor for a judicial recount in cases where there was reason to believe that a union election had been rigged (Craig and Solomon, 1996:181–182).

Union democracy isn't an easy concept to define. Anderson (1979) has suggested that it means, essentially, the ability to influence decisions that are important to members and to participate effectively in its affairs. A more comprehensive definition by Edelstein and Warner (quoted in Chaison, 1982:166) has described democracy as:

> … a decision-making system in which the membership actively participates, directly or indirectly through its representatives, in the making and implementation of policy and in the selection of officials, for all levels, on the basis of political equality and majority rule. Furthermore, the system operates on the basis of the accountability of officials, the legitimacy of opposition, and due process for the protection of the rights of individuals and minorities.

It doesn't take a Ph.D. in political science to appreciate that doing all these things amounts to a tall order for any union. Indeed, a close reading of the definition reveals significant tension between a number of the objectives, such as operating through majority rule while still respecting the rights of individuals and minorities. If this is what is expected of unions, no wonder their actual achievements in the area of democratic operation often fall short of expectations. Indeed, one reason for some perceived lapses in union democracy—not to say that actual lapses do not occur—is the tremendously high expectations people have for it. In part, this is the result of the way unions position themselves among the few democratic institutions in society willing and able to stand up to big business and other powerful and moneyed interests. And in part it's because, at the national or societal level, as the union impacts section of the next chapter will explain in more detail, trade unionism is clearly and closely related to democracy. With respect to unions' internal operations, however, things may turn out to be a bit different. Usually, union constitutions will provide that everyone be treated equally. In practice, though, some members and, particularly, officials, may turn out to be more equal than others. In the sub-sections that follow, we'll try to provide some explanations for this apparent paradox, closing the discussion with a comparison of evidence of union democracy in Canada and the United States.

Components of Union Democracy

A review of the Edelstein-Warner definition just quoted reveals a number of key components, including membership participation, selection of officials, legitimacy of opposition, and due process. In addition, we might add freedom from outright corruption and fraud, since this is the aspect of union democracy (or the lack thereof) that has the potential to arouse the greatest public concern. Since this last point is so important, let's begin with it.

Freedom from Corruption

At a bare minimum, unions should operate within the law. They should hold regular meetings, and treasurers should provide regular reports of how members' dues are spent. Officials should not resort to violence, intimidation, or other bully-boy tactics either in their dealings with their own members or in dealings with others (such as members of other unions or prospective members they are trying to organize). They should avoid having anything to do with organized crime, and they should not make "sweetheart" deals with employers behind their members' backs. Nor should they refuse to carry a member's grievance forward simply because the grievor or his or her father may happen to have run for office against a member of the current executive.

Any union (or any other organization) that cannot abide by these rather minimal standards is not only acting undemocratically, it is violating the most basic precepts of morality and common decency. The *Landrum-Griffin* legislation was passed precisely to avoid further instances of such essentially criminal union behaviour, which the record shows was quite common in the United States during the 1940s and early 1950s. This type of unionism has fortunately been rare in Canada, with the notable exception of American import Hal Banks and his Seafarers' International Union, who regularly resorted to beatings and intimidation (Morton, 1995:147). Perhaps because this type of behaviour has been rare in Canada, there seems to have been little pressure for a "Landrum-Griffin North" (Craig and Solomon, 1996).

Membership Participation

No two observers agree on exactly what proportion of union members attend meetings regularly; all agree that that proportion is very low. Two older sources quoted by Strauss (1991:213) estimate 2 to 6 percent and 5 to 7 percent, respectively, while a more recent estimate cited by Chaison (1982:166) is in the 10 to 15 percent range. Why is attendance at most meetings so low? And what do these low attendance figures really mean?

It's common to attribute such poor attendance to apathy, or to union leaders' tight control over meeting agendas, which leads members to believe they will have little chance to provide meaningful input even if they do attend (see Chaison, 1982).

Certainly many members do feel, if not apathetic, at best instrumental towards their union; it's there if they need it, and they will turn out for strike votes and elections, but they have no wish to become involved in the organization's day-to-day operations. As for the issue of leaders' control over agendas, there is no doubt that this happens on occasion. However, we have no way of knowing how frequently it happens. Anecdotal evidence suggests that apathy (or instrumentalism) is a more significant factor here than any attempt by leaders to control the agenda. Indeed, many leaders would dearly love to have better attendance; it would make them look better and also give them a better "read" on what their members are thinking.[18] The problem is, how to get better attendance without resorting to tactics that members might regard as undemocratic.

A brief comparison of today's situation to that prevailing in many unions in the nineteenth century may be instructive. It appears that few of these unions had attendance problems; the Nova Scotia carpenters' union described by McKay (1991:169) boasted average turnouts of more than 150—an extraordinary record by today's standards. In this case, peer pressure and a strong craft tradition apparently helped ensure good attendance. Moreover, like most unions of its time, the Carpenters was a fairly small, homogeneous group of men, most of whom worked together during the day and would have welcomed the opportunity to socialize with their work mates in the evening. Being men, few would have had to worry about who would look after the children during their absence.

Many of today's unions are large, heterogeneous organizations representing people doing many different jobs. The person one sits next to at a union meeting may be someone one doesn't know. This fact alone is enough to explain why modern North American unions, especially big industrial and public service unions, would find it difficult to play the same role as that played by the Nova Scotia carpenters' union. Especially in the public sector unions, many members are women, which means they *do* have to worry about who will look after the children.[19] Beyond that, for women and men alike, there is the problem of overcommitment. The nineteenth-century unionist likely participated in just two organizations: his union and his church. Today's unionist, especially if he or she has children, often belongs to or participates in a staggering number of organizations, ranging from Home and School associations and children's sports teams to civic improvement groups, musical and cultural organizations, and church groups. As if all that were not enough, even people of modest means now have access to an array of home entertainment technology that their grandparents could only have dreamed of. Given what the union meeting must compete against in modern workers' crowded schedules, is it really any wonder that it often loses out?

Moreover, attendance figures alone may not mean all that much. As Anderson suggests (1979:488), what's most important may not be the number of bodies in the chairs, but whether those who have come feel free to participate actively and without fear of being suppressed if their ideas don't happen to agree with those of the leadership. Given members' crowded schedules and the child-care problem, there may be no realistic way for today's unions to ensure high attendance at ordinary meetings, although this author has heard of at least one imaginative idea, used by a nurses' association in Newfoundland, that tied the granting of scarce travel funds to satisfactory attendance. If attendance is high when important business such as strike votes or contract terms is being discussed, and if members who do attend feel free to participate fully in the discussions, this may be the best anyone can hope for. The evidence suggests that turnout generally is high when important issues are at stake (Godard, 1994:241) and that, contrary to popular belief, leaders do their best to get as much membership input as they can, particularly on those important issues.[20] Whether members always feel free to participate in the way they would wish is another question, one to be taken up in the next section.

Selection of Officers and Legitimacy of Opposition

In a democratic union, at a minimum there should be regular election of officers. Those opposing the "official" or incumbent slate should have the opportunity to express their views to members through official union publications and in other ways. Finally, there should be at least a certain degree of turnover in union presidents and other officials, to ensure that the organizations receive the benefit of fresh thinking and prevent ruling cliques from becoming unduly entrenched. While we would not expect incumbent union presidents to be defeated often, given the inherent advantages incumbents possess in unions as in most other political organizations, a situation in which they were never defeated would not augur well for union democracy.

More research is needed on the question of what opportunities are provided to opposition slates to express their views through union publications and other channels. As for the matter of turnover, the evidence is mixed. A study conducted by Gary Chaison and Joseph Rose (1977) showed that Canadian union presidents were defeated for re-election less than 15 percent of the time. However, between 1963 and 1972 nearly 80 percent of both national and international unions experienced at least one presidential turnover (Chaison and Rose, 1977; Chaison, 1982). Far more common than defeat at the polls were retirements attributed to age, health, union rules against successive terms in office (which some would argue are themselves a healthy sign of union democracy), or changes to other positions (Chaison, 1982:165). The fact that nearly four-fifths of the unions surveyed changed presidents in a decade suggests that a healthy degree of renewal may well be taking place, although we would need to know what influence the outgoing president had in the choice of his or her successor before making such an assertion with any degree of certainty.

Due Process

Unions possess a considerable degree of power over their members, including the power to discipline them. Penalties can include loss of union membership, which in turn can lead to loss of one's employment and livelihood in situations where only union members can be employed, or where hiring is conducted through the union, as in the building trades (Craig and Solomon, 1996:180–181). Organizations that have such great power over their members have the responsibility to use it wisely and fairly, especially in situations where someone's livelihood may be at stake. Ideally, those disagreeing with their union's disciplinary action should have the right to a prompt and fair hearing before a neutral third party or parties. In practice, it would appear that this ideal is seldom realized. The Canadian Auto Workers appears to be among the few Canadian unions that have established an impartial panel made up entirely of people from outside the organization to hear members' complaints about internal union actions (Craig and Solomon, 1996:181; Murray, 1995:182). What appear to be more common are internal procedures for handling such complaints, procedures that start at the local level and if not resolved there may end up before the union's executive board or even at its annual or biennial convention. Such a procedure is apt to be extremely time-consuming, to put it mildly (Craig and Solomon, 1996:181). What is not clear is the extent to which unions may have developed speedier, more informal internal dispute resolution processes comparable to the expedited arbitration systems found in a number of industries and jurisdictions. (These are discussed in some detail in the grievance chapter.) Given the bad press unions could receive from disgruntled individuals who had suffered lengthy delays in getting their cases heard, some sort of "expedited review" system would appear to be in their enlightened self-interest.

Limitations on Union Democracy

There are a variety of reasons why unions generally find it impossible to fully achieve the lofty democratic ideal suggested in the Edelstein and Warner definition discussed earlier. One argument often advanced (see Godard, 1994 and Murray, 1995) is the "iron law of oligarchy," one originally formulated by the political theorist Robert Michels. This theory argues that as political leaders stay in power, they become increasingly less responsive to their constituents and more concerned with simply staying in power. Godard (1994:238) points out that the "iron law of oligarchy" may be of particular relevance to union leaders, who unlike business leaders may have little or nothing to fall back on if they lose their jobs, except perhaps a shop-floor job, and for whom staying in office would thus appear to be of great importance.

Certainly there are some Canadian union leaders who may well be more concerned with getting re-elected than with formulating the wisest possible long-term policies for their organizations. At the same time, there is at least modest evidence to suggest that the "iron law" may not be working very strongly in Canada. As noted earlier, most Canadian union presidents appear to serve for fairly limited periods; as we will point out below, the same is generally true at the national level, at least for CLC presidents—in stark contrast to the situation prevailing in the United States within the AFL-CIO. Moreover, it is also worth noting that any union or federation wishing to prevent the "iron law" from taking effect has a number of

One of today's most visible union leaders is Ontario Public Service Employees Union President Leah Casselman, shown here addressing a group of several hundred striking Ontario government employees on the first day of the OPSEU strike, March 13, 2002.

options at its disposal, including term limits for leaders or stipulations that new people be regularly rotated onto their executives.

Other limitations to union democracy may be rather more intractable, since they have to do with the inherent nature of a union as a collective majoritarian political organization in which, at least occasionally, the wishes of the minority must be sacrificed to those of the majority. For example, an individual may feel hard done by because the union has refused to carry a grievance on overtime pay forward. But the union is perfectly within its rights to do so, providing it has considered the case on its merits and its decision is not the result of discriminatory treatment. After all, a union cannot possibly carry all or even most grievances through to arbitration. The union official handling the case may have decided that the case was not winnable, or may simply have felt that scarce union funds might be better used to try to save a member's job in a dismissal grievance than to try to recoup $50 in overtime pay. Subject to the broad limitations of duty of fair representation provisions, union officials must be given latitude in matters of this sort if their organizations are to represent the bargaining unit as a whole effectively.

Strikes are an even better example of situations where the wishes of the individual must often be subordinated to the needs of the union as a whole. At such times, strict discipline is generally necessary. In particular, it is absolutely essential that a striking union be able to call its members out on picket duty and that those members obey the picket captain's orders. Failure to maintain an adequate picket-line presence could lead to the collapse of the strike; failure to follow a picket captain's orders could in certain situations lead to arrest, injury, or possibly even loss of life. Similarly, if enough members crossed a picket line and continued working, the strike could also collapse. This explains the fines and other forms of discipline that unions sometimes impose on members who cross picket lines, as well as the ostracism with which such workers are often greeted by co-workers once the strike is over.

Collective bargaining is yet another core union process that is arguably impossible for any union to conduct in a fully democratic fashion. A union may go to great lengths to solicit members' input on the initial bargaining package; almost all Canadian unions submit their tentative agreements to the membership for an up-and-down ratification vote. But bargaining itself is, as we'll see in the negotiation chapter, a delicate process often very heavily dependent on the personal chemistry of the chief union and management negotiators. If a union had to go back to the membership every time a demand was dropped or a position changed, the flow of negotiations would be seriously interrupted, and it's unlikely a settlement could ever be reached.

One other point must be made concerning limitations on union democracy arising from the nature of unions as political organizations. Most of us probably think of democracies as also being meritocracies, in which the best person for any given job is assigned that job regardless of whom he knows, how long he has been with the organization, or what sort of socio-economic background she comes from. Unions don't seem to function entirely as meritocracies. Seniority within the organization does appear to matter, as does knowing officials or other important members. To a degree, at least, individuals have to "work their way up" the union ladder. Someone generally also has to become known by key senior members and officials before being entrusted with a leadership position, no matter what skills and abilities he or she has. To a degree, this sort of "internal seniority system" keeps unions from acquiring fresh ideas and new perspectives. The question here is, to what degree do unions' "internal seniority systems" prevent genuinely talented people from working their way into leadership positions as quickly as they should?

Here, at least modest light has been shed by a study of Canadian union presidents by Solomon, Andiappan, and Shand (1986). These researchers sought to relate the time it took individuals to rise to the presidency of Canadian national unions to such personal characteristics as the individual's age and educational background, as well as to such organizational characteristics as the union's size. Solomon and his associates found that, on average, it appeared to take a fairly long time (about eight years after assuming elected or appointed office within the union) for someone to be elected president. Though university graduates still took a fairly long time (just under seven years) to reach the presidency, this was significantly less time than the ten-plus years it took non-university graduates to do so. Presidents of larger unions and those deriving most or all of their income from their union salaries also took longer to "reach the top," indicating that seniority and trust factors may be more important in leadership situations where there is more at stake.

Taken together, these findings suggest that while seniority definitely matters, so do a person's qualifications. It would be interesting to compare the characteristics of union officials with the characteristics of officials of political parties or civic organizations with an eye to determining the relative mix of seniority and education or other qualifications in each case. Very possibly unions are not alone among voluntary organizations in placing importance on personal connections and seniority within the organization.

Safeguards for Democracy

Although there are a number of limitations to how democratic a union can be, there are also a number of safeguards that, taken together, help to ensure active membership participation, the legitimacy of opposition, and the upholding of due process.

First, as noted earlier, many leaders not only permit but encourage active participation on the part of their membership. As Godard (1994:240) notes, it's often in their enlightened self-interest to do so, since committed members are likelier to support strikes and a union with a reputation for encouraging member participation may have an easier time recruiting new members.

Second, members who are unhappy with their leadership have a number of options available to them. Most obviously, they may vote an incumbent slate out at the next election. In this regard, if an executive has been in office for a long time, even a close election (say, of 55:45 proportions) can serve as a kind of "warning shot across the bows" and make the executive more responsive to the membership after the election.[21] Disgruntled rank-and-filers can also reject tentative contracts, engage in **wildcat strikes** (Godard, 1994:241), or (in extreme instances) move to have the union decertified. All of these actions can have serious consequences both for the leadership and for the union as a whole; thus the threat of any of them is something a wise union official will not take lightly.

Third, there are a number of legislative safeguards for union democracy, in addition to those contained in union constitutions and those of labour federations such as the CLC. Most jurisdictions have in place a duty of fair representation provision that has the practical effect of requiring unions to consider each member's grievance seriously. While such provisions don't mean that a union must carry every grievance through to arbitration (a practical impossibility, as we'll see when we get to the grievance chapter), it does mean that any possible bias in a union's handling of grievances (i.e., refusal to carry forward grievances filed by "dissident" members) is likely to be scrutinized rather thoroughly by the labour board. In most cases, the effect of these duty-of-fair-representation provisions is to induce union officials to bend over backwards not only to be fair, but to be perceived as fair. A number of jurisdictions also have in place provisions that require unions to conduct secret strike votes before calling any strike. But indeed, it appears most Canadian unions already require such votes as a matter of course.

Union Democracy in Canada and the United States

Overall, Canadian unions appear to be significantly more democratic than their American counterparts. To begin with, there has been far less outright corruption here than in the United States. Thugs of the Hal Banks variety have been mercifully rare here—and far too common south of the border. For example, a succession of presidents of the Teamsters Union, which was expelled from both the American AFL-CIO and CLC for corruption (Craig and Solomon, 1996:86–87), were convicted of serious criminal offences, and for years it was routine for Teamster officials to use gangsters to protect themselves (Craig and Solomon, 1996). Corruption was also rampant in some of the building trade unions and in the longshoring unions, at least one of which was also expelled from the AFL-CIO.

One reason why labour leaders of the Hal Banks type have been rare in Canada may be most Canadian jurisdictions' duty-of-fair-representation provisions—something that does not exist in American legislation. The possibility of an aggrieved member taking the union before the labour board very likely acts as a brake on seriously undemocratic union conduct. In contrast, under a system where a member's only recourse is a cumbersome internal review procedure, followed by the courts, leaders might be more willing to engage in undemocratic behaviour, knowing there is little likelihood they will be called to account.

Most important of all is an issue that has rarely been treated in the union democracy literature, though it is noted by Edelstein and Warner: union democracy at the national level. Here there are profound differences in the ways in which the Canadian and American labour movements have operated, at least since the creation of the CLC in 1956. CLC presidents function as just that—presidents. That is to say, they are elected, serve for a relatively short period of time, and then move on to other things. In contrast, the "presidency" of the major American federations (first the AFL, now the AFL-CIO) has in practice functioned more as a monarchy. At least two long-serving AFL presidents (Samuel Gompers and William Green) died in office. The first president of the merged federation, George Meany, died shortly after his last convention, at which he was so ill that he had to be wheeled on and off the convention floor (A. Robinson, 1981). Only in 1995, when Meany's successor, Lane Kirkland, was replaced by John Sweeney, did one witness a change in the federation's presidency resulting from some cause other than the incumbent's death or disability. And even Kirkland served for 15 years and was well into his seventies when he retired.

With no serious possibility of an electoral challenge, AFL and AFL-CIO presidents have often conducted themselves in quite high-handed fashion. For example, under Gompers, the strong minority of AFL members favouring socialism and comprehensive industrial democracy was always ruthlessly suppressed (Galenson and Smith, 1978).[22] Despite such strong rumblings from the rank-and-file, Gompers appears never even to have considered the possibility of forming a labour party in the United States (Galenson and Smith, 1978). Later, under Meany, the AFL-CIO placed a low priority on organizing, despite many executive council members' obvious desire to expand the federation's efforts in this area (Goulden, 1972; Reuther, 1976; Winpisinger, 1989). As well, during the Vietnam era, Meany almost single-handedly put the federation firmly behind the government's policies (Goulden, 1972; Dulles and Dubofsky, 1984). When unionists dared oppose the Johnson administration's Vietnam policies, Meany not only cut them off at AFL-CIO conventions, he publicly attacked them as traitors and Communist sympathizers (Goulden, 1972).

Not only was the conduct of Gompers and Meany extremely undemocratic; there is reason to believe that it did not serve the country's union members and other working people at all well. For example, had the American labour movement established its own political party, as almost all other Western labour movements have, it might have been in a better position to combat the extreme anti-unionism of the Reagan administration. Meany's support of the Vietnam War and other reactionary foreign policies effectively severed the labour movement's ties to Congressional liberals (Peirce, 1995) as well as alienating young people from the labour movement (I. Robinson, 1990). And had Meany devoted more money and resources to organizing, American union membership might well not have declined as sharply as it did even during the relatively prosperous 1960s and 1970s (see Table 5.1), which again would have left it in a better position to withstand the neoconservative assault of the 1980s. It is hard to imagine any CLC president persisting in such misguided and undemocratic actions as those engaged in by Gompers and Meany, given the very real likelihood of defeat at the next election.[23]

More research is clearly needed on specific aspects of Canadian versus American union democracy at the national level. It would, for example, be useful to know what happens to "unofficial" resolutions at AFL-CIO and CLC conventions, and more generally how policy is made in both federations. For now, even the brief discussion we have provided should suffice to show that the Canadian labour movement has generally functioned a good deal more democratically at the national federation level than has the American one, and that this more democratic functioning appears to have benefitted the Canadian labour movement.

QUESTIONS FOR DISCUSSION

1) If you are a union member, how do you feel about how your union is serving you? If you are not a union member, how would you feel about joining one?

2) At which points did Canadian union membership increase significantly? At which points did it decrease? What were the reasons?

3) How have union membership rates by industry been changing in recent years?

4) In which provinces is union membership highest? In which is it lowest? Why, do you think?

5) Thirty-five years ago, Canadian union membership rates were roughly the same as those in the United States. Now Canadian rates are more than twice those of the United States. Why has this situation changed? Do you think Canadian rates will continue to be significantly higher than American rates in the future?

6) What are some of the main effects of Canada's fragmented union structure? Are there signs that this situation is starting to change?

7) Discuss the role played by union locals, municipal and district labour councils, and provincial labour federations.

8) Discuss the role played by provincial and national labour federations, particularly the CLC.

9) How does union structure in Quebec differ from that in all other Canadian provinces?

10) How would you define union democracy? Do you think the standards set by Edelstein and Warner in the definition discussed in the text are too high? Are Canadian unions more or less democratic than American unions, in your view? Are there inherent limitations to union democracy? If so, how can unions be more democratic within those limitations?

SUGGESTIONS FOR FURTHER READING

Chaison, Gary. (1996). *Union mergers in hard times: The view from five countries*. Ithaca and London: Cornell Univ. ILR Press. A thought-provoking study of recent union mergers in the United States, Britain, Australia, and New Zealand, as well as Canada. Chaison's prediction is that in years to come Canadian union fragmentation will be greatly reduced and that large conglomerate unions such as the CEP and CAW will become "centers of mergers of activity and will come to rely on absorptions for continued growth."

Strauss, George. (1991). "Union democracy." In G. Strauss et al. (Eds.). *The state of the unions*. Madison: IRRA Press. A useful discussion of a difficult concept.

CHAPTER 6

UNION ACTIONS AND IMPACTS

Union member votes on the employer's final offer as a steward looks on.

Building on the discussion of the previous chapter, this chapter examines the kinds of actions unions take in support of their objectives and the economic and social impacts they have, both at the workplace and in Canadian society as a whole. We begin with a brief overview of union actions, and the way in which these actions have changed in recent years. We then take a more detailed look at a broad range of union activities, from traditional ones such as collective bargaining and political action, to modern ones such as the creation of union-sponsored venture capital corporations and joint participation with management in a variety of employee involvement schemes. Next, we examine unions' wage impacts, both on employers and on other, non-unionized workers. After a brief look at the ways in which unions

achieve their wage goals, the chapter goes on to consider unions' productivity impacts and effects on the management of organizations, before concluding with a discussion of their broader effects on Canadian society as a whole.

UNION ACTIONS

The question of the methods or actions that unions use to achieve their objectives has been of interest to industrial relations experts for more than 100 years. In a classic 1897 work entitled *Industrial Democracy*, Sidney and Beatrice Webb suggest that unions rely primarily on three methods: mutual insurance, collective bargaining, and legal enactment.[1]

As was pointed out in the labour history chapter, the mutual insurance function of unions was extremely important in the days before unemployment insurance, publicly funded health care, and sick and disability leave. Union benefit funds could help tide unemployed workers over periods of cyclical depression and support the families of workers killed or injured at work, or incapacitated due to illness. By representing themselves as "mutual benefit societies" or "friendly societies," unions were also able to get around harsh nineteenth-century legislation banning them as criminal conspiracies in restraint of trade (Forsey, 1982; Heron, 1989; Craig and Solomon, 1996). Much of the unions' traditional mutual insurance function has been taken over by government. However, some elements of it survive, such as the Supplementary Unemployment Benefits contained in auto workers' collective agreements, which top up government EI payments to a level near the worker's normal wage (Craig and Solomon, 1996:78). With continuing cutbacks to government social programs, unions may start returning to some of their older mutual insurance activities more frequently.

Unions' collective bargaining activities are still generally carried on more or less as the Webbs envisaged, though the range of issues brought to the table is now often considerably greater. As for legal enactment, unions have been among the strongest supporters of higher minimum wages, health and safety legislation, anti-discrimination laws, and a broad range of social programs of benefit to all working people— not just union members. Again, this emphasis on working on behalf of all working people is in line with the Webbs' original emphasis.

Even today, the Webbs' three methods are at the core of what most unions spend a good deal of their time doing. But the range of union activity has expanded a good deal over the past century, and to some degree its character has also changed. In the area of collective bargaining, for example, while most bargaining continues to be adversarial, a growing number of unions have entered into more cooperative arrangements with management. In some cases, unions have taken on what amounts to something approaching joint governance of the workplace—a role that would have been totally foreign to the unionist of 50 years ago and that continues to arouse considerable controversy within the Canadian labour movement even now (CAW, no date; CPU, 1990; USWA, 1991).[2] In the political arena, unions have also expanded their role, moving beyond support for specific pieces of labour-related legislation to more or less permanent alliances with parties such as the NDP, and less formal arrangements with women's, environmental, anti-poverty, and church groups and other progressive organizations and the creation of "humanity" or "justice" funds to support specific causes (Godard, 1994:218). They have also become adept at using publicity campaigns to help achieve their objectives and at using their members' savings and pension funds to promote local and regional development and job creation through a broad range of labour-sponsored venture capital corporations and pension pools (Boivin and Déom, 1995:459–460; Jackson and Lamontagne, 1995; Jackson, 1997 and 1998). Finally, Canadian unions have long been and continue to be involved in a broad range of educational ventures (CWC, 1990; CUPE, no date; Fisher and Peirce, 1995; White, 1995).

Thus, while their general objectives remain the same as those of unions in the past, today's unions tend to operate within a far broader context. They also have available to them strategies and technologies that the unionists of, for example, the 1940s could only dream about. The discussion that follows takes into account both that broader context and some of those strategies and technologies.

Collective Bargaining

Overall, the Canadian industrial relations system can fairly be described as voluntarist. This means that in unionized workplaces, most outcomes are left to be negotiated between the union and management rather than being established through legislation, as is the case in some European countries such as France (Goetschy, 1993). As a result, collective bargaining is, almost by definition, a core activity for virtually all Canadian unions.

The bargaining process itself will be considered in some detail in the chapter on negotiation, and thus need not be discussed here. But it may be worth taking a brief look at some of the ways in which that process has changed in recent years.

First, collective bargaining now addresses a far broader range of issues than it generally did early in the century, when agreements might be just one or two pages long and were usually limited to such core issues as wages, hours of work, holiday and overtime pay, and union security provisions (see Giles and Starkman, 2001). During the early postwar period, as was noted in Chapter 4, unions began to negotiate a broad range of **fringe benefits** such as paid vacations, sick leave, pensions, and medical and hospitalization insurance (Heron, 1989; Giles and Starkman, 2001). More recently, demands from an increasingly diverse work force containing growing numbers of women have caused unions to negotiate maternity and paternity leave provisions, flexible schedules, workplace day-care centres, and in some cases anti-discrimination and anti-harassment provisions that go beyond the requirements of human rights legislation. At the same time, the introduction of labour-saving technology into workplaces has caused unions to seek (albeit often unsuccessfully) to negotiate protection against job or income loss resulting from such technology. The introduction of new chemicals and other potentially hazardous substances has led to the negotiation of clauses regarding their use, as well as the employer's responsibility to provide appropriate safety equipment and training in the handling of such substances (see Giles and Starkman, 1995:367). Finally, growing concern for members' well-being both on and off the job has led many unions to negotiate employee assistance programs to help employees with drug, alcohol, financial, or other personal problems. The addition of this broad range of issues to such core issues as wages and hours of work has tended to make bargaining a longer and more complex process than it was in the past.

Second, while most collective bargaining continues to be adversarial, or **distributive**, a growing proportion of it is now of an **integrative**, or problem-solving nature (Downie, 1982 and 1989; Craig and Solomon, 1996). Integrative bargaining's most obvious use is in cases involving clear "win-win" issues, such as health and safety (Chaykowski, 1995:237); however, this type of bargaining has sometimes been more widely applied, even in cases involving monetary issues (Downie, 1982:323). A recent, essentially integrative approach developed by Robert Fisher and William Ury and known as **principled bargaining** (see Chaykowski, 1995:247) emphasizes the separation of issues from personalities, a focus on the parties' underlying interests, and the invention of options that give rise to mutual gain rather than win-lose situations. There is evidence to suggest that principled bargaining has been adopted by a number of major companies and prominent unions (Chaykowski, 1995:247–248).

Clearly, any move towards principled bargaining entails a significant shift in attitude. Whereas in conventional bargaining, mistrust of the other side and a focus on short-term tactics designed to give one's own side the advantage are the norm, principled bargaining requires a good measure of trust and a willingness to take the long view in dealings with the other side. To union leaders trained to distrust management, as many have traditionally been, it may be extremely difficult to make the necessary attitudinal change.[3]

Joint Union–Management Ventures at the Workplace

The same types of challenges posed by a shift from distributive to principled bargaining apply, to an even greater degree, to unions' participation in joint ventures with management designed to increase worker morale and productivity. Such ventures can range from single-issue labour–management committees to broad **gainsharing plans** such as the Scanlon Plan (see Downie, 1982:330–332). They can also include quality circles, self-directed work teams, and employee stock ownership plans (Verma, 1995).

In a few cases, unions and management have negotiated joint governance arrangements whereby the union becomes, in effect, a full partner in management of the organization (Verma, 1995:299–300). Such arrangements entail a radical transformation of the union's role, from that of workers' advocate to that of administrator and perhaps even manager of discontent. They also open up far greater possibilities for direct communication between management and employees—possibilities that run the risk of reducing the union's influence in the workplace (see Lemelin, 1989:452–455) and may even conflict with its advocacy role. If, for example, in its role as co-manager, a union has agreed with management on the need to cut costs, but rank-and-file members are pushing hard for immediate, up-front wage increases, what will union negotiators do at the bargaining table, and how will the demand for wage increases affect the union's continued participation in the joint governance scheme?

Moreover, participation in such schemes often requires union members and officials to learn new skills. Traditionally, motivational and political skills were most important for union leaders. But if a union is co-managing an organization, its officials and those of its members involved in joint governance committees will also need to learn business-related skills such as finance, economics, and accounting (see Verma, 1995:299).

Union participation in joint cooperation and employee involvement schemes has often proven quite controversial, both within individual unions, in the Canadian labour movement as a whole, and among IR academics. Some regard increased employee involvement as inevitable, given globalization and increased competitiveness. Such writers argue that unions have no choice other than to participate in employee involvement programs. If unions don't participate, they suggest, management will introduce the programs anyway, and the interests of neither individual workers nor the union will have been well-served.[4] Others (i.e., Godard, 1991) are more skeptical, while still others (i.e., Wells, 1993) oppose any union participation in such ventures, basically on the grounds that for a union to assume any significant co-management role amounts to a conflict of interest with its core role as the workers' advocate. Within the labour movement, some unions (i.e., CAW, no date) have adopted policies of outright opposition to joint cooperation schemes, while some of the schemes' strongest supporters, such as the CEP and Steelworkers, have insisted on being given a major role as a condition of participation (Verma, 1995:297).[5] Arguably the recent economic environment, which has seen many large-scale layoffs even in highly profitable organizations, has made such joint ventures a dicier business from the unions' perspective. With large-scale layoffs occurring despite unions' best efforts to increase productivity, even former supporters may wonder what's in the schemes for them. At a minimum, such continuing layoffs could serve to strengthen the hand of union "hawks" opposing cooperation, thus making it more difficult for unions to enter into any new programs, as well as weakening the internal political position of leaders disposed towards cooperation.

Joint Participation Outside the Workplace

Canadian unions are also involved in a variety of joint ventures with management outside the workplace. Among other things, unions and management groups have formed a number of sectoral councils to address such issues as training, economic restructuring, trade policy, and labour–management cooperation on an industry-wide basis. One of the first such councils was the Canadian Textile Labour–Management Committee (CTLMC), formed in 1967 in the wake of a bitter strike at the Dominion Textile plant in Quebec (Thomason, Zwerling, and Chandra, 1992:264). Comprising nine management representatives and nine from the textile unions, the committee has not formally involved itself in collective bargaining as such but has sought to improve the bargaining process by ensuring that the parties are provided with accurate information about the real state of the industry (Thomason et al., 1992:266). In addition, the CTLMC has involved itself with issues ranging from domestic and foreign trade policies to productivity, occupational health and safety, and education and training. The committee appears to have been at least partly responsible for a major improvement in labour–management relations and a significant reduction in strike incidence in the textile industry (Thomason et al., 1992:264–266).

Another important sectoral initiative is the Canadian Steel Trade and Employment Congress (CSTEC), formed jointly by the major steel companies and the United Steelworkers of America (USWA) in 1985 (Verma and Warrian, 1992:124). Since its formation, CSTEC has been heavily involved in trade issues, a special concern being the targeting of unfair foreign competition. The Congress's other major concern has been providing employment assistance for displaced steelworkers, of whom there have been a great many due to ongoing restructuring in the industry. Such assistance is provided under CSTEC's HEAT (Helping Employees Adjust Together) program, which (under an agreement with the federal government since 1987) has been provided with the same amount of per capita funding to assist displaced workers as would otherwise have been given to the Industrial Adjustment Service (Verma and Warrian, 1992). HEAT's services have included provision of job market information, training in starting a business, relocation assistance, and personal financial planning and retraining (Verma and Warrian, 1992:125).

Canadian unions have also been involved in a number of tripartite, or labour–management–government initiatives, although **tripartism** has never been as strong here as in many European countries, such as the Netherlands and Sweden (Adams, 1995:506). While a fair number of tripartite consultative bodies were established during the 1960s and 1970s, in 1976 the labour movement withdrew its representatives from most of them, including the Economic Council of Canada, in protest over the federal government's imposition of wage-price controls (Craig and Solomon, 1996:138).[6] More recently, however, unions have joined with management and the federal government in launching the Canadian Labour Market and Productivity Centre (CLMPC) (Adams, 1995; Murray, 1995), recently renamed the Canadian Labour and Business Centre (CLBC). Much of this body's work has been on relatively uncontentious issues such as training and labour market information (Adams, 1995); however, over the past few years it has broadened its focus, doing important research on issues as varied as work hours (CLMPC, 1997), the impacts of labour-sponsored venture capital corporations (Jackson and Lamontagne, 1995), changing demographics, and women in the workplace (Craig and Solomon, 1996:54).

Political Action

Almost all unions engage in some kind of political action. To a large extent, unions' ability to achieve their objectives depends on the types of legislation and government policies in place. They can't possibly hope to influence legislation or government policy without in some way becoming involved in the political process, whether through lobbying government on specific issues or through more formal connection with a political party.

This said, the form of political activity taken varies greatly within the Canadian labour government. Unions and labour federations differ particularly with respect to affiliation with a political party. The Canadian Federation of Labour, for example, was always strongly opposed to any such affiliation (McCambly, 1990); in Quebec, a similar position has been taken by the Centrale des syndicates démocratiques (CSD), which during the '70s broke away from the CSN over this very issue (Boivin and Déom, 1995).

In the Canadian context, however, labour organizations such as the CFL and CSD have been probably the exception rather than the rule. Most Canadian unions are explicitly committed to **social unionism**, a type of unionism that believes that the role of unions is to further workers' well-being as a whole, outside the workplace as well as within it (Godard, 1994:217). Almost by definition, a commitment to social unionism entails some kind of affiliation with a political party, since acting on behalf of the working class as a whole necessitates winning passage of a broad range of legislation that will benefit workers and lower-income Canadians. This is something that is extremely difficult to do through ad hoc lobbying on specific issues. While affiliation with a political party is no guarantee of success, it does arguably improve unions' chances, by providing them with an experienced partner to assist them in their political ventures on a steady basis.

In English Canada, the labour movement has most often chosen the NDP or its forerunner party, the CCF, as its political partner. In general, the links between the labour movement and the NDP have become closer over the past 25 years. Unions are allowed a given number of delegate slots at NDP conventions (Godard, 1994:218), and many choose to affiliate directly to the party, a decision that allows them to play an active role in formulating its policy (Murray, 1995:189). In Quebec, most labour activists support the Parti Québécois, or the federal Bloc Québécois party (Boivin and Déom, 1995:458–459). The support, however, is typically of a more individual and ad hoc nature than the formal affiliation of unions with the English NDP. Only one Quebec central labour organization, the Quebec Federation of Labour, or provincial wing of the CLC, has formally endorsed the PQ (Boivin and Déom, 1995).

There's little doubt that the NDP-CCF and PQ have often been of great benefit to the labour movement. As we pointed out in the labour history chapter, the threat of a CCF victory was arguably the major factor responsible for passage of Canada's first collective bargaining legislation, *PC 1003*. Later on, the NDP's balance-of-power position in a minority Liberal government was crucial in winning passage of the *Public Service Staff Relations Act*. More recently, NDP and PQ provincial governments have been responsible for a variety of pro-labour laws ranging from the removal of restrictive exclusions from unionization rights and the liberalization of certification procedures[7] to anti-strikebreaker bills, first-contract arbitration, and technological change provisions.

But there have also been many strains between the labour movement and the NDP or PQ, particularly when these parties have formed a provincial government and have been forced to make unpopular spending cuts directly affecting some of their union supporters. In 1982, the PQ government unilaterally imposed a 20 percent public sector salary reduction for the first three months of 1983, then unilaterally extended the existing agreements until the end of 1985 (Hébert, 1995:222). This action infuriated the public schoolteachers and other public sector workers, who had been among the PQ's strongest supporters, and caused much of the province's labour movement to withdraw support from the party in the 1985 election, which the PQ lost. Similarly, in 1993, Ontario's NDP government infuriated public sector unions by imposing a "Social Contract" providing for a three-year public sector wage freeze and unpaid days off. Public sector and many private sector unions withdrew their support from the NDP, which went down to disastrous defeat in the 1995 Ontario election, following an even worse performance in the 1993 federal election, for which the "Social Contract" legislation was largely blamed (Morton, 1995). Indeed, the party has not yet recovered its former strength in Ontario, faring even worse in the 1999 provincial election than it did in 1995. More recently, relations between the PQ and Quebec's labour movement have again been severely strained by the government's large-scale cutbacks in health care and other social areas. These conflicts and other recent developments, such as the federal NDP's move toward the centre, have led the labour movement to start reconsidering its role vis-à-vis its longtime political partners.

Not all politics is carried out in parliaments and legislative assemblies. As the economic environment becomes more globalized, many Canadian unions are finding themselves increasingly concerned with international development issues and with related problems of workers' rights, child labour and the like, as well as with issues such as child poverty, hunger, and regional underdevelopment at home. To help address these issues, a number of unions have established social justice or humanity funds. The Canadian Auto Workers' Social Justice Fund requires participating employers to donate one cent for each straight-time hour worked by each bargaining unit worker to a designated charity, food bank, or international relief effort (Godard, 1994:218). The Steelworkers' Humanity Fund, established on a similar checkoff basis, addresses itself to international labour issues, including support for core labour rights such as workers' freedom of association and reduction of child labour. As globalization increases, such funds could well become a more prominent aspect of Canadian union activity, since they are potentially very useful vehicles for linking Canadian and overseas labour organizations.

Publicity Campaigns and Member Communication

Like most modern organizations, today's unions are finding that they have to spend an increasing amount of their time and energy communicating, both with their members and with the public at large. To keep members abreast of what they are doing, unions send out regular newsletters and other publications such as special pre-strike bulletins, develop telephone trees, post notices on union bulletin boards, and occasionally use other mediums such as the Internet. To tell their story to the general public, they use the full range of modern media, from traditional newspaper and magazine ads, to radio, TV, and (once again) the Internet.

Union publicity efforts serve a variety of purposes. In some cases, the purpose is to inform both the union's own people and sympathetic members of the general public about what the union is doing on a particular issue such as shorter work hours or health and safety. In other instances, the aim is to build coalitions with other stakeholders. In still other cases, like those of the Ontario Secondary School

Parents, teachers, education workers, and unions have demonstrated their support for public education in Ontario and across the nation.

Join local and school based campaigns to protect our students' future.

Ontario Secondary School Teachers' Federation
Fédération des enseignantes–enseignants des écoles secondaires de l'Ontario
www.osstf.on.ca

OSSTF/FEESO

The Ontario Secondary School Teachers' Federation urges citizens to join their campaign to protest education cutbacks in the province.

Teachers' Federation against education cutbacks or the CUPE ad against Ontario's two-tier health care, the aim is to protest government policy. While many union ads tend to be negative, at least insofar as they are critical of existing economic and political conditions and seek to change them, unions also run a variety of positive ads. For instance, a number of the union ads appearing in the *Ontario New Democrat* do not address specific issues but are designed merely to emphasize the unions' general support for the NDP.

The strongest and most controversial type of union publicity campaign is the **boycott**, or negative publicity campaign designed to induce the public not to purchase the goods or services of the company in question. Boycotts are frequently though not always launched in the context of a strike or lockout or union recognition dispute. Perhaps the best-known

Let us never return to the days when the wealthy enjoyed the best of care and the poor entered through the back door.

Treatment for the POOR Only
No patients received for clinics after 9:30 A.M. and 2:30 P.M. Doors will be locked at these hours

Yes to Canada's Health Care system, with quality services for all.

Canadian Union of Public Employees

CUPE ad offers Canadian Forum readers a stark reminder of what two-tier health care could be like.

United Farmworkers' grape and lettuce boycott was one of the most successful boycotts ever undertaken and was widely credited with helping the union win bargaining rights for California farm workers.

example is the grape-and-lettuce boycott undertaken by the late Cesar Chavez and his fledgling United Farm Workers (UFW) union in the United States during the late 1960s. The boycott, generally regarded as highly successful, was widely credited with helping the UFW win bargaining rights for thousands of farm workers, mainly Mexican-American immigrants, who up to that point had been working under wretched conditions for extremely low wages. A more controversial and perhaps less successful campaign was one launched by the Ontario English Catholic Teachers' Association against firms found to have donated money exclusively to the governing Conservative party, to which the teachers were opposed because of the education cutbacks leading to the fall 1997 Ontario teachers' strike (Lakey, 1998).[8] The teachers' union boycott was particularly controversial because it was a secondary boycott (a boycott of an ally of one's adversary rather than the adversary itself)[9] and because, in the eyes of some, it amounted to punishing people for their political beliefs.

UNIONS IN BUSINESS

The severe recession of the early 1980s caused many labour organizations to start working proactively to create jobs and promote local and community development. It was at this time that labour-sponsored venture capital corporations (VCCs) began to appear.

Among the first, and by far the largest of the labour-sponsored VCCs, was the Quebec Solidarity Fund, launched in 1984 with support from the Quebec government (Jackson and Peirce, 1990:42; Boivin and Déom, 1995:460). Like other labour-sponsored VCCs, the Solidarity Fund offers investors a variety of tax credits, including an RRSP deduction as well as a provincial equity tax credit (Boivin and Déom, 1995:460). By 1993, the Fund had attracted just under 200 000 investors, nearly half of whom were QFL members, and was accounting for about half of all risk capital invested in Quebec (Boivin and Déom, 1995). It is generally recognized that the Fund has been responsible for creating or saving many thousands of jobs in the province. Since its inception, the Fund has invested in a broad range of small and medium-sized enterprises in such sectors as communications, EDP software and service, and forest products, and has created specialized sectoral funds in biotechnology, environmental industries, and aerospace (Jackson and Peirce, 1990; Boivin and Déom, 1995). Among its more recent ventures, the Fund helped finance Entourage, a new employee-owned firm launched by former Bell Canada technicians in the Ottawa region who are CEP members (Jackson, 1998).

The Solidarity Fund is far from being the only such organization in Canada. Other such VCCs include Working Ventures, founded by the Canadian Federation of Labour (Jackson and Peirce, 1990:43; Murray, 1995:188), First Ontario Fund, the Manitoba Federation of Labour's Crocus Investment Fund, and B.C.'s Working Opportunities Fund (Jackson, 1998:4). The last three of these funds have been particularly interested in supporting employee-owned firms (Jackson, 1998). In addition, the Solidarity and Crocus Funds and B.C.'s Working Opportunity Fund have, since the 1980s, directly supported a broad range of community economic development projects. For example, the Working Opportunity Fund invests in community loan funds serving small business (Jackson, 1998:10).

Unions and labour federations have also been heavily involved in social housing. Nationally, the CLC played a key role in establishing the Cooperative Housing Foundation; at the local level, many local labour councils sponsored cooperative housing projects during the 1970s and 1980s. In Cape Breton, the non-profit Cape Breton Labourers Development Corporation funds the construction of affordable homes for International Labourers Union members. In B.C. during the 1980s, the labour movement supported a progressive board of directors at Vancouver City Savings Credit Union, which resulted in a number of innovative affordable housing projects (Jackson, 1998:11).

Through their members' pension funds, unions control many hundreds of millions of dollars. An idea that has lately been gaining increasing currency both in the United States and, to a lesser degree, in Canada is that of using these funds to promote such socially desirable objectives as community development, affordable housing, and small-business growth (Jackson, 1997). The vehicle normally used for this purpose is an Economically Targeted Investment (ETI), a pooling mechanism that allows pension funds to channel a certain portion of their assets into such worthwhile ventures (Jackson, 1997).

Vancouver's Greystone Properties is a good example of a Canadian ETI. This organization, sponsored by 28 pension plans jointly trusteed by construction unions and construction companies, has become a major investor in affordable housing in Vancouver. The fund is used to finance construction projects that provide jobs for union members affiliated with the participating pension plans, and also to provide mortgages for low- and middle-income people in a city whose housing costs are among the country's highest. In addition to achieving these worthy social objectives, Greystone has provided above-average returns to its sponsors (Jackson, 1997). In the eyes of at least one observer (Jackson, 1997:2), Greystone represents a model that could be replicated across Canada, especially with construction union pension funds.

In some cases, unions and their members have also bought significant or even controlling interests in the firms for which members work. Most often, this strategy has been used in single-industry resource towns where the corporate owners want to pull out even though the enterprise remains viable (Jackson, 1998:3). While many unions are critical of employee buyouts, arguing that it isn't the union's or workers' job to save management from the consequences of its own mismanagement, the Steelworkers have been a notable exception (Jackson, 1998:5). Since the early 1990s, this union has encouraged viable buyouts, both directly and through venture capital funds. By now, it has had enough experience to be able to provide support for those locals contemplating a buyout (Jackson, 1998). Its most notable success was in the case of Algoma Steel in Sault Ste. Marie, Ontario. Here, a firm on the brink of collapse (Verma and Warrian, 1992:121–124) was rescued and turned around, thanks to an employee buyout that saw the firm's 6000 workers acquire a 60 percent interest in the company (Steed, 1994; Jackson, 1998:3). Although Algoma Steel is again facing severe difficulties, there can be little doubt that the Steelworkers' efforts kept the firm viable longer than it would otherwise have been. Other buyouts of note have occurred in the pulp and paper industry, at Spruce Falls in Ontario and Tembec in Quebec. In these cases, unionized workers represented by the CEP bought major interests in their mills and managed to keep most of their jobs (Jackson, 1998:3–4).

The preceding discussion has touched on only a few of the ways in which unions have begun to function, in effect, as business organizations, mobilizing their members' capital and in some cases using it to leverage other funds to create and save jobs, build affordable housing, and promote community development. Given government's growing reluctance to fund direct job creation schemes, this aspect of union action seems likely to expand in the coming years and will bear close observation by students of industrial relations.

Education

The labour movement has a long and proud record of involvement in education. As we noted in the labour history chapter, nineteenth- and early twentieth-century union halls often served as libraries, forums for public lectures and seminars, and venues for a broad range of educational and cultural activity. The tradition of union education has continued to the present day. Although there is not space in a general industrial relations textbook to do more than skim the surface on the subject of unions' educational ventures, even a cursory look will suffice to give some idea of the extent of their involvement.

While many union-sponsored courses focus on technical issues of immediate concern such as organizing, bargaining strategy and shop steward training, others have addressed broader issues such as women in the labour movement and unions and the environment (CUPE, no date; Fisher and Peirce, 1995). Over the years, the CLC has run weekend institutes and week-long summer programs covering a broad range of subjects (R. White, 1995). In Newfoundland, the Newfoundland Association of Public Employees (NAPE) has been a major player in this area, as has the Canadian Union of Public Employees (CUPE). NAPE's offerings have included training in public speaking and leadership, which has gone a long way towards building up members' confidence when placed in situations requiring them to speak in public (Fisher and Peirce, 1995). CUPE's courses, many offered in French as well as English, have included ones in political action, pay equity, technological change, and assertiveness training. The union has placed special emphasis on health and safety training; among its offerings, in addition to general health and safety courses, are specialized courses aimed at health-care workers, municipal sewage-treatment-plant workers, social-service workers, and those who must deal with asbestos in the workplace (CUPE, n.d.).

A number of unions have begun to offer courses on contemporary political and economic issues of special relevance to their members. CUPE's offerings have included "Contracting Out and Privatization—Ways of Winning," a subject of obvious interest to the union's members given the wave of privatization that has taken place over the past 15 years (CUPE, n.d.). The Communications Workers of Canada (CWC) and its successor union, the Communications, Energy, and Paperworkers Union (CEP) have also offered courses and developed educational materials on various "hot topics." During the early 1990s, the CWC conducted ongoing education on the subject of free trade (CWC, 1992). More recently, the CEP has developed a series of articles, videos, and other materials on work hours for insertion into its leadership development and steward training courses (J. White, 1997b).

Unions' Expanded Scope of Action

As we have seen in the preceding pages, Canadian unions have greatly expanded their scope of action beyond such core activities as negotiating collective agreements, handling members' grievances, and seeking to achieve passage of pro-labour legislation. To begin with, they have entered into a broad range of partnerships with management, both within workplaces and beyond the workplace. Politically, their sphere of interest has widened, to encompass coalitions with anti-poverty and other social justice groups at home and with foreign unions and Canadian NGOs promoting economic development and human and labour rights overseas. And particularly over the past 15 years, many have entered the world of business, learning how to use available funds such as pension monies to promote job creation, community development, affordable housing, and other social objectives. In the field of labour education, a number of unions have expanded the labour "curriculum" beyond traditional core subjects such as collective bargaining and grievance handling, to encompass highly technical courses in specific areas of occupational health and safety and employment law and personal development courses in areas such as stress management and retirement planning (CUPE, n.d.). Supporting all these efforts has been an increasingly sophisticated publicity apparatus that makes use of the full gamut of media approaches, from traditional newspaper and magazine ads to direct mail campaigns and the establishment of Web sites on the Internet.

This new, expanded scope of union action has not been uncontroversial, either within the labour movement or outside of it. As noted earlier, some unionists feel a union has no business affiliating with a political party. A fair number might argue against a checkoff-based fund such as the Steelworkers' Humanity Fund, on the grounds that it should be up to the individual union member to decide which charities and non-profit organizations he or she will support. At least one major Quebec labour federation, the Centrale des syndicats démocratiques, has been skeptical about the merits of the Solidarity Fund (Boivin and Déom, 1995:460), and more national unions than not seem to be opposed to employee buyouts, even in cases where the rank-and-file strongly support the buyout (Jackson, 1998:5). Economically targeted investment vehicles for employee pension plans have been no less controversial (Jackson, 1997).

While the debates over these issues seem unlikely to end any time soon, the fact remains that most Canadian labour organizations have expanded their scope of action in one or more of the areas just mentioned. The areas into which a union or labour federation chooses to expand will depend on a variety of factors, including the organization's traditions and history, its membership composition, its members' interests, and the economic pressures facing the industry in which it operates. Some may wish (or need) to expand into more "new" areas than others. But in today's highly volatile economic and political environment, few if any unions can afford the luxury of simply burying their heads in the sand and concentrating solely on "minding the shop." While Canadian union membership rates have not declined anywhere near as sharply as those in the United States have, the pressures on Canadian union membership are nonetheless real (Murray, 2001; Lipsig-Mumme, 1995). In the coming decades, the ability to mount effective publicity campaigns and to use members' accumulated funds to create or save jobs may become increasingly critical to a union's survival. Our prediction, therefore, is that the scope of union action will continue to expand.

UNION IMPACTS

Not surprisingly, given the broad range of activities in which we have just seen that they engage, unions have an equally broad range of impacts on their members' wages and working conditions, on the productivity and overall performance of the firms in which their members work, and on the Canadian economy and Canadian society as a whole. Many of these impacts, especially the wage impacts, have been studied extensively. A 1986 U.S. review article (Lewis, 1986) considered more than 200 studies on wage impacts alone. Gunderson and Riddell (1993) review 11 Canadian studies on the same subject.

To a large extent, the union impacts likely to be of greatest interest to any given industrial relationist will depend on that person's overall perspective on IR (discussed in detail in Chapter 1). Pure economists and others of a neoclassical persuasion are apt to be most interested in unions' wage impacts. Students of organizational behaviour and other managerialists are likely to focus on the way unions affect management and overall firm productivity. Institutionalists may be most interested in positive productivity effects resulting from unionized workers' having a greater say in how firms are managed. For their part, reformists and people taking a political economy perspective are apt to emphasize unions' macro-level effects on Canadian society as a whole. Our view is that one must take *all* the above effects into account to have a good understanding of how unions operate in Canada today.[10]

Wage Impacts

Direct Union Wage Impact

While unions are certainly about more than just money, it's unlikely that most people would remain members for very long if their unions could not negotiate a higher wage than they would otherwise receive. In simplest terms, a **direct union wage impact** is the premium a worker receives for union membership. It can be expressed as the difference between the wage a unionized worker and an otherwise equally qualified non-unionized worker would receive for doing the same job, as the following equation shows: DUWI = W(uw)–W(nuw), where W(uw) is the average wage for unionized workers doing any given job, and W(nuw) is the average wage for non-unionized workers doing that same job.

To be sure, the question of how large any direct union wage impact is will typically be much more complex than the previous discussion would suggest. The whole assumption behind the calculation of direct union wage impacts is that other things, such as workers' experience and skill levels, are equal. Often they are far from equal. Because unionized firms generally offer higher pay and sometimes better working conditions as well, they tend to attract (and are able to hire) more highly qualified people than non-unionized firms. It may, therefore, be difficult to say to what extent a "union" wage impact is a simple premium for union membership, and to what extent it is a premium for greater skill or experience (Gunderson and Riddell, 1993:390–391).

Over the years, advances in statistical techniques have made it possible for researchers to "control" for differences in labour quality and job characteristics (Gunderson and Riddell, 1993; Gunderson and Hyatt, 1995:323; see also L. Reynolds, 1982:133–135). While there are still significant methodological problems[11] in determining the precise direct union wage impact for any country as a whole, the 11 Canadian studies reviewed by Gunderson and Riddell (1993:394–396) found that impact to be in the 10 to 25 percent range, a finding generally in line with earlier U.S. studies (L. Reynolds, 1982:485–486; Lewis, 1986).

Since about 1990, however, the size of those impacts appears to have been decreasing. One recent study (Renaud, 1997) suggests that by 1990, the Canadian direct wage impact had declined from a peak of about 25 percent at the end of the 1970s to around 10 percent. Similarly, a 1999 study by Gunderson, Hyatt, and Riddell found that in 1997, Canadian workers covered by a collective agreement earned about 8 percent more than those not covered.[12] Gunderson and Hyatt (2001:393) suggest that the declining size of the direct union wage impact may be due either to unions' declining power or their reorientation toward other, less costly objectives such as employment, job security, or union voice mechanisms. We, however, are by no means convinced that unions are any less interested in wage increases for their members than they were in the past. A more persuasive explanation to us may be found in the increasingly large public sector share of

Canadian union membership. Given that public sector wages, particularly in lower-end jobs, tend to be significantly higher than comparable private sector wages (Gunderson, Hyatt, and Riddell, 1999), there is less room for a high union wage impact in that sector. As well, as we point out in more detail in the public sector chapter, public sector bargaining was severely restricted during much of the 1990s, making it extremely difficult for public sector unions to achieve significant wage gains for their members during that period. In this connection, it will be interesting to see whether the public sector union wage impact increases as something approaching free collective bargaining returns to most Canadian public sector jurisdictions.

In any event, it's clear that direct union wage impacts are not the same for every worker, or in every industry. In general, these impacts tend to be greater for blue-collar than for white-collar and for less skilled than for more-skilled workers (Gunderson and Hyatt, 1995:325; Gunderson and Riddell, 1993:397; Reynolds, 1982:496–497). The impacts may be especially high in industries such as construction (Guderson and Riddell, 1993:397; Reynolds, 1982:485–486). In the United States, the evidence suggests that the impacts are greater for black workers and women than for white male workers (Reynolds, 1982:486); in Canada, there is some evidence of greater impacts for those women covered by collective agreements, though this is effectively cancelled out because fewer women than men are covered by collective agreements (Gunderson and Hyatt, 2001:393). Studies from both countries suggest that direct union wage impacts are generally greater in the private than in the public sector (Gunderson and Riddell, 1993; Gunderson and Hyatt, 2001).[13]

Impact on Fringe Benefits

Most workers do not receive all their pay as up-front wages. Usually a portion of the total compensation package is paid in fringe or non-wage benefits for such things as pensions, vacations, medical and dental insurance, holidays, and sick leave (Gunderson and Hyatt, 2001). Unionized establishments generally pay a greater portion of the total compensation package in fringe benefits than do non-unionized ones; thus their impact on fringe benefits is typically greater than their impact on up-front wages (Gunderson and Riddell, 1993:406–407). There are a number of reasons for this. For one thing, the average unionized worker is likely to be older and in a higher tax bracket than the average non-unionized worker, and hence more apt to favour deferred forms of compensation, such as pensions, which are non-taxable. These benefits may be particularly attractive because, due to economies of scale, they can be purchased relatively inexpensively, especially in larger establishments (Gunderson and Riddell, 1993:407). Again, since unionized workers are older and in most cases would have had the chance to save up money over the years, they tend to prefer to take more of their total compensation in the form of increased leisure (i.e., longer vacations and holidays) than as up-front pay (Gunderson and Riddell, 1993:230).

Their greater average age also helps explain their relatively greater interest in medical insurance and pension plans.

Unionized firms also tend to favour pensions and other forms of deferred payment because they help "lock workers in," thereby reducing costly turnover. In addition, pensions and other work benefits serve as work incentives, since older workers who stand to lose a lucrative pension if they are let go will likely work harder than they otherwise would to prevent that from happening (Gunderson and Riddell, 1993:408).

Indirect Union Wage Impacts

Indirect union wage impacts are the effects unions have on the wages of non-unionized workers. As various commentators point out (Gunderson, 1989; Gunderson and Hyatt, 2001:393–4), unions can affect the wages of non-unionized workers through a broad range of market, institutional, and legislative mechanisms. Economic theory would suggest that over the longer term, unions should reduce wages in the non-unionized sector, as employees from the unionized sector who are laid off when the unionized wage rises above the equilibrium level "spill over" into the non-unionized sector, thereby reducing wages there as well (Gunderson and Riddell, 1993:325–328). In practice, it's quite difficult to determine the overall impact of unions on non-unionized workers' wages in Canada. In general, the consensus is that this effect has been modest—probably less than 3 to 4 percent (Gunderson and Hyatt, 1995:327; Gunderson and Riddell, 1993:401). But it would be misleading to think of the indirect union wage effect as being uniform across the economy. Some non-unionized workers have lower wages due to unionization, while others, including most notably white males, may see their wages rise (see Gunderson and Hyatt, 1995:327).

What we're really talking about here are two quite different kinds of indirect union wage impact, impacts that pull wages in different directions and apply to different types of workers. The depressing or so-called "crowding" effect predicted by economic theory (Gunderson and Riddell, 1993:385–386) will typically apply to lower-skilled workers with little labour market power. The so-called "threat" effect applies in situations where non-unionized employers increase their employees' pay, often to levels at or near those paid to unionized workers, in order to forestall a unionization drive or prevent employees with scarce skills from quitting and going to work in a unionized firm (Gunderson and Riddell, 1993:387–389). This type of indirect wage impact, also sometimes known as the "as-if-unionized" impact, most often applies in situations involving highly skilled workers such as professionals or skilled technical staff. The reasoning here is that if the firm pays workers the same or nearly the same wages as they would receive if unionized, they will have less incentive to join the union; particularly if, along with higher wages, the workers receive union-style benefits and some kind of in-house grievance system. In effect, this type of indirect union wage impact is a soft union-avoidance tactic since the primary aim is to reduce workers' demand for union services.

Unions and Wage Dispersion

In addition to increasing their members' wages relative to those of non-unionized workers, unions may affect national income distribution in various ways. Because unions tend to reduce wage differentials related to skill, age, experience, and seniority, there's less wage dispersion among unionized than among non-unionized workers (Gunderson and Riddell, 1993:402). To put it another way, there appears to be significantly less difference between the best-paid and worst-paid unionized workers than between the best-paid and worst-paid non-unionized workers. At the same time, unionization tends to increase overall dispersion by creating a wage differential between unionized and non-unionized workers (Gunderson and Hyatt, 1995:325). A number of studies from both Canada and the United States have shown that the former effect is stronger, which means that overall, unions tend to reduce wage dispersion throughout the economy as a whole (Gunderson and Hyatt, 1995; Gunderson and Riddell, 1993:402). Other things being equal, we would expect similar results from unions' efforts in the political arena, since they generally tend to support redistributive economic and social policies such as progressive taxation policies, high levels of unemployment insurance and welfare benefits, and pay and employment equity programs.[14]

How Unions Achieve Their Wage Goals

In the section on union actions, we noted that unions use a variety of approaches to achieve their objectives, approaches that can range from collective bargaining to work for a labour-oriented political party or publicity campaigns. Here, we focus in slightly more detail on the methods unions use to achieve their wage objectives.

In Canada, collective bargaining is the major method used by most unions to achieve their wage objectives. This is not, however, the only method Canadian unions use. Some seek to keep wages up by restricting entry to the trade or profession (as by increasing entrance requirements for professional training or denying accreditation to those licensed in other jurisdictions). Others seek to fix non-union wages (as by supporting higher minimum wage or equal pay legislation) to reduce the relative cost of union as opposed to non-union labour, thereby maintaining or increasing the demand for union labour. Still others seek to change the environment within which bargaining is conducted (as by supporting changes in labour legislation that make union certification easier or supporting changes to a more centralized structure that will make it easier for the union to call an effective strike).[15]

Union Impact on Productivity

There is considerable disagreement within the industrial relations profession as to whether, on balance, unions serve to increase or decrease firms' productivity. The arguments on both sides have been usefully summed up by Freeman and Medoff (1979 and 1984).

Neoclassicists and others primarily interested in unions' economic impacts (the "monopoly" perspective described by Freeman and Medoff) argue that unions reduce productivity by raising wages above competitive levels, by reducing output through the strikes they call, and by forcing management to agree to restrictive work rules that result in the substitution of capital for labour, and hence increased unemployment (Freeman and Medoff, 1979:75; Gunderson and Hyatt, 1995:328). Institutionalists and others primarily interested in workplace equity or equity within society as a whole argue that far from reducing productivity, unions often have positive effects on it. These include reduced quit rates and improved morale and worker–management cooperation resulting from union grievance processes and other mechanisms that give workers a sense that they have some say in what goes on in the workplace. Unions can also induce management to use more efficient production methods and even, perhaps, more effective personnel policies. In addition, they can increase productivity by collecting information about the preferences of all workers, information that can help the firm select better personnel policies and a more appropriate mix of wages and fringe benefits (Freeman and Medoff, 1979:75). For their part, managerialists as well as some institutionalists argue that unions can have either positive or negative productivity effects, since what is most important is whether a union helps or hurts relations between workers and management. From this perspective, what may be of greatest interest are management's policy towards unions and the union's willingness to enter into a cooperative relationship with management (Godard, 1994:374–375). For example, if a union opposes an employee involvement initiative, the program's chances of success will clearly be reduced (Verma, 1995:297–298).

Which position is closest to the truth? The one thing almost everyone can agree on is that the question is an extremely difficult one to answer. As the previous discussion has suggested, some union effects are clearly positive, while others are clearly negative, and still others can be either positive or negative depending on the particular situation. Complicating matters still further is the fact that in many situations, particularly where what is being "produced" is a service rather than a tangible good, it may be extremely difficult if not impossible to measure productivity as such. In such cases, asking whether unions increase or decrease productivity may not be at all useful. Here (assuming we were trying to determine the effects of unionization in a recently unionized establishment), it might be far more useful to start by asking workers whether they found they were getting along better or worse with their supervisor than they were before the union came in, or whether they felt more or less confident than before about their ability to do their job. Even where productivity can be measured, the union's impact on the labour–management relationship may still be much the most important factor. Where this is positive, it can lead not just to improved bargaining and communications (Gunderson and Hyatt, 1995:329), but to a broad range of problem-solving behaviour in all areas of workplace life, which in turn can result in reduced accident and illness rates, lower grievance and strike rates, and even reduced down time and spoilage. Conversely, where the union's impact on the labour–management relationship is negative, the results can include greatly increased sickness, accident, and industrial conflict rates and increased down time and spoilage. At the end of the day, both positive and negative impacts of this kind may turn out to be more important than the generally modest union wage impacts discussed earlier in the section.

Union Impacts on Management of the Organization

People from all different perspectives on IR agree that union impacts on the management of organizations are substantial. Where they disagree is on whether such impacts are beneficial. From a comparative perspective, these impacts appear to be greater in North America, with its detailed collective agreements regulating many different aspects of workplace behaviour, than in Europe, where agreements are apt to be more general (see Giles and Starkman, 1995:340) and unions do not generally have a significant effect on firms' day-to-day operations, a fact that may help explain North American managers' greater opposition to unions (Adams, 1995a:502). It is also worth noting that in many European countries, alternative mechanisms, such as works councils, are available to handle day-to-day problems on the shop floor.

In North America, unionization constitutes a significant limitation on management's freedom to run the enterprise as it sees fit. Here, management authority is specifically limited by any collective agreement provision; to counter such limitations, almost all management organizations insist that collective agreements contain management rights clauses, which generally have the effect of referring to management any matter not specifically addressed in the agreement. In Canada, unionization invariably brings with it a grievance process, since all jurisdictions' labour legislation requires collective agreements to include a process for the handling of disputes arising over the interpretation of the agreement (Carter, 1995:63).

Unions' most important impacts on the management of firms come through the aforementioned grievance processes, work rules laid out in collective agreements, and joint participation with management on various committees. For the average worker, and perhaps for management as well, it's the grievance process that is of greatest importance. Most significantly, the grievance process offers an avenue of redress for any worker who feels she or he has been unjustly dismissed. The chances of reinstatement following a dismissal grievance are more than 50 percent (McPhillips and England, 1995:81), whereas the non-unionized worker has no chance of reinstatement, except in the few jurisdictions offering the equivalent of a dismissal grievance process to certain non-unionized workers. The wish to avoid a costly and possibly embarrassing dismissal grievance process undoubtedly deters many managers from engaging in arbitrary dismissals. If managers are unduly timid, fear of a dismissal grievance may even keep them from firing people who should be let go. In lesser matters, as well, the grievance process serves as a brake on what might otherwise be capricious or arbitrary management behaviour.

Indeed, the threat of possible grievances typically causes management to operate in a very different way in a unionized establishment than it would in a non-unionized one. Now it must operate in accordance with two sets of rules: company policy and the collective agreement. As we noted in the management chapter, this makes the whole process of managing more formal and more legalistic. To the extent that the collective agreement brings a degree of certainty to what might otherwise be a confused, chaotic management process, the firm will likely benefit. To the extent that its work rules stifle creativity and innovation and cause people to become more concerned about legalistic observance of the contract than about doing their jobs better, the firm is likely to suffer. No theory can tell us whether the positive or negative effects are more likely to prevail; the only way to tell is to go to individual workplaces and do detailed case studies. Here again, the nature of the individual labour–management relationship may be pivotal. Where there is a positive relationship, both sides may be willing to exercise some discretion in interpreting the collective agreement. Where the relationship is bad, both sides are more apt to "go by the book" in almost every instance, a process that can prove extremely counterproductive or even paralyzing if carried to extremes.

The work rules contained in collective agreements address a broad range of issues. Unless limited by legislation (as in the case of many public sector organizations) or by management rights provisions stating that layoffs and promotions are totally within management's discretion, collective agreement provisions are apt to use **seniority** as a criterion (if not *the* criterion) for promotion, and reverse seniority as the criterion for layoffs. Unions generally like seniority-based promotion and layoff provisions because they prevent management from promoting or laying people off in an arbitrary fashion (Godard, 1994:319–320). Without seniority provisions, employers facing an economic downturn might lay off more senior workers, because they would normally be earning higher wages, or might simply lay off any workers management didn't like. While the use of seniority to govern promotions is more controversial, relatively few collective agreements use seniority as the sole basis for promotion; much more common are provisions that state that seniority will be one criterion along with skills and ability (Giles and Starkman, 2001).

Other union work rules may apply more specifically to the work process. In some cases, workload itself may be limited. This was the case with the longshoring agreements of the 1960s, where a minimum gang size and maximum allowable load size might well be stipulated (see Picard, 1967). More recently, it has often been the case with agreements in education. Public schoolteachers' agreements have sometimes limited class size; university professors' agreements have sometimes stipulated a normal or maximum number of courses a professor will be expected to teach.

Another important group of work rules has to do with procedures governing work force reduction. In addition to provisions requiring that layoffs be in reverse order of seniority, unions may negotiate total or partial restrictions on management's ability to contract out work to outside firms. They may also negotiate restrictions on management's ability to implement technological change, such as requirements that the union be given a period of advance notice or that affected workers be provided with retraining opportunities. Finally, contracts may provide for a layoff notice period greater than that required by employment standards legislation or for training, job search assistance, or other benefits for employees facing layoff. In the federal public service, many agreements contain a separate work force adjustment appendix outlining detailed procedures to be used in the event of large-scale reorganization or restructuring.

In addition to the impacts resulting from grievance procedures and the work rules contained in collective agreements, unions also affect the management of organizations through their joint participation, with management, in a number of committees or other forms of joint governance mechanism. The most important of these committees are the joint health and safety committees required in all jurisdictions. Here, unions often play a key role, both by educating and informing workers on the issues and by helping to ensure that the committee is not just a token. Unions also play an important role in the pay equity process through their involvement in job-evaluation procedures (Gunderson and Hyatt, 1995:330). Beyond that, collective agreements often provide for a variety of labour–management committees. Many agreements provide for a general labour–management committee; less common, but far from unheard-of, are more specific committees designed to address such issues as technological change (ECC, 1987; Peirce, 1987). While the scope and powers of these committees vary greatly, they do involve a good many workers, at least to some degree, in the day-to-day management of the organization—a development that most industrial relationists and many managers probably regard as healthy.

Union Impacts on Society as a Whole

The previous discussion suggests that within the workplace, unions can have both positive and negative effects. For society as a whole, the situation is rather more clear-cut. Here, particularly in the social and political spheres, the impacts appear to have been almost entirely positive. It is largely thanks to unions, through their participation in politics, that Canadians have publicly funded medical care, unemployment insurance, public pensions, and other worthwhile social programs. Note here that the labour movement could not have achieved these results without a political partner (today the NDP, formerly the CCF), nor could the NDP or CCF have achieved them without the labour movement's active support. Earlier, we noted that the CCF and NDP have not only passed legislation providing for pro-labour legislation and social programs when they have been in government, they have also forced governments from other parties to pass such legislation when they have held the balance of power in minority governments, or when there has been a serious threat that those governments would lose to the CCF or NDP in the next election. It's important to note as well that the CCF, in particular, did not really get off the ground until it started attracting strong support from unionists during the Second World War

(Heron, 1996). More recently, the NDP was strengthened by the increased support it started receiving from the CLC and affiliated unions beginning with the 1979 federal election (Morton, 1995; Murray, 1995). In the four federal elections held starting in 1979, the party posted some of the best results it had ever achieved. The critical role played by the labour movement within the NDP is also shown, in a negative way, by the party's appalling showing in the 1993 federal election, in which organized labour withdrew much of its support, particularly in Ontario. Without strong, steady support from the labour movement, the NDP has little chance of remaining viable as a national political party.

The labour movement has made other important contributions to Canadian society. Over the years, it has done a great deal to raise the profile of health and safety issues, educating members, managers, and the general public alike. While Canadian workplaces are still far from safe, as the employment law chapter will show in more detail, they are safer than they would be without the work of unions, which have played a particularly important role in the joint health and safety committees required in all Canadian jurisdictions. Unions have also worked to bring in affirmative action, pay equity, anti-discrimination legislation, and other human-rights measures benefitting all Canadians. Overall, we can only agree with Desmond Morton (1995:154), that "[m]uch that has made Canada a humane and civilized society has come from the social vision of its labour movement."

One other point about unions' broader impacts should be made: their effect on the members who participate in their day-to-day operation and governance. More than 50 years after they had left the Knights of Labor (Kealey and Palmer, 1981), former members recalled their time in the Order as one that transformed their lives, giving them new vision and new hope. More recently (Murray, 1995:183), union activists have spoken highly of the impact that participation in the union has had on their personal development and understanding of society.[16] In some cases, union participation has marked the beginning of a worthwhile political career. In many more, union activists have taken the skills and self-confidence that they have learned through their participation and applied them to the problems faced by civic organizations such as school boards, zoning boards, or hospital boards. It would be an exercise in futility to attempt to measure the value of these activists' previous union participation through any sort of conventional cost-benefit calculus, but almost certainly that participation has helped make a difference to their communities.

ARE UNIONS STILL NEEDED?

Often, one hears the argument that while unions were very much needed in the late nineteenth and early twentieth centuries, when most workers were wretchedly paid and forced to work under appalling conditions, they have outlived their usefulness. Today, so the argument goes, almost all workers are well-paid, management has become totally enlightened, and working conditions everywhere are first-rate, thus making unions essentially redundant.

Those who have read the previous chapters with any care will immediately recognize the erroneous factual basis for such arguments. Chapter 2, on the economy, showed that many workers' earnings and overall economic situations are declining. Chapter 3, on management, showed that in many cases management practice is becoming less, rather than more, enlightened than in the recent past. In addition, the health and safety section of Chapter 7, on employment law, will reveal some of the many health and safety problems continuing to face Canadian workers. All of this is hardly evidence supporting the thesis that unions have outlived their usefulness.

Even more significant than such blatant factual errors is the implicit assumption that Canadian society would somehow be better off without unions. It seems appropriate, in the circumstances, to ask what Canadian society would be like without unions, and what kinds of societies do not have free trade unions, in the sense in which we would understand them.

Since the second question is somewhat simpler, let's begin with it. Virtually every country we would consider democratic has free trade unions that advance their members' interests and, usually, those of the country's working people as a whole. On the other hand, fascist and other authoritarian regimes and military dictatorships generally do not allow unions at all, or at the very least constrain their activities severely (Kuwahara, 1993:223; Pellegrini, 1993:131; Fuerstenberg, 1993:178; Bean, 1994); while in Communist countries, such as the former Soviet Union, unions have most typically been absorbed into the larger state apparatus and given no independent role of their own in the IR system (Héthy, 1991). Quite simply, it would appear that free trade unions go hand-in-hand with democracy.

As for what Canadian society would be like without unions, the most immediate and obvious differences would be noticed at the workplace. To start with, many fewer Canadians would enjoy any real protection against dismissal or other arbitrary action by their employers. And many fewer would have any part in setting the terms and conditions of their employment. This would become a privilege enjoyed only by a select group of professionals, athletes, and middle- to upper-level managers. Health and safety laws would be less strictly enforced, even if the laws themselves did not change; the same would likely be true for human rights laws. Moreover, the already strong trend towards less secure work and more part-time, temporary, and contractual work would very likely accelerate without the brake now placed on it by union collective agreement provisions.

In addition to losing unions' workplace representation, working people would also lose political representation, since the one national party pledged to advance their interests, the NDP, would almost certainly cease to exist without a labour movement to support it. Publicly-funded health care might not disappear immediately, but support for it would certainly diminish, as would support for EI, social assistance, and other social programs, and public arts funding. Supporters of health care and public arts funding would definitely find their job much harder if they were forced to operate without the labour movement's financial support and the NDP's political support.

In a more general way, the question is perhaps best answered by two more. If there were no Canadian labour movement, what other group in contemporary Canadian society would be big enough and strong enough to provide a significant check to the economic and political clout of big business and the political right (Crispo, 1982)? And what other group would be in a position to advance the economic and political interests of the broad spectrum of ordinary working Canadians? Such questions are, admittedly, far from new or original. Expanded only slightly, they form much of the basis of the institutionalist perspective on industrial relations described earlier. They are nonetheless worth asking, given that the advocates of a union-free society have thus far had little to say in response to either one.

Fortunately, such questions are likely to remain purely hypothetical. As we pointed out earlier, the practical need for unions appears if anything to be increasing, rather than decreasing. From a broader perspective, a society without free unions would almost certainly be one in which few Canadians would care to live.

QUESTIONS
FOR DISCUSSION

1) If you are in a union, what kinds of activity does it engage in? What kinds have you, personally, been involved with? If you aren't in a union yourself, ask a friend or relative who is and find out what sort of things their union has been doing.

2) How has the range of union activities been expanding in recent years? Do you think this expansion has been healthy, overall?

3) Should unions affiliate with political parties? If not, how should they pursue their political objectives?

4) Should unions engage in business ventures such as labour-sponsored venture capital corporations? Why, or why not? What about employee buyouts of failing businesses?

5) Why do public sector unions place such heavy reliance on publicity campaigns?

6) What are unions' major impacts on wages? In what ways, and why, have some of these impacts been changing in recent years?

7) What are some problems in evaluating union wage impacts?

8) What are unions' major impacts on productivity and management of the organization? Why are these impacts often extremely difficult to measure?

9) What are some of the major impacts unions have on society as a whole? How do they achieve these impacts?

10) Do you agree with those who argue that unions have outlived their usefulness in Canada? Why, or why not?

SUGGESTIONS FOR FURTHER READING

Freeman, Richard, and James Medoff. (1984). *What do unions do?* New York: Basic Books. Classic study of unions' impacts that implicitly argues that most economists have looked at union impacts from far too narrow a perspective. The comparison between the "monopoly" and "collective voice" perspectives on unions is particularly useful.

Jackson, E.T., and François Lamontagne. (1995). "Adding value: The economic and social impacts of labour-sponsored venture capital corporations on their investee firms." Ottawa: CLMPC. Useful study of this important new mechanism.

CHAPTER 7

EMPLOYMENT LEGISLATION

Family and friends of the Westray Mine victims march from the mine site in Plymouth, N.S. to the Westray Memorial Park in nearby New Glasgow to mark the fifth anniversary of the disaster in Plymouth, N.S.

Employment legislation applies to most workers, but is of special interest to those who don't belong to unions, since they aren't covered by labour relations legislation. In this chapter, after a brief discussion of employment legislation's (EL) general significance and the groups of workers to whom it applies, we start by considering work standards legislation governing such matters as minimum wages and overtime regulations. Next, we look at dismissals and the non-unionized worker. From there, we go on to consider human rights legislation, one of the areas of employment legislation that has been changing rapidly of late. We continue with a discussion of health and safety legislation. This discussion emphasizes the joint labour–management safety committees that are a distinctive feature of the Canadian legislative framework. We conclude with a consideration of workers' compensation legislation and a broad look at overall trends in Canadian EL.

EMPLOYMENT LEGISLATION: AN OVERVIEW

Why EL Is Needed

There are a number of reasons why legislation covering the broad spectrum of workers,[1] not just those belonging to a union, is needed. First, as we noted earlier, only about one-third of all Canadian workers belong to a union. Many workers who do not belong to a union don't even have the legal right to join one (Beatty, 1983). Considerations of fundamental equity suggest that some kind of legislation is needed to protect certain basic rights for all workers. For example, it seems unduly harsh to suggest that a worker should be required to join a union to be assured of a safe workplace.

In addition, a number of important workplace issues, particularly human rights issues such as sexual harassment and religious discrimination, may be inherently difficult to regulate through collective bargaining alone. As we point out in Chapter 10, much collective bargaining is based on the notion of a settlement zone, or the range of overlap between union and management positions. Inherent in the notion of the settlement zone is the possibility of some kind of compromise, which in turn strongly implies that the issue in question can be quantified. Thus, while we can apply the notion of a settlement zone to monetary issues, it is virtually impossible to apply it to issues such as health and safety or sexual harassment. Where, realistically, is the basis for compromise on issues of this type? Will the collective agreement provide for a workplace free from harassment on Mondays, Wednesdays, and Fridays, but grant no protection on Tuesdays and Thursdays? Will it offer health and safety protection to those working in the plant but not to its office workers? At a minimum, collective bargaining over such issues needs to be supplemented by a process that applies to all workers.

Nor is the lack of a settlement zone the only difficulty likely to arise. By definition, collective bargaining is a majoritarian political process.[2] A union made up mainly of men might well decide that wages and benefits were more important than a sexual harassment provision, and vote to have their negotiators pursue the former at the expense of the latter. Then, too, what's gained at the bargaining table can also be lost there, particularly in a difficult economic climate like the present one. Once again, a largely male-dominated union, forced to choose between loss of wages and benefits or dropping of a sexual harassment provision, could well opt for the latter. While the minority female membership might not think much of the male members' concept of solidarity, under current labour legislation they would have little recourse, other than perhaps splitting off and forming their own union at the next available opportunity.

With human rights legislation in place, the likelihood of problems such as these is greatly reduced. Moreover, since human rights issues are generally handled by a specialized body, such as a human rights commission, they may well be addressed more effectively by such a commission than if they are left solely to union officials, who often do not have the time or resources to become experts in such a specialized area. This is not to say that unions don't still have a role to play in addressing human rights issues covered by specific legislation. They do, and as we shall soon see, that role is and continues to be an important one. But it is also a more limited and, arguably, more manageable one than unions would have in the absence of such legislation.

Jurisdiction and Administration of EL

Like most labour relations legislation, most employment legislation falls under provincial jurisdiction. Here again, the major exception is workers employed in undertakings of a clearly federal nature, such as the railroads, airlines, telephone companies, and chartered banks. These workers fall under federal jurisdiction and are covered by the relevant sections of the *Canada Labour Code* and *the Canadian Human Rights Act*.[3] As for administration, work standards (employment standards) legislation is typically handled by a branch of the labour ministry, as is health and safety legislation. Human rights issues are generally handled by separate commissions, as is workers' compensation.

Coverage Under EL

Employment legislation applies to most, but by no means all, Canadian workers. Some jurisdictions exclude certain groups completely from coverage under their employment standards acts, while others do not apply particular provisions to certain groups.

Overall, exclusions are not as broad as for labour relations legislation, nor do they appear to be quite as broad as they were in the early 1980s, when England (1987) found large numbers of workers falling outside the protection of many jurisdictions' employment standards laws. Still, the remaining exclusions raise significant equity concerns, particularly given that some of those excluded are among the country's least fortunate workers and some are also excluded from unionization rights under labour relations legislation. In Nova Scotia, the Governor-in-Council may exempt the members of certain professions from coverage under the province's labour standards code. He or she may also exempt specified employees or classes of employees from the province's pregnancy leave and parental leave provisions. In Prince Edward Island, farm labourers, salespeople, and home care workers are exempt from the application of most sections of the employment standards act. Home care workers are also exempt in Quebec, as are senior managers, while in Saskatchewan, employment standards legislation does not apply to management or to those employed primarily in farming, ranching, or market gardening. (The above list of exclusions should be considered suggestive rather than definitive.) As McPhillips and England note (1995:75), there is always the possibility that Section 15 of the Charter could be used to find such exclusions unconstitutional. The fact that these exclusions have remained in place for nearly 20 years after the Charter took effect is anything but comforting. However, the Supreme Court's recent ruling striking down Ontario's agricultural exclusion from labour relations legislation (discussed in more detail in the next chapter) may offer hope in the area of EL, as well.

The Significance of EL

As you'll see throughout this chapter, EL applies to virtually every aspect of the employment relationship, from the preparation of job application forms and conducting of job interviews to the handling of layoffs and outright dismissals. Employment legislation is so important and so pervasive in its application that the IR or HR practitioner who isn't familiar with at least its broad outlines cannot be considered fully qualified. There have been far too many cases where lack of familiarity with this legislation has led otherwise sensitive and knowledgeable practitioners to do things such as continue to use application forms calling for photos,[4] or ask job applicants whether or not they are married. At best, such actions do a firm's reputation no good; at worst, they can be a serious embarrassment or even a legal liability.

EL's practical importance, then, should be obvious. Managers need to know it to be sure they and their organizations are operating legally. Workers need to know it to be sure they are obtaining everything they are entitled to. Beyond that, employment legislation bears an interesting relationship to labour relations legislation. While the two operate in quite different ways, there are also important ways in which they complement each other. In particular, EL (sometimes referred to as minimum standards legislation) serves to establish a kind of floor below which unions cannot go in collective bargaining. A union can't legally enter into an agreement paying a wage below the provincial minimum, nor can it legally bargain an agreement requiring workers to work a seven-day week or take only one week of vacation. On the other hand, unions are perfectly free to negotiate terms and conditions of employment more favourable to their members than those prescribed by the relevant employment legislation, and in most cases, they do just that.

In addition, unions may serve as useful "enforcement agents" for the legislation, which government often fails to enforce sufficiently, due to a lack of resources or political will. A union may play this role directly, through the grievance process, or indirectly, by educating its members about their rights under EL. The health and safety system, discussed in more detail below, offers an excellent illustration of this point. Instances of workers exercising their legal right to refuse to work in situations they consider unsafe are rare in non-unionized workplaces (McPhillips and England, 1995:91), a fact that suggests that unions' role in enforcement may be critical.

Recently, EL and labour relations legislation have come to intersect in another important way. Grievance arbitrators have increasingly been expected to apply human rights legislation, such as bans on discrimination against people with disabilities, in the course of resolving collective agreement disputes (Carter, 1997:185). The duty to accommodate such workers, or those of religions requiring special work schedules, has been more and more broadly imposed on employers and unions, even to the point where modifications to the collective agreement have been required in order to bring agreement provisions in line with human rights legislation (Carter, 1997:196–198). As Carter points out (1997:202–204), this new obligation to interpret collective agreements in the light of human rights legislation has significantly changed the role of arbitrators. It has also begun to change collective bargaining itself, as employers and unions alike take the duty to accommodate into account in fashioning collective agreement provisions.

WORK STANDARDS LEGISLATION

Work standards legislation[5] covers what might broadly be referred to as terms and conditions of employment, with the notable exception of health and safety issues. Among the provisions found in most Canadian work standards laws are those governing minimum wages, maximum permissible hours of work, overtime pay, minimum annual vacation entitlements, paid holidays, termination notice periods, and maternity leave. Provisions found in some, but not all, Canadian legislation include those governing paternity or family leave, adoption leave, clothing or special apparel payments, child employment laws, minimum-age levels for employment, bereavement and sick leave, and maximum permissible board and lodging charges (McPhillips and England, 1995:76; McPhillips, 2001). Overall, there is a good deal of variation within Canadian jurisdictions.

Some Specific Provisions

Minimum Wages

As of November 2001 (see Table 7.1), the general minimum wage ranged from $5.50 per hour in Newfoundland to $8.00 per hour in British Columbia. Three provinces had separate rates for workers under 16 or under 18, all roughly 10 percent below the adult minimum.[6] Nunavut and the Northwest Territories require an additional 50 cents per hour in areas distant from the highway system, and B.C. and to a lesser degree Alberta have special rates for workers in non-traditional settings, such as crop harvesters and camp counsellors. There are special rates for homeworkers and domestics in Ontario and Quebec. (Special rates not shown in table).

Table 7.1
SPECIAL FEATURE: SELECTED EMPLOYMENT STANDARDS PROVISION IN CANADA

Jurisdictions

Subjects	Federal	Alberta	British Columbia	Manitoba	New Brunswick	Newfoundland
Hours of work and Overtime pay	Maximum: 48 in a week. Overtime at 1 1/2 times the regular rate after 8 in a day and 40 in a week.	Maximum: 12 in a day. Overtime at 1 1/2 times the regular rate after 8 in a day and 44 in a week.	Employer must not directly or indirectly require or allow an employee to work "excessive hours or hours detrimental to the employee's health or safety." Overtime at 1 1/2 times the regular rate after 8 in a day and 40 in a week, and at 2 times the regular rate after 11 in a day and 48 in a week.	No maximum. Overtime at 1 1/2 times the regular rate after 8 in a day and 40 in a week. Employees can refuse to work any overtime after these hours.	No maximum. Overtime at 1 1/2 times the minimum wage after 44 hours in a week.	Maximum: 16 in a day. Overtime at 1 1/2 times the minimum wage after 40 in a week.
Minimum wages	Same as general adult minimum wage rate in each provincial or territorial jurisdiction.	Generally: $5.90 per hour (01/10/99).	Generally: $8.00 per hour (01/11/01) $6.00 per hour for those with no paid work experience prior to Nov. 15, 2001, and fewer than 500 hours' experience since.	Generally: $6.25 per hour (01/04/01).	Generally: $5.90 per hour (01/07/01).	Generally: $5.50 per hour (01/10/99)
Annual vacations with pay (Length of employment is with the same employer.)	Two weeks with 4% of earnings; Three weeks after 6 years with 6% of earnings.	Two weeks with 4% of earnings; Three weeks after 5 years with 6% of earnings.	Two weeks with 4% of earnings; Three weeks after 5 years with 6% of earnings.	Two weeks with regular pay; Three weeks after 4 years with regular pay.	Two weeks with 4% earnings.	Two weeks with 4% of earnings. Three weeks after 15 years with 6% of earnings.
General holidays with pay	New Year's Day Good Friday Victoria Day Canada Day Labour Day Thanksgiving Day Remembrance Day Christmas Day Boxing Day	New Year's Day* Alberta Family Day* Good Friday* Victoria Day* Canada Day* Labour Day* Thanksgiving Day* Remembrance Day* Christmas Day*	New Year's Day Good Friday Victoria Day Canada Day Labour Day Thanksgiving Day Remembrance Day Christmas Day British Columbia Day	New Year's Day Good Friday Victoria Day Canada Day Labour Day Thanksgiving Day Remembrance Day Christmas Day	New Year's Day Good Friday Canada Day New Brunswick Day Labour Day Christmas Day	New Year's Day Good Friday Memorial Day Labour Day Christmas Day

* means no requirement that employees be paid if they are not normally scheduled or required to work on that day

Table 7.1
(continued)

	Northwest Territories and Nunavut	Nova Scotia	Ontario	Prince Edward Island	Quebec	Saskatchewan	Yukon Territory
	Maximum: 10 in a day and 60 in a week. Overtime at 1 1/2 times the regular rate after 8 in a day and 40 in a week.	No maximum. Overtime at 1 1/2 times the minimum wage after 48 in a week.	Maximum: 8 in a day and 48 in a week. Overtime at 1 1/2 times the regular rate after 44 in a week.	No maximum. Overtime at 1 1/2 times the regular rate after 48 in a week.	No maximum. Overtime at 1 1/2 times the regular rate after 40 in a week.	Maximum: 44 in a week unless the employee agrees otherwise. Overtime at 1 1/2 times the regular rate after 8 in a day and 40 in a week.	No maximum. Overtime at 1 1/2 times the regular rate after 8 in a day and 40 in a week.
	Generally: $6.50 per hour; and $7.00 per hour in areas distant from the highway system. (01/04/91) Under 16: $6.00 per hour; and $6.50 per hour in areas distant from the highway system. (01/04/91). (This is not an oversight!)	Generally: $5.80 per hour (01/10/01)	Generally: $6.85 per hour (01/01/95). Students under 18 working no more than 28 hours in a week or during a school holiday: $6.40 per hour (01/01/95).	Generally: $5.80 per hour (01/01/01).	Generally: $7.00 per hour (01/02/01) $6.25 per hour for employees who usually receive gratuities (01/02/01)	Generally: $6.00 per hour (01/01/99).	$7.20 per hour (01/04/98).
	Two weeks with 4% of earnings; Three weeks after 5 years with 6% of earnings.	Two weeks with 4% of earnings.	Two weeks with 4% of earnings.	Two weeks with 4% of earnings.	Two weeks with 4% of gross wages; Three weeks after 5 years with 6% of gross wages.	Three weeks with 3/52 of earnings; Four weeks after 10 years with 4/52 of earnings.	Two weeks with 4% of earnings.
	New Year's Day Good Friday Victoria Day Canada Day First Monday in August Labour Day Thanksgiving Day Remembrance Day Christmas Day	New Year's Day Good Friday Canada Day Labour Day Remembrance Day Christmas Day	New Year's Day Good Friday Victoria Day Canada Day Labour Day Thanksgiving Day Christmas Day Boxing Day	New Year's Day Good Friday Canada Day Labour Day Christmas Day	January 1st Good Friday* (or Easter Monday*) Dollar Day* (i.e. Victoria Day) National Holiday July 1st Labour Day* Thanksgiving Day* December 25*	New Year's Day Good Friday Victoria Day Canada Day Labour Day Thanksgiving Day Remembrance Day Christmas Day Saskatchewan Day	New Year's Day Good Friday Victoria Day Canada Day Discovery Day Labour Day Thanksgiving Day Remembrance Day Christmas Day

Source: Drawn from Employment Standards Legislation of HRDC website, http://labour.hrdc.drhc.gc.ca/psait_spila/lmnec_esla/index.cfm/doc/english on Nov. 30, 2001.

Hours of Work and Overtime Pay

Here there is a great deal of variation among the different jurisdictions. About half the jurisdictions have no maximum number of hours an employer can have employees work without first obtaining a labour ministry permit (see Table 7.1; also see Gunderson and Reid, 1998). In those provinces that do have daily maximums, the range is from 8 (Ontario) to 16 (Newfoundland). The point at which overtime must be paid varies from 40 to 48 hours in a week. Normally, overtime must be paid at 1.5 times the employee's regular wage rate; however, three provinces, all in the Atlantic region, have set overtime at 1.5 times the provincial minimum wage. In three provinces (Ontario, Manitoba, and Saskatchewan), employees have the right to refuse to put in any overtime after working a given number of hours within any day or week (Gunderson and Reid, 1998). Under the new Ontario *Employment Standards Act*, which came into force in 2001, employers and employees may 'agree' to work weeks of up to 60 hours.

Vacation Entitlement

Every province except Saskatchewan requires a minimum of two weeks of paid vacation per year, with 4 percent of earnings. In Saskatchewan, the minimum is three weeks with 3/52 of earnings. Many, but not all, jurisdictions require three weeks' paid vacation for more senior workers; the threshold for the longer vacation kicks in after anywhere from four to 15 years' service with the same employer. In Saskatchewan, employers must give employees four weeks' paid vacation after ten years of service (see Table 7.1).

Paid Holidays

The various jurisdictions provide employees with anywhere from five to nine holidays per year. Usually employees must be paid for these days; however, in a few cases, there is no requirement that employees be paid if they are not normally required to work on that day (see Table 7.1).

Notice of Individual Termination

In general, the notice that an employer must provide to a worker being terminated is quite short (not shown in table). In the federal jurisdiction, the notice period is two weeks for all employees. In seven provinces, it can be as short as one week for recent hires. Typically, an employee must have worked at least three months to be eligible for any required notice at all. Except for the federal jurisdiction, most jurisdictions have a "sliding scale" for notice periods, which generally increase to eight weeks for employees with 10 or more years' service. In the Yukon, individual termination provisions do not apply to unionized workers; in New Brunswick, they do not apply to workers covered by a collective agreement. About half of all jurisdictions require an employee who wishes to quit to give notice.

Group Termination Provisions

Every Canadian jurisdiction except Prince Edward Island has special group termination provisions that take effect when a large number of workers are terminated in a short period of time, most often as a result of a plant closure or major downsizing (not shown in table). The special provisions are designed to take into account the hardship that may be faced not just by the affected workers individually, but by the entire community, particularly when the business being closed or downsized is the community's only or major employer. Given the large number of plant closures that have occurred in recent years, these group termination provisions are of increasing importance to workers and their unions, and have also attracted growing interest from the academic industrial relations community (Gunderson, 1986).

Notice periods for group terminations are frequently a good deal longer than those for individual terminations, and in many cases the length increases on a sliding scale based on the number of workers affected. Depending on the jurisdiction and the number of employees involved, the notice period may be as short as the individual termination period or as long as 18 weeks; however, most notice periods fall in the 8- to 16-week range. Normally, in addition to notifying affected employees, the employer must notify the Minister of Labour (or the equivalent) and the union if the establishment is unionized. In five provinces, notices must contain specific information such as the number of employees being terminated, the names of the employees, the effective date of the terminations, and the reason for the terminations. The federal jurisdiction, British Columbia, Manitoba, Ontario, and Quebec all require or may require the employer to set up a joint planning committee to address the issue of re-employment for the workers being terminated. The federal jurisdiction provides for severance pay in addition to the required notice period. Here, employers must give the employees being terminated notice about the amount of severance pay, vacation benefits, wages, and any other pay and benefits to which they are entitled.

Pregnancy and Parental Leave

Provisions include the right to paid or unpaid leave during pregnancy and after the birth or adoption of a child (not shown in table). They also generally stipulate that the worker be reinstated into her old position following her return to work. Under the new *Employment Standards Act*, Ontario now allows up to 17 weeks' pregnancy leave and 35 weeks' parental leave if the employee took pregnancy leave, 37 if she did not. British Columbia allows up to 32 weeks' combined leave, but will grant five more weeks for the parent of a child whose physical, psychological, or emotional condition requires additional care.

How Effective Is Work Standards Legislation?

In today's economy (discussed in Chapter 2), work standards legislation is of increasing importance, particularly to younger workers, part-timers, and those in low-end jobs in the private-service sector, for whom unionization is generally not a realistic prospect. Given the importance of this legislation, the question that should be asked is how effectively it addresses the needs of Canadian workers. Does it provide coverage for the least fortunate workers? Are its provisions adequate to meet workers' basic needs? And are enforcement mechanisms sufficient to ensure that workers can obtain their rights under the legislation?

Complete answers to these questions would require a detailed examination of every Canadian jurisdiction's work standards legislation and of the mechanisms through which that legislation is enforced. Such an examination must await other hands. However, on the evidence now available, the answers to the preceding questions are far from reassuring.

Coverage for All

Basic equity considerations suggest that work standards legislation should apply to all workers, or at a minimum all workers whose exclusion from certain provisions (i.e., overtime pay) is not compensated for by above-average pay and status, as in the case of most managers. Nonetheless, a number of groups of workers other than managers continue to be excluded from all or part of various jurisdictions' work standards acts. Members of some of these groups, such as domestic workers, farm workers, and home care workers, are among the country's least fortunate workers. Some are also excluded from labour relations legislation, a situation that leaves them with no protection at all. With the growth of "atypical" employment situations described in Chapter 2, it is becoming increasingly important for governments to provide protection for part-timers, homeworkers, and others in such "atypical" employment relations. Thus far, however, most Canadian governments appear to have done little along these lines.

Granted, the special conditions under which some of these groups work make it difficult to apply the same work standards laws that would be applied in a more conventional industrial setting. The nature of home care work, for example, makes it very difficult to apply conventional hours of work and overtime regulations; the same could be said of vacation pay with respect to farm workers. But such difficulties should not lead to the blanket exclusion of entire groups from protection under work standards legislation. While exclusion of certain groups from the operation of specific provisions may well be necessary, such exclusions should be accompanied by separate codes outlining appropriate standards for the occupation in question. In this regard, the special minimum wage provisions for homeworkers in Ontario and groups such as homeworkers, camp counsellors, and farmworkers in B.C. are a step in the right direction. Clearly, however, far more needs to be done.

Adequacy of Protection

Considerations of basic equity suggest that the minimum wage should be enough to enable a worker to provide basic necessities for himself or herself, a partner, and an average-sized family of two children. Similarly, hours of work and vacation provisions should ensure workers adequate rest and time to themselves or with families, while overtime pay provisions should offer adequate compensation for the loss of time and rest and for the extra stress that overtime work entails.

Even a cursory examination of the minimum standards required under various work standards laws suggests that existing legislation (even if enforced) is a long way from providing most workers with the basic necessities of life or sufficient free time. At the beginning of 1983 (LLCG, 1984:4–29), minimum wages ranged from $3.50 to $4.25 per hour. Shortly before that, a study by the National Council of Welfare (LLCG, 1984:4–37) had found the net minimum wage income falling well below the income one could expect from social assistance for units of three people and more in every province except Quebec. Between 1975 and 1987, real minimum wage income fell by more than 30 percent in Alberta, B.C., and Quebec and by more than 20 percent in the remaining provinces (Gunderson, Myszynski, and Keck, 1990). Over the past decade, the situation has worsened still further, except in B.C., Manitoba and Quebec, where NDP or PQ governments have legislated increases that have at least allowed workers to hold their own. But even these provinces fall well below the $5.15 U.S. minimum when exchange rates are taken into account (*Time Almanac*, 2002). Moreover, the U.S. minimum itself has fallen sharply in constant dollar terms, dropping from over $6 in constant (1996) dollars during the 1960s and '70s to $4.72 in 2000 (*Time Almanac*, 2002:633). In Ontario, the minimum has not increased for seven years despite a substantial increase in the cost of living, particularly in the Toronto area. In the Northwest Territories, the rate has remained the same since 1991, while throughout the Atlantic region, the rate remains below $6 an hour. And in Saskatchewan, despite the presence of an NDP government throughout the past decade, the rate has increased by only 65 cents an hour during that period—or just over 1 percent a year (HRDC, 2001).

Regarding hours of work, paid vacations, and holidays, the situation is little better. The two weeks' vacation required under most jurisdictions' work standards legislation is a fraction of the amount available to most European workers (Owen, 1989; *Better Times*, 1997 and 1998). Restrictions on long hours (see Table 7.1; also Gunderson and Reid, 1998) are minimal. An ominous portent for the future is the new Ontario employment standards provision allowing employees and workers to agree to work weeks of up to 60 hours.

As we pointed out earlier, only three jurisdictions give workers the right to refuse overtime. About half of all jurisdictions have no maximum number of hours a worker can be allowed to work in a day or week, and even those jurisdictions that have maximums generally set them at a very high level (12 hours a day in Alberta, 16 in Newfoundland). Overtime pay provisions are also seriously inadequate. In some cases workers cannot receive overtime until they have worked 44 hours in a week, and in three Atlantic provinces (New Brunswick, Newfoundland, and Nova Scotia), overtime is based on the provincial minimum rather than on the worker's actual wage, a situation that could lead to a worker's receiving less for overtime than for regular hours. Even in jurisdictions where the 50 percent overtime premium is "fairly" based on the worker's regular wage, the premium is generally acknowledged to be insufficient to prevent many employers from making heavy use of regularly scheduled overtime rather than hiring additional workers to meet increased demand. The result has been, for many workers, increased physical and emotional stress and increased difficulty in meeting family and personal needs.

Adequacy of Enforcement

Enforcement of minimum standards legislation has been a problem ever since such legislation was first introduced, as minimum wages for children and female workers (see McCallum, 1986). Then and now, inadequate funding for inspectors, lack of political will, and a desire on the part of those administering the legislation to accommodate rather than prosecute all but its most intransigent violators appear to have been the norm.

Roy Adams' 1987 study of the Employment Standards branch of the Ontario Ministry of Labour found no effective procedure available to help unorganized employees resolve disputes with their employer over the application of the Employment Standards Act.[7] Routine inspections of workplaces were rare, dropping significantly between 1980 and 1986, and even rarer were cases where an employer was prosecuted for victimizing employees seeking to exercise their legal rights under the act. Adams also found a high level of non-compliance with provincial minimum wage provisions and notes that most awards under the act occurred after the employee had left employment (LLCG, 1991:982). Similarly, Ontario's work hours legislation also appears to have been enforced quite laxly. A 1987 Ontario Task Force report on hours of work and overtime found that in 1985, more than 140 000 workers in the province had worked weeks of more than 60 hours on a regular basis (LLCG, 1991:995) and that for every overtime hour worked with a permit, 24 had been worked without one (LLCG, 1991:995–996). Since then, as we noted in Chapter 2, the overtime situation has almost certainly worsened.

Overall, work standards enforcement mechanisms in Ontario have been so weak that they appear to have given employers little real incentive to comply with the law (LLCG, 1991:996). Such lax enforcement is in sharp contrast to the generally strict and effective enforcement of unfair employer labour practice provisions under most Canadian jurisdictions' labour relations legislation (discussed in the next chapter), and it raises serious questions about governments' commitment to maintaining effective work standards legislation.

With regard to enforcement, some new provisions of Ontario's revised *Employment Standards Act* seem reasonably promising. Most importantly, the act contains a new general anti-reprisal provision that can be enforced by an employment standards officer's order for reinstatement or compensation. Officers can also issue a notice of contravention against an employer found in violation of the law. As well, corporations are now subject to a minimum fine of $100 000 for a first offence, and even larger fines for subsequent offences. But while the new provisions do appear to point toward stricter enforcement of the act, what remains to be seen is whether there is the political will to provide such enforcement.

THE INDIVIDUAL EMPLOYMENT CONTRACT

Non-unionized workers are under individual employment contracts (whether or not the contract has ever been written down). An individual contract of employment, which is essentially "a contract for the payment of compensation for service" (LLCG, 1984:2–1), confers obligations on both employee and employer. The employee must report for work regularly, perform his or her duties honestly and faithfully, obey lawful and safe orders, and avoid gross misconduct such as drunkenness or insubordination (McPhillips, 2001:216). For professional and managerial employees, avoiding any conflict of interest (as would be created if an employee solicited his or her employer's customers) may be an important element of the express or implied contract (McPhillips and England, 1995:77).[8] Employers, in addition to abiding by any relevant statutes such as employment standards or human rights laws, must pay employees regularly and cannot change their duties, status, or level of pay significantly without the employees' consent. Most important of all, they can only dismiss employees for just cause or with sufficient notice (McPhillips, 2001:217). A firm's economic difficulties do not constitute just cause. Any dismissal for just cause must be well founded in the conduct of the employee (Christie, 1980:362). As for the question of what constitutes "sufficient notice" for any given employee, this is an important, but sometimes difficult, issue that will be discussed in more detail shortly.

Dismissals and the Unorganized Worker

Perhaps the single most important difference between collective bargaining legislation and the legislation governing non-unionized workers is in the area of protection against dismissal. A unionized worker who has been dismissed may seek redress (up to and including reinstatement with full pay for any time lost between the termination and the arbitration award) under the grievance procedure of his or her collective agreement. Though other types of grievance often do not get carried forward to arbitration, in most cases dismissal grievances will be if the worker insists, if only so that the union can avoid a possible duty of fair representation complaint for failing to do so. Ordinarily in dismissal cases, the onus of proof is on the employer to demonstrate that the employee should be discharged; the standard of proof required by most arbitrators is high. Given these facts, a discharged worker stands more than an even chance of being reinstated (McPhillips, 2001; Christie, 1980). The substantial protection that union membership thus provides against arbitrary dismissal has frequently been cited in union-membership-joining and union-growth studies as a major reason why workers wish to join unions.

Dismissals may be of two types: express (outright) or **constructive**. A "constructive" dismissal occurs when the employer unilaterally makes a major alteration in an employee's pay, status, or workplace responsibilities, such that the employee believes she or he is no longer being asked to do the same job on the terms initially agreed upon, and feels invited, if not compelled, to resign. If, for example, a middle-level manager found herself assigned to sweep floors, she would logically interpret the reassignment as a demotion and consider it a constructive dismissal. In a case involving the Burns Foods Company,[9] a foreman named Baker was suddenly advised that his position had become redundant and offered alternative work at lower pay as a beef boner or security guard. When he refused, he was dismissed. The court ruled that Baker's removal from the position he had held for nearly 30 years constituted a constructive dismissal, since at no time did the company argue his work was unsatisfactory. But the notion of constructive dismissal does not apply to minor, or sometimes even fairly significant changes, such as lateral transfers, providing they do not involve lower pay or a demotion. In a case involving Lloyd's Bank,[10] a manager sued for constructive dismissal after being transferred from the bank's Vancouver branch to an equivalent position, at higher pay, at the bank's smallest branch in New York. The court ruled this a lateral move rather than a demotion in denying the plaintiff's constructive dismissal suit.

Whether a dismissal is express or constructive, the non-unionized employee has two options available: an action under work standards legislation (discussed in the previous section) or redress at common law, through the courts. Either way, reinstatement is normally not available (Christie, 1980), except in the three jurisdictions (mentioned below) that offer some kind of equivalent to the grievance procedure for non-unionized employees, or, in Ontario, where an employment standards officer has found that an employer has seriously contravened the *Employment Standards Act* (as by not allowing an employee returning from maternity to leave to resume her former job). Elsewhere, the best the aggrieved non-unionized employee can hope for is reasonable notice, or money in lieu thereof. Under work standards legislation (see above), the notice period is extremely short, even for employees with many years' service. For more recent hires, it is all but non-existent. Unjust dismissal actions at common law can lead to substantially larger awards (sometimes from six to 24 months of salary[11] in the case of professional or managerial employees or those with very long service). However, when a worker goes to court, the outcome is never certain, the process is normally quite long and stressful, and lawyers' fees can eat up a large portion of the award. The courts may not, therefore, be a realistic option for most workers other than professionals, managers, top-level athletes and entertainers, or those with extremely long periods of service. Still, awards have been increasing in recent years. Awards of 12 to 24 months' salary are no longer uncommon (McPhillips, 2001).

Given the large amounts of money that may be at stake and the potential of damaging a firm's reputation and hurting the morale of other employees, it behooves employers to exercise extreme care when discharging employees. Dismissal is an extremely stressful experience in the best of circumstances. Employers and managers must take care not to aggravate an already emotionally loaded situation by such ill-advised and heartless actions as termination in the presence of fellow workers, personal abuse, or false accusations of serious misconduct such as theft.

In determining the size of awards, judges still rely quite heavily on a 1960 case involving an advertising director named Bardal and *The Globe & Mail*.[12] While there was never any allegation of improper conduct or unsatisfactory performance, Bardal was summarily dismissed after refusing to resign with six months' notice and one month's salary. The factors used by the court in arriving at an award of a year's salary included the nature of the employment, the employee's length of service, his age, and the availability of similar employment, as well as his experience, training, and qualifications. In addition to the "Bardal" factors, courts take into account whether the employee has made any attempt to mitigate (lessen) the damages by seeking other, substantially similar work. Employees have the duty to mitigate; however, in these cases the onus is on the employer to prove that the employee has not made an attempt to find suitable work.

Dismissal Adjudication for Non-Unionized Employees

Three jurisdictions (Nova Scotia, Quebec, and the federal jurisdiction) provide some kind of arbitration or adjudication in dismissal cases for non-managerial, non-bargaining-unit employees with more than a certain length of service. The qualifying period for application of the laws (ten years in Nova Scotia, three in Quebec, and one in the federal jurisdiction) sharply reduces the number of cases brought under the adjudication procedures.

The adjudication process most studied is that carried out under the *Canada Labour Code*, which provides for adjudication of dismissal grievances of non-managerial, non-bargaining-unit employees with more than a year's service. Under this procedure, the adjudicator can either reinstate or award damages in lieu of reinstatement (McPhillips and England, 1989:50–51). A study by Genevieve Eden (1993) suggests that experience under this section of the *Code* has been more or less similar to experience in the unionized sector. Of 279 dismissal cases decided under this section of the *Canada Labour Code* between 1978 and 1989, 61 percent were sustained, a figure roughly comparable to that for dismissal grievances. In general, it appears that the same concepts of progressive discipline being applied by arbitrators in the unionized sector are being adhered to by adjudicators under the *Code* (Eden, 1993).[13]

It's not entirely clear why more jurisdictions have not followed the lead of the federal jurisdiction, Nova Scotia, and Quebec by providing some kind of adjudication procedure for non-unionized workers' dismissal grievances. Some writers have suggested that opposition from unions may be one reason, given that the availability of a dismissal grievance procedure for non-unionized workers might reduce workers' incentives to join unions. On the other hand, workers in various European countries (such as Germany) have a variety of options for handling grievances (including dismissal grievances), some of which also do not involve the union (Fuerstenberg, 1993:181); there is little evidence that these countries' union membership rates have declined as a result. Given the fundamental importance to workers of having some kind of protection against arbitrary dismissal and the very real likelihood of stable if not declining Canadian union membership rates for the future, the issue warrants further investigation.

HUMAN RIGHTS LEGISLATION

The basic purpose of human rights legislation is to prevent discrimination. Such legislation, in force in every Canadian jurisdiction, prohibits workplace discrimination on a broad range of grounds. For example, the federal human rights act bars discrimination on the basis of race, national or ethnic origin, colour, religion, age,[14] sex, sexual orientation, marital status, family status, disability, and criminal convictions unrelated to the work the person would be doing (CCH, 1998b; McPhillips, 2001).[15] Most provinces' grounds are fairly similar, but there are some minor variations. For example, certain provinces, such as Newfoundland, include political opinion as a prohibited ground.

Every province exempts bona fide occupational qualifications (to be discussed in more detail below). In addition, a number of jurisdictions, including most of the Atlantic provinces, exclude occupations of a religious or philanthropic nature. For example, a Catholic school may require that its staff be Catholic or adhere to traditional Catholic values (i.e., staff cannot live together outside marriage).

Human rights legislation is normally enforced on the basis of individual complaints to the appropriate commission or council (McPhillips, 2001), although in a few cases proactive investigations may be conducted.

Bona Fide Occupational Qualifications

A bona fide occupational qualification (BFOQ) allows employers to discriminate for legitimate business reasons. Most Canadian legislation specifically allows discrimination on this basis (McPhillips and England, 1989:55). Obvious examples include physical strength requirements for police and firefighters, vision requirements for pilots and air traffic controllers, and appearance requirements for clothing models. A less obvious example would be a clause in an employment contract barring a spouse or close relative of the current employee from employment at the same firm, on the basis that nepotism, or even the perception of nepotism, is bad for morale and thus constitutes a legitimate business reason for the prohibition. Given recent case law on the subject, contract clauses of the latter type are now quite difficult for employers to enforce.[16]

There have been two broad and somewhat interrelated trends in the use of BFOQs. The first has been towards an increasingly narrow construction, on the part of courts and adjudication tribunals, of what constitutes a legitimate business reason for discrimination. A generation ago, airline flight attendants were always female. As well, they normally had to be within a certain, quite narrow, size range and were generally grounded on reaching a certain age. Airlines justified these requirements on the basis that their customers wanted a certain type of image in flight attendants. The flight attendants successfully countered with the argument that they had serious work to do (including providing emergency first aid as well as serving coffee and drinks) and that the gender, age, and size requirements had nothing to do with that work and should thus be eliminated. Now, there are often older flight attendants on airplanes, as well as an increasing number of men working in this position. There is little evidence that the quality of service has suffered as a result.

Tests of an employee's ability to meet a bona fide occupational requirement must directly address that requirement, not its second cousin. While courts and tribunals generally continue to allow police forces and fire departments to require strength as a condition of employment, they are no longer allowed to impose minimum height and weight requirements. Such tests, it was found, had the effect of systematically discriminating against most women and even many male members of certain minority groups. They also might not be a totally reliable predictor of a person's strength, since a small person who works out every day may well be stronger than a giant couch potato.

The second trend has been the application of the duty to accommodate those who cannot comply with legitimate business requirements because of their sex, religion, or some other factor that constitutes a prohibited ground of discrimination. This duty applies up to the point where an employer would suffer "undue hardship" by making the required accommodation (see Carter, 1997). As we note elsewhere in this chapter and in the next one, the duty to accommodate has, in recent years, been construed increasingly broadly. In the now well-known case of *Bhinder v. CNR*,[17] the Supreme Court of Canada ruled that the railroad's hard-hat rule discriminated against a Sikh electrician who was required by his religion to wear a turban, even though the requirement had not been made for discriminatory reasons. At that time, the Court also ruled that though the rule was discriminatory, it could be considered a BFOQ since its aim was to protect workers' safety. However, in the later *Central Alberta Dairy Pool* case,[18] the Court changed its direction, indicating that Bhinder would have incurred only a minimal added safety risk by working without a hard hat and that the employer could have accommodated him by placing him in a different job (LLCG, 1991:1007–1019). Since then, employers have been expected to modify jobs, buildings, and work schedules to accommodate people with disabilities and those of different ethnic and religious backgrounds who cannot work regular hours (see Carter, 1997). What remains unclear from the cases reported to date is exactly what constitutes "undue hardship" under the duty to accommodate.

Application of Human Rights Legislation

Human rights legislation applies to all stages of the employment relationship: from initial application and interviewing to the job itself to eventual retirement or

termination. It's crucial for human resource, personnel, and IR staff to know this legislation, since they must use it on a daily basis. As we noted at the beginning of the
chapter, failure to act in accordance with this legislation can cause a firm embarrassment or even lead to legal action.

Hiring Process

In some jurisdictions, including the federal jurisdiction, there are specific provisions
that prohibit, on job application forms or at job interviews, the inclusion of questions
related to any of the forbidden grounds of discrimination. In jurisdictions whose
human rights legislation does not contain the provisions, such questions should still
not be asked by employers. However, someone who feels that information related to
a prohibited ground of discrimination was the reason he or she was not hired must
prove that the information was the basis for the decision in jurisdictions without
express job application provisions (McPhillips and England, 1995:83). The ban, it
should be noted, applies not only to questions intended to elicit information directly
(i.e., asking a person's date of birth), but also to those intended to elicit it indirectly
(i.e., asking when a person graduated from university, from which it would usually
be easy to infer an age range). Job applicants who don't want prospective employers
to know information related to a prohibited ground of discrimination should not
include it on their resumes. If such information is necessary for legitimate business
reasons (i.e., date of birth for company benefit plans), it can be obtained once the person is on payroll (see McPhillips and England, 1989).

On the Job

At the most obvious level, human rights legislation bars such grossly unequal treatment as paying men and women different rates for the same work, or establishing
separate locker room facilities for people of different races. With regard to pay, a
number of jurisdictions have moved beyond equal pay for equal work to adopt the
more sophisticated concept of equal pay for work of equal value (see the discussion
of pay equity below).

Employers have the duty to do everything in their power to prevent harassment
on any of the prohibited grounds and, where it occurs, to find the offenders and
deal with them appropriately, to minimize the likelihood of any recurrence. Under
the federal act, hate messages on the basis of any prohibited ground of discrimination are specifically barred. In a 1988 case involving the Canada Employment
and Immigration Commission,[19] a black employee who received racist notes
through interoffice mail was awarded $4000 [20] when the human rights tribunal
found that the employer had done nothing to try to bring the perpetrators to justice. Among other things, the head of security had not informed police, sought
legal advice, or asked other black employees if they had been the target of similar
hate mail (LLCG, 1991:1054–1058).

A special focus in recent years has been sexual harassment. A number of juris-dictions include special human rights provisions on this form of harassment, and many organizations have established sexual harassment policies, perhaps driven by the fear that if they do not establish and enforce such policies, they may be held liable not just for harassment of subordinates by supervisors, but also that of co-worker by co-worker (McPhillips and England, 1995). A growing trend has been to the recognition that a "poisoned climate," created through such actions as post-ing magazine pin-ups on office walls or telling crude, sexually oriented jokes, may make women feel unwelcome and should thus be considered a form of harassment, even if the actions are not directed against a particular individual (McPhillips and England, 1995).

Ending the Employment Relationship

Termination of an employee on the basis of any prohibited ground of discrimination is illegal in all jurisdictions. Human rights commissions' remedies (discussed below) include the right to reinstatement in such cases. A major exception is mandatory retirement, legal in all jurisdictions except Quebec and Manitoba, which have barred it as a form of age discrimination. For example, Ontario's *Human Rights Act* has placed a cap of age 64 on its age discrimination provision (Reid and Meltz, 2001). It is not clear whether many of the assumptions under which mandatory retirement policies were initially established still apply today; also, at a time of growing strain on the public pension system, mandatory retirement policies appear increasingly counterproductive from a practical perspective. For these reasons, we should expect to see these policies challenged in the near future.[21]

Remedies for Human Rights Violations

Human rights commissions generally have a broad range of available remedies. If an employer has not hired someone for discriminatory reasons, or has terminated some-one for such reasons, the employer may be made to hire or reinstate that individual with back pay. In addition, the worker may be given compensation for any expenses resulting from the discriminatory practice, such as legal costs (LLCG, 1991:1019). As noted earlier, where discrimination has led the victim to suffer a loss of self-respect or hurt feelings, the commission may order compensation. The commission may also order the employer to change the discriminatory practices in question.

Under the Ontario act (Swinton and Swan, 1983, in LLCG, 1984:4–137–138), if the initial investigation of a complaint by an officer does not result in a settlement, conciliation is used. Where this is unsuccessful, the commission may convene a board of inquiry. Board findings may be appealed to the courts on issues of facts or law. With the consent of the Attorney General, offenders may also be prosecuted in the courts; however, this method is rarely used, as the commission normally prefers to seek an accommodation (Swinton and Swan, 1983, in LLCG, 1984).

Human Rights Legislation for Unionized Workers

Unionized workers have additional protections available to them, beyond those already discussed. For example, human rights codes apply specifically to unions, which can be subjected to human rights complaints if they discriminate against any of their members (McPhillips and England, 1995:87). As well, the duty of fair representation provisions found in most jurisdictions' labour acts bar bad faith and arbitrary or discriminatory behaviour, on penalty of a complaint to the labour board. Finally, collective agreements often contain non-discrimination provisions, as well as provisions specifically pertaining to such areas as sexual harassment.[22] Such provisions can be enforced through the grievance procedure, which may well be a more efficient and effective process than those provided under human rights legislation (see Carter, 1997; LLCG, 1991:1007).

Pay and Employment Equity

Pay Equity

Despite the improved workplace conditions brought about by human rights legislation, women and members of ethnic minority groups continue, in many cases, to be at a severe disadvantage on the job. The average female worker in Canada receives only about 81 percent of the average male's pay (Stats Can, 1998). It appears that a significant portion of the gap still results from outright discrimination. Another significant portion is due to job segregation, which results in women being clustered in typically lower-paying traditionally "female" occupations such as child care and secretarial work (McPhillips, 2001) and finding it difficult to enter traditionally "male" occupations that pay more.

Pay equity legislation, providing that workers be given equal pay for work of equal value, is now in place in seven jurisdictions. In three jurisdictions (Quebec, Ontario, and the federal jurisdiction), it has been applied to both public and private sectors (HRDC, 2001(b)); in the other four (Manitoba, New Brunswick, Nova Scotia, and P.E.I.), it applies only to the former. Such legislation resulted from the growing recognition that traditional "equal pay for equal work" provisions could be easily evaded and in any case were not doing enough to close the male–female wage gap. Under the federal pay equity legislation, the criterion to be used in assessing the value of work performed by employees in the same establishment is the "composite of the skill, effort, and responsibility required in the performance of the work and the conditions under which the work is performed" (LLCG, 1991). Furthermore, separate establishments maintained primarily to allow for the continuation of male–female differentials are treated as the same for purposes of the legislation, and employers are also barred from reducing anyone's salary to eliminate pay discrimination (LLCG, 1991).

For many years, pay equity has been a major source of friction between the federal government and its employees. As early as 1979, the Professional Institute (PIPSC) filed pay equity complaints against the government with the Canadian Human Rights Commission. Five years later, the Public Service Alliance (PSAC) followed suit. In 1995, the PIPSC and Treasury Board negotiated a settlement; however, the PSAC complaint remained unresolved (Fryer, 2000:28). After much further bickering, the Canadian Human Rights Tribunal in 1998 ordered the government to pay retroactive adjustments, with interest, to nearly 200 000 current and former employees in the groups represented by the PSAC. The government's decision to appeal the Tribunal's decision sparked nationwide protests and was in any case unsuccessful, as the Federal Court of Appeal rejected the government's appeal of the Tribunal's decision. Finally, in 1999, the Treasury Board and the PSAC negotiated a settlement whereby affected employees received over $3 billion in retroactive adjustments and interest. But the Treasury Board-PSAC settlement did not apply to employees of the separate employers and agencies that employ an increasingly large proportion of the federal government work force. The issue thus remains a 'live' one for the many affected employees of those separate employers and agencies (Fryer, 2000:28). Some have argued that at a time when the federal government is having increasing difficulty attracting and retaining talented professionals and other "knowledge workers" (see Fryer, 2000 and 2001 and Duxbury, Dyke and Lam, 1999), its continued intransigence on the pay equity issue is quite counterproductive.

Employment Equity

The purpose of pay equity is to correct pay imbalances for women already working (Robb, 1987). Employment equity seeks to break down patterns of occupational segregation that have, in the past, made it difficult for women or, sometimes, members of various other groups such as ethnic minorities or people with disabilities, to enter certain occupations. In 1986 (LLCG, 1991:1047), the federal government enacted the *Employment Equity Act*, designed to apply both to federally regulated employers and to all employers receiving federal government contracts of more than $200 000 (LLCG, 1991; also McPhillips and England, 1995:86). The four groups to whom this act specifically applies are women, Aboriginal people, people with disabilities, and visible minorities. The act does not impose specific hiring quotas (McPhillips and England, 1995), but does require affected employers to implement employment equity (i.e., fair representation of the four designated groups within the work force) by identifying and eliminating employment barriers against members of those groups (LLCG, 1991:1047–1048; CCH, 1998b). Beyond simply removing discriminatory barriers, employers are expected to initiate positive hiring policies and practices to help ensure that members of the designated groups are fairly represented in their work forces.[23] They are also required to monitor and report on employment equity progress on an ongoing basis and to consult with employees and, where the organization is unionized, the union regarding the implementation of their employment equity programs (CCH, 1998b). There are limits to how far employers are expected to go in implementing employment equity. Specifically, the legislation provides that they will not be expected to assume undue hardship,[24] hire or promote unqualified people, or create new positions to ensure equitable representation of designated group members (CCH, 1998b).

HEALTH AND SAFETY LEGISLATION

As Giles and Jain (2001:309) have aptly pointed out, "Work kills, maims, and sickens at a horrifying rate." For many, the seriousness of the situation with regard to occupational health and safety in Canadian workplaces was brought home by the 1992 Westray Mine disaster, in which 26 miners were killed in a coal mine explosion in Pictou County, Nova Scotia (Richard, 1997:I, vii). Judge Peter Richard, commissioner of the provincial board of inquiry looking into the causes of the tragedy, found "a complex mosaic of actions, omissions, mistakes, incompetence, apathy, cynicism, stupidity, and neglect," with a few "well-intentioned but misguided blunders" added to the mix (Richard, 1997:I, viii). Richard's report concluded that mine management disregarded critical safety factors and "appeared to regard safety-conscious workers as...wimps" (Richard, 1997:I, ix). While the report was severely critical of mine management on many counts, it came down especially hard on it for failing to take proper measures to control coal dust, a primary cause of the explosion (Richard, 1997:I, 347). Despite several previous "near-misses," management had done little or nothing to remove coal dust from the mine, or to collect and test coal dust samples to monitor their combustibility, thus ignoring its own policies as well as violating the requirements of the provincial *Coal Mines Regulations Act* (Richard, 1997). The report was also severely critical of the provincial government, in particular its Labour Department, for making no effort to enforce its demands that management correct the numerous safety violations

As the Westray Mine disaster demonstrated, unsafe working conditions remain a fact of life in far too many Canadian mining operations.

that government inspectors had found at the mine, some as recently as 10 days before the explosion (Richard, 1997:I, 347–348).

To what extent is the Westray pattern of willful employer neglect of employees' safety and government's inability or unwillingness to enforce its own safety regulations typical of Canadian workplaces as a whole? The issue of occupational health and safety is a complex one, as Judge Richard himself admits in his report. Many occupational accidents do not have any single or simple cause. There are also many conscientious employers who recognize that safety is in their own as well as their workers' best interests, and do what they can to make their workplaces safer. Finally, some workers are the authors of their own misfortune.[25] Sometimes an injury or death is the result of simple carelessness or ignorance on the part of employees, and sometimes it is the result of "macho" practices (driving without a seat belt, operating welding equipment without goggles, going out on a boat without life preservers) that may have been perpetuated for any number of reasons.

Whatever the reasons, Canada's record in occupational health and safety is and has long been appalling. Between 1976 and 1981, Canada ranked worst in work injury incidence in a group of eight countries studied by the ILO, with an average rate of about 11 injuries per 100 workers and second only to West Germany in a group of nine ILO countries in workplace fatalities, with a yearly average of about 10 per 100 000 workers (Digby and Riddell, 1986, in LLCG, 1991:1071-2). The situation hasn't improved much since then. In 1997, over 800 Canadian workers died on the job, almost 800 000 were injured, and over 17 million person-days of work were lost due to workplace injury and illness (HRDC, 1999). The economic as well as human toll of unsafe work is clearly staggering.

The Canadian approach to health and safety is twofold: prevention where possible, compensation where prevention doesn't succeed (McPhillips, 2001; McPhillips and England, 1989:58). The two main preventive methods used are the "external system," whereby specified health and safety standards are established legislatively, and the "internal system," which provides for joint labour–management safety committees (required in all Canadian jurisdictions)[26] as a means of promoting safer workplace practices. The legislation is often contained in a specific health and safety statute applicable to all employers. It is sometimes supplemented by various statutes applicable to certain industries only, and administered by different government departments (McPhillips and England, 1989).

The External System

There are two main components to the external system. The first is detailed laws, often geared to the circumstances of particular industries, compelling employers to operate in a safe manner. The second is a general "performance duty" imposed on both employers and workers, obliging them to promote health and safety at work (McPhillips and England, 1989).

Safety legislation is often extremely detailed, specifying how many parts per million of a given substance may legally be discharged into the air or water, or at what temperatures and under what conditions certain foods must be stored in restaurants. It also covers such issues as required sanitary facilities, the qualifications needed by workers to work in a given industry, and the manufacture and use of equipment. In some cases, it imposes specific obligations on workers, as by requiring that restaurant workers wash their hands after visiting the washroom or that construction workers wear hard hats on job sites. Legislation may also require training or successful completion of a test before workers are allowed to perform potentially hazardous work, such as operating certain types of heavy equipment or working on high construction scaffolds. In other cases, it requires periodic inspection of equipment, such as elevators.

Under the "performance duty," employers are obliged to ensure the health and safety of all workers on the site, whether they employ them or not. Employers are also obligated to notify the government of any serious accidents or illnesses that occur, as well as of any hazardous substances in use on the work site (McPhillips and England, 1989:58–59). Workers, for their part, are obliged to take reasonable care to protect their own health and safety and that of their co-workers while on the job. In certain occupations, particularly those involving frequent contact with the public, "taking reasonable care" entails obtaining a periodic medical examination to ensure one does not have a contagious disease that could easily be spread at the workplace. In some jurisdictions, the performance duty also confers an obligation on the suppliers of tools and equipment to ensure that the tools and equipment are in good condition and comply with the statutory safety standards (McPhillips and England, 1989:59).

Though external legislation has undoubtedly helped make Canadian workplaces safer than they would otherwise be, the system is far from perfect. Ultimately, any system of external legislation can only be as good as its enforcement mechanism. To suggest that health and safety legislation has typically been haphazardly enforced in Canada may be putting the matter charitably. In general, governments have preferred to accommodate employers rather than prosecute them for safety violations. Another problem is that inspectorates have been inadequately staffed, and inspectors have historically been reluctant to issue stop-work orders on large or politically sensitive projects, particularly those (like Westray Mines) backed by the provincial government, preferring to leave the hard decisions to their superiors. In Ontario at the end of the 1980s and beginning of the '90s, only one workplace in five was being inspected at all (LLCG, 1991:1104), and fewer than one percent of all findings of health and safety violations resulted in a prosecution or conviction (LLCG, 1991).

In recent years, provincial governments appear to have been taking a somewhat tougher line on chronic safety violators. Both in Ontario and elsewhere, the level of fines has increased. By the early 1990s, Ontario had begun to issue fines in excess of $100 000 in extreme cases, and criminal prosecutions, though rare, had occurred (McPhillips and England, 1995:93). But the Westray disaster shows just how much further Canadian jurisdictions have to go in enforcing health and safety standards.

Inadequate enforcement isn't the only problem. Another is the failure of legal standards to address the hazards that contribute to the majority of occupational injuries (LLCG, 1991:1101), a problem that becomes more serious all the time as new substances and equipment are introduced into Canadian workplaces. Still another problem is that the safety standards may be set too low to provide adequate protection against certain hazardous substances. As Edward Tucker (1986, in LLCG, 1991:1099–1100) points out, regulatory practice in Ontario has generally entailed bringing worst-practice firms in line with the industry average, thus serving to sanction existing exposure levels rather than improving them when new evidence suggests a tougher standard would be warranted. The main thrust of Ontario's regulatory concern is suggested, in Tucker's view, by the fact that the Labour Ministry has rarely selected standards that would lead to significant compliance costs for industry (Tucker, 1986, in LLCG, 1991).

The Internal System

While external safety legislation is important, no legislation can cover every possible workplace situation. An important feature of Canada's health and safety system is, therefore, its "internal responsibility system," whereby management and labour both assume responsibility for workplace safety. A key assumption here is that prevention is more likely to occur when workers are actively participating in the process; the worker who operates a particular machine is often the one who best knows that machine's potential hazards and how to get around them (Swinton, 1983, in LLCG, 1991:1126). While the internal system is normally intended to work in tandem with the external one, Nova Scotia's health and safety act contains a unique provision stating that the internal system (encompassing all workplace parties) is the foundation upon which the act is based (CCH, 1998c:551–1 to 551–2). The internal system's three major components, as outlined in Ontario's 1978 *Occupational Health and Safety Act*,[27] are joint health and safety committees, the right to refuse unsafe work, and the right to be informed about workplace hazards (CCH, 1998c:1125–1126).

Joint Committees

Joint labour–management health and safety committees are required in all jurisdictions in workplaces of more than a certain size—20 employees being the usual minimum (McPhillips and England, 1995:89). In workplaces below the minimum-size threshold for a committee, a workplace health and safety representative is generally required.

Committees are normally expected to have equal numbers of worker and management representatives. In many jurisdictions, their maximum size is 12 (CCH, 1998c:1805). On average, they meet once a month, though they are sometimes not required to do so more than quarterly. Their powers and functions are established through provincial legislation; in general, those powers are merely advisory, in that an employer cannot normally be forced to comply with a committee's recommendations unless mandated to do so by a government official (CCH, 1998c:1801). What the committee can do is call in a government inspector, who may issue a stop-work order or other directive if the work practice appears sufficiently dangerous. In most jurisdictions, employers are required to pay committee members for time spent preparing for and attending meetings and doing committee business (see CCH, 1998c:1922). In Ontario, an employer is obliged to respond within 21 days to any written committee recommendation (CCH, 1998c).

Committees are usually given a fair degree of latitude. In most jurisdictions, they have the power to handle employees' health and safety complaints, to establish health and safety training and education programs, to take part in health and safety-related inquiries and investigations, to access government and employers' reports relating to employees' health and safety at their work site, and to request any information necessary from an employer to identify existing or potential workplace safety hazards (CCH, 1998c). There is some variation in committees' functions in different jurisdictions. Under the *Canada Labour Code*, they are obliged to maintain records pertaining to the disposition of employees' health and safety complaints and to cooperate with any occupational health service established at the workplace. Other specific duties include accompanying government safety inspectors on "walkaround" inspections of work sites, investigating serious accidents, and helping to resolve work refusal cases (discussed in more detail below). In Quebec, committees have the additional responsibilities of designating a physician in charge of health services and working with the provincial Occupational Health and Safety Commission to develop recommendations for safe work practices (CCH, 1998c:1811).

How effective are the joint committees? A number of commentators (i.e., Bryce and Manga, 1985; McPhillips and England, 1989, 1995) have indicated that the presence of a joint committee seems to lead to a significant reduction in workplace injuries. Others, including Robert Sass (1993), a pioneer in introducing joint committees during the 1970s, have concluded that the committees are ineffectual. An obvious problem here is that many workplaces simply don't have committees. As McPhillips and England argue (1995:89), a minimum threshold of 20 employees may be too large, especially at a time when many jobs are in small and medium-sized businesses. A single representative may not be as effective as a committee in representing workers' health and safety interests—particularly a representative hand-picked by management. Second, it is generally recognized that committees need the active cooperation of top management if they're to operate effectively. While enlightened managers may be prepared to recognize that a strong health and safety committee is in their best interest, as well as their workers', not all managers are enlightened. Those opposed to committees may flout the law by simply refusing to establish one (McPhillips and England, 1989), by holding meetings infrequently, or by not granting the committee any budget or any real power.

Overall, the evidence to date suggests that the committees can work, but only when management gives them a fairly free hand. The minimum establishment size required in most jurisdictions raises the question of whether some alternative mechanism is needed to ensure adequate protection of workers' safety in small businesses. Perhaps where there are a number of similar businesses (i.e., restaurants) within a given city or town, there could be a committee for all the restaurants in that area, including at least one representative from each area restaurant.

Right to Refuse Unsafe Work

A key component of any internal safety system is allowing workers the right to refuse any work they honestly consider unsafe, pending an investigation by a neutral third party (normally a provincial health and safety inspector). This right is granted to workers in all Canadian jurisdictions. Most jurisdictions require "reasonable" grounds or the "likelihood" of risk; in Alberta and Newfoundland, the right is more narrowly applied to situations of imminent or immediate danger (McPhillips and England, 1995:91). In most jurisdictions, anyone refusing unsafe work must formally report the situation to management (CCH, 1998c:601). Under the *Canada Code*, the worker must also notify the health and safety committee, or representative where no committee exists. If management intervention fails to resolve the situation, the next step is for either the worker or employer[28] to notify a government safety inspector (CCH, 1998c). If the safety inspector upholds the worker's decision, she or he can continue to stay off work until the situation is corrected to the inspector's satisfaction; otherwise the employee must return to work. The one major exception, under both the *Canada Code* and provincial legislation, is that no one can refuse to work where the refusal would put someone else's life, health, or safety directly in danger (CCH, 1998c:1315). In some cases (police or correctional services work, for instance), a certain amount of risk is assumed to "come with the territory."

Though workers in most jurisdictions run the risk of loss of pay if no alternative work is available to them after a refusal, the worker is normally protected from discharge or other disciplinary action for exercising a legal right to refuse work under the health and safety act (CCH, 1998c:1316), providing the worker has duly notified the employer and, where appropriate, a government inspector. However, several studies (i.e., LLCG, 1984:4–359; McPhillips and England, 1989:62) find that, at least in Ontario, the vast majority of refusals to work occurred in unionized settings. Failure to exercise the legal right to refuse work in non-unionized settings could result from a (possibly justified) fear of employer reprisal, simple ignorance of the law, or both. Whatever the reasons, the evidence suggests that unions have an important role to play in ensuring the adequate enforcement of safety legislation. It also suggests the need for stronger mechanisms to protect non-unionized workers, such as the equivalent of a dismissal grievance procedure in cases where a refusal to work triggered the dismissal. Possibly the new Ontario employment standards reprisal provision discussed earlier in the chapter could be extended to health and safety cases, as well.

It is important to point out that in some cases, workers have not only the right but the duty to refuse unsafe work. If, for example, a worker were ordered to dump toxic waste into a stream, she or he would legally be required to refuse, on the basis that workers are obliged not to break any law. (To be sure, it would normally be the employer, rather than the employee, who would be prosecuted for this illegal action [CCH, 1998c:2316]). Similarly, Alberta's health and safety act requires workers not to operate any tool, appliance, or equipment if they have reason to believe that the equipment will cause an imminent danger to them or anyone else on the work site (CCH, 1998c:2317).

Notification of Hazardous Materials (WHMIS)

The third and far from least important component of the internal system is the right to know (Swinton, 1983), specifically, the right to be informed about the actual or potential danger posed by various hazardous substances that may be used in the workplace. Each jurisdiction has its own Workplace Hazardous Materials Information System (WHMIS) provisions. Under the federal *Hazardous Products Control Act*, suppliers are required to classify the products they sell according to the amount of risk entailed in handling those products. They are also required to provide appropriate labels that will enable workers to tell at a glance what kind of substance they are working with (CCH, 1998c:60, 560). These labels must include the product's brand or generic name, that of the supplier, appropriate hazard symbols indicating the type of hazard potentially posed by the product, information on how to handle the product safely, and any appropriate first-aid measures (CCH, 1998c). Material safety data sheets (MSDS) must provide detailed descriptions of the product's chemical composition, any hazardous ingredients it contains, its fire or explosion hazard, its toxicological properties, and appropriate preventive and first-aid measures (CCH, 1998c:60, 820).

For their part, employers must ensure that controlled substances are labelled, must obtain and distribute material safety data sheets, and must educate workers about any hazardous substance used or produced at the workplace (CCH, 1998c:100). They are also required to provide workers and supervisors with a copy of the regulations (McPhillips and England, 1995:92). Under Ontario's law and that of most other jurisdictions, trade secrets can be exempted from WHMIS regulations. In Ontario (CCH, 1998c:14:700), employers may apply to the Hazardous Materials Information Review Commission for an exemption for information contained on a label or MSDS that they believe to be confidential business information. However, even if the exemption is granted, the confidential information must be released to a doctor in a medical emergency (CCH, 1998c).

Workers' Compensation

Workers' compensation legislation is the major mechanism used to compensate the victims of workplace accidents or work-induced illness.[29] Normally, **workers' compensation** is under the control of a provincial board whose primary responsibilities are to collect levies from employers and pay benefits to disabled workers. The basic principle of the system is that it is "no-fault." This means that a worker need not prove employer negligence to be eligible for benefits, but is also precluded from seeking further remedies through the courts. To be eligible for benefits, the worker must have suffered an accident or disease that arose out of and during the course of employment, disabled him or her beyond the day of the accident, and was not the result of his or her own willful misconduct, except in cases of death or serious disablement (CCH, 1998c:15.403).

Funds used to pay compensation benefits are drawn from a levy on employers, based on the nature of the industry and the size of the employer's wage bill (McPhillips and England, 1995:94). In high-risk industries, employers pay higher rates than in low-risk ones. In the past (see McPhillips and England, 1989), the tax was based on the number of claims filed by the industry as a whole. Such a system may actually have served as a disincentive to safe practice, since conscientious employers who did their best to maintain safe workplaces were forced to pay the same amount of tax as laggard or negligent ones. To correct this problem, most jurisdictions now use a system of "experience rating" whereby employers whose claims are above the industry average must pay higher premiums (CCH, 1998c:15,103), while those with good safety records pay less.

Workers may qualify for either temporary or permanent disability benefits. The main basis for compensation is the level of disability sustained by the victim; benefit levels generally range from 75 to 90 percent of the victim's regular salary. Every jurisdiction has imposed a cap on the maximum earnings covered by workers' compensation; in 1997, these ranged from $35 900 in Prince Edward Island to $56 100 in Ontario, with most falling within the $40 000 to $50 000 range (CCH, 1998c:15, 502).

A problem in the past was that employers were under no obligation to rehire disabled workers, either in their old position or a different one, in situations where a worker recovered from an injury or illness. Prior to experience rating, they would have had little incentive to do so. In some jurisdictions, however, this situation has begun to change. In Ontario, the *Workers' Compensation Act* was amended in 1989 to require reinstatement of workers medically able to perform their previous duties. In cases where the worker cannot perform his or her previous duties, but can do some job within the organization, the employer is expected to offer the worker the first available opportunity of suitable employment. A duty to accommodate (for example, by redesigning the workplace) applies here as in the case of other workers with disabilities (McPhillips and England, 1995:95).

In Newfoundland, which up until the 1990s had the country's highest workers' compensation levies, the provincial compensation board has recently taken a number of measures to improve the situation. These have included a reduction of benefit levels, including elimination of the "employer top-up" whereby employers would make up the difference between employees' benefit levels and their regular wages, in an attempt to provide disabled workers with more incentive to get back into the workplace (English, 1995, 1996). Other changes have included the introduction of individual employer experience rating and of a rehabilitation program whereby a disabled worker is assigned to a single workers' compensation caseworker throughout his or her disability (English, 1995, 1996). The idea here is that workers are more apt to be rehabilitated if they form a close working relationship with a single caseworker.

In redesigning compensation systems to encourage rehabilitation, workers' compensation boards must walk a fine line. The problem is to provide those who want and are able to return to work with appropriate incentives to do so without denying those who cannot their legitimate benefits, or pressuring them to return to work before they are really ready.

A RAPIDLY CHANGING FIELD

Unlike labour relations legislation (discussed in the next chapter), which has seen few major changes over the past 25 years, employment legislation has been changing constantly throughout most of that period. Human rights legislation, pay equity and employment equity, and joint health and safety committees are but a few of the more important innovations. Generally, the legislative changes have, from the workers' perspective, been positive, in that they have provided workers with additional protections against discrimination and poor working conditions. However, this has not always been the case. The Ontario government, for example, in line with its general policy of deregulation and of shifting power in the direction of business and employers, passed *Bill 136*, weakening pay equity and the *Employment Standards Act*. More recently, the

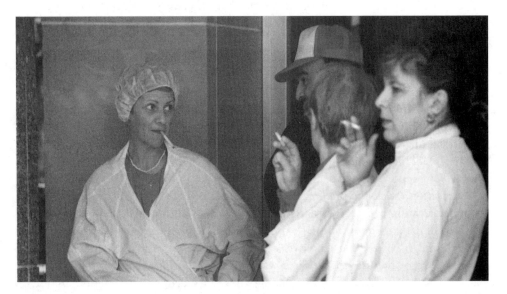

"Puff the Magic Dragon—Not!" Smoke in the workplace is becoming an increasingly divisive and difficult issue for workers and managers alike.

changes to the 2000 *Employment Standards Act* would allow employees to 'agree' to work a week of up to 60 hours.[30] Along similar lines, changes to workers' compensation legislation reduced benefit levels, limited appeals to the compensation board's decisions,[31] and limited compensation for mental stress, except in cases where the stress was a reaction to a "sudden and unexpected traumatic event" (*Canada Labour Views*, 1997).

New areas of legislative concern have been emerging almost every year. Recent efforts in various jurisdictions have sought to provide protection for gays and lesbians under human rights legislation, same-sex benefits for the partners of gays and lesbians, ergonomic workplace designs, improved indoor air quality, rights for non-smokers, and protection against workplace violence. In connection with non-smokers' rights, the City of Ottawa has recently (August 2001) put into effect a non-smoking policy believed to be the toughest in Canada. Under the city's new anti-smoking bylaw, smoking is prohibited inside all businesses, including restaurants and bars, though the two latter may establish separate outdoor patio areas reserved for smokers. A key objective of this legislation was protection of workers' health, especially in places such as bars where second-hand smoke has long been recognized as a serious health hazard. Anti-smoking bylaws have been passed in a number of other cities, as well, though few appear to be as strict as Ottawa's. There has also been growing recognition of the problems faced by certain groups, such as the problems faced by the obese on the score of their appearance[32] (Zwerling, 1997). Unfortunately, considerations of space preclude a more detailed treatment of these emerging areas of human rights legislation. Suffice it to say that the collective creativity shown by Canadian legislatures in coming up with solutions to both old and new problems is really quite extraordinary.

There remain, however, two serious concerns. First, despite the *Charter of Rights and Freedoms*, which has now been in force for about twenty years, many individuals and groups of workers continue to be excluded from even basic protection, particularly under work standards legislation. Second, enforcement mechanisms have not only failed to keep pace with the onrush of new legislation; they have proved inadequate to enforce existing legislation, such as work standards provisions governing minimum wages and overtime hours. Here, the most damning evidence is the extreme rarity with which the right to refuse unsafe work appears to be exercised in non-unionized establishments. If some of the same creativity already applied to drafting legislation could now be used to design adequate enforcement mechanisms, Canadian workers would be much better served. Perhaps the new anti-reprisal provision contained in the most recent revision of Ontario's *Employment Standards Act* will serve as at least a small first step in that direction.

QUESTIONS
FOR DISCUSSION

1) What are some practical consequences of knowing (or not knowing) employment legislation? Have you ever experienced any of these consequences, whether positive or negative?

2) Why, in general, is EL needed? What is its significance?

3) What are some major areas covered by work standards legislation, and what are three major problems with this legislation?

4) What protection does a non-unionized worker have against arbitrary dismissal in most jurisdictions? In practice, do most non-unionized workers have a meaningful remedy? Why, or why not?

5) What are the main grounds of discrimination prohibited under human rights legislation, and to which aspects of the employment relationship does HRL apply?

6) What is the purpose of bona fide occupational qualifications (BFOQs), and how can employers test for them? What are some recent trends with regard to BFOQs?

7) Distinguish pay equity from employment equity. Why do many people argue that both are needed?

8) Distinguish the external system from the internal system. What role do joint committees play within the latter?

9) How does workers' compensation operate within most Canadian jurisdictions? What are some problems with it?

10) What are some emerging areas within EL?

11) How does EL "intersect" labour relations legislation?

12) What are some important differences between EL and labour relations legislation?

SUGGESTIONS
FOR FURTHER READING

Eden, Genevieve. (1993). "Industrial discipline in the Canadian federal jurisdiction". *Relations Industrielles*, 48(1). A study of adjudication of dismissal grievances in the federal jurisdiction that suggests that experience under this system is roughly comparable to that under grievance arbitration in unionized establishments.

Richard, K. Peter (Commissioner). (1997) *The Westray Story: A Predictable Path to Disaster.* No place of publication given: Province of Nova Scotia. Not for the faint of heart! A chilling indictment of Westray management's callous disregard for workers' safety, and the Nova Scotia government's appalling lack of political will in enforcing its own legislation.

CHAPTER 8

LABOUR RELATIONS
LEGISLATION

Union and management representatives meeting with a conciliator from the labour ministry. Compulsory conciliation has been a prominent feature of Canadian labour legislation since the early years of this century.

Labour relations legislation (LRL) is of pivotal importance in any industrial relations system. It addresses such issues as how a union can become certified, when a strike or lockout may legally occur, and what constitutes an unfair employer or unfair union labour practice. In this chapter, we start by considering the rationale for LRL. Next, we take a brief look at the development of LRL in Canada, including the role played in recent years by the Charter of Rights and Freedoms. From there, we go on to examine some of the major features of Canadian LRL and to compare it to labour relations legislation in the United States. We then discuss some of LRL's main functions, illustrating our discussion with specific provisions from various Canadian laws. This discussion is followed by an

examination of some key variations in different provincial acts, and by a brief look at Quebec's special system of legislation. We conclude the chapter with a discussion of how LRL is administered. Note that, in this chapter, we generally confine ourselves to private sector labour relations legislation. Public sector legislation is considered in the next chapter.

THE RATIONALE FOR LRL

Legal scholars, philosophers, historians, and industrial relations experts have all written quite extensively on the rationale for labour relations legislation (LRL). Probably the simplest and most compelling explanation for having such legislation is to prevent the suffering, chaos, and injustice that would almost certainly occur in its absence. This is not a theoretical or hypothetical statement. For more than 100 years, significant industrial activity was carried out in Canada without any legislation to protect workers' right to bargain collectively or to strike. Some of the results of this lengthy "experiment" were discussed in Chapter 4 (labour history). They included frequent loss of life, serious injury, and extensive property damage resulting from strikes; an almost total lack of protection for workers against even the most arbitrary actions on the part of their employers; grossly inadequate protection of workers' health and safety; and a very low standard of living for most ordinary Canadians.

In a world in which most people must work and relatively few work at jobs they would voluntarily undertake, conflict between employers and workers is all but inevitable. The question is not whether there will be conflict; it is rather what form it will take (see Hebdon, 1992; Godard, 1994:75–83). In the absence of legislation regulating industrial conflict or providing workers with the right to join unions, many strikes take on the character of pitched class warfare (see Kervin, 1984). Through the nineteenth century and most of the first half of the twentieth, as the labour history chapter shows, this kind of strike was far too common. It has remained common, even in the postwar period, in countries where governments don't legitimate industrial conflict or accept workers' right to organize and bargain collectively.[1]

Under labour relations legislation, the possibility of violence leading to serious injury or loss of life still exists, but it is greatly reduced. Disputes are easier to settle, since most are over specific terms and conditions of employment rather than more intractable issues such as the union's right to exist (see Kervin, 1984). In most cases, employers and unions are able to maintain reasonably effective long-term working relationships despite the occasional strike. Thus regulated and with severe limits put on unfair practice by either side, a strike becomes less like class warfare and more like, say, a hockey game: rough, occasionally dangerous, but not usually anarchic. Most conflict will eventually be resolved through collective bargaining, strikes, and other activities of the IR system (Barbash, 1984). Indeed, there are those (i.e., Dubin, 1959) who would argue that conflict comes to play an essentially constructive role, once it has been regulated and limited by labour relations legislation.

Another important rationale for LRL and the collective bargaining it supports is the opportunity the latter provides for a degree of worker input into management decisions, indeed for some measure of worker self-government. As Paul Weiler (1980:29–32) notes, under collective bargaining, "[m]anagement must spell out its workplace rules; employees must be given a vehicle for collectively voicing their objections when their rights seem to be under siege." To Weiler, such an exercise in self-government is of value in and of itself, above and beyond the superior economic results it is likely to produce when compared to what most individual workers could likely obtain through individual negotiations with their employers. Essentially similar arguments have been advanced by other institutionalists, such as Alan Flanders (1970, in LLCG, 1991:153–164).

To be sure, not everyone would agree with Weiler's positive assessment of collective bargaining. Over the years, it has often been criticized from both the right and the left. Neoclassicists like Milton Friedman (1962, in LLCG, 1991:30–32) see unions as an intrusion on individuals' freedom to choose. Managerialists (discussed in Freeman and Medoff, 1979, in LLCG, 1991:168–182) primarily resent the loss of control unions mean to employers and managers. On the left, reformists such as David Beatty (1983) criticize collective bargaining for leading to a tyranny of the majority and taking little, if any, account of the needs of the "worst-off" classes in industrial society, such as domestics and farm workers. Further left, radicals such as Leo Panitch and Donald Swartz (1988, in LLCG, 1991:59–60) suggest that "free collective bargaining" is pretty much an oxymoron, given the coercive way in which the state has used its power in recent years, and its pronounced bias towards capital and business interests throughout the postwar period.

Despite these and other criticisms such as the belief that unions gave away too much by giving away the right to strike during the life of the agreement (see Adell, 1988a), most Canadians, inside the labour movement and out, would probably agree that labour relations legislation and collective bargaining have helped produce a society where workers are economically better off and have more workplace rights than did those of their grandparents' generation. Imperfect though the Canadian system of LRL doubtless is, most believe that both workers and Canadian society as a whole are better served with it than they would be without it.

THE EVOLUTION OF CANADIAN LRL

As we noted in the labour history chapter, Canada was slow to develop collective bargaining and to pass collective bargaining legislation. Indeed, Canada was among the last industrialized countries to grant private sector workers the right to join a union, doing so only in 1944, several decades later than countries such as Sweden and Denmark, and about a decade later than the United States.[2] In the case of Canadian public sector workers, most of whom did not receive full bargaining rights until the late 1960s or early 1970s, the lag was generally even greater. Among the major reasons for the slow evolution of unionism and collective bargaining in Canada were the country's comparatively late industrialization; its linguistically, regionally, and religiously fragmented labour movement; determined employer opposition; and a particularly unsympathetic federal government.

Through much of the nineteenth century, unions were regarded as conspiracies in restraint of trade in Canada and in many European countries (Adams, 1995:496). This notion ended with the *Trades Union Act* of 1872, which declared that the purposes of unions were not to be considered unlawful simply because they might be in restraint of trade (Carter, 1989:30). However, the protection applied only to those unions that took the trouble to register with the government, which few if any apparently did, thereby rendering it all but meaningless in practice (Morton, 1990:27). Overall, the act offered unions few positive benefits. Employers could still harass, dismiss, and blacklist union activists without fear of government reprisal.

Conciliation Legislation

The rest of the century saw little major change to Canadian labour legislation, although an 1877 amendment to the *Masters' and Servants' Act* meant that employees could no longer be sent to jail for striking or leaving their employers' service (Morton, 1990:34).[3] A much more significant development was the introduction of conciliation legislation around the turn of the century. In 1900, the government created a Department of Labour with a conciliation service (Heron, 1989:46). At the same time, it passed the *Dominion Conciliation Act*, allowing the labour minister to appoint a conciliation board either at one of the parties' request or on his own initiative (Carter, 1989:30). The idea behind the conciliation process, which initially was voluntary, was that once people became aware of the issues of labour disputes from reading the conciliation board's published report, public pressure would compel the two sides to settle those disputes (Carter, 1989). Similar principles were written into the *Railway Labour Disputes Act* of 1903 (Carter, 1989). In 1907, with the passage of the *Industrial Disputes Investigation Act*, conciliation became compulsory. Now, no union in a transportation, resource, or utilities industry could strike nor could an employer lock workers out until the conciliation board's report had been published and a further "cooling-off" period had elapsed (Heron, 1989:47). Compulsory conciliation has remained a cornerstone of most Canadian LRL to this day, although three-person board reports are now rare and the process has evolved into something much more closely resembling mediation in most cases (Carter, 1989).

The *IDI Act* seemed to favour the labour movement and initially won the Trades and Labour Congress' cautious support (Morton, 1990:89). Its greatest benefit to unions may have been in legitimizing very weak unions, which would otherwise have had little hope of getting their point across to the general public (Morton, 1990).

More often, though, the time delays simply gave employers the opportunity to stock-pile production, fire and blacklist union activists, or hire strikebreakers and private police (Morton, 1990; Heron, 1989). The act did little to promote union growth. Since it did not provide such basic rights as the right to join a union or go on strike, it didn't put an end to the kind of bitter, violent recognition disputes that had led to its enactment in the first place.

The Wagner Act

If anything, bitter strikes over recognition became more frequent through the 1930s and 1940s, an added source of frustration being that, by this time, American private sector workers enjoyed the right to bargain collectively and to strike, thanks to the New Deal *Wagner Act*[4] passed in 1935. A key feature of the *Wagner Act* was its specific prohibition of such unfair employer labour practices as intimidation or harassment of union members or the formation of a management-dominated company union. Another important feature was the establishment of a separate agency, the National Labor Relations Board, to administer and enforce the act (Carter, 1989:32). The NLRB mechanism was particularly welcomed by unionists since, in the past, labour matters had customarily been dealt with by the courts, which in general were not well disposed towards unions (Carter, 1989).

Between 1937 and 1943, a number of Canadian jurisdictions did adopt certain features of the American legislation, the most comprehensive of these being Ontario's Labour Court, which came into effect in 1943. This act was in many ways similar to Wagner but didn't fully meet with the labour movement's approval because administration was left to the courts rather than being turned over to a separate administrative agency, as in the United States (Carter, 1989:32–33).

PC 1003: Basic Bargaining Rights for Canadian Workers

During the war, the lack of basic bargaining rights became an issue uniting the long-divided Canadian labour movement, which had grown considerably stronger due to wartime labour shortages (Carter, 1989; Heron, 1989:78). By 1943, one Canadian union member in three was on strike—a rate that exceeded that of 1919, the year of the Winnipeg General Strike (Heron, 1989:78). Alarmed at the situation, Prime Minister Mackenzie King commissioned a report from the National War Labour Board. The report, written by Justice Charles McTague, told the government in no uncertain terms that only full union bargaining rights comparable to those granted American workers would put an end to the wave of strikes and violence (Morton, 1990:182–183). Not until the next year, however, faced with the very real possibility of a CCF victory in the next election (Heron, 1989:78–80; Morton, 1995:143) did King grant Canadian workers these rights. He did so through a wartime order-in-council, *PC 1003*, which contained most of the Wagner protections and mechanisms, including a separate board to administer the act as well as the right to bargain collectively and to strike. Now, employers could not refuse to bargain with a legally certified union that had demonstrated to the labour board it could command majority support in any given workplace (Heron, 1989:80). The Canadian act's major difference from the Wagner model was its incorporation of IDI's compulsory conciliation, an incorporation apparently made at King's insistence (Morton, 1989:168). When labour legislation returned to provincial jurisdiction with the end of the war, the federal government passed a permanent statute, the *Industrial Relations and Disputes Investigation Act* (1948), which incorporated most of the wartime order's major features. Within the next two years, most provinces had passed their own labour acts guaranteeing basic union rights (Heron, 1989:86), though some provincial acts, especially in Alberta and the Atlantic region (Finkel, 1986; Forsey, 1985), were far more restrictive than the federal one.

Unlike most previous Canadian labour bills, *PC 1003* and its offspring did help promote union growth, since employers were now specifically forbidden from interfering with unions in any way. The 1945 *Rand Formula* guaranteeing union security may also have contributed, since unions now had a firm financial basis to help ensure their survival (Heron, 1989:85). Nonetheless, as we noted in the labour history chapter, many Canadian workers, including most of the country's female workers, still could not join a union. This situation did not change until after 1967, when the federal government passed the *Public Service Staff Relations Act (PSSRA)*. Among other things, the *PSSRA* legalized collective bargaining for federal government employees and gave them the right to choose between binding arbitration and the traditional conciliation-strike route. Within a few years, provincial public sector workers across Canada were covered by some kind of collective bargaining act. Some, like the *PSSRA*, included the right to strike; others, like the administrative model adopted in Ontario[5] and Alberta, substituted binding arbitration. During the late 1960s and early 1970s, collective bargaining rights were also extended to other public sector workers, such as teachers and nurses. Again, some jurisdictions gave these groups the right to strike, while others forced them to submit their disputes to arbitration. (This issue is covered in more detail in the public sector chapter.)

The Impact of the Charter

Since the passage of public sector bargaining legislation, Canadian LRL has seen few important changes and no fundamental ones. This is not what most would have predicted following the enactment of the *Canadian Charter of Rights and Freedoms* in 1982. Many observers believed that the Charter would significantly affect the fundamental balance between legislatures and courts (see Carter, 1989:40–41). Some, notably David Beatty (1987; also Beatty and Kennett, 1988) thought the effect would be positive, as the courts used the Charter to strike down unjust labour laws. Others feared that unions would be the losers and that they would fare less well before the courts than before labour boards, whose activities courts might now severely circumscribe, reversing a long-term trend towards granting more power to labour boards and less to the courts (Arthurs, 1988; see also Carter, 1982). Neither the enthusiasts' hopes nor the skeptics' fears have been realized. The Charter's overall effect on Canadian LRL might best be described as underwhelming. If its freedom of association clause has not been used to provide workers with positive protection for the right to join a union, to strike, or to picket (England, 1988; Fudge, 1988), neither has the document been used to reduce labour boards' jurisdiction or to reduce unions' ability to use members' dues for political as well as collective bargaining objectives.[6] In general, courts have been reluctant to use the Charter to reshape the IR system (Carter, 1995:70; Swinton, 1995). What is perhaps most surprising is that the Charter was not, until 2001, used to provide even minimal "defensive" protection for freedom of association, as by striking down exclusion laws (discussed in more detail later in the chapter) that bar domestics, farm workers, and professionals from union membership in several Canadian jurisdictions. In the year 2001, the Supreme Court of Canada struck down Ontario's longstanding exclusion of agricultural workers on Charter-based grounds. Though this is certainly good news for workers and unions, it is not yet clear to what extent the Ontario case might form the basis for successful Charter-based challenges to the other remaining exclusions (aside from those of management and confidential IR personnel). The wording of the Supreme Court's ruling also strongly suggests that the Ontario exclusion was ruled unconstitutional because it was too sweeping. By implication, more targeted agricultural exclusions (such as Quebec and New Brunswick's exclusion of agricultural workers in groups of fewer than five) might survive a Charter challenge.

The Duty to Accommodate

Though Canadian LRL's content has not changed much of late, its interpretation is changing dramatically. This is primarily the result of the passage of various types of employment legislation (discussed in detail in the previous chapter), in particular, human rights legislation. Thus far, the new human rights legislation has had its greatest effect on the grievance procedure, where arbitrators have been obliged to interpret collective agreements in the light of anti-discrimination provisions contained in human rights acts. Ever since the landmark *O'Malley v. Simpson-Sears* case (1986), intent to discriminate need not be proved for a finding of illegal discrimination to be reached. Now, a concept of "constructive" or "systemic" discrimination applies, under which workplace rules and collective agreement provisions can be found discriminatory, regardless of their intent, if they have a disproportionate effect on an individual employee (Carter, 1997:188). Since the advent of "constructive" discrimination, both unions and employers have been required to accommodate such adversely affected employees up to the point of "undue hardship." The requirement has been construed to extend far beyond the protection of women and minority group members from sexual, religious, and racial harassment, to the provision of special treatment such as the drawing up of different work schedules for members of religious groups whose beliefs forbid work on certain days, or the redesign of jobs to allow individuals with disabilities to perform them more easily (Carter, 1997:190–197). As Carter has shown (1997:197–198), the duty to accommodate may even extend to rewriting collective agreement provisions or agreeing to waive their application. This kind of requirement would seem to fly in the face of core collective bargaining principles, such as equal application of all collective agreement provisions and the barring of special treatment for individual workers without the union's express consent and approval (Carter, 1997:186). As the arbitral jurisprudence in this area grows and workers become more aware of their rights under human rights legislation, the duty to accommodate will likely pose increasing challenges for employers, unions, and arbitrators alike.

MAJOR FEATURES OF CANADIAN LRL

Legislative Fragmentation

To those familiar with other industrial relations systems, the most notable feature of the Canadian system of labour relations legislation is its extreme fragmentation. Unlike the situation prevailing in the United States, where private sector labour law is under federal jurisdiction, most Canadian private sector workers fall under provincial jurisdiction, thanks to a British Privy Council decision in the 1926 Snider case (discussed in the labour history chapter), which placed labour relations in the provinces' constitutional domain. As a result, each province has had to write its own private sector labour relations act.

The one exception to the general pattern of provincial jurisdiction is workers in enterprises of a clearly federal or interprovincial nature, such as the railroads, airlines, chartered banks, and telecommunications companies. These workers, who together make up about 10 percent of the country's union members, are governed by the *Canada Labour Code*. Federal government employees fall under the *Public Service Staff Relations Act*; provincial government employees and most other public sector workers, such as teachers and nurses, fall under a broad array of provincial public sector laws, which we discuss in the next chapter.

In all, there are about three dozen different pieces of labour relations legislation in effect in Canada. Such extreme legislative fragmentation poses a number of difficulties, not least of which is the simple confusion of keeping all these laws straight (Carter, 1989:28). For the practitioner, mastering all the different acts can pose a formidable challenge, although there are, as we'll see, broad patterns of similarity among many of the acts that make this task a bit less formidable than it might at first seem. As

Carter (1995:55–56) notes, labour boards and courts sometimes find it difficult to decide whether a given enterprise should fall under provincial or federal jurisdiction. As well, provincial jurisdiction has definitely contributed to the emergence of a highly decentralized bargaining structure (see Anderson, 1982; Rogow, 1989a), for example by making it more difficult for an industry to conduct negotiations at the national level (Carter, 1995). Given that Canada's decentralized bargaining structure has often been implicated as a cause of its relatively high incidence of strikes, the implications of provincial jurisdiction may be more profound than many realize. Moreover, in an economy that is becoming increasingly globalized, the lack of a single clear national standard in labour relations legislation could prove a barrier to international trade and global competitiveness.

On the positive side, the existence of many different sets of labour legislation may well contribute to innovation and change, as in the case of the many new dispute resolution procedures introduced in British Columbia while Paul Weiler (1980) was head of that province's labour board.[7] Whether the advantages of a system that allows for comparatively low-risk legislative innovation and experimentation outweigh the disadvantages posed by Canada's decentralized bargaining structure and lack of a single national standard for labour relations legislation is a question each reader must answer individually.

Emphasis on Processes

A key assumption behind Canadian LRL is that it should operate primarily through free collective bargaining between employers and unions (Godard, 1994:278). It follows, then, that LRL should not normally prescribe outcomes (i.e., a given wage level or set of working conditions), but should rather confine itself to laying out processes that will allow free and fair collective bargaining to take place. The idea here is that the parties, who know each other and must work with each other and with the collective agreement on a daily basis, are in a better position to fashion an agreement that meets their particular needs than a group of legislators or a labour board would be.

Two types of provisions would seem to represent an exception to this emphasis on processes rather than outcomes. The first of these are first-contract arbitration provisions allowing for the imposition of an initial collective agreement in cases where the labour board believes an employer has not bargained in good faith with an eye to concluding an agreement. The second are provisions, now found in almost every labour act except Ontario's, which eliminated that right in 1998 (G. Adams, 1998; R. Jackson, 2001), that allow labour boards to certify a union with less than majority support in situations where the board believes that the employer's unfair labour practices have prevented the employees' true wishes from becoming known. At first glance, both types of provision may seem like heavy-handed government intervention in the collective bargaining process. Closer inspection, however, reveals that, far from serving to stifle free collective bargaining, these provisions are designed to further it, by serving as a deterrent to grossly unfair labour practice. In this respect, it may not be too far-fetched to compare them to the penalty kicks occasionally imposed in soccer matches. Such drastic measures are not put into effect every day; nor was it anyone's intention that they should be. Generally, labour boards will impose a first agreement or certify with less than majority support only as a last resort. Indeed, at least one observer (Godard, 1994:290–292) suggests that even these remedies may be inadequate, and that given what amount to rather minimal disincentives to unfair employer labour practice, it is surprising more unfair practices are not committed.

Closely related to Canadian LRL's emphasis on processes is its voluntarism, or belief in the ability of employers and unions to resolve disputes on their own, without compulsory government intervention (Godard, 1994:278). A belief in voluntarism clearly underlies the development of several innovative new dispute resolution methods, such as grievance mediation. Here, the consent of both parties is normally required before the process can go forward (Joyce, 1996). The major exception to Canada's generally voluntarist approach to dispute resolution is the retention of compulsory conciliation provisions in most jurisdictions' labour acts. One study (Gunderson, Myszynski, and Keck, 1989) did find the provisions to be associated with a somewhat lower level of strike incidence. Nonetheless, as we note in Chapter 11, Canada continues to lose many person-days to strikes by international standards. In any event, it is debatable whether there is justification for such widespread government intervention into the bargaining process, particularly in private sector disputes without a substantial public interest component (see Godard, 1994:349–50).

One other point should be made. The parties are not absolutely free to write any provisions they wish into collective agreements, because they are bound to abide by any relevant legislation, such as employment standards and human rights laws. Normally it is illegal for an agreement to contain any terms less favourable to employees than those found in the jurisdiction's employment standards act. For example, the parties cannot agree to a wage less than the provincial minimum or a shorter vacation period than that provided under the employment standards act. They also cannot agree to provisions that discriminate against any group, such as separate pay scales for women and men.

No Mid-Term Strikes

Another key tenet of Canadian labour relations legislation is the "peace obligation" imposed on both unions and employers during the life of the agreement. While the agreement is in force, a union cannot strike and an employer cannot lock out its employees. Every jurisdiction's labour act stipulates that disputes over contract interpretation must be settled through a grievance process culminating, if need be, in binding arbitration. While the parties are free to devise their own process, they are not free to do away with it (Carter, 1995:64).

Broad Worker Protection

Overall, Canadian LRL provides workers and their unions with a reasonably broad range of protection in a number of areas. As noted earlier, first-contract arbitration provisions and provisions allowing labour boards to certify with less than majority support give workers and unions at least some protection against employers' unfair labour practices. Union security and dues checkoff provisions, required in a number of jurisdictions, have helped unions establish a firm financial footing. And striking workers enjoy a number of safeguards, ranging from Quebec's and British Columbia's absolute prohibition of replacement workers to most provinces' guarantee that they can get their jobs back once the strike is over (Carter, 1995:65). On the other side of the ledger, the duty of fair representation provisions found in most Canadian juris-dictions afford workers a good measure of protection against arbitrary treatment at the hands of union leaders, which may make hesitant workers feel more comfortable about joining unions.

Canadian Versus American Legislation

Canadian LRL originally evolved out of the American *Wagner Act* (1935). In many ways, it still strongly resembles its American ancestor. In other ways, it has taken some quite different directions.

The fact of provincial jurisdiction may well have helped Canadian legislation to change more and more often than has been the case in the United States, where the legislation is under federal jurisdiction and any change can affect many millions of workers. Both countries' laws tend to emphasize processes rather than outcomes and to be relatively voluntarist in their overall orientation. However, the American legis-lation has remained truer to its voluntarist heritage. First, almost all Canadian juris-dictions have compulsory conciliation provisions. Second, Canada's compulsory grievance arbitration, which is not part of the Wagner model,[8] represents a signifi-cant degree of government intervention into the IR system. Third, the United States has no equivalent of Canada's first-contract arbitration or anti-scab laws. Indeed, U.S. law allows for the permanent replacement of striking workers (Carter, 1995), except in cases where a dispute has arisen over illegal activities, such as the employ-er's attempt to get rid of the union. In these cases, permanent replacements are illegal and strikers have a right to get their jobs back (Sims, 1996:Chapter 9).

In other areas as well, Canadian law offers workers and unions significantly greater protection than U.S. law. For instance, union security is generally stronger in Canada, which has no equivalent to the "right-to-work" provisions of the 1947 *Taft-Hartley* amendments to Wagner. Where the card count still exists, union certifi-cation is significantly easier in Canada than in the United States. Even in those juris-dictions that have moved to the vote, the 'quickie' (5–10 day) voting process normally used in Canada offers less chance for employer interference in the process than do the U.S.'s lengthy campaigns, and thus there is probably less likelihood that the union will lose the campaign. In addition, laws against unfair employer labour practice appear to be more strictly enforced here (Bruce, 1990).

MAJOR FUNCTIONS OF CANADIAN LRL

Certification and Decertification

Overseeing the **certification** process is arguably the single most important function of Canadian labour relations legislation. Before *PC 1003*, a Canadian union could win bargaining rights only through voluntary recognition or a strike (Craig and Solomon, 1996:213). As was noted earlier, strikes over recognition tended to be long and bitter and often resulted in bloodshed; thus the establishment of a procedure through which unions could obtain legal recognition of bargaining rights was crucial to bringing about some measure of labour peace.

The certification process begins with an application from a union to the labour board to represent the workers in a proposed bargaining unit. The application, a copy of which is normally delivered to the employer (see *OLRA*, sec. 7[2]), must include a written description of the proposed bargaining unit and an estimate of the number of individuals in the unit. It generally must also include a list of the names of the individual workers in the proposed bargaining unit and their status as union members; however, this information is not given to the employer (see *OLRA*, sec. 7[13]).

At this point, the labour board has two jobs to do: (a) determine the appropriate bargaining unit, and (b) ascertain the union's level of support. To assist it in determining the appropriate bargaining unit, the board will allow employers or, in some cases, individual workers who object to the union's proposed unit to submit a proposal for a unit they prefer (*OLRA*, sec. 7 [14]).[9] In making its determination, the labour board will take into account both the union's and employer's wishes (*OLRA*, sec. 8); in Ontario, it may conduct a special poll of employees to determine their wishes in the matter (*OLRA*, sec. 9[1]). The board may also consider such factors as the community of interests of the workers involved, traditional or customary bargaining units in the industry in question, and the way in which the proposed bargaining unit would fit into the employer's administrative set-up (Godard, 1994:281–282; Craig and Solomon, 1996:213–214), with the workers' community of interest normally being of greatest importance (Craig and Solomon, 1996:214).

To become certified, unions in all Canadian jurisdictions must reach two threshold points: (a) a level of support that will entitle them to apply for certification (whether this is determined through a card count or a formal election), and (b) a level that will entitle them to become officially certified as the representative for the bargaining unit in question. Typically, the level of support required to apply for certification is lower than that at which certification will be granted. In Alberta and Ontario, where a vote is always required, it will be triggered if the union can produce evidence that 40 percent of the proposed bargaining unit have joined the union. To reduce the chances of employer interference, most Canadian labour acts requiring a vote also require that the vote be held very soon (within 5 to 10 working days) after the certification application has been filed. In Manitoba, whose arrangements are fairly typical of provinces that do not normally require a vote, 40 percent support is needed to apply for certification. With signed membership cards from 65 percent or more of the proposed bargaining unit members, the union will automatically be certified. If support is between 40 and 65 percent, a vote must be held (*Manitoba Labour Relations Act*, Sec. 40(1)).

Where a vote is required, simple majority support is always enough to certify the union. However, various jurisdictions differ as to whether the union must receive votes from a majority of the bargaining unit or simply a majority of those voting. Most jurisdictions, including Ontario and the federal jurisdiction, allow certification based on a majority of those voting; a few jurisdictions, including Quebec and P.E.I., require support from a majority of bargaining unit members—a situation that in effect allows abstentions to count as negative votes. Newfoundland has come up with a compromise whereby the union must receive support from a majority of those voting in situations where at least 70 percent of the proposed bargaining unit have voted (*Nfld. Labour Relations Act, Sec. 38[2]*).

Traditionally, labour boards made their decisions about the appropriate bargaining unit before deciding whether a union would or would not be certified as that unit's representative. This has changed with the growing trend towards the prehearing or "quickie" vote aimed at minimizing employer interference in the certification process where a vote is required.[10] Such a vote will normally be granted if either party requests it, and in Ontario, it has become standard (see *OLRA*, sec. 8[5,6]). In cases where the proposed bargaining unit is in dispute, the board may direct that one or more ballots be segregated and that the ballot box be sealed until after it has decided on an appropriate bargaining unit. If a hearing is necessary, the board will conduct it after the certification vote is held, but before the ballots are counted. In some jurisdictions, including Ontario (*OLRA*, sec. 9[2]) and Manitoba, the board may certify the union pending final determination of the bargaining unit, providing it is satisfied that any dispute over the bargaining unit cannot affect the union's right to certification.

Decertification is a process whereby union members who are unhappy with the way in which their union has represented them can get rid of that union in favour of a different one, or no union at all. Any bargaining unit employee may apply to the board for decertification; however, the application will normally be entertained only near the collective agreement's expiry date,[11] or in cases where the union has not managed to negotiate a collective agreement within a reasonable length of time after certification (one year in Ontario). From this point, the process is quite similar to the certification process. Again, a copy of the application must be delivered to the employer and the union. If a sufficient percentage of the bargaining unit applies for decertification (40 percent in Ontario), the board will direct that a decertification vote be taken and will set about determining the appropriate bargaining unit for the purpose of that vote. Normally the percentage requirements for decertification are identical to those for certification. In Ontario and many other jurisdictions, if a majority of those voting favour decertification, the union will be decertified (see *OLRA*, sec. 63[14]).

As Craig and Solomon note (1996:223), decertification provisions are an essential element of public labour policy. Among other things, such provisions help enhance union democracy by providing workers with a way of getting rid of unions that have been ineffective, or that have treated them unfairly or arbitrarily. At the same time, high levels of decertification activity are hardly a sign of a healthy IR system. Most typically, they are associated with a rise in employer anti-union tactics and unfair labour practice activity (see Godard, 1994:139 and Barbash, 1988), though as Godard notes, decertification may also be linked to increased union raiding (discussed in detail in Chapter 5).

Remedying Unfair Labour Practice

An inadequately enforced labour act would not amount to much. Accordingly, a major purpose of Canadian LRL is to set standards for **unfair labour practice** and provide remedies for it. Unfair labour practice provisions apply both to employers and unions. In some cases, they also apply to individuals.

Employers are barred from participating in or interfering with a trade union, from discriminating against union members, or from seeking to induce employees not to join a union. In some jurisdictions, including Ontario (see below), the hiring of professional strikebreakers is specifically defined as an unfair labour practice. When a union has been certified, an employer cannot refuse to bargain with it or engage in mere "surface" bargaining not aimed at concluding a collective agreement (see *OLRA*, sec. 17). Once bargaining begins, an employer cannot alter wage rates or other terms and conditions of employment until the conciliation process has run its course (see *OLRA*, sec. 86[1]). During organizing drives, employers are barred from issuing any threats or promises to workers or attempting to influence the unionization process by hiring additional workers, who, in most cases, would likely vote against unionization (Godard, 1994:286–287). They are also barred from closing down and relocating all or part of their operations in an attempt to avoid or get rid of a union; indeed, in some jurisdictions *(see Saskatchewan Trade Union Act, Sec. 11[1(i)])*, the mere threat of doing so is an unfair labour practice.

For their part, unions are barred from interfering with the formation and operation of employers' organizations (*OLRA*, sec. 71), as well as from interfering with other unions that have won the right to represent given groups of workers. In most provinces, including Ontario (*OLRA*, sec. 74), they are bound by a duty of fair representation provision, which forbids them from acting in an arbitrary or discriminatory manner, or in bad faith in representing bargaining unit members. Unions cannot use intimidation or coercion to seek to compel people to join (*OLRA*, sec. 76), and are specifically barred from trying to persuade employees to join at the workplace during regular working hours (sec. 77).[12] They are also forbidden from suspending or otherwise disciplining members for refusing to engage in unlawful strikes.

As will be noted in more detail in the "Administration" section, labour boards are primarily responsible for administering and enforcing labour relations acts. They have a broad range of remedies available, including the power to issue cease and desist orders, the power to order unfairly discharged employees reinstated with or without compensation (*OLRA*, sec. 96[4]), and the ability, where appropriate, to alter a bargaining unit determined in a certificate or defined in a collective agreement (*OLRA*, sec. 99[7]). In extreme cases, they may certify a union with less than majority support in almost all jurisdictions except Ontario (G. Adams, 1998; R. Jackson, 2001) or impose a first collective agreement through arbitration in those jurisdictions that make first-agreement arbitration available. Many labour acts also stipulate that violators can be prosecuted through the criminal courts. However, it would appear that criminal prosecution is seldom used, as labour boards generally prefer to take a more accommodative approach (Carter, 1995:68; Sommer and Saxe, 2001).

Maintaining Union Security

Without protection for their right to carry out legitimate activities in the workplace and a regular source of income, few unions would last for very long. Protection is provided in all jurisdictions through provisions stating that no employer or employers' organization shall participate in or interfere with the formation, selection, or administration of a trade union or with the union's activities (see *OLRA*, sec. 70), and similar provisions barring employers or other unions from interfering with a duly certified union's bargaining rights. Income protection is assured in most jurisdictions through some version of the *Rand Formula* (discussed earlier in the chapter). In Ontario, section 47(1) of the *Labour Relations Act* provides for the regular deduction of union dues from all bargaining unit members, whether or not they are union members. Non-members will have their deductions reduced to take account of pension, insurance, and other benefit plans available only to members (sec. 47[2b]), and those with a religious objection to joining a union or paying union dues may have their dues money paid to a recognized charity (sec. 52[1]).

Regulating Industrial Conflict

Strikes

Canada generally regulates strikes more strictly than do most other countries. As we note in more detail in the strike chapter (Chapter 11), most jurisdictions require the appointment of a conciliator before a strike can become legal. American private sector labour law does not require conciliation prior to strikes, nor does that of most other countries (Bean, 1994:116–7). Generally a strike will be legal only after the conciliator has reported his or her lack of success to the minister and a certain length of time (normally 7 to 14 days) has elapsed. While this is now becoming less common, some jurisdictions maintain a second stage of conciliation, culminating in a public report. Most jurisdictions require a secret strike vote. Two jurisdictions (Saskatchewan and Ontario) give the employer a say in whether or not a strike will continue. In the former, the employer may ask the labour board to conduct a vote on the employer's last offer; in the latter, the employer may make a similar request of the minister (*OLRA*, sec. 42[1]). Saskatchewan's *Trade Union Act* (Sec. 45) also allows the union, or the lesser of 100 workers or 25 percent of the bargaining unit members, to apply for a mediator who may among other things conduct such a vote, in cases where a strike has lasted 30 days.

Although this isn't the Canadian norm, two jurisdictions (Alberta and B.C.) have special provisions for handling emergency disputes in the private sector, in cases where the government believes the public health or welfare is being seriously endangered. The Alberta legislation provides for the establishment of a public emergency tribunal to mediate the dispute and, where necessary, hand down a binding arbitration award *(Labour Relations Code, Secs. 110-111)*. The B.C. legislation allows the government to block a planned strike or lockout and substitute mediation, designation of essential employees, and appointment of a public interest inquiry board (Craig and Solomon, 1996).

There are also restrictions on employers' conduct during a labour dispute. Just as unions cannot strike, employers cannot legally lock out until the conciliation process has been exhausted and the appropriate time delays have passed. Quebec and British Columbia ban the use of replacement workers, within certain limits, while Ontario (*OLRA*, sec. 78[1]) bans professional strikebreakers, as does Alberta. Most Canadian jurisdictions provide for the reinstatement of workers following a legal strike. Manitoba specifically bans the use of permanent replacement workers (Carter, 1995:65).

Grievances

As we pointed out earlier, a distinctive feature of Canadian labour legislation is that strikes during the life of the collective agreement are illegal. Instead, every Canadian jurisdiction's labour act requires that collective agreements establish a grievance process, culminating in final and binding arbitration, to settle disputes over the interpretation or application of the agreement (e.g., *OLRA*, sec. 48[1]). Most provinces also have a provision in their labour acts stating that if a collective agreement does not make specific reference to a grievance procedure, it shall be deemed to contain such a provision (e.g., *OLRA*, sec. 48[2]).

VARIATIONS IN PROVINCIAL LEGISLATION

Over the years, different provinces' labour relations acts have begun to vary a good deal in a number of ways. While the basic core of the acts is usually quite similar, there are now a number of differences in such important areas as eligibility for coverage under the legislation, certification procedures, duty of fair representation provisions, first-contract arbitration, technological change, replacement worker provisions, and the availability of alternative dispute resolution procedures such as grievance mediation and expedited arbitration.

To the beginning student, labour relations acts seem to present a great welter of minute, confusing detail, often written in highly technical language. It is definitely not our intention to drown readers in a sea of mind-boggling detail. At the same time, we would like to offer some guidance on the question of which types of provisions and which acts seem to offer the greatest (or least) protection to workers and their unions. To this end, we consider a number of provisions with an eye to determining their relative impact on unions and employers. The provisions we will be examining include those governing exclusions from coverage under labour relations legislation, certification procedures, first-contract arbitration, expedited arbitration, technological change, duty of fair representation, the use of replacement workers in strikes, management's right to communicate, and labour boards' ability to certify with less than majority support as a remedy for unfair labour practice. The results of this examination are summarized in Table 8.1. In the discussion below, "liberal" provisions are those generally favourable to workers and their unions, while "restrictive" provisions are those favourable to employers (or unfavourable to workers and unions).

As Table 8.1 reveals, the most liberal labour act overall appears to be that of British Columbia, where seven of the nine laws considered here are liberal and only two are restrictive. Clustered behind B.C. are Manitoba (six liberal and two moderately liberal), the federal jurisdiction (six liberal and one moderately liberal law), and Saskatchewan and Quebec (five liberal and one moderately liberal). But because the method of union certification is such an important issue, and B.C. has moved to a vote instead of a traditional card count, one could argue that in practice unions enjoy more rights in Manitoba and in the federal jurisdiction, where a card count is still used for certification, than they do in B.C. Alberta is the most restrictive jurisdiction, with only one moderately liberal provision, followed closely by Nova Scotia, with one liberal and one moderately liberal provision. The remaining jurisdictions (New Brunswick, Newfoundland, Ontario, and P.E.I.) fall in the middle of the pack. It may be of interest that all the liberal jurisdictions except the federal jurisdiction have had an NDP or PQ government for at least two full terms. Of the remaining provinces, only Ontario has ever had such a government, and then for just one term.[13]

Exclusions

In many European countries, the right to join a union has been written into freedom of association provisions in national constitutions. This is not the case in Canada, where the Supreme Court has ruled that the *Charter of Rights and Freedoms'* guarantee of freedom of association does not apply to workers' rights such as collective

Table 8.1
VARIATIONS IN PROVINCIAL LABOUR LAWS

Jurisdiction	Laws								
	1	2	3	4	5	6	7	8	9
Federal	L	L	L	L	NA	L	ML	R	L
Alberta	R	R	ML	R	NA	R	ML	R	NA
B.C.	L	R	L	L	L	L	L	R	L
Manitoba	L	L	ML	L	L	L	ML	R	L
New Brunswick	ML	L	NA	R	L	L	R	R	L
Newfoundland	L	R	L	L	NA	R	R	NA	L
Nova Scotia	R	R	ML	R	NA	R	R	R	L
Ontario	R	R	L	L	L	R	ML	R	R
P.E.I.	R	L	NA	L	NA	R	R	R	L
Quebec	ML	L	L	L	NA	R	L	NA	L
Saskatchewan	L	L	ML	L	L	L	R	NA	R

Notes: NA = not applicable, because in the author's judgment the law in question cannot meaningfully be classified as either liberal or restrictive.
L = Liberal; ML = Moderately Liberal; R = Restrictive.
Law 1: Exclusions
Law 2: Certification procedure
Law 3: Union's duty of fair representation
Law 4: First-contract arbitration
Law 5: Expedited arbitration
Law 6: Technological change
Law 7: Replacement workers
Law 8: Employer's freedom to communicate
Law 9: Labour board's ability to certify with less than majority support as remedy for unfair labour practice.

Sources: Statutes found on HRDC Web site; CCH (2001); Adams (2001).

bargaining, striking, or **picketing** (Adell, 1988b; Arthurs, 1988; Cavalluzzo, 1988; England, 1988). Far from providing positive protection for workers' right to join a union, Canadian LRL has continued to exclude the members of a number of occupational groups from coverage.[14]

Aside from their philosophical significance, exclusion provisions are of considerable practical relevance to the labour movement, since they can play an important role in union membership growth. Other things being equal, provinces with more liberal exclusion policies should have higher union membership rates than those with restrictive policies simply because they will have a larger pool of potential members to draw from. The evidence suggests that this has indeed been the case. In 2001 (see Table 8.2), the five provinces with the highest union membership rates,

Newfoundland, Quebec, Manitoba, Saskatchewan, and British Columbia, all had liberal or moderately liberal exclusion policies. Of the five provinces with the lowest rates, four had restrictive policies. Significantly, Ontario and Alberta, whose exclusion policies are the country's most restrictive, with the largest number of groups excluded, had by far the lowest membership rates.[15]

While some writers (i.e., Beatty, 1983) disagree, most Canadian industrial relations experts would justify the exclusion of management and confidential labour relations personnel, found in almost all Canadian jurisdictions, on the grounds that their inclusion in unions could create a conflict of interest. The real questions here may be who is a manager and what proportion of an employee's time is spent on confidential labour relations matters (on the latter, see Sommer and Saxe, 2001). In the case of professionals, however, most would likely agree that the rationale for their continued exclusion is at best unclear (LLCG, 1984:3–25), given that many now work not as independent practitioners but as salaried employees. Nonetheless, four provinces continue to exclude members of the legal, medical, dental, and architectural professions, and three exclude professional engineers.[16] Even less defensible is the exclusion of agricultural workers and domestic workers, the former being excluded

Table 8.2
PROVINCIAL EXCLUSION POLICY AND UNION DENSITY RATES, 2001

Jurisdiction	Union Density (%)	Exclusion Policy	No. of Exclusions
Newfoundland	39.4	L	0
Quebec	36.6	ML	1
Manitoba	35.6	L	0
Saskatchewan	34.1	L	0
British Columbia	33.1	L	0
P.E.I.	29.7	R	5
New Brunswick	28.6	ML	2
Nova Scotia	28.4	R	5
Ontario	26.1	R	10
Alberta	22.5	R	7

Sources: For provincial exclusion laws, as in Table 8.1. For union density rates, Akyeampong (2001). Number of exclusions refers to number of different groups excluded. The agricultural exclusion is divided into two parts: exclusion of small units and exclusion of the rest of the agricultural labour force. Jurisdictions having only the former in effect are counted as having one exclusion; those with a comprehensive agricultural exclusion are counted as having two. The table does not include exclusions of management or confidential IR personnel; it also does not include the exclusion of small numbers of government officials and magistrates (Ontario and Quebec).

"No place in the sun." Though they're among the country's poorest workers, agricultural workers are exclud-ed from unionization rights in several Canadian provinces, including Ontario. To make matters worse, sever-al provinces also exclude them from coverage under employment standards law.

in four provinces and the latter in three. Industrial relations experts have been calling for the abolition of these exclusions ever since the 1968 Woods Task Force Report (LLCG, 1984:3–27), with some going so far as to describe the agricultural exclusion, in particular, as blatantly political.[17] Until December 2001, their pleas fell largely on deaf ears. Indeed, exclusion laws changed far less in the 20 years after the Charter took effect than they had in the previous 20 years. Then, in a landmark decision, the Supreme Court of Canada overturned Ontario's agricultural exclusion on Charter-based grounds.[18] This decision should also spell the end for Alberta's comprehensive agricultural exclusion. But it is not as yet clear whether it will be used to strike down other exclusions (i.e., those of domestics and professionals) as well, or whether the less sweeping exclusion of small groups of agricultural workers in Quebec and New Brunswick would survive a Charter-based challenge.[19]

The federal jurisdiction and four provinces (B.C., Saskatchewan, Manitoba, and Newfoundland) can be said to have "liberal" exclusion policies, since their legislation excludes only management and confidential labour relations personnel (see Table 8.1). Two provinces (New Brunswick and Quebec) can be characterized as having "moderately liberal" policies, since their acts exclude small numbers of workers other than managers or confidential personnel. (New Brunswick excludes domestic workers and farm workers in units of less than five, while Quebec excludes farm workers in units of less than three.) The remaining provinces' exclusion policies can be described as "restrictive," since they exclude large numbers of workers beyond the basic management-confidential exclusion. Alberta, P.E.I., and Nova Scotia continue to exclude members of all five professions listed above; in addition, Alberta excludes domestics and most agricultural workers. Ontario excludes domestics, most agricultural workers, horticultural workers, professionals (except for engineers), and those engaged in trapping and hunting.

Certification Procedures

As we indicated earlier, Canadian jurisdictions' certification procedures vary significantly. Of greatest importance here is whether a jurisdiction requires a vote for all certifications, or will allow certification based on a count of signed membership cards except in cases where the number of workers supporting and opposing unionization is close enough that the labour board is in legitimate doubt as to whether the union enjoys majority support. Some analysts argue that the card count allowed in many Canadian jurisdictions is one of the reasons why Canada has higher union membership rates than the United States, where a vote has always been required since 1947 (see Bruce, 1990; Ng, 1992). Where a vote is required, such analysts argue, there is more opportunity for employers to influence the process, as by suspending, transferring, or harassing union activists or by warning employees of the dangers of unionization (Weiler, 1983). However, with B.C.'s recent switch from the card count to a vote, the card count can no longer be said to be the norm in Canada, since more workers now live in provinces using a vote than in provinces still relying on a card count.[20]

The federal jurisdiction and five provinces (New Brunswick, P.E.I., Quebec, Manitoba, and Saskatchewan) have liberal certification procedures, since they allow certification through a card count providing certain conditions are met. The five remaining provinces have restrictive certification procedures, since they require a vote for certification in all cases.

In recent years, the tendency has been for more jurisdictions to require a vote. Until 1984, when B.C. began to require a vote (Craig and Solomon, 1996:215), certification through card count was the norm throughout Canada. After 1984, other provinces began to follow suit. For example, Alberta moved to the vote in 1988 (Craig and Solomon, 1996), while Newfoundland did so in 1994, followed by Ontario in 1995 and B.C. in 2001. Another recent tendency has been towards greater "politicization" of the certification process. For example, B.C.'s NDP government dropped the previous Social Credit government's requirement of a vote in its 1992 revisions to the province's labour code, only to reinstate it when the Liberals replaced the NDP in 2001. Likewise, when a Conservative government replaced the NDP in Ontario in 1995, one of its first acts was to amend the labour relations act so as to require a vote (CCH, 1998d).

Duty of Fair Representation

At first glance, one would think duty of fair representation (DFR) provisions might be detrimental to unions, since they impose certain definite obligations on them. We would argue that DFR provisions likely benefit unions, since they can help reassure potential members that they have some protection against arbitrary or discriminatory treatment by union officials and thereby induce more people to join. Some DFR provisions, such as Ontario's, forbid the union from showing bad faith or acting in an arbitrary or discriminatory fashion towards any bargaining unit member, whether or not that individual happens to be a union member. The Quebec provision also forbids the union from displaying "serious negligence" towards any bargaining unit member.

Five jurisdictions (Ontario, Quebec, B.C., Newfoundland, and the federal jurisdiction) could be characterized as having "liberal" DFR provisions, since their provisions apply to the negotiation process as well as to contract administration. Four other jurisdictions (Saskatchewan, Manitoba, Nova Scotia, and Alberta) could be said to have "moderately liberal" provisions, since their DFR clauses apply only to unions' handling of grievances.

First-Contract Arbitration

First-contract arbitration provisions may be of considerable help to unions, since (at least in principle) they can deter employers in a first-contract situation from refusing to bargain seriously to prevent the union from achieving a collective agreement. A 1987 study by Jean Sexton finds that the provisions had a positive effect in helping Quebec unions achieve an initial collective agreement.

Eight jurisdictions (the federal one and the provinces of British Columbia, Manitoba, Newfoundland, Ontario, Prince Edward Island, Quebec, and Saskatchewan) have some kind of first-contract arbitration provision in effect. While there is quite a bit of similarity to most of these provisions, there is some variation regarding the length of contract that will be imposed. Four jurisdictions will impose an agreement for only one year, but in three (the federal jurisdiction, Ontario, and Saskatchewan), the agreement must be for at least two years, a period of time that commentators such as Weiler (1980) suggest may be necessary if the union is to achieve a lasting bargaining relationship with the employer. In Quebec, the duration may range from one to three years. There is also some variation in the conditions under which the board or an arbitrator acting under the board's direction will impose a first agreement, although most jurisdictions allow considerable ministerial discretion on this point.

We would classify the eight jurisdictions having first-contract arbitration provisions in place as "liberal," and the three remaining jurisdictions as "restrictive" in that they offer no special protection to unions in the delicate first-contract situation.

Expedited Arbitration

The purpose of **expedited arbitration** (to be discussed in more detail in the grievance chapter) is to achieve a speedier and more informal resolution of grievances. It can benefit unions in a number of ways. First, it can significantly reduce the cost of arbitration (Rose, 1986). Second, by speeding up the dispute resolution process, it can help make union members feel better about the kind of service the organization is providing them. Third (and not unrelated to the two previous points), by offering an inexpensive alternative to conventional arbitration, it allows for the resolution of a greater number of workplace problems. Again, this should have the effect of increasing members' satisfaction with their unions, since a common criticism of conventional arbitration is that it allows for the final resolution of only a tiny proportion of the total number of grievances filed.

Five provinces (B.C., Manitoba, New Brunswick, Ontario, and Saskatchewan) have some kind of expedited arbitration procedure in effect. In B.C., Manitoba, and Saskatchewan, expedited arbitration can be combined with some form of grievance mediation, thereby further reducing the costs of arbitration and increasing the number of cases resolved (Rose, 1996; see also Weiler, 1980). We would classify those provinces having expedited arbitration provisions as "liberal." Interestingly, this is one case where a gain for the union is not necessarily a loss for the employer. Employers as well as unions can benefit from lower arbitration costs, quicker resolution of problems, and the resolution of a greater number of workplace difficulties. Indeed, one reason for the growing popularity of expedited arbitration may well be that it offers a "win-win" situation for all concerned.

Technological Change

Technological change is of serious concern to unions, both because it is sometimes used specifically to weaken unions (Godard, 1994:137) and because it can have the effect of destabilizing workplace relations and undermining collective agreement protections (Godard, 1994; Peirce, 1987). Five jurisdictions (B.C., Manitoba, New Brunswick, Saskatchewan, and the federal jurisdiction) have in place some kind of technological change provision requiring employers to give notice before making a technological change that will affect workers' jobs or incomes.

In practice, legislated technological change provisions haven't afforded workers and their unions much protection, in large measure because labour boards have been reluctant to enforce the legislation even in cases where an employer is in clear violation (see Economic Council of Canada, 1987; Peirce, 1987). Still, the provisions may encourage otherwise reluctant employers to bargain over the issue, and, therefore, are probably better than no provision at all. Therefore, we would classify the five jurisdictions with some kind of technological change provision in place as "liberal," and the remaining provinces as "restrictive," in that they offer workers no legislative protection against the adverse effects of this change.

Use of Replacement Workers

One of the most hotly debated issues in industrial relations is whether employers should be allowed to replace striking workers. Those taking a neoclassical or managerial perspective generally argue in favour of this right, on the grounds that management should be free to run enterprises as it sees fit, and that to take away the right would be to tilt the balance of power too much in the union's favour (see Godard, 1994:295). Others point out that the practical effect of allowing replacement workers is to undermine the union's legal right to strike, particularly in the case of low-skilled jobs, where workers can easily be replaced (Godard, 1994:295–296; Beatty, 1983). Still others are concerned that the use of replacement workers could lead (as it often has) to picket-line violence, or even loss of life.[21] In this regard, the Giant Gold Mine case, where nine workers were killed in an explosion in a replacement worker situation, is but one of many painful illustrations from recent Canadian labour history.

Quebec, which pioneered anti-scab legislation in 1977 following a picket line confrontation that led to loss of life, prohibits the use of replacement workers hired after negotiations begin, but before the end of a strike, or who are supplied by another employer or by a contractor. The legislation also bans multi-establishment employers from using a worker at a struck or locked-out establishment elsewhere, or from bringing employees from other establishments into the struck or locked-out one. British Columbia's legislation is similar, but also bars employers from bringing in someone from outside to substitute for a non-bargaining unit employee temporarily performing the work of a striking bargaining-unit employee. Ontario had similar legislation on the books during the early 1990s, but it was repealed when the present Conservative government came to power in 1995.

The two jurisdictions that prohibit the use of replacement workers should be classified as "liberal" on this issue. Alberta and Ontario, which ban the use of professional strikebreakers, and Manitoba, which does that and also prohibits replacement workers from being hired permanently after the strike, can be classified as "moderately liberal." So should the federal jurisdiction, since recently enacted changes to the *Canada Labour Code* provide protection against the use of replacement workers where the purpose of bringing in those workers was to undermine the union, rather than to pursue legitimate bargaining objectives. The remaining jurisdictions should be classified as "restrictive," as they offer striking workers no protection against replacement workers.

Employer's Freedom to Communicate

Eight jurisdictions (Alberta, B.C., Manitoba, New Brunswick, Nova Scotia, Ontario, and P.E.I. as well as the federal jurisdiction) have in place provisions specifically granting employers the right to communicate with their employees, within certain limits. These provisions appear to be on the increase; in 1984, the *Labour Law*

Casebook (3–67) indicated that they were in place only in B.C., Manitoba, and Ontario, the latter being where the first such provision came into effect, in 1975.

Alberta's provision is typical; it states that an employer can express his or her views "so long as (s)he does not use coercion, intimidation, threats, promises, or undue influence." Manitoba's and Ontario's provisions specifically exclude interference with unions from permissible employer communications. The P.E.I. provision differs in that it specifically allows employers to express their views on "collective bargaining, or terms and conditions of employment," so long as they do not use coercion, intimidation, threats, or undue influence. In B.C., the provision allows employers to communicate to an employee "a statement of fact or opinion reasonably held with respect to the employer's business."[22]

Defenders of the provisions argue that granting employers the right to communicate with employees is little more than a fair balance of the rights given to unions to make their case. They also point out that unions have more than sufficient protection from other legislative provisions (found in all Canadian acts) barring employers from having a hand in the formation or operation of a union or from interfering with its operations. Critics, for their part, argue that, whatever other legislative provisions might say, these provisions open the door to employers wishing to influence the unionization process—a process in which employers should have no say whatever. Of particular concern to the critics are employer free speech provisions in the four jurisdictions that also require a vote for certification (Alberta, B.C., Nova Scotia, and Ontario), and the P.E.I. provision, which specifically permits direct communication on collective bargaining issues and might, therefore, be seen as encouraging employers to make an "end run" around unions by communicating with employees directly on these issues.

Our view is that although these provisions will not necessarily lead to increased employer interference with unions, they have the potential to do so, particularly in provinces requiring a vote for union certification. We would therefore classify all jurisdictions having such provisions in place as "restrictive."

Labour Board's Right to Certify With Less Than Majority Support

Eight of eleven jurisdictions give their labour boards the power to certify a union with less than majority support in cases where the board believes that an unfair employer labour practice has prevented employees' true wishes from becoming known. In Ontario, where a certification vote is always required, the labour board has only the power to order a further vote. In Saskatchewan, where certification by card count is the norm, the board has the power to order a vote. Alberta's labour act is silent on this issue. As we noted earlier in this chapter, the Ontario government removed this power from its labour board in 1998 finding a highly controversial 1997 case in which the Steelworkers' union was certified at a Windsor

Wal-Mart store, despite receiving fewer than one-quarter of employees' votes in the election (*Canada Labour Views*, 1997).

In our view, labour boards require the power to certify with less than majority support as an adequate remedy for particularly egregious employer unfair practices such as those engaged in by Radio Shack (described in R. Jackson, 2001) and other notoriously anti-union employers. Merely ordering further votes will not suffice. If a strongly anti-union employer knows it doesn't risk having the union certified as a result of its unfair practices, it will have little incentive to refrain from those practices. We would therefore classify all jurisdictions that allow the labour board to certify with less than majority support in such circumstances as 'liberal,' and the remaining jurisdictions as 'restrictive.'

Other Provisions

Six jurisdictions (the federal jurisdiction and all provinces from Ontario westward) allow individuals with religious objections to joining a union or paying union dues to apply to the labour board for exemption in situations where they would otherwise be expected to join the union or pay dues. Normally, the amount of money that would have been paid in dues is then remitted to a charity agreed upon by the worker and the union. Some argue that such provisions weaken unions by depriving them of potential members and revenue. Our view is that such provisions are unlikely to do much harm since only a very small number of workers will likely wish to avail themselves of them. In any case, it could also be argued that both individual unions and the Canadian labour movement as a whole will, in the long run, be better off for not forcing workers' consciences in such matters. We have, therefore, not included these provisions in our "liberal/restrictive" classification scheme.

With regard to unfair labour practices, several jurisdictions have written specific "reverse onus" provisions into their legislation. These provisions, which apply particularly when an employee is dismissed or otherwise disciplined during a certification drive, state that during critical periods like certification drives, the employer will be assumed to have disciplined the employee for reasons relating to union activity unless and until the employer proves otherwise. There would be a strong argument for classifying jurisdictions with such reverse onus provisions in place as "liberal," except that there is some reason to believe labour boards may operate in the same way even when specific reverse onus language is not in place.[23] Research is needed to determine whether there are significant differences in the handling of unfair labour practice cases in provinces with and without reverse onus provisions in their labour acts.

LRL in Quebec

Special mention should be made of Quebec's labour relations legislation, since in some ways that province's collective bargaining procedures and administrative mechanisms differ quite markedly from the rest of Canada's. Here, we focus mainly on private sector legislation; features applying to the public sector will be discussed in the next chapter.

While Quebec is best known to the English Canadian IR community for pioneering anti-strikebreaking legislation and the strike-right for public sector workers, the most distinctive feature of its legislative regime is arguably its decree system, whereby collective agreements are extended to the non-unionized sectors of an industry. Common in Europe (see Chapter 13 for more details), the decree system has been in effect since 1934 (Boivin and Déom, 1995:476). It was established to encourage collective bargaining and to eliminate competition over wages and working conditions among firms in the same industry (Boivin and Déom, 1995). Decrees are found mainly in low-wage industries comprising large numbers of small and medium-sized firms, such as men's and women's clothing, security guards, garages, bread distribution, hairdressing, and waste removal (Boivin and Déom, 1995:477). Agreements resulting from decrees are normally narrower in scope than standard agreements, since permissible provisions for an extension are limited to wages, hours of work, working days, vacations with pay, and classification of operations and of employers and employees.[24] Quebec law also provides for special, highly centralized arrangements in the construction industry, formerly a decree sector but now subject to sector-wide bargaining (Adams, 2001).[25]

Perhaps because of the decree system, which encourages a good measure of sector-wide negotiation, employers' associations play a much more prominent role in

Signs like the warning to potential strike breakers shown in the above picture aren't needed in provinces, such as Quebec, which have banned the use of replacement workers during strikes.

Quebec than they do elsewhere. The province has about 90 such organizations representing some 25 000 employers, mainly in construction or the decree sectors. Many of them are directly engaged in negotiating with unions. In 1969, most of those associations joined forces to create a confederation of employer associations known as the Conseil du patronat du Québec (CPQ). The CPQ does not engage in collective bargaining as such, instead focussing its energies on legislative lobbying, public relations, and research (Boivin and Déom, 1995:468). The existence of such a federation has arguably enabled the Quebec business community to speak with one voice to a far greater extent than would be possible in any other province.

Another unique feature of Quebec LRL is its Essential Services Council, established in 1982. The Council's main function is to ensure that sufficient employees are designated as essential to protect the public health, safety, and welfare during labour disputes affecting public services (Boivin and Déom, 1995:471). Since its activities apply mainly to the public sector, they will be discussed in more detail in the next chapter.

Finally, Quebec has differed significantly from other provinces in the way it administers LRL. In 1969, it replaced its labour relations board with a three-tier system including certification agents, labour commissioners, and general commissioners to deal with certification and unfair labour practice issues. A Labour Court was also established to handle appeals from commissioners' and general commissioners' decisions and to deal with criminal prosecutions brought under the Labour Code (Boivin, 1989:424–425). While similar to labour boards in many ways, the Labour Court has had exclusive jurisdiction in penal prosecutions brought under the Labour Code, a power not possessed by labour boards, which are administrative tribunals (Carrothers, et al., 1986). The idea was that such a specialized tribunal, staffed with IR and human resource specialists, would reduce recourse to the courts on labour-related matters. It proved unable to achieve this objective and was also widely criticized for its lengthy delays in rendering decisions (Boivin, 1989:425). Also, appeals from the Labour Court's decisions have been much more frequent than appeals from labour board decisions (Carrothers, et al., 1986:183). As a result, the government in 1987 passed legislation replacing the court with a labour relations board that would function in basically the same way as other provinces' boards (Boivin, 1989). However, for reasons not clear to the author, the legislation was never proclaimed in force. Similar legislation was passed in 2001 (Adams, 2001), but it likewise has not yet been proclaimed.

HOW LRL IS ADMINISTERED

Labour Boards

As Donald Carter (1995) notes, Canadian labour relations legislation is administered through three different institutions: labour relations boards, arbitrators (working either singly or in panels), and the courts. Of the three, labour relations boards are by far the most important. Found in every province except Quebec, which for the past three decades has used a labour court instead (see above), these boards are administrative tribunals that derive their authority from the collective bargaining law they administer (Carter, 1995:65). Their major functions are overseeing union certification and decertification and policing unfair labour practice; however, in recent years their jurisdiction has expanded to include the power to issue directives concerning illegal strikes and lockouts and to determine whether the parties are bargaining in good faith (Carter, 1995:66). As well, a number of boards, including Ontario's (*OLRA*, section 43[4]), can arbitrate first-contract disputes.

Labour relations boards normally report to the government through the labour ministry, but are regarded as having some autonomy from that ministry (Carter, 1995:65). In general, they are tripartite. Most comprise independent chairpersons and representatives from both management and the labour movement (Carter, 1995). Ontario (*OLRA*, section 110[2]) also provides for one or more vice-chairs. In larger jurisdictions, labour board appointments are full-time; in smaller ones, they are more apt to be part-time. Generally, labour boards employ a staff of professionals to perform research and various other functions (*OLRA*, section 110[2]). Normally, a panel of three, headed by a chair (or vice-chair) and containing at least one member from the union and management sides is considered a quorum. However, when necessary, the chair or a vice-chair may sit alone in a number of jurisdictions (see *OLRA*, section 110[12–14]).

Labour relations boards have quite extensive powers. In Ontario, these include the power to subpoena witnesses and compel them to give evidence under oath; to require any party to produce documents; to accept such evidence as the board deems proper, whether or not that evidence would be admissible in the courts; to require employers and unions to post board notices; to enter workplaces to inspect work processes and interrogate workers and managers; to conduct representation, strike, and ratification votes; and to bar unsuccessful applicants for certification for a period up to one year (*OLRA*, section 111[2]). They also have a broad range of remedies available to them, including (as noted above) the power to issue cease and desist orders, to certify a union with less than majority support (except in Ontario) where an unfair labour practice has prevented employees' true wishes in the matter from being made known, and to order unfairly discharged employees reinstated with or without compensation. While most labour acts provide substantial fines for violation,[26] labour boards rarely resort to criminal prosecution, even for serious and willful violations of the labour act, generally believing that prosecution will do little good and will likely only serve to embitter the parties even further (Godard, 1994:291). Instead, the approach they generally take is the non-punitive "make-whole" one from civil law (Godard, 1994:289), which requires the guilty party to right past wrongs and to restore the victim to the position he or she would have been in had the offence in question not been committed. This means that instead of fining or jailing an employer for unfairly discharging an employee during a union organizing drive, the board would normally order the employee reinstated with back pay (Godard, 1994:289–290). In some cases, unions have been awarded damages to compensate them for the extra expenses resulting from the employer's breach of the labour act (Carter, 1995:69). Where a board has found that the closing of an establishment was motivated at least in part by anti-union animus, it has ordered employers to make cash settlements with displaced employees and/or offer them equivalent jobs in the employer's other establishments (Godard, 1994:290).

Typically, labour board proceedings are more informal and less legalistic than proceedings before a court, though some have suggested that the gap between the two has narrowed of late (Arthurs, 1988:30). There is no requirement that parties to a labour board proceeding be represented by a lawyer (Carter, 1995:65), although an increasing number are (see Arthurs, 1988:30). In general, labour boards are more concerned with finding practical and workable solutions that will win broad acceptance in the industrial relations community than with laying down long-term legal precedents. To this end, they usually take an accommodative approach in addressing workplace problems. Often a labour relations officer is assigned to a dispute, in the first instance, to help the parties resolve the problem on their own. If an accommodation is reached, the board will not hear the matter (Arthurs, 1988:68). As well, the board will sometimes refuse to act if the conduct in question has ended by the time of the hearing; in Ontario, it has had a policy of not issuing an order to remedy illegal strike or lockout action if the strike or lockout has ended before the hearing, except in cases where there has been a clear pattern of such misconduct (Arthurs, 1988).

For the labour movement and many academic industrial relationists, labour boards have a number of advantages over the courts. In general, problems are resolved more quickly and expeditiously by boards. Since unions often have fewer resources than employers, this greater speed of resolution may be critical. In addition, labour boards, which normally include both union and management representatives, have tended to be more even-handed than the courts, which overall have tended to favour employers far more often than labour (Arthurs, 1988:20; England, 1988:169). Some have also noted that because labour boards are made up of IR practitioners and have expert staff available to them, they tend to be more knowledgeable about IR and more sensitive to its implications than do most judges, who may or may not have special training and expertise in the field. At the same time, there have been concerns that in their quest to be accommodating, labour boards have failed to take sufficient steps to prevent employers from committing unfair labour practices (Godard, 1994:289–292), and that existing penalties don't serve as much of a deterrent against such practices (Godard, 1994:290–291).

Arbitrators

While labour boards are the most important of the institutions that administer LRL, they are by no means the only ones. It is arbitrators who are chiefly responsible for interpreting and administering collective agreements. At one time (Carter, 1995:69), three-person panels comprising a union nominee, a management nominee, and a neutral chair were the norm for grievance arbitration. Now, however, single arbitrators are increasingly being used, as many on both sides of the union–management divide have come to the conclusion that their decisions are just as good and arrived at more quickly and at less expense than those reached by three-person panels (Carter, 1995; see also Rose, 1986).

Initially, the expectation was that collective agreement arbitration would be essentially a private arrangement between the parties. Over the years, however, it has become more of a mixed or hybrid public-private system (Carter, 1997). There have been two reasons for this evolution. First, as Carter notes (1997), arbitrators have for some years been expected to apply external legislation, such as employment standards and human rights provisions. For example, in Ontario, section 48(12[j]) of the *Labour Relations Act* specifically requires arbitrators and arbitration panels to "interpret and apply human rights and other employment-related statutes, despite any conflict between these statutes and the terms of the collective agreement." The trend towards interpreting collective agreements in the light of external legislation has accelerated in recent years with the growth of the "duty to accommodate" arising out of human rights legislation (Carter, 1997). Second, in a number of jurisdictions government has become increasingly involved in the arbitration process through expedited arbitration or mediation-arbitration systems utilizing a single arbitrator or mediator-arbitrator chosen by the Labour Minister. Such systems were set up largely to remedy some of the deficiencies long apparent with the conventional arbitration process, such as its costliness and lengthy time delays (Thornicroft, 2001). As we will note in more detail in Chapter 12, the evidence to date (i.e., Rose, 1986) suggests that expedited arbitration systems have indeed managed to achieve significant time and money savings without (apparently) resulting in any decline in the quality of awards.

Courts

The third institution through which LRL is administered is the court system. Prior to LRL, all labour-related legal matters were dealt with in the courts. As noted above, the outcomes were seldom favourable to workers, given that judges, in the words of Harry Arthurs (1988:19), proved "singularly inventive" in finding remedies to help protect employers against workers and labour unions, including a broad range of injunctions, severe limitations on picketing and union organizing, and convictions on both civil and criminal conspiracy charges. Even during the early postwar period (Carter, 1995:66), courts continued to exercise substantial power in regulating strikes, picketing, and bargaining-table behaviour. As the role of labour boards has expanded, that of the courts has diminished. While in principle the courts continue to play an important role, given their power to review arbitral and labour board decisions, enforce provincial labour acts, and interpret the Canadian Constitution (Carter, 1995:69), in practice their only remaining function of any importance is issuing injunctions limiting or, in some cases, barring picketing altogether (see Godard, 1994:297).[27] As was noted earlier in the chapter, fears that the *Charter of Rights and Freedoms* would be used to return control over most labour-related matters to the courts have thus far proved largely unfounded, as the courts have generally been reluctant to use the document to reshape the IR system (Carter, 1995:70). However, there is always the possibility that the courts could start to assume a more activist role, justifying it on Charter-related grounds.

RECENT TRENDS IN LRL

As we noted earlier, there has been little *fundamental* change in Canadian labour relations legislation since the passage of the *Public Service Staff Relations Act* in 1967. Even the *Charter of Rights and Freedoms*, which came into effect in 1982, has had but limited impact on labour-related matters. Nonetheless, subtler changes of a more incremental nature *have* been occurring, and the pace of these changes appears to have picked up over the past five years or so.

One of the most significant recent developments has been a growing tendency to apply external legislation, particularly human rights legislation, to the interpretation of collective agreements. The duty to accommodate minority group members, people with disabilities, and others inadvertently discriminated against by workplace arrangements or collective agreement provisions has been held to apply up to the point of undue hardship. In some cases, arbitrators have held that this duty entails providing special work schedules for people whose religion forbids them to work on certain days; in others; it has led to the rewriting of collective agreement provisions or the waiving of their application (R. Jackson, 2001; Carter, 1997).

This trend toward the convergence of individual employment legislation and the collective agreement interpretation has generally not benefitted unions. As Joseph Rose and Gary Chaison (2001:57) have noted, one major result of the trend is that "[W]orkers increasingly receive or expect to receive industrial justice (e.g., protections against discrimination, layoffs or wrongful discharge) through the law as individuals rather than as group members during collective bargaining." This in turn may lead workers to feel less need for and commitment to unions than they did in the past.

Other trends in LRL have likewise been moving in the direction of a greater individualization of collective bargaining. Of particular note here are the recent moves, in many jurisdictions, away from a card count toward a mandatory vote for union certification, and the growth in employer freedom to communicate provisions. Taken together, these policy shifts suggest that labour boards today may now be prepared to entertain a more active role for employers in the union certification process and a greater degree of communication between employers and individual employees, even at times on subjects that have customarily been addressed between employers and unions at the bargaining table. In addition, at a time when there is clearly increasing pressure to harmonize Canadian to American labour relations standards, these policy shifts represent a discernible, albeit gradual move in the direction of American-style regulation of labour relations—a style marked, in particular, by aggressive employer campaigning against unions during certification drives, and by a willingness to engage in officially proscribed labour practices if that is what it takes to become or remain union-free. Thus, while it would be premature to speak of convergence of the Canadian and American legislative regimes as a short-to-medium term possibility, the recent evidence suggests that long-term moves in that direction may already have begun.

QUESTIONS FOR DISCUSSION

1) Get a copy of your province's labour relations act. Read it. Pay special attention to its preface or introductory paragraphs explaining its purpose. Does its purpose seem to be more closely related to maintaining industrial peace and promoting collective bargaining or to promoting economic growth?

2) What's the rationale for labour relations legislation (LRL)?

3) Describe the main stages in the evolution of Canadian LRL.

4) What are some important provincial variations? Which ones may be of particular importance to union membership growth or decline?

5) What are some distinctive features of Quebec LRL? Do any aspects of the Quebec system seem worth adopting elsewhere?

6) How is LRL administered in Canada?

7) How much effect has the Charter had on Canadian LRL?

8) What has been the impact of the duty to accommodate on the interpretation of Canadian LRL? What don't we yet know about that impact?

9) Discuss some of the ways in which Canadian LRL has become more oriented toward the individual in recent years. Do you think this evolution has been healthy, overall?

10) What are some issues which in your view Canadian LRL in general (or your province's act in particular) should be addressing but isn't?

SUGGESTIONS FOR FURTHER READING

Adell, Bernard. (1988). Law and industrial relations: The state of the art in common law Canada. In G. Hébert et al. (Eds.) *The state of the art in industrial relations*. Kingston and Toronto: Queen's Univ. IRC and the Univ. of Toronto Centre for Industrial Relations. Contains a very useful discussion of perspectives on labour law.

Beatty, David. (1987). *Putting the 'Charter' to work: Designing a constitutional labour code*. Montreal: McGill-Queen's Univ. Press. Few labour lawyers or academic industrial relationists share Beatty's faith in the Charter, but he makes a compelling case nonetheless.

Carter, Donald. (1997). "The duty to accommodate: Its growing impact on the grievance arbitration process." *Relations Industrielles, 52(1)*. An important article that shows just how far human rights legislation has affected arbitrators' interpretation of collective agreements.

Weiler, Paul. (1980). *Reconcilable differences: New directions in Canadian labour law*. Toronto: Carswell. A lucid, often witty, and always thought-provoking discussion by a man who, as chair of the B.C. labour relations board during its glory days, was "present at the creation" of many major innovations in Canadian labour law.

CHAPTER 9

LABOUR RELATIONS AND COLLECTIVE BARGAINING IN THE PUBLIC SECTOR

"Blackboard Jungle."
Thousands of teachers could
well lose their jobs in ongoing
educational restructuring
across Ontario.

The public sector is of critical importance in the Canadian IR system because of the often essential nature of the work it performs and because public sector strikes can have severe consequences for the general public. It is also important because roughly half the country's union members work there, and because it has recently been under severe stress due to government cutbacks and restructuring. After noting these points and indicating who should be considered a public sector employee, we begin with a discussion of the evolution of public sector collective bargaining, an evolution quite different from that of collective bargaining in the private sector, paying special attention to the difficulties of the past decade. From there, we go on to consider some special features of public sector bargaining, including

employee and employer differences, legislative differences, the narrower scope of bargaining generally permitted there, and special dispute resolution methods such as conventional and final-offer arbitration and the controlled strike. We conclude the chapter with a look at future prospects for collective bargaining in the public sector.

THE IMPORTANCE OF THE PUBLIC SECTOR

The public sector is important to IR students for a variety of reasons. First and perhaps foremost is the often essential nature of the work it performs. Public sector workers teach our children, care for our sick, and look after the needs of social assistance recipients, in addition to performing a host of other jobs ranging from garbage collection and snow removal to issuing driver's and marriage licences. In many cases, there is no readily available substitute for the services provided through the public sector (Gunderson and Reid, 1995:158). If a shoe factory goes on strike, it is normally easy enough to obtain another brand of shoe. But if public schoolteachers go on strike (as happened in 1997 and 1998 in Ontario), parents can't simply turn around and find another school. If public transit workers go on strike (as happened several times in 2001 in various Alberta and B.C. cities), people can try to get to work or to medical appointments some other way, but the result is a serious inconvenience for many, real hardship for some, and frayed nerves, snarled traffic, and fouled air all around. Thus the effects of public sector strikes tend to be more severe than those of private sector ones (Gunderson and Reid, 1995), and also more readily apparent.

The public sector is also important because it makes up a sizeable share of the country's work force and a very large share indeed of its union membership. In recent years, public sector unions and leaders have played an increasingly important role in the Canadian labour movement (Rose, 1995:47). With their high proportion of female members, the public sector unions have become leaders in the fight for paid maternity leave and employment and pay equity (Swimmer and Thompson, 1995).

Finally, the public sector is important to IR students because of the state of crisis it has been in, not just in Canada but throughout most of the industrialized world (Beaumont, 1995). During the 1990s, faced with growing and seemingly intractable deficits, and increasingly unable or unwilling to balance the books by increasing taxes, governments everywhere sought to reduce the one cost seemingly within their control: that of public sector workers' compensation. Although there were some exceptions, cost reductions were generally not obtained through collective bargaining (Swimmer and Thompson, 1995; Swimmer, 2000). Across the country, governments resorted to legislation freezing public sector pay or even reducing it, sometimes by as much as 8.5 percent (Fryer, 1995).[1] In addition, Canadian governments have adopted such strategies for reducing public sector labour costs as privatization, contracting out, downsizing, reorganization of work, and a greater use of "atypical" work arrangements such as part-time or temporary work, fixed-term contracts, homework, and even volunteers (Rose, 1995:35).

Though the deficits of the 1990s have now turned into surpluses in most jurisdictions, the restructuring, cutbacks, and public sector pay restrictions have largely continued. Public sector workers have also been angered by the heavier workloads resulting from governments' failure to replace colleagues let go in the earlier wave of downsizings. Not surprisingly, such government tactics have led to increased union militancy and a rash of public sector strikes all across Canada. The year 2001 saw a cross-country wave of health care disputes extending from Nova Scotia and New Brunswick to British Columbia. The same year also saw a series of transit strikes in Calgary and various B.C. cities (including one in Vancouver that lasted four months) and a wave of one-day federal public service strikes conducted by the Public Service Alliance (PSAC), as well as a longer Alliance strike at two major federal museums in Ottawa (this strike is described in more detail in Chapter 11). While the prospect of a full-scale public service

Tensions were high by the end of the sixth week of Calgary's transit strike in 2001. Here, a Calgary police officer (right) is shown moving two striking transit workers from the front of a bus being driven by management, on one of three routes on which the transit company was offering limited service.

strike was averted, largely due to the terrorist events of Sept. 11, 2001, the underlying problems leading to the earlier strikes have remained. At the federal government level, one of the most severe of those problems was the government's apparent lack of credibility in maintaining a restrictive 2.5% wage offer for its employees at a time when senior bureaucrats and members of Parliament had just received large increases.[2] The inconsistency of the government's position was used as the basis for extensive publicity campaigns by both the Alliance and the Professional Institute (PIPSC), the two biggest federal public service unions. During the fall of 2001, all outstanding Alliance groups ratified their tentative agreements with the government, and a number of

PIPSC groups reached tentative agreements as well. But public service workers' underlying dissatisfaction with their employer clearly remains.

Aggravating the situation is the aging of the public sector work force. Across Canada, employers are increasingly being faced with the problem of replacing aging workers due to retire (CLBC, 2000). This problem is likely to be even more severe in the public sector, given that in many jurisdictions, the public sector work force is older than the overall work force (see Lowe, 2001; Auditor General, 2000 and 2001). As a result, issues of recruitment and retention have come increasingly to the fore. Public sector managers, as well as union officials, have warned that continuing labour–management friction can only hurt recruitment at a time when government is facing increasingly severe competition from the private sector for talented employees (see Fryer, 2000 and 2001). But it remains to be seen to what extent governments are prepared to move beyond traditional adversarial views of public sector industrial relations and to start to create a climate conducive to the recruitment and retention of talented Canadians. The issue is one we shall revisit at the end of the chapter.

Who Is a Public Sector Worker?

For the purposes of this discussion, the public sector includes the federal and provincial civil services, municipalities, health care, and education.[3] Between 1977 and 2000, the percentage of working Canadians employed in the public sector remained relatively steady at between 21 and 24 percent; however, this apparent stability masks important changes occurring in many parts of the public sector. Since the mid 1980s, certain parts of that sector, notably health care, education, and municipal work, have grown more rapidly than others (Rose, 1995:31; see also Table 9.1). Between 1984 and 1994, provincial government employment grew only modestly, while federal government employment was largely stagnant (Rose, 1995). Since 1991 (see Table 9.1), there has been a gradual but steady decline in the percentage of Canadians employed by the public sector, a decline driven mainly by an ongoing decline in public administration (direct government employment), which now has fewer employees than it did two decades ago despite the growth in the Canadian population since then. During that same period, the number employed in education increased by about one-third, while the number employed in health and welfare increased by about 60 percent. Whereas in 1977, the three sub-sectors (public administration, education, and health care) were of roughly equal size, by 2000 health care employed almost half of all Canadian public sector workers, with education accounting for slightly over one-quarter and public administration, slightly under.

Because union density rates are far higher in the public than in the private sector— 71 percent as compared to 18 percent in 2001 (Akyeampong, 2001), public sector workers make up a much larger share of the country's union members than of its work force. Rose (1995:24) estimates that in 1992, public sector unionists accounted for almost 55 percent of the country's union membership, a significant increase from its 43 percent share in 1984 (Rose, 1995:23). Since 1991, as we noted above, there have been declines in employment in public administration, due mainly to downsizing, privatization, and contracting-out. These declines have led to drops in membership in a number of public sector unions, particularly in the federal public service. As Rose (1995:25) notes, the PSAC had been in a decline for more than a decade even before the major restructuring exercises of the mid 1990s, which reduced its membership still further. Still, high density rates allowed the public sector to account for over half the country's union membership in 1998 (Akyeampong, 1999). While this rate could decline owing to continuing public sector cutbacks in some jurisdictions such as British Columbia (to be discussed later in the chapter), public sector unionists are almost certain to remain a critical element of the country's labour movement for the foreseeable future.

THE DEVELOPMENT OF PUBLIC SECTOR UNIONISM

Why Public Sector Unionism Developed Slowly

Two important facts about the growth of Canadian public sector unionism should be noted at the outset. First, it came a good deal later than private sector unionism. Most

Table 9.1

EMPLOYMENT (IN THOUSANDS), CANADIAN PUBLIC SECTOR AND VARIOUS SUB-SECTORS SELECTED YEARS 1977–2000

Year	Pub. Adm.	Education	Health/ Welfare	Total Pub.	Total	Pub. as % of total
1977	723.8	716.9	796.2	2236.9	9978.2	23.4
1981	793.3	732.1	931.2	2456.6	11 398.0	21.6
1987	769.4	788.4	1148.5	2706.3	12 320.7	22.0
1991	846.3	860.7	1312.7	3019.7	12 850.6	23.5
1996	810.2	908.4	1393.5	3112.1	13 462.6	23.1
1997	795.3	914.1	1390.6	3100.0	13 774.4	22.5
1998	781.2	935.0	1426.3	3142.5	14 140.4	22.2
1999	774.2	982.6	1444.4	3201.2	14 531.2	22.0
2000	761.7	974.8	1526.4	3262.9	14 909.7	21.9

Pub. Adm. = Public Administration
Total Pub. = Total public sector employment (sum of public administration, education, and health and welfare). Government enterprise employees are not included.
Data used are unadjusted annual averages for the various years.
Note: There are some relatively minor differences in employment figures between the 1996 and 2000 editions of Historical Labour Force Statistics used in this table. These differences do not affect the overall trends shown above.

Source: Statistics Canada, Cat. No. 71-201-XPB (Historical Labour Force Statistics), 1996 edition (for 1977 and 1981); 2000 edition (for all other years).

Canadian public sector workers did not acquire the right to join unions until after the passage of the *Public Service Staff Relations Act (PSSRA)* in 1967—23 years after private sector workers acquired that right through *PC 1003* (discussed in the labour history and labour law chapters). Such a time lag between the granting of private and public sector union rights is quite normal in Western industrialized countries. In the United States, the lag between the *Wagner Act* and President Kennedy's executive order granting federal government employees limited bargaining rights was 26 years (Mills, 1989:536–537). Likewise, there was a lag of several decades between private and public sector bargaining rights in such European countries as France (Lorwin, 1954) and Sweden (Johnston, 1962).[4] The reason for such a lag is that the problem of providing essential public services under an IR regime that permits public sector workers to strike is one that few governments seem ready to confront until they have had substantial experience with private sector disputes.

The second important fact about Canadian public sector unionism is that, in contrast to private sector unionism, which developed rather slowly, it "emerged full-blown in a very compressed time span" (Ponak, 1982:343). In 1960, aside from some outside municipal workers, public schoolteachers (Ponak, 1982:344), and those in the province of Saskatchewan, very few public sector workers had joined unions. By the mid to late 1970s, the vast majority had (Ponak, 1982:350). The extremely rapid evolution of public sector collective bargaining meant that certain growing pains were inevitable. In particular, finding appropriate bargaining structures and dispute resolution procedures proved (and continues to prove) extremely difficult (Ponak, 1982).

The Early Years: Public Employee Associations

The late emergence of Canadian public sector collective bargaining should not be taken to mean that public sector employees never engaged in any form of collective action before 1967. There was some form of public sector employee organization as early as the late nineteenth century (Rose, 1995:31), and by the end of the First World War, associations of public employees had become fairly prominent (Ponak, 1982:345; Fryer, 1995:347). These associations operated quite differently from trade unions. Among other things, they sought to avoid confrontation with employers, had no compulsory membership requirements, did not affiliate with labour federations, and included management personnel up to the most senior levels (Ponak, 1982:345). While the associations undertook various social activities, they also played a consultative role by presenting to government employees' concerns about wages and working conditions (Fryer, 1995:347).

Throughout the pre-war period and well into the postwar period, such consultation marked the limit of permissible collective action for the vast majority of Canadian public sector employees. Before the Second World War, with even most private sector workers effectively barred from joining unions due to employer opposition and the lack of protective legislation, any significant degree of public employee organization was out of the question.[5] After the war, labour relations legislation in every jurisdiction except Saskatchewan continued to exclude public sector workers, other than some municipal workers (see Graham, 1995) and a few public school-teachers. Public employers were generally opposed to unionism on the grounds that collective bargaining would inevitably lead to strikes and thus to disruption of essential services and possibly even threats to public safety (Ponak, 1982:347). Another, even more fundamental basis for opposition to public employee unionization was the sovereignty notion (see Fryer, 1995), whose proponents maintain that government bodies such as legislatures are vested with certain powers, especially over fiscal matters, that cannot be shared or taken away. Collective bargaining would, it was argued, be unconstitutional in that it would diminish those powers by forcing revisions in government budgets (Ponak and Thompson, 1989:376–377). The clearest statement of the doctrine was made in 1964 by Quebec Premier Jean Lesage: "The Queen does not negotiate with her subjects!" (Ironically, just a year after issuing this lofty pronouncement, Lesage found himself essentially doing just that, as his province became the second, after Saskatchewan, to grant public sector workers full collective bargaining rights, including the right to strike.)

In addition, many public sector workers, particularly white-collar and professional ones, didn't like what they saw traditional unionism as representing. Many were skeptical about the possibilities of collective action and most disliked the adversarial tone characteristic of union–management relations in industrial settings. Professionals generally believed collective action, especially strikes, to be unprofessional; historically most had worked under a collegial system whereby their views were incorporated into management decisions (Thompson, 1982) and could rely on professional associations to protect their economic self-interest. Others believed that the nature of their public service obligations, including particularly the need to maintain continuous service, ruled out collective bargaining (Ponak, 1982:346). It should also be noted that, prior to the Second World War, most government departments and other public sector organizations were generally quite small. For the most part, those working in such organizations would have known their co-workers and immediate superiors and subordinates quite well. In such small, intimate organizations, it may have been easier to work out problems informally than it would be later on, when government departments and other public sector organizations grew into large, impersonal bureaucracies (see Heron, 1989).

Association-Consultation: The NJC Experience

Through the early 1960s, the most common form of public employee action was association-consultation, whereby members of employee associations would consult, either formally or informally, with public sector management to express employees' concerns regarding pay, working conditions, and other aspects of the employment relationship. Perhaps the best-known consultative body was the National Joint Council (NJC), established in 1944 to address the needs of federal government employees. Comprising representatives from about a dozen civil service staff associations (the Staff Side) and senior government officials (the Official Side), the NJC would meet when necessary to consider such issues as recruitment, training, hours of work, promotion, discipline, tenure, pay, health, welfare, and seniority (Ponak, 1982:348). When the two sides managed to reach agreement on an issue, a recommendation would be made to Cabinet. Since the Council included senior government officials, the idea was that its recommendations would be quickly accepted by the government. All too often, this did not happen. For one thing, the scope of discussable issues was narrower than the Staff Side had expected. Most notably, wages were outside the NJC's jurisdiction, which forced the associations to submit salary briefs directly to the government (Ponak, 1982). Another serious problem was the lack of any mechanism to resolve disputes between the two sides. If the Official Side said "No," the matter was determined unilaterally by government (Ponak, 1982). These and various other inherent weaknesses had the effect of breeding considerable frustration on the part of federal government employees (Ponak, 1982:349).[6]

By the 1950s, the NJC's lack of any real power had caused an increasing number of staff associations to question its value. Throughout the 1950s and into the 1960s, the lack of wage increases, the rapid growth of government departments into large, impersonal bureaucracies, and a general climate of social change and questioning of authority helped move most government employees away from association-consultation and towards conventional trade unionism (Heron, 1989; Ponak, 1982:349). Recognizing that consultation wasn't meeting their members' needs, the associations began deleting no-strike clauses, excluding management personnel, hiring full-time staff, and affiliating with major labour federations such as the CLC (Ponak, 1982). The "last straw" was when John Diefenbaker's minority Conservative government rejected an NJC-recommended wage increase as inflationary (Swimmer, 1995:368–369). After his government fell (over a different issue), public service bargaining rights became a major issue in the ensuing election campaign, and the Liberals, under Lester Pearson, promised that, if elected, they would grant those rights with binding arbitration (Swimmer, 1995:369).

Transition to Collective Bargaining

Elected in 1963, Pearson and his Liberals had struck a commission to develop a model for public service bargaining when they were overtaken by a series of events, of which the most important was an illegal nation-wide postal strike in 1965 (Swimmer, 1995). The strike, to which most Canadians were reasonably sympathetic (Swimmer, 1995), apparently made government officials realize that, for many public employees, arbitration would no longer suffice. Also propelling the Liberal government towards granting fuller public service bargaining rights was its tenuous minority position, with the balance of power held by the pro-labour NDP. When, after the success of the postal strike, many of the old associations began demanding the right to strike, the government (as a matter of political expediency) came up with the then-novel choice of procedures mechanism (Swimmer, 1995), which it later enshrined in the *Public Service Staff Relations Act (PSSRA)*.

The *PSSRA* and Its Impacts

Passed in 1967, the *PSSRA* gave federal government employees the right to join unions. The unions were given the right to choose between binding interest arbitration and the conventional conciliation-strike route at the start of each bargaining round. To protect the public safety, union members designated as essential are not allowed to strike. To compensate for this limitation on the right to strike, the employer is not allowed to lock workers out. The legislation also created the Public Service Staff Relations Board (PSSRB) to administer the act. One of the Board's major functions was to determine appropriate public service bargaining units. The PSSRB determined those bargaining units along occupational rather than departmental lines, which meant a complicated system of 76 bargaining units (*PSSRA*, section 78[1]).[7]

After passage of the *PSSRA*, public sector unionization grew very quickly. There were three reasons for this. First, the existing associations proved an ideal membership base for the public service unions. For the most part, association members joined one of the public service unions en masse, eliminating the need for extensive membership campaigns (Ponak, 1982:350). Second, since public employers generally accepted unionization, certification could proceed quite rapidly once the unions had signed up the old association members. Finally, the *PSSRA* was to set in motion a wave of legislation providing first provincial government employees (Fryer, 1995:343) and then other public sector workers, such as teachers and nurses, with collective bargaining rights. By the early 1970s, every province had granted its employees the right to join unions (Fryer, 1995). Some provinces adopted a variation of the *PSSRA*, providing the right to strike; others (including Alberta and Ontario[8]) adopted an administrative model with binding arbitration as the dispute resolution procedure (Fryer, 1995:345–346).

Public sector unionization had a dramatic effect on both the size and character of the Canadian labour movement. Between 1965, when Quebec gave its employees the right to unionize, and 1978, the end of the great wave of public sector legislation, Canadian union membership more than doubled from 1.59 million to 3.28 million. The country's union density rate also increased sharply, from 29.7 percent to 39.0 percent (Chaison, 1982:149). No less dramatic was the change in the labour movement's character. In 1960, most union members were male and blue-collar (Ponak and Thompson, 1995:423). By the 1970s, many were women and many of the male members were white-collar workers or professionals. The Canadian Union of Public Employees (CUPE) had become the country's largest union (Morton, 1995:149). Its heavily female membership and those of other public sector unions would push demands for maternity leave, flexible work hours, and anti-discrimination provisions, while professionals and white-collar workers pushed professional development issues, such as support for in-service education and travel to conferences (see Ponak, 1982:351).

From the 1960s through 1975, public sector unions negotiated significant improvements in wages and working conditions. Special attention was paid to the correction of long-standing salary anomalies in lower-paid, largely female-dominated job classifications (Fryer, 1995:349). Throughout most of this period, public sector collective bargaining operated quite well with only moderate government interference in the form of back-to-work legislation, much of that being in Quebec (Ponak and Thompson, 2001:435).[9]

End of the Golden Age

This "Golden Age" of public sector collective bargaining, as it has since become known, ended abruptly on Thanksgiving Day 1975, with the federal government's imposition of a three-year program of wage and price controls. (These were discussed extensively in the labour history chapter.) While the controls applied to all workers, they appear to have demonstrated to government the political advantages of restraining public sector compensation (Ponak and Thompson, 1995:444).

At this time, as well, a number of governments began to take a harder line in their approach to labour issues generally and public sector labour issues in particular.[10] At least in part, they may have been responding to growing public outrage at the frequent, lengthy strikes in the Montreal Transit system and the post office, a feeling that the highly publicized "public be damned" attitude of certain postal union leaders did little to diminish (Swimmer, 1995:385–386). In 1978, as inside postal workers were negotiating their first agreement after the end of controls, the federal government passed legislation to extend their contract until after the upcoming federal election (Swimmer, 1995), confident that the postal workers would find little sympathy from a public that had been deprived of mail service for six weeks three years earlier. The late 1970s also saw sharp reductions in federal government employment levels, which up till then had been increasing steadily since the beginning of the decade (Swimmer, 1995:377, Table 3). On another front, the government moved to restrict government employees' bargaining rights substantially in a series of amendments to the *PSSRA* introduced in 1978. While the amendments, including restriction of the right to strike, extension of managerial exclusions, introduction of the lockout right, and the tying of arbitration awards to private sector compensation norms, were eventually withdrawn in the face of strong public opposition (Thompson and Ponak, 1995:427), they pointed the direction for future federal public service labour policy. In Quebec, the government took the first steps towards the comprehensive essential services legislation it passed in 1982 (Hébert, 1995:214).

Perhaps not surprisingly, public sector unions responded to these developments with a show of increased militancy. For example, they were among the leaders in the labour movement's nationwide protest against the Trudeau government's wage and price controls. Beginning in 1976, the public sector share of total person-days lost to strikes began to increase (Gunderson and Reid, 1995:138–139). Starting around 1980, the percentage of disputes settled through arbitration began to decline, suggesting, among other things, a preference for strike action as opposed to arbitration on the part of public sector workers (Ponak and Thompson, 1995:437). The public sector also began to feature high grievance rates (Ponak and Thompson, 1995:429). Overall, public sector union members were starting to behave more like their private sector counterparts, due to an increasingly difficult economic environment, as well as the growing restrictions placed on their activities by governments across Canada.

The 1980s: Wage Controls and Restraint

In 1982, the federal government responded to a second wave of inflation by imposing another round of controls. This time the controls were applied exclusively to wages and only in the public sector. By 1983, every province had followed Ottawa's lead and limited public sector compensation in some way or another (Ponak and Thompson, 1989), six provinces adopting formal control programs of their own (Fryer, 1995:350). The harshest measures were taken in Quebec, where public sector workers saw their pay rolled back by about 20 percent (Hébert, 1995:222), and in British Columbia, where a right-wing government not only imposed a public sector wage freeze, but also made drastic (25 percent) cuts in government employment levels (Morton, 1989:177; Thompson and Ponak, 1992:308). In Alberta, where government employees and many other public sector workers did not have the right to strike, arbitrators were ordered to take the government's ability to pay into account in fashioning public employee arbitration awards (see Haiven, 1995:246).

The wave of retrenchment wasn't limited to compensation issues. In 1982, in the wake of a disagreement over designation levels in an air traffic controllers' dispute, the Supreme Court of Canada ruled that the government had the sole right to determine the level of service to be provided (Swimmer, 1995:381). The decision in effect removed most of the PSSRB's adjudicative role and led to a sharp increase in federal public service designation levels after 1982 (Swimmer, 1995:379–381). In 1983, the Alberta government passed legislation outlawing hospital strikes in the province (Haiven, 1995:254). Meanwhile, in Quebec, a government weary of the public sector strikes that it had often been forced to end through legislation, in 1982 established an Essential Services Council to manage and maintain essential services during public sector disputes (Boivin and Déom, 1995:471). Among other things, the essential services legislation compels the parties to come up with an agreement on the definition of essential services before any strike can become legal. Three years later, the Quebec government placed further restrictions on public sector unions with its 1985 *Act respecting the process of negotiation of the collective agreements in the public and parapublic sectors*. This act gave the Treasury Board all but complete control over the collective bargaining process (Boivin, 1989:429), significantly increasing restrictions on public sector strikes and removing the right to strike completely for all matters negotiated at the local as opposed to provincial level (Boivin, 1989:429). While the legislation was bitterly opposed by the province's unions (Boivin, 1989:430), their opposition was unavailing, although they did have the satisfaction of seeing the government that had introduced it defeated in the December 1985 provincial election.

The attack on public sector unions went farthest in British Columbia where, in 1987, a sweeping revision of labour relations legislation sought to shift the balance of power away from workers and unions and towards employers (Shields, 1990). Though the B.C. government's attack on labour was not confined to the public sector, its effects were felt most sharply there. Among other things, Bill 19, passed by the Social Credit government of William Vander Zalm, replaced the province's tripartite labour relations board with an Industrial Relations Council headed by a commissioner selected by the government (Shields, 1990:52). This "labour czar" was given sweeping powers to impose mediation, binding conventional or final-offer arbitration, or a public interest inquiry board on the bargaining process (Shields, 1990:58). With regard to essential services, the Labour Minister was given the power to declare a category of workers essential whenever a dispute posed a threat to the province's economy or to residents' health, safety, and welfare. In the public sector, collective bargaining was subjected to the "ability to pay" clause, which made the government's ability to pay the primary consideration in all public sector settlements. In effect, this marked the abolition of free public sector collective bargaining over wages and its replacement with a state of permanent[11] wage controls, with compensation levels to be determined unilaterally by Cabinet (Shields, 1990).

The 1990s: Retrenchment and Restructuring

The 1990s were to prove even more difficult for public sector workers than did the 1980s. In addition to continuing the previous decade's public sector wage freezes and rollbacks and (in many cases) suspension of collective bargaining (Fryer, 1995:350), governments across Canada reduced the scope and size of their operations, driven partly by massive deficit and debt levels and partly by an ideological shift back toward free market economics. As a result, public sector bargaining systems all across Canada faced their most severe stresses since the beginning of wide-scale public sector collective bargaining (see Swimmer, 2000; Ponak and Thompson, 2001). Starting in the late 1980s, such developments as privatization, contracting-out, and the use of short-term and temporary contracts all served to put public sector workers' jobs increasingly at risk (Rose, 1995:35). Not surprisingly, given the growing lack of job security and what Joseph Rose has described as governments' "uncanny ability to provoke public sector unions" (Rose, 1995:47), those unions began to take an increasingly militant line, urging their members to vote against governing parties in elections, waging aggressive publicity campaigns against the government policies that were costing members their jobs, and accounting for an increasingly large share of the country's strike incidence, even in the face of severe restrictions on their right to strike.

The Federal Government and the 1991 Public Service Strike

Once again, the federal government set the tone for public sector bargaining across the country. On February 26, 1991, Finance Minister Michael Wilson told federal government employees that any wage increases could only be achieved at a proportional cost in jobs (Fryer, 1995:351; Swimmer, 1995:398).[12] Moreover, annual wage increases greater than 3 percent would not be considered for the next three years (Swimmer, 1995:398). This hard-line stance would lead to a full-scale public service strike, the first in the country's history, in September of 1991. Though in one sense federal government employees could be said to have lost the strike, since the government legislated them back to work and unilaterally extended their old agreement with a wage freeze for the first year and a 3 percent increase for the second (Swimmer, 1995:399–400), in another sense they and their union, the Public Service Alliance of Canada (PSAC), may have come out ahead. Prior to the strike, many members of the general public appear to have shared government officials' prevailing view of government employees as underworked, overpaid "fat cats."[13] Thanks to an astute public relations campaign and a conciliation board report that recommended a 6 percent increase for PSAC's administrative group in the first year and a smaller amount in the second, the union was able to correct that misperception and demonstrate to the public that the vast majority of federal government employees were hardworking men and women attempting to get by on modest salaries (Swimmer, 1995). The union was also helped in its PR campaign by a PSSRB finding that the government had not bargained in good faith, which demonstrated to the public that the government had in effect provoked the strike it was now trying to outlaw (Swimmer, 1995:400).

The New Liberal Government: Different People, Same Policies

While the union's tough stance may have won it both respect and improved pension and work-force adjustment benefits (Swimmer, 1995), it didn't change the government's wage control policy. Indeed, in November of 1992, just slightly over a year after the massive public service strike, the government took an even harder line in unilaterally extending the wage freeze for a further two years. This meant that federal government employees had a wage increase of only 3 percent over a four-year period (Swimmer, 1995:401), a rate far below inflation even in the recessionary 1990s. The new wage freeze destroyed what little credibility the government had left with the public service unions. Abandoning its traditional stance of political neutrality, the PSAC vowed to work for the Conservatives' defeat in the 1993 federal election (Swimmer, 1995:400). But the Liberal victory in that election would provide government employees little solace. Although they had pledged during the campaign to restore free collective bargaining in the public service, once the Liberals took office, their prescription for the public service was more of the same medicine provided by the Conservatives. Wages were unilaterally frozen for a further two years, until 1997; worse still, the government axed 45 000 civil service jobs, or nearly one-quarter of all federal public employment (Swimmer, 1995:405; Craig and Solomon, 1996:362). Those who remained have had to work harder to do both their own work and that of their now-departed colleagues. In addition, thanks to changes resulting from the 1992 *Public Service Reform Act (PSRA)*, it became much easier for the government to replace full-time, permanent employees with short-term, temporary, or casual ones who would receive no benefits and not be eligible for union membership (Swimmer, 1995:397–398). In the face of these and other developments, not least of which was the government's appropriation of the entire federal public service pension surplus (see Fryer, 2000 and 2001), federal government employees found themselves beleaguered on almost every front as the millennium approached.

The Provincial Scene

Federal public service employees have not been alone in facing wage freezes, major downsizing and restructuring initiatives, and more difficult working conditions for those who have managed to keep their jobs. So extensive did the scope of unilateral government action become that across Canada during the 1990s free public sector collective bargaining was the exception rather than the rule.

In the generally depressed Atlantic region, federal cuts to transfer payments hit particularly hard, leaving already hard-pressed provincial governments with little or no room to maneuver. In Newfoundland, the provincial government imposed a one-year wage freeze in 1991, later extending the freeze for a further three years. In 1994, the government's actions in slashing pension fund payments to teachers, closing schools, and reducing teachers' job security provoked a three-week province-wide teachers' strike. Pension contributions to other public employees were reduced that same year, and those employees were required to take 1.5 days off without pay in each of the two succeeding years (Fryer, 1995:353–354). Elsewhere in the region, governments took even harsher measures. In Nova Scotia, after a two-year wage freeze beginning in 1991, the government unilaterally imposed five unpaid days off on all public sector workers in mid-contract, following this action in 1994 with a further 3 percent cut to the pay of all public sector workers earning more than $25 000 per year (Fryer, 1995:354). In Prince Edward Island, the government imposed an 8.5 percent rollback on all public sector compensation in 1994, even though public sector workers had voluntarily agreed to a 6 percent reduction for four months just two years earlier (Fryer, 1995:355).

In Quebec, governments got into the habit of unilaterally extending public sector collective agreements. Successive extensions in 1991, 1992, and 1993 meant that no collective bargaining was conducted over a six-year period, and public sector workers received only a 3 percent wage increase throughout those six years

(Hébert, 1995:226–227). In addition, the 1993 extension was accompanied by legislation ordering all public employers to reduce their wage bill by 1 percent in each of the next two years. As in the case of the Ontario "social contract" discussed below, the reduction was to be achieved by means of unpaid holidays, unless the unions were prepared to agree on other ways of achieving the savings (Boivin and Déom, 1995:476).

While the parties negotiated a three-year agreement in 1995 providing modest pay increases and reduced actuarial penalties on pension plans to encourage early retirements (Déom and Boivin, 2001:500), the agreement was quickly eclipsed by the province's sudden move toward a zero budget deficit in the wake of the PQ government's narrow referendum defeat. The government demanded an $800 million annual reduction in unionized public sector workers' labour costs. Not wishing a repeat of the backlash that followed its imposition of legislation in 1983, the government eventually negotiated a deal with the public sector unions whereby its cost savings would be achieved through voluntary retirements. For the most part, this deal was implemented without resort to legislation (Déom and Boivin, 2001:501). Nonetheless, the government's pursuit of its zero deficit target caused it to embark on widespread cutbacks in health care and education. Along with an extremely unpopular series of municipal restructurings, these cutbacks appear to have cut significantly into the PQ government's popularity, as evidenced by a number of by-election losses in longtime PQ strongholds in October 2001.

In Ontario, an NDP government under Bob Rae, faced with ballooning budget deficits, initially sought to recoup more than $2 billion in savings from its 900 000 public employees without resorting to layoffs (Craig and Solomon, 1996:362). Rather than unilaterally imposing legislation, the government first sought to achieve this objective through a "social contract" to which it hoped the public sector unions would agree (Fryer, 1995:357). When the unions did not agree, the government passed its "Social Contract Act" in 1993. The act, bitterly opposed by the province's labour movement and also by three of the party's own backbenchers, provided for a three-year wage freeze and up to 12 days of unpaid leave per year in the event the wage freezes did not achieve sufficient savings.[14] For the most part, varying numbers of unpaid "Rae Days" proved necessary throughout the public sector (Craig and Solomon, 1996:363). Throughout the life of the social contract, the term would be used contemptuously to refer to what many public sector workers regarded as their betrayal by the party that had come to office with their support and pledged to defend their interests. Probably the legislation's main effect was to seriously weaken, if not destroy, the relationship between the province's labour movement and the NDP. The party failed to win a single Ontario seat in the 1993 and 1997 federal elections and was soundly defeated by Mike Harris' Conservatives in the 1995 and 1999 provincial elections. Not until 2000 did it again win a federal seat in a province once considered one of its strongholds.

Draconian though it may have seemed in 1993, the Rae government's approach now appears almost benign when compared to that of the Conservative government

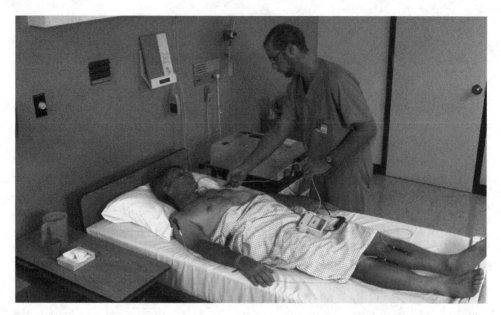

Health care workers like this nurse are coming under increasing stress due to cuts in health care budgets across Canada.

that succeeded it. Abandoning a 50-year tradition of pragmatic, consensus-oriented conservatism in Ontario, the Harris government took office committed to implementing its strongly ideological "Common Sense Revolution" featuring large tax cuts, massive cuts in government spending, and major restructuring in health care and education. In 1996 and early 1997, public service cutbacks led to a series of province-wide one-day general strikes (*Collective Bargaining Review*, 1996–1997). Later in 1997, the province ushered in a new era of educational restructuring when it passed Bill 160. The bill eliminated local school boards, effectively concentrating control over the province's educational system in Toronto. The government's education agenda also includes shorter vacations, longer school days, and more classes with less preparation time for teachers (see Galt, 1998). In protest over these changes, the province's teachers staged a series of strikes in 1997 and 1998 (Green, 1998). The government's changes in health care have been no less dramatic. Major restructuring initiated by the provincial government has led to the closure of many hospitals, the merger of others, a reduction in the services offered patients, and the deinstitutionalization of many long-term patients (Marshall, 1998). Many services formerly provided in hospitals will now be provided through home care of various kinds, and the government has shown itself interested in contracting out much of the home care service now provided by public sector workers (Marshall, 1998). Even as this book is being written, the Ontario government's cutbacks in health care and education are continuing.

The Prairie provinces responded in various ways to the economic crisis of the 1990s. In Manitoba, the government froze public sector wages for a year in 1991. Though normal negotiations took place in 1992, resulting in a three-year contract (Fryer, 1995:356), the government did not allow that agreement to stay in place for long. In February 1993, the Finance Minister asked the public sector unions to accept a "voluntary" reduction in pay and benefits. When the unions did not agree, the government legislated 10-day unpaid layoffs for each of the next two years.

In Alberta, an ideologically driven far-right government under Premier Ralph Klein sought, in effect, to balance the provincial budget on the backs of public sector workers, cutting public expenditures by 20 percent to balance the budget over a three-year period ending in 1997. Cuts ranged from 8.3 percent in social services to 12.4 percent in education and 17.6 percent in health care (Fryer, 1995:360; Thomason, 1995:303). In education, the budget cuts resulted in the complete elimination of adult education funding, a 50 percent reduction in kindergarten funding, and a 5 percent cut in teachers' salaries (Thomason, 1995:303–304). These moves were accompanied by a major consolidation of public school boards and elimination of those boards' taxing authority (Thomason, 1995:280, 303).[15] In health care, still deeper cuts were made without consultation with the unions involved and with little consultation even with management (Haiven, 1995:268). Eventually the government would close two large Calgary hospitals, physically demolishing one of them (Ponak and Thompson, 2001:418). Not surprisingly, health care professionals have long been on a collision course with the government. Meanwhile, the government was equally hard on its own employees, initially forcing them to accept a 5 percent pay reduction comprising unpaid days off and a freeze on increments (Fryer, 1995:360), and later taking away four statutory holidays as well.

Initially, public sector collective bargaining fared better in Saskatchewan, where an NDP government took over in 1991. After a series of rotating strikes by government employees, their union agreed to accept a five-year agreement providing for modest wage increases and a cost-of-living adjustment in its late stages. The agreement expired in September 1996 (Fryer, 1995:359–360). Even here, however, with a government committed to maintaining free public sector collective bargaining, public sector workers have not been immune from restructuring, such as that resulting from the widespread closure of rural hospitals (Ponak and Thompson, 2001:418), or from frequent back-to-work orders when they have gone on strike.[16] Indeed, by the late 1990s, the frequent imposition of back-to-work legislation together with the continuation of rigid, top-down management practices had put even this province, the first to grant its employees the right to bargain collectively (in 1944), into a full-blown public sector labour relations crisis (see Cameron, 2001).

In British Columbia, also an NDP province since 1991, a genuine social contract was arrived at through collective bargaining in the health care sector (Fryer, 1995; Haiven, 1995; Marshall, 1998). The "social accord" in health care, which was negotiated in 1993, broke new ground in Canadian public sector bargaining. Though the agreement provided for a reduction of 4800 acute-care jobs, the reductions were to be achieved through attrition, early retirement, and a reduced work week rather than layoffs (Haiven, 1995:268). Additional features included a modest (1.5 percent) wage hike, an early retirement fund, job security provisions, a labour adjustment program to help workers being transferred to community-care facilities, a guarantee of no expansion in contracting-out, and the involvement of workers in decision making, including decision making regarding new community health programs (Haiven, 1995:268–269; Marshall, 1998). Later, the B.C. government negotiated a new agreement with its own employees that didn't provide for a general wage increase, but did give the union considerable authority in improving work systems and redesigning service delivery (Fryer, 1995:363–364).

With the defeat of the NDP government and its replacement by a right-wing Liberal government in June of 2001, public sector labour relations in B.C. took a hard turn back toward the adversarial mode that had dominated during the 1980s. With the passage of Bill 18 in August 2001, the Labour Minister is entitled to direct the Labour Relations Board to designate education as an essential service without waiting for an investigation. This move could severely restrict teachers' right to strike (Lancaster, 2001, 25:7/8). At about the same time, the government passed legislation ending an overtime ban by the province's nurses (ibid.). In November of 2001, the government announced that the size of the civil service would be reduced by one-third over the next three years, a move expected to cost some 11 500 jobs (B.C. Govt., 2001). The cuts are even deeper than those made during the 1990s by Ontario, Alberta, and the federal government.

DISTINCTIONS BETWEEN PUBLIC AND PRIVATE SECTOR BARGAINING

By now, it should be clear that public sector bargaining differs from bargaining in the private sector in a number of important ways. In this section, we consider in more detail some of the many important differences between collective bargaining in the two sectors. The distinctions we focus on include employer differences, employee and union differences, and legislative and policy differences, including those in dispute resolution mechanisms.

Employer Differences

Government's Dual Role

The single most important employer difference between public and private sector bargaining is the dual role government plays, as the employer of public sector workers and as legislator. This dual role gives it a degree of power that private sector employers can only dream of possessing. Particularly in times of economic crisis, governments often find it irresistibly tempting to pass legislation to achieve objectives they haven't been able to achieve at the bargaining table (Haiven, 1995:243–244; Swimmer and Thompson, 1995:6). As we noted earlier in the chapter, government's desire to reduce inflation or the deficit has often led it to introduce public sector wage controls, freezes, or rollbacks. Government's desire to protect Canadians from the effects of public sector work stoppages has also caused it to make frequent use of back-to-work legislation, particularly since 1975. From 1950 through 1999, the federal and various provincial governments resorted to such legislation on 76 occasions, 54 of them between 1975 and 1994 (Ponak and Thompson, 2001:435). Even when government has not intervened, the threat of such intervention has often been enough to induce unions to accept a settlement proposed by the government, as in the case of the 1991 Toronto Transit strike (Craig and Solomon, 1996:412–413).

The vast power government possesses in its dual role as employer and legislator can be a source of considerable frustration to public sector workers and unions, who often spend months in painstaking negotiations, only to see their hard-earned results overturned by a single stroke of the legislative pen. Government's power may also be a source of frustration to public sector managers, who sometimes find themselves forced to administer a government-imposed solution they don't like and had no hand in fashioning. In this connection, it is worth noting that a 1989 study by David Zussman and Jak Jabes found a significantly higher degree of frustration and lower degree of job satisfaction among public than among private sector managers.

Diffusion of Management Authority

Another key difference between private and public sector collective bargaining is the far greater diffusion of management authority in the latter. In most private sector organizations, management responsibility is well defined and clearly established (Ponak and Thompson, 1995:424). Unions can usually come to the table knowing whom they are bargaining with and (for the most part) where those negotiators stand.

In the public sector, on the other hand, there is typically a "bewildering fragmentation of authority among numerous management officials" (Ponak and Thompson, 1995). In some cases, this fragmentation is inherent. Government departments, for example, normally have both an administrative and a political role. While federal and provincial government employees typically spend most of their time on their administrative functions (i.e., program delivery or policy analysis), reporting to the deputy minister, they ultimately report to the minister, who may assign them to political chores having little to do with their administrative work or even in direct contradiction to it. Given that few ministers are likely to want to give up the power to use government employees more or less as they see fit, this situation seems unlikely to change any time soon. Even where public sector workers do not potentially have political responsibilities, there is still typically a division of management authority between elected officials and the line management who administer public sector organizations on a daily basis (Swimmer and Thompson, 1995:5). Often this division of authority is not a happy one, as elected officials' political agendas or lack of labour relations and administrative experience may lead them into more or less serious conflict with line management (Swimmer and Thompson, 1995).

Such fragmentation is exacerbated by the fact that many public bodies are funded from several different sources, each of which is likely to want to influence how the money is spent. In urban transit, for instance, local transit commissions are generally financed through a combination of user fees, municipal subsidies, and provincial grants. Provincial governments, various municipal governments, citizen groups, and the transit commissions' management all seek to play some role in the collective bargaining process (Swimmer and Thompson, 1995). These groups' objectives may well differ. Citizen groups may be primarily interested in improving or at least maintaining the level of service, while provincial and municipal governments may be more concerned with keeping costs down. The existence of so many different claimants inevitably makes decision making and the collective bargaining process much more complex (Swimmer and Thompson, 1995) Not infrequently, the internal or intraorganizational bargaining that must take place before the union's proposals can be seriously addressed is as complex, if not more so, as the bargaining between the management and union sides (Swimmer and Thompson, 1995:425; also see Walton and McKersie, 1965).

To bypass the difficult and time-consuming multilateral bargaining that normally ensues in such situations, public sector unions may seek (sometimes successfully) to do an "end run" around the management bargaining team to deal directly with a public official they believe will be more sympathetic to their cause, such as a mayor or provincial premier (Ponak, 1982:354–355). While such intervention can bring an end to the particular dispute in question, it may also impose excessive long-term costs on taxpayers in addition to being a source of frustration for public sector managers, who not unjustifiably resent the loss of authority and lack of trust implied by such actions. Even in cases where elected officials do not intervene in such a direct way, political competition between officials of different parties or representing different levels of government can aggravate the problem of management fragmentation still further (Ponak and Thompson, 1995:425), again making bargaining more complex and increasing the frustration of public sector workers and the unions representing them.

Where negotiations haven't been centralized at the federal or provincial level, a common phenomenon over the years has been phantom bargaining (Ponak, 1982:354), whereby formal negotiating authority is ostensibly vested in a management group, such as a health care employers' association, but the key player, in this case the provincial government, that controls the purse strings, is not represented at the table. The absence of parties with any real authority from the bargaining table in such situations has sometimes led unions to refer to the government as the "phantom at the bargaining table" and to complain that without direct government representation, collective bargaining amounts to little more than going through the motions (Ponak, 1982).

In attempting to get around these various difficulties, Canadian governments have tried a number of different approaches. Quebec has customarily taken a highly centralized approach to public sector bargaining (Hébert, 1995; Haiven, 1995:240), although in recent years large-scale disputes resulting from that centralization have induced the government to bring in a degree of decentralization through a two-tier (provincial and local) bargaining system (Hébert, 1995; Boivin and Déom, 1995; Grant, 2000). In health care in that province, and also in New Brunswick, the government actually sits at the bargaining table as the management representative (Haiven, 1995:244). For its part, Saskatchewan has taken a middle-of-the-road position, allowing the employers' association to represent management, but also having a government observer sit at the bargaining table (Haiven, 1995).

Perhaps the most significant recent changes have taken place in British Columbia, where the government has provided for negotiations in seven different public sub-sectors (Ponak and Thompson, 1995:445). Under the 1993 *Public Sector Employers' Act*, each sub-sector other than the provincial civil service has its own employers' association responsible for coordinating human resource activity within the sub-sector, including collective bargaining (Fryer, 1995:362). The government is directly represented in these employer associations and has representatives in each sub-sector's governing body and the power to approve bylaws (Fryer, 1995:362–363). But although the highly centralized B.C. arrangements generally resulted in constructive negotiations, including those leading to the social contract in health care discussed earlier in the chapter, it remained to be seen, at the time of writing, whether these arrangements would survive the change in government that followed the previous NDP government's defeat in the election of June 2001.

Overall, it appears that Canadian governments and public sector employers are as far from consensus as ever about the most appropriate arrangements for public sector bargaining. After several decades of varied experience, most are still "groping for the right organizational form for labour relations" (Ponak and Thompson, 2001:423).

Economics Versus Politics

It's only a slight oversimplification to suggest that the currency of private sector bargaining is money, while that of public sector bargaining is political power. While private sector employers and unions are far from unconcerned about politics, at the bargaining table their major battles tend to be over monetary issues such as wages, benefits, hours of work, and levels of employment. In contrast, though public sector employers and unions are certainly concerned about money, particularly at a time of continuing government budget cutbacks and work force reductions, public sector bargaining itself remains primarily an exercise in political rather than economic power (Swimmer and Thompson, 1995:2).

In private sector strikes, the union's aim is normally to induce employers to make a better offer out of fear of losing business and perhaps permanent market share. In public sector strikes, the aim is more often to turn public opinion against the government, with an eye to pressuring the government into changing those policies that the union feels are hurting its members.

Notably, the costs of disagreement tend to be quite different in the private and public sectors. While private sector strikes almost invariably impose monetary costs, in terms of lost profit and longer-term market share, strikes may actually benefit public sector employers economically, since their revenues remain the same, but their expenses are reduced by the amount of the striking employees' forgone wages and benefits (Ponak and Thompson, 1995:425–426). Here the costs are mainly political ones, particularly in the case of disputes that seriously inconvenience the public for a lengthy period of time, such as postal or transit strikes or strikes of municipal garbage collectors. Irate at the loss of the service in question, angry residents will deluge ministers' or municipal officials' offices with letters, phone calls, faxes, and e-mails demanding the restoration of the service at any cost and threatening to vote the government out of power at the first possible opportunity. Politicians' fear of not being re-elected may help explain why, in good times, striking public sector workers have sometimes received extremely, perhaps even overly generous settlements—and why in bad times they have often been legislated back to work.

A point perhaps not often enough made (see Gérin-Lajoie, 1993) concerns the lack of an economic "bottom line" in public sector bargaining and the effect such a lack may have on union–management relations and the bargaining process. In the private sector, if a firm is losing profits and market share, management and the union may not agree on the cause of the problem, but at least they'll be able to agree there is a problem. The recognition of this common problem and of a common interest in keeping the enterprise afloat may just be enough to get the parties to start thinking about innovative possible solutions. In the public sector, where there normally is no economic bottom line, and where revenues typically have no direct link to either the quantity or quality of the good or service produced (Ponak and Thompson, 1995:426), it's often much harder for the parties to agree on what their problems are, or even necessarily that there is a problem. With no decline in profit or market share to serve as a "wake-up call," public sector managers in times of crisis may see their employees coming into work and apparently doing their jobs as usual, without recognizing that serious morale problems resulting from government restructuring or downsizing have seriously affected the quality of service these employees are providing to the public.

Employee and Union Differences

Employee Differences

By and large, and increasingly so in today's tough economy, public sector workers have the same concerns as private sector ones (Ponak and Thompson, 2001). Job security, the maintenance of real income levels, work hours, and workload are of prime importance in both sectors.

This said, there *are* a number of significant differences between public and private sector employees, and also between the ways in which public and private sector unions tend to operate. Public sector union members are much more likely than their private sector counterparts to be female, professional, and white-collar. In 1998, 58 percent of all public sector union members were female, compared to 22 percent in the private sector (Akyeampong, 1999). In addition, the public sector contains more than its share of unionized white-collar workers, and virtually all the country's unionized professionals (Ponak and Thompson, 2001:424). The high proportion of female members in most public sector unions has led pay and employment equity issues to be of prime concern for these unions. It also helps explain these unions' outrage at the slow settlement of their longstanding pay equity dispute with the government—a settlement reached only in 1999 after 15 years of bickering and several court cases (Thompson and Ponak, 2001: Fryer, 2000).[17] The high proportion of professionals in many public sector unions helps explain these unions' concern with intrinsic issues around the nature of work. Teachers' unions have often bargained (or attempted to bargain) over such issues as class size and preparation time, the latter a key issue in the 1998 Ontario teachers' strike discussed earlier. Likewise, reimbursement of professional dues and fees is an important issue to many public sector unions. Several agreements negotiated by the Professional Institute (PIPSC) with the government, including those of tax auditors, make provision for such reimbursement. As well, the PIPSC's new agreement with its own staff association contains a provision reimbursing employees for membership dues in legal or industrial relations organizations.

Union Differences

THE IMPORTANCE OF PUBLICITY While public sector unions are obviously concerned with specific issues of particular relevance to their members (class size for teachers, shift schedules for nurses), overall their bargaining agendas tend to be fairly similar to those of private sector unions—when they can bargain at all. What's different is the way in which they attempt to achieve their objectives. Given that members of the general public are important stakeholders in all public sector activity, both as consumers of public services and as taxpayers, public sector unionism is inherently political, with many of its efforts directed towards winning and maintaining public support both for public sector unions' specific rights and for the government spending that undergirds the services public sector workers provide. During the 1990s the relative importance of political action and publicity campaigns increased dramatically, due mainly to government restrictions on public sector bargaining activity.

As Swimmer and Thompson (1995:2) note, the media are far more important in public sector than in private sector bargaining, as both sides seek to win the hearts and minds of everyday citizens. This is particularly true during labour disputes. The media played a prominent role both in the 1991 federal public service strike

(Swimmer, 1995:400) and in more recent disputes such as those involving Ontario's teachers and National Gallery employees. But public sector unions' publicity efforts are not confined to times when there is a work stoppage. Most are regularly involved in campaigns aimed both at the general public and their own membership (Lawson, 1998; Marshall, 1998). For example, in 1996 PSAC responded to the federal government's privatization and contracting-out of national parks with an article in the union's magazine, *Alliance* (Mitchell, 1996), following it up later in the year with a direct mail campaign featuring articles that showed the public, in a humorous way, some of the possible effects of the government privatization campaign. More recently, CUPE ran a series of hard-hitting magazine ads (see Chapter 6) dramatizing its attack on Ontario's health care restructuring plan by suggesting that the plan is likely to lead to a two-tier health care system comparable to that of Victorian England. More recently still, during the summer and fall of 2001 both the PSAC and the PIPSC ran ads on Ottawa buses and bus shelters condemning the federal government for its hypocrisy in offering its workers only 2.5% pay increases after granting deputy ministers and Members of Parliament far larger increases. While some observers, such as Warrian (1996), argue that political protest and other such pressure tactics will generally be futile, so long as restrictions on public sector bargaining prevent public sector unions from bringing many of their major concerns to the bargaining table, it is difficult to see what alternative they have.

UNION FRAGMENTATION   Union representation can be quite fragmented in the public sector, particularly in health care and education. In large, industrial settings like auto plants and steel mills, a single union typically represents all employees or at least the great majority of them (Haiven, 1995:241). For the most part, the industrial union model also holds in government departments, although in the federal government, the large number of occupational groupings under the *PSSRA* has led to fragmentation of a different sort (see Swimmer, 1995). This is not the case in health care. In hospital settings (Haiven, 1995), there are normally at least three unions representing health care workers: a nurses' union, a general service union for maintenance and support staff, and a "paramedical" unit for skilled technical staff like dietitians, X-ray technologists, and physiotherapists. To make matters even more complicated, several different unions may be competing for the right to represent the same group of workers (Haiven, 1995:241–242)—a phenomenon likely to become even more common in the near future because of hospital closures and mergers (Marshall, 1998). CUPE represents many hospital maintenance and support staff, but it is far from being the only union in the field. The Service Employees International Union (SEIU), International Union of Operating Engineers, and various government employee unions also represent many of these same workers (Marshall, 1998; see also Haiven, 1995:241–242). The result of this kind of "balkanization" is that bargaining becomes more difficult, since there is a rarely a single union that can come to the bargaining table representing all employees in a provincial sub-sector (Haiven, 1995:241–242). Similar if less pronounced fragmentation exists in the education sector. For example, at the university level, professors are generally represented by a certified independent staff association, while support staff are most often represented by a union such as CUPE or SEIU.

Legislative and Policy Differences

There are a good many legislative and policy differences between the private and public sector. The two most important ones are the far greater degree of fragmentation and variation in dispute resolution methods found in the public sector, and the significantly greater extent to which governments restrict public sector unions' rights with respect to such matters as bargaining-unit determination and the scope of bargainable issues.

Table 9.2

	PUBLIC SECTOR COLLECTIVE BARGAINING LEGISLATION			
Jurisdiction	**Municipal**	**Police**	**Firefighters**	**Hospitals**
FEDERAL	Can. Code	None (RCMP)*	PSSRA	PSSRA
B.C.	Gen. lab. act; Pub. Sec. Employers' Act$	Gen. lab. act; Police/ Fire Act	Gen. lab. act; Police/ Fire Act	Gen. lab. act; Pub. Sec. Employer's Act
ALBERTA	Gen. lab. act	Police Act	Gen. lab. act	Gen. lab. act#
SASK.	Gen. lab. act	Police Act	Fire Dept. Act	Gen. lab. act
MANITOBA	Gen. lab. act	Gen. lab. act; Police Act;	Gen. lab. act; Fire Dept. Arb. Act.	Gen. lab. act; Essential Services Act
ONTARIO	Gen. lab. act	Police Act; Pub Service Act (OPP) Pub. Sector Dispute Resolution Act	Fire Act; Pub. Sector Dispute Resolution Act	Gen. lab. act; HLDAA+
QUEBEC	Gen. lab. act;	Gen. lab. act; Police act++	Gen. lab. act	Gen. lab. act; Pub. Serv. Act
N.B.	Gen. lab. act;	Gen. lab act++	Gen. lab. act++	Pub. Serv. Act Nursing Homes Act

Table 9.2
(continued)

Jurisdiction	Municipal	Police	Firefighters	Hospitals
N.S.	Gen. lab. act	Gen. lab. act	Gen. lab. act	General lab.act
P.E.I.	Gen. lab. act	Gen. lab. act Police Act	Gen. lab. act	Gen. lab. act
NFLD.	Gen. lab. act;	Gen. lab. act Royal Nfld. Constabulary Act	Gen. lab. act; St. John's Fire Dept. Act	Pub. Serv. Act

Jurisdiction	Teachers	Civ. Service	Govt. Enterprise
FEDERAL	*PSSRA*	*PSSRA*	*Can. Code*
B.C.	Gen. lab. act Education Act; Pub. Sector Employers' Act$	Pub. Serv. Act Gen. lab. act	Gen. lab. act;
ALBERTA	Gen. lab. act; Education Act	Pub. Serv. Act	Gen. lab. act
SASK.	Education Act	Gen. lab. act	Gen. lab. act
MANITOBA	Education Act; Gen. lab. act	Gen. lab. act; Civ. Serv. Act	Gen. lab. act
ONTARIO	Education Act; Gen. lab. act	Civ. Serv. Act	Civ. Serv. Act;
QUEBEC	Gen. lab act; Pub. Serv. Act	Gen. lab. act; Pub. Serv. Act; Civ. Serv. Act	Gen. lab. act; Pub. Serv. Act; Civ. Serv. Act
N.B.	Pub. Serv. Act	Pub. Serv. Act	Pub. Serv. Act
N.S.	Education Act	Civ. Serv. Act	Gen. lab. act
P.E.I.	Education Act	Civ. Serv. Act	Geb. lab. act
NFLD.	Education Act	Pub. Serv. Act	Pub. Serv. Act

Division 16 contains specific provisions for hospital employees.
* The RCMP are excluded from unionization rights under both the Canada Labour Code and PSSRA.
+ HLDAA=Hospital Labour Disputes Arbitration Act
++ Subsection 80.1 contains specific measures for municipal and regional police and municipal firefighters.
$The Public Sector Employers' Act, providing for public sector employer associations, applies to all public sector collective bargaining in the province except for the provincial civil service.
‡ Unlike those covered by the main part of Quebec's Code du Travail, police and firefighters are forbidden to strike and must submit disputes to binding arbitration.
Note: Public service acts are general acts applying to several different branches of the public sector. Civil service acts, where applicable, apply only to the provincial civil service or (occasionally) to employees of certain government enterprises.

Source: Applicable statutes from HRDC as of November 1, 2001. http://labour.hrdc-drhc.gc.ca/psait_spila/lmric_irlc/index.cfm/doc/english.

Legislative Fragmentation

For the private sector, each province has a single labour act more or less closely modelled after the American *Wagner Act* (Ponak and Thompson, 1989). While there are some relatively minor differences in dispute resolution procedures, almost all jurisdictions require some type of conciliation before a strike or lockout can become legal.

In contrast, jurisdictions vary greatly with respect to the coverage of particular groups under public sector legislation. At one extreme is Ontario, with separate laws for almost every public sector group, including government employees, teachers, hospital workers, police, and firefighters. At the opposite extreme are the federal jurisdiction and New Brunswick, each of which has a single private sector act and a single public sector one. In between are provinces such as Saskatchewan and British Columbia, which apply their general labour acts to a number of different public sector groups, but have special acts for teachers (in both provinces), for police and firefighters (in Saskatchewan), and for provincial government employees (in B.C.). Quebec (see Hébert, 1995:201 and Boivin and Déom, 1995:473–474) has a hybrid system whereby all groups fall under the jurisdiction of the general labour act, but many groups also have specific legislation governing such things as bargaining structure, the scope of collective agreements, and in particular the maintenance of essential services (see Table 9.2).

The variation in dispute resolution procedures (see Table 9.3) is equally great. Most provinces do not permit police and firefighters to strike, but all grant that right to municipal employees and most grant it to employees of government enterprises. In between, there is little consensus. Seven jurisdictions permit their employees to strike; four (Alberta, Manitoba, Nova Scotia, and P.E.I.) do not. Eight jurisdictions permit teachers to strike, while three (Manitoba, Saskatchewan, and P.E.I.) do not. Likewise, eight jurisdictions allow hospital workers to strike while three (Alberta, Ontario, and P.E.I.) do not.

Most jurisdictions offer little in the way of consistent policy rationale for their choice of public sector dispute resolution methods. P.E.I., which has long had one of the most restrictive labour acts in Canada (Forsey, 1985; Peirce, 1989), does not allow any public sector workers except municipal employees to strike. At the opposite extreme are the federal jurisdiction, where all workers who have the right to bargain collectively have, at least in principle, the right to choose strike action (see Table 9.3), and B.C., where all public sector workers have the right to strike, subject in most cases to essential service designations. In between, New Brunswick and Quebec allow all groups except police and firefighters to strike—an exclusion that would probably make sense to most Canadians given the essential nature of the work performed by these groups. Elsewhere, however, the right to strike seems to have been applied more or less randomly. Alberta, for example, allows teachers to strike, but not its own employees or hospital workers (see Table 9.3). Manitoba is just the opposite; there hospital workers can strike, but teachers and provincial government employees cannot. Ontario allows both teachers and provincial government employees to strike, but not hospital workers; in Nova Scotia, teachers and hospital workers as well as police can strike, but not provincial government employees.

Table 9.3

DISPUTE RESOLUTION PROCEDURES IN VARIOUS PUBLIC SECTOR JURISDICTIONS

Juris.	Municipal	Police	Firefighters	Hospitals	Teachers	Civ. Service
FED.	Strike (Yukon/NWT)	NA	COP*	COP*	COP*	COP*
B.C.	Strike*	Strike*	Strike*	Strike*	Limited Strike*	Strike*
ALB.	Strike	Arb.	Arb.	Arb.	Strike	Arb.
SASK.	Strike	Strike	Strike or Arb.+	Strike	COP$	Strike
MAN.	Strike	Strike++	Arb.	Strike*	Arb.	Arb.
ONT.	Strike	Arb.	Arb.	Arb.	Strike	Strike*
QUE.	Strike*	Arb.	Arb.	Limited Strike*	Limited Strike*	Strike*
N.B.	Strike	Arb.	Arb.	Strike*	Strike	Strike*
N.S.	Strike	Strike	Strike§	Strike#	Limited Strike**	Arb.
P.E.I.	Strike	Arb.	Arb.	Arb.	Arb.	Arb.
NFLD.	Strike	Strike&&	Strike++	Limited Strike§§	Strike	Limited Strike

Note: Most provinces permit government enterprise employees to strike. Arbitration is required in PEI and, for the most part, Alberta. Some provinces subject government enterprise employees to essential service designations.

* Essential services provisions stipulate that certain employees will be or may be required to continue working during a strike.

$ Union choice of arbitration at the request of either party or strike.

+ Arbitration requested by either party is binding only if the constitution of the local union prohibits strikes.

++Except for the city of Winnipeg, where the method is arbitration at the request of either party.

‡ In Quebec, health care and education workers are not permitted to strike over local and regional issues.

§ It should be noted that, at least according to Jackson (1995:317), there have been no recorded strikes by firefighters in Canada. Strikes by police have occurred, but only extremely rarely.

According to Thompson and Swimmer (1995:11), two large hospitals use arbitration instead.

** Nova Scotia schoolteachers are not permitted to strike over local and regional issues.

&& Arbitration is used for members of the provincial police force, the Royal Newfoundland Constabulary.

♯ Arbitration in St. John's, strike elsewhere.

§§ The union can demand arbitration if more than 50 percent of a bargaining unit is designated as essential and thus prohibited from striking. The same is true in the Nfld. civil service. Arbitration may be imposed if there is a state of emergency and the House of Assembly forbids a strike. Hospital employees may not engage in rotating strikes.

Source: Labour Law Analysis, Strategic Policy and International Affairs, Labour Branch of HRDC, as of Nov. 1, 2001. http://labour.hrdc-drhc.gc.ca/psait_spila/lmric_irlc/index.cfm/doc/english.

How has such a fragmented, convoluted, and inconsistent system of public sector bargaining been allowed to evolve? At the end of the day, one can only speculate on the reasons for this evolution. Given the otherwise irrational, even contradictory nature of many of the provisions we have been discussing, it seems likely that local political considerations have played an extremely important if not pivotal role in that evolution (see Drache and Glassbeek, 1992:344).

Bargaining Unit Determination

Another key difference between public and private sector collective bargaining has to do with the way in which bargaining units are determined. In the private sector, as we pointed out in the previous chapter, this determination is normally made by the labour relations board, generally with considerable input from the parties involved (see Ponak and Thompson, 1989:387). Indeed, where the parties agree, the labour board will not normally interfere. Where they do not agree, the board will base its decision largely on what seems likely to make for the most harmonious union–management relationship.

In contrast, public sector bargaining units are most often spelled out in public sector legislation (Fryer, 1995:345). Under the *PSSRA*, federal government employees were initially divided into some 76 different occupational groups (Swimmer, 1995:370), leaving the PSSRB little if any authority to determine bargaining units (Ponak and Thompson, 1989:387).[18] New Brunswick followed the federal government's lead, authorizing a number of occupationally based province-wide bargaining units (Fryer, 1995:345). In contrast, B.C.'s public service act spells out three bargaining units, and a single province-wide unit is named in the legislation of Alberta, Manitoba, Nova Scotia, Ontario, and P.E.I. (Fryer, 1995). Some statutes go even farther, spelling out the only union that can legally represent government employees. While some analysts (i.e., Fryer, 1995:345) suggest that legislative determination of the bargaining agent appears to go against the Charter's "freedom of association" provision, various Supreme Court cases have made it clear that "freedom of association" does not include the right to choose one's own bargaining agent (Thompson and Ponak, 1995:432; Cavalluzzo, 1988).[19]

In an attempt to correct this problem, at least within the federal public service, the Fryer Committee (Fryer, 2001) has recommended that after a two-year 'freeze' on changes in bargaining unit structure, subsequent bargaining unit determination in the federal public service be made by the Canada Industrial Relations Board (CIRB). At the time of writing, however, it remained to be seen whether the government was prepared to implement this recommendation.

Scope of Bargainable Issues

Yet another important difference is the scope of issues that may be negotiated in the private and public sectors. In the private sector, the parties are free to negotiate pretty well any provision they want pertaining to the terms and conditions of employment, so long as it is not illegal. In most public sector acts, the scope of bargainable issues is severely limited. A modified form of the old sovereignty doctrine would appear to apply in some cases. For example, the *PSSRA* does not allow bargaining over any issue that would require parliamentary legislation, except for the appropriation of funds (Swimmer, 1995:371). What this means in practical terms is that many issues that are central to private sector bargaining become management rights in the public sector more or less by default (Swimmer, 1995). These issues include the criteria for appointments, promotions, layoffs, job classification, and technological or organizational change (Swimmer, 1995:371–372). While some of these restrictions may be understandable, given the federal government's need to apply the merit principle to prevent favouritism in appointments and promotions, the merit principle does not explain the government's refusal to allow its employees to bargain over technological change. Even less does it explain the government's refusal to allow its employees to bargain over pensions (Swimmer, 1995:371), a position also taken by every province except Saskatchewan (Fryer, 1995:345).[20]

Most provincial public sector acts are only slightly more liberal than the *PSSRA* with respect to the scope of bargainable issues. Many do allow bargaining over technological and organizational change (Swimmer, 1995:372), but most prohibit bargaining over employee training programs, appointments, and promotions (Fryer, 1995:345). Somewhat more justifiably, perhaps, given the paramilitary nature of fire and police departments, both, in particular the latter, often forbid their employees to bargain over disciplinary issues and superior-subordinate relations (Jackson, 1995:319; Ponak and Thompson, 1995).

As Ponak and Thompson note (1995:431), such severe restrictions on the scope of bargaining may well hurt the bargaining process by creating frustration on the part of unions, thereby preventing trust from emerging. (See also Fryer, 2000 and 2001.) Indeed, the restrictions can themselves be a source of increased conflict, in that the parties may wind up wasting a good deal of time and energy bickering about what can and cannot legally be bargained over, rather than engaging in productive negotiations (Ponak and Thompson, 1995). Nor does restricting the scope of bargainable issues eliminate conflict over these and other issues. For example, during a period in the 1980s when wage controls applied to the federal public service, effectively eliminating government employees' ability to bargain over money, the number of grievances under the *PSSRA* increased sharply (*Current Scene*, 1991), a finding very much in line with the theory of public sector conflict advanced by Hebdon (1992).

Dispute Resolution Procedures

To most Canadians, the single most important difference between public and private sector collective bargaining lies in the different procedures for resolving disputes in the two sectors. As noted earlier, the conciliation-strike routine is all but universal in the private sector. Only very rarely are other procedures, such as back-to-work legislation or the imposition of binding arbitration, invoked, and then only in large federal-jurisdiction strikes with a substantial public interest component, such as railway or airline disputes.

In contrast, the essential (or allegedly essential) nature of much public sector work has led policy-makers to devise a broad array of special dispute settlement procedures for that sector. As these procedures are dealt with in more detail in Chapter 11, they are discussed only briefly here. The alternative public sector procedures discussed here include conventional interest arbitration, final offer arbitration, choice of procedures, and the controlled strike. Other procedures, such as med-arb and back-to-work legislation, have been left to Chapter 11.

Conventional Interest Arbitration

Conventional interest arbitration is the method normally used for resolving disputes involving police, firefighters, and other public sector workers whose services are considered so essential to the public health, safety, or welfare that they cannot be allowed to withdraw them. In addition, as noted earlier, it is also used for many government employees, teachers, and other public sector workers whose work may or may not be truly essential, but whom the government has nonetheless, for whatever reason, forbidden from striking.

Under conventional interest arbitration, arbitrators are normally free, within certain broad limitations, to fashion an award comprising the union's position, the management's position, or their own (Ponak and Thompson, 1989). Starting in the 1980s, some jurisdictions, notably Alberta (Ponak and Thompson, 1995:427), required arbitrators to take the government's ability to pay into account in arriving at public sector awards; however, it is not clear what effect, if any, such statutory provisions had on arbitration awards (Rose, 2000). In general, ability to pay has been held in low repute within the arbitral fraternity (see Sack, 1991), both on the score of its subjectivity and because most arbitrators feel it ties their hands too much in fashioning awards.[21]

The major advantage of conventional, as opposed to final-offer arbitration (discussed below) is that, because arbitrators can "split the difference" in fashioning their awards, those awards are likely to be more acceptable to both sides (Ponak and Thompson, 1989:394). A major disadvantage is that, particularly in cases where parties use arbitration frequently, they can lose their ability to bargain, preferring to leave hard decisions to the arbitrator rather than making them themselves. Most evidence suggests that conventional arbitration systems lead to lower rates of negotiated settlement than systems that allow strikes and lockouts (Ponak and Thompson, 1989, 1995). While final-offer arbitration (FOA) appears to offer a way around this difficulty, it has not thus far been widely adopted in Canada.

The Conservative government in Ontario has made a sustained and multi-pronged attack on interest arbitration since its election in 1995, in the belief that controlling arbitration outcomes would help it achieve its objective of downsizing the public sector and slashing government spending. In 1996, Bill 26 established ability to pay as a permanent feature of public sector pay determination (Rose, 2000:261). In 1997, a new *Public Sector Dispute Resolution Act* went even further, specifying that arbitrators must take into account clauses of the act including those encouraging "best practices that ensure the delivery of quality and effective public services that are affordable to the taxpayer" (ibid., 263). In its initial form, the act would also have replaced mutually acceptable arbitrators chosen in the usual way with a Dispute Resolution Commission staffed by government appointees. This provision was dropped after strong protest from the labour movement (ibid., 263–4). However, the government's next move, the appointment of retired judges in cases where the parties could not agree on an arbitrator, would prove nearly as controversial. The use of these retired judges, who have not necessarily possessed any qualifications in labour law or industrial relations, has led veteran arbitrator Kevin Burkett (quoted in Rose, 2000:264) to complain that the government doesn't trust mutually acceptable arbitrators to come to the 'right' result. Although CUPE was initially unsuccessful in a court challenge to the appointment of a retired judge as arbitrator in a major hospital case,[22] the Divisional Court later quashed an arbitration award involving the Service Employees International Union on grounds that the retired judge chairing the arbitration board had created an "apprehension of bias" and denied the union a fair hearing (Rose, 2000:268).

In public education, the Ontario government imposed even more severe restrictions on arbitration through Bill 62, the legislation ending the second wave of province-wide teacher strikes in 1998. In addition to allowing either party applying to have all remaining issues in dispute settled through mediation-arbitration, the bill restricted arbitral discretion in a number of important ways. Most notably, the bill stipulated that arbitral awards cannot result in a school board incurring a deficit and required the mediator-arbitrator to demonstrate how the school board could meet any increased compensation costs resulting from an award. The bill also precluded awards from interfering with the scheduling of classroom instruction and required arbitrators to accommodate the new funding formula, average class size, and increased instructional time. Finally, it allowed the Labour Minister to appoint the mediator-arbitrator if the parties couldn't agree on one, which again meant the appointment of retired judges (Rose, 2000:275–6). School board officials interviewed by Rose (2000:278) admitted that the arbitral restrictions established through Bill 62, together with the appointment process, clearly favoured them, while arbitrators (ibid., 281) likewise described the process as severely constrained. Rose's stark conclusion is that ". . .the magnitude and restrictiveness of the statutory requirements stripped arbitrators of their independence. . .Driven by statutory requirements, the arbitration process appeared to start and end with appraising the parties' costing models to determine whether a budget deficit was probable" (ibid., 283).

Unionists and others interested in preserving the independence of the arbitration process may draw some comfort from a recent decision of the Ontario Court of Appeal that overturned the Divisional Court's ruling in the CUPE case cited above. In *CUPE and SEIU vs. the Minister of Labour for Ontario* (Nov. 21, 2000), the Court of Appeal(COA) ordered the government to refrain from appointing chairs of boards of arbitration under the *Hospital Labour Disputes Arbitration Act (HLDAA)*, unless such appointments were made from the established roster of experienced arbitrators or involved individuals mutually acceptable to the parties. In its ruling, the COA cited that same "apprehension of bias" which Divisional Court had found in the SEIU case. But the issues raised in the case remain 'live' ones because the Ontario government has since requested, and been granted, leave to appeal the case to the Supreme Court of Canada.

Final-Offer Arbitration (FOA)

Under **final-offer arbitration (FOA)**, arbitrators have no discretion in fashioning their awards. They must choose either the union's or employer's position for the entire package, if that is how the award is being made, or for each issue. The idea behind FOA is that because the risk of "losing" is so great, particularly when the award is being made as a package rather than issue by issue, most parties would rather settle on their own (see Godard, 1994:353–354). FOA has been fairly widely adopted in American public sector legislation, and the evidence suggests that it generally achieves a significantly higher rate of negotiated settlements than does conventional arbitration (Ponak and Thompson, 1995:438). Nonetheless, it has seldom been adopted in Canada, although it was used in 2001 to settle Nova Scotia's health care dispute. One major criticism of this approach is that it can lead to bad collective agreements, at least in cases where both sides submit unreasonable proposals (Ponak and Thompson, 1995). Another is that it can foster a damaging win-lose mentality that will hurt the parties' efforts to build a more constructive relationship. In the Nova Scotia case, where arbitrator Susan Ashley gave the registered nurses their demand of 17 percent over three years but other health care workers received only the government's proposal of 7.5 percent plus a lump sum payment (Lancaster, 2001 (25:7–8)), there is concern that the award, however justified from an economic perspective,[23] would lead to lasting bitterness and resentment within hospitals and other health care facilities.

Choice of Procedures (COP)

Under choice of procedures (COP), one party or the other (in Canada, normally the union) is given the right to choose between the traditional conciliation-strike route and binding arbitration. Initially devised for the *PSSRA*, COP soon spread to a number of provinces and U.S. states (Ponak and Thompson, 1989:396–397). In Canada, the federal government's intention was to come up with a system that would give public service unions the right to strike, yet lead to arbitration in most cases. For the first decade or so of public service bargaining, COP generally fulfilled this expectation. However, after 1976, the public service unions' growing militancy and anger at the government's wage-price controls led them to choose strikes rather than arbitration most of the time (see Fryer, 2000). In addition, experience with arbitration boards and conciliation boards suggested that the latter were willing to address a broader range of issues, including some technically beyond the permissible scope of bargaining (Swimmer, 1995:375–376). For these reasons, the Public Service Alliance no longer allows its bargaining units to choose arbitration (Swimmer, 1995:377).

More recently, the federal government has tended to take a dim view of arbitration, fearing that arbitral awards could lead to costs it was not prepared to bear. When collective bargaining resumed in 1996, following a five-year hiatus, the government suspended interest arbitration for a period of three years. In 1999, the suspension was renewed for a further two years (Fryer, 2000 and 2001; Swimmer, 2000). While the suspension expired and was not renewed, leaving federal government unions free, at least in principle, to opt for arbitration or the conciliation-strike route, it is not clear at this writing how freely the federal government is prepared to allow interest arbitration to operate in practice.

Controlled Strikes

The controlled strike, based on the designation of certain employees who must remain on the job to provide essential services, has become the most common option in jurisdictions that permit public sector workers to strike. Indeed, every jurisdiction except Saskatchewan that permits public sector strikes now has some kind of designation procedure in place. Under the *PSSRA*'s revised procedure, Treasury Board designates those positions that are considered essential. If the parties cannot agree, a review panel makes recommendations for the designation of positions. If after that the parties still do not agree, the PSSRB makes a final and binding decision (Fryer, 2001:24). Elsewhere, the usual procedure is for the union and public sector employer to negotiate acceptable levels of designation, with the final decision left to a labour board or some other impartial tribunal in the event of a dispute (Thompson and Ponak, 1995:439). Often the negotiations over designation are long and difficult, sometimes as difficult as the actual collective agreement negotiations themselves (Thompson and Ponak, 1995:439–440). In the federal public service, the process is so cumbersome that unions sometimes feel compelled to agree to the government's position on designations in order to allow conciliation to proceed in timely fashion (Fryer, 2001:24).

In principle, the controlled strike should often be the most attractive option for governments, because it ensures the continuation of essential public services without removing unions' right to strike. In practice, administering such strikes has often been fraught with difficulties.[24] The most serious problem, particularly in hospital settings where the approach has most often been used (see Haiven, 1995), is knowing how many employees to designate as essential. If the figure is set too low, public health and safety could be at risk. If it is set too high, the union may not be able to carry on an effective strike (Thompson and Ponak, 1995). Often, labour tribunals ruling on designation levels have erred on the side of caution, in some cases ludicrously so. During a 1989 hospital strike in B.C., one hospital saw 110 percent of its usual nursing complement designated as essential (Haiven, 1995:256)! An option already in place in Newfoundland (see Table 9.3) that might prevent public sector employers from designating excessive numbers of employees as essential, is to allow the union to take the dispute through to binding arbitration in cases where designation exceeded a certain level, such as 50 percent. The reason such an option could work is that, in recent years, governments have been increasingly reluctant to submit public sector disputes to arbitration, disliking the loss of control and possible expense entailed in arbitrated settlements.[25]

THE FUTURE OF PUBLIC SECTOR BARGAINING: IS A TRANSFORMATION POSSIBLE?

As this chapter has shown, public sector labour–management relations have become extremely conflict-ridden over the past two decades or so. Wage freezes, rollbacks, and restrictions on collective bargaining have generally reduced public sector workers' real incomes, particularly since 1990. At the same time, workloads have increased and employees have come to feel far less secure in their jobs due to the ongoing wave of downsizing, restructuring, privatization, and contracting-out described earlier in the chapter. While most Canadian governments are in a far stronger financial position than they were ten years ago, the pressure on public sector compensation continues, more or less unabated, as evidenced by the B.C. government's proposed massive cutbacks in its public service. Canadian governments' tough stance on public sector compensation is underscored by a growing unwillingness to submit public sector disputes to arbitration, or (as in the case of Ontario), by an insistence on controlling the process so tightly that the outcome is all but pre-determined. By and large, the result has been an escalation of the already severe tensions between governments and public sector workers (see Rose, 2000 for examples). Aggravating the situation still further is the aging of the public sector work force, which means that most Canadian governments are or will soon be faced with significant recruitment and retention problems, particularly in nursing and other health care areas where they face severe competition for employees from the United States.

Given the current set of circumstances, it would seem self-evident that governments should be turning themselves into more attractive places to work, with an eye both to attracting bright young recruits and to keeping the talented, experienced people they already have. And indeed a number of Canadian governments, the federal one in particular, have begun to talk about turning themselves into "employers of choice" willing and able to attract and retain "the best and brightest." Thus far, however, the rhetoric of progressive change has far outstripped the reality. A 1999 survey of the federal public service (PSES, 1999) found a high level of dissatisfaction with heavy workloads, long work hours, and limited career development possibilities. The same survey also revealed that many believed the selection, classification, and promotion systems to be unfair and that federal government employees felt they had little say in decisions affecting their work. Along similar lines, a 1999 survey of federal public service professionals found only about one-third of all respondents highly committed to the public service and revealed that three-quarters had considered leaving the service (Duxbury, Dyke and Lam, 1999). More recently, a survey of local-level union-management relations conducted for the Fryer Committee revealed that many employees fear reprisal if they file a grievance and suggested that union representatives don't believe management really listens to their views (see Fryer, 2000:33–35).

In 1999, Treasury Board established the Fryer Committee,[26] a tripartite task force made up of equal numbers of government managers, union officials, and academics, to see what could be done to improve the deteriorating state of union–management relations in the federal public service. In its first report (Fryer, 2000), the committee found a serious lack of trust and respect between the parties, resulting in large measure from the government's suspension of bargaining and arbitration during the 1990s as well as from the restrictive legislative framework under which federal public service bargaining is conducted. The committee concluded that unless these problems were addressed, the federal public service labour–management relations system would not likely be sustainable into the 21st century. In its final report (Fryer, 2001), the committee concluded that the government and the public service unions will have to work together collaboratively if the system is to improve. The committee's unanimous recommendations are based on a number of core principles, including government employees' right to form unions and engage in collective bargaining, the need to promote cooperative solutions to labour–management problems, support for the fundamental values of trust, honesty, and mutual respect, and the need for fair, credible, and efficient recourse procedures (Fryer, 2001:13). Chief among the recommendations is that of a new institutional framework for labour–management relations, one that operates through institutions that involve employees, through their unions, in redesigning employment systems (ibid., 12) and that provide for effective dispute resolution systems.

More specifically, the committee recommends revising and simplifying the *PSSRA*, expanding the scope of public service bargaining, and the consultation and co-development of policies at the service-wide, departmental, and workplace levels. The committee also recommends streamlining of the process of designating essential employees, and a major reduction in the exclusion of employees from collective bargaining rights. And the public service unions would become more responsive to their members through a provision allowing them to hold meetings at the workplace, during working hours. To aid in the resolution of grievances and other workplace disputes, the committee recommends replacing the 20-odd mechanisms currently in use by a single board comprised of management and union representatives as well as neutrals. In addition to adjudicating grievances and complaints, the board would be able to use mediation and other forms of alternate dispute resolution (see Chapter 12 for more details).

With an eye to reducing the government's legislative intervention in collective bargaining, the committee recommends creation of a Public Interest Disputes Resolution Commission.[27] The commission would replace the current "choice of procedures" mechanism for resolving public service bargaining disputes. To help preserve its political impartiality, the commission would report directly to Parliament, rather than to a government minister. It would have a broad array of powers, including fact-finding, mediation, referral back to the bargaining table, issuance of a preliminary report outlining the reasonableness of the parties' positions, and issuance of a report outlining possible terms of settlement. Under specified conditions (as, for example, when a union had such a large proportion of its members designated as essential that it could not conduct a meaningful strike), a union would have the unilateral right to request imposition of the commission's terms. With such a commission in place, the government would retain its right to legislate and the union, its right to strike; however, the

Fryer Committee believes that the existence of such a body, with a broad array of powers available to induce the parties to work out their own settlements to disputes, would turn both back-to-work legislation and strikes into unpalatable alternatives.

At this writing (January 2002), it is not clear to what extent the government is prepared to implement the Fryer Committee's recommendations. At least one observer (Lancaster, 2001:16,5/6) has described the government's initial response as "noncommital." Just as the Fryer Committee was issuing its final report, the government established a new task force, chaired by senior deputy minister Ranald Quail, with the mandate to prepare new public service collective bargaining legislation. While the Quail Task Force professed to be open to hearing employees' suggestions for improvements, its credibility with the public service unions was severely damaged by its failure to include even one union representative. Also of concern is the Task Force's unwillingness to consider the large and growing number of separate employers and agencies, which now employ nearly half of all civilian federal government employees, as being within its mandate.

What can be said is that, whether the federal government adopts the Fryer Committee's recommendations or not, the committee has provided a model for collaborative public sector labour–management relations, the lack of which has long been bemoaned by Canadian industrial relations practitioners. At a time of continuing friction in nearly all areas of public sector labour–management relations, the model is one that might well be considered by provincial governments and other public sector organizations, as well as by the federal government. In the absence of the type of fundamental change toward a more collaborative approach to labour relations that has been proposed in the Fryer Committee report, the outlook for the Canadian public sector can only deteriorate still further, as conflict increases and those who are able to do so vote with their feet for higher salaries and a less turbulent working environment.

QUESTIONS FOR DISCUSSION

1) How (if at all) does work in the public sector differ from work in the private sector?

2) Based on what you have learned so far, would you like to work in the public sector? Would you recommend that a friend or relative apply to work in that sector? Why, or why not? Do you think the situation is likely to change in the near future?

3) Why is the public sector important to any study of IR?

4) Discuss the main stages of the evolution of public sector collective bargaining.

5) What was the significance of the *Public Service Staff Relations Act*?

6) What are the main employer differences between the public and private sectors?

7) What are the main employee and union differences between the two sectors?

8) What are their major legislative and policy differences?

9) Why are special dispute resolution methods needed for the public sector? Discuss some of these methods, indicating which appear to you to be most promising, and which most problematic.

10) How (if at all) do you think governments can meet their commitments to deficit and debt reduction while maintaining free collective bargaining in the public sector? Does the approach taken by the Fryer Committee seem to offer promise? Do you think this approach is likely to be generally adopted? Why, or why not?

SUGGESTIONS FOR FURTHER READING

Fryer, John (chair). (2001). *Working Together in the Public Interest: Final Report of the Advisory Committee on Labour Management Relations in the Federal Public Service.* Ottawa: Treasury Board of Canada. This report, based on thorough and detailed consultation with government managers and union officials, outlines a new, collaborative approach to federal public service labour–management relations. Together with the committee's first report, *Identifying the Issues* (2000), it offers insight into the problems affecting public sector labour relations across Canada, in addition to providing potential solutions for many of those problems.

Swimmer, Gene, and Mark Thompson (Eds.). (1995). *Public sector collective bargaining in Canada.* Kingston: Queen's IRC Press. An indispensable book for anyone with an interest in the public sector. It should be required reading for all staff and management at Treasury Board. Contains articles on subjects ranging from collective bargaining to compensation and pay equity. Of particular note are the papers on health care, by Larry Haiven; on public sector union growth, by Joe Rose; on provincial public service issues, by former NUPGE president John Fryer; and on comparative public sector issues, by P.B. Beaumont.

Swimmer, Gene (ed.). (2000). *Public Service Labour Relations in an Era of Restraint and Restructuring* Toronto: Oxford University Press. Detailed case studies of how different Canadian jurisdictions (including the federal government) handled public service labour relations during the economic crisis of the 1990s. The studies show that jurisdictions which retained collective bargaining fared as well as those resorting to legislation.

Zussman, David, and Jak Jabes. (1989). *The vertical solitude: Managing in the public sector.* Halifax: Institute for Research on Public Policy. This study on public sector management deserves to be better-known than it is. It provides significant research evidence in support of its thesis that managing in the public sector is a different, and in many ways more difficult, job than managing in the private sector.

CHAPTER 10

BARGAINING STRUCTURE,
THE NEGOTIATING PROCESS, AND
THE COLLECTIVE AGREEMENT

"And that's our final offer!" Negotiators often try to make it look as if their settlement was achieved only at the last minute, after a frenetic all-night session. This way, their constituents will be convinced that the negotiator "gave it her best shot."

The negotiating process is critical in the IR system since in unionized workplaces, most outcomes are established through collective bargaining. We start this chapter with a consideration of bargaining structure, which may have a good deal to do with determining the relative balance of power between the parties, and may also be a factor in the ease or difficulty of negotiations. Next, we look at the negotiating process itself. An important part of this examination will be a discussion of the concept of a settlement zone, and the issues to which the settlement zone concept does and does not apply. The chapter ends with a look at collective agreements, which are an important record of negotiation results.

COLLECTIVE BARGAINING: A BRIEF OVERVIEW

Collective bargaining may be defined as "the determination of terms and conditions of employment through negotiations between employers and representatives of employees" (Rogow, 1989b:44). Our concern here is with the negotiation process itself, as well as with the structure of collective bargaining and the collective agreements that are its direct results. In the two subsequent chapters (strikes and grievances), we'll focus on the two types of conflict most commonly arising out of the collective bargaining process.

Bargaining Structure

Bargaining structure is of considerable importance to any discussion of collective bargaining because particular types of structure have been related to higher strike levels, higher levels of inflation, and even conflict within unions (Anderson, 1989b). In addition, structure has been associated with bargaining power, the types of issues that are negotiated, and the internal politics on both sides of the bargaining table (Anderson, 1989b; Chaykowski, 1995:230–231).

At its simplest level, "collective bargaining structure" answers the question "Who bargains with whom?" (Rogow, 1989a:132). A more detailed definition is offered by Thomas Kochan (1980:84), who defines bargaining structure as "the scope of employees and employers covered or affected by the bargaining agreement." Kochan goes on to distinguish between the formal structure, which is the negotiation unit (i.e., those employees and employers legally bound by the terms of the agreement), and the informal structure (i.e., other employees or employers affected by the results of a negotiated settlement through **pattern bargaining** or some other process that is not legally binding). In this section, our main concern is with formal structures, though informal structures will be briefly discussed in connection with pattern bargaining.

It's also important to distinguish between the certification unit, or the group of employees designated by a labour board as appropriate for collective bargaining, and the negotiation unit, or the grouping of employees that actually takes part in such bargaining (Anderson, 1989b; Rogow, 1989a). The actual negotiation unit may comprise several different certification units, assuming the parties agree (Anderson, 1989b:212).[1] Joint or coordinated bargaining by several different unions has been far more frequent in the public sector, as in the case of Quebec's 1972 Common Front, which as we noted earlier was formed by the CSN, QFL, and the CEQ (provincial teachers' federation) to bargain with the provincial government on behalf of the province's teachers, hospital workers, and government employees (Boivin, 1989:416). Likewise, multi-employer bargaining is comparatively rare outside the public sector and the construction industry (Rose, 1986, 1992), where it has often been legislatively mandated to help promote greater labour–management stability.

Types of Bargaining Structure

The most basic distinction is between centralized structures (involving relatively few sets of negotiations per jurisdiction or industry with each covering relatively large numbers of workers), and decentralized structures (those involving large numbers of negotiations per jurisdiction or industry with each covering relatively few workers). By international standards, Canadian bargaining structure is quite decentralized (Chaykowski, 1995; Anderson, 1989b; Rogow, 1989a), with negotiations most often occurring between a single employer and a single union, unlike the situation prevailing in many European countries, such as Germany and Sweden (Adams, 1995a). Moreover, at least in the private sector, this tendency toward decentralization has been increasing in recent years, owing mainly to the breakdown of traditional multi-employer or pattern bargaining arrangements in several major industrial sectors (see Rose, 1986; Forrest, 1989).

Six basic types of bargaining structure have been identified in the literature (Chaykowski, 1995:231–232; Anderson, 1989b). These structures are differentiated from each other according to (a) the number of employers involved (one or many); (b) for single employers, the number of establishments or specific places of businesses involved (one or many); and (c) the number of unions involved (one or many).

The single-plant, single-union, single-employer structure, which is among the most common in Canada, involves negotiations at a single workplace. It often occurs because the employer operates at one location only, has only one unionized establishment, or has different unions at different locations (Chaykowski, 1995:231). Another reason for its frequency is labour boards' tendency to use workers' "community of interest" as a major criterion in certification unit determination. This criterion generally pushes labour boards in the direction of smaller and more homogeneous units (Rogow, 1989a:139; Anderson, 1989b:221). Another quite common structure is the single-employer, multi-establishment, single-union type, which involves the negotiation of a single collective agreement across several different workplaces by the same employer and union. Offering useful economies of scale for both employers and unions in situations where the employer runs an integrated operation across a number of generally similar establishments (Chaykowski, 1995:232), it is most common in public administration, transportation, and communications (Anderson, 1989b).

Two less common structures are the single-employer, single-establishment, multi-union and single-employer, multi-establishment, multi-union types. The former involves a negotiating partnership between two or more unions within the same workplace, as when production workers represented by an industrial union negotiate together with maintenance workers represented by a craft union. It is quite rare in Canada (Chaykowski, 1995; Anderson, 1989b:214), probably because in most situations where workers from different occupations within the same establishment feel they have enough in common to bargain together, they will already have joined the same union. The latter occurs mainly in the railway industry where operating union coalitions bargain as a group with each of the major railways (Chaykowski, 1995:232), and in certain other industries made up of a few very large employers and a larger number of small craft unions. As for the multi-employer, multi-establishment, single-union type of structure, it is most apt to be found in industries characterized by large numbers of relatively small employers and a single dominant industrial or craft union, such as trucking, fishing, and forestry (Chaykowski, 1995; Anderson, 1989b:214). It is also found in health care, especially in bargaining with registered nurses, who typically are represented by a single, province-wide union (Chaykowski, 1995:232; Haiven, 1995).

The highly centralized multi-employer, multi-establishment, multi-union type of bargaining structure is rarely one that parties choose for themselves. It's most often found in the construction industry, where it has generally been imposed by governments in a bid to bring labour peace following major disputes (Chaykowski, 1995:232; Rose, 1992:190; Boivin and Déom, 1995). Under this type of structure, bargaining is normally conducted through a certified employers' association rather than by individual employers (see Rose, 1992:190). In some cases, as in B.C.'s construction industry prior to the new government's recent repeal of sector-wide construction structures, bargaining may be conducted by a province-wide council of trade unions—the union equivalent to an employers' association (Rose, 1992; Anderson, 1989b:215).

Reasons for Canada's Decentralized Structures

A key reason for Canada's generally decentralized bargaining structures is the fact of provincial jurisdiction over most labour relations matters. This tends to make national-level bargaining quite difficult (Chaykowski, 1995:231), except in interprovincial industries under federal jurisdiction, given that such things as certification procedures and bargaining unit determination criteria tend to differ significantly from province to province.

A second important reason is labour boards' tendency to determine bargaining units according to IR "community of interest" criteria that generally favour the creation of relatively small, homogeneous bargaining units rather than larger, more heterogeneous, more broadly based ones (Rogow, 1989a). Except in the construction industry and in British Columbia prior to 2001, where broader-based bargaining was often promoted as a matter of public policy, the creation of "communities of interest" has generally been given greater weight than the reduction of conflict or creation of viable longer-term bargaining relationships (Rogow, 1989a:140–141). For example, the historical tendency of both Ontario and federal boards has been to create separate units for office and production workers (Rogow, 1989a:141).[2] Another criterion often used by boards, that of facilitating unionization whenever a majority of employees wish it, has also tended to lead to the creation of small and relatively homogeneous bargaining units, since smaller units are generally more cohesive and easier to organize (Rogow, 1989a:139).

A third reason has to do with the attitude of North American employers, many of whom seem, on principle, to oppose broader-based bargaining, particularly any sort of multi-employer bargaining that would require them to surrender some of their control over bargaining to an employers' association (see Adams, 1995a). The fact that certain employers object to broad-based bargaining even in good times when it might help them by reducing unions' ability to whipsaw suggests that, at least for some, opposition to this type of bargaining may be rooted in something deeper than economic calculation (see Rogow, 1989a).[3] Nonetheless, the state of the economy *has* been the major reason for employers' growing support for more decentralized structures, which in turn has been one of the most important reasons for the increase in such structures in recent years.

Increased competition, driven sometimes by trade liberalization and sometimes by other factors, has led to the breakup of many previously centralized bargaining structures and pattern bargaining arrangements over the past two decades. Sometimes, one of the weaker firms in a centralized or pattern bargaining arrangement finds it can no longer meet the industry standard and remain competitive, with the result that it withdraws from the centralized arrangement. Soon other firms are likely to find themselves in a similar position and likewise withdraw. Once that starts happening, the centralized arrangement's demise is virtually inevitable. In other cases (as in the case of General Motors' unsuccessful attempt to do away with pattern bargaining in its 1996 negotiations with the Canadian Auto Workers), an industry leader sets out with the avowed intention of ending the arrangement. Among the industries in which growing competitive pressures have led to the dissolution of employer associations or pattern bargaining arrangements are the railways, pulp and paper, trucking, and meatpacking (Rose, 1986a:3; Forrest, 1989).

One of the few major industries that has so far been able to resist the shift to decentralized bargaining structures has been the auto industry (Kumar and Meltz, 1992). One reason why the industry has been able to retain its long-standing pattern bargaining arrangement has been a bilateral Canada-U.S. Auto Pact, which created an integrated continental market in auto products and parts manufacturing while maintaining previous levels of Canadian production and employment (Kumar and Meltz, 1992). However, in recent years even this most venerable of pattern bargaining arrangements has been put to the test. Only a determined struggle by the Canadian Auto Workers (CAW) in its 1996 strike against General Motors (discussed in detail in Chapter 12 of the first edition) allowed pattern bargaining to survive that round of negotiations. The big auto companies will doubtless make further attempts to eliminate pattern bargaining in the future, although the CAW, one of Canada's strongest and most militant unions, will do its best to preserve it.

The Canadian IR system has by no means been alone in this trend towards greater decentralization. All across the industrialized western world, "decentralization" and "flexibility" have become "industrial relations catchwords" over the past two decades (Scheuer, 1992:168). In the United States, a change in the product market and increased competition from non-unionized firms helped lead to the break-up of pattern bargaining arrangements that had prevailed in the rubber tire industry since shortly after the Second World War (Kochan, McKersie, and Cappelli, 1984), whereby the agreement negotiated between the United Rubber Workers and its chosen target among the four largest tire companies became the agreement for all four, and thus most of the industry.[4] In Sweden, employers seeking more flexibility pushed bargaining from the national to the industry level, and even in some cases to the company level (Adams, 1995a; Hammarstrom, 1993; Kjellberg, 1992). Similar moves have taken place, generally at the behest of employers, in such countries as Denmark (Scheuer, 1992; Ferner and Hyman, 1992b) and Italy (Ferner and Hyman, 1992a). Even the German system, long considered among Europe's most stable, has made certain moves, albeit smaller ones, in the same direction (Jacobi, Keller, and Muller-Jentsch, 1992).[5] The impacts of these moves toward more decentralized bargaining are discussed in some detail in the comparative chapter (Chapter 13).

In the public sector, a more difficult economic climate tends to lead toward more centralized bargaining structures, as provincial governments increasingly concerned with holding down public sector compensation costs seek to play a more and more direct role in the negotiation process (Muir, 1971). For example, in elementary and secondary education, bargaining has, over the past three decades, moved from the local to the provincial level in Quebec, New Brunswick, Nova Scotia, and Saskatchewan (see Gallagher and Wetzel, 1980). More recently, centralized teacher bargaining has been adopted in British Columbia, in a move strenuously opposed by the provincial teachers' federation (Thomason, 1995:286–287), and in Ontario, where, as we noted in the first edition of this book, the centralization was one of the causes of teachers' strikes in 1997 and 1998. Teachers' federations' almost universal opposition to centralized bargaining is sometimes based on the belief their members can get a better deal at the local level, and almost always on the belief that they and their members will have more control over their jobs and more say in educational policy decisions affecting them and their students.

One way around the problem of local control is two-tier bargaining whereby items of general applicability such as wages and retirement benefits are negotiated provincially and issues of purely local significance are left for local-level negotiators to hammer out. Such systems have been devised in Saskatchewan (Anderson, 1989b; Gallagher and Wetzel, 1980) and, more recently, in Quebec (Boivin and Déom, 1995:429) and appear to be working reasonably well in both cases.

Effects of Different Bargaining Structures

In general, bargaining structures' effects on different parties tend to be different depending on whether the economy is weak or strong. In good times (i.e., high parts of the business cycle marked by low unemployment and relatively high inflation), private sector unions generally favour decentralized bargaining structures. Under such structures, at times when the demand for labour is high and employers are very much interested in maintaining labour peace, they can often **whipsaw** employers, that is, use one settlement with one employer as the basis for obtaining similar or (generally) better terms with others (Gallagher and Wetzel, 1980). At such times, many employers are willing to give up some degree of control and enter into multi-employer bargaining agreements, because these will combat whipsawing by establishing a common wage scale throughout the industry (Gallagher and Wetzel, 1980). Indeed, some well-known centralized bargaining arrangements, including most notably the national-level bargaining that prevailed in Sweden from the 1950s through the 1980s (Kjellberg, 1992:96), have actually been started at the employers' behest, with an eye to moderating wage settlements. Other benefits employers may seek from multi-employer bargaining include a reduction in work stoppages and scale economies in negotiations and contract administration, as well as reduced uncertainty about labour costs and, therefore, about product pricing (Rogow, 1989a:146).

In bad times, (again confining ourselves to the private sector), it is unions who usually favour centralized bargaining arrangements, while employers often seek to escape from them. Now, whipsawing is often done by employers, who may obtain concessions from the union in one negotiation and use this initial set of concessions as the basis for even greater ones in another negotiation. So long as the bargaining structure remains centralized, it is harder for an employer to force concessions on a union, and the costs of a strike are apt to be considerably greater. As well, employers have a harder time getting rid of their unions altogether under centralized than under decentralized bargaining (see Kochan et al., 1984; Rose, 1992). Ending centralized arrangements also means that employers are free to bargain based on their own particular circumstances, rather than having to take into account the circumstances of other firms that may not be as efficient or as well-run and that may thus serve to "drag them down" under centralized bargaining. At a time of ever-increasing competitiveness, this kind of flexibility means a good deal to many employers.

With regard to wages, market-driven decentralized structures generally lead to greater dispersion between higher and lower-paid workers and greater union–non-union wage differentials (Anderson, 1989b). For example, in Sweden, the devolution of bargaining from the national to the industry level during the late 1980s and early 1990s was accompanied by increased wage dispersion (Kjellberg, 1992). In good times, decentralized structures generally lead to higher wage settlements, since unions can whipsaw employers into accepting their terms (Anderson, 1989b; Gallagher and Wetzel, 1980; Rogow, 1989a). In bad times, such structures typically lead to lower compensation levels, as employer whipsawing (Rogow, 1989a:151) and increased competition from non-union firms allow employers to force unions to agree to productivity improvements, wage freezes, or even outright pay cuts (Anderson, 1989b:229; Forrest, 1989; Rose, 1986a).[6] In contrast, centralized structures, which are marked by a significantly greater degree of government involvement both in the bargaining process and in any subsequent dispute settlement processes (Rogow, 1989a:154), generally lead to greater similarity of wages, benefits, and other terms of employment across industries or jurisdictions (Rogow, 1989a:152).

At the macro-economic level, centralized systems have been associated with lower levels of inflation than decentralized ones (Tarantelli, 1986), at least in good economic times.[7, 8] Again, more moderate settlements are likely to result at least in part from unions' loss of the ability to whipsaw. In addition, there is often a different political dynamic at work in centralized systems, many of which have traditionally been found in countries with strong labour or social democratic parties with a good chance of forming the government, such as Sweden, Denmark, and Austria (see Tarantelli, 1986). When such a party forms the government, the labour movement will often be able to achieve much of its agenda politically and may well be induced to agree to lower wage settlements in return for pension and tax reform, price controls, a full employment guarantee, or other government policies favouring workers and unions (Adams, 1989). The promise of favourable government policies can also induce unions to call fewer strikes than they otherwise would (Adams, 1989; Tarantelli, 1986).

An argument often advanced in favour of more centralized bargaining structures is that they lead to fewer strikes and less time lost due to those strikes (Anderson, 1982 and 1989b; see also Rogow, 1989a). Such a finding seems almost axiomatic, given that such structures involve many fewer sets of negotiations at any given time than decentralized ones. In addition, larger negotiations with more at stake are likely to be conducted by more skillful and experienced negotiators (Rogow, 1989a:149). Managers with real decision-making authority are more likely to be at the table or at least in close contact with the management negotiating team (Rogow, 1989a:146, 151). And because of the relatively greater importance of centralized negotiations, governments are more apt to intervene both to prevent strikes and to end them quickly should they occur (Rogow, 1989a:154).

Internationally (see Adams, 1989, 1995a), the evidence strongly suggests that centralized systems result not just in fewer strikes, but in the loss of less working time. However, for Canada, a study by Gunderson, Kervin, and Reid (1986) finds a higher probability of strikes in bargaining units of greater than 1000 employees. A study by Rose (1986a) of construction industry disputes finds that, although strike frequency decreased in larger bargaining units, the number of workers involved and average strike duration both increased, while another study cited by Anderson (1989b:230) finds a lower probability of strikes in single-plant units than in multi-plant, single-employer structures.

Why has centralization led to a reduction in working time lost to strikes internationally, but not in Canada? The likeliest explanation is that here, centralized structures have not been accompanied by a widespread shift of conflict from the bargaining table to the political arena, as they generally have in European countries such as Sweden and Germany. That is primarily because labour or social democratic parties such as the NDP or PQ, with which unions might make such political bargains, have never formed the government federally, and have only occasionally done so at the provincial level. Lacking the political option that many European unions possess, Canadian unions have used the increased strike power that centralized structures undeniably provide (see Rogow, 1989a:146) to help them achieve their ends through the collective bargaining process. Thus it is not centralization itself, but the shift in the locus of conflict that often accompanies it that seems to be the main reason for reduced industrial conflict levels in European countries with centralized structures (see Mishel, 1986 for more detail).

As for the bargaining process itself, the effects of greater centralization are somewhat mixed. On the one hand, centralization seems to make negotiations go more smoothly because of the superior negotiators generally conducting them and the presence or availability of senior management with real authority. On the other hand, because in centralized bargaining each side represents a greater number of union or management factions, internal or intraorganizational bargaining becomes more complex, with the result that negotiations as a whole tend to go more slowly (Mishel, 1986:151). There is also evidence that centralized negotiations may increase local union negotiators' and rank-and-file members' feelings of alienation from the negotiations and from the centralized negotiators, who are less likely to be closely attuned to specific local conditions and issues (Mishel, 1986:153). This, together with the fact that centralized negotiations by their very nature tend to encompass issues of general importance, thereby omitting issues of local concern, may well be a factor in the higher incidence of wildcat strikes found in centralized structures (Mishel, 1986; Anderson, 1989b:231). Again, two-tier bargaining systems (described earlier) may be a way around this problem. These systems have long been used successfully in Europe, though in Canada they're confined mainly to the public sector (see Adams, 1989; Gallagher and Wetzel, 1980; Hébert, 1995). While they are no panacea, the evidence suggests they can help reduce a number of the problems associated with centralization, particularly when the union is careful to solicit local input throughout the bargaining process.

THE NEGOTIATION PROCESS

A study of the negotiation process is an important part of any IR course because collective bargaining, through which collective agreements are concluded, involves detailed, often highly complex negotiations between unions and management organizations. While these negotiations have certain things in common with more conventional commercial negotiations, they also differ from commercial negotiations in a number of important respects. In this section, we take a brief look at the significance of negotiation in general before looking at some special features of union–management negotiations. The discussion then turns to the stages of negotiations and the concept of a settlement zone (including situations in which the settlement zone may not apply). We then take a closer look at the role played by bargaining power and at specific negotiating strategies. The section concludes with a brief discussion of ways to improve the bargaining process.

Negotiation in Everyday Life

The collective bargaining simulations that many instructors include in introductory IR courses are designed to give students a taste of the negotiating process. Not all introductory IR students will earn their living as union or management negotiators. But almost everyone, other than those pledged to live their lives as hermits or ascetics, will need negotiating skills. Among other things, such skills are important in obtaining a job, getting a promotion or transfer, or buying a house or a car. A recent study showed that job seekers who negotiate over salary and benefits before signing up earn an average 3 to 4 percent more in compensation than those who do not—a difference that can add up to many thousands of dollars over a working lifetime (Kunde, 1998). Nor is the need for good negotiating skills confined to the business world. In modern, two-career marriages, with husband and wife often heavily overcommitted both at home and at work, frequent negotiation is needed to ensure domestic duties are apportioned fairly, children are adequately looked after, and the husband and wife get enough "quality time" both together and alone. And in divorce cases, good negotiating skills can mean the difference between a reasonably amicable and modestly priced separation agreement, essentially crafted by the parties themselves, and the sort of nightmarish scenario involving lengthy court proceedings where the parties each spend many thousands of dollars and have nothing to show for it other than a relationship that's even more embittered than it was prior to the divorce.

All in all, it's not going too far to suggest that negotiating ability is one of the most critical life skills a person can possess. Those who possess it are far likelier to succeed professionally, make and keep friends, and have happy and successful marriages and family lives than those who don't.

The Qualities of a Good Negotiator

What are the qualities possessed by most good negotiators? It's probably best to start this discussion by recognizing that negotiation has often been misrepresented in the media, giving members of the general public a false impression of the process. Some, when asked what qualities a negotiator should bring to the table, would undoubtedly reply: "The ability to lie, cheat, and deceive and manipulate others for one's personal benefit." Others would probably include: "A willingness to engage in crass, boorish, or aggressive behaviour aimed at intimidating one's opponents." People taking such views fail to recognize that, particularly in labour negotiations, there's usually a long-term relationship to consider. While a negotiator might succeed in taking unfair advantage once, in the long run, such behaviour doesn't pay. Professionals know they'll likely have to face the same negotiator sitting across from them at some point in the future, and govern their conduct accordingly. As Lewicki, Saunders, and Minton (1997:232) note, negotiators will readily justify resorting to an ethically dubious "hardball" strategy when facing people whose behaviour they have previously experienced as exploitative, arguing that anticipatory self-defence legitimizes their actions. Similarly, loud-mouthed, aggressive behaviour, outbursts of temper, personal attacks on opponents, and attempts to deceive the other side are the mark of the amateur;[9] more experienced negotiators are less likely to resort to threats (Kervin, 1989:205). In the long run, the most successful negotiators are generally those who behave like the negotiator they would like to face on the other side of the table.

While even experts sometimes disagree as to the precise qualities a good negotiator needs, most would agree that, to start with, a negotiator needs to like both people and the practice of negotiation. Beyond that, negotiators must possess empathy, persuasive ability, persistence, courage, honesty and integrity, and a willingness to take risks (Fisher and Williams, 1989:187–9, 202–3). Most important of all, are good speaking and listening skills, the latter being of particular importance because it's only by careful listening that the negotiators pick up cues from the other side. Often what is not said may be even more important than what is said, as issues that had previously seemed important to the other side simply fade from the table (Fisher and Williams, 1989:203). A sense of humour is also important because humour can be an excellent way to defuse the tension bound to arise during long and difficult bargaining sessions.

Special Features of Union–Management Negotiations

People observing a union–management negotiation for the first time are often bewildered by its length and complexity. As Fisher and Williams note (1989:190–191), many commercial negotiations are concluded in half an hour or less. In many labour–management negotiations, it may be weeks or even months before the parties so much as raise monetary issues, let alone settle them. For much of this time, they may be arguing over comparatively minor issues. Why spend so much time bickering over a whole slew of peripheral issues when anyone could predict the whole thing will come down to wages and job security in the end (as probably happens at least 90 percent of the time)? Moreover, the process often involves lengthy set speeches, threats that neither party has any intention of carrying out, and numerous other rituals and posturings (Sass, 1989) that would be more appropriate in a theatrical performance than in what is, after all, a business transaction. Why can't the parties simply "talk turkey" from the outset and get the job done quickly, the way most commercial negotiators do (Fisher and Williams, 1989:191)?

There are at least four reasons for the generally far greater length and complexity of union–management negotiations. First, such negotiations typically address a far broader range of issues than do most commercial negotiations, and the issues themselves are often more complex than those raised in the average commercial transaction. If, for example, two parties are negotiating over the sale of 1000 desks, only three issues are normally of concern: the quality of the desks (which can generally be ascertained directly through an inspection), the price, and the delivery date. In contrast, union–management negotiations typically cover a broad range of issues including wages, many different benefits, job security, hours of work, vacation leave, work rules, procedures for layoff, transfer, and promotion, and various health and safety issues, in addition to the rights and responsibilities of the union and management organization (see the section on the collective agreement for more detail). Such a broad range of issues can't be addressed in an hour or even a day. Given the many possible tradeoffs, costing alone can be an extremely time-consuming process. Moreover, some issues, such as regulating the use of hazardous chemicals in the workplace or changing a pension plan, may be so complex technically as to require many hours of study by joint committees or even reliance on outside expertise. One can't expect to resolve such complex issues in a single afternoon. Finally, because of the breadth and complexity of issues involved in most labour–management negotiations, more is often at stake here than in commercial negotiations, and emotions can run high on both sides, particularly as the strike deadline approaches. This too can complicate bargaining, not just between the parties, but within each of the negotiating teams.

Second, union–management negotiations are quite strictly regulated by statute (Fisher and Williams, 1989), and this too has an effect on the bargaining process. For one thing, a union's need to ensure that it is complying with its statutory duty to represent all its members fairly may lead it to introduce a broader range of issues than it otherwise would, and to spend a fair amount of time on seemingly peripheral issues that it knows are unlikely to form part of the eventual settlement. For another, the various dispute resolution processes imposed by labour relations legislation may slow negotiations down considerably. As we noted in Chapter 8, even in the private sector no union can strike or employer lock out until the agreement has expired and, in most cases, until some kind of conciliation process has been attempted and certain time limits have passed. This compulsory conciliation process may simply have the effect of delaying serious bargaining until after the conciliator has issued his or her findings. And as we noted in Chapter 9, public sector legislation often imposes additional restrictions, such as further time limits or extra steps to the dispute resolution process. In some cases, strikes are barred altogether, forcing the parties to take their disputes to binding arbitration. When this happens, the result is often the so-called chilling effect whereby the parties refuse to make concessions in the expectation, or at least hope, that the arbitrator will arrive at a middle position, thereby relieving them of the need to make hard decisions on their own (Godard, 1994:353). Whether strikes are permitted or not, the various dispute resolution processes often make negotiations take far longer than they otherwise would.

Third (and not unrelated to the previous point) union–management negotiations are representative negotiations, at the end of which negotiators must emerge with a settlement acceptable not just to them but to their principals (senior executives on the management side, the membership on the union side), who have the ultimate say as to whether the tentative agreement is accepted or rejected (Fisher and Williams, 1989). Both union and management negotiators generally represent diverse constituencies, whose interests are often conflicting. For instance, older workers in higher tax brackets may seek pensions and other forms of deferred payment. Younger male workers typically seek more in up-front wages, while female workers will often push for maternity benefits and flexible hours provisions allowing them more time for family matters (Fisher and Williams, 1989). All of this means that intraorganizational bargaining within the teams is often fierce—sometimes as difficult for chief negotiators as the negotiations with the opposing party.[10] Not only does intraorganizational conflict lengthen the bargaining process, it may also increase the likelihood of a bargaining impasse or even a strike (Gunderson, Hyatt & Ponak, 1995:393). As well, members of the various management or union factions will often be part of the bargaining team, leading chief negotiators to "put on a good show" with an eye to convincing those team members that they have genuinely expended their best efforts on their behalf (Fisher and Williams, 1989). In the eyes of observers like Bob Sass (1989:170–172), it is the need to meet constituents' psychological as well as economic needs that explains much of the otherwise irrelevant or even ludicrous ritual and ceremony often connected to the negotiation process. Such ritual and ceremony can also serve broader strategic purposes, since they can help conceal one's own bottom line while one is busily probing for that of the other side (Sass, 1989:172).

Fourth, union–management relationships are generally long-term in nature (Fisher and Williams, 1989). Most have a history; most will also have a future. In arriving at a settlement, union and management negotiators must try to come up with solutions that will not merely meet the parties' immediate needs today, but will help them build or maintain an effective working relationship over the medium to long term. Since such a process involves making projections and educated guesses about the future and gets into the parties' feelings and perceptions as well as objective economic issues, it will almost inevitably be more complex than a commercial negotiation that addresses only economic issues and that is often set at a single point in time, or at most involves projection over a time span of a year or two. Where the relationship has been troubled in the past, there may be debris from previous battles to clean up and hurt feelings to assuage before the parties can move on to constructive negotiations over current issues.

The Role of Bargaining Power

Even the most cooperative union–management relationship will almost certainly feature a significant degree of competition over money (Kervin, 1989). In less cooperative relationships, competition is likely to permeate most, if not all, aspects of the bargaining process. Where competition is present, what chiefly determines bargaining outcomes is the extent to which each side is able to exert bargaining power over the other.

The literature offers a number of definitions of the term "bargaining power." One widely quoted definition is that of Leap and Grigsby (1986): the ability to resist another's proposal in favour of a proposal more favourable to one's own side. Godard's definition (1994:339) is not dissimilar, but has a slightly different emphasis. In his view, each side has bargaining power, and therefore is likely to win concessions from the other side, to the extent that a work stoppage imposes direct and indirect costs on the other side.

As Godard sees it, the direct sources of union bargaining power result from the union's ability to impose losses on management during a strike. In the private sector, these losses will take the form of lost profit and market share. In the public sector, they take the form of increased public sympathy for the strikers (and their cause) and a corresponding loss of confidence in the government (Godard, 1994). This explains why public sector unions, as we noted in previous chapters, generally devote so much of their time and effort to publicity campaigns. The greater the union's ability to impose such strike costs on management, the likelier management is to make concessions that will end the strike (Godard, 1994).

The indirect sources of union bargaining power "entail the costs to management of increased exit and recalcitrance due to worker discontent and adversariness after a strike" (Godard, 1994).[11] At the most obvious level, this refers to the costs management incurs when any significant number of workers quit, particularly highly skilled ones who may be difficult to replace, and in situations involving highly complex and capital-intensive technologies (Godard, 1994). But such costs can also include increased grievances, increased absenteeism and sick leave, and in more extreme cases even an increase in spoiled goods, vandalism, and sabotage, as workers seek to get back at an employer they feel has treated them unfairly in any way they can. Finally, the indirect costs to the company may include a loss of public faith that can lead to reduced profit and market share. Such a loss of public faith is most apt to occur in situations where the conflict has been a bitter and lengthy one, and the union has used negative publicity campaigns or a boycott.

The direct sources of management bargaining power relate to the economic cost, to workers, of a strike or lockout (Godard, 1994). Such direct bargaining power is reduced to the extent that lost income can be replaced by temporary or part-time work, or by strike pay (Godard, 1994). However, in most cases strike pay replaces only a small proportion of workers' regular wages or salaries, and temporary jobs rarely pay anything like as much as regular full-time ones. Therefore, this source of management power is likely to remain a potent one except in very good economic times, when striking workers may find it relatively easy to locate a new full-time job, and when a firm may need to make up for production losses after a strike with large amounts of overtime (see Godard, 1994). The greater management's ability to impose costs on workers through a strike or lockout, the likelier management will be to extract concessions, such as wage and benefit reductions or the easing of rigid work rules, at the bargaining table (Godard, 1994).

The indirect sources of management bargaining power relate to the possibility of job losses resulting from lost business following a strike, and the possible imposition of harsher working conditions, such as heavier workloads or stricter discipline (Godard, 1994:339–340). Again, this latter source of power can be reduced, to the extent that the union is successful in fighting heavier workloads or stricter discipline through its grievance process.

As the history of the Canadian labour movement illustrates, bargaining power can shift quite quickly. Often, such shifts in bargaining power are the result of large-scale economic and political trends. During the Great Depression, for example, with production severely curtailed and jobs at a premium, bargaining power swung very markedly towards employers. Once war was declared and most able-bodied young male workers were sent to the front, power shifted quite markedly in the opposite direction, although the government did what it could to mitigate the effects of this shift by imposing wage controls, freezing workers in essential employment, and limiting employees' right to quit or shift jobs (Morton, 1995:142–143). Through the 1970s, workers and their unions generally continued to enjoy a fair degree of bargaining power; however, things shifted quite quickly as a result of the recessions that came in the wake of the two major energy shocks of the 1970s, particularly the major recession of 1981–1983. In Canada, unemployment has generally been quite high, by earlier postwar standards, ever since, and collective bargaining settlements have been correspondingly modest. Now, with the impending retirement of large numbers of "Baby Boomer" workers, the balance of power may be about to shift again, particularly in highly-skilled professional, managerial, and technical fields and in much of the public sector (see Galt, 2000; Lowe, 2001; Auditor General, 2000 and 2001).

The Stages of Negotiation

One can think of negotiations as passing through four major stages: settling in, consolidation, finalization, and mopping-up (Fisher and Williams, 1989:189). It's generally best, when negotiating, to take one's time and try to go through all the stages. Attempts to push the other side too fast can result in unnecessary resistance; overly rapid concessions can lead to trouble on one's own side, and perhaps even to rejection of the tentative agreement if constituents don't believe you've fought hard enough on their behalf.

Settling in, the first stage, is a time for opponents to feel each other out and get to know each other (Fisher and Williams, 1989), particularly if the chief negotiators haven't been to the table together before. Normally it's best to begin with some noncommittal pleasantry about the weather or something else other than the bargaining agenda. It's also usually best to negotiate items in reverse order of their importance, because less important items are generally easier to settle. A particularly good idea may be to start with an item that can be seen as a "win-win" for both sides, like a health and safety issue. Once a few minor items have been settled, teams are more likely to have developed the momentum needed to tackle the more major items, like wages and job security.

The second stage, consolidation, is normally by far the longest. It's here that each side puts forward its positions and arguments and learns about the other side's priorities (typically through the simple dropping of certain less important demands). The consolidation stage often requires several caucuses (team meetings) to allow each side to assess the other side's demands and priorities and come up with an appropriate response to them. It is generally considered good strategy not to agree to anything important without calling a caucus (Fisher and Williams, 1989:203). The overall aim of this stage is to hone one's own bottom line—the least your team is prepared to agree to—as well as to develop an understanding of the other side's bottom line. While bottom lines may change in response to information exchanged at the table or changes in the economic or political environment within which negotiations are being conducted (Fisher and Williams, 1989:189), changes in a team's bottom line should not be made lightly. Particularly in the later stages of negotiations, it's important for the chief negotiator to remind team members periodically of the bottom line to which they have committed themselves (Fisher and Williams, 1989:199).

Where two teams' bottom lines (in terms of wages or the overall cost of the agreement) intersect, then a settlement zone (see Figures 10.1A and 10.1B) can be said to exist (Fisher and Williams, 1989:189). Where they do not intersect, then there is no settlement zone. If management prefers to hold the total compensation increase to 1 percent, but can live with an increase up to 3 percent, while the union would prefer an increase of 4 percent but can live with an increase as low as 2 percent, then the settlement zone is between 2 and 3 percent. Assuming the teams have good negotiators and allow the process to work as it should, they'll very likely come in with a settlement somewhere in that range. If, on the other hand, management's bottom-line range is from -1 to +1 percent but the union's is still between 2 and 4 percent, then no settlement zone exists, and the parties will reach a bargaining impasse unless one or both gives in on the monetary package, or on some non-monetary issue (such as work rules or job security) that's considered important enough to allow some relaxation of the other side's monetary bottom line.

More important, perhaps, are those cases where a settlement zone does not exist, not because the parties have not moved far enough, but because the issue over which they disagree is one of fundamental principle, not quantifiable, and thus not amenable to the sort of trade-off inherent in the very notion of a settlement zone (Kervin, 1984). For this reason, disputes over such issues tend to be longer, more bitter, and far harder to settle than disputes over monetary issues. Often such disputes are only resolved after some kind of direct government intervention (Kervin, 1984). A union's right to exist is such an issue; one can't realistically agree that the plant will operate with a

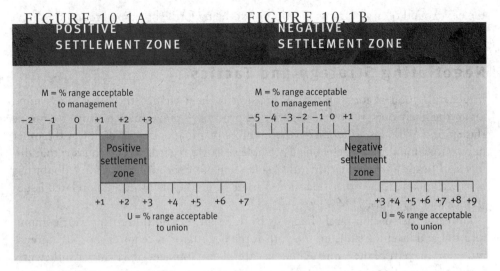

FIGURE 10.1A
POSITIVE SETTLEMENT ZONE

FIGURE 10.1B
NEGATIVE SETTLEMENT ZONE

Source: Prepared from sketch by author.

union from January through June, then be union-free the rest of the year. Health and safety and human rights issues also involve matters of fundamental principle, which explains why, as we pointed out in Chapter 7, they are regulated primarily through legislation, rather than being left to the vagaries of collective bargaining.

Where a settlement zone does exist, it is discovered during finalization, or the actual reaching of a settlement (Fisher and Williams, 1989:189). Unlike consolidation, which usually lasts for a long time, finalization is normally quite quick. The experience of reaching a settlement is difficult to describe in words, though most people who have ever negotiated will know intuitively what that experience feels like.[12] Sometimes agreement is reached only after the parties have all but given up hope. It's apparently common for negotiators to report feeling quite depressed just prior to this stage (Downie, 1984). Often the final settlement is triggered by a corridor or washroom meeting of the two principal negotiators, followed by a last-minute concession or repackaging that makes a previously unpalatable package at least marginally acceptable to the other side. In this regard, a prudent negotiator is like a wise parent, who will always hold a goodie or two in reserve for use in truly desperate situations (Williams, 1982, Lewicki et al., 1997).

Mopping up generally means drafting specific language for provisions to which the chief negotiators have agreed in principle. It may also entail attending to letters of intent or troubleshooting issues subsequently raised by one's constituency or principals (Fisher and Williams, 1989:189). It's important to attend to this stage carefully. Contract language that is not carefully drafted or does not reflect the true intent of the principals at the time of agreement can come back to haunt all concerned in the next round of negotiations, in addition to being fertile breeding ground for grievances and other types of union–management conflict during the life of the agreement.

Negotiating Strategy and Tactics

In general, good negotiators use persuasion to help change the other side's mind about the likely outcome of the negotiating process. A powerful persuasive technique (Fisher and Williams, 1989:187–189) involves planting a seed of doubt in the other negotiator's mind, as by depicting a credible scenario regarding a given issue that differs significantly from what the other side seems to expect. If the seed of doubt has been well planted, the other side should come to modify its position on related issues (Fisher and Williams, 1989:189).

Effective persuasion rarely happens by accident. In addition to superior communication and listening skills on the part of the negotiator, it requires thorough preparation on the part of the entire team, the careful development of a firm yet sufficiently flexible bottom line, and the judicious use of a number of specific negotiating tactics.

Preparation for Bargaining

Often success in negotiations can be attributed to a team's superior preparation. A good starting point is to canvass one's constituency or principals to determine what issues they would like to resolve from bargaining, the relative importance of those issues, and how long a lawful work stoppage they are prepared to stage or take (Fisher and Williams, 1989:199).

With the team's general objectives established, detailed preparations can begin. On the management side, this may well include monitoring workers' attitudes and concerns, getting a read on the overall economic and political environment within which negotiations will be conducted,[13] monitoring the union's developments, monitoring local or industry wage developments to get a sense of a reasonable "ballpark" figure for the final settlement,[14] and conducting background research aimed at developing proposals for non-wage issues (Godard and Kochan, 1982:128–130). Such background research may in turn entail conducting interviews or soliciting written submissions from line managers (Godard and Kochan, 1982:129–130), reviewing company policies and the administration of the current agreement, and examining any outstanding grievances or arbitration decisions resulting from the previous agreement, in addition to examining data drawn from suggestion boxes or employee exit interviews (Williams, 1982:213). With this broad range of information in hand, the management team can start developing and costing specific wage and benefit proposals (Godard and Kochan, 1982:129).

For the union team, the overall objective of preparation is pretty much the same as it is for management: to obtain as thorough a knowledge of the general and specific economic and political environments as possible to arrive at bargaining proposals that are realistic and stand a reasonable chance of acceptance, in addition to

Researcher pores over past settlements in her industry. In negotiations, good preparation is often half the battle.

meeting as many of the needs of the union's members as possible. But because of the union's statutory obligation to represent members fairly, and because unions generally operate in a far more public and open fashion than do management organizations, the *process* of preparation may be somewhat different. Like the management team, the union will solicit members' written input on contract proposals, and will conduct background research into comparable settlements in the area and industry. Then, both to receive further input and to help ensure members buy into any tentative settlement eventually negotiated, the union will typically hold one or more general membership meetings at which both general and specific bargaining objectives are discussed. It has been this author's experience that, unlike most typical union meetings (see Chapter 5), this type of meeting is generally very well attended.[15] At these meetings, the union leadership and negotiating team will normally take pains to ensure that proposals are put forward to address the needs of all major constituencies within the union. After these meetings, still further written input may be solicited, and the union may also inform members of ongoing developments through e-mail messages or a series of "Negotiation Newsletters."

Developing the Bottom Line

For both sides, the bottom line is normally developed at prenegotiation meetings. It's important that, by the end of these meetings, all issues be divided into three categories: bottom-line issues, over which the team is prepared to strike or take a strike;

trading issues, which are important but that can be bought by the other side in return for an equivalent concession; and "throwaway items," or items of less importance that will be given up after a good fight (Fisher and Williams, 1989:200). Within these categories, individual issues should be rank-ordered. Also, to the extent possible, the opponent's anticipated demands should be classified in similar fashion (Fisher and Williams, 1989).

In addition to helping teams develop their bottom line, such meetings may serve as "dress rehearsals," where the other side's expected positions are examined in preparation for the actual negotiations (Fisher and Williams, 1989:202). Another purpose of the prenegotiation meeting is to build teamwork and esprit des corps with an eye to ensuring that all team members remain committed to the team's agreed issue positions. At such meetings, team members are assigned roles such as the taking of notes, collection of data, costing, or observing the other side's reactions (Fisher and Williams, 1989). Part of these meetings may also be devoted to tactical decisions such as how to begin negotiations, or whether the chief negotiator will be the team's sole spokesperson and, if not, under what conditions others should speak. Most teams usually find it best to allow the chief negotiator to do all the talking, except in the case of specific technical issues, such as costing, where the team member assigned to the role may be better informed and thus better able to help the team's cause (see Fisher and Williams, 1989:203).[16]

Specific Negotiating Tactics

Researchers such as Kervin (1989:186) have identified five different types of bargaining move: concessions, trade-offs, promises, threats, and procedural moves. The ability to use all five judiciously is critical to almost any negotiator's success. In addition, good negotiators generally have the ability to find a critical focal point for a settlement, and to package items in a way that both constituents and opposing negotiators find acceptable. As well, they know how to make opening moves that are far enough away from their intended bottom line to allow a fair amount of room to maneuver, but not so far away, or so unreasonable, as to lead the other side to believe that they aren't really interested in striking a deal.

OPENING MOVES "What's a reasonable opening position?" is a question that instructors who use collective bargaining simulations in their introductory IR courses are probably asked more than any other. The question is never an easy one to answer. But among the relevant factors would surely be inflation levels, one's own level of experience and that of one's opponents, and (in classroom simulations), the amount of time available for the exercise. As a general rule, a union team could do worse than set an initial target of twice what it expects to receive for the monetary package, while management teams might start by offering half what they expect to give eventually. You might also consider how many moves you expect to take before reaching your bottom line, and how much you are willing to "give in" at each stage (Teplitsky, 1992:42). In addition, both sides should initially put forward far more issues than they expect to be on the table at the end of negotiations. The main reason for this strategy, often termed the "blue sky" or "large demand" approach (Craig and Solomon, 1996:272), is to allow ample room for trade-offs along the way.

One of the few things all negotiation experts agree on is that the initial position should not be the same as the bottom line. Again, many bargaining novices tend to wonder why so much time is wasted on the seemingly meaningless if not irrational ritual of arriving at a final settlement when to a great extent the terms are known before negotiating even starts (Craig and Solomon, 1996:203). Why doesn't manage-ment simply make a "firm, fair, and final offer" on a take-it-or-leave-it basis, and end all the palaver right there? One reason is that the *process* of collective bargaining, as distinguished from its economic outcomes, is considered by most citizens of democ-ratic societies to be of value in and of itself. The use of Boulwarism[17] (to give the aforementioned take-it-or-leave-it approach its official name) essentially prevents col-lective bargaining from occurring, which is why it has been ruled illegal in both Canada and the United States (Craig and Solomon, 1996:204; Godard, 1994:288). A related reason is that serious negotiations seem, for whatever reason, to help people both appear and feel more competent. By eliminating the negotiating process as such, Boulwarism eliminates a potentially important source of satisfaction (Godard, 1994, Lewicki et al., 1997:47). Beyond that, various studies have found that those who make more extreme initial offers get better settlements than those who make more modest ones (Lewicki et al., 1997:45).

Initial offers shouldn't be overly precise. Far better for a union to demand 3 percent than 2.89 or 3.11 percent. Indeed, it's not uncommon for a union, in mak-ing its initial demands, to call simply for a "substantial increase" or an increase "suf-ficient to allow our members to catch up with five years of inflation." Phrasing a demand in this way can be an effective technique, since it forces management to start thinking about just what would constitute a "substantial" increase, and may thus lead to a quicker meeting of minds than a more rigid numerical demand would.

CONCESSIONS AND TRADE-OFFS   A **concession** is a move that entails taking a position closer to, or even identical with, the other side's latest position. One might at first think rapid concessions the key to success in negotiation; however, the litera-ture indicates otherwise. A pattern of a tough opening position followed by gradual concessions appears to be much more successful most of the time (Godard, 1994:204).[18] For one thing, such a pattern convinces constituents that one has done one's best in their behalf, and thus reduces the likelihood of rejection of the tentative deal. For another, it allows the opposing negotiator to feel he or she has had some influence on the process (Kervin, 1989). From a psychological perspective, it is also better to start tough and gradually ease up than to start soft and be forced to toughen up after criticism from team members. In the latter instance, opponents are apt to get their backs up, and a strike may well be the ultimate result. Where concessions are made, they're generally more effective if done conditionally, in the form of a "tit-for-tat" or possible trade-offs (i.e., making a concession on one item in return for the opponent's roughly equal concession on another) than if done unconditionally (Kervin, 1989), perhaps because they suggest the concession maker is dealing from a position of strength rather than from one of weakness.

THREATS AND PROMISES   A threat suggests some action that will hurt the opponent (i.e., going on strike) if or unless the opponent makes a certain move. A promise, though sometimes unconditional, typically offers the opponent some benefit in return for a move on its part (Kervin, 1989:186). While threats are not uncommon (Kervin, 1989:205), experienced negotiators tend to use them sparingly, since they're likely to evoke hostility and lead to counterthreats and reduced joint outcomes (Kervin, 1989). Given that most labour–management negotiations are conducted under strict deadline pressure and that normally a work stoppage can occur should negotiations reach an impasse, it is usually best to let this fact speak for itself, rather than getting an opponent's back up unnecessarily. The impact of promises is less clear. What can be said is that negotiators who make promises are perceived by opponents to be more trustworthy and cooperative, which suggests that their use could lead to a quicker settlement so long as the negotiator is perceived to have the authority to fulfill them (Kervin, 1989).

PROCEDURAL MOVES   Procedural moves include actions such as suggesting or making a change in the bargaining process (Kervin, 1989:186). Such a change could take the form of a request for a caucus, a request for a change in the time or place of the next negotiating session, or a request for mediation (Kervin, 1989). On the surface, such moves appear to be neutral, like a baseball hitter's request for time from the umpire. As in the case of the baseball example, however, such requests can throw an opponent's timing off and generate considerable uncertainty, and they can also seriously impede the flow of negotiations. For this reason, when such changes are initiated unilaterally, especially if they're at all frequent or occur during the late stages of negotiations when timing is everything, they are often interpreted as hostile acts. Significantly, the use of such procedural moves has been associated with an increased rate of bargaining impasses and strikes (Kervin, 1989:202). But where a procedural move, such as a request for mediation, is initiated jointly, it may signal increased willingness to work together and thus help lead to a quicker settlement.

FOCAL POINTS   Experienced negotiators have the knack of proposing settlement terms that "seem to make sense" to opponents because of their symmetry, simplicity, or obviousness, or because they are in line with previous, well-known settlements (Kervin, 1989:204). In the words of Thomas Schelling (1957:435): "The

Would you want this man as your chief spokesperson? Most collective bargaining specialists say frequent use of threats is typically the mark of the amateur.

'obvious' place to compromise frequently seems to win by some kind of default, as though there is simply no rationale for settling anywhere else." From this perspective, much of the negotiator's skill may lie in finding just what that obvious place is and pointing it out to constituents and the other side. Settlements that can be expressed in round numbers or that split the difference between the two sides' most recent offers seem to possess "focal quality," to use Schelling's terminology. So, too, do settlements that rely on common, generally accepted indicators. Far better, in devising a cost-of-living formula, to rely on the Consumer Price Index than on some other possibly more accurate, but definitely more obscure inflation index. In this case, any possible benefits to be derived from using the alternative index would likely be far outweighed by the greater difficulty of using that index.

PACKAGING   Packaging is the art of combining several different positions into a comprehensive final offer. Often it entails the use of several different types of move at once (concessions, trade-offs, promises, threats). Research has found that the packaging of issues leads to a higher rate of settlement than dealing with issues one at a time (Kervin, 1989:206). There are a number of possible reasons for this. For one thing, a package is generally offered at the end of negotiations. At this stage, it offers the opportunity to end the proceedings once and for all—an opportunity that the other side may well be glad to avail itself of, if it can do so without loss of face. For another, it presents a clearer and more immediate picture of the bargaining scenario as a whole than do deals pieced together issue by issue. This can be helpful in convincing constituents or principals that their issues have been addressed in some way, even if not entirely to their satisfaction. Finally, and quite simply, a skillfully prepared package has the ring of authority about it. Far more than further movement on individual issues, a package suggests that the negotiator offering it is serious about settling. This note of finality also carries with it an implicit threat—that of withdrawing from negotiations if the package is not accepted—that can likewise encourage the other side to settle.

Desire to Settle

The previous discussion has focussed on a number of generally accepted techniques for reaching settlement. Implicit in this discussion has been the assumption that both sides want to settle and possess the ability to do so (Godard, 1994:342). While it *seems* obvious that both sides should want to settle, this isn't always the case. Moreover, even when both sides do want to settle, one or both may be prevented from doing so by factors at least partly beyond their control. For example, a management group might genuinely want to offer workers more money, but be unable to do so because of strict cost-control measures coming out of the head office. Similarly, a union local might be willing to accept management's demand for a relaxation of certain work rules, but be prevented from doing so by national union policy.

When a settlement isn't reached and any mandatory third-party intervention proves unavailing, a strike or lockout is the usual result. To the pure economist, most strikes are irrational, particularly in times of low inflation. But as we point out in more detail in Chapter 11, strikes serve more than simply economic functions. Many a strike that is economically irrational may be quite rational from a political perspective. Management may want to push the union into a strike it knows it can't win, as a means of asserting more control over the workplace and possibly even getting rid of the union at a later date.[19] A union may feel the need to call a strike to build its members' internal solidarity, or even to serve as a reality check on some members' extravagant expectations (Gunderson, Hyatt, and Ponak, 1995:382–383). And either or both sides may view such a strike as an investment in longer-term bargaining power vis-à-vis the other side—a case of "short-term pain for long-term gain" (Fisher and Williams, 1989:197).

To sum up, and at the risk of belabouring the obvious, if both sides don't want to settle, then they probably won't settle. No amount of persuasion, repackaging of offers, or jawboning by a conciliator or mediator is likely to be of much use so long as either or both parties are operating on the basis of a different agenda.[20]

Ways of Improving the Bargaining Process

In a situation where a union and management group may have a history of acrimonious negotiations, but be sincerely interested in turning things around, there are a number of options open to them for improving the bargaining process.

One approach that has been tried and often found to be effective is that of early negotiations, or prebargaining (Downie, 1989:265–266). Normally, most negotiations are conducted under extreme time pressure due to the imminent threat of a strike or lockout. While the threat of a work stoppage can lead to a settlement, it can also generate tension and hard feelings. Starting negotiations well ahead of time can remove most of that tension and lead to a more productive, problem-solving atmosphere. Early-bird negotiations seem to work best when there is a target date and a well-thought-out time frame for negotiations (Downie, 1989:266).

Another well-known approach is single-team bargaining (a variation of integrative bargaining, discussed in the union impacts chapter), which has union and management representatives seated next to each other at a round table rather than across from each other at a rectangular one in a bid to promote joint problem-solving. When the approach was tried out at Labatt Breweries, a pioneer in single-team bargaining during Tom Crossman's time as personnel director, it not only involved the use of a round table (or sometimes no table at all), but also the elimination of single spokespersons for the two sides, a strategy normally recommended (including here) as being the most efficient and effective way to proceed (Downie, 1989:267).

Even where the parties prefer not to sit at a round table, they can still move away from traditional confrontational bargaining marked by distrust, high levels of conflict, and an emphasis on "win-lose" outcomes, towards what Fisher and Ury (1983) have described as **principled bargaining**. This approach focusses on the parties' underlying interests rather than on the positions they may take at the bargaining table (Chaykowski, 1995:247). It works by separating team members' personalities from the problems under discussion, developing objective criteria for negotiating outcomes that involve fairness in both standards and procedures, and devising options that give rise to "win-win" or mutual gains situations rather than to "win-lose" or zero-sum ones (Chaykowski, 1995). While it is not clear how widely principled bargaining has been adopted in Canada, Chaykowski (1995:247–248) notes that it has been adopted by a number of major corporations and unions; two of the unions that appear to have adopted it most widely are the Steelworkers and Communications, Energy and Paperworkers (CEP).

Yet another possibility may be to substitute voluntary arbitration for the threat of a strike or lockout. While mandatory interest arbitration, as we note elsewhere in the book, generally hurts the bargaining process, a substitute dispute resolution process voluntarily selected by both parties can sometimes help it (Downie, 1989:264–265). Such an approach has been taken in such varied industries as the U.S. steel industry and the clothing industry in Ontario. In the latter, the number of disputes actually referred to arbitration was extremely low, suggesting that the voluntarily chosen mechanism may indeed have improved the bargaining process (Downie, 1989:265).

Again, we must emphasize that the use of mechanisms like those just described pre-supposes a certain degree of trust, as well as a joint willingness to settle. Where the trust isn't there, the parties may wish to work specifically on improving their relationship, using either an organizational development technique, such as one of those described by Downie (1989:268–270), or one of the preventive mediation programs now run by most provincial governments. (These are described in more detail in Chapter 12.)

THE COLLECTIVE AGREEMENT

Collective agreements—the tangible result of the negotiation process—are central to the Canadian IR system (Giles and Jain, 1989). These documents are of such importance because, in unionized establishments, they regulate many aspects of the day-to-day relationships between workers, unions, and employers (Giles and Starkman, 1995), including such important matters as workers' rates of pay and hours of work, their working conditions, and (at least in the private sector),[21] the processes for layoffs, promotions, and transfers. They also spell out specific management and union rights and provide a mechanism (normally some kind of grievance procedure) for handling any disputes that may arise during their lifetime.

By European standards (see Adams, 1995a:503), most Canadian and American agreements are quite long and detailed. There are a number of reasons for this. Perhaps the most important is that, due in large measure to the relative political weakness of these two countries' labour movements (Giles and Starkman, 1995:341), they've concentrated most of their attention on collective bargaining and detailed regulation of work at the individual workplace level, rather than on political action, as is often the case in Europe. In addition, alternative mechanisms such as works councils, through which many workplace-level matters are regulated in European countries such as Germany and the Netherlands (Adams, 1995a:506), are rare here. As a result, the collective bargaining process takes on more importance and is forced to address a considerably broader range of issues than is generally the case in other industrialized countries.

Some Functions of Collective Agreements

The primary function of the collective agreement, at least from a legal point of view, is to set out the terms and conditions of employment to be followed by the union and management organization for a given period of time (Giles and Jain, 1989). But collective agreements mean different things to different people, depending upon their perspective and their role in the IR system. To the dedicated unionist, the agreement is a bible to which he or she will almost invariably refer in time of need or doubt. To most IR and HR managers, on the other hand, it's probably somewhere between a nuisance and a necessary evil. As for IR academics, institutionalists generally look on collective agreements very favourably, as being, in effect, mini-constitutions that bring some measure of self-government and industrial democracy to the workplace (Giles and Jain, 1989:320).[22] On the other hand, neoclassicists and managerialists often view collective agreements, particularly their work rule provisions, as both inefficient and wasteful and an infringement on management's right to run enterprises as it sees fit (Godard, 1994:315). At the other end of the spectrum, those taking a radical/political economy perspective (i.e., Panitch and Swartz, 1988) see collective agreements as doing little to rectify the fundamental power imbalance between workers and management.

Evolution of Canadian Collective Agreements

In 1901, as Giles and Jain (1989:318) note, Local 713 of the Carpenters' Union signed an agreement with Niagara Falls contractors that contained only eight brief clauses governing such basic issues as wage rates, hours of work per day, holiday and overtime pay rates, and security of employment for union members. Today, many collective agreements are far longer, often reaching 100 pages or more and not infrequently containing a variety of appendices, letters of understanding, and wage schedules in addition to the main text (Giles and Jain, 1989:321). Also, unlike the Carpenters' agreement, written in plain English, many of today's agreements are written in complex, even convoluted legal jargon that makes them barely understandable to the workers and supervisors who must live by them on a daily basis (Giles and Jain, 1989). Why have Canadian agreements become so long and involved? And why must they be written in such complex language that the people who work with them most closely have difficulty understanding them?

One reason, particularly for the greater length of today's agreements, lies in the growth of larger and more bureaucratic workplaces employing many different types of worker, including many unskilled and semi-skilled ones, and the industrial unionism that arose in response to this development. This has meant that collective agreements often must contain work rules and pay schedules applying to a dozen or more groups of workers, instead of just one as in the case of the Carpenters' Union.

In recent years, Canadian workplaces have made increasing use of a broad range of new technologies and chemical substances of various kinds. The increasingly rapid pace of technological change has led unions to negotiate provisions seeking to protect workers against the adverse effects of such change, such as loss of employment or income (see Economic Council of Canada, 1987; Peirce, 1987). A growing emphasis on human rights in the workplace has also led some unions to negotiate clauses regulating such things as testing for AIDS and substance abuse and the monitoring of employees' e-mail (Giles and Starkman, 2001). Meanwhile, the introduction of many new, potentially hazardous substances into Canadian workplaces has led unions to negotiate a variety of health and safety provisions governing procedures for using such substances, protective equipment, and the like. Again, these provisions, sometimes addressing quite complicated technical issues, have helped add to Canadian agreements' length and complexity.

Globalization and increased foreign competition have recently put considerable additional stress on the IR system. The growing numbers of layoffs arising from widespread downsizing and restructuring have led most unions to make job security a priority, negotiating employment and income security provisions when they can, and when they can't, negotiating severance pay provisions or other ways of at least partially cushioning the impact of layoffs. The current environment has also led unions to demand greater control over pension plans (Giles and Starkman, 1995:349), and to negotiate increased involvement in the new forms of work organization that employers have often introduced in an attempt to make their firms more competitive (Giles and Starkman, 1995:343).

Another important source of collective agreement length and complexity has been the Canadian work force's growing diversity. As large numbers of women entered the work force and signed union cards, unions began negotiating maternity leave and family leave provisions, anti-discrimination and anti-harassment clauses, and in some cases provisions establishing on-site workplace child care centres.[23] The entry of large numbers of professionals into unionized workplaces, many resulting from the widespread unionization of the public sector during the 1960s and '70s, resulted in provisions reimbursing employees for professional society memberships and committing employers to promote these employees' career development opportunities. Similarly, the entry of large numbers of ethnic and religious minorities into unionized workplaces has required unions to place additional emphasis on negotiating anti-discrimination and anti-harassment provisions, as well as provisions requiring employers to accommodate those of different religious backgrounds by providing time off for major religious observances, or creating a different work schedule when necessary. And the hiring of increased numbers of people with disabilities, spurred by human rights legislation, led unions to negotiate special provisions governing building accessibility, or in some cases even redesigning jobs to allow them to be performed by those with disabilities (see Carter, 1997).

The prevailing Canadian doctrine of **residual management rights**, under which it's generally accepted by most arbitrators that any right not specifically granted to the union in the collective agreement is reserved to management (Giles and Starkman, 2001:274), constitutes yet another source of collective agreement complexity. Particularly in view of many employers' continuing resistance to unions, unions have, in order to protect their members' interests, been forced to negotiate extremely detailed and comprehensive collective agreement provisions limiting the rights of management in the areas of greatest concern to those members. As well, because grievance arbitration (discussed in Chapter 12) has become highly legalistic, contract language must be drafted with great care—undoubtedly further adding to the documents' complexity in many cases (Giles and Jain, 1989). A related development is the explicit incorporation into collective agreements of legal requirements from work standards, health and safety, and human rights legislation to which the parties are required to conform (Carter, 1997). This too has become a source of collective agreement complexity.

MAIN TYPES OF COLLECTIVE AGREEMENT PROVISION

An Overview of Collective Agreements

One's first reaction, on looking at a typical Canadian agreement, is apt to be one of bewilderment or even despair at the array of clauses, sub-clauses, schedules, and letters of intent. After one has examined a number of collective agreements, one comes to see that, in many ways, most agreements resemble each other quite closely. Most begin with a brief statement outlining the agreement's general purpose and, if the document is at all complex, with a list of relevant definitions (Giles and Jain, 1989:321). Next comes a group of clauses outlining the rights and obligations of the parties (**management rights** and union recognition clauses), defining the bargaining unit, and, typically, providing for grievance procedures or (in some cases) other means of resolving conflict such as joint committees (Giles and Jain, 1989; Godard, 1994:305).

The second major group of clauses typically covers wages and hours of work. Included here are wage and hours schedules governing different groups of workers, provisions governing overtime pay, shift premiums for work at night, vacation allotments, and provisions for both paid and unpaid leave (Giles and Jain, 1989:321).

A third group of provisions (not always grouped together in the agreement) governs work rules, broadly defined. Here, in addition to rules governing how work is assigned and performed, one finds provisions governing technological change and the methods used for layoffs, transfers, and promotions (Giles and Jain, 1989). The fourth and last major group of provisions concerns the work environment, again broadly defined (Giles and Jain, 1989). Such provisions may include disciplinary procedures, health and safety clauses, and anti-discrimination and anti-harassment clauses of various kinds.

If wage schedules are at all detailed and complicated, they are generally placed in an appendix, along with other issues considered too lengthy to be included in the main text (Giles and Jain, 1989). The agreement's back pages may also contain letters of intent or memoranda of understanding typically intended to spotlight issues to be addressed more fully in subsequent rounds of negotiations. A good example of such a letter of intent is the one on employees' use of frequent flyer points accumulated while on business-related travel contained in the 2000 agreement between the Canadian Commercial Corporation and the Professional Institute.

Union and Management Rights and Conflict Control Provisions

These "ground rule" provisions, found in virtually all Canadian agreements, delineate the respective workplace rights of management and the union and provide for the handling of disagreements over interpretation, normally through a grievance procedure, but also sometimes through joint committees or other more proactive means. In addition, provisions in this group often specify the bargaining unit and members to whom the agreement applies, either directly or by listing members of excluded groups, such as management or in some cases professional staff or part-time employees.

Of greatest importance here are management rights and union rights and security provisions. Management rights provisions refer to clauses affirming management's right to run the enterprise as it wishes, subject to the limitations of the collective agreement. Such clauses may be either general or specific. In the latter case, they may spell out specific rights management reserves to itself, such as the right to hire, promote, transfer, or lay off workers, as well as to dismiss or suspend them, as in the case of Article 8.01 of the agreement between Bell Canada and the Communications Workers of Canada.

Union rights and security provisions officially recognize the union's place in the enterprise. In addition, they grant specific rights for union officials, such as stewards, and address the rather controversial issue of how dues are to be collected. The vast majority of Canadian agreements contain a provision stating that the employer recognizes the union as the workers' official bargaining agent. Many such provisions also state which employees are to be considered members of the bargaining unit.

Beyond contract language generally recognizing their right to exist, unions need more specific provisions to ensure their presence is felt in the workplace on an ongoing basis. This means that their officials, in particular their stewards, need to be free to represent members' interests without management harassment. With this in mind, unions will frequently seek to negotiate provisions allowing them access to company facilities, such as offices or bulletin boards, to enable them to carry out their duties. Along similar lines, stewards' rights provisions have become fairly standard features of Canadian agreements. In some cases (Giles and Starkman, 1995:349), the company will reserve the right to limit the amount of time stewards can devote to union duties if it deems the time taken for such duties excessive.

Union security provisions address the issue of whether employees are required to be union members and if so, within what time frame. A number of types of union security clause are found in Canadian agreements. The strictest are the so-called **"closed shop" provisions** stating that the employer will hire only individuals who are already union members. Closed shops are most typically associated with the existence of hiring halls, organized and run by unions to provide employers with the number of workers they may need at any given time. Such arrangements are commonest in industries like construction and longshoring, where the work is temporary in nature and the workers' real attachment is to their trade and union rather than to the firm. **"Union shop" provisions** do not require union membership as a condition of employment, but do require all employees to join within a specified time period after being hired. A **"modified" union shop provision** requires all those hired after a given date to join the union. The weakest type of union security provision, the so-called **"maintenance of membership" provision**, does not compel anyone to join the union or pay dues, but does require anyone who has already joined or joins in the future to remain in the organization (Giles and Jain, 1989:326). "Rand formula" clauses (discussed in Chapters 4 and 8) do not require anyone to join a union, but do require all bargaining unit members to pay union dues, on the basis that non-members benefit just as much from the union's efforts in their behalf as do members. Where no union security provision is in place, the situation is referred to as an **open shop**.

As of 1999 (Giles and Starkman, 2001:284–5), about 53 percent of all Canadian agreements imposed some type of union membership requirement. The commonest types were the union and modified union shop, each with about 20 percent. Closed shop provisions were found in fewer than 10 percent of all agreements, and maintenance of membership provisions, in less than 3 percent. Rand formula arrangements were the commonest of all, found in more than 31 percent of all agreements. Open shops, common in the United States because of the "right-to-work" provisions of the *Taft-Hartley* amendments to that country's labour relations act, are less common here, though not the rarity they once were. In 1999, they occurred in over 16 percent of all agreements, compared to just 6.5 percent in 1994. The increase in open shop provisions has been largely at the expense of Rand formula ones, which in 1994 were found in 39 percent of all agreements (see Giles and Starkman, 1995). Since Rand formula clauses provide unions with a cash flow and simplify their bookkeeping procedures (Giles and Starkman, 2001:285), they are of considerable benefit to unions. The recent move away from such provisions to outright open shop ones should, therefore, be of concern to the labour movement.

CONFLICT-CONTROL PROVISIONS Conflict-control provisions address the issue of how disputes arising during the life of the agreement will be handled. In some instances they also establish preventive mechanisms, such as joint committees, designed to reduce or redirect labour–management conflict. Such provisions include "no-strike" clauses whereby the union agrees it will not strike during the life of the agreement and management agrees it will not lock out and provision for grievance arbitration as the mechanism for resolving mid-term contract disputes. Both types of provision are found in the vast majority of Canadian agreements. In many cases, grievance procedures are quite specific. Many agreements specify a list of acceptable arbitrators. Others provide for a single arbitrator instead of a three-person panel; still others name a standing umpire or establish various types of expedited arbitration procedure (Gandz and Whitehead, 1989:250–252).

Grievances, as we point out in more detail in Chapter 12, are costly and time-consuming for both unions and management organizations. Recognizing this, thoughtful unions and management organizations often make provision for joint committees, with an eye to addressing ongoing problems on a proactive basis, thereby preventing them from becoming formal grievances. As of 1999, such committees were found in about 70 percent of all agreements, covering more than three-quarters of all employees (Giles and Starkman, 2001:288). In a few cases, unions and management organizations have gone beyond committees to negotiate broad, framework-style agreements, variously known as joint governance arrangements or social contracts (Verma, 1995; Giles and Starkman, 2001), normally involving a trade-off whereby the union agrees not to strike for a fairly lengthy period (typically in the vicinity of five years) and to moderate its wage demands in return for job security and increased involvement in organizational decision-making. These agreements mean that the union becomes, in effect, a full partner in managing the organization (Verma, 1995), and thus entail a fundamental transformation away from its traditional role as workers' advocate. Historically they have been particularly popular in Quebec, where they have been actively promoted both by provincial governments and by unions seeking to play a more proactive role in the workplace change process (Déom and Boivin, 2001:497-8).

Wage and Hours Provisions

Since most people work primarily for the pay they receive, wages and hours are at the heart of the collective agreement. Compensation issues are normally among the more difficult items to negotiate and are typically left to the end of the negotiation process, after less contentious issues have been settled (see Fisher and Williams, 1989).

Wages

Most agreements contain various wage schedules detailing hourly, weekly, bi-weekly, monthly, or sometimes even annual pay rates for workers in different groups. Production and other blue-collar workers are normally paid on an hourly basis, while office, white-collar, and professional workers are typically paid on a weekly or monthly basis (Giles and Starkman, 1995:357). Premium wages (most often 50 percent above the usual rate) are normally paid for overtime work (typically anything beyond 40 hours in a week or 8 in a day); sometimes an extra premium (normally at least twice the usual rate) will be paid for work on Sundays or holidays. Premium wages may also be paid for shift work, for work performed at night, or for unusually onerous or unpleasant work, such as unloading animal carcasses from ships' holds (Picard, 1967). In some cases, special clauses will provide "standby pay" for those who must remain on call or carry cell phones when off-duty, or **"reporting pay"** or **"call-back pay"** for those called into work for short periods (Giles and Starkman, 1995:353).

In addition to accounting for different jobs, wage schedules often take workers' length of service into account. Such "step increments" become particularly important in situations where there is little opportunity for promotion (as in the case of much public sector work in recent years). Schedules often contain four to six steps within each job category, with workers normally receiving a one-step raise each year providing their performance remains satisfactory (Giles and Starkman, 1995:356).

When inflation was high, as it was in the late 1970s and early 1980s, many unions sought to protect their members' real wages by negotiating cost of living allowance (**COLA**) **clauses**. The basic idea behind such provisions is to adjust wages to the inflation rate so workers' purchasing power is maintained through the life of the contract. COLA clauses typically provide some, though not complete, protection against inflation. Often they are triggered only at a certain rate of inflation (i.e., 3 percent). Also, some COLA clauses don't cover the full contract period, while others provide for less than full adjustment to the inflation rate. With the sharp decline in inflation since the early 1980s, COLA clauses have become far less common in Canadian agreements, accounting for only about 14 percent of all Canadian agreements in 1998 compared with 30 percent in 1981 (Giles and Starkman, 2001:296). Another consequence of the drop in inflation has been that few of the remaining COLA clauses have been triggered (Giles and Starkman, 1995).

While most unionized workers are paid a regular wage or salary, some are under incentive systems whereby they are paid wholly or partially on the basis on the amount of work performed. Unions generally dislike incentive systems, particularly individual systems that they typically criticize as "pitting worker against worker." As well, piece-work systems are often difficult and costly to administer and can lead to considerable workplace conflict (Giles and Starkman, 1995:357). For these reasons, they have generally been uncommon in Canadian agreements, occurring in only about 5 percent of all Canadian agreements (Giles and Starkman, 2001:295), a significantly lower percentage than in the late 1980s (Fawcett, 1998). Where such arrangements do occur, it's most often in the clothing industry (Grant, 1992:233) or in logging and other parts of the forest sector (Radforth, 1982; Giles and Starkman, 1995:357).[24] Though individual incentive arrangements have become less common, it should also be noted that "team-oriented" incentive plans such as gain-sharing, group incentive plans, and, in particular, profit-sharing plans, have increased since the late 1980s (Fawcett, 1998).

Still another form of compensation system is the "pay-for-knowledge" system whereby workers are paid a different hourly, weekly, or monthly rate depending on the number of skills they have mastered (see Halpern, 1984). Normally, mastery must be demonstrated by passing specific tests covering the skill or skills in question. Such systems are most common in socio-technical systems environments and other workplaces using self-directed work teams, where it is necessary for workers to have a broad range of skills to function effectively as team members. An example of a pay-for-knowledge pay schedule may be found in the now well-known Shell Sarnia socio-technical systems arrangement (see Table 10.1).

Benefits

In addition to wages, compensation packages in collective agreements generally include a variety of benefits such as pension plans, disability and medical insurance, sick leave, extended health care, life and accident insurance, and dental insurance.

Table 10.1

BASIC MONTHLY SALARIES

Team Members (Shift)	Basic Monthly Salaries	Hourly Rate Equivalents
Phase 12	$1 698	$10.47
Phase 11	$1 643	$10.13
Phase 10	$1 588	$ 9.79
Phase 9	$1 536	$ 9.47
Phase 8	$1 483	$ 9.14
Phase 7	$1 429	$ 8.81
Phase 6	$1 376	$ 8.48
Phase 5	$1 322	$ 8.15
Phase 4	$1 269	$ 7.82
Phase 3	$1 215	$ 7.49
Phase 2	$1 162	$ 7.16
Phase 1	$1 124	$ 6.93
Team Members (Craft) Journeymen	$1 551	$ 9.56

Source: Halpern, 1984, Basic Monthly Salaries, Pay-for-Knowledge Progression, Shell Sarnia Plant.

Nationwide, such benefits comprise more than 30 percent of total compensation costs (Giles & Starkman, 2001:296), which makes the traditional term, "fringe benefits," something of a misnomer. In unionized establishments, the figure is almost certainly higher than 30 percent, since (as we noted in earlier chapters), many unionized workers are older and in higher tax brackets and therefore prefer to take as much as possible of their compensation in the form of non-taxable benefits rather than taxable wages, and employers also like to use such benefits (particularly pension plans) as a means of reducing costly turnover. Aside from benefits of the type listed above, some agreements also contain provisions entitling workers to a given number of days off a year for religious or unspecified personal reasons. Agreement provisions normally spell out the details of the various plans, the eligibility rules (often linked to **seniority**, especially in the case of pension plans), and the respective contributions to be made by the employer and employees towards the cost of the various plans.

In recent years, there have generally been few new benefits, as cost-conscious employers have sought to reduce benefits or shift more of their costs to employees (Giles and Starkman, 2001). However, one new benefit that has been introduced with some regularity is prepaid legal services (Giles and Starkman, 2001). Another, perhaps in recognition of the growing stresses faced by workers in today's difficult economy, is the **Employee Assistance Program (EAP)**, which enables workers to receive counselling on a broad range of issues, from alcohol- and drug-related problems to marital and financial ones.

Work Hours

Hours of work have been of enormous importance to the Canadian labour movement since the nineteenth century, when, as we noted earlier, demands for a shorter work day were a rallying cry around which the entire movement could unite.[25] Hours provisions have taken on renewed importance in recent years, with the increased family responsibilities being shouldered by many workers and the growing recognition that shorter hours may be the best solution to persistent demand-deficient unemployment (Gunderson and Reid, 1998; Peirce, 2000(b)).

Most agreements stipulate normal working hours per week for those working on different jobs. The most common arrangements are still weeks of 35 to 40 hours during regular daytime hours; however, various alternative arrangements such as shift work and shorter or longer hours have been growing more frequent in recent years (Giles and Starkman, 2001). In the case of shift work, agreements may provide for the rotation of shifts among employees or the scheduling of shifts by seniority (Giles and Starkman, 2001), which typically means that more senior employees can pick preferred daytime shifts. Other provisions stipulate the length of time allowed for lunch breaks, coffee breaks, and washroom breaks. Vacation and holiday pay provisions state how much vacation workers at given seniority levels will be entitled to, which days will be considered paid holidays, and how much of a premium will be paid to those required to work on those holidays. Finally, the growing presence of women in the work force has led to clauses providing maternity leave beyond the minimum provided through unemployment insurance, the right to accumulate seniority while on maternity leave, and to take time off to care for sick family members or attend parent-teacher interviews at school (Giles and Starkman, 1995:354).

The growing presence of women in the workplace has also led to demands for more flexible working hours to allow working mothers (and sometimes fathers) to attend to family responsibilities. Flexible hours provisions allow employees to choose which hours they will work within a given core period (say between 7 a.m. and 6 p.m.), so long as they put in the requisite number of hours each day. **Compressed work weeks** most often give employees a day off every week or two weeks. In return, the employee puts in a slightly longer day, so that he or she works the regular number of hours over a one- or two-week period. Both are now common in the federal government. Such arrangements are often extremely popular with employees (see CLMPC, 1997 for examples), since they allow periodic long weekends as well as providing needed time during business hours to attend to family matters. However, they sometimes meet with management resistance, either because they complicate scheduling and create difficulties in maintaining service (CLMPC, 1997) or simply because the managers in question don't feel comfortable with anything other than orthodox "nine-to-five" scheduling, particularly in situations where employees may be working without supervision.

In a bid both to reduce unemployment and to allow workers to better attend to family responsibilities, European labour movements have been pushing shorter hours increasingly hard in recent years(see Peirce, 2000). The Canadian labour movement has been somewhat ambivalent on the issue of shorter work hours (A. Jackson, 1997), in part because it represents many lower-paid workers who feel they need overtime pay to help make ends meet. For this reason, it has generally been reluctant to push for legislation reducing work hours, except to a certain extent in Quebec. However, a number of unions have taken the lead in negotiating agreements providing for reductions in either regular work hours or overtime hours or both in return for job creation. The unions that have done the most along these lines in recent years include the Canadian Auto Workers (CAW), United Steelworkers of America (USWA), and Communications, Energy and Paperworkers' Union (CEP). For a number of years, the CEP has promoted a broad-brush approach to reduced hours including longer leaves, reduced and flexible hours for workers with family responsibilities, and a shorter work week or shorter work year featuring longer vacations and increased family and educational leaves (Peirce, 2000 (b)). The union has also called for "time banking," which would allow workers to defer part of their regular or overtime salary and take it as paid leave time at a later date. As well, a number of CEP locals have negotiated reduced overtime or shorter work weeks in return for agreements to create or save jobs (White, 1997a:170). Overall, however, recent evidence suggests that Canadian unions are generally putting a fairly low priority on shorter work hours. A survey conducted by Kumar, Murray, and Schetagne (1998: Table 9) found that reducing work hours was an extremely important priority for only 20 percent of the responding unions.

Work Rules and Job Control Provisions

Without unions, management would have complete control over how work was organized and performed. At the bargaining table, unions seek to wrest some degree of control over **work rules** stating how work is to be done, as well as over the criteria for layoffs, transfers, promotions, technological change, and larger-scale work force reductions. Since workers' belief that they are entitled to basic job rights almost inevitably conflicts with management's desire to maximize flexibility and control, job control and work rules provisions can be among the most bitterly contested in the entire agreement (Giles and Starkman, 1995 and 2001).

Hiring Process and Job Assignment

The strongest protection a union can achieve for its members is a "closed shop" provision (discussed earlier in the chapter) allowing only its members to be hired. Another, related form of control over job assignment may be obtained through the joint union–management dispatch systems that have often been used in longshoring (see Picard, 1967; Shipping Federation, 1972). Unions may also obtain a measure of control over hiring and, in some cases, over the number of people admitted to the trade through provisions establishing union–management apprenticeship programs, requiring vacancies to be filled from within the organization when possible, and preventing supervisors and other non-bargaining unit employees from performing jobs normally done by their members (Giles and Starkman, 1995:360). Management's strongest weapon here is the **probationary period,** found in about two-thirds of all major Canadian agreements (Giles and Starkman, 2001). Workers on probation, which normally lasts less than five months but may run for up to a year, can easily be let go should management deem their work to be unsatisfactory. A probationary period thus allows management considerable control over the hiring process, even if the union has negotiated other sorts of restrictions (Giles and Starkman, 2001).

Work Rules

Work rules provisions get at the very heart of the production process. They regulate such things as the speed of assembly lines and production processes, the number of people who must be assigned to a given job, the maximum allowable workload, and the question of who is to be allowed to do certain jobs. In longshoring in the Port of Montreal (Shipping Federation, 1972; Picard, 1967), collective agreement provisions traditionally sought to protect employment by placing a maximum on the size of sling loads, requiring a given number of certain classes of worker for each gang in addition to a given minimum overall gang size, and requiring certain numbers of relief men under certain circumstances (Picard, 1967, Rules 11 and 12). Workload restrictions

In longshoring, prior to modernization, unions tried to use work rule provisions to protect their members' jobs and prevent injures from lifting loads that were too heavy.

are also an important part of bargaining in education. Teachers and university professors say that in order for them to provide quality education, there need to be restrictions both on the numbers of students they are asked to teach and on the numbers of classes or courses to which they are assigned. Such restrictions are needed, they argue, so that they will not be swamped with marking and preparation work. Additionally, public school teachers say they need time to "recharge themselves" during the school day. Workload was a major issue in both the 1997 and 1998 Ontario teachers' strikes (see Peirce, 2000:121). It has remained a hot issue since then, as teachers have protested being forced to assume compulsory extracurricular duties such as coaching.

Job Control

Job control provisions govern the criteria to be used for changes in the firm's internal labour market, especially promotions, transfers, and layoffs. Like workload and work rule provisions, they are often the source of considerable conflict between workers and management, since management generally prefers to retain its control over such decisions, while workers and their unions fear that such decisions may be made arbitrarily and thus often prefer that such decisions be made on the basis of seniority (Giles and Starkman, 1995:362). The rationale behind seniority is that long-serving workers, who have invested much of their working lives in the organization, should be entitled to preferential consideration for promotion and transfers and greater security against layoffs (Giles and Starkman, 2001). Another argument in favour of seniority is that by providing an objective, impersonal standard for personnel decisions, it eliminates the possibility of arbitrary or unfair management actions, which in turn can increase workers' morale and productivity (see Freeman and Medoff, 1979). However, seniority provisions have come under increasing attack in recent years. For one thing, seniority-based layoff provisions may inadvertently discriminate against women, minority group members, and people with disabilities, who, as the "last hired," would of necessity be the first laid off and the last recalled under most existing layoff arrangements (Giles and Starkman, 1995 and 2001). For another, the negative efficiency implications of such provisions, especially when applied to promotions, may be more severe now than in the past when, in many large industrial plants, workers and jobs might be more or less interchangeable. With fewer and fewer interchangeable jobs and more and more "knowledge-based" work in the economy as a whole, length of service has come to be a less reliable indicator, in many cases, of a worker's ability to do a new or different job. These are two reasons that may help explain why seniority provisions have become less common in Canadian agreements since the mid 1990s (Giles and Starkman, 1995 and 2001).

Seniority provisions are used in two different ways: to determine a worker's status with respect to accrued benefits such as vacation time, severance pay, and pensions; and to determine his or her status relative to other workers in situations involving promotions, transfers, layoffs, choice of shifts, and the like (Godard,

1994:315–316). The first type of provision, known as benefit status provisions, is generally uncontroversial; the second type, known as competitive status provisions, is often anything but, for reasons that will be discussed presently.

Within the "competitive status" group, provisions applying to layoffs and recalls are the most common. Such provisions, typically stating that layoffs will be made in reverse order of seniority and that recalls will be in direct order of seniority, were found in about 65 percent of all major Canadian agreements in 1999 (Giles and Starkman, 2001:302). Such provisions are favoured by almost all workers and may be preferred even by some managers, since they spare managers the necessity of making painful individual decisions as to who will be let go during economic downturns.

The use of seniority as a criterion for promotions is more controversial. Nonetheless, provisions of this kind remain quite common in Canadian agreements. In 1999, such provisions were found in about 55 percent of all major Canadian agreements, as compared to 60 percent in 1986 (Giles and Starkman, 2001:302). Seniority-based promotion provisions run the gamut from those that use seniority alone to clauses stating that it will be used only to break a tie in situations where the workers' skills and abilities are equal. In between, there is a broad range of provisions stipulating that some mix of ability and seniority will be used. Not atypical is the Coca-Cola Company provision described in Godard (1994:316) that the employee in question must possess the ability to do the job. Managers often dislike seniority-based promotion provisions because they mean that the individual promoted is often not the best person for the job, which over time may lead to reduced efficiency. Indeed, some workers also dislike these provisions, because they sense that an individual's ability, motivation, and effort do not matter as much as his or her length of service. For this reason, seniority-based promotion provisions have often been criticized as demotivating.

Many collective agreements also contain **bumping** rights that allow senior workers who have been laid off to take the jobs of more junior workers, who in turn may take the jobs of even more junior workers and so on down the line (Godard, 1994). Such bumping provisions were found in about 45 percent of all major collective agreements in 1999 (Giles and Starkman, 2001). Managers generally dislike bumping provisions, particularly those that set up lengthy organization-wide bumping chains, since they can lead to considerable uncertainty as to who will be doing which jobs within the organization.[26] As a result, most bumping provisions restrict bumping rights in some way or other, either by limiting them to certain locations or departments or by requiring that "bumping" employees possess the ability to do the job within a minimal period of time (Godard, 1994:318–319).

Technological Change

Workers and employers have battled over technological change from time immemorial (Peirce, 1987). On the whole, the Canadian collective bargaining system has not handled issues related to technological change very well. This really isn't too surprising, given that the purpose of collective bargaining is to fix terms and conditions of employment for a given period of time, whereas technological change is by its very nature destabilizing and often serves to change the balance of workplace power both between management and workers and among different groups of workers (Peirce, 1987; Cardin, 1967). Among the major consequences of such change can be layoffs, loss of income, and deskilling of jobs. In extreme cases, it can even lead to plant closures.

A study from the mid 1980s (Peirce, 1987) found that slightly over half of all Canadian agreements covering 500 or more workers contained some kind of techno-logical change provision. However, in most cases the protection afforded was rather minimal. On average, these "large agreements" contained less than two of the six technological-change-related provisions most commonly coded by Labour Canada. Provisions calling for advance notice or consultation before bringing in technological change were found in slightly less than 40 percent of the "large agreements." Training and retraining provisions related to technological change were found in about 30 per-cent of those agreements, and employment security provisions, in just over 20 per-cent. Far less common were clauses providing for technological-change-related labour–management committees, relocation allowances, and notice of layoff related to technological change (Peirce, 1987, Table 1). Moreover, agreements covering fewer than 500 workers were only about half as likely to contain technological change pro-visions as were those in the "large agreement" pool (Peirce, 1987).

A more recent review (Giles and Starkman, 2001:305) suggests that not much has changed since the mid 1980s with respect to the handling of technological change through collective bargaining. As was the case in 1985, more than 45 per-cent of all agreements still contain no technological change provisions at all. Advance notice and consultation provisions are still found in fewer than half the major agreements, and training provisions (at about 20 percent) are now even less frequent than they were fifteen years ago. These findings lend credence to Giles and Starkman's contention (2001:305) that Canadian employers have remained "stead-fast in their determination to preserve their control over the process of technologi-cal change." So do the findings of a survey by Pradeep Kumar and associates, which show only about 14 percent of all responding unions reported a high degree of suc-cess in this area in their last bargaining round, while another 42 percent reported moderate success (Kumar et al., 1998:Table 11).

However, there is also reason to believe Canadian unions may not always have done enough to raise the issue at the bargaining table. The Economic Council's "Working with Technology" survey (Betcherman and McMullen, 1986; Peirce, 1987:59–60) found that, while technological change had occurred in 80 percent of the unionized establishments surveyed in the five years prior to the survey, negotia-tions over such change had occurred in only 46 percent of the unionized establish-ments. When unions did raise technological change issues, they were successful about half the time, a finding that suggests that if unions were to raise these issues more often, collective agreement provisions addressing workers' interests would probably become more frequent (Peirce, 1987).[27]

Some (i.e., Cardin, 1967) have suggested that issues like technological change may be handled better under centralized bargaining systems that allow for political bargaining.[28] Others (Task Force on Microelectronics, 1982; Adams, 1985; ECC, 1987; Peirce, 1987) have suggested that collective bargaining over this issue should be replaced (or at least supplemented) with joint committees that would apply in all workplaces, unionized and non-unionized alike, and that would have the power to take issues through to arbitration if the committee were unable to arrive at a consensus. But despite the frequency with which this recommendation has been made, there has thus far been little sign that any Canadian government is prepared to act on it—nor does greater centralization of bargaining seem a realistic prospect in the near future.

Work Force Reductions

With the large-scale restructuring, downsizing, and layoffs that have been taking place in many industries in recent years, job security has become a top priority for unions. An issue of particular concern for many unions is contracting out, or the hiring of an outside firm to do a given job, rather than using existing employees or hiring new ones (Giles and Starkman, 1995:361). In many (perhaps most) cases, the firm to which the work is being contracted will be non-union, which may pose a threat to union membership levels as well as to members' jobs and incomes. In almost all cases, these firms pay their workers substantially lower wages than do the organizations that have contracted out the work to them. Contracting out has been a particularly hot issue in the public sector, as government departments, hospitals, and universities (to give just a few examples) have contracted out food operations, snow and garbage removal, and cleaning services with increasing frequency (Rose, 1995:36). Understandably, contracting out is an issue of considerable importance to many unions. Indeed, Kumar et al. (1998) found restricting it to have been the responding unions' fourth most important priority overall in their most recent round of bargaining. About 48 percent of all responding unions placed a high priority on this issue, while another 27 percent gave it moderate priority (1998:Table 10).

To help protect their members against the effects of contracting out, unions have negotiated a variety of prohibitions against the practice. Complete prohibitions are rare (Giles and Starkman, 2001:305; Peirce, 1987). Much commoner are prohibitions against moves that may lead to job loss, or prohibitions against contracting out of work to non-union firms. Other agreements contain provisions barring the contracting out of work so long as there are enough regular employees available to do that work. In recent years, unions have been moderately successful in negotiating **contracting-out** prohibitions, which were found in about 53 percent of all major collective agreements in 1999 (Giles and Starkman, 2001:305), a substantial increase from their 31 percent frequency in 1985 (Peirce, 1987, Table 7). Where unions are not successful in preventing job loss (as through the negotiation of contracting-out prohibitions), they will, at a minimum, seek to cushion the impact of job loss through provisions requiring the employer to give employees notice of impending layoffs or to give severance pay packages to those being laid off. As of 1994, notice of layoff provisions were found in slightly over half of all Canadian agreements (Giles and Starkman, 1995).

Severance pay packages are a way of giving laid-off employees time to find a new job or adjust to retirement. They take on particular importance when a large number of employees are laid off simultaneously in a community, making new jobs hard to find. In some cases, the severance package may be a lump sum; more often, however, it is based on the number of years of service (Peirce, 1987:9), a typical formula being one week's pay for each year of service to a maximum of 26 weeks. In some cases, those being laid off may also receive career counselling, time off for job searches, or permission to use the employer's facilities in searching for a new job. Unions may also seek to negotiate the continuation of employer-paid benefits after layoffs have occurred (Giles and Starkman, 1995:361).

Work Behaviour and Work Environment Provisions

Work behaviour and work environment provisions address issues relating to the social and physical environment in which work is performed (Giles and Jain, 1989:340). General rules governing work behaviour and disciplinary methods and more specific prohibitions on certain types of harassment relate to the social environment. Health and safety provisions are concerned with the physical environment.

Most collective agreements permit management to discharge or suspend employees provided there is "just cause" (Giles and Starkman, 1995:366). (Whether the employer has in fact shown just cause is something the union will usually dispute, particularly in discharge cases.) Some agreements stipulate special, expedited hearings for discharge cases; others state that an employee's disciplinary record may be "cleared" after a specified period of time (Giles and Starkman, 1995:366–367). While unions normally prefer not to incorporate specific disciplinary procedures into the collective agreement (Giles and Starkman, 1995:366), in some cases there will be specific rules or penalties for offences such as absenteeism (i.e., verbal warning for a first offence, written warning for a second offence, suspension for a third offence, layoff and possible dismissal for a fourth offence).

The handling of discharge and discipline cases by arbitrators represents the one significant modification to the doctrine of residual management rights that otherwise governs the interpretation of Canadian collective agreements. Though most agreements contain a provision that states that arbitrators do not have the power to alter an agreement term or substitute a new provision for an existing provision (Giles and Starkman, 1995:367), in discipline and discharge cases, arbitrators have broad discretion to substitute their own penalties for those imposed by the employer. In such cases, especially discharge cases, the onus of proof rests with the employer, and the standard required by arbitrators is generally high (Giles and Starkman, 1995). Except in cases where an employee has been discharged for a single, extremely serious offence such as theft or assault, arbitrators normally expect employers to have imposed progressive discipline (discipline in steps, as indicated in the previous paragraph) to give the employee a chance to mend his or her ways. Where progressive discipline has not been applied, the discharge will normally be overturned at arbitration. Of those workers filing discharge grievances, slightly more than half are reinstated, many with some back pay (McPhillips and England, 1995:81). Collective agreements' grievance procedures thus offer workers quite substantial protection against arbitrary disciplinary action by employers.

A recent trend, resulting from the growing number of women in the workplace and their increasing prominence within many unions, has been the inclusion of sexual harassment provisions in collective agreements. While human rights legislation (discussed in Chapter 7) provides protection against such behaviour, incorporating harassment provisions into the agreement allows women who believe they have been sexually harassed to avail themselves of the agreement's grievance procedure as an alternative to the often cumbersome and time-consuming procedures established by the legislation. Similarly, the growing number of workers from ethnic and religious minorities has spurred demands for other kinds of anti-discrimination provisions, likewise enforceable through the grievance procedure.

As for health and safety, unions have long been leaders in pushing for safer workplaces. Their contributions in this area are among the most important ones they have made. Even though health and safety issues are the subject of legislation in every Canadian jurisdiction, unions continue to have an important role to play here, as we noted in Chapter 7, both through their role in enforcing legislation that governments might otherwise lack the resources or political will to enforce at all adequately, and through their ability to enhance legislative standards at the bargaining table. In many cases, unions will insist on the inclusion of provisions allowing workers to be informed about, or to refuse, unsafe work (Giles and Starkman, 1995:367). While such provisions would seem to be redundant since these rights are provided in provincial and federal health and safety legislation, they again allow unions to avail themselves of their agreements' grievance procedures, which in practice may afford a speedier and more appropriate remedy than legislatively established procedures. Beyond that, unions can negotiate any number of industry- or firm-specific clauses, such as provisions requiring employers to cover all or part of the cost of safety equipment (see the Bell-CWC agreement discussed below for a good example) or establishing safety programs or training procedures governing the use of potentially hazardous equipment (Giles and Starkman, 1995).

Collective Agreements and the Union–Management Relationship

A collective agreement provision can tell a knowledgeable reader a good deal about the nature of the relationship between the union and management that have negotiated that provision. For example, provisions laying out harsh disciplinary procedures or rigid limitations on who can perform certain jobs or the number of people required to perform them are often found in highly adversarial union–management relationships, where there has been a long history of mistrust between the parties. Such provisions also appear to be characteristic of declining industries, such as longshoring and coal mining, where management's need to curb labour costs comes into direct conflict with the union's need to preserve its members' jobs and income.[29] Conversely, provisions that allow the parties a greater degree of latitude, or suggest some significant sharing of workplace power or responsibility, are generally characteristic of more positive union–management relationships. Such provisions are more likely to be found in industries that are growing, or at least stable, such as telecommunications. The point here is that where collective agreement provisions impose increased costs on management (as many such provisions do), they are less apt to lead to serious union–management conflict in situations where at least part of the increased costs may be compensated for by a growth in revenues and profits.

Adapting and elaborating on some terminology devised by Godard (1994) to classify management attitudes towards unions, we would describe provisions in which the delineation of the union's and management's respective territory and rights is extremely detailed or minute as characteristic of an exploitive relationship between the parties. Here, the focus is quite simply on how much each side can extract from the other; there is generally little concern about the impact agreement provisions will have on the overall union–management relationship or even on the enterprise's long-term viability. Quite a number of these kinds of provisions can be found in collective agreements between the Shipping Federation of Canada, representing shipping company owners in the Port of Montreal, and Local #375 of the International Longshoremen's Association, representing the port's longshoring workers. For instance, Rule 44 of the Picard Commission Report, which for a time served as the agreement between the parties, actually stipulated that toilets and washrooms be provided in sheds, and close to the docks where there were no sheds (Picard, 1967)! Such a provision points to an appalling level of mistrust between the longshoremen and the shipowners, ample evidence of which may be obtained from examining the history of that relationship (see Picard, 1967).

Agreement provisions that, without in any way suggesting a fundamental change in the nature of the employment relationship, are phrased in more general terms and allow some latitude in interpretation may be thought of as characteristic of accommodative union–management relationships. In such relationships, while the parties' interests may still diverge sharply in many cases, particularly when it comes to monetary issues, both are also concerned with the viability of the enterprise and with maintaining a good long-term relationship. In general, the parties to such relationships would tend to agree that extremely detailed and minute delineation of union and management "territory" in agreement provisions is not the best way to achieve such a relationship. A number of examples of such accommodative provisions may be found in the agreement between Bell Canada and the Communications Workers of Canada. For example, Article 12.01, on health and safety, states: "Both parties...recognize the need to ensure the safety and protect the health of all employees." Article 12.02 states that it is the company's responsibility to introduce "reasonable procedures and techniques" to provide for workers' health and safety, while for its part the union may make suggestions for improvements in this area. Article 12.05 stipulates that the company will pay for all required safety equipment except safety footwear, for which the company will contribute a substantial share of the cost, depending on the type of shoe or boot required. While leaving no uncertainty as to who is in charge of running the enterprise (as Article 12.02 in particular indicates), the provisions just cited point to a willingness on the part of Bell to accommodate workers' reasonable needs in the area of safety equipment and rest breaks for computer operators. Even more important, Article 12.01 suggests a willingness to share responsibility for health and safety issues and provides at least implicit recognition that here may be a "win-win" area for both parties. Normally the degree of trust needed to arrive at this kind of recognition must be built up over a number of years. Provisions of this kind are, therefore, generally characteristic of mature and stable bargaining relationships.

Occasionally (though rarely in Canada), one finds agreements that go beyond the accommodative approach just described to adopt an egalitarian approach. In place of detailed "control" provisions, such agreements tend to feature broad, rather general statements of principle. The best-known and most-studied Canadian agreement of this kind, that between the Shell Chemical Plant in Sarnia, Ontario, and Local 9-148 of the Oil, Chemical and Atomic Workers Union, does not contain a management rights provision or a formal grievance procedure (Halpern, 1984). The agreement also contains no specific work rules or job control provisions, beyond a stipulation that layoffs will be made in order of reverse seniority, providing that the remaining employees are capable of meeting all job requirements (Halpern, 1984:73). A foreword making up about one-fifth of the agreement's very modest length states that its purpose is "to establish an enabling framework within which an organizational system can be developed and sustained that will ensure an efficient and competitive world-scale Chemical Plant operation and provide meaningful work and job satisfaction for employees" (Halpern, 1984:70). The agreement also reflects the management's and union's mutual commitment to a number of key principles, such as a belief that employees are responsible and trustworthy and are capable of making proper decisions related to their work arrangements "if given the necessary authorities, information and training" (Halpern, 1984). Such an agreement was adopted because both sides recognized that a collective agreement "composed of tight rules and regulations" would be inconsistent with the plant's workplace design, based on "minimal specification," encouragement of exploration, and a high degree of mutual trust (Halpern, 1984:51).

Beyond explicit contract provisions, the way in which parties interpret an agreement can offer important insights into their relationship. In mature, accommodative relationships, management and the union will tend to interpret the agreement judiciously and will not always seek to turn every apparent "violation" of the agreement into a formal grievance. Indeed, such relationships often feature proactive, problem-solving mechanisms like joint committees whose aim is to prevent most workplace problems from developing into grievances. In exploitive relationships, in contrast, each apparent "violation" of the contract is seen as a way to score political points against the other side. In extreme cases (like the highly conflictual relationship between Canada Post and the Canadian Union of Postal Workers), grievances may be used as a political weapon by both sides (Gandz and Whitehead, 1989; Stewart-Patterson, 1987; Godard, 1994:360). For example, a union may file large numbers of grievances just before or during negotiations as a means of putting pressure on management. For its part, management may "stonewall" on settling grievances, refusing to settle as a means of proving its toughness and resolve to the union. Such politicization of the grievance process, of which an excessively formal and legalistic interpretation of the collective agreement is often part and parcel, has frequently been associated with poor overall organizational performance (see Gandz and Whitehead, 1989:244).

COLLECTIVE AGREEMENTS AND COLLECTIVE BARGAINING: AN OVERALL ASSESSMENT

The excessively legalistic interpretation of collective agreements that appears to be characteristic of exploitive union–management relationships is just one of the problems associated with such agreements. Another is that even the most detailed agreement cannot possibly cover all possible workplace situations. In particular, as we noted already, technological change, plant closures, and other large-scale changes over which the union may have very limited control may alter the ground rules quite considerably. The recent trends toward globalization and fiercer international competition that we described in earlier chapters lead one to wonder how collective bargaining can realistically be expected to operate in an increasingly global economy marked by almost instantaneous transmission of information, rapid movement of goods, services, and capital across international borders, and constant fluctuations in exchange rates (Giles and Starkman, 1995:342–343).[30]

Another more fundamental criticism of collective bargaining is that it assumes at least rough equality between the parties. In practice, this doesn't always exist, particularly not in bad economic times, when (as in recent years) the balance of power tends to shift strongly in the direction of employers. Where such a balance of power does not exist, it becomes harder for unions to negotiate effectively, and the collective bargaining process does less well at defusing workplace conflict than it otherwise would. Should the power imbalance continue for any length of time, the conflict may well resurface in the form of increased grievance rates, higher quit rates (as in the case of many nurses), higher levels of official or unofficial strike action (as in the case of Ontario's teachers), or increased absenteeism and sick leave (see Shellenbarger, 1998), all of which may have severely negative consequences for both the organization and its employees. Yet another issue relates to the evolution of collective agreements into long, detailed, often highly legalistic documents. Many, particularly management-oriented industrial relationists, tend to regard this evolution as unhealthy, citing among other things the increased cost of negotiating and administering detailed and complex agreements and such agreements' tendency to reduce trust.

Nonetheless, despite the validity of these criticisms and others pointing out the lack of real workplace democracy achievable through collective bargaining under the current system (see Giles and Starkman, 1995:368), most workers are generally better off with collective bargaining than they would be without it. As we noted in Chapter 6, unionized workers' wages are generally higher than those of their non-unionized counterparts. As well, unionized workers enjoy significantly more workplace voice, thanks mainly to the grievance process. Thus, while it is far from perfect, collective bargaining is probably the best system available for determination of pay and working conditions. While the adversarial nature of the process and the length and complexity of most collective agreements are regrettable, they are likely inevitable so long as management continues to resist unions fiercely, and as long as bargaining remains highly decentralized, thus forcing most conflict to be worked out at the bargaining table rather than in the political arena. Unless and until either or both of these things change, collective bargaining seems likely to remain adversarial and conflict-ridden, and the collective agreements resulting from it will likely continue to be, for the most part, long, complex, and highly legalistic documents reflecting, to a considerable degree, the often bitter power struggles that have accompanied their drafting.

QUESTIONS
FOR DISCUSSION

1) Have you ever been part of a union–management negotiation? If so, what was the experience like? Do you think it's something you would enjoy doing again? If you haven't been part of a union–management negotiation, have you had any other sort of negotiating experience, either individually or as a member of a group? What was that experience like?

2) Distinguish between centralized and decentralized bargaining structures, and explain why private sector unions generally prefer decentralized structures in good times, but centralized ones in bad times. Also explain why Canadian private sector bargaining structures have generally become more decentralized in recent years.

3) Discuss the role of bargaining power in negotiations.

4) List the four stages of negotiation, and explain why it's important to go through all of them.

5) Discuss the concept of a settlement zone, and identify some issues to which this concept would, and would not, apply.

6) Why do seasoned negotiators seldom make threats? What are some tactics they would be more likely to use?

7) Get a collective agreement. Read through as much of it as you can. Are you able to make sense of it? If not, why are you having difficulty?

8) Try to determine, from some key clauses of the agreement, what kind of union–management relationship the parties have.

9) Discuss the evolution of Canadian agreements. What has contributed to their growing length and complexity? In your view, has this evolution been healthy?

10) List the four main types of agreement provisions and, using the agreement you read for questions 7 and 8, try to identify one or more provisions of each type in that agreement.

11) How does seniority play a role in Canadian agreements? Overall, is that role healthy or not, in your view?

12) Discuss some problems with collective agreements. Might there be ways to get around some of those problems?

SUGGESTIONS
FOR FURTHER READING

Kumar, Pradeep, Gregor Murray, and Sylvain Schetagne. (1998). "Adapting to change: Union priorities in the 1990s." *Workplace Gazette*, fall. Extremely comprehensive study on Canadian union behaviour and priorities. It contains detailed survey evidence showing that, by and large, Canadian unions have been adapting to change by taking a defensive, bread-and-butter-oriented stance at the bargaining table, while at the same time seeking to organize new industries and groups of workers.

Lewicki, Roy, David Saunders, and John Minton. (1997). *Essentials of negotiation.* Chicago and Toronto: Irwin. A thorough and very readable study of negotiation that moves beyond traditional negotiation contexts into such emerging areas as multilateral, cross-cultural, and international negotiations.

Schelling, Thomas. (1957). "Bargaining, communication, and limited war." *Journal of Conflict Resolution*, 1(1). This classic (and beautifully written) study, which is not limited to union–management negotiations, explains the crucial concept of the focal point. A must for anyone with a broader interest in negotiating theory.

Tarantelli, Ezio. (1986). "The regulation of inflation and unemployment." *Industrial Relations*, 25(1). A masterful study in comparative political economy that links bargaining structures to inflation and unemployment.

CHAPTER 11

STRIKES

Members and supporters of the Sudbury Mine, Mill & Smelter Workers' Union, Local 598/CAW take part in a solidarity rally in Sudbury, Ontario on January 27, 2001, almost six months after their strike against Falconbridge Mines began. However, scenes like this are rare. In most years, well over 90 per cent of Canadian agreements are negotiated without a work stoppage.

In this chapter we discuss the significance of strikes in the Canadian industrial relations system, as well as considering the causes of strikes and some of the policy measures used to control them. We start by defining the term "strike" as it is used in various labour relations acts. Next, we consider different types of strikes and discuss some of the problems involved in measuring strike incidence. From there, we go on to consider the causes of strikes, including both economic and non-economic causes. This analysis includes a discussion of some recent Canadian strikes that have attracted widespread public attention. We conclude with a discussion of some of the dispute resolution methods used to help prevent strikes or reduce their impact, and with an explanation of recent trends in strike activity in Canada.

THE SIGNIFICANCE OF STRIKES

Partly for the wrong reasons, strikes tend to be the aspect of the industrial relations system with which the average person is most familiar. Media coverage of industrial relations developments undeniably centres mainly on strikes, particularly the bitter, emotional type featuring violent picket-line confrontations. Quite simply, stories about conflict sell more newspapers and attract more viewers to TV screens than do stories about negotiation and compromise. As well, many journalists lack the training, the time, or the support from their superiors needed to provide in-depth coverage of industrial relations developments other than strikes (Hannigan, 1986).

While perhaps inevitable, such media emphasis on violent confrontation can obscure the fact that in most years, well over 90 percent of Canadian agreements are negotiated without a work stoppage. Moreover, even when there is a work stoppage, most employers do not attempt to bring in replacement workers, and the majority of strikes are conducted peaceably. Sensationalist media coverage also tends to obscure the innovative preventive mechanisms being developed all across Canada, of which the various provincial preventive mediation programs are an excellent example.

The media's emphasis on strikes also gives uninformed readers and viewers the mistaken impression that strikes are the only significant form of industrial conflict. As will be emphasized throughout this chapter, strikes are but one of many ways used by workers to send management the message that they aren't happy with what is going on in the workplace. Other forms of conflict range from active ones such as grievances (to be discussed in Chapter 12), vandalism, and sabotage, to more passive ones such as heavy use of sick leave or disability leave, unexcused absenteeism, alcohol or drug abuse, slacking on the job, or quitting. All result in reduced productivity; some (such as alcohol abuse or absenteeism) may arguably lead to far greater productivity losses than do strikes, which have never cost the country as much as one percent of total working time, even in tumultuous years like 1919 (marked by the Winnipeg General Strike) and 1976 (marked by a nation-wide Day of Protest against federal wage controls).

Clearly, then, strikes should not be considered as an isolated phenomenon. Rather, they should be viewed in the larger context of industrial conflict as a whole, of which they are just one manifestation, though certainly a dramatic one. This said, there *are* reasons why strikes are central to industrial relations. As was noted in the labour history chapter, Canadian labour relations law has developed largely in response to bitter, bloody strikes, with an eye to preventing the recurrence of such disputes, or at least making them less bloody. The *Industrial Disputes Investigation Act* of 1907, which made conciliation compulsory for the first time, was a direct response to a lengthy Alberta coal-miners' strike the previous winter (Morton, 1989). Similarly, *PC 1003*, the bill that, in 1944, granted basic collective bargaining rights to Canadian workers, can be linked to bitter wartime strikes in the gold mining and steel industries (MacDowell, 1978, 1982). A sizeable portion of all Canadian labour relations acts is devoted to strikes: what constitutes a strike, when it can take place, which groups (if any) cannot strike, what types of picketing are and are not legal, whether employers can replace striking workers, what procedures the government may use to help the two sides arrive at a settlement, and what special restrictions may be placed on strikes in certain sectors. Indeed, it is probably not going too far to say that a central purpose of labour relations legislation is to regulate strikes with an eye to protecting the public interest and maintaining public peace and order.

This emphasis is not misplaced. While strikes today are generally less violent than the pitched battles of the early twentieth century (Heron, 1989), they can still have extremely severe consequences—including injury or loss of life. Property damage can be extensive. Third parties can be seriously inconvenienced or in some cases injured, especially in public sector disputes. Striking workers may lose their homes or be forced into bankruptcy. And in the aftermath of a strike, particularly a lengthy one, firms may lose customers and market share,[1] or in extreme instances be forced to shut down part or even all of their operations. Strikes may also lead to lasting bitterness between unions and management, or sometimes even within unions. Given such a broad array of potentially serious consequences, strikes pose some difficult challenges for policy-makers. Particularly in the case of public sector disputes (P. Weiler, 1980), they may be faced with balancing workers' right to strike in support of their demands with the public's need to continue receiving such essential services as health care.

To be sure, strikes may also have positive effects. Not only may they, in some cases, serve the "cathartic" function discussed by Gunderson, Hyatt, and Ponak (2001), allowing workers to release pent-up frustration; they can also serve as a kind of "wake-up call" to both union and management. Both in Canada and in other countries, a number of creative joint problem-solving mechanisms have been introduced in the wake of strikes that convinced both sides they would need to restructure their relationship to prevent further strikes from occurring in the future.[2] Without the spur of the strike to prod them into action, the parties might never have developed those mechanisms.

WHAT IS A STRIKE?

No one can hope to understand the causes of strikes or the best ways of preventing them without understanding what a strike is. Moreover, from a practical perspective, such knowledge is extremely important both for unionists and for IR and HR managers.

In general, a strike must be a "concerted" (i.e., planned) activity, involving a collective refusal to work. Thus an individual worker's refusal to work would not be considered a strike, whether or not that refusal was legal.[3] On the other hand, the stoppage need not be a complete one to be considered a strike. In general, Canadian labour relations acts state that a slowdown or other "concerted activity" designed to limit output is a strike. Specifically, the *Canada Labour Code* (section 3[1]) defines a strike as "a cessation of work or a refusal to work or to continue to work by employees, in combination, in concert, or in accordance with a common understanding, and a slowdown of work or other concerted activity on the part of employees in relation to their work that is designed to restrict or limit output." A virtually identical definition may be found in Ontario's *Labour Relations Act* (section 1[1]).[4] Under federal and provincial labour acts, such varied work actions as union-imposed overtime bans (Snyder, 1995:29), rotating Canada Post strikes (Snyder, 1995:29—30), **work-to-rule** campaigns by railway employees, and a postal union's threat to order its members to stop verifying whether letters bore sufficient postage (Snyder, 1995:30) have all been deemed strikes. So, too, have unions' refusal to cross picket lines, even in cases where the refusal was based on a "fear of picket line violence" (Randazzo, 1995:11), and a union's refusal to handle work that was the subject of a legal **lockout** between a different employer and a sister local (Randazzo, 1995). All of this suggests that unions should be exceedingly cautious in calling actions such as work-to-rule campaigns, slowdowns, and other partial withdrawals of service.

When May a Legal Strike Occur?

In Canada, legal strike activity is tightly constrained by a variety of what Godard (1994:294) has referred to as "timeliness restrictions." First, the collective agreement must have expired. Second, both sides must have made a "good faith" effort to obtain a settlement. Third, in almost all Canadian jurisdictions, a legal strike cannot be conducted until the government has appointed a third party (usually called a conciliator, but sometimes called a mediator) in an attempt to settle the dispute. In most jurisdictions, a strike will be legal only after the conciliator or mediator has reported his or her lack of success to the government and a certain length of time (normally seven to fourteen days) has elapsed.[5] In some cases, though less often now than in the past, the parties must also have passed through a second stage of conciliation, involving the creation of a tripartite board and the issuance of a public report. In addition, a number of jurisdictions, including British Columbia, require a supervised strike vote to be held, while five jurisdictions, including Quebec, Alberta, and B.C., require a brief (48- or 72-hour) notice period before any strike or lockout can become legal.

Strike Restrictions in the Public Sector

The previous discussion has been concerned only with strikes in the private sector. It's important to bear in mind that in Canada, as in many other industrialized countries (Beaumont, 1995), public sector strikes are generally much more severely restricted than private sector ones.

As we pointed out in the public sector chapter, several jurisdictions, including Alberta, do not allow government employees to strike, instead requiring binding arbitration. Some also bar strikes among other public sector groups such as health-care workers and teachers. Of those provinces that do permit public sector workers to strike, all but one (Saskatchewan) have established a designation process whereby some employees are designated essential and must, therefore, remain on the job in the event of a strike.

Another significant feature of Canadian public sector strikes is the frequency with which legislation is used to end them. Between 1950 and 1999 (Ponak and Thompson, 2001), federal and provincial governments resorted to such legislation 76 times—24 times in Quebec alone. Such legislation is not unheard-of in Canada's private sector, but is rarely used there, and then normally only in the case of disputes involving large, heavily regulated industries in the federal jurisdiction, such as the ports and the railways, where there is reason to believe that a lengthy dispute could cause innocent third parties serious harm.

The numerous restrictions on public sector strike action have not prevented public sector unions from engaging in strike action—sometimes with great frequency. Indeed, some of the most serious recent Canadian strikes have been public sector ones. Later sections of this chapter consider why this has been the case.

MEASURING STRIKE ACTIVITY AND INTENSITY

It's generally agreed that Canada's strike record compares poorly to that of most other Western industrialized countries. But what, exactly, is meant by this assertion? On what basis can we compare relative strike intensity in different countries, or, for that matter, in different jurisdictions or industries within Canada?

The most basic measure of strike activity is *frequency*, or the number of strikes occurring in any given jurisdiction during any given period of time (normally a year). While it is useful to know how many strikes have occurred in a jurisdiction, by itself this statistic is of relatively little significance. Of particular importance are the size, or number of workers involved in any given dispute, and the *duration*, or the length of time workers remain off the job. The more workers involved and the longer the dispute lasts, the greater its impact will be.

Both size and duration have varied greatly over the years since the First World War (see Table 11.1). One reason for the variation is that both measures have sometimes been greatly affected by single, large disputes. For instance, the average size of strikes in 1976 was more than three times what it had been the year before, in large measure because of the Day of Protest in October. That one-day political strike also resulted in a duration figure (7.3 days) only about one-third of the previous year's (21.6 days). Similarly, lengthy Canada Post strikes in 1975 and 1981 were key factors in unusually long average strike durations for those years.

Multiplying the number of strikes, or frequency, by size, or number of workers, times duration, gives us the total number of person-days lost in any given jurisdiction or industry. As Table 11.1 shows, this figure has fluctuated greatly over time. In 1975 and 1976, more than 10 million person-days were lost due to strikes and lockouts—more than 100 times as many as were lost in 1930, during the Great Depression. Part of the difference results simply from an increase in the size of the Canadian work force. Part of the difference can also be attributed to rising union membership rates, since only unionized workers are counted in strike data. In 1976, Canada's union density stood at 37 percent, or nearly three times the rate (13 percent) it had been in 1930. We must also take into account inflation, the 1976 "Day of Protest," labour's generally stronger political position in 1975–1976, and the addition of large numbers of public-sector workers to the ranks of workers eligible to strike.

One more piece of information is needed before we can meaningfully compare relative strike intensity in different jurisdictions or industries. Other things being equal, larger industries and jurisdictions lose more person-days due to strikes simply because there are more collective agreements expiring than in smaller industries and jurisdictions, and because these agreements cover a greater number of workers. Yet the number of person-days lost compared to the number worked may be minuscule in a large jurisdiction. It is, therefore, usual to divide the number of person-days lost by the number of person-days worked, so that the former can be expressed as a percentage of time worked.

With this figure in hand, we can compare relative strike intensity in different industries and jurisdictions. Granted, different countries' data are seldom totally comparable. To begin with, there is the issue of whether "strike" data includes only strikes, or also includes lockouts, as in the case of Canada. For the period 1977 to 1985 (Labour Canada, 1982, 1986), about 10 percent of the workers involved in disputes were involved in a lockout rather than a strike; during this same period, lockouts accounted for about 16 percent of the total person-days lost.[6]

Even more important is the size threshold that must be crossed before a country will say that a dispute constitutes an official strike. In Canada, all disputes in which ten or more person-days of work are lost are counted as strikes. In the United States, only disputes involving 1000 or more workers are counted. The immediate result of these two countries' different size thresholds is that the United States's record looks far better than it would were the Canadian definition of an official strike applied. It is also possible (Gunderson, Hyatt, and Ponak, 1995) that the large work stoppages, which are the only ones officially reported in the United States, have different causes than the smaller ones that make up the lion's share of Canadian disputes. But despite

Table 11.1

MEASURES OF STRIKE ACTIVITY, CANADA, 1919-2001

Year	Frequency*	Avg. Size	Duration‡	Person-Days Lost**	As Percentage of Working Time
1919	336	443	22.8	3 400 942	0.60
1920	322	187	13.3	799 524	0.14
1921	168	168	37.1	1 048 914	0.22
1922	104	421	34.9	1 528 661	0.32
1923	86	398	19.6	671 750	0.13
1924	70	490	37.7	1 295 054	0.26
1925	87	333	41.2	1 193 281	0.23
1926	77	310	11.2	266 601	0.05
1927	74	301	6.8	152 570	0.03
1928	98	179	12.8	224 212	0.04
1929	90	144	11.7	152 080	0.02
1930	67	205	6.7	91 797	0.01
1931	88	122	19.0	204 238	0.04
1932	116	202	10.9	255 000	0.05
1933	125	212	12.0	317 547	0.07
1934	191	240	12.5	574 519	0.11
1935	120	277	8.7	288 703	0.05
1936	156	223	8.0	276 997	0.05
1937	278	259	12.3	886 393	0.15
1938	147	139	7.3	148 678	0.02
1939	122	336	5.5	224 588	0.04
1940	168	361	4.4	266 318	0.04
1941	231	377	5.0	433 914	0.06
1942	354	322	4.0	450 202	0.05
1943	402	543	4.8	1 041 198	0.12
1944	199	378	6.5	490 139	0.06
1945	197	488	15.2	1 457 420	0.19
1946	226	614	32.4	4 515 030	0.54
1947	234	442	22.9	2 366 340	0.27
1948	154	278	20.7	885 790	0.10
1949	135	347	22.1	1 036 820	0.11
1950	160	1 200	7.2	1 387 500	0.15
1951	258	392	8.9	901 620	0.09
1952	219	513	24.6	2 765 510	0.29
1953	173	315	24.1	1 312 720	0.14
1954	173	327	25.3	1 430 300	0.15
1955	159	378	31.2	1 875 400	0.19
1956	229	387	14.1	1 246 000	0.11
1957	245	329	18.3	1 477 100	0.13
1958	259	425	24.4	2 816 850	0.25
1959	216	440	23.4	2 226 890	0.19
1960	274	180	15.0	738 700	0.06
1961	287	341	13.6	1 335 080	0.11
1962	311	239	19.1	1 417 900	0.11
1963	332	251	11.0	917 140	0.07
1964	343	293	15.7	1 580 550	0.11
1965	501	342	13.4	2 349 870	0.17

Table 11.1
(continued)

Year	Frequency*	Avg. Size	Duration‡	Person-Days Lost**	As Percentage of Working Time
1966	617	667	12.6	5 178 170	0.34
1967	522	483	15.8	3 974 760	0.25
1968	582	385	22.7	5 082 732	0.32
1969	595	514	25.2	7 751 880	0.46
1970	542	481	25.0	6 539 560	0.39
1971	569	421	11.9	2 866 590	0.16
1972	598	1 180	10.9	7 753 530	0.43
1973	724	484	16.4	5 776 080	0.30
1974	1 218	487	15.6	9 221 890	0.46
1975	1 171	431	21.6	10 908,810	0.53
1976	1 040	1 525	7.3	11 544 170	0.53
1977	806	270	15.3	3 320 050	0.15
1978	1 057	379	18.4	7 357 180	0.32
1979	1 049	441	16.9	7 819 350	0.33
1980	1 028	427	20.8	9 129 960	0.37
1981	1 049	325	25.9	8 850 040	0.35
1982	679	684	12.3	5 702 370	0.23
1983	645	511	13.5	4 440 900	0.18
1984	717	261	20.8	3 883 000	0.15
1985	825	196	19.3	3 125 560	0.12
1986	748	647	14.8	7 151 470	0.27
1987	668	871	6.5	3 810 170	0.14
1988	548	377	23.7	4 901 260	0.17
1989	627	709	8.3	3 701 360	0.13
1990	579	467	18.8	5 079 190	0.17
1991	463	547	9.9	2 516 090	0.09
1992	404	371	14.1	2 110 180	0.07
1993	382	267	14.9	1 516 640	0.05
1994	374	216	19.9	1 605 580	0.06
1995	328	455	10.6	1 582 320	0.05
1996	330	865	11.8	3 339 560	0.11
1997	284	907	14.1	3 573 374	0.12
1998	381	642	10.0	2 443 876	0.08
1999	413	384	15.4	2 445 770	0.08
2000	377	381	11.6	1 661 650	0.05
2001#	318	642	9.4	1 968 265	0.08

Data for 2001 are for January–September only.

* Number of strikes in existence during the year in question, whether they began that year or earlier.

"Avg. Size" is obtained by dividing the total number of workers on strike during the year by the frequency figure described in the previous note.

‡ Average days lost per worker on strike is found by dividing total person-days lost by the number of strikers involved.

** Product of frequency (number of strikes) times size and duration.

Sources: 1919–1975, Labour Canada, *Strikes and Lockouts in Canada,* various issues; 1976–1997 data provided by Work Stoppage Bureau, Workplace Information Directorate, Human Resources Development Canada. 1998–2000 data are from *Workplace Gazette* (Summer, 2001), p. 29. 2001 data are from HRDC Web site. Note: 1997 data have been modified slightly from 1st edition of this text, using new data from the above issue of *Workplace Gazette*.

these and other measurement problems,[7] one can generally make reasonably accurate international or inter-industry strike comparisons using a measure such as percentage of working-time lost.[8]

Recent Trends in Canadian Strike Activity

As we noted in the first edition (see p. 435) 1996 and 1997 were years that marked a dramatic reversal of a number of long-term trends in Canadian strike activity. In general, Canadian strike intensity had been declining steadily since the mid 1970s. But in 1996, the proportion of working-time lost due to strikes was more than that double that of the previous year, at 0.11 percent of working time lost. The following year, the figure increased again, to 0.12 percent. In both of these years, a high rate of public sector strikes helped fuel higher overall strike intensity. In 1996, 42 percent of all person-days lost to strikes in Canada were in the public sector. The following year saw the public sector accounting for an even larger proportion (55 percent) of person-days lost due to strikes (see Table 11.2). Between 1998 and 2000, the proportion of person-days lost to strikes in the public sector declined somewhat, ranging from 26 to 42 percent. However, the public sector still accounted for a majority of strikes and of workers involved. The private sector accounted for more person-days lost because its strikes were generally of much longer duration.

In both 1998 and 1999, the percentage of working-time lost to strikes stood at 0.08 percent—higher than in the early 1990s, but lower than in 1996 and 1997 (see Table 11.1). The year 2000 saw a drop to 0.05 percent, or the same as in 1995. Although data for 2001 are only available through September, the trend for that year is back up. Through the first nine months of 2001, the percentage of working-time lost to strikes was 0.08 percent—the same as in 1998 and 1999. Just under 2 million person-days were lost to strikes during that nine-month period.

Trends by Industry

In 1999 (see Figure 11.1A), community and business services and transportation, communication and other utilities accounted for the largest share (about 28 and 27 percent, respectively) of person-days lots due to strikes. The former reflects the impact of large health care strikes in Quebec and B.C. and a public school strike by support staff in Toronto (*Workplace Gazette*, spring 2000), while the latter reflects the impact of even bigger strikes at Bell Canada and Hydro-Quebec. Other sectors accounting for a sizeable proportion of person-days lost included manufacturing (just over 20 percent), primary industries (11 percent), and public administration (just over 8 percent). Though manufacturing saw the largest number of strikes (31 percent of the total), it did not account for as many person-days lost because many fewer workers were involved in its strikes than in those of the two leading sectors. The data for 2000 (see Figure 11.1B) show that community, business and personal services

Table 11.2

STRIKES AND LOCKOUTS, CANADA, BY PUBLIC VERSUS PRIVATE SECTOR STATUS, 1976–2000.

Public Sector

Year	Frequency (% of total)	Size	Duration (Days)	PDL	% Time Lost (% of total)
1976	226 (22)	393 427	5.6	2 219 400	0.10 (19)
1977	191 (24)	61 409	13.0	800 800	0.04 (24)
1978	212 (20)	148 697	8.0	1 188 810	0.05 (16)
1979	208 (20)	234 022	10.2	2 385 420	0.10 (30)
1980	244 (24)	227 616	14.0	3 193 820	0.13 (35)
1981	271 (26)	110 121	20.1	2 210 430	0.09 (25)
1982	121 (18)	273 020	3.3	895 230	0.04 (16)
1983	95 (15)	215 841	9.9	2 129 160	0.09 (48)
1984	108 (15)	31 334	18.3	571 970	0.02 (15)
1985	158 (19)	51 466	12.2	628 470	0.02 (20)
1986	128 (17)	214 209	3.7	795 650	0.03 (11)
1987	105 (16)	397 558	2.2	884 750	0.03 (23)
1988	76 (14)	93 592	23.2	2 166 800	0.08 (44)
1989	139 (22)	340 718	4.9	1 657 820	0.06 (45)
1990	119 (21)	60 820	12.9	785 760	0.03 (15)
1991	115 (25)	215 576	6.6	1 429 050	0.05 (57)
1992	80 (20)	73 930	6.7	496 390	0.02 (24)
1993	85 (22)	56 155	6.3	355 210	0.01 (23)
1994	55 (15)	26 169	15.8	413 830	0.01 (26)
1995	55 (17)	44 125	4.1	182 882	0.01 (12)
1996	76 (23)	76 088	18.3	1 389 198	0.05 (42)
1997	56 (20)	184 626	10.6	1 948 070	0.07 (55)
1998	119 (31)	183 741	3.5	642 070	0.02 (26)
1999	135 (33)	99 413	10.4	1 037 920	0.03 (42)
2000	100 (27)	81 493	7.2	586 290	0.02 (35)

Private Sector

Year	Frequency (% of total)	Size	Duration (Days)	PDL	% Time Lost (% of total)
1976	814 (78)	1 192 794	7.8	9 324 770	0.43 (81)
1977	615 (76)	156 238	16.1	2 519 250	0.11 (76)
1978	845 (80)	251 925	24.5	6 168 370	0.27 (84)
1979	841 (80)	228 364	23.8	5 433 930	0.23 (70)
1980	784 (76)	211 387	28.1	5 936 140	0.24 (65)
1981	778 (74)	231 211	28.7	6 639 610	0.26 (75)
1982	558 (82)	191 108	25.2	4 807 140	0.20 (84)
1983	550 (85)	113 631	20.3	2 311 740	0.09 (52)
1984	608 (85)	155 582	21.3	3 311 430	0.13 (85)
1985	671 (81)	110 867	22.5	2 497 090	0.10 (80)
1986	620 (83)	270 046	23.5	6 355 820	0.24 (89)
1987	563 (84)	184 324	15.9	2 925 420	0.11 (77)

Table 11.2 (continued)

Year	Frequency (% of total)	Size	Duration (Days)	PDL	% Time Lost (% of total)
1988	472 (78)	113 204	24.2	2 734 460	0.10 (56)
1989	488 (78)	104 029	19.6	2 043 540	0.07 (55)
1990	460 (79)	209 651	20.5	4 293 430	0.15 (85)
1991	348 (75)	37 758	28.8	1 087 040	0.04 (43)
1992	324 (80)	76 010	21.2	1 613 790	0.06 (76)
1993	296 (78)	45 629	25.5	1 161 430	0.04 (77)
1994	319 (85)	54 687	21.8	1 192 750	0.04 (74)
1995	273 (83)	105 034	13.3	1 399 439	0.05 (88)
1996	252 (77)	207 656	9.4	1 950 362	0.07 (58)
1997	223 (80)	69 066	23.5	1 625 304	0.05 (45)
1998	262 (69)	60 661	29.7	1 801 810	0.06 (74)
1999	278 (67)	59 199	23.8	1 407 820	0.05 (58)
2000	277 (74)	62 077	17.3	1 075 340	0.03 (65)

PDL = person-days lost
Percentage of time lost due to strikes was calculated against time worked by total non-agricultural paid workers.
Source: Work Stoppage Bureau, Workplace Information Directorate, HRDC.

continued to account for the largest proportion of days lost (about 28.5 percent of the total) with manufacturing not far behind at 26.5 percent. But transportation, communication and utilities dropped sharply, to just over 6 percent of the total. On the other hand, primary industries' share of the total was up sharply, to 17 percent, and public administration increased, as well, to 13%. The unusually high figure for primary industries, which as we noted in Chapter 2 employ only a very small percentage of the nation's work force, can probably be attributed largely to the lengthy Falconbridge Mine strike, described below.

At the industry level, it is difficult to uncover strike trends over time, because a few large disputes can account for the lion's share of person-days and work-time lost in any given year, thus "skewing" the longer-term data considerably. However, an examination of that data over the past decade (years other than 1999 and 2000 not shown)[9] does suggest that the relative number of strikes and proportion of person-days lost appears to be increasing in public administration and service industries (including health care and education), and decreasing in other industries. As was noted in Chapters 2 and 4, relatively fewer Canadian workers than in the past are employed in manufacturing, and that sector's union density rates have also declined, meaning that a smaller proportion of those Canadian workers legally entitled to strike are in manufacturing. The same is even more true of construction, a tradition-ally strike-prone industry that in both 1999 and 2000 accounted for less than

Figure 11.1A

Figure 11.1B

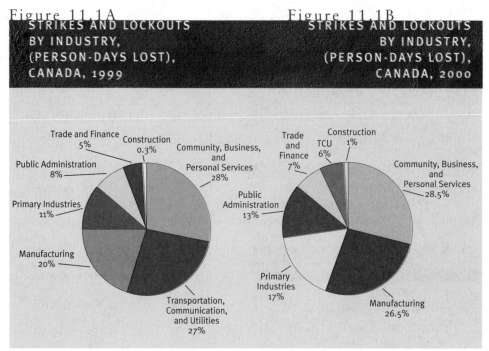

STRIKES AND LOCKOUTS
BY INDUSTRY,
(PERSON-DAYS LOST),
CANADA, 1999

STRIKES AND LOCKOUTS
BY INDUSTRY,
(PERSON-DAYS LOST),
CANADA, 2000

Source: HRDC, *Workplace Gazette*, various issues in 2000 and 2001.

1 percent of person-days lost to strikes. In addition, various legislative changes, including most notably the Ontario government's granting of strike rights to its employees in 1993, have meant that a greater proportion of those legally entitled to strike are in public administration. The increasing proportion (more than half) of Canadian union members employed in the public sector is also an important consideration here.

Trends by Province

Historically, Quebec, British Columbia, and Newfoundland have generally seen the highest levels of strike intensity. Through the 1980s, these three provinces generally had at least double the rate, in terms of person-days lost per paid worker, of any other (Labour Canada, various years). As recently as 1986, Quebec and B.C. alone accounted for about three-quarters of the workers involved in all Canadian strikes, and 70 percent of the person-days not worked (Workplace Information Directorate, 1998). Ontario's levels were typically far lower, in part because government employees and many other public employees were not allowed to strike, as they were in the other three provinces just mentioned. As well, as we noted in Chapter 5, Ontario has had significantly lower union membership rates than the other three provinces. But in both 1996 and 1997, having granted its employees the right to strike a few years earlier, Ontario accounted for more than two-thirds of the workers involved in strikes and half the person-days lost to strikes (Peirce, 2000:438).

In 1999, Ontario still accounted for a substantial 34 percent of person-days lost to strikes, as well as 35 percent of the total number of strikes and workers involved. But Quebec now accounted for a larger share of both strikes and person-days lost (36 and 35 percent respectively), while B.C. (13 percent of person-days lost) and Newfoundland (3 percent)[10] showed signs of returning to their old positions at the high end of the strike spectrum (*Workplace Gazette*, spring 2000). Because Quebec underwent three very large public sector strikes that year, it is too early to tell whether 1999 marks the end of what had been a downward trend of strike activity in Quebec (Peirce, 2000). Data for 2000 (*Workplace Gazette*, summer 2001), which show Quebec accounting for only about 19 percent of person-days lost due to strikes, suggest that for that province, at least, 1999 may have been something of an aberration. A rather alarming finding is the exceptionally high level of strike activity in B.C., which in 2000 accounted for over 28 percent of all striking workers and 24 percent of person-days lost to strikes (see Table 11.3).

Table 11.3

STRIKES AND LOCKOUTS IN CANADA, BY JURISDICTION, 2000

Jurisdiction	Number (% of total)		Workers Involved (% of total)		Person-Days Lost (% of total)	
Newfoundland	13	(4)	3 640	(3)	29 270	(2)
P.E.I.	NONE		—		—	
Nova Scotia	5	(1)	259	(*)	10 250	(1)
New Brunswick	4	(1)	1 232	(1)	24 270	(1)
Quebec	119	(33)	25 188	(18)	312 580	(19)
Ontario	141	(39)	52 492	(37)	647 590	(39)
Manitoba	10	(3)	1 448	(1)	40 890	(2)
Saskatchewan	5	(1)	433	(*)	12 710	(1)
Alberta	11	(3)	8 500	(6)	59 380	(4)
B.C.	46	(13)	40 767	(28)	399 180	(24)
Territories	1	(*)	420	(*)	1 260	(*)
Multi-province	1	(*)	84	(*)	2 450	(*)
Federal (Can. Code)	21	(6)	9 107	(6)	121 820	(7)
TOTAL	**377**	**(100)**	**143 570**	**(100)**	**1 661 650**	**(100)**

* Less than 1%. Totals may not add up to 100% due to rounding.
Source: *Workplace Gazette*, Vol. 4, No. 2 (Summer, 2001), p. 28.

Trends by Type of Strike

It's useful to know whether a given strike has occurred during the negotiation of a first agreement, during renegotiation, or during the life of the contract. Typically, these three different types of strike have a different dynamic.[11] First-agreement strikes often centre on the fundamental issue of the employer's willingness to bargain with the union. Renegotiation disputes are more often about money, while wildcat strikes, or strikes occurring during the life of the agreement, often revolve around a very specific issue, such as the actions of a particular supervisor or anger over a co-worker's suspension. Wildcat strikes may also be a sign of rank-and-file discontent with the union's leadership.

As Table 11.4 indicates, renegotiation strikes have almost always resulted in the greatest number of person-days lost. During the 1970s, wildcat strikes sometimes involved a greater number of workers than renegotiation disputes; however, because they are illegal in almost all Canadian jurisdictions and frequently not sanctioned by union leaders, these disputes are generally very short relative to other strikes. Both their relative frequency and their proportion of person-days lost appears to have diminished, although in this connection it's important to bear in mind that Workplace Information Bureau data by type of strike cover only disputes involving 500 or more workers, and hence we lack information on smaller disputes, which might reveal different trends. There are a number of possible explanations for the decline in wildcats.

First, health and safety legislation in all Canadian jurisdictions (McPhillips and England, 1995) allows workers to refuse to continue working in conditions they consider unsafe. Such legislation has essentially eliminated what was formerly a major cause of wildcats. Second, a number of organizations have come up with innovative and speedy forums for resolving grievances, such as the dockside arbitration used in the Port of Vancouver (J. Weiler, 1984). While such innovative dispute resolution methods may not have eliminated wildcats altogether, they do appear to have reduced their incidence (J. Weiler, 1984). Finally, there is reason to believe that employers and managers may well be taking a harder line on wildcats. Knowing that they will likely be held legally accountable should they walk out during the life of the agreement, workers and unions may be more reluctant to do so than they were at times when management might have been more willing to look the other way.

Overall Trends

Looking more generally at the pattern of Canadian strike activity since the end of the First World War, it is by and large true, as economically oriented analysts have suggested, that strike activity tends to rise and fall with the business cycle, rising in inflationary periods and declining in times of recession or depression. This would appear to have been particularly the case with respect to strike frequency, perhaps somewhat less so with respect to size and duration. Certainly a desire to keep pace with rising

Table 11.4

STRIKES AND LOCKOUTS IN CANADA INVOLVING 500 OR MORE WORKERS, BY CONTRACT STATUS, VARIOUS YEARS

1976

Status	Number (% of total)	Size (% of total)	PDL (% of total)
First Agreement	2 (1)	1 543*	79 100 (1)
Renegotiation	134 (76)	608 111 (41)	7 995 000 (88)
Wildcat	40 (23)	879 755 (59)	1 013 980 (11)
Other	1 (1)	750*	750*
TOTAL	**177 (100)**	**1 490 159 (100)**	**9 088 830 (100)**

1981

Status	Number (% of total)	Size (% of total)	PDL (% of total)
First Agreement	1 (1)	1 242 (1)	890*
Renegotiation	66 (67)	189 585 (79)	6 061 120 (98)
Wildcat	32 (32)	49 625 (21)	107 140 (2)
Other	——	N/A	N/A
TOTAL	**99 (100)**	**240 452 (100)**	**6 169 150 (100)**

1986

Status	Number (% of total)	Size (% of total)	PDL (% of total)
First Agreement	——	N/A	N/A
Renegotiation	71 (80)	412 770 (96)	5 635 450 (99)
Wildcat	17 (19)	16 016 (4)	27 460*
Other	1 (1)	1 300*	10 400*
TOTAL	**89 (100)**	**430 086 (100)**	**5 673 310 (100)**

1991

Status	Number (% of total)	Size (% of total)	PDL (% of total)
First Agreement	——	N/A	N/A
Renegotiation	32 (88)	215 577 (99)	1 447 890 (100)
Wildcat	4 (13)	2 800 (1)	4 510*
Other	——	N/A	N/A
TOTAL	**36 (100)**	**218 377 (100)**	**1 452 400 (100)**

1996

Status	Number (% of total)	Size (% of total)	PDL (% of total)
First Agreement	2 (6)	2 800 (1)	70 500 (3)
Renegotiation	26 (76)	125 159 (49)	2 286 090 (88)
Wildcat	4 (12)	46 934 (18)	144 496 (6)
Other	2 (6)	83 000 (32)	83 000 (3)
TOTAL	**34 (100)**	**257 893 (100)**	**2 584 086 (100)**

* = less than 1%

PDL = person-days lost

N/A = not applicable

Percentages may not add up to 100, due to rounding.

Source: Work Stoppage Bureau, Workplace Information Directorate, HRDC.

inflation was an important factor in the wave of strike activity that followed the two world wars and also occurred in the middle and late 1970s and very early 1980s. Along similar lines, it is worth noting that strike frequency fell off very sharply starting in 1982, a recessionary year that marked the end of the last significant wave of inflation seen in this country—and the beginning of a second round of wage controls for most public sector workers.

At the same time, it is important not to overlook the various pieces of labour legislation, especially *PC 1003* (1944) and the *Public Service Staff Relations Act* (1967), which granted collective bargaining rights to large numbers of new workers. The increase in strike intensity immediately following the passage of these two pieces of legislation should not be considered simply a response to inflation. In part it was a reflection of the fact that more workers were now legally entitled to go on strike. In part, as well, it may have reflected pent-up frustration over non-economic as well as economic issues, to which the newly unionized workers could now, for the first time, legally respond by striking.

But it would probably be a mistake to attribute growing public-sector strike intensity solely to structural factors. As a number of observers (Ponak and Thompson, 1995) point out, and as we pointed out in the public sector chapter (Chapter 9), the decade of the 1990s was one marked by large-scale privatization, contracting-out of government work, service cuts, and layoffs of public sector workers. Such developments were obviously the source of extreme frustration and stress for many public sector workers. One should also not overlook provincial and federal governments' all but nationwide imposition of public sector wage controls, which had the effect of removing many public sector workers' ability to bargain over money. In the short run, the wage controls may have reduced public sector strike intensity, as appears to have been the case for the early '90s. But the wave of public sector strikes in 1996 and 1997 and the nationwide wave of health care and transit strikes in 2001 suggest that when added to the other frustrations and stresses of public sector worklife in the 1990s, the period of prolonged wage controls has been a spur to renewed militancy, as public sector workers seek to make up some of the ground lost through years of wage controls, freezes, or in some cases even actual rollbacks (see Fryer, 2000 and 2001). At the same time, the relatively low level of private sector strike intensity suggests that innovative new bargaining arrangements such as Quebec's "social contracts," in which unions have signed long-term collective agreements containing no-strike clauses in return for job security and a guarantee of government investment in plant modernization, may be improving labour–management relations at least to a degree (see Déom and Boivin, 2001; Chaykowski and Verma, 1992).

SOME RECENT DISPUTES

In this section, we stop to take a closer look at four Canadian strikes that have occurred since 1999. While this section does not pretend to offer a representative treatment of all recent Canadian strikes, the four disputes we have chosen should provide some sense of the kinds of issues of greatest concern to Canadian workers and their unions.

CFB Goose Bay (1999)

In the previous edition of this book (see pp. 449–450), we noted the importance of community support in response to the contracting-out of support services at the Canadian Forces Base at Goose Bay, Labrador, to Serco, a British-based multinational company. That support, which included a one-day general strike, helped cushion the effects of the contracting-out, though it did not prevent substantial job losses. In 1999, community support was instrumental in winning the remaining workers better terms and conditions of employment after a bitter 46-day strike.

The strike began June 11, 1999. Conciliation broke down after Serco tabled an offer that did not address such important issues as staffing, seniority, Isolated Post Allowances, and hours of work (*Alliance*, fall 1999). After the strike began, the company attempted to hire local contractors to take over tasks normally performed by the strikers, such as garbage collection and grass-cutting, but all refused (ibid.). In addition, the contractors refused to rent the company equipment that would allow it to do the work itself. Although the Public Service Alliance and Serco had already signed an essential services agreement guaranteeing services in the event of an emergency, the company then started using military personnel to do the strikers' normal work, a development that increased friction between the military and civilians (PSAC News Release, June 14, 1999). Union officials and community members were also upset that large aircraft such as 727s and Hercules were being allowed to land for refueling stops without the protection of striking firefighters—a situation one official described as "a time bomb ready to explode" (PSAC News Releases, June 14 and 17, 1999).

Negotiations eventually resumed after union officials called the company president and the Department of National Defence and warned them to expect a long strike if the company didn't come to the table with "a fair and reasonable offer" (*Alliance*, fall 1999). The eventual four-year agreement, signed July 27, 1999 but retroactive to April 1998, provided the 260 remaining workers with job security for the duration of the agreement and also increased wages, benefits, and shift premiums for firefighters (PSAC News Release, July 27, 1999).

After the end of the strike, PSAC local union president Randy Ford said, "The working environment is getting better every day. When we first came back it was 'shaky' because there was a lot of mistrust. That is improving with time." (*Alliance*, fall 1999). PSAC regional executive vice-president Paul Ducey suggested that the new contract with its improved wages and benefits would provide an economic boost to the community, which stood behind the base workers during their strike (PSAC News Release, July 27, 1999).

Falconbridge Ltd. and CAW/Mine Mill Local 598 (2000–1)

Corporate mergers and shifting union structures played an important role in the seven-month strike between nickel giant Falconbridge Ltd. and CAW/Mine Mill Local 598, one of the longest and most bitter in recent Canadian history.

The strike began August 1, 2000, just weeks after Brascan Corporation took over majority ownership of Falconbridge's parent company, Noranda. In a bid to reorganize its business into two separate divisions—mining and smelting—the company sought to strip "entire sections" from the collective agreement, reducing the document by over 80 pages (OPSEU, 2000b). Among the areas in which the company was seeking major concessions were bumping and recall rights, union representation, and workplace committees, including health and safety (ibid.). A management negotiator's reference to union members as "scumsuckers and bottomfeeders" at the last round of negotiations left members feeling they had no choice but to go on strike (ibid.).

Breaking with a 75-year tradition, the company employed replacement workers to enable it to maintain at least partial production (SCSJ, 2001). While many striking workers would normally have had the opportunity to work for other contractors for the duration of the strike, Falconbridge blocked off this option by informing contractors that they would be blacklisted from future contracts with the company if they hired the strikers, which led contractors to demand a separation certificate before they would hire them (OPSEU, 2000b).

Viewing the strike as a "community crisis" that was inflicting serious economic and social harm on both the workers and the Sudbury Community, Sudbury Regional Council passed a resolution (OPSEU, 2000a) calling on the parties to resume bargaining, with the help of a provincial mediator if necessary. Regional Council was particularly upset at the company's use of replacement workers—a "practice not accepted by the Sudbury community"—and called on the company to reverse its decision to employ such workers. Undeterred, the company not only continued to use the replacement workers but threatened to resume full production—with or without its striking workers (Lowe, 2001). Initially content merely to delay production vehicles and buses loaded with replacement and supervisory workers, frustrated strikers eventually forced a complete 12-day halt to production, whereupon the company responded by applying for, and being granted, an injunction limiting the number of picketers to 20 per plant gate. After a late January confrontation between strikers and their allies from other unions and local and Ontario Provincial Police riot squads armed with tear gas, pepper spray, attack dogs and truncheons, a second injunction in early February limited the number of pickets to five per line (Lowe, 2001).

The new collective agreement, ratified February 20, 2001 by 87% of those voting, provided the 1250 mine, mill, and smelter workers with a signing bonus, a wage increase, and various other economic improvements. But it also gave the company increased contracting-out rights and the ability to eliminate certain job classifications and to force employees to do more than one job in different classifications. After the strike, the company announced that the total Falconbridge work force would be reduced by 10%, but through retirements and attrition rather than layoffs (SCSJ, 2001).

The union declared that the end of the strike would not mean the end of the Falconbridge workers' struggle—merely that the struggle would take another form as the workers dealt with the implications of the new contract language (SCSJ, 2001). Meanwhile, at least one observer (Lowe, 2001) suggested that neither side emerged a winner. On the one hand, the company, despite its deep pockets, use of force, and numerous allies in powerful places had failed to break the union's spirit. On the other hand, the new realities of globalized production meant that Falconbridge was able to maintain some production, obtaining 'feed' for the strikebound Sudbury nickel smelter from a non-striking unit in Quebec and then shipping it to Norway for refining, a production chain that required the collaboration of half a dozen other unions including the Steelworkers, railway unions, and various longshoring and seafaring unions. A key factor here may have been the CAW's "pariah" status within the Canadian Labour Congress (the recent conflict between the CAW and the CLC was discussed in Chapter 5). Because of that "pariah" status, the CAW was unable to invoke the assistance of CLC unions in obtaining a "hot goods" declaration that would have broken the international production chain and very likely allowed the strike to end much sooner than it did (Lowe, 2001). In Lowe's view, globalized production requires more rather than less solidarity among unions, and the price the CAW paid for its departure from the CLC was probably too high.

National Gallery of Canada and PSAC (2001)

Employees in the federal government's artistic community demonstrated considerable creativity during the course of a lengthy dispute with the National Gallery of Canada and the Museum of Contemporary Photography. Their efforts eventually bore fruit in a three-year agreement providing substantial wage and benefit increases.

The two-month strike, conducted against the backdrop of the Gallery's exhibition of the paintings of Gustav Klimt that opened on June 15, was preceded by a work-to-rule campaign and a variety of colourful protest tactics, including a lunch-hour march by employees and their dogs at which National Gallery management were requested to "Throw us a bone!" (PSAC Release, April 6, 2001). On May 10, the museum workers launched a full-scale strike after the failure of both conciliation and mediation (PSAC Release, May 10, 2001). The 2% salary increase that management had last offered was substantially below the regional inflation rate, and also below the 2.5% achieved, without a work stoppage, by their colleagues at the nearby Science and Technology and Aviation museums (ibid.).

During the strike, the museum workers kept up their colourful protest tactics. Most notable were the piles of red shoes frequently on display in front of the museums as well as in strike posters. Though the protests were entirely peaceful and the difference between the union's demands and management's salary offer was relatively small, the

Gallery management took various legal actions against the strikers and made repeated requests for judicial injunctions to restrain the union's picketing, an aggressive tactic that did little to improve the already strained relations between the parties (PSAC Release, June 27, 2001). Nonetheless, on July 10 the parties reached a tentative agreement that was ratified three days later. The agreement provided a signing bonus, wage increases of up to 10.25% over a three-year deal, and improved vacation leave and parental benefits, as well as an assurance that there would be no reorganization during its life. It also included a back-to-work protocol assuring employees that an "inclusive, respectful and supportive work environment" would await them upon their return. A key element of the protocol was the Gallery's agreement to withdraw all civil suits launched against its staff during the strike (PSAC Release, July 13, 2001).

Government of Nova Scotia and NSGEU (2001)

The year 2001 saw an almost unprecedented wave of strikes in the health care sector, from Nova Scotia to British Columbia. Fuelling these strikes were years of real income loss resulting from government-imposed wage freezes and rollbacks in the public sector (many of these were described in the first edition of this book). But frustration over increased workloads, bed closures, and what the health care workers have come to perceive as a lack of respect and recognition from politicians were also factors. Aggravating the situation is the higher pay being offered to nurses by recruiters from other countries, such as the U.S. and Britain, as well as other provinces.[12]

The most bitter of these disputes took place in Nova Scotia, whose premier, ironically, is a former physician—Dr. John Hamm. Ironically as well, the dispute started to heat up just as a similar strike was winding down in Saskatchewan. To make up for a decade of frozen wages, nurses belonging to the Nova Scotia Government Employees' Union (NSGEU) and their counterparts with the Nova Scotia Nurses' Union were demanding pay increases of between 20 and 25 percent over three years. This was far higher than the 8.3 percent the government was prepared to offer (Home Excite, June 18). Fearful of the possible effects of a province-wide health care strike, the Hamm government on June 14 introduced a bill to take away health care workers' strike rights. Beyond that, the bill would also have given Cabinet the power to impose settlements, prevented arbitration of health care disputes, and barred court challenges of any Cabinet-imposed settlement (Home Excite, June 14).

The government cited a $500 million deficit and $12 billion debt as its reasons for imposing the legislation. But unionists, nurses, and health care policy analysts said the legislation would only aggravate the already severe shortage of nurses in the province (Home Excite, June 15). Clearly, the legislation aggravated the friction between the parties, leading the NSGEU to reject a tentative settlement reached with the help of a mediator, and causing another public sector union, CUPE, to order its members to work to rule even though it hadn't yet started bargaining (Home Excite, June 15 and 16). After a rally featuring national union leaders, the NSGEU's support workers (such as radiologists and lab technicians) launched full-scale strike action on

June 27, supported by the union's nurses who honoured their picket line (Home Excite, June 27). When the NSGEU members were ordered back to work, most complied, but continued their protest by resigning *en masse*. Finally, the government withdrew the controversial legislation that had been the source of so many of the problems, and on July 5 it agreed to send its dispute with the NSGEU and NSNU to final offer selection. On July 17, local arbitrator Susan Ashley was appointed to settle the dispute. Ashley's ruling awarded the province's registered nurses, who had been the most poorly paid in the country prior to the award, their final demand of 17 percent over three years. But other health care workers received only the government's offer of 7.5 percent plus a lump sum payment (Lancaster, 2001 (25:7-8)).

Some Common Themes

Wages were clearly a factor in all four of the above disputes. This was particularly true in the case of the public sector disputes, where workers had seen their wages frozen for many years during the 1990s and as a result had experienced a significant decline in real income.

By the same token, lack of respect and recognition must also be considered a significant factor, not just in the two public sector disputes but also in the Falconbridge strike. We've already referred to the name-calling indulged in by a Falconbridge management negotiator. Along similar lines, insinuations by the Nova Scotia health minister to the effect that nurses were prepared to neglect patients in need of care infuriated many nurses (Home Excite, June 14). The use of injunctions and other hard-nosed legal tactics by the National Gallery's management had a similar effect.

Government restrictions on unions' bargaining rights were a prime factor in the Nova Scotia health care dispute, and may also have been at least an indirect factor in the National Gallery strike. Had the Nova Scotia government not introduced its legislation removing both the strike right and arbitration, the NSGEU might have accepted the tentative mediated settlement. As it was, union president Joan Jessome noted that even some of those voting to accept felt they were doing so "with a gun to their head," while those who voted to reject told her their dignity wasn't for sale (Home Excite, June 16). Workers at the National Gallery, in common with other federal government employees, were frustrated after years of suspension of bargaining, continuing suspension of interest arbitration, and numerous other restrictions on their rights as employees (see Fryer, 2000 and 2001).

Globalization and increased competition were clearly important factors in both the Goose Bay and Falconbridge disputes. As readers of the first edition will recall, it was the contracting-out of base support services to the British multinational firm Serco that had led to all the problems at the base in the first place. In the Falconbridge dispute, a series of mergers and reorganizations led the company to try to 'strip' the contract. Its globalized production chain also enabled it to maintain at least partial production despite the union's most valiant efforts.

While the four strikes discussed above are all quite different from one another, it's worth noting that management took a tough line in all four cases. This was most evident in the Falconbridge strike, where the company brought in professional strikebreakers and used force to attempt to maintain production, but was also illustrated by Serco's use of military personnel as strikebreakers, the Nova Scotia government's bill banning both strikes and arbitration, and the National Gallery's repeated use of injunctions and other legal manoeuvres against the strikers.

WHAT CAUSES STRIKES?

Having looked in some detail at four recent Canadian strikes, and the causes for those strikes, we can now step back a bit and consider the issue of strike causes more generally. In few cases, other than certain wildcat strikes, is the cause likely to be single or simple. Leaving aside for the moment strongly inflationary periods, where strike action is often necessary to prevent rapid erosion of workers' real wages, experience suggests that most Canadian strikes appear to require: (1) serious medium- or long-term worker frustration, typically the result either of poor labour–management relations or an extremely difficult economic environment, or both, and (2) a triggering incident or incidents that can serve to channel that frustration, and around which union leaders can mobilize broad support for strike action. In the case of a now-famous Canada Post strike staged by CUPW in 1981, frustration had arisen from the long-standing poor relationship between management and the union and, in the eyes of some observers (Morton, 1989), the corporation's mismanagement. The triggering incident for the lengthy dispute appears to have been Canada Post's refusal to meet the union's demand for a maternity leave provision. In some unions, such an issue might not have proved of sufficiently broad appeal to have led to strike action. Here, it undoubtedly helped that about 40 percent of CUPW's members were women (Craig and Solomon, 1996, 53). More often, wages are likely to be the triggering issue. In many cases, wage issues by themselves might be insufficient to provoke a strike, particularly in deflationary periods. But given that almost everyone could use more money, an employer's refusal to meet a union's wage demand will often prove to be the "last straw" when antagonistic relationships marked by large accumulations of grievances or employer attempts to diminish the union's influence have already sown the seeds of conflict.

Beyond this, there is now a large body of literature relating strikes to various economic causes such as unemployment, inflation, nominal and real wage levels, and profits. A smaller, but still significant, literature exists on such socio-political and cultural determinants as community cohesion, union leaders' values and ideologies, decision-making authority, and intraorganizational conflict within unions and management organizations. Some attempts have also been made to link strikes to bargaining unit size and to the bargaining history of particular organizations. While much of this literature is interesting and important, space precludes a detailed consideration of most of it here.[13] It should also be noted that a good deal of the literature, especially the more economically oriented portion of it, presumes a background in econometrics and statistics and, in general, gets into research issues that are too complex for most beginning students.

Strike causation is undeniably a complex issue. Realistically, an introductory text can do little more than scratch the surface. Here, we propose three fairly generic approaches that provide some tools for understanding strike causes without getting into heavy-duty statistics or complex research methodology issues. In applying these approaches, readers should be aware that, in the last analysis, each bargaining relationship and set of strike issues is unique. To fully understand the causes of any given strike, one must know the players and the history of their interactions with each other, in addition to understanding the economic, political, and cultural environment within which those interactions are and have been conducted. This said, the generic or "framework" approaches discussed below can make readers aware of some of the more common patterns of strike causation.

Avoidable vs. Unavoidable Strikes

Lloyd Reynolds (1982:427) makes a useful distinction between *avoidable* and *unavoidable* strikes. The former are those in which the true positions of the parties overlap (i.e., there is a settlement zone), so that with sufficient information, a mutually acceptable solution can be found. The latter are those in which there is no settlement zone, and the parties will undergo a work stoppage rather than make further concessions.

Within any given negotiation, an unavoidable strike may result from fundamental disagreement over an issue of principle (maternity leave in the 1981 Canada Post strike, the union's continued right to exist in other cases). A settlement zone doesn't exist in the case of such issues because they are really not quantifiable, and hence any numerical compromise is impossible. One cannot have a union shop on Tuesdays and Thursdays, but a non-union shop the rest of the week. As well, when strikes do arise over such issues of fundamental principle, they are apt to be longer and more bitter than those over less fundamental issues such as money (Kervin, 1984). Other unavoidable strikes may result from either party's desire to change the bargaining framework or structure (as in the 1996 GM strike discussed in the first edition [see Peirce, 2000:444–5]), or from intraorganizational conflict within the union or management group. In the latter case, the strike, though perhaps irrational from an economic perspective, may be seen as necessary to help maintain internal cohesion within the union or management group. Speaking of the need some unions have to call occasional strikes for this purpose, Reynolds notes (p. 428) that "[u]nused weapons become rusty." Strikes are also extremely difficult to avoid in situations where, typically because of a history of bad relations, one party feels driven to use a strike to punish the other.

Mistakes or Collective Voice?

John Godard's (1994) distinction (similar but not identical to Reynolds's) is between strikes that result from mistakes, generally in the negotiation or ratification process, and those more appropriately regarded as unions' expressions of their members' collective voice. In the former group (Godard, 1994:343–346) he includes disputes resulting from immature or flawed bargaining relationships, as well as those caused by negotiators' lack of skill, inexperience with each other, or inability to get along. Another cause, often related to union intraorganizational conflict, can be individual workers' miscalculations, which may lead them to reject tentative agreements that their leaders know are probably the best they can realistically hope for. The complexity of the situation itself can also be the source of mistakes that lead to strikes. Here again, intraorganizational conflict may lead to negotiating errors. More fundamentally, such errors are more apt to occur in situations where difficult issues are at stake, where bargaining structures are complex, or where many different occupations and classes of worker are being represented.

The "strikes as mistakes" perspective also covers disputes resulting from an **asymmetry of information**. Typically, this takes the form of the management's possessing more complete and up-to-date financial information than the union. The union may then be caught in the position of not knowing whether or not management is telling the truth when it claims it cannot afford to meet the union's demands, and thus being forced to call a strike in order to call the management's bluff.[14] Godard (1994:343–346) argues that while the "strikes as mistake" approach has its uses, it's wrong to view strikes only as mistakes, given the conflict he sees as inherent in employment relationships generally. In his view, it is generally more useful to view strikes as expressions of unions' collective voice. With this approach, what primarily determines whether or not a particular situation will lead to a strike are the extent and intensity of worker discontent, union leaders' ability to mobilize that discontent, the union's strike power, and management's willingness and ability to "buy off" discontent through generous wage settlements or progressive human resource policies. Also relevant are the availability of other means of expressing discontent (especially quitting) and the presence or absence of cohesive community support, which may prove necessary, particularly in the case of a lengthy or bitter strike.

Both Godard's and Reynolds's approaches help explain why, despite the existence of a formidable array of dispute resolution mechanisms (discussed below), Canada has continued to have relatively high strike intensity by international standards. As the reader will observe, a number of Canadian dispute resolution mechanisms, such as back-to-work legislation, are reactive. Most of those that are proactive, such as conciliation and mediation, are approaches designed to prevent mistakes from occurring in the negotiation process. The assumption here is that if the parties can communicate reasonably effectively, behave decently towards each other, and convey accurate information at the table, a strike should not be necessary. Often, such interventions are useful in preventing strikes or at least in reducing their length and severity. But they are of little value where a settlement zone simply does not exist (in many cases involving intra-organizational conflict), or in situations (as in the "industrial conflict" perspective described by Kervin [1984]) where the conflict extends beyond the workplace and permeates virtually all aspects of the workers' lives, as in strikes occurring in single-industry mining towns. It would be naive to view such strikes as "mistakes." Here, a strike is almost always an overt expression of serious long-term discontent—discontent of the same variety, normally, which led the striking workers to unionize in the first place.

The one key question left largely unanswered, even in Godard's more comprehensive discussion, is why worker discontent takes the form of strikes under some circumstances but not others. Why, in particular, do some countries (and provinces within Canada) appear to have consistently lower strike intensity than others?

Strikes and Workplace Conflict: The Big Picture

In attempting to answer the questions just posed, it's important to bear in mind, once again, that strikes are just one of many possible forms of workplace conflict. Such conflict may find either individual or group expression. Moreover—and this is key to the discussion that follows—some IR systems' arrangements for handling "alternative" types of conflict, such as worker grievances, seem far likelier than others to reduce the sort of worker frustration that's likely to lead to strike action later on.

Let's suppose our job is to find out why Canada has normally had higher strike intensity than Germany. Even if we confine our investigation to strikes that are the result of mistakes, there are some good reasons, as the literature (Adams, 1995a; Bamber and Lansbury, 1993) has already established, why the Canadian system should lead to more such mistakes than the German one. Most important, within the highly centralized German system, bargaining is normally conducted at the national industry level between an employers' association and an industrial union. This means there are many fewer sets of negotiations going on whose failure could lead to a strike. It also means that negotiators on both sides are apt to be highly experienced, and therefore less apt to make mistakes than the inexperienced negotiators who often hammer out deals in Canada. As well, German collective agreements themselves are simpler and cover a smaller range of issues than Canadian ones, since in Germany a good many issues are left to be resolved at the enterprise level. This also reduces the likelihood of negotiating error.

A final point concerns information asymmetry. In Canada, as noted above, unions may well be forced to call strikes to find out the true state of affairs from employers who may or may not be telling the truth. In Germany, this would seldom if ever be necessary. Most corporations have worker directors and works councils, whose officers are generally active unionists, and who are legally entitled to full and accurate information about the firm's performance (Adams, 1995a). Union negotiators thus go to the table with pretty much the same information about the firm as their management counterparts.

Less often discussed in the literature is the question of how grievance arrangements may increase or decrease the likelihood of strike action, assuming now that we are dealing with strikes as collective expressions of union members' frustration and discontent. An aggrieved German worker (Adams, 1995a) has a broad range of avenues for possible redress, including his works councillor, his local union officer, his immediate supervisor, or the union's local office. If these approaches fail, the worker may take his case to a Labour Court. The Labour Court has jurisdiction over a far broader range of issues than does a Canadian arbitration panel (Adams, 1995a), and hence the likelihood of a complaint's being heard by the court is that much greater. All in all, the German approach to grievances suggests a desire to see individuals' workplace complaints resolved as quickly as possible. By allowing the individual worker to retain "ownership" of his grievance, the German system also seeks to "uncouple" individual workers' frustrations from the sort of collective frustrations that can lead to strikes. The works councils, which can legally take disputes through to arbitration, can also help to defuse at least some of the collective frustrations arising at the shop-floor level.

With its broad range of options, then, the German approach to grievances probably serves to defuse a large portion of individual workers' frustrations and discontents. Here it is in sharp contrast to the Canadian approach, which relies almost exclusively on a single mechanism: the formal grievance process. Under this procedure, the grievance is filed by the union, not by the individual worker. Ultimately it is the union that will decide whether or not the grievance gets carried forward. While there have been many improvements in recent years (see Chapter 12 for details), the process is still generally costly, legalistic, and extremely slow. A minuscule proportion of all grievances are carried through to arbitration (Gandz, 1979); most are either settled by the parties or withdrawn. It is not generally considered a breach of the union's statutory duty of fair representation for it to use individuals' grievances for political purposes, trading off the possibility of individual redress for the organization's larger collective aims. As well, many grievances are filed for avowedly tactical or political purposes. In unhealthy organizations, it's common for unions to file large numbers of grievances during or just before negotiations. At the extreme, as in the case of Canada Post, the existence of huge numbers of unsettled grievances may itself be a possible cause of strike action. Even in less extreme cases, unsettled grievances add to everyone's frustrations and tend to make negotiations that much more difficult.

Overall, Canadian approaches to grievances seem likely to increase both individual and collective frustration. The major sources of frustration for individuals are the slowness of the process and their loss of control over it. For unions, serving as their members' collective voices, the major sources of frustration are probably the slowness and costliness of the process and its likelihood of leading to intraorganizational conflict. For example, aggrieved individuals whose cases haven't been heard may, at negotiation time, put severe pressure on union executives and negotiating teams—possibly pressing them to go in directions they would rather not take and that the organization as a whole would benefit from not taking.

The German approach to grievances appears to be based on two important assumptions: (a) the individual's right to have his case heard, and (b) the desirability of defusing workplace conflict at an early stage. In contrast, the Canadian approach seems to be founded on a pluralistic desire to balance unions' power with that of management. The idea here appears to be that if unions are given the greatest possible latitude with respect to worker grievances, subject of course to the limitations of duty of fair representation provisions, this will be another "weapon" that can help them get to a level playing field with management. Both systems' aims are worthy. The question is whether Canadian society as a whole, or even the Canadian labour movement, is best served by grievance arrangements that offer individual workers little guarantee of a hearing, while increasing union–management conflict by allowing individuals' frustrations to feed into and exacerbate that conflict, personalizing it, as it were. Arguably, Canadian grievance arrangements have helped make strikes longer and more bitter, a conclusion that receives at least modest support from the long average duration (by international standards) of Canadian strikes in most years.

The preceding discussion does not pretend to be a complete analysis of comparative Canadian and German strike intensity. Hopefully it has given readers some insight into the complexity of strike causation, and into some of the many different ways in which strikes are related to other kinds of industrial conflict. Clearly, here is an area where further research is badly needed.

DISPUTE RESOLUTION METHODS

Canadian jurisdictions have developed a variety of dispute resolution methods for use in helping to prevent strikes, or, in some cases, as alternatives to strikes. Virtually all involve the use of a neutral third party. These methods work in various ways. In mediation and, increasingly, in conciliation as well, the neutral assumes a more interventionist role, working actively with the parties in an attempt to reach a settlement. In arbitration, normally used after one or more other methods have failed, the neutral actually establishes the terms and conditions of the new agreement. In establishing an arsenal of dispute resolution methods and in deciding which ones to use on any given occasion, Canadian governments seek to strike a balance between allowing the parties as much freedom as possible to settle their own disputes and protecting the public interest. For example, **compulsory arbitration** is virtually unheard-of in the private sector. Its main use is with groups such as police and firefighters whose services are deemed so essential to public welfare and safety that they can't be allowed to go on strike. Similarly, conciliation boards are now all but unknown in private sector disputes, though they are still used from time to time in high-profile public sector ones (Craig and Solomon, 1996; Godard, 1994).

In one important respect, Canadian government intervention in the IR system appears to go beyond "striking a balance." The compulsory conciliation provision found in most Canadian labour acts seems both highly interventionist by international standards, and inconsistent with the general principle of voluntarism underlying the Canadian IR system, which was discussed in some detail in the labour law chapter (Chapter 8). While there may be some rationale for retaining the procedure in disputes with a substantial public interest component, it is not at all clear why a conciliator should be used to help resolve disputes in, say, shoe factories. It's also not clear, as Godard (1994:352) points out, whether the process actually winds up doing more good than harm. Undoubtedly some strikes have been averted as a result of compulsory conciliation. On the other hand, it's entirely possible that without it, unions and management organizations would have become more creative in thinking up their own ways to resolve disputes, and thus averted other strikes in that way.[15]

Compulsory Conciliation

Compulsory conciliation was first introduced into Canadian labour legislation in 1907, when it was written into the *Industrial Disputes Investigation Act (IDI Act)*. Some version of compulsory conciliation continues to be part of every Canadian labour act except that of Saskatchewan.

Under compulsory conciliation, a government official, normally someone from the labour ministry, meets with the parties to determine the possibilities of settlement. Increasingly, conciliators have come to play active roles in attempting to resolve disputes, functioning more and more as mediators in fact if not name. Indeed, in two jurisdictions, British Columbia and Alberta, mediators are used instead of first-stage conciliators. As noted earlier in the chapter, a conciliator must report his or her lack of success to the labour minister and, in addition, a certain length of time must generally have elapsed before a strike or lockout can become legal.

The second stage of the conciliation procedure, still "on the books" in most Canadian jurisdictions, is the conciliation board. Under this procedure, a tripartite board comprising a neutral, a management representative, and a union representative meets. Where used, the board operates more formally than a single conciliation officer, eliciting presentations from the parties and making recommendations as to the appropriate terms of settlement (Godard, 1994). However, as noted above, conciliation boards are increasingly rarely used, primarily because of the delays they cause and their tendency to interfere with the parties' willingness to negotiate a settlement on their own (the so-called "chilling effect"). A number of jurisdictions have substituted mediation for the second stage of the conciliation process; the *Canada Labour Code* allows for a mediator or conciliation commissioner in addition to the traditional officer and board (Craig and Solomon, 1996). Quebec and British Columbia have done away entirely with second-stage conciliation.

Mediation

In theory, **mediation** involves more active intervention on the part of the third-party neutral than does conciliation, though the boundaries between them are becoming increasingly blurred in practice. Unlike conciliation, mediation is usually voluntary, although as noted above, it has been incorporated as the first stage of the conciliation process in two Canadian jurisdictions and as the second stage in several others.

Depending on the nature of the negotiations and the experience of the negotiators, the mediator may be called on to do such things as meeting with the parties to determine what their key issues are, discovering where the "settlement zone" lies, acting as a go-between, actively pressuring the parties to compromise so that an agreement may be reached, and dealing with the media both during negotiations and after a tentative agreement has been reached (Craig and Solomon, 1995; Downie, 1989; Godard, 1994). Experience suggests that there is no one "best way" to mediate; people with varying backgrounds and personal styles have proven successful. It is, however, generally agreed that effective mediators must be honest and impartial, have good listening skills, know how to keep a secret, and have a good sense of timing (Craig and Solomon, 1996).[16]

Mediation of various types is being used quite frequently, both within the IR system and for other purposes, such as resolving child custody disputes in divorce cases. A survey of the Ottawa-Hull "Yellow Pages" for 2001 found 48 active mediation practices in the English section and another 6 in the French section. The ad for one of those practices put the matter most succinctly: "Mediate, Don't Litigate." While there are many reasons for mediation's growing popularity, the two most important are probably its significantly lower cost compared to formal litigation, and its less adversarial nature. Those using mediation seem to find the process less traumatic than going to court would be. The trend towards using mediation to resolve a wide range of disputes is a far-reaching one that will bear careful observation in the coming years.

Arbitration

Interest arbitration, in which a neutral acceptable to both sides or a tripartite panel chaired by such a neutral establishes the terms and conditions of the new collective agreement, is often used in Canada's public sector, normally after the failure of one or more of the methods described above. Note that interest arbitration should not be confused with **rights** or **grievance arbitration**, which has to do with interpreting the existing contract. (This type of arbitration will be discussed in Chapter 12, on grievances.) Note as well that compulsory interest arbitration is virtually never used in the private sector. In general, both management and unions prefer to negotiate their own contracts rather than turning the decision over to a third party. On occasion, however, **voluntary arbitration** is used. Not uncommon in the United States, where it has been tried in industries as varied as steel and major league baseball, it is rarer in Canada. However, it has been used in the Ontario clothing industry (Downie, 1989) and in some university settings such as the University of Ottawa (Craig and Solomon, 1996).

Binding interest arbitration is the normal method of resolving contract disputes involving essential employees such as police and firefighters, whose services are generally considered so crucial that they cannot be allowed to strike.[17] Without the ability to present their case before a neutral third party, these groups would be at a severe disadvantage in bargaining. Aside from such clearly essential workers as police and firefighters, arbitration is substituted for the usual conciliation-strike route in varying ways across Canada. The approaches taken here range from that of Quebec, which specifically rejects arbitration except in the case of police and firefighters (Hébert, 1995), to those of Alberta, Manitoba, and P.E.I., where government employees continue to be denied the right to strike and must, therefore, submit to binding interest arbitration. In certain jurisdictions, other groups, such as teachers and nurses, must likewise go to arbitration. In the federal public service under the *PSSRA* and in certain provinces under similar acts, government employees may choose either binding interest arbitration or the traditional conciliation-strike route. However, the federal government has been increasingly unwilling to use arbitration in recent years. The arbitration option was suspended for three years in 1996 when public service collective bargaining was restored, and for a further two years in 1999. Although the Fryer Committee, whose report was discussed in Chapter 9, has recommended restoration of a form of arbitration through its Public Interest Dispute Resolution Commission, it is not clear at this writing whether the government will act on the Fryer Committee recommendation.

The federal government's unwillingness to allow its employees to take bargaining disputes to arbitration appears to be part of a broader trend. Earlier, the province of Ontario granted its employees the right to strike in 1993, in the process removing their right to take disputes to arbitration. Governments' reluctance to take disputes to arbitration has been based on the fear that arbitrators will impose awards whose costs they will be unable to bear. Such a fear may have been understandable during the tough time of the early-to-mid 1990s. It is less understandable now, given that most Canadian governments are now in a balanced budget or even surplus position.

There are two major types of interest arbitration: conventional and **final-offer (FOA)**. Under **conventional arbitration**, the arbitrator is given considerable latitude in fashioning an award. He or she may, and often does, pick and choose among the positions submitted by the parties. With FOA, there is no such latitude. The arbitrator must choose either the management's position or the union's. FOA may be used either on a total-package basis, or issue-by-issue. An intriguing variation (see Craig and Solomon, 1996:319) is tri-offer FOA, where, in addition to the positions advanced by management and the union, the arbitrator may pick the recommendations of a fact-finder.

Conventional arbitration has been criticized on a number of counts. Some have been concerned at its cost, others at the slowness with which settlements are achieved through it compared to settlements achieved in other ways. The two most common criticisms are (a) that groups that use it regularly may become so dependent upon arbitrators that they lose their ability to fashion their own settlements (the so-called **"narcotic effect"**) and (b) that it inhibits genuine bargaining by removing the incentive for the parties to make hard choices, since they know the arbitrator is there to make the choices for them at the end of the day. This latter effect is commonly known as the **"chilling effect."** While there is no consensus in the literature on the extent to which such effects exist in Canada, there is at least some reason to believe they may be significant problems.

The use of FOA, especially in its total-package form, would seem to provide a good way around any possible chilling or narcotic effects. In principle, the possibility of having an arbitrator reject one's entire package and select that of the other side should be a very severe disincentive to unreasonable behaviour, and an equally strong incentive for the parties to settle on their own. Some evidence cited by Ponak and Thompson (1989:394–396) suggests that, under FOA, the rate of freely negotiated settlements is a good deal higher than under conventional arbitration. Nonetheless, FOA has found little favour in Canada, though it has become relatively common in U.S. public sector bargaining.[18] The one notable exception is the Nova Scotia health care dispute of 2001, where, as noted above, it was imposed after the provincial government withdrew its legislation suspending health care workers' right to arbitration.

Mediation-Arbitration (Med-Arb)

Med-arb, as it is commonly known, is a hybrid form of dispute resolution that has not often been used in Canada, but has lately become more prominent because of its use in certain high-profile public-sector disputes such as the 1997 postal strike. As the name suggests, this approach involves the neutral's functioning first as a mediator, then, if the parties are unable to settle on their own within a given period of time, as an arbitrator. Judge Alan Gold, who for some years was standing arbitrator for the Port of Montreal and who often used med-arb (Gold, 1993), suggests that med-arb may work best where there is a standing arbitrator or umpire who knows the industry and the players extremely well.

Among the criticisms of med-arb, perhaps the most serious is that having acted as a mediator could prejudice a person's decision as an arbitrator (Craig and Solomon, 1996). Judge Gold, however, indicates (1993) that this had not been a problem, at least in his experience. Given the relatively small amount of experience Canada has had with med-arb, it may still be premature to pass judgment as to its effectiveness.

Fact-Finding

Fact-finding is a type of dispute resolution less often used now than in the past. The idea behind fact-finding is that if the neutral has issued a report outlining the key issues, particularly if that report is made public, the parties will be more likely to settle. The process, which is more formal than mediation, typically involves the presentation of briefs by the parties and a hearing where they present their cases (Gunderson, Hyatt, and Ponak, 2001:341). The fact-finder then issues a report with recommendations; the report is often released to the public as well as to the labour relations board. However, the recommendations are never binding.

Fact-finding was previously used extensively by Ontario's Education Relations Commission. Since the abolition of that body's separate dispute resolution functions, it has been used relatively infrequently in Canada. But fact-finding is one of many options available in the "toolkit" approach to public service dispute resolution recommended by the Fryer Committee (Fryer, 2001). Should this recommendation be adopted by the government, a time-honoured form of dispute resolution could get a new lease on life.

Back-to-Work Legislation

Back-to-work legislation is used to end public sector strikes that have reached a point where government officials believe that, if they continued, they would pose significant risk to the public health, safety, order, or welfare. Such legislation has often been used to end strikes at Canada Post and in the Quebec public sector. Sometimes (as in the most recent Canada Post strike), it is followed by a referral to med-arb or straight arbitration, or even by the imposition of a settlement. While occasional use of back-to-work legislation is perhaps inevitable in any country that allows public sector workers to strike, the frequency with which this legislation has been used in Canada (see above) suggests there is something seriously wrong with existing public sector bargaining arrangements.

SUMMARY

Overall, there appears to have been a gradual but significant trend away from formal investigative mechanisms such as second-stage conciliation, and in the direction of more informal facilitative mechanisms such as mediation. The conciliation process itself has evolved into something very much like mediation in most jurisdictions. Within the public sector, arbitration, initially envisaged as the normal option under *PSSRA*'s "choice of procedures" approach, has recently found less favour. A number of jurisdictions (notably Ontario) that formerly used arbitration to resolve disputes with their public servants have moved to the conciliation-strike route. Meanwhile, med-arb, though still relatively uncommon, is becoming more prominent because of its occasional use in high-profile public sector situations. Also in the public sector, federal and provincial governments continue to make frequent use of back-to-work legislation.

A NEW WAVE OF STRIKE ACTIVITY?

During the 1990s, some observers (i.e., Gunderson, Hyatt, and Ponak 1995) were predicting an end to what they saw as a 35-year wave of Canadian strike activity. That prediction may have been premature. The two years after that prediction was made— 1996 and 1997—saw strike intensity revert to its highest levels since 1990. Since then, strike levels have continued to be higher than in the early 1990s, except for the year 2000. Data for the year 2001 are not complete, but figures for the first nine months indicate a level of strike intensity roughly comparable to that of 1998 and 1999, which is still significantly higher than the levels generally experienced during the early 1990s.

One reason for Canada's low strike intensity in the early 1990s may have been the prevalence of public sector wage controls, which almost certainly led to a reduced incidence of public sector strikes during those years. To the extent that earlier public sector strike levels were held artificially low, the rise in public sector strike activity

Members of the Public Service Alliance walk the picket lines in front of a federal building in Peterborough, Ontario on Wednesday, August 15, 2001. The strike was one of many called across Canada in a series of "Workless Wednesdays" designed to draw public attention to federal government workers' contract demands.

during the mid 1990s could be considered, at least in part, a statistical artefact. But it would be a mistake to write off the recent strike resurgence as solely a statistical artefact. In Ontario, where strike activity during that period included a number of one-day community-wide "general strikes," the phenomenon almost certainly reflected broad and continuing anger at provincial government policies, especially at cutbacks in health care and education. The recent rash of health care and other public sector strikes reflects anger over years of pay freezes, increased workloads due to downsizing and restructuring, and job insecurity, as well a perceived lack of respect from politicians and government bureaucrats.

From an economic perspective, the recent resurgence of public sector strike activity is entirely logical. Members of many public sector groups have seen a substantial erosion in real purchasing power over the past decade. The resurgence is also consistent with the theory of conflict developed by Hebdon (1992) and with the view of conflict that has been advanced here. Due to the restrictions that have been placed on it recently, the collective bargaining process has been far less able to defuse conflict than was the case in the past. The result seems to have been that frustrations have risen to the point where they are likelier to result in strike action.

In the private sector, Quebec's social contracts in the steel and pulp and paper industry seem quite promising. It isn't entirely clear to what extent such contracts have penetrated other sectors of the economy; however, the presence of many elements of the social contracts in agreements under the Quebec Federation of Labour's Solidarity Fund (Boivin and Déom, 1995) suggests that the approach has probably been more generally applied. Further research is needed on the extent to which the social contracts and similar arrangements have lowered strike intensity in Quebec. Still, given that Quebec has, except for the apparently anomalous year of 1999, seen a major reduction in its levels of strike activity, the social contracts and other elements of the province's approach to reducing labour–management conflict will bear closer observation elsewhere in Canada.

Within the IR profession, a great deal of research and practical activity have focussed on the development of dispute resolution methods designed to prevent strikes or at least minimize their impact on "innocent" third parties. Many of these methods have proven useful. However, Canada's continued relatively high strike intensity suggests that, by themselves, dispute resolution methods are not enough. This chapter has suggested that, in addition, attention must be paid to broader institutional factors, such as Canada's generally decentralized bargaining structure and the ways in which the grievance procedure feeds into and aggravates existing sources of union–management conflict. In the public sector, the recent resurgence of strike activity coupled with governments' frequent use of back-to-work legislation suggests the need for a fundamental rethinking and retooling of that sector's collective bargaining arrangements.

QUESTIONS FOR DISCUSSION

1) Have you ever been on strike? What was the experience like? If you haven't been on strike, try to find a friend or relative who has been, and ask that person what the experience was like.

2) What's special about the way unions operate during and immediately before a strike?

3) Legally speaking, what is a strike?

4) What is the most accurate way of comparing strike intensity across different jurisdictions, industries, or countries?

5) At which points in history was Canadian strike activity highest and lowest? Why?

6) Why does public sector strike activity now appear to be on the increase again, after a number of years of very low strike incidence? Why might public sector strike rates be increasing at the same time as private sector rates are decreasing?

7) What were the major causes of the four recent strikes discussed in the mini-cases? How do they relate to the various theories of strike causation discussed in the chapter? Does the "strikes as mistakes" theory do much to explain any of these strikes?

8) What are some methods of dispute resolution used to prevent strikes or lessen their impact once they've started? Which ones are used mainly in the public sector? Which seem most effective? Are there serious problems with any?

9) Assume you have been appointed provincial labour minister. What steps would you take to reduce strike intensity in your province? Would these steps involve any curtailment of basic union rights? If so, how would you justify that?

10) Assume you are member of a job action committee for a teachers' union. You and your colleagues are all extremely frustrated at the slow pace of negotiations, and you have reached a legal strike position and taken a strike vote. At this juncture, someone says, "Maybe we aren't ready for a full-scale strike yet, but we could just not grade the final exams." Comment on the wisdom of this strategy.

SUGGESTIONS
FOR FURTHER READING

Adams, Roy. (1995a). "Canadian industrial relations in comparative perspective." In M. Gunderson and A. Ponak (Eds.), *Union-management relations in Canada*. 3rd edition. Don Mills, ON: Addison-Wesley. Contains a useful discussion of industrial conflict that suggests conflict may depend more on structures than on processes (such as dispute resolution systems).

Hebdon, Robert. (1992). "Ontario's no-strike laws: A test of the safety valve hypothesis." In *Proceedings* of the 28th Conference of the Canadian Industrial Relations Association, held in Kingston, Ontario, in 1991. Quebec City: CIRA. Fascinating discussion of conflict that strongly suggests that suppressing conflict in one way (as by making strikes illegal) merely causes it to resurface in other ways. An article that should be much better-known than it is.

Kervin, John. (1984). "Strikes: Toward a new typology of causes." In *Proceedings* of the 21st Annual Meeting of the Canadian Industrial Relations Association, held in Guelph, Ontario. Offers an extremely helpful classification scheme for different types of strikes, including a discussion of policy approaches suitable for each. A useful corrective to the Panglossian optimism of those who think that all we need to do to prevent strikes is to be of good will and learn how to communicate better.

CHAPTER 12

GRIEVANCES:
FUNCTION, RESOLUTION, AND PREVENTION

Grievance mediation can bring smiles to the faces of both sides—as well as lower bills.

The grievance process is important in that it provides a way other than the traditional mid-term strike to resolve problems arising out of the interpretation of collective agreements. It is also important in that it provides workers with a certain measure of workplace voice and a forum through which they can express discontent about workplace conditions without fear of employer reprisal. In this chapter, we begin by examining the overall significance and functions of the grievance process. After a look at a specific case, we go on to examine grievance procedures and outcomes. We then consider some criticisms of the conventional arbitration process and some innovative new dispute settlement mechanisms that have arisen in response to those criticisms, before closing with a broad look at grievances in the overall context of workplace conflict.

GRIEVANCES AND THEIR SIGNIFICANCE

As we've pointed out throughout this book, worker–management conflict is a fact of life in most workplaces. Strikes, which are perhaps the most dramatic manifestation of such conflict, were discussed in the previous chapter. Here, we are concerned with grievances, a less dramatic, but often equally profound, manifestation of worker–management conflict.

What Is a Grievance?

Strictly speaking, a grievance (Gandz, 1982:289) is an allegation that one or more provisions of a collective agreement has been violated, and a claim for redress for any damages resulting from that violation. While one could apply the term to most types of employee complaint, such as those resulting from arbitrary or excessively harsh supervisory practices or the behaviour of co-workers (Gandz, 1982), using the term in its more general sense could result in ambiguity. It is, therefore, probably wiser, for purposes of this course, to apply the term "grievance" only to allegations of collective agreement violation.

The Function and Significance of Grievances

The grievance process is of great significance in the Canadian IR system because it provides a forum for the resolution of disputes arising out of the collective agreement. Under Canadian legislation, mid-term strikes are banned,[1] although individual workers are, as we noted in Chapter 7, allowed to refuse work they believe unsafe. Otherwise, the rule is "Work now; grieve later" (Godard, 1994:363). As we noted in the labour law chapter, collective agreements in every Canadian jurisdiction must contain procedures, culminating in binding arbitration, for the resolution of disputes over the interpretation and application of the agreement. For example, section 48(1) of the *Ontario Labour Relations Act* states that every collective agreement shall provide for the final and binding settlement by arbitration, without a work stoppage, of all differences between the parties arising from the interpretation, application, administration, or alleged violation of the agreement, including any question as to whether the matter is arbitrable. Where such procedures are not explicitly written into an agreement, the labour board will normally deem them to have been included.

Because of the "Work now, grieve later" rule, it's vital that aggrieved employees have a quick and relatively inexpensive mechanism for obtaining redress. It has been well established (see Rose, 1986b) that failure to address grievances quickly can lead to more serious labour relations difficulties (including wildcat strikes and other forms of industrial conflict) later on. Initially, in both Canada and the United States (Thornicroft and Eden, 1995; Nolan and Abrams, 1997), grievance arbitration appears to have resolved most problems fairly expeditiously. However, since the early postwar period, it has tended to become lengthier, more formal, more highly legalistic, and a good deal costlier (Nolan and Abrams, 1997; Arthurs, 1988). The reasons for these developments are discussed later in the chapter, along with a number of remedies that have been worked out in recent years.

In addition to maintaining the integrity of the agreement by providing a mechanism for ensuring that its terms are adhered to (Godard, 1994:359), the grievance process serves a number of other functions. First, and perhaps most important, it provides a system of industrial jurisprudence under which individuals can seek redress without fear of reprisal from superiors (Godard, 1994:360–361). By thus protecting workers from arbitrary treatment from superiors, the grievance process serves as an important mechanism of individual and group voice (Godard, 1994:360; Freeman and Medoff, 1984). Next to the higher wages that unions normally provide workers, the grievance process may well be the most compelling reason for people to join unions. Beyond that, the process can provide a forum for supplementary negotiations over items left vague in the agreement (Godard, 1994:359–360). It can also serve as a political mechanism for resolving intraorganizational conflict within both management and union sides. As Godard notes (p. 360), a union official may pursue a grievance more to satisfy a certain faction within the organization than because she or he believes the case has merit as such. Likewise, lower-level managers may encourage the union to pursue a certain grievance in the hopes it will persuade senior management to change a policy they dislike or find unworkable. Management may also "hang tough" on a particular grievance or set of grievances to prove a point to the union or to their superiors.

Finally, the grievance process can be used as a pressuring device in an attempt to induce management to address issues not covered by the collective agreement. As Godard notes (1994), an agreement may contain no provision on contracting out— an issue that could cost union members jobs or income. Though they cannot grieve over this issue where there is no relevant agreement provision in place, what they can do is file a large number of grievances over other provisions contained in the agreement, thereby causing management considerable inconvenience, if not disruption, and possibly getting them to rethink their position on contracting out.[2] While this is a perfectly legitimate use of the grievance process, it is also a controversial one, since (particularly around negotiation time) it can lead to large accumulations of grievances not arising out of the complaint of any individual union member. Habitual use of the grievance process for this purpose, as has often been the case in organizations such as Canada Post (Stewart-Patterson, 1987), is generally a sign of very poor labour–management relations overall. Indeed, high grievance rates can seriously affect a firm's bottom line. A number of studies, such as those by Ichniowski (1986), have found that establishments with high grievance rates perform more poorly in terms of both labour efficiency and product quality than those with lower grievance rates.

Types of Grievances

It's useful to distinguish between individual, group, and policy grievances. As the name implies, an **individual grievance** involves the application of the agreement to one member. An example would be a grievance by Mary Jones alleging that her three-day suspension for chewing gum in the company cafeteria violated the collective agreement in that the suspension was not imposed for just cause. A **group grievance** results from a combination of similar individual grievances seeking a common redress (University of Ottawa, 1994). For example, a group of workers might file a grievance alleging that the company had failed to pay overtime pay for work after regular working hours. A **policy grievance** involves a question of the agreement's general application or interpretation (University of Ottawa, 1994). Such a grievance might be initiated over large-scale technological or organizational change or a change in the pension plan. While such grievances are relatively infrequent, they are generally quite serious because they may involve millions of dollars or hundreds of jobs. For this reason, policy grievances are often initiated at a late stage of the grievance procedure, where they can be dealt with by senior management and union officials (Gandz and Whitehead, 1989:241).[3]

Before we go any further, it might be helpful to look at an actual grievance case. We suggest that you read the following case now, then again when you have finished the chapter. See how your view of the case changes as a result of what you've learned.

Work-Family Conflict*

THE DENISON MINES CASE[4]

When domestic problems cause an employee to miss work and fall asleep on the job, what is the employer's responsibility? The following case may shed some light on this matter. Please read the case thoroughly, then answer the questions at the end.

In a case involving Denison Mines Ltd. and the United Steelworkers of America, one company policy stated that any employee planning to take an unscheduled absence should phone security. A second policy read as follows.

It is not the desire of Denison Mines to discipline employees for unauthorized absence. The Company recognizes that the vast majority of employees wish to give a fair measure of work. . .It is the very small minority of others for whom it is necessary to set forth guidelines concerning absence without leave.

When an employee returns from an absence without an acceptable reason for the absence being known to his Supervisor, the Supervisor, or another Supervisor in some circumstances, will, in discussion with him, give him an opportunity to explain his absence. If the employee is unable to provide an acceptable reason for his absence, the Supervisor will warn him against a repetition of such conduct.

If the same employee cannot provide an acceptable reason for another absence within 90 days of the first one, a Supervisor will, again after discussion with him, warn him again of the need to improve his work attendance or face further discipline.

* This case is Re Denison Mines and U.S.W.A., 9 L.A.C. (3rd) 97–104. Individual's names have been changed and deletions made to save space; otherwise, the case is as originally published. Used by permission.

A further repetition of absence without an explanation acceptable to the Company will, after the employee has been given the chance to explain his conduct, result in a registered letter being sent to his place of residence. This will warn him that a repetition within 90 days will lead to termination of his employment.

The foregoing relates to situations where only an absence problem is involved. However, discipline for unexcused absence cannot be treated on a purely isolated basis. The foregoing is for use in the majority of cases, but the total disciplinary record of an employee and his length of absence will be considered when discipline for an unexcused absence is being weighed. No two people are alike and circumstances are seldom exactly the same twice. Supervisors are expected to take this into consideration and use their best judgment accordingly.

When, because of unforeseen circumstances, an employee is absent from work without having first obtained permission from his Supervisor, it becomes his responsibility to ensure that his Supervisor is notified as soon as possible concerning the reason for the absence and its expected duration. Please note, however, that such notification does not free the employee of the obligation to justify his absence nor will it be regarded as. . .permission to be absent.

A "Doctor's slip" is acceptable proof of illness only when he has actually treated the illness.

If an employee is absent without permission for more than five of his scheduled consecutive shifts or does not return to work within five days of his completion of an unauthorized leave of absence, he will be considered to have terminated his employment and the Company will feel no obligation to interview or contact him.

The grievor, Jean Grenier,[5] was first employed by the company February 24, 1978. He was terminated November 18, 1982. At the time of his discharge he was classified as a rock breaker operator. He is 41 years of age, married and has two small children. He. . .was recruited by the company from Rouyn, Quebec.

The evidence revealed the grievor's most recent absenteeism problems stemmed from a severe domestic problem. On December 4, 1981, while the grievor was at work, his wife left their home with their two small children and departed by bus. He sought the assistance of the local police to no avail. He learned the following day she had gone to Quebec City, but it took him three months to locate her exact whereabouts. On an earlier occasion his wife had taken the two children to Ottawa "in order to speak to the Prime Minister" and subsequently was committed to the North Bay Psychiatric Hospital. The evidence was that she was committed to the same facility a second time and that she had previously taken an overdose of sleeping pills. The grievor gave evidence about the effect of these problems on his life and his work.

After his wife had deserted the family home to go to Quebec City, the grievor became very concerned about the welfare of his two children. The family had lived in a three-bedroom house leased from the company in Elliot Lake but he found them in a one-bedroom apartment in Quebec City. His little girl also missed her father very much and he, in turn, missed his family.

In February of 1982 he failed to stop at an intersection while driving a taxi as a second job and he further failed to stop when police signalled him to do so. He was later arrested, charged, and subsequently convicted of related offences. At the time of the incident, the police advised him to see his doctor and his doctor attributed the situation to acute anxiety brought on by his domestic crisis. . .He was hospitalized for a few days at that time and, on the advice of his doctor, he then went to see his children in Quebec City. He received sickness benefits under the collective agreement for his time off.

Despite the wishes of his children, his wife refused to return to Elliot Lake. Thus, to see his family at all, he had to drive the 700 miles from Elliot Lake to Quebec City. From March of 1982, he was working for the company, maintaining his three-bedroom home, holding down a second job, and wishing to see his children as much as possible. His daughter, he testified, was particularly insistent on "wanting to see her daddy."

Throughout his two-week vacation in July he was trying to resolve his problems with his family in Quebec. The problems, however, remained unresolved and caused him to be absent from work for two days in July when a leave of absence was refused. Up to this point in time and after, the grievor was using weekends to travel to Quebec City to resolve his problems and see his children. The July absences constituted the first step of the absenteeism policy. I might add that his first-line supervisor was fully aware of the grievor's domestic problem in that he too was experiencing a marital difficulty at the time and they discussed their marital problems two or three times a week.

The second step arose out of an absence on August 18, 1982. According to the grievor, he had been fined and his driving licence suspended. . .as a result of the February traffic incident. He appealed the sentence and the matter came before the courts on August 18, 1982. He testified that he told his supervisor two or three days before that he would be away on the day in question and was wished "the best of luck in court." When he received the third step notice he did not grieve but refused to sign the warning because he felt it was unjustified. He explained that he did not appeal because he would have to reveal to the company and union all the embarrassing details associated with the February incident. He indicated the necessity of attending court to have the suspension set aside so he could lawfully drive to see his family and advised that, in fact, the suspension was removed subject to the imposition of a more substantial. . .fine.

His progress to the third stage of the policy came with an absence on August 30, 1982. His cage time for the Monday evening shift was 7:50 p.m. and he had travelled to Quebec City that weekend. He left his wife at 7:00 a.m. on the Monday morning and drove the 700 miles to Elliot Lake that day. Because of traffic he concluded he would be 20 minutes late and telephoned to determine if he could come in on this basis. He was told he might as well not come in under the circumstances. He was subsequently interviewed and received the following 90-day letter dated September 14, 1982. It reads:

Dear Mr. Grenier:

You have been counselled on your unacceptable absenteeism by various levels of supervision, and have received ample warning and briefing of the Company policy pertaining to unacceptable absenteeism.

As a result of your excessive and unacceptable absenteeism, it is necessary to inform you that a further absence, unacceptable to the Company, within ninety (90) days of August 30, 1982 will result in your being discharged.

He filed a grievance dated September 9, 1982, which was ultimately rejected by the company on November 29, 1982, at the third stage of the grievance procedure.

In October he was issued a two-day suspension for allegedly sleeping on the job. The incident occurred on a Friday. When he learned on the following Tuesday that the suspension was to be imposed for the Wednesday and Thursday he approached his supervisor to see if he could take it on the Thursday and Friday to facilitate a trip to Quebec City. However, he was told that he could not take a suspension at his convenience and, accordingly, he did not go to see his family. He testified that this meant he would have to use the time around Remembrance Day to visit them. [I]t should be noted that the grievor approached a more senior company official, Sean Yeats, with respect to his request to move the suspension. He explained why and Mr. Yeats suggested that he ask his supervisor for the Friday off as a leave of absence but. . .refused to intervene. Had the request been granted, the grievor would have had three days in addition to the weekend to visit his children. As it turned out, his second line supervisor, Ellis Kinder, refused the request.

The fourth stage incident. . .arose around the time of Remembrance Day. . .a Thursday. He was asked to work this day and agreed only on the condition he be given the Friday off. This was refused. At about the same time he received a telephone call from his little girl who repeated over and over again "Are you coming daddy?" He was worried that she was delirious. The grievor testified he was depressed and felt great tension between his job and his family. So great was this conflict, he said he did not fully make up his mind until he had travelled to North Bay on Remembrance Day. Rationalizing that he had grieved his 90-day letter, he decided to press on. At that point, he obviously had no intention of returning to Elliot Lake on the Friday. This shift was therefore missed. His next regular shift was on the Monday and he missed it as well as the Tuesday shift.

He explained these absences on the basis of a doctor's appointment in Quebec City on the Monday, his mental state, and a concern for the health of his little girl. When he returned to work on the Wednesday he produced a "return to work slip" from a Dr. Laurent Bouchard. . .in Quebec City. The slip appears to have its date altered but the grievor denies having done this and, on the evidence, I am not prepared to find he altered the document. A further slip was introduced into evidence purportedly over the signature of the same doctor and dated December 28, 1982. It reads: "Patient seen at the office on November 15, 1982 at 1600 hours. . .History of state of depression. Felt able to return to work."

He testified that he could see the doctor only on the Monday and that the appointment was made because of concern for his own health and the well-being of his little girl. He was candid in acknowledging, however, that "a big purpose" was to have something to give to the company on his return.

At the interview during which he was discharged, his personal problems were not reviewed and no offer was made for him to participate in the employee assistance plan. His wife has commenced divorce proceedings and he has access to his children pursuant to a court order. His next access to the children will be during his vacation in July (if he is reinstated. . .) And he testified that his claim for custody has been impaired by the loss of his job. However, if he gets his job back he is going to seek their custody. The only time he will need to go to Quebec is for court proceedings.

I would note that in October Ellis Kinder overlooked a lateness because of a concern that the incident might have been construed as a fourth-stage absence. Kinder also interviewed [Grenier] when the fourth stage occurred in November. He said his investigation revealed that the grievor had called in on the Monday or Tuesday, that the grievor's 90-day letter was active, and that "he was due for discharge." He, however, did not make the decision to terminate. This was done by Sean Yeats. Kinder, in cross-examination, acknowledged he was aware of the grievor's domestic problems but not in detail. He was also aware that the 90-day letter was under grievance. He was not aware that the grievor was away from work in February for acute anxiety. Yeats did not appear to have been told of the family problems and Kinder made no effort in his interview with the grievor to relate his knowledge of the grievor's family problems to the incident he was inquiring into. Yeats made his decision without interviewing the grievor and did not testify at the hearing.

Kinder testified that he was aware of the employee assistance program at the time of his dealings with the grievor and may even have mentioned the program to him at the third stage interview in September. However, he said he thought the program was to deal with alcohol and drug problems, although he had seen nothing in writing describing the program for supervisors or employees.

CASE QUESTIONS

1) Comment on the company discipline policy under which Grenier was discharged. In what ways does it fit in with the notion of "progressive discipline" discussed later in this chapter (you may have to read that section of the chapter to answer this question). In what ways doesn't it fit in?

2) What do you expect the result of this case to be at arbitration? Why?

3) How might Ellis Kinder and Sean Yeats have handled this case differently?

4) How might Jean Grenier have handled things so as to improve his case with the company?

5) Do you agree with Kinder's view of the role of an employee assistance program (EAP)? If you do, defend your position. If not, what do you think the EAP's role should be?

GRIEVANCE PROCEDURES

Collective agreements generally spell out grievance procedures in fairly considerable detail. A 1978 study by Jeffrey Gandz (quoted in Gandz and Whitehead, 1989) found that Ontario grievance procedures had anywhere from two to seven steps, with three being the most common number. A verbal stage involving a discussion between the grievor (often accompanied by a union steward) and the supervisor appeared in about two-thirds of the procedures, either as the official first stage or as a step preceding the official first stage (ibid.). If the problem could not be resolved verbally, the grievance would then be reduced to writing and submitted to the next level of management above the supervisor. Most grievance procedures contained strict time limits for each stage; however, almost all procedures also contained provisions allowing the parties to opt out of those time limits by mutual consent. A common feature was a semi-official "extra step" in which senior management and union officials would meet on a regular basis to review cases pending arbitration (ibid.). In some instances, this "extra step" was incorporated as an official stage of the procedure.

Since 1978, despite growing delays in the time it takes cases to be sent to arbitration and some evidence that suggests that at least some of the stages in the typical grievance process achieve few settlements and are thus of little practical use (Brett and Goldberg, 1983), the typical grievance process doesn't appear to have changed much. Most grievance processes that the author has examined contain either three or four official stages; many contain an additional unofficial stage either at the beginning or end of the process. The procedure in the University of Ottawa agreement discussed earlier is slightly more expeditious than some others the author has examined in that it contains only one step between denial of the initial written grievance and referral to arbitration: a meeting between the grievor (accompanied by a union representative) and the Dean to explore the possibilities of settlement. However, by allowing the parties to opt out of the grievance procedure's time limits at any stage, the procedure has failed to address one of the major causes of delay noted in the literature. Another potential source of delay arises from the possibility of using a three-person panel rather than a single arbitrator (see Thornicroft, 2001; Ponak and Olson, 1992; Rose, 1986a), although the latter would seem to be the norm.

The procedure outlined in Table 12.1, based on one described by Trotta (1976), would not be atypical, even today.

Table 12.1

A SAMPLE GRIEVANCE PROCEDURE

STEP 1   **(oral discussion, filing of grievance).** Meeting between supervisor and aggrieved employee, accompanied by shop steward. If problem not satisfactorily resolved in three working days, then grievance to be reduced to writing and Step 2 taken.

STEP 2   **(discussion between shop steward and department head).** Shop steward to discuss grievance with department head. If grievance not satisfactorily adjusted within three working days, then Step 3 shall be taken.

STEP 3   **(discussion between senior management and union officials).** Grievance committee consisting of four members appointed by the union to meet with plant manager or his or her appointed representative. The aggrieved employee and a representative from the international union may also be present.

STEP 4   **(referral to arbitration).** If grievance not settled, dispute may be taken to arbitration providing either party has given written notice requesting arbitration within 15 working days after the end of the Step 3 meeting. The parties designate a mutually satisfactory arbitrator. If they cannot agree on one within three days after the arbitration request, then the appropriate government agency shall, at the request of either party, provide both parties with a list.

ISSUES MOST COMMONLY GRIEVED

Discharge and discipline are the issues most commonly grieved by unions. A study by Gandz and Whitehead (1989) of grievances in a basic steelworks found that about half of all grievances were of a disciplinary nature. Seniority accounted for another 15 to 20 percent of the grievances, the remainder being related to such issues as job postings, overtime, health and safety, and the performance of bargaining unit work by supervisors. For Ontario as a whole, a more comprehensive study quoted by Adams (1978:40) found that discharge and discipline cases constituted 37 percent of all grievances sent to arbitration.[6] While management grievances against the union are rare, they do exist. Most typically (as in the case of the steelworks described by Gandz and Whitehead), such grievances would result from an illegal work stoppage. As for the causes of dismissal, both Adams (1978) and Barnacle (1991) found dishonesty, poor work performance, insubordination, poor attendance, alcohol, failure to get along, and union activity[7] to be the seven types of behaviour most commonly leading to dismissal. The two studies found relatively little difference in the percentage of cases related to each cause, and in both, dishonesty, work performance, poor attendance, and insubordination were the four commonest causes of discharge.

THE ARBITRATION PROCESS

Panels Versus Single Arbitrators

Arbitration decisions may be made either by single arbitrators or three-person panels. If a three-person panel is used, the union and management each select one member, and the agreed-upon third party neutral serves as chairperson of the board. This effectively makes the chair the decision-maker, since the panel need only reach a majority decision, not a unanimous one (Thornicroft and Eden, 1995:260). Indeed, even if neither nominee agrees with the neutral's decision, the chair's decision will generally be deemed to be the final award (Thornicroft and Eden, 1995; Craig and Solomon, 1996:340).

Numerous studies have found that single arbitrators reach their decisions more quickly than three-person panels, and that the single-person process generally costs a good deal less (Goldblatt, 1974; Rose, 1987; Button, 1990; Thornicroft and Eden, 1995). Other studies (i.e., Barnacle, 1991) have found little difference in grievance outcomes whether a panel or a single arbitrator was used. No doubt as a result, in recent years a decreasing percentage of cases have been heard by three-person panels. For example, in Ontario between 1980 and 1984, about 58 percent of conventional arbitration cases were heard by panels (Rose, 1986a). By 1985–1986, panels were being used in only about a third of those cases (Rose, 1991). Still, a surprising number of organizations continue to rely on the panels. As late as 1985–1988, panels were being used in three-quarters of all Alberta arbitration cases (Ponak and Olson, 1992). Moreover, as we noted earlier, even grievance procedures (like the University of Ottawa's) that allow for a single arbitrator may offer the option of a three-person panel. Given the obvious time and cost savings to be achieved from use of a single arbitrator, it is not at all clear why panels have remained so popular, particularly at a time when companies and unions alike are finding it necessary to cut costs in almost every area of their operations.

The Arbitration Hearing

Arbitration hearings are normally held in neutral settings (most often hotel meeting rooms (Gandz and Whitehead, 1989:249). While there is no requirement that parties be represented by legal counsel, unions and, especially, management organizations have been using legal counsel increasingly in recent years (Arthurs, 1988; Barnacle, 1991). When the union does not use legal counsel, the case is most often presented by a business agent or a national or international representative (Gandz and Whitehead, 1989:249).

Often there will be preliminary objections to a grievance. These include allegations that the agreement's time limits have been breached, that the arbitrator lacks jurisdiction because the provision breached is not in the collective agreement but rather in a subsidiary document such as a letter of intent, or that the grievance has already been withdrawn, abandoned, or settled (Sack, 1994:75–76; Gandz and Whitehead, 1989:249–250). While the respondent may argue that the arbitrator should adjourn the hearing until the preliminary objection has been decided, the normal practice is for the arbitrator to reserve judgment on the preliminary objection and proceed to hear the grievance proper, including his or her ruling on the preliminary objection in the final award. In this way, delay and expense can be avoided (Sack, 1994:69–70,75–76).

Once any preliminary objections have been dealt with, the hearing normally proceeds as follows.

1. Each party makes an opening statement in which the nature of the grievance and issues in dispute are raised (Gandz and Whitehead, 1989:249). Since the union is normally the party filing the grievance, the union will normally speak first. However, in discharge and discipline cases, where the onus of proof is on the employer, the company will normally present first (Sack, 1994:70–71; Peach and Kuechle, 1975:248). The party making the first opening statement has the opportunity to reply to new points raised by the other party (Sack, 1994:77). The grievor's opening statement should include the remedy sought (i.e., reinstatement in the case of dismissal) and the amount of income she or he has lost since the discharge, to guide the arbitrator in making a back pay award (Sack, 1994:79).[8]

2. The party on whom the onus of proof rests (normally the union, except in discharge and discipline cases) calls witnesses, who give evidence, generally under oath (Gandz and Whitehead, 1989:250). Each witness is cross-examined by the other party and then re-examined by the first party. Witnesses may also be questioned by the arbitrator, and by the panelists if there is a three-person panel (Gandz and Whitehead, 1989). It's important to bear in mind that the rules about what kind of evidence an arbitrator can accept are much less strict than those applied to formal court cases. In general, labour relations legislation empowers arbitrators to accept any evidence they consider proper, whether or not such evidence would be admissible in a court of law (Sack, 1994:81–82). It's also important that no witness be "badgered" in cross-examination to the extent that that witness feels unfairly harassed (Sanderson, 1976:66). Should this happen, the other side's representative or the arbitrator may intervene, and the arbitrator's ultimate decision may be negatively influenced (Sanderson, 1976).

    In evaluating the evidence before them, arbitrators will generally hold the parties to different levels of proof, depending on the nature of the grievance (Thornicroft and Eden, 1995:258). In most cases, the standard of civil trials, proof on "a balance of probabilities," is required (Thornicroft and Eden, 1995; Sack, 1994:81). This simply means that the side bearing the burden of proof must establish that its version of the facts is likelier to be true (Sack, 1994:81). However, in discharge cases, particularly those involving allegations of serious misconduct such as theft or dishonesty, a higher standard of proof is usually required. Here, arbitrators will often apply the standard normally used in criminal cases: proof beyond a reasonable doubt (Thornicroft and Eden, 1995:258).

3. The responding party also calls witnesses, who then give evidence and are cross-examined and re-examined as in the case of the first party's witnesses.

4. Each side then presents its closing argument, normally in the same order as the initial presentation (Gandz and Whitehead, 1989:250; Peach and Kuechle, 1975:247). Such closing arguments will frequently cite arbitration decisions made in similar cases (Gandz and Whitehead, 1989:250).

5. The arbitrator then adjourns the hearing. If sitting as the chair of a three-person panel, he or she confers with the nominees. If acting as a sole arbitrator, he or she then prepares the award. If there is a panel, he or she prepares a draft award and seeks input from the panelists. In a number of jurisdictions, there are time limits that the arbitrator or panel must observe. In Ontario, a single arbitrator must issue an award within 30 days after the end of the arbitration hearing, while a panel must do so within 60 days (*OLRA*, section 48[7–8]). However, these deadlines may be extended with the consent of the parties or at the arbitrator's discretion, so long as reasons are given in the award for the extension of the deadline (*OLRA*, section 48[9]). The final written award is then sent to the parties (*OLRA*, section 48[9]). The arbitrator's or panel's decision is binding on the parties and on the employees covered by the agreement affected by the decision (see *OLRA*, section 48[18]).

Enforcement

Most labour acts lay out a procedure for enforcing arbitration awards where either party refuses to comply (Sack, 1994:141). In Ontario, the award may be filed in the General Division of the Ontario Court (*OLRA*, section 48[19]) and enforced in the same way as any other court judgment, through contempt proceedings for continued non-compliance (Sack, 1994:141). Thus, if a party continues to ignore the arbitrator's award after it has been filed with the court, he or she risks a fine or even imprisonment (Thornicroft and Eden, 1995:262).

Judicial Review of Awards

In general, Canadian jurisdictions are reluctant to use the courts to overturn arbitrators' decisions. A number of provinces attempt to limit judicial review of arbitration awards through a privative clause (Thornicroft and Eden, 1995). An example is section 101 of B.C.'s labour act, which provides that except as noted in the act, any arbitration award or decision is final and not open to question or review in a court on any grounds whatever. Another section of the same act does grant the labour relations board limited power to review an arbitration award where a party has been denied a fair hearing or where the award is inconsistent with the principles of the labour act (Thornicroft and Eden, 1995; Sack, 1994:141–142). To date, most other provinces have not granted their labour boards this power (Sack, 1994:142).

In general, requests to appeal an arbitration decision are rarely granted. They are most likely to be granted in cases where the arbitrator has shown bias, denied a party a fair hearing, or made an incorrect interpretation of a common law principle or a statutory provision lying outside his or her "core area of expertise" (Sack, 1994). Appeals will also be granted in cases where the arbitrator has made a jurisdictional error (i.e., an error relating to a legislative provision limiting his or her remedial powers).[9]

ARBITRATION OUTCOMES

To date, there has been no single, comprehensive study on all aspects of arbitration outcomes. There have, however, been a great many studies of a more limited nature seeking to relate arbitration outcomes to such factors as arbitrator characteristics, grievor characteristics, the type of issue grieved, and the use of legal counsel by the two parties.[10] Overall, the evidence appears to be fairly inconclusive as to whether arbitrator and grievor characteristics such as age, gender, education, and experience significantly affect the outcomes of arbitration cases (see Thornicroft and Eden, 1995:268–270). A much more significant issue may be the extent to which women, non-lawyers, and younger people find it possible to enter the profession at all. A 1988 survey by Brian Bemmels (see Thornicroft and Eden, 1995:264) revealed that only 7 percent were women, 63 percent held a law degree, and the average age was nearly 56. Similar results were obtained in several other studies reviewed by Thornicroft and Eden (1995). In principle, it would seem desirable to have a cadre of arbitrators whose demographic characteristics more closely approximated the diversity of the work force. To the extent that the various provincial arbitrator development programs allow more women, non-lawyers, and younger people to enter the field, they will be performing a very useful service indeed.[11]

Discharge Cases

Because the impact of discharge cases both on individual workers and on organizational morale can be so dramatic, these cases are of special importance in industrial relations. This may explain why they have been more intensely studied than other types of grievance case. For the most part, except in cases involving a single extremely serious offence such as theft, assault, or sabotage, arbitrators expect employers to have applied **progressive discipline**, whereby the penalties have increased for each succeeding offence and the employee has been made aware of the possibility of further penalties up to and including discharge for any further offences (Adams, 1978; Thornicroft and Eden, 1995).[12] The purpose here is twofold. First, it informs employees that their conduct is unacceptable and states what the consequences will be should such conduct continue. Second, it allows them to correct the offending behaviour, where this is possible. The development of progressive discipline as the accepted norm for most dismissals arguably represents the single most important modification of the otherwise dominant doctrine of residual management rights. Slightly over half of all discharged employees who grieve their dismissals are reinstated, many with back pay (McPhillips and England, 1995:81).

Progressive discipline has always had a rehabilitative aspect to it (see Adams, 1978:29–30). In recent years, this aspect of progressive discipline has come increasingly to the fore, particularly in cases involving unexplained absenteeism and drug and alcohol use. A growing trend in such cases is for arbitrators to expect employers to have offered employees the chance to rehabilitate themselves, as by referring them to counselling or an **employee assistance program (EAP)**. No employee is required to accept counselling or employee assistance. On the other hand, should an employee not be willing to do so, the employer is then entitled to conclude that the employee in question is either unable or unwilling to be helped, and to proceed with appropriate disciplinary measures up to and including discharge.

Somewhat surprisingly, one's likelihood of reinstatement doesn't seem to depend very heavily on the type of offence one has allegedly committed. In George Adams' 1978 study, 53.5 percent of grievors were reinstated. The proportion of employees reinstated for different categories of misconduct ranged from 38 percent for attendance and 39 percent for poor work performance and dishonesty to 58 percent for union activity and 55 percent for alcohol-related offences. A later (1991) study by Peter Barnacle yielded essentially similar results. Some 54 percent of all grievors were reinstated, and slightly over half (51 percent) of all dismissals for dishonesty were sustained, as compared to 25 percent of those for union activity and 35 percent of those for alcohol-related offences. Only 12 percent of all those discharged were exonerated (i.e., awarded full compensation).[13]

Of far more significance than the type of offence allegedly committed was the grievor's previous disciplinary record. Adams found that a full 94 percent of those with no previous disciplinary record were reinstated, as compared to just under 60 percent for those with a good record or a prior disciplinary warning, and only 39 percent for those with a previous suspension. Similarly, Barnacle found that dismissals were sustained for 68 percent of those with a prior record related to the dismissal offence, and 47 percent of those with some kind of prior record, but for only 23 percent of those with no prior disciplinary record. These findings point strongly towards arbitral use of progressive discipline as a criterion in determining the appropriate penalty for a given offence (see Thornicroft and Eden, 1995:269).

An all-too-familiar criticism of the IR system concerns the length of time it takes to bring most cases before an arbitrator. Adams's study in particular lends some support to this criticism. He found that the longer it took arbitrators to hear cases, the less likely a grievor was to be reinstated or to receive any back pay. In cases heard within three months of discharge, only 29 percent of the dismissals were sustained and 29 percent of the grievors were exonerated. However, in cases heard more than six months after the discharge, 62 percent of the dismissals were sustained and only

10 percent of the grievors exonerated (1978:50–51). Such findings lend support to the hypothesis, discussed in the labour law chapter, that expedited arbitration systems can be of considerable benefit to workers and unions. It should also be noted that in recent years, the situation seems to have been getting worse rather than better. Thornicroft (2001:371) notes that one study found that between 1976 and 1996, the average elapsed time from initial filing to issuance of the arbitrator's award doubled.

Use of Legal Counsel

The use of legal counsel by management and unions has frequently been cited as the cause of delays in arbitration cases (Rose, 1987; Elliott and Goss, 1994; Thornicroft and Eden, 1995). Since lawyers are also expensive, the question naturally arises, why do parties continue to use them? The answer, as revealed by a number of studies (i.e., Goldblatt, 1974; Barnacle, 1991), is quite simple. If you have a lawyer and your opponent doesn't, you are more likely to win the case. If, on the other hand, your opponent has a lawyer and you don't, you're more likely to lose. Therefore, if there is any chance at all that your opponent will be using legal counsel, you would be well advised, from a purely practical perspective, to follow suit. In this regard, Barnacle (1991:163) found that, in cases where dismissals were sustained, employers used lawyers 85 percent of the time, but unions used them only 45 percent of the time. On the other hand, where full or partial compensation was awarded, the difference was much narrower, with employers using lawyers 78 percent of the time and unions, 69 percent.

An interesting observation is that lawyers appear to make little difference to arbitration outcomes when neither party uses them or when both parties do (Thornicroft and Eden, 1995:265). This in turn suggests that both sides could achieve substantial time and money savings simply by agreeing not to use legal counsel at all.

Lawyers as Arbitrators

As we noted earlier, both in Canada and the United States, the vast majority of arbitrators come from the legal profession (Barnacle, 1991; Thornicroft and Eden, 1995). This raises the question of whether lawyer-arbitrators arrive at different outcomes than do arbitrators from other professions, such as economics or industrial relations. While space does not permit a detailed discussion of this issue, Barnacle's findings[14] suggest that the differences between lawyers and arbitrators from other backgrounds are generally rather slight. Similarly, Terry Wagar's 1994 study and Thornicroft and Eden's review of eight studies (1995:268) found little difference in outcomes between cases decided by lawyers and those decided by people from different backgrounds, a finding which lends further support to the notion that the quality of arbitration decisions would probably not suffer from opening up the profession to individuals from a broader range of backgrounds.

Other Outcomes

Dastmalchian and Ng (1990) found that grievances were more likely to be granted in organizations with a positive industrial relations climate than in those with a negative one. In another study, this one of the Canadian federal public sector (Ng and Dastmalchian, 1989), the same two authors found that grievances were more often settled at early stages of the internal grievance procedure, and that higher-status employees were more apt to have their grievances granted than lower-status employees.

A number of studies, including most notably one by Brett and Goldberg (1983), have found that grievances are rarely settled at the middle stages of internal grievance procedures. In effect, what seemed to be happening was that middle-level managers and union officials were simply rubber-stamping their subordinates' decisions and passing the matter up to someone with real power to decide the case. This finding, as we will point out in more detail shortly, has important implications for the development of grievance mediation systems and other alternatives to conventional arbitration.

CRITICISMS OF CONVENTIONAL ARBITRATION

There is by now a substantial literature on the failings of the conventional arbitration process. Most of this literature (i.e., Nolan and Abrams, 1997; Button, 1990) laments the transformation of grievance arbitration from an informal, speedy, and relatively inexpensive process to a slow, costly, and highly legalistic one. Another major criticism is that, because arbitration has become so slow and so costly, only a very small percentage of all grievances filed—2 percent or less, according to various studies (i.e., Foisy, 1998; Gandz and Whitehead, 1989:240)—are actually heard by an arbitrator. Still another criticism is that because the union "owns" the grievance process and individual workers cannot, for the most part, file their own grievances, the individual worker has little redress if the union decides not to file his or her grievance (Godard, 1994:360).

In this section, we examine the time delays, costs, legalism, and inaccessibility of conventional arbitration, leaving the broader and more systemic question of union ownership of the process to a concluding section.

Time Delays

If good labour–management relations are to be maintained, it's essential that grievances be resolved as quickly as possible. As the well-known case of Canada Post (see Stewart-Patterson, 1987) attests far too clearly, large backlogs of unsettled grievances often represent industrial relations "time bombs" waiting to explode. Though most managers and union officials would agree about the importance of settling grievances quickly, the time required to settle grievances under conventional arbitration seems to be increasing. Earlier, we pointed out that the length of time it takes arbitration cases to be resolved appears to have increased substantially since the mid 1970s. Various studies reviewed by Thornicroft and Eden (1995:267) found the total length of time from the action that inspired the grievance to the issuing of the arbitration award to be anywhere from six to fourteen months, with delays of eight to twelve months most common. At Canada Post, delays of more than a year have often been the norm, with delays of more than two years not uncommon (Stewart-Patterson, 1987). For obvious reasons, lengthy delays are of particular concern in discharge cases; an employee who has lost his or her job and cannot find another will almost certainly undergo considerable hardship. In addition, as was noted above, the longer the arbitration process takes, the less likely employees are to be reinstated. While it is workers who most obviously suffer as a result of slow grievance processes, delays can also come back to haunt employers, as other employees file their own grievances to "protest" inaction on earlier cases, or in some instances even engage in illegal work stoppages (Rose, 1986b).

Costs

Though arbitration may indeed be relatively inexpensive compared to litigation in the courts, it is still far from cheap. Arbitrators' fees (split between the parties, along with other expenses such as the rental of hotel suites and photocopying) typically range from $500 to $2000 per day (Thornicroft and Eden, 1995:261). Their total fees for a case where the hearing itself is finished in one day typically range from $2500 to $5000 (Thornicroft and Eden, 1995); when the hearing is longer, the fees will obviously be proportionally higher. Where there is a three-person panel, panelists must also be paid, lodged, and fed. And when parties use legal counsel, they must pay lawyers' fees that can range from $100 to upwards of $300 per hour (Thornicroft and Eden, 1995). To get the complete picture regarding costs, one must also include the value of the many hours of union and management personnel's time devoted to preparing and presenting arbitration cases. By the late 1980s, one well-known arbitrator was "conservatively" estimating the costs of a single case to be $4400(not including the value of the time spent on the case (see Button, 1990:6). Since then, costs have increased further, so that for a one-day case involving legal counsel and using a three-person panel, the total bill could be as high as $15 000 per side when the value of people's time was taken into account (Elliott and Goss, 1994:9).

Legalism

As Elliott and Goss (1994:12) have noted, arbitration hearings are all too likely to become bogged down in technical legal arguments, rather than concerning themselves with the merits of the grievance at issue. In their view, the problem has been exacerbated by the growing use of legal counsel in recent years and by the excessive number of cases that arbitrators and arbitration panels are forced to read, digest, and incorporate into their awards. Because of this excessive reliance on precedents, arbitrators take significantly longer to write their awards than they otherwise would, and the costs to the parties are greater. Moreover, when at long last awards are issued, they are often so weighted down with legal citations as to be very difficult for anyone but a lawyer to understand.

Accessibility

Given the time delays, costs, and legalism of conventional arbitration, it isn't really surprising that so few cases are taken through to arbitration. With most arbitration cases running to four figures if not five, few management organizations and fewer unions could ever hope to take more than a tiny fraction of all grievances to arbitration. On this point, Kenneth Thornicroft (2001:365-6) speaks for many in expressing the fear that "[A]rbitration has become the preserve of those large unions and employers that have the resources to arbitrate contentious disputes—small employers and unions are constrained to find some other way to resolve their disputes." While some grievances may be resolved informally, many grievors, including some with very legitimate complaints, simply do not obtain a hearing for their cases. Such workers are likely to feel considerable frustration, and they can pose serious problems both for management and for their own union officials.

ALTERNATIVES TO CONVENTIONAL ARBITRATION

Growing awareness of the problems of conventional arbitration has led to the development of a number of innovative alternatives. The three most important for our purposes are **expedited arbitration**, which speeds up the arbitration process and reduces its cost, **grievance mediation**, where a third-party neutral helps the parties negotiate a solution to the grievance to prevent it from going to arbitration, and **preventive mediation**, where the parties seek to improve communications and develop proactive problem-solving mechanisms that will improve their overall relationship and thus prevent most problems from becoming formal grievances.

Expedited Arbitration

Most of the delay in arbitration cases results from cumbersome internal grievance processes, the use of three-person panels, dickering over the choice of an arbitrator or chairperson, the use of legal counsel at hearings, and long waits between the hearing and the issuing of an award. To counter these difficulties, a number of expedited (speeded-up) arbitration systems have been developed both by governments and by unions and management working on their own. Though there are certain differences between the various systems, most observe the principles in Table 12.2.

The Canadian Railway Office of Arbitration (CROA) is a good example of a private sector arbitration system that has earned its spurs. This system, which has been in effect since 1965 (Button, 1990:30), uses a standing umpire who normally hears cases starting on the second Tuesday of each month (Button, 1990:36). The umpire will sit for up to three days if necessary (Button, 1990:39), hearing on average 13 cases at a sitting (Button, 1990:36). The grouping of cases means that where there is a delay in one case (as when the parties decide to try to settle the matter themselves) the umpire can

Table 12.2

THE WAY TO QUICKER ARBITRATION DECISIONS[15]

1) Always use a single arbitrator rather than a three-person panel.

2) Where possible, have a standing umpire who will hear cases at the same time each week or month (i.e., the third Thursday). This allows him or her to hear a number of cases on the same day. It also ensures that the arbitrator "knows the business" and eliminates dickering over fees, since the umpire will be on monthly or annual retainer.

3) If a standing umpire isn't possible, then draw from a list you have agreed on in advance in an order you have agreed on in advance (i.e., alphabetical order), so as to eliminate dickering over the choice of an arbitrator.

4) Agree not to use legal counsel, or at least to restrict its use to complicated policy grievances.

5) Eliminate steps of the internal grievance procedure that don't seem to be producing any significant number of settlements, and consider replacing them with grievance mediation (discussed below).

6) Adhere strictly to time limits in any remaining steps.

7) Simplify procedural requirements as much as possible, by allowing oral decisions in straightforward cases, reducing the use of precedents, and requiring short written decisions very soon after the hearing.

simply move on to the next and return to the first when the parties are ready to proceed. Cases are presented in the form of written briefs, which reduces (though it hasn't completely eliminated) the use of legal counsel at hearings (Button, 1990:37).[16] A CROA umpire, M.G. Picher, has suggested that the use of written briefs saves time by helping the arbitrator to focus on the material at hand and reducing the need for rambling, long-winded oral argumentation (Button, 1990). In 1987–1988, the CROA simplified its procedures further by deciding to limit the use of counsel to discharge cases, unless the parties agreed otherwise (Button, 1990). The system has resulted in significant cost savings. For 1987–1988, the average cost per case was $1295 (Button, 1990:41), or 29 percent that of cases heard under conventional arbitration in the province (Rose, 1987). Best of all, the system has succeeded in doing what arbitration was originally intended to do: provide a quick, relatively inexpensive mechanism for resolving disputes over the interpretation of the collective agreement (Rose, 1987:43).

Though the CROA system of expedited arbitration is perhaps the country's best-known private sector system, it is not the only one. An essentially similar grievance commissioner system was adopted in 1972 by Inco and two United Steelworkers locals (Thornicroft and Eden, 1995:273). And in Vancouver, the once strike-plagued longshoring industry has long relied on a "dockside arbitrator" who is on call 24 hours a day and, travelling by motor launch or helicopter if necessary, can be on the site anywhere in the port within an hour or two to render an instant on-the-spot decision orally (J. Weiler, 1984).[17] At various times, other expedited systems have been used in the garment, motor transport, and auto industry in Canada, as well as in numerous American industries (Gandz and Whitehead, 1989:251–252).

As we noted in the labour law chapter, public expedited arbitration systems are in place in four provinces (B.C., Manitoba, Ontario, and Saskatchewan). In all four, expedited arbitration can be combined with prior grievance mediation,[18] further reducing costs and increasing the number of cases resolved. Section 49 of the Ontario act sets out that province's expedited arbitration procedure. Under the *OLRA*, either party may apply to the Labour Minister for appointment of a single arbitrator. The arbitrator, drawn from a list maintained by the ministry, must schedule a hearing within 21 days of the request (section 49[7]) and issue an award within 21 days of the hearing. If both parties agree, the arbitrator may deliver an oral decision immediately after the hearing (section 49[8]). The Ontario legislation also makes provision for prior grievance mediation through a med-arb procedure (section 50).

Over the years, expedited arbitration has become increasingly popular in Ontario. By 1992–1993, some 45 percent of all arbitration awards in the province were of the expedited variety, as compared to 19 percent in 1981–1982 (Thornicroft and Eden, 1995:272). The system has been shown to save both time and money. According to Rose (1991), between 1980–1981 and 1985–1986, expedited arbitration alone saved $2.2 million; prior grievance mediation saved a further $6.4 million. Time savings were even greater, as the average elapsed time between the incident giving rise to the grievance and an expedited award was only four months, compared to eleven months under conventional arbitration (Thornicroft and Eden, 1995:272).

Grievance Mediation

One criticism of all arbitration systems, even the best-designed expedited ones, is that they serve to foster an adversarial mentality by establishing a "winner" and a "loser," thus damaging ongoing relationships (Elliott and Goss, 1994). Grievance mediation, used either on its own or in conjunction with a system of expedited arbitration, can get around this difficulty by helping the parties to resolve their own differences. Instead of damaging the ongoing relationship, it can actually strengthen it by developing problem-solving skills that can later be applied to other areas of the relationship. In addition, its costs are quite low compared to those of arbitration.[19] Arbitration is still available should the parties fail to resolve their dispute on their own. The process is confidential in that, unless both parties consent, nothing said or done there can be used as evidence in subsequent legal proceedings (Thornicroft and Eden, 1995:273). Normally no formal record of the proceedings is kept, except to record any agreement reached (Elliott and Goss, 1994:32). As well, settlements are without prejudice to either party, which means that no precedent created by the settlement can be used in any future cases (Thornicroft and Eden, 1995:273).

Mediation focusses on effective communication and negotiation skills (Elliott and Goss, 1994:27). The mediator's role is not to "settle" the dispute, but to help the parties communicate and negotiate more effectively, thus increasing the likelihood they will reach agreement on their own (Elliott and Goss, 1994). A typical mediation session might consist of the following four stages (Elliott and Goss, 1994:27–29):

1) Introduction. Here, the mediator explains the process and his or her role and seeks to create an atmosphere in which the parties feel free to speak openly. It is at this time that the ground rules for mediation are laid out.

2) Creating an agenda. Where the parties have not agreed on an agenda beforehand, one is established, normally through brief presentations by the parties outlining the issues they would like to see resolved. After the presentations, which would normally be followed by clarifying questions from the other side and the mediator, key points are identified to form the agenda.

3) Discussing interests. Here, each party has the opportunity to present its side of the story. The mediator will seek clarification of anything that appears unclear and will also seek to ensure that each party hears and understand the other's perspective, whether or not they agree with it. At this stage, common ground and agreed-upon facts are identified, in addition to any facts that may be in dispute. It is at this stage that the mediator seeks to reduce the dispute to its basic elements and to focus on the parties' underlying needs and interests.

4) Problem solving. Here, the mediator takes the information obtained in the previous stages and uses it to help the parties find a mutually agreeable solution, initiating suggestions for a possible solution where appropriate (Thornicroft and Eden, 1995:273). This may be done on either an issue-by-issue or "total package" basis.

The decision as to the best time to use mediation is often a judgment call. Ideally, it should be used at the earliest possible point in the dispute; where a relationship is very poor, it may even be used before the usual Stage 1 grievance meeting (Elliott and Goss, 1994:29). Often, the best stage can be determined empirically, from an examination of settlement rates at different points of the agreement's internal grievance process. If there is any step where settlement rates are particularly low, that would be a good place to insert grievance mediation (see Elliott and Goss, 1994:29–30). The Brett-Goldberg study cited below suggests that this place may well be somewhere in the middle of the process, where currently few cases are being resolved.

Grievance mediation has been used in four provinces, most often as a first stage in an expedited arbitration process. In Ontario, Rose (1991) found that voluntary grievance mediation had saved some $6.4 million between 1980–1981 and 1985–1986. As of the early 1990s (Craig and Solomon, 1996:351), about

80 percent of all expedited arbitration cases were being resolved through mediation. Unfortunately, the Ontario government has since discontinued this most useful and innovative program. However, it remains in effect in Alberta, Manitoba, and B.C., where similar results have been obtained (Elliott and Goss, 1994:41–52), and in the private sector in the United States.[20] For example, in the American bituminous coal industry (Brett and Goldberg, 1983), an industry long notorious for its poor labour–management relations, 153 grievances were mediated between 1980 and 1982. Of these, 89 percent were resolved without arbitration. Likewise, of 2220 grievances mediated by the Chicago-based Mediation Research and Education Project between 1980 and 1982, about 85 percent were resolved without arbitration (Elliott and Goss, 1994:52).[21]

Preventive Mediation

While it is good to reduce the costs and time delays of arbitration through an expedited arbitration process, and better to use grievance mediation to prevent grievances from even being taken through to arbitration, it's best of all, where possible, to improve the labour–management relationship so that problems are handled proactively, as they arise, before they become formal grievances. This is where preventive mediation comes in. Designed to overcome the problems resulting from mutual mistrust and poor communications, preventive mediation programs in the federal jurisdiction and most provinces seek to help management and unions build and maintain constructive and cooperative working relationships (HRDC, 1994). To this end, a number of the programs, including those of Ontario (Bergman, 1988) and the federal jurisdiction (HRDC, 1994) use Relations by Objectives (RBO) workshops to help the parties hone their communications and joint problem-solving skills. A key principle of all preventive mediation programs is that they are purely voluntary (HRDC, 1994; Joyce, 1996).

The federal program includes six components: establishing a labour–management committee, negotiation skills training, committee effectiveness training, relationship by objectives, grievance mediation, and facilitation. The various provincial programs appear to have a fairly similar emphasis, although there are certain differences; for example, the Newfoundland program includes joint supervisor-steward training in collective agreement administration (Joyce, 1996).

Unfortunately, there has thus far been little in the way of evaluation of the various preventive mediation programs. However, some anecdotal evidence (i.e., Joyce, 1996) suggests that the programs have been effective and have found favour with both management and unions. On the RBO workshops that are an important component of many preventive mediation programs, a study by Bergman (1988) found that union–management relationships had improved after the workshops and that participants attributed at least some of the improvement to the RBO experience (Bergman, 1988; Downie, 1989:270).[22]

GRIEVANCES AND INDUSTRIAL CONFLICT: THE BIGGER PICTURE

The grievance procedure is a crucial element of the Canadian IR system since it provides workers with some measure of workplace voice and a certain degree of protection against arbitrary dismissal or disciplinary action. While the grievance system appears generally to have worked reasonably well during the early postwar period, since then it has often been criticized for its slowness, costliness, and growing legalism, which taken together have meant that only a very small proportion of all grievances are ever taken through to arbitration. In response to these serious criticisms of the conventional arbitration process, governments, unions, and management have developed a broad range of innovative new dispute settlement mechanisms, of which the most important are expedited arbitration, grievance mediation, and preventive mediation. The evidence suggests that grievance mediation has helped resolve a large proportion of grievances without the need for arbitration, and that expedited arbitration has helped to provide a speedier, less legalistic, and less expensive forum for the disposition of unavoidable grievances. While we lack hard evidence on the success of preventive mediation programs, anecdotal evidence to date indicates that these programs have generally had at least some success in improving union–management relations.

Though these and other innovative new dispute settlement mechanisms[23] have contributed significantly to reducing workplace conflict in Canada, major sources of conflict remain unaddressed. One important source of conflict is unions' "ownership" of the grievance process. As noted earlier, an individual cannot normally file a grievance independently; only a union can do so. Inevitably, unions' ownership of the process means that a certain number of grievances will be used for political purposes— perhaps to be traded off for other grievances or even for certain collective agreement provisions. Particularly where labour–management relations are already poor, it also means that large numbers of grievances may be filed not because people feel their collective agreement rights have been violated, but simply as a pressure tactic, perhaps to protest the slow pace of negotiations or an arbitrary management action on some other front.[24] For its part, management may respond by stonewalling, that is refusing to deal with outstanding grievances for a more or less indefinite period of time. While perfectly legal, this kind of use of the grievance process increases labour–management conflict in a number of different ways. First, it overloads the grievance process so that legitimate (perhaps even serious) problems may not be addressed for far too long. Second, particularly when management stonewalls, it becomes extremely difficult to distinguish individual problems from broader political issues. Third, to the extent that individuals' grievances are not addressed in timely fashion, it decreases individuals' satisfaction with both the employer and the union, leading both to increased worker-management conflict and increased intraorganizational conflict within the union.

One could also argue that in the Canadian IR system, the grievance process is simply asked to do far too much. Not only does it serve as a vehicle for individual workplace voice; it must also serve as a vehicle for group and in some cases collective voice. In addition, as we noted earlier, it often serves as a forum for informal union–management negotiations and as a mechanism for helping to resolve intra-organizational conflict within both unions and management groups. Perhaps all this is really more than should be asked of any single process.

One way to reduce some of the strain on the seriously overloaded grievance process might be to allow any worker to file a dismissal grievance independent of his or her union, on condition he or she was willing to bear half the costs. Beyond that, unions, management, and governments alike will need to continue to search for flexible, creative, and low-cost mechanisms for defusing workplace conflict.

*   *   *

Before we leave the subject of grievances, you are probably wondering what happened to our old friend, Mr. Grenier. Here is how the arbitrator ruled.

. . . .It is my view that this case reveals an entirely too mechanical application of the absenteeism policy. The fourth-stage procedure before me here has had its application approved by a number of arbitrators, including myself. We have agreed that suspensions need not be employed to bring home the importance of regular attendance and, on a case-by-case basis, we have acknowledged that four intentional violations may indicate little prospect for rehabilitation by an employee and sufficient tolerance by the company. However, in all of these cases, the arbitrator has had regard to the peculiar facts giving rise to the absence, the grievor's seniority, and his overall work record.

It has also been acknowledged by other arbitrators that employers are not benevolent societies who need to involve themselves endlessly in the personal problems of their employees. But this does not mean an employer has no responsibility in this area. The instant case is a classic example of the need and obligation for a more sensitive employer approach to the personal problems of its employees.

Elliot Lake is a small northern community centring on two large employers. Many employees have come to work in this community and therefore were not born and raised locally. The result is that a network of friends and family to help in a time of personal crisis is not always available. For the same reasons, domestic turmoil can also mean separations involving considerable distance as in this case. I cannot agree that an employer can limit its concern for the personal welfare of its employees to the more well-defined problems of drug and alcohol abuse. [Numerous resources]. . . are available in northern Ontario to deal with the emotional, legal and economic problems arising from marital difficulties. Large employers and their trade unions have an obligation to facilitate access to these resources where there is a reasonable prospect for meaningful assistance. Moreover, employers and trade unions must not be timid in making assessment about the relationship of workplace problems to personal difficulties. Mr. Kinder said he was hesitant to ask about the grievor's problems but the cause of certain workplace problems can only be ascertained by intelligent probing and encouragement. There is therefore a need for a blend of understanding and warning. Assistance and understanding need not be indefinite and need not involve an undue burden on the employer. Limits on the time for improvement or adjustment can also be . . . set out.

However, in the instant case the grievor's personal problems were all but ignored by the employer. No attempt was ever made to refer him to legal assistance or a social worker. And no serious effort was made to accommodate his difficulties with the interests of the company. Indeed, the company made no serious attempt to ascertain and consider the reasons for his absenteeism problem. In a real sense, the failure to grant him a one-day leave in October may have led to the difficulty in November. Given the grievor's crisis, I believe some accommodation could easily have been made and, based on Mr. Yeats' advice to the grievor, I suspect he thought so too.

I also point out that the grievor's absence on August 18, 1982 appears to be justifiable and his failure to grieve somewhat understandable. No evidence was called to rebut his contention that he told his supervisor about his court appearance a few days beforehand.

On the other hand, the grievor's conduct in November was not entirely blameless and no expert medical or other professional evidence was called to support his testimony or to interpret what the future holds. In the circumstances, I have decided to reinstate the grievor to his former position and direct that the company and the grievor share his economic losses equally. (Note: Since the arbitration ruling was issued about five months after Grenier's termination, this means he received an unpaid suspension of two and a half months.) I would also direct the company and the trade union to make the employee assistance program available to the grievor to whatever extent is reasonable in the circumstances.

QUESTIONS FOR DISCUSSION

1) If you are in a union, read your collective agreement's grievance procedure. How many steps does it contain? Can time limits be waived? If a grievance is sent to arbitration, will there be a single arbitrator or a three-person panel? If you aren't a union member, find and read a collective agreement and answer the same questions.

2) What are some benefits of the grievance process to workers, unions, and organizations? In your view, do the benefits outweigh the drawbacks?

3) Why has grievance arbitration become a lengthy, costly, and legalistic process?

4) List the steps in a "typical" grievance procedure.

5) Describe a typical arbitration hearing.

6) What seem to be the key factors in determining whether someone filing a dismissal grievance is reinstated or not?

7) Discuss some ways in which Canadian unions, management organizations, and governments have tried to speed up the arbitration process and reduce the number of grievances being sent to arbitration.

8) The arbitrator in the Denison Mine case criticized the employer for a 'mechanical' application of its absenteeism policy. How might it more appropriately have applied that policy?

9) Would you be more or less likely to reinstate Jean Grenier than you would have been after you first read the Denison Mine case? If your position has changed, explain why.

10) What lessons does the Denison Mine case have to teach about the relationship between grievances and organizations' overall management practice?

SUGGESTIONS
FOR FURTHER READING

Barnacle, Peter. (1991). *Arbitration of discharge grievances in Ontario: Outcomes and reinstatement experiences*. Kingston: Queen's IRC Research and Current Issues Series No. 62. Not hammock reading by any means, but an astoundingly thorough and systematic analysis of discharge outcomes and reinstatement experiences in more than 800 Ontario discharge cases. Similar studies are badly needed for other jurisdictions.

Brett, Jeanne, and Stephen Goldberg. (1983). "Grievance mediation in the coal industry: A field experiment." *Industrial and Labor Relations Review*, 37. A groundbreaking early study of grievance mediation in one of the United States's most conflict-ridden industries.

Elliott, David, and Joanne Goss. (1994). *Grievance mediation: How and why it works*. Aurora, ON: Canada Law Book Co. A bit evangelical at times, but contains a wealth of information about how to conduct grievance mediation and the results of grievance mediation in both Canada and the United States.

Rose, Joseph. (1986b). "Statutory expedited grievance arbitration: The case of Ontario." *Arbitration Journal*, 41:4. Important early study of the results of Ontario's expedited arbitration system.

Weiler, Joseph. (1984). "Grievance arbitration: The new wave." In J. Weiler and P. Gall (Eds.), *The labour code of British Columbia in the 1980s*. Calgary and Vancouver: Carswell. Interesting and well-written discussion of a number of alternatives to conventional arbitration, including the Port of Vancouver's "dockside arbitration" system, by a man who served for many years as the port's arbitrator.

CHAPTER 13

INDUSTRIAL RELATIONS
AROUND THE WORLD

This Brazilian street vendor is one of many Third World people forced to earn a living outside the formal labour force. Throughout much of the Third World, the number of people forced to earn their living in this way has risen sharply in recent years.

In today's increasingly globalized economy, it is impossible to obtain a full understanding of the Canadian IR system without understanding developments in other countries. Over the past three decades, the changes on the international IR scene have been profound, especially in the developing world. The chapter begins by examining some traditional IR models. It then considers the special situation of the developing world, where in many cases large segments of the population do not even participate in the formal labour force as such. Special emphasis is placed on the growth of informal workers' associations and informal associations of micro-entrepreneurs, and on the relationships some of these associations have formed with more formal bodies in their own countries, and

with unions and other organizations in developed countries. The chapter concludes with a brief examination of the question of whether traditional IR terminology and methodology can usefully be applied in the developing world.

INTRODUCTION: A NEW WAY OF LOOKING AT IR

Previous chapters have illustrated some of the ways in which the Canadian IR system has been changing over the past two decades. For example, we have pointed out, in the management chapter, how the balance of workplace power has shifted from workers and unions toward employers and managers. We've also noted (see Chapter 2) that significantly fewer Canadians than in the past hold secure, full-time jobs, and have pointed out the increasing difficulties public sector unions are having representing their members in today's hostile economic and political environment.

Canada has by no means been alone in experiencing these kinds of changes. Most of them have been occurring around the world, in both developed and developing countries. In some cases, the changes have been significantly more severe and more abrupt elsewhere than they have here. In others, the impacts have been aggravated by extreme poverty, crushing debt loads, disease, or political instability (see Loxley, 1998).

Such developments pose serious questions as to the adequacy of our traditional industrial relations tools, particularly in the world's poorer countries. Up until now, few would have disagreed with Keller's (1991) characterization of workers and trade unions; managers, employers and their associations; and the state as the three key actors in virtually all IR systems. But such a characterization assumes, almost by definition, a society in which a fair amount of industrialization and economic development has taken place, in which a sizable share of the population work in more or less traditional employer-employee relationships, and in which the state has built up regulatory capacity sufficient to allow it to ensure that unions are able to function as workers' official representatives, as well as to administer employment-related legislation. In much of the developing world, none of these would necessarily be safe assumptions. In some countries, less than one-third of the population may even be in the formal employment sector, let alone officially employed (ILO, 1997:Table 7).[1] In others, a large number of self-employed workers or micro-entrepreneurs operate more or less illegally, without registering or paying taxes, either because they are ignorant of the regulations or because they simply can't afford the costs of complying with them (ILO, 1997:184–5). In still other cases, a large proportion of the population may be working without pay in family-run businesses, in which the distinction between 'employer' and 'employee' is virtually meaningless.

Such situations impose very real constraints on the ability of the traditional industrial relations actors to function as they would in a developed country. How, for example, can 'official' unions effectively represent workers, such as rickshaw drivers or street vendors, who have neither an employer nor a regular workplace, and who may in some cases be operating illegally or even in such a way as to undercut the union's 'regular' members (see ILO, 1997:203)? Even leaving aside the very real issue of resource constraints, how can governments regulate the wages, hours, or working conditions of such workers through employment legislation or health and safety laws? With respect to child labour, where do unions and other workers' organizations draw the line between work necessary to support the family and outright exploitation—and are they prepared to allow different standards in family-run businesses than in other types? And how can governments regulate family-run businesses employing unpaid workers in such a way as to prevent the abuse and exploitation of these workers, while at the same time respecting local or national traditions regarding the role of the family and not imposing such high regulatory costs that the businesses go under?

At a minimum, understanding these situations will require a new and broader conception of what industrial relations is. It also requires an appreciation of the role played by a broader range of actors than we are used to studying within the field of IR, including informal workers' associations, sector cooperatives, and associations of micro-entrepreneurs. As we'll see later in the chapter, while in many cases such organizations operate independently of the 'official' IR institutions, such as trade unions or employers' associations, in others they have been incorporated into the larger, more formal organizations.

A key objective of this chapter, then, will be to describe in some detail the new, more complex model for international IR, whose outlines we have briefly sketched in the preceding paragraphs. Another will be to show how and to what extent the various IR actors—formal and informal alike—have succeeded in adapting to today's harsher global environment, and what problems and challenges remain, in both developed and developing countries. But before we do either of those things, it will be necessary to consider a more traditional model of international IR, as well as to indicate some of the major forces that have served to undermine that model over the past two decades or so. Without an understanding of that model, we will find it difficult to appreciate the full significance of all the recent changes.

A TRADITIONAL IR MODEL

Unfree Systems

Traditionally, IR systems were divided into three groups: unfree, partially free, and free. Unfree systems were those in which unions had no effective role to play. In some cases, such as that of the Axis powers before and during the Second World War, this was the result of the outright dissolution of unions or a ban on their activities (see Kuwahara, 1993:223; Pellegrini, 1993:131; Fuerstenberg, 1993:178). Communist countries such as the former Soviet Union could hardly ban unions, since in theory these countries operated on the basis of control by the working class. At the same time, they were in no way prepared to accept a challenge to central state authority. In these countries, therefore, unions were not at all the independent workers' advocates we are used to. Rather, they generally served as a kind of "transmission belt," communicating official government policy to workers (Héthy, 1991:125–7) or at best carrying out modest social welfare functions.

With the gradual political liberalization that took place in Eastern Europe during the 1970s and '80s, the traditional Communist model loosened up somewhat. In countries like Hungary, public enterprises acquired a degree of autonomy from the government, and there began to be an appreciation of the need for separate roles for employers and trade unions (Héthy, 1991:130). Elsewhere, in countries like Bulgaria and Poland, worker participation through self-management became more common (ibid., 129). Nonetheless, there was little real collective bargaining until after the collapse of the Soviet Union. Despite a general trend toward economic and political liberalization, governments remained reluctant to loosen their grip on wage determination, particularly in times of economic crisis, and there were few mechanisms available for solving labour disputes (ibid., 137).

Partially Free Systems

In general, partially free systems were found in the developing countries of Africa and Asia, particularly those that had only recently obtained their independence from a colonial power. They were also (and to a degree still are) found in a number of Latin American countries. In general, such systems allowed unions and labour centrals some freedom of maneuver, but would often limit that freedom, whether through legislation or through some form of outright repression (Fashoyin, 1991:118).

Often the leaders of newly-independent countries found themselves in a delicate position vis-à-vis their countries' unions. On the one hand, the unions had in many cases played a key role in the independence movement. On the other hand, unions and their leaders were sometimes perceived as a political threat to ruling elites. Moreover, once unions began operating more freely, engaging in collective bargaining and going on strike to support their demands, they were seen as interfering with national economic policies designed to attract outside investment and featuring wage moderation and an absence of labour conflict (Fashoyin, 1991:117–8; Gladstone, 1980). Whether rightly or wrongly, free collective bargaining and strikes were often seen as luxuries that developing countries could not afford (see Peirce, 1996).

As a result, the governments of developing countries have at various times adopted strategies ranging from the substitution of compulsory arbitration and government wage-price controls for the right to strike to the co-optation of key unions and central labour bodies, even to the extent of giving union leaders important positions in the government (see Kassalow, 1963; Peirce, 1996; Park and Lee, 1995:31; Beng and Chew, 1994:64–5). Other countries have weakened their labour movements through fragmentation (as by refusing to allow a single major labour federation) or by failing to pass legislation protecting union organizers against arbitrary dismissal (see Kuruvilla and Arudsothy, 1995:172–3; Manusphaibool, 1993; Brown and Frenkel, 1993:90). Still others, such as Greece, have banned all political strikes (Fashoyin, 1991:119).

While not all developing countries have resorted to such drastic measures as the arrest and detention of union leaders and activists or the de-registration of unions found to be behaving in ways not to the government's liking, many have done so at least on occasion. For example, military governments in Brazil and Argentina have routinely trampled on workers' and unions' rights (Fashoyin, 1991:111). In Singapore (Leggett, 1993:131), 1963 saw over 100 left-wing labour opponents of the government detained without trial and several unions deregistered.[2] In the Philippines (Jimenez, 1993:233), after President Marcos declared martial law in 1972, strikes and picketing in most key industries were banned. Violators were arrested and detained for the duration of the national emergency.

Free Systems

Free IR systems have, with some limitations, allowed unions to function as independent advocates for workers. The most important mechanism used by unions has been collective bargaining, whether at the national, industry, or enterprise level. But the unions of North America and Western Europe, where the lion's share of free systems are located,[3] have by no means confined themselves to collective bargaining. As we noted in the union actions chapter (Chapter 6), political action through both formal and informal channels has been an important part of most Canadian unions' agendas. Political action has played an even more prominent role in many European countries (i.e., Sweden, Austria, and on occasion Germany) where the labour movement has been instrumental in helping to elect a sympathetic government and, once that government has been installed, in providing it with advice on appropriate social and economic policies.

It should be noted that many countries, particularly European ones, provide for workplace representation through some mechanism other than unions. In Europe, these mechanisms are generally known as works councils. In Canada, they are known as joint committees. (As we noted in Chapter 7, these are normally mandatory in the case of health and safety.) It would be inaccurate to suggest that these mechanisms have no connection with unions. In Germany, for example, though works councillors are elected from the ranks of all employees, in practice most have been active trade unionists (Adams, 1995:503). In Canada, workers' representatives on joint committees are drawn from the union in all unionized establishments; indeed, such committees are generally referred to as joint union–management committees. What can be said is that works councils and joint committees normally operate in a different way than unions do. For the most part, the aim is to work out problems through consensus. The strike is virtually never used as a means of resolving disputes within the workplace-level body. Instead, disputes are normally resolved through arbitration, or, in the case of Canadian health and safety committees, through referral of the matter in dispute to a government safety officer, normally from the labour ministry.

Types of Free Systems

Over the years, several different types of free IR system have evolved. In decentralized systems, government normally plays quite a limited role, and unions' major activity is collective bargaining, most often at the enterprise level. In centralized systems, government's role is much more extensive. In addition to collective bargaining, most often at the national or industry level, unions are extensively involved in political action. Where the major thrust of bargaining is at the nation-wide or industry level, it is often supplemented with a second tier of bargaining over local-level issues. As noted above, a prominent feature of most (though not all) such systems is a more or less consensual workplace-level mechanism such as a works council. Hybrid systems contain some features of each of the two preceding types. In the following paragraphs, we describe each of these three types in turn.

DECENTRALIZED SYSTEMS Countries with decentralized IR systems include the U.S., Canada, and, to a lesser extent, the U.K. Economic activity is determined largely by market forces, and collective bargaining is normally conducted at individual workplaces (Lipsig-Mumme, 2001). In the U.S. and Canada, the collective agreements that result from this bargaining are generally extremely detailed and impose significant restrictions on employers' ability to manage. For this reason (although there are others as well), employers in these countries, the U.S. in particular, tend to be more anti-union than their counterparts from European countries, where bargaining is more apt to be at national and industry level and collective agreements are less detailed (see Adams, 1995).

While unions certainly go in for political activity in decentralized systems, their involvement is often of a more sporadic and ad hoc nature than in centralized systems; this is particularly true in the U.S. In Canada, much of the English Canadian labour movement is formally affiliated with the social democratic New Democratic Party. However, the NDP has never possessed anything like the power of Labour and social democratic parties in Britain and on the Continent, and in practice the labour movement's ties to it don't mean a great deal; on election day many rank-and-file members wind up voting for other parties, particularly the Liberals. Formal consultation is sporadic and carried out at the will of particular governments (Lipsig-Mumme, 2001:525).

In decentralized systems, union membership rates range from low (the U.S.) to moderate (Canada and the U.K.). There is also a significant amount of exclusion with respect to the lack of protection of certain groups under labour relations and employment standards legislation. For example, farmworkers are excluded from unionization rights in the U.S. and several Canadian provinces (see Chapter 8, and also Peirce, 1989). Professionals are also barred from joining unions in several Canadian provinces, including Ontario. In the U.S., the *Taft-Hartley Act*, passed in 1947, effectively removed union security from many Southern and Midwestern states. It is thus extremely difficult for workers in these states to be able to join unions.

Table 13 .1

Year	Country	Union Density Rate (%)*
1995	Argentina	25.4
1995	Australia	28.6
1995	Austria	36.6
1995	Belgium	38.1
1991	Brazil	32.1
1993	Canada	31.0
1993	Chile	15.9
1995	China	54.7
1995	Egypt	29.6
1995	Finland	59.7
1995	France	6.1
1995	Germany	29.6**
1995	Greece	15.4
1991	India	5.4
1993	Ireland	36.0
1995	Japan	18.6
1995	Korea (South)	9.0
1991	Mexico	42.8
1995	Netherlands	21.8
1995	New Zealand	23.2
1995	Norway	51.7
1994	Pakistan	5.5
1996	Russia	74.8***
1995	South Africa	21.8
1994	Spain	11.4
1994	Sweden	77.8
1995	Thailand	3.1
1995	U.K.	26.2
1995	U.S.A.	12.7

Source: ILO, (1997), Table 1.2.

* Union density refers to the percentage of the non-agricultural labour force belonging to unions. This figure is generally lower, often significantly so, than the percentage of wage and salary-earners belonging to unions.

Please note that the data for Canada are not the most recent available and do not necessarily correspond to those used in earlier chapters, because the aim here was to make data as comparable as possible between countries.

** 'Germany' includes both the former West Germany and East Germany.

*** Data for Russia are for the Russian Federation.

Within the group of countries with decentralized IR systems, the U.S. stands out for a number of reasons. Its union membership rates, particularly in the private sector, are extremely low. The opposition of its employers to unions is particularly fierce, and the enforcement of labour legislation generally quite lax—so much so that many employers appear to be willing to commit unfair labour practices confident in the knowledge they probably won't be caught, or that even if they do get caught it probably won't matter since the damage to the union will already have been done and the union left without any meaningful remedy (Bruce, 1990). Some, notably Selig Perlman (1966), have attempted to explain the extraordinarily individualistic character of American labour relations as a result of the U.S.' 'exceptional' nature. Unlike most European countries, Perlman says, the U.S. was never faced with the problem of winning the suffrage or the rights to a basic education for workers, and therefore the American labour movement never had to develop any sort of class-consciousness and tended to avoid politics, instead focussing itself more narrowly on bread-and-butter issues at the workplace. While there is undoubtedly some truth to Perlman's theory, there is a great deal that it does not explain, including most notably the fact that Canadian unions, facing roughly the same general conditions as their American counterparts, have often displayed quite considerable class-consciousness and have generally been more heavily involved in political activity (see Peirce, 1993).

CENTRALIZED SYSTEMS Centralized systems feature significant government involvement in the economy and IR system. In such systems, bargaining is normally conducted at the national level, as was traditionally the case in Sweden, or at the industry level, as in the case of Germany. The fact that collective bargaining isn't conducted at the workplace level and that in most cases supplementary mechanisms (works councils or multi-tier bargaining) are available to deal with workplace problems has had the effect of reducing industrial conflict in centralized systems well below its customary level in decentralized ones (see Adams, 1989). In effect, much conflict that would occur at the workplace in North America is moved into the political arena under centralized systems, thus accounting, in part, for these systems' lower level of conflict. Another reason for their lower level of industrial conflict is that because so much more typically rides on them than is the case with enterprise-level negotiations, negotiators are more expert, and generally senior management with real power will be at the table. Given how much is at stake in such negotiations, there is also an increased likelihood of government intervention if negotiations break down.

Unions in centralized systems normally devote much of their effort to electing a favourable (labour or social democratic) government. Once such a government is elected, it will often establish tripartite (union-employer-government) consultation mechanisms that allow unions a significant voice in the formation of national social and economic policies. Often the unions will be induced to accept lower wage settlements and refrain from striking in return for pension and tax reform, a full employment guarantee, price controls, or other government policies favouring workers and unions (Adams, 1989). Such accords may be one reason for the generally superior economic performance found in centralized systems through the 1980s.

Economically, countries with centralized IR systems tend to be more egalitarian and have a good deal less wage dispersion than countries with decentralized ones—in part because of the practice, in many European countries, of extending the wages negotiated in formal collective agreements to non-unionized firms, as a way of taking wages out of competition. For this reason, many European countries have a far higher rate of collective agreement coverage than union membership. In connection with the issue of wage dispersion, it's interesting to note that when Sweden, during the late 1980s and early '90s, moved away from its traditional national-level bargaining to bargaining at the industry level, wage dispersion in that country increased significantly (Kjellberg, 1992).

A number of researchers (see among others Tarantelli, 1986) have found that centralized systems generally perform better than decentralized ones with respect to unemployment and inflation, as well as industrial conflict. Nonetheless, such systems have been falling into disfavour in recent years, largely because of the opposition of employers, who prefer the greater flexibility offered them under decentralized systems. As we will see later in the chapter, even in Northern Europe, much bargaining has been devolved to lower levels, while in North America, many earlier centralized arrangements, such as pattern bargaining in the meatpacking and rubber industries (discussed in Chapter 10), have broken down due to employer opposition.

HYBRID SYSTEMS Several IR systems do not fit neatly into either the centralized or decentralized category. These systems, including those of Japan, Australia, and Quebec, are perhaps best described as hybrid systems.

The most distinctive features of the Japanese system are its system of enterprise unions, whose membership is limited to employees of the individual firm or plant (Matsuda, 1993), and the "lifetime employment guarantee" provided to key employees of large, core firms—a group that never made up more than one-third of the Japanese work force (Matsuda, 1993:192 and 201).[4] Under this system, in return for loyalty to the firm and a willingness to work very long hours by Canadian standards, employees are effectively guaranteed a job until mandatory retirement at age 60 (Matsuda, 1993; Adams, 1995). While the government is heavily involved in economic planning, it plays little role in the IR system as such, and unions are not normally involved in the planning of social or economic policy.[5] Rather than serving as workers' advocates either in the political arena (as in centralized systems) or in the workplace (as in decentralized ones), Japan's enterprise unions play primarily an integrative role (see Tannenbaum, 1921 and 1950),[6] helping to link employees to the corporate culture (Lipsig-Mumme, 2001) and generally concerning themselves more with the company's productivity and profitability than with the problems of individual employees.[7]

Over the years, the Japanese IR system has been much studied and widely admired by western observers. However, it must be said that the favourable conditions of employment it has provided for the few have been achieved only at the cost of harsh and insecure working conditions for the many, including most of society's more vulnerable members. It should also be noted that over the past few years, Japan's lingering recession and the Asian economic crisis have led to massive layoffs (Lipsig-Mumme, 2001:526).

Australia's is another system that is difficult to classify. While its economy has remained market-oriented, labour market shortages in the early twentieth century led the government to establish quite a centralized IR system as a means of ensuring labour peace. A cornerstone of that system was the establishment of an arbitration court to set wages and resolve disputes. In an attempt to block low-cost foreign competition, the government also imposed severe immigration restrictions and provided tariff protection for manufacturers who could show they were paying "fair and reasonable" wages (Frenkel, 1993(a):251). Unions thus had a strong incentive to register and seek members, so they could avail themselves of the arbitration tribunals. The tribunals encouraged unions to centralize their power at federal and state levels and facilitated generally high union membership rates (sometimes over 50 percent of the work force). By world standards, Australian workers enjoyed very good working conditions, being among the first to achieve the 40-hour workweek (Frenkel, 1993(a):252). The system held up remarkably well until the late 1980s, when continuing economic deterioration led to the dismantling of tariff barriers, a weakening of the arbitration tribunals, and devolution of bargaining to industry and workplace levels (Frenkel, 1993(a); Lipsig-Mumme, 2001).

Yet another hybrid system is that of Quebec. Like the rest of Canada, Quebec operates within a primarily market-oriented economy, and has a system of labour legislation derived from the American *Wagner Act*. But there are important differences between IR in Quebec and in the rest of Canada. For one thing, Quebec governments have historically been far more prone than other Canadian governments to intervene actively in the economy (Déom and Boivin, 2001:487). For another, the Quebec labour movement plays a major role in social and economic planning in the province (ibid., 488), unlike other provinces' labour movements, which have generally been marginalized except under NDP provincial governments.

Perhaps most important for our purposes, Quebec's IR system contains a number of features normally characteristic of European rather than North American systems. The most prominent and longstanding of these is the decree system, in effect since 1934, whereby the labour minister has the power to extend parts (especially monetary clauses) of collective agreements to non-unionized firms in the same sector. While the extension of collective agreements is not as common in Quebec as in many European countries (see Table 13.2), over 11 000 employers and 110 000 employees were covered by decrees at the end of 1998 (ibid.), the latter representing just under 5 percent of the province's labour force. Other distinctive features of Quebec's IR system include its multiple labour federations, a direct legacy of the confessional unions set up by the Catholic Church early in the twentieth century to keep Quebec workers under the

Table 13.2

COLLECTIVE AGREEMENT COVERAGE VS. UNION DENSITY RATES, SELECTED COUNTRIES

Country	Year	Collective Agreement Coverage (%)*	Union Density (%)**
Australia	1995	65	29
Canada	1996	37	31
France	1995	90	6
Germany	1996	90	30
Greece	1994	90	15
Ireland	1994	90	36
Japan	1994	25	19
Netherlands	1996	80	22
New Zealand	1995	23	23
Spain	1996	82	11
Sweden	1995	85	77
U.K.	1994	26	26
U.S.A.	1995	11	13

Sources: ILO (1997), Tables 3.1 and 1.2.
* Collective agreement coverage refers to the percentage of employees covered by collective agreements.
** Union density figures are defined as in Table 13.1, and the figures and years on which they are based are the same as in that table. Please note that there may be minor differences in the labour forces used for the calculation of union density and collective agreement coverage, as well as in the years from which data are drawn. However, these differences should not affect the main thrust of the table.

Church's sway, and the organization of large numbers of employers into formal employers' associations.[8] It should also be noted that Quebec has made more use than other provinces of European-style tripartite social accords (normally called social contracts) as a means of dealing with economic crises in particular industries. Under the typical Quebec social contract, in return for a long-term pledge of labour peace, unions are provided with a guarantee of employment security and joint administration of the agreement, and employees are provided with full information about the firm's financial situation (Boivin and Déom, 1995; Verma and Warrian, 1992).

In recent years, there have been threats to certain aspects of the Quebec system. Most seriously, pressure from employers' associations has led the government to abolish decrees in two sectors and to consider abolishing them in others (Déom and Boivin, 2001:489–490). Nonetheless, despite severe economic pressures over the past decade, in particular, most of the Quebec system's distinctive features have remained largely intact.

FORCES FOR CHANGE

Few if any of the 'traditional' IR systems we have just been describing have remained entirely intact; some have changed beyond recognition. In certain cases, most notably that of the former Soviet bloc countries, change has resulted from major political upheaval (in this case the breakup of the former Soviet Union). More often, though, the change has been driven by a combination of macroeconomic and local political forces, with the former coming to assume an increasingly prominent role.

Arguably the single greatest force driving change in national IR systems has been the globalization of the world's economy. As we'll see in the following sections, globalization is a far-reaching phenomenon, which includes increasing trade, capital mobility, and the internationalization of product and labour markets. In its wake, globalization has left a world characterized by fewer steady, full-time jobs, more precarious employment, weaker national governments with reduced ability to regulate their domestic economies and IR systems, and reduced union membership rates. Firms, on the other hand, have significantly increased their autonomy in recent years. Globalization has also led to smaller public sectors and the widespread devolution of bargaining from the national or industry to the enterprise level.

In the next sections of this chapter, after taking a close look at globalization itself, we will examine the other developments described in the preceding paragraph. Special emphasis will be placed on seeing how different types of 'traditional' IR system have managed to adjust to today's harsher global economic and political environment.

Globalization

Though the global economy has been interdependent for many centuries, the extent of this interdependence has increased sharply since the end of the Second World War. To take one of the more obvious measures, global trade increased 60-fold in current dollar terms, or at least sixfold in real terms, between 1950 and 1992. Spurred by financial liberalization resulting largely from the abolition of exchange controls in the U.S. and Britain, global capital flows have increased no less sharply. By 1992, these flows were amounting to some $250 billion (or roughly $1 billion per business day)—a four-fold increase over their levels just six years previously (Loxley, 1998:8). This rapid expansion of world trade is closely linked to the development of multinational enterprises (ILO, 1997:89). By the mid 1990s, it was estimated that these enterprises were accounting for about one-quarter of total world production, even though they employed just 3 percent of the world's labour force (Giles, 1996:6). The ILO (1997:89) has estimated that about one-third of trade occurs within multinational enterprises and another third among them, meaning that at most one-third of international trade is conducted "in conditions of true independence."

As we noted earlier in the book (see Chapter 2), globalization has also affected the way in which goods are produced. 'Modular' production processes in which goods are assembled at one location from components produced at several other locations have now become commonplace (see Giles, 1996).

Globalization has had a profound effect on labour markets. Liberalized trade, largely the result of the dismantling of tariff barriers, has meant that employers have been forced to place far greater emphasis on controlling labour costs, since they are no longer able to rely on protective tariffs to shield them from low-cost foreign competition (Gunderson and Riddell, 1993). With 'modular' production processes of the sort just described in place, it has become much easier for firms, particularly multinational ones, to shift all or part of their production to countries whose labour costs are lower (Giles, 1996). For example, a recent *Toronto Star* article by Linda Diebel (2001) focussed on the plight of Third World garment workers, mostly young women. In the late '80s, major structural changes in the garment industry cost the Canadian garment manufacturing industry over 30 000 jobs, which were relocated to countries like Mexico where labour was cheaper. Now, a further transformation has resulted in "the constant shuffle of large orders from country to country or state to state, turning the ensuing jobs into checkers on a global board." The women working in the Mexican garment plants can't afford to buy the bras they make.

Nor need a firm actually shift production to a lower-cost country to achieve substantial labour cost savings. In many cases, the mere *threat* of relocating or contracting out production is enough to dampen unions' wage demands at the bargaining table, or even to rid the firm of the union altogether (ILO, 1997:76).[9] And firms can have the same effect on national governments seeking to raise corporate taxes or increase social welfare spending. In Germany, for example, where corporate taxes have fallen by 50 percent over the past two decades despite a 90 percent rise in corporate profits, a group of corporations including Daimler-Benz and Deutsche Bank thwarted the Finance Minister's bid to raise corporate taxes by threatening to move investment or production to other countries if the government's policy didn't suit them. Instead of a tax increase, the result was a further cut in the corporate tax rate (Hertz, 2001).

Regrettably, globalization has been linked to actual slavery in West Africa and other extremely poor regions (Bales, 2001). International attention was focussed on the issue in April 2001 when a ship was found transporting children who had been trafficked to work in the West African country of Gabon. The United Nations' children's agency, UNICEF, has estimated that more than 200 000 children are trafficked in West and Central Africa each year (Bales, 2001). Elsewhere, as in Thailand, young girls are often sold into forced prostitution (ibid.). As globalization has driven rural people in poor countries into debt and into cities, they have become unable to support their children. In such circumstances, they are easy prey for slave-traders, who offer them a small amount of money and say their children will work on plantations and send the money home. Then the children disappear, never to be seen again (Bales, 2001).

Stung by the criticisms of globalization, First World leaders have recently been attempting to put a human face on it. In a keynote address to world leaders at the recent "G-20" world trade summit in Ottawa, Canadian finance minister Paul Martin insisted that globalization can and will be made to help the world's poorest people and countries. Thus far, however, the record does not seem to have borne him out. Between 1950 and 1992, developing countries' share of world trade declined from 32 percent to just over 25 percent (see Table 13.3). There were even greater declines in the shares of trade carried out by the world's most heavily indebted and least developed countries. Between 1980 and 1992, the rate of growth of export earnings in developing countries was less than half the rate for industrialized countries (Loxley, 1998:Table 2.4). In heavily indebted countries, the growth rate over the 12-year period was 41 percent, or just over one-third the rate for industrialized countries. In the least developed countries, the growth rate was a minuscule 6 percent (or half a percent per year). More recently, another study, by Center for Economic and Policy Research (CEPR) economists Mark Weisbrot and Dean Baker (*CCPA Monitor*, 2001), has found that the era of globalization has brought less economic progress than was achieved in the preceding 20 years.[10] The CEPR study finds no evidence that globalization improved economic outcomes for developing countries, and suggests that, in fact, recent structural and policy changes arising from globalization may be at least partly responsible for social and economic deterioration in these countries.

Regional Economic Integration

Closely related to globalization is the trend toward economic integration within specified geographic regions of the world. Over the years, a number of different patterns of regional economic integration have emerged, the aim being to promote liberalized trade within those regions. The two most important of these patterns, for our purposes, are the North American Free Trade Zone and the European Union (EU).

Table 13.3

TRENDS IN GLOBAL TRADE, 1950–1992

	1950	1960	1970	1980	1990	1992
World Exports, Current $b	61	129	315	1998	3447	3662
Share of Exports (%)						
Industrial Capitalist Countries	66.1	72.5	75.7	69.1	65.5	69.9
E.Europe/USSR	6.8	10.1	9.8	7.7	5.0	2.5
Developing Countries, *of which:*	32.4	24.0	19.3	29.7	23.5	25.1
Oil Exporters	6.3	6.8	6.3	16.4	6.1	5.4
Exporters of Manufactures	8.8	5.1	4.8	7.3	11.7	13.6
Heavily Indebted	10.9	7.4	5.8	6.5	4.6	4.2
Least Developed	2.8	2.3	1.6	0.6	0.4	0.4

Source: Loxley (1998), Table 2.2

In 1994, the trilateral North American Free Trade Agreement (NAFTA) between Canada, the U.S., and Mexico took effect, following on the heels of an earlier (1989) bilateral agreement between Canada and the U.S. (Reid and Meltz, 2001). Since then, several other Latin American countries have been invited to join the agreement, and the intention is to extend the agreement throughout the Americas within the next few years.

It's difficult to measure the precise effects of the NAFTA agreement on the Canadian economy, because it has taken effect at the same time as other major macroeconomic developments, including the economic recession of the 1990s, the implementation of the GST, and exchange-rate fluctuations (Reid and Meltz, 2001:170). Moreover, one must also consider what might have happened had the agreement not been implemented. It is entirely possible that in the absence of something like a NAFTA agreement, the U.S. would have put up additional trade barriers that would have made it more difficult for Canadian firms to sell their goods in that country's markets.

Still, there is at best little evidence that either agreement has benefitted the Canadian economy. Through the 1990s, unemployment was generally higher than it had been during the '80s. During that decade, hundreds of thousands of well-paid manufacturing jobs were lost. Nor is it clear that export growth has made up for the loss of those jobs. A recent Industry Canada study (see CCPA *Monitor*, 11/01) found that between them, the earlier Canada-U.S. FTA and NAFTA have accounted for only 9 percent of the growth of Canada's exports to the U.S. Most of that growth, the study says, was due to the country's weak dollar, and would thus have occurred in any event. In addition, the country's social safety net is significantly weaker than it was ten or fifteen years ago. EI benefits are provided to fewer people, replace a smaller share of regular earnings, and run for a shorter period of time, and there have also been major cuts to health care, social assistance, and other social programs.

The EU, which began in 1950, is the world's oldest system of regional integration. While it has traditionally favoured economic integration (including, now, a common currency) over the harmonization of social issues (Lipsig-Mumme, 2001:531), it has nonetheless achieved some success in the latter area. Adjustment processes resulting from integration have generally been less painful in the EU than under NAFTA because the disparities between member countries are less extreme in the EU.

Increasingly it is being recognized (see Lipsig-Mumme, 1995:218) that the union movement must start to form transnational alliances if it is to have any hope of countering the massive power of multinational corporations. It is within the EU that unions have gone furthest in this direction, working through organizations like the European Trades Union Congress, which has become a respected player in social and economic policy formation in the region (Lipsig-Mumme, 2001:531). As well, the Maastricht Agreement makes possible Europe-wide collective bargaining and includes protection for the region's most vulnerable workers (ibid.). Other hopeful developments include a 1994 EU Directive providing for European works councils in multinational enterprises with at least 1000 employees, including at least 150 in each of two member states (ILO, 1997:139). It was expected that by the year 2000, the directives would apply to some 20 million workers, or nearly 15 percent of the EU's working population. Such developments offer the hope that at least some measure of social protection will accompany economic integration within EU countries.

Growing Importance of Management and Employers

Few would dispute the ILO's contention that managers have effectively taken the initiative in reshaping industrial relations in the workplace, and that individual firms are tending to exert greater influence in the conduct of industrial relations and in personnel management decisions. An example of management's more prominent role is the growing use of progressive human resource management policies (discussed in Chapter 3) such as profit-sharing pay schemes, merit-based pay, direct communication with workers, and total quality management (ILO, 1997:97-8). In such varied settings as India, Korea, Japan, Latin America, the U.S., and Britain, these progressive HRM policies have been found to increase workers' identification with management and reduce their desire to join or remain in unions (ibid., 96–99). While progressive HRM policies haven't always been found to weaken unions (in Europe, they generally do not), they are nonetheless often a threat to traditional job-control unionism (ibid., 97). At a minimum, they have forced unions to redefine their roles quite substantially.

The growing importance of individual firms has had a number of significant effects on IR systems. Particularly given the trend toward an increase in the number of small and medium-sized enterprises (SMEs), one impact has been a generally reduced role for formal employers' associations, which have tended to enjoy relatively good relations with unions in most countries.[11] Many small firms don't join the associations because they don't think the associations will be able to address their particular needs (ILO, 1997:61). The SMEs' relative growth in importance has been related to the decline in union density rates in some countries, given that these firms are significantly less likely to be unionized than larger firms. At the other end of the spectrum, a growing number of large, highly diversified firms that work in networks have also been breaking away from employers' associations. The major reason here appears to be that firms that work in networks find it difficult to take part in sectoral negotiations, a primary concern of most employers' associations (ibid., 62). Overall, the main reason for the apparent decline in employers' associations is that in the current environment of heightened competition, most employers prefer to act autonomously, particularly in the export business (ibid.). The same desire has prompted many firms to move toward decentralized bargaining structures (discussed below).

At the macro level, a major consequence of firms' growing importance is the weakening of national governments' ability to regulate their domestic economies and IR systems as they otherwise might. This has been a particularly important phenomenon in Western Europe, where pressure from firms has by and large prevented a return to the Keynesian macroeconomic policies used to stabilize economies and keep unemployment down from the end of World War II through the early 1970s (ILO, 1997:11). Increasingly, the fear is that such expansionist macroeconomic policies, which generally depended on high levels of taxation, could trigger a "capital strike" that saw firms moving to countries where taxes and labour costs were lower, or at least outsourcing a sizable share of their production. Fearing such a "capital strike," governments of all political stripes have made price stability their major economic objective, leading many to adopt austerity policies that work real hardship on workers and their families (ibid., 11). With even social democratic governments, which have normally been labour's political partners, unable to implement policies that benefit working people, the labour movement has, in effect, been left "without a viable macroeconomic programme" (ibid.). This in turn weakens the labour movement at the national political level.

If smaller enterprises have come to play an increasingly important role, so too have the multinationals, which as noted earlier now control an estimated two-thirds or more of all international trade (ILO, 1997:89). Since they are ultimately answerable to no national government, these enterprises pose a particularly serious challenge to national governments seeking to regulate their economies and IR systems. A recent trend within the multinationals has been the rationalization of product lines. Instead of attempting to produce the firm's full range of goods and services at each location, the multinationals now are increasingly setting up establishments specializing in specific production activities at each location (ibid., 91). This new approach has reduced the autonomy of national affiliates. So too has the growing tendency of multinationals to use the new information and communications technology to compare the economic performance of their different affiliates, with an eye to 'disciplining' the bargaining behaviour of local management and work forces alike (ibid., 93). For example, AusCo, an Australian appliance company which in 1992 established a joint venture that saw some of its appliances being manufactured in China, used the threat of closure and relocation of all production to China to extract major concessions from its work force, including a 50 percent reduction in employment and a speeding-up of the assembly line as well as the introduction of teamwork and continuous improvement techniques in production (ibid., 92). Nor is AusCo an isolated example. A survey of 176 multinationals with headquarters in Britain revealed that 70 percent of them make economic comparisons between their affiliates, and a number of major multinationals such as Digital, IBM, and Analog Device have adopted a corporation-wide approach to human resource management (ibid., 93). Needless to say, such developments have further increased the stress on workers and the unions representing them.

Precarious Employment

Largely as a result of the sort of cost-cutting business strategies described in previous sections, employment has in recent years become more precarious in developed and

Table 13.4

TRENDS IN UNEMPLOYMENT* RATES, 1980 AND 1995, VARIOUS COUNTRIES

Country	1980 rate (%)	1995 rate (%)	1995 rate as % of 1980 rate
Argentina**	2.3	18.8	817.4
Australia	6.1	8.5	139.3
Canada	7.5	9.5	126.7
Chile	10.4	4.7	45.2
Finland	4.7	17.4	370.2
France	6.4	11.6	181.3
Japan	2.0	3.2	160.0
Norway	1.7	4.9	288.2
Philippines	4.8	8.4	175.0
Spain	11.4	22.9	200.9
Sweden	2.0	7.7	385.0
U.S.A.	7.0	5.6	80.0
Venezuela	5.9	10.3	174.6

Source: ILO (1997), Table 8. 1980 data for Canada were drawn from Table 2.4 in Peirce (2000).
* Unemployment is defined as percentage of the labour force unemployed.
** Figures for Argentina are for the Buenos Aires metropolitan area only.

developing countries alike. Throughout the world, fewer and fewer workers hold what could be called steady, full-time jobs. In manufacturing, firms have moved in the direction of "just-in-time" employment, with a small group of 'core' permanent workers being supplemented by a larger group of peripheral workers brought in only at periods of peak demand. In the burgeoning private service sector—for example, in retail—just-in-time employment often takes the form of split shifts, whereby employees must in effect spend twelve hours in order to be paid for eight hours of work.

The trend toward increasingly precarious employment has had a number of different manifestations. First, throughout most of the world, unemployment rates have increased. In some cases, such as those of Argentina, the Scandinavian countries, France, and Spain, the increase has been dramatic. Second, in industrialized countries generally, as in Canada (see Chapter 2), a larger share of work is being done on a temporary, part-time, or contractual basis, or out of employees' homes rather than at a formal workplace. Third, in developing countries, labour force participation has declined. A growing number of people support themselves through activities in the largely unregulated 'informal' sector of the economy, working mainly for themselves or a family member, generally for extremely long hours and often under very poor, sometimes hazardous conditions. As Tables 13.5 and 13.6 show, not only does the informal sector account for a large proportion of labour force activity in the developing world; its influence is growing. While comparative data from the 1980s and

Table 13.5

FORMAL SECTOR WAGE EARNERS AS A PERCENTAGE OF THE NON-AGRICULTURAL LABOUR FORCE, BY REGION					
Year	Country	Percentage	Year	Country	Percentage
Africa			**Americas**		
			1995	Argentina	.39
1995	Botswana	.60	1994	Bolivia	.27
1995	Cote d'Ivoire	.17	1991	Brazil	.49
1995	Ethiopia	.18	1993	Chile	.48
1995	Kenya	.51	1995	Colombia	.41
1995	Mauritius	.71	1995	Costa Rica	.48
1995	Senegal	.40	1995	Ecuador	.44
1995	South Africa	.42	1995	El Salvador	.67
1995	Tanzania	.34	1994	Guatemala	.57
1995	Uganda	.57	1994	Honduras	.22
1995	Zambia	.23	1991	Mexico	.43
1995	Zimbabwe	.64	1995	Nicaragua	.49
1995	*11–country average*	.43	1991	Panama	.49
			1995	Paraguay	.19
Asia			1991	Peru	.41
1995	China	.78	1993	Uruguay	.57
1991	India	.24	1995	Venezuela	.46
1995	Indonesia	.54	1990s	*17–country average*	.44
1994	Pakistan	.19	**Europe**		
1995	Thailand	.60	1995	Azerbaijan	.75
1990s	*5–country average*	.47	**1990s**	**34-COUNTRY AVERAGE**	**.45**

Source: Derived from ILO (1997), Table 1.2.

Table 13.6

FORMAL SECTOR WAGE-EARNERS AS A PERCENTAGE OF THE NON-AGRICULTURAL LABOUR FORCE, SELECTED COUNTRIES & YEARS				
Year	Country	F.S. as % NALF	Year	F.S. as % NALF
1985	Kenya	.70	1995	.51
1985	Mauritius	.72	1995	.71
1985	South Africa	.68	1995	.42
1989	Uganda	.76	1995	.57
1985	Zambia	.47	1995	.23
1985	Zimbabwe	.76	1995	.64
1988	Venezuela	.58	1995	.46
1980	India	.25	1991	.24
1980s	*AVERAGE (UNWEIGHTED)*	*.62*	*1990s*	*.47*

Source: Derived from ILO (1997), Table 1.2

1990s are available for only eight countries, these data show that on average in those eight countries, formal sector participation declined by about one-quarter between the two decades (Table 13.6). From this fact, we can infer that there has likely been a corresponding increase in the informal sector, and other evidence seems to bear this out. In Latin America, the informal sector accounted for over 80 percent of all new jobs created between 1990 and 1994, while in Africa it was estimated that by 1990 the informal sector accounted for over 60 percent of all existing jobs and that it would account for some 90 percent of all new jobs created during the 1990s (ILO, 1997:178-9). The rapid growth in the informal sector in Africa and Latin America has been mainly at the expense of growth in the formal sector (i.e., the regular labour force) and has been linked to economic stabilization and restructuring programs that led to declines in public sector employment and large-scale downsizings by private sector firms (ILO, 1997:181).

Declining Union Representation

Throughout most of the world, except in certain newly-industrializing Asian countries and a few countries like South Africa and Chile that have only recently emerged from authoritarian regimes, the proportion of workers represented by unions has declined over the past two decades. The sharp decline in union membership rates in countries such as Britain, the U.S., Australia, and New Zealand is by now fairly well-known. Less well-known, perhaps, but equally dramatic have been the rates of decline in Southern European countries such as Greece and Portugal, in African countries such as Kenya, Uganda, and Zambia, and in Latin American countries such as Argentina, Colombia, Costa Rica, Mexico, and Venezuela. It is worth noting that all regions of the world experienced declines in union density; out of 62 countries for which comparative 1980s-1990s data were available from the ILO, 52 saw their union density rates decline while only 10 experienced an increase.[12] As Table 13.7 notes, the average decline for the 62 countries surveyed was 7.9 points (17.7 percent).

The biggest average decline in points (see Table 13.7), 10.7 points, occurred in Europe. However, Europe's rates during the 1980s were generally far higher than in most of the rest of the world. For this reason, the Americas' 24.6 percent drop in percentage between the two periods is probably more significant. The smallest average declines in both points and percentage (4.0 and 14.2, respectively) occurred in Asia, where certain newly-industrializing countries such as Hong Kong, the Philippines, and South Korea actually saw their density rates increase.

Overall, union density rates have held up relatively well in Canada and most Northern European countries (particularly the Scandinavian ones). But these countries are exceptional. In 48 of 92 countries for which data were available, union density rates were less than 20 percent in 1995 (ILO, 1997:7). The rate exceeded 50 percent in only 14 of those countries. Between 1985 and 1995, density rates dropped by more than 20 percent in 35 of the 66 countries for which comparative data were available (ibid.).

Table 13.7

CHANGE IN UNION DENSITY RATES, VARIOUS COUNTRIES, 1980s & 1990s, IN POINTS AND IN PERCENTAGES

Country	Period	Change (points)	Change (percentage)
Egypt (Africa)	1985-95	-9.3	-23.9
Kenya (Africa)	1985-95	-25.0	-59.6
Mauritius (Africa)	1985-95	-8.9	-25.7
South Africa (Afr.)	1985-95	+6.3	+40.7
Uganda (Africa)	1989-95	-3.9	-49.9
Zambia (Africa)	1985-95	-6.3	-33.5
Zimbabwe (Africa)	1985-95	+2.3	+20.1
7-country average	*1980s-90s*	*-6.4*	*-18.9*
Argentina (Americas)	1986-95	-23.3	-47.9
Canada (Americas)	1985-93	-0.2	-0.6
Chile (Americas)	1985-93	+4.3	+37.2
Colombia (Amer.)	1985-95	-4.2	-37.3
Costa Rica (Amer.)	1985-95	-9.8	-42.6
Dom. Republic (Americas)	1989-95	-1.6	-8.6
El Salvador (Amer.)	1985-95	-0.6	-8.0
Guatemala (Amer.)	1985-94	-3.7	-45.6
Mexico (Amer.)	1989-91	-23.1	-42.7
U.S.A. (Amer.)	1985-95	-2.3	-15.2
Uruguay (Amer.)	1990-93	-8.2	-41.4
Venezuela (Amer.)	1988-95	-11.0	-42.5
12-country average	*1980s-90s*	*-7.0*	*-24.6*
Australia (Asia)	1985-95	-12.0	-29.6
Bangladesh (Asia)	1985-95	-11.0	-71.9
China (Asia)	1985-95	-4.6	-7.8
Hong Kong (Asia)	1985-94	+4.4	+30.8
India (Asia)	1980-91	-1.2	-18.2
Japan (Asia)	1985-95	-4.0	-17.7
(South) Korea (Asia)	1985-95	+0.4	+4.7
Malaysia (Asia)	1986-95	-1.8	-13.4
New Zealand (Asia)	1986-95	-23.9	-50.7
Pakistan (Asia)	1987-95	-0.9	-13.4
Philippines (Asia)	1985-95	+4.4	+24.1
Singapore (Asia)	1984-95	-3.5	-20.4
Taiwan (Asia)	1987-95	-2.3	-7.6
Thailand (Asia)	1987-95	-0.2	-7.4
14-country average	*1980s-90s*	*-4.0*	*-14.2*
Austria (Europe)	1985-95	-15.1	-29.2
Azerbaijan (Eur.)	1985-95	-24.6	-24.6
Belarus (Eur.)	1985-95	-3.9	-3.9
Belgium (Eur.)	1985-95	-3.9	-9.2
Bulgaria (Eur.)	1991-93	-10.5	-17.0
Cyprus (Eur.)	1985-95	-9.1	-14.5
Czech Rep. (Eur.)	1990-95	-40.5	-52.8
Denmark (Eur.)	1985-94	+0.8	+1.2

Table 13.7
(continued)

Country	Period	Change (points)	Change (percentage)
Finland (Eur.)	1985-95	-1.7	-2.8
France (Eur.)	1985-95	-5.5	-47.4
Germany* (Eur.)	1991-95	-1.1	-3.5
Greece (Eur.)	1985-95	-8.1	-34.5
Hungary (Eur.)	1985-95	-21.6	-29.2
Iceland (Eur.)	1985-94	-6.0	-7.8
Ireland (Eur.)	1985-93	-5.0	-12.3
Israel (Eur.)	1985-95	-76.9	-76.9
Italy (Eur.)	1985-94	-2.3	-7.0
Luxembourg (Eur.)	1987-95	-8.5	-17.7
Malta (Eur.)	1985-94	+12.4	+27.3
Netherlands (Eur.)	1985-95	-1.6	-6.7
Norway (Eur.)	1985-95	+1.0	+2.0
Poland (Eur.)	1989-95	-20.0	-42.6
Portugal (Eur.)	1986-95	-21.8	-53.7
Romania (Eur.)	1991-93	-10.0	-19.8
Slovakia (Eur.)	1990-95	-24.5	-31.9
Spain (Eur.)	1985-94	+4.1	+56.2
Sweden (Eur.)	1985-94	-2.1	-2.7
Switzerland (Eur.)	1985-94	-5.4	-21.2
U.K. (Eur.)	1985-95	-9.8	-27.2
29-country average	1980s-90s	-10.3	-16.4
62-country global average	**1980s-90s**	**-7.9**	**-17.7**

Source: ILO (1997), Table 1.3
* Germany refers to the united former West and East Germany.

What explains the sharp drop in union membership rates in so many countries over the past two decades? Certainly tougher economic conditions are an important factor. But it is difficult to see how economic conditions alone explain declines as severe as the 50 percent drop in New Zealand, 47 percent drop in France, and 30 percent drop in Australia (Table 13.7)—all relatively prosperous countries by world standards. Nor do economic conditions explain the sharply different union membership and density rates exhibited by countries such as the U.S. and Canada, whose economies are heavily integrated and which have experienced quite similar economic fortunes in recent years.

Most sophisticated union growth analysts would probably agree, with Robert Price (1991), that in order to get a full and accurate picture of union growth or decline, one must understand the relevant legal and sociopolitical factors at work as well as economic ones. Thus in New Zealand and Australia, the decline in union membership rates was driven in large measure by deliberate government policy aimed at reducing the size of the public sector and at making it more comparable to the private sector (see Warrian, 1996) and by the replacement of collective bargaining with a system of individual contracts of employment (see Haworth, 1993; Dannin, 1995). In Britain, a succession of Conservative governments took policy measures quite deliberately aimed at weakening that country's union movement, such as legislation restricting strikes and making union recognition more difficult (Ferner and Hyman, 1992; Lipsig-Mumme, 2001:525). In the U.S., relatively weak legislation protecting unions' rights has been combined with a failure to enforce even that legislation (see Meltz, 1989; Bruce, 1990). In addition, one must consider the U.S.'s lack of a social democratic or labour party to advance unions' interests in the political arena (Bruce, 1989), American employers' particularly virulent opposition to unions (Adams, 1995:502–3), and the American labour movement's longstanding lack of interest in organizing unskilled and semi-skilled workers (Peirce, 1995; Lipsig-Mumme, 1989). In Eastern and Central European countries formerly belonging to the Soviet bloc, widespread privatization of previously state-owned enterprises (ILO, 1997:44–5) together with the removal of compulsory membership requirements go far toward explaining declining membership rates.[13]

In developing countries, reductions in the size of the public sector, which is almost invariably far more heavily unionized than the private sector, have been a major factor in declining union membership rates. An equally important factor is the drop in employment in the formal sector, since employment in that sector is normally a prerequisite for union membership (ILO, 1997:17). In some Asian countries, the explanation may be a bit different. There, it is believed that the rapid growth of the economy and rise in real wages may have reduced unions' ability to grow and members' desire to join them (ibid.).

A phenomenon closely related to declining union membership is the decentralization of collective bargaining from national or industry levels to the level of the individual enterprise. In general, more centralized systems such as that of Sweden have higher union density rates and have dropped less sharply than decentralized systems such as those of the U.S., Britain, or Australia (see Table 13.7 and also Lipsig-Mumme, 2001). For one thing, concerted employer anti-union initiatives tend to fare less well against a united labour movement (see Kochan, et al., 1984). As well, labour movements in centralized systems generally have significantly more ability to influence national policy on issues such as taxation and hours of work.[14] Because decentralization of bargaining is such an important issue, it will be treated in a separate section.

Decentralization of Bargaining Structures

The movement toward bargaining at the level of the firm, rather than at national or industry levels, was already well underway by the early 1980s (Kochan, et al., 1984);

however, the trend has accelerated significantly since then. Driving this trend has been employers' desire for greater flexibility, a desire that also appears to have led to some weakening of employers' associations in the traditionally centralized European countries (ILO, 1997:62).

In a group of 63 countries surveyed by the ILO (1997, Table 3.1), 18 saw an increase in bargaining at the national or sectoral (industry) level during the ten years preceding the survey. Eleven saw a decrease in bargaining at these levels, while in 23 bargaining at these levels remained relatively stable. Eleven countries provided no data for these levels. At the company level, 46 countries experienced an increase in bargaining, 3 saw a decrease, and 7 remained stable, the same number providing no data. Only in Africa was there an overall trend toward more bargaining at national or sectoral levels.[15] Elsewhere, the vast majority (87 percent) of countries providing data experienced an increase in company-level bargaining. Only 23 percent of responding non-African countries saw an increase in national or sectoral bargaining during the study period.

Moreover, even within those countries that the ILO lists as stable at national/sectoral levels, there has been some devolution of bargaining to lower levels. In Sweden and Denmark, for example, bargaining has recently devolved from the national to the industry level, although in the latter employers' associations are still required to submit their draft industry-wide agreements to their central organization for approval (ILO, 1997:120,126). Likewise, in Germany, industry unions are more willing than in the past to accept some degree of enterprise-level bargaining (ibid., 126). An increasing number of German industry-level agreements contain "opening clauses" allowing works councils and employers to negotiate enterprise-level amendments to those agreements. In the chemical industry, a 1997 agreement provided for the possibility of enterprise-level negotiation of a variable portion of wages that may be increased or reduced according to local economic conditions (ibid., 119). In France, a country where collective bargaining has historically been underdeveloped at the enterprise level (Goetschy and Jobert, 1993), the number of enterprise-level agreements increased by about one-third between 1990 and 1995 (ILO, 1997:121). In that country, legislation passed in 1995 allows employers to sign agreements with works councils under certain conditions.

Throughout much of Europe works councils are playing an increasingly important role in IR systems—another sign of the growing importance attached to enterprise-level consultation. Sweden and Finland are now the only continental European countries without works councils. Greece established works councils in 1988; Switzerland introduced mandatory participation in the private sector in 1994; and in the Netherlands, a 1996 act extended works councils to the public sector. In France (see above) as well as in Austria and Spain, the scope of works councils' activities has recently been widened (ILO, 1997:121).

Perhaps because of the important role played by works councils in continental European countries, and because in practice most works councillors are active union

Table 13.8

Country	Trend over 1985–95 period National/Sectoral Level	Trend over 1985–95 period Company Level
Africa		
Egypt	Increasing	Increasing
Eritrea	Stable	Decreasing
Kenya	Stable	Increasing
Mali	Increasing	Increasing
Mauritius	Increasing	Stable
South Africa	Increasing	Increasing
Swaziland	Stable	Decreasing
Uganda	Increasing	Increasing
Zambia	Stable	Increasing
Zimbabwe	Increasing	Decreasing
Americas		
Argentina	Stable	Increasing
Brazil	Increasing	Increasing
Canada	Decreasing	Increasing
Chile	N/A	Increasing
Colombia	Increasing	Increasing
Cuba	Increasing	Increasing
Guyana	Stable	Increasing
Mexico	Stable	Stable
Nicaragua	Stable	Increasing
Peru	Decreasing	Increasing
United States	Decreasing	Increasing
Uruguay	Stable	Increasing
Venezuela	Decreasing	Increasing
Asia		
Australia	Decreasing	Increasing
Bangladesh	Increasing	Increasing
China	N/A	Increasing
India	Stable	Increasing
Japan	Stable	Increasing
New Zealand	Decreasing	Increasing
Philippines	N/A	Increasing
Singapore	Stable	Stable
Thailand	N/A	Increasing
Europe		
Austria	Stable	Increasing
Azerbaijan	N/A	Stable
Belgium	Stable	Increasing
Bulgaria	Increasing	Increasing
Cyprus	Increasing	Stable
Czech Republic	Stable	Increasing

TRENDS IN BARGAINING STRUCTURES, 1985–95, SELECTED COUNTRIES

Table 13.8
(continued)

Country	Trend over 1985–95 period National/Sectoral Level	Trend over 1985–95 period Company Level
Denmark	Stable	Increasing
Estonia	Increasing	Increasing
Finland	Stable	Increasing
France	Stable	Increasing
Germany	Stable	Increasing
Greece	Decreasing	Increasing
Hungary	Decreasing	Increasing
Ireland	Increasing	Stable
Italy	Stable	Increasing
Netherlands	Stable	Increasing
Poland	Decreasing	Increasing
Portugal	Increasing	Increasing
Russian Federation	Decreasing	Increasing
Slovenia	Stable	Stable
Spain	Increasing	Increasing
Sweden	Stable	Increasing
Switzerland	Increasing	N/A
Ukraine	Increasing	Increasing
United Kingdom	Decreasing	Increasing

Source: ILO (1997), Table 3.1
N/A= No data available

members (see Adams, 1995), the devolution of bargaining to lower levels recently experienced in those countries does not seem, thus far, to have had the effect of lowering union membership rates significantly, or of undermining overall worker representation there. In general, the same cannot be said elsewhere. Leaving aside the former Soviet bloc countries as a special case (to be discussed in the next section of this chapter), Canada was the only country, among those seeing a decrease in national or industry-level bargaining between 1985 and 1995, not to experience a sharp decline in its union density rates. And even in Canada, the labour movement has less political clout than it had 15 or 20 years ago; the same is even truer of labour movements in the U.S., Britain, and Australia. Overall, the evidence suggests that unless decentralization of bargaining is accompanied by an increase in formal enterprise-level mechanisms such as works councils, it is very likely to lead to weaker labour movements and a decline in workers' ability to solve workplace problems collectively.

Workers and students demonstrate against clothing retailer "The Gap" in New York City as part of a January 2002 protest against the globalization of industry.

Liberalization of Former Soviet Bloc IR Systems

With the collapse of the former Soviet Union and the transition of former Soviet bloc countries from planned to market economies, these countries' IR systems have undergone a profound transformation. As noted earlier (see Héthy, 1991), some liberalization was already occurring, particularly in Hungary, prior to the collapse of the Soviet Union. Still, for the most part, unions continued to be closely tied to the state, serving largely as the transmitters of state policy and distributors of its largesse rather than as independent advocates for workers' interests (ILO, 1997:149), while for their part, employers other than the state had very little role to play.

Over the past decade, the role of all three major partners in the IR system has changed markedly, though there are variations in the type and rate of change due to such factors as differing rates of privatization of previously state-owned enterprises in different Central and Eastern European countries. The state's role in these countries' IR systems has been reduced, though it continues to be a major player in its new role as legislator and administrator of labour law, and as the continuing owner of at least some business enterprises.

The unions have for the most part shifted from a patronage role to a more conventional (in Western terms) collective bargaining role. Since the early 1990s, collective bargaining has increased dramatically if unevenly throughout the region. In Central Europe, in particular, most of that bargaining is now done at the enterprise level. An ILO survey of union branches (ILO, 1997:149) found that in Poland, over 96 percent of all wage bargaining was conducted at this level, while for the Czech Republic, Hungary, and Slovakia, the figures were 72 percent, 65 percent, and 60 percent, respectively. At the same time, industry-level bargaining has declined throughout most of the region (ILO, 1997:148).

With the advent of collective bargaining, the role of employers has become more important. Nonetheless, employers continue to be the weak link in the IR system. One reason is the continuing underdevelopment of the private sector in several of those countries, resulting from the continued existence of large numbers of state-owned enterprises ILO, 1997:146). Another reason is that, compared to unions, which are now accustomed to serving both as political movements and workers' advocates, employers as a whole tend to be poorly organized. Also, there tends to be a fundamental conflict of interest between the owners of small and medium-sized businesses, who have little interest in regulating labour relations and see little benefit from being more organized, and the managers of state enterprises, who may have a great deal to gain from continuing regulation and from being on good terms with the unions (ibid., 145–6). One result of this split within the employers' ranks is that, to date, collective bargaining remains minimal in the private sector, which is dominated by small and medium-sized firms. To date, it has been introduced primarily in large state-owned firms (ibid., 149–150).

Perhaps because collective bargaining is still so new in the former Soviet bloc countries, national tripartite (government-employer-union) agreements have assumed special importance there. Often a response to a wave of major strikes, these tripartite agreements have served a variety of functions, from setting minimum wages and establishing an economic and social council to protecting workers' claims in the event of insolvency of formerly state-owned enterprises (ILO, 1997:151). In several countries, tripartite agreements have resulted in major reforms in the laws governing collective bargaining and social protection. In Hungary, for example, the National Council for Reconciliation of Interests, founded during the last years of Communism, in early 1997 achieved an agreement aimed at promoting collective bargaining, facilitating the settlement of industrial disputes, and strengthening the application of labour legislation (ibid., 152–3). Tripartite committees were also responsible for settling major strikes in Hungary and the Russian Federation (ibid., 151).

The weakness and disorganization of employers is one reason for the particular importance of tripartite agreements in the former Soviet bloc countries. A number of case studies carried out in the Czech Republic, Bulgaria, and Hungary have found that tripartite agreements are an essential first step if collective bargaining is to develop within enterprises (ILO, 1997:150; see also p. 155, Note 10).

Summary

The preceding sections have illustrated some of the changes to IR systems and to the actors within those systems resulting from today's tougher, more uncertain economic climate. Driving these changes has been a wave of globalization and trade liberalization that has led to intensified competition between firms, particularly with respect to labour costs. Overall, the major impacts of these changes have included a shift in the balance of workplace power toward employers and managers, a reduction in national governments' ability to regulate their domestic economies and IR systems as they see fit, more precarious employment, a decline in the public sector, labour movements that are weaker both numerically and in terms of their political clout, and a devolution of collective bargaining away from national and industry levels to the level of the enterprise. Though these changes have affected the different actors in varying ways and to varying degrees, it would be fair to say that they have made life more difficult for almost everyone concerned.

In the next section, we look at strategies that different players have adopted in an attempt to adapt to the new, harsher environment. These include union recruitment and retention strategies aimed at women, the unemployed, and atypical workers generally, the formation of informal workers' associations, the creation of liaisons between workers' associations and the formal trade union movement, the growth of transnational unionism, the formation of associations of self-employed entrepreneurs, and publicity campaigns aimed at improving working conditions by inducing consumers not to buy from firms engaging in child labour or other exploitive practices. The chapter concludes with a brief assessment of the adequacy of traditional IR concepts in the current environment.

NEW STRATEGIES FOR A NEW WORLD ORDER

Unions

Confronted by steep declines in employment and membership in their traditional power bases, manufacturing and the public sector, unions are now looking more and more to groups with low levels of unionization, including women, young people, those employed in the private service sector, part-time workers, and even the unemployed, in an effort to bolster their ranks (ILO, 1997:31–2). In some cases, as we note in more detail in a later section, they have begun attracting members from the informal sector as well, or forming alliances with informal sector workers' organizations. They are also offering their members a broader range of services and starting to engage in transnational campaigns aimed at correcting abuses such as child labour (IlO, 1997:40–44).

New Sources of Members and Methods of Organizing

Even in Canada, where unionization rights are relatively well-protected by world standards, those seeking to organize private-service sector workers face formidable obstacles. As we noted in Chapter 2, employer opposition to unionization in this sector is particularly strong, and the typically small size of bargaining units makes them expensive for unions to organize and service. Other obstacles include the low pay and high rate of turnover characteristic of this sector and in certain cases legal obstacles, such as bargaining structures that make it extremely difficult for a union to win certification or the outright exclusion of certain groups.[16] In developing countries, the obstacles are often far more severe. In general, the private service sector employs mainly women, and there are many developing countries in which women are far from enjoying equal rights in society at large—or even within the labour movement (ILO, 1997:32).

Despite these obstacles, there have recently been a number of successful efforts to increase union organization in the private service sector. In Canada, many of these efforts have resulted from the diversification of old industrial unions such as the Auto Workers and Steelworkers into general or conglomerate unions. The Steelworkers, for example, now represent security guards and hotel and restaurant workers (Murray, 2001:99). In the U.S., there has been a growing recognition that the organization of women and ethnic minority group members requires different strategies than the recruitment of traditional male members in manufacturing. The Service Employees' International Union (SEIU), which represents large numbers of janitors and others in the highly unstable building services industry, has made significant use of those new strategies to bring in large numbers of women and minority group members, particularly Mexican-Americans in Texas and California. A study cited by Bronfenbrenner (1994) found that the union was far more successful in achieving certification of new units comprised mainly of women and minority group members when it (a) used women, many whose experience was primarily in community development organizations rather than the labour movement, as organizers; and, (b) stressed empowerment and dignity rather than possible economic benefits in its organizing campaigns. Increasingly, too, the SEIU has realized that the site for organization must be the community as a whole, rather than the enterprise. Of particular note, in this connection, was its "Justice for Janitors" campaign, which bypassed National Labor Relations Board rules on bargaining structure and resulted in the city-wide organization of workers in such cities as Los Angeles, Portland, Denver, and Seattle (ILO, 1997:45–6).

A number of efforts have been directed specifically at women. In the Netherlands, for example, there are now separate women's trade unions that include equality of opportunity and treatment on their bargaining agendas (ILO, 1997:32–3). In Canada and the U.S., some unions have made particular efforts to organize women (ibid., 33). Unions and labour federations in Canada, France, Britain, and Italy have reserved certain management positions for women, and other unions have set up special women's departments. Other countries whose unions have made a special effort to take account of women's concerns or to integrate them into the union's management structure include Sweden, Uganda, the Netherlands, and Germany (ibid., 32–3).

Still other efforts have been targeted at specific groups of 'atypical' workers. Unions in France, Germany, Japan, and Britain have made special efforts to reach out to part-time workers, while homeworkers have been targeted in Canada, Britain, the Netherlands, and Australia. Unions have also managed to conclude collective agreements for temporary workers sent out by agencies and other casual workers in Germany, France, and the Netherlands, as well as Canada. In Canada, certain artists and performers in the federal jurisdiction can now bargain collectively under the *Artists and Producers Professional Relations Act*. Since the act was passed in 1993, a number of collective agreements have been concluded by groups such as the Periodical Writers' Association of Canada. The act has been held up as a model for collective representation of freelance workers offering their services to a variety of different clients, but on essentially similar terms (Sims, 1995:241). Artists and performers have also achieved collective representation in France and Japan (ILO, 1997:35). In Canada, as well, certain types of self-employed individuals such as taxi drivers and fishers have been able to obtain collective representation under "dependent contractor" provisions in various jurisdictions' labour relations legislation. In France, there are collective agreements between oil companies and the tenant managers of service stations and interoccupational agreements for commercial travellers and sales representatives (ILO, 1997:35).

Collective representation of retirees and the unemployed has been uneven, in part because of legal restrictions on union membership for members of these groups in countries such as Chile (ILO, 1997:35). Europe offers a more favourable environment for such representation, since all organizations affiliated to the European Trade Union Federation allow workers who have lost their jobs to retain their membership. The role of the unemployed within the labour movement is particularly significant in such countries as Belgium and Denmark, where the unions play a key role in administering jobless benefits and other services for the unemployed (ILO, 1997; Price, 1991:47), and may have accounted for rising union membership rates in these countries during periods of high unemployment. In several northern European countries, union confederations have set up special departments to address the needs of the unemployed and have launched programs aimed at other target groups such as migrants and young people. In addition, they have attempted to stay in touch with their retired members (ILO, 1997:35).

New Union Services

In an attempt to retain existing members, unions have begun offering these members a broader range of direct assistance. The supplementary unemployment benefits found in many collective agreements are a direct legacy of unions' "mutual insurance" function, as described by the Webbs (see the beginning of Chapter 6). Other unions have begun providing their members legal and financial services and career counselling and other kinds of employment advice (Murray, 2001:101; ILO, 1997:31). An increasingly common benefit of union membership is the 'affinity' credit card, whereby members pay lower fees and receive reduced interest on outstanding balances. Such cards are now available to union members in Britain, the U.S. and Canada (see ILO, 1997:31). Some British and American unions also offer their members discounts on loans and insurance premiums and run their own travel agencies and even retirement homes. In Japan, the "trade union identity" movement has established "total well-being" programs (ibid.).

Transnational Unionism

The emergence of multinational enterprises and the formation of regional economic blocs have made it increasingly important for unions in different countries to work together. Often, such international collaboration is difficult to achieve. To begin with, there are the obvious linguistic, religious, and cultural barriers. Beyond that, in several African countries (Nigeria, Cameroon, and Kenya), legislation either prohibits or severely restricts unions from affiliating to international confederations (ILO, 1997:37). In Britain, the U.S., and Brazil, the scope of international union action is limited by legislation restricting secondary boycotts; in other countries, it is limited by restrictions on sympathy and solidarity strikes (ibid., 38). Elsewhere (as within the European Union), the diversity of national labour relations regimes may prove a barrier to international cooperation. Differing degrees of protection of the right to strike, the different levels at which bargaining is conducted in different countries, and the fact that collective agreements can be extended to non-unionized enterprises in some countries but not others are but a few of the divergences that can hinder transnational collective bargaining (ibid.).

Despite these barriers, international cooperation between unions has been increasing. Such cooperation has been most prominent in Europe, where regional economic integration has the longest track record and where the European Trade Union Congress (ETUC) plays a prominent role as a coordinating body (ILO, 1997:44). There, too, the International Trade Secretariats (ITSs) for different sectors have played an important role in bringing together the unions of the subsidiaries of multinationals, such as Honda and Fiat, into committees to exchange information or prepare for negotiations with the company's central management. Like other regional and international labour organizations such as the ETUC and International Confederation of Free Trade Unions (ICFTU), the ITSs also help facilitate bilateral relations between national trade unions and represent these unions in bodies such as the ILO (ILO, 1997:39).

Genuine international collective agreements are rare, but examples do exist. In 1988, the Danone Company and the IUF (International Union of Food, Agricultural, Hotel, Restaurant, Catering, Tobacco and Allied Workers' Associations) signed an agreement covering the promotion of equality between the sexes, skill training and development, and union rights (including unions' access to information). In 1995, the same union signed an agreement with the Accor Hotel group guaranteeing full freedom of association in all the group's establishments (such as the Novotel Hotels). There have also been agreements at the sectoral level (ibid., 43). For example, in 1995, the ETUC organization for the textiles, clothing, and leather sector and the European Confederation of the Footwear Industry signed an agreement whereby the Confederation's member companies undertook not to employ children in manufacturing anywhere in the world, either directly or through indirect subcontracting arrangements (ibid., 44).

Where international collective agreements have been reached, they've often been the result of broad-based publicity campaigns involving a broad range of partners such as religious, consumer, women's, and students' organizations as well as labour groups (see ILO, 1997:43 (Box 2.3)). Such campaigns are of particular importance in developing countries, where repressive labour legislation may make it extremely difficult for workers to form unions, or for them to assert their rights in any meaningful way even if they do manage to form a union. In such cases, particularly when confronting a multinational enterprise, appealing to those enterprises' customers may be the only way to bring about positive change.

Recently, heightened competition has made many multinational firms more concerned than before about their public image. For this reason, the threat of loss of business can often bring about results more effectively than traditional union action at points of production. As Box 13.1, below, indicates, modern publicity campaigns are often multifaceted exercises involving a variety of different players.

Box 13.1

JUST ONE OF MANY CODES OF CONDUCT

When workers at the Korean-owned Mandarin clothing factory in El Salvador sought to put an end to harsh and degrading treatment that included being forbidden to talk while working, beatings and sexual abuse, their attempts to form a union were suppressed. Over 350 workers, most of whom were women, were fired.

In the United States, a pressure campaign directed at Mandarin's biggest customer, the United States retailer The Gap, was mounted by trade unions and religious, consumer, women's and students' organizations. At first, The Gap, which is one of the largest apparel companies in the world, sought to deny that its subcontractor was guilty of such acts. But in the face of overwhelming evidence that the charges were true, and mounting pressure including from shareholders and politicians, The Gap announced that it would pull out of El Salvador. The campaigners demanded that The Gap reconsider this decision and instead use its influence to ensure that workers' rights were protected.

The Gap agreed to remain in El Salvador, to translate its hitherto ignored code of conduct into the languages of the 47 countries where clothing is produced for the company and to make sure that the code is posted prominently in each country. The Gap also accepted responsibility for the working conditions where its products are made and agreed to the independent monitoring of its subcontractors by a third party.

Source: International Textile, Leather and Garment Workers' Federation (ITLGWF), from ILO, 1997 (Box 2.3).

There are a number of different types of trade union publicity campaign, and various roles that a union may take in such campaigns. In some cases, the aim is to assist an affiliated union, typically though not always in a developing country. Here, the union may coordinate local demands, enter into partnerships with other international unions, lobby politicians, apply pressure on targeted companies, or even threaten to apply trade sanctions based on workers' rights provisions of national trade law. In the Dominican Republic, it was the threat of Generalized System of Preferences (GSP) sanctions, along with pressure applied on overseas corporate customers of Dominican apparel firms, that ultimately induced the country's government to change its labour code to allow trade unions in the country's export processing zones. This in turn enabled workers in apparel factories located in those zones to sign collective agreements (ILO, 1997:40).

In other cases, the objective may be broader, such as the abolition of child labour or the overall improvement of working conditions in a particular country (1997:43). Here, a tactic sometimes used is the awarding of a "social label," as a sign that the goods in question have been manufactured under acceptable conditions. As an example, in 1997 several major American clothing firms, including Nike and L.L. Bean, concluded an agreement with trade unions and human rights groups in which they agreed to implement basic rules governing wages and working conditions and apply them to sub-contractors, as well as their own subsidiaries. The agreement provided for a label, to be attached to clothes manufactured by the companies' subsidiaries and sub-contractors, and established an association to verify implementation (ibid., 41, 43).

WORKERS' ASSOCIATIONS

We noted earlier that in many developing countries, a majority of workers do not belong to the formal sector, but rather work in the informal sector of the economy. The ILO has identified six different types of informal sector worker: owners or employers of micro-enterprises with a few paid employees or apprentices; self-employed workers; wage labourers employed in micro-enterprises; unpaid family workers; paid domestic workers; and wage workers who work in a place of their own choosing—normally at home (ILO, 1997:181). Many such workers do different categories of informal sector work during a given year. For example, they may work as paid labourers during peak agricultural harvesting seasons, then spend the rest of the year as self-employed entrepreneurs, selling goods they have made at home (ibid.). Although there is considerable variation from country to country in the relative importance of the different classes of informal sector worker, the ILO (1997:182) suggests that the self-employed, either working alone or aided by unpaid family members or apprentices, make up the largest group.

While it was formerly believed that the informal sector was a "transient phenomenon destined to disappear with economic modernization" (ILO, 1997:217), more recent evidence suggests that far from disappearing, the informal sector is growing. As we noted earlier, the informal sector has grown significantly, at the expense of the formal sector, particularly in Africa and Latin America. By 1995, the former comprised more than half the non-agricultural labour force in 14 of 17 Latin America countries (ILO, 1997:237, Table 1.3).

There are major barriers to the organization of informal sector workers, including the diversity of their employment status, which makes it difficult for them to find common cause; the fact that family or ethnic loyalties are often more important than working-class solidarity; and the small size and instability of informal sector units (ILO, 1997:181–3).[17] Yet another problem, which makes it particularly difficult for governments to regulate informal sector activities, is the blurring of the usual employer-employee distinction. Organization is also hindered by these units' tendency to operate on the fringes of, if not outside the law, and by their lack of access to credit, training, and sometimes even such basic public services as sanitation, electricity, and running water (ibid., 184–6, 192–3). While it is difficult to estimate the extent of informal sector organization, it appears to be extremely low; estimates range from 1 percent in Bogota, Colombia, to 20 per cent in Dar-es-Salaam, Tanzania. Moreover, existing organizations don't appear to be growing very rapidly (ibid., 195).

Typically informal workers' associations are made up primarily of self-employed (own-account) workers or micro-entrepreneurs, who are generally in a stronger negotiating position than casual labourers or unpaid family workers (ibid.). The associations may be either trade- or neighbourhood-based. Examples of the former include a rickshaw-pullers' union in Nagpur, India, which has achieved some improvements in the legislation governing rickshaw licences, and a Tanzanian association of repair service businesses, which was formed to provide collective guarantees. The latter has developed codified skills profiles for its various trades in order to be able to regulate access to business and contract negotiations collectively. In this way, the association has reduced competition from ill-qualified newcomers (ILO, 1997:198–200).

Neighbourhood-based or area-based multi-trade associations may be more cohesive than trade-based ones, as their members tend not to be competing for the same business (ILO, 1997:197). In some cases, they may play something of the same role as business associations in North America, ensuring that surroundings are kept clean and seeking to create an attractive environment for business while avoiding official harassment or theft (ibid.:198). But they also may play a more overtly political role, as in certain Latin American and African cities, where they helped coordinate protest riots against increases in the price of staple foods (ibid.). In the Philippines, the Apitong Neighbourhood Association (ANA) managed, despite some setbacks, to develop the land it had acquired through a government-sponsored community mortgage program for housing in urban areas. In addition to developing road, drainage, and water systems, ANA provided management training and helped obtain credit for members seeking to set up small businesses (ibid., 197).

Women have played a key role in many informal workers' associations. As the ILO notes (1997:195), these organizations have often been of particular benefit to impoverished women workers, since they have provided services that have helped increase

women's opportunities in the labour market and made them more aware of their legal rights. It has also been observed that governments tend to regard women's organizations as less politically threatening than male-dominated groups, and that the former are less vulnerable to corruption because they have less experience in dealing with public institutions (ibid.). For example, the Cissin-Natanga Women's Association of Burkina Faso was initially organized by a group of women attending a literacy course. In 1985, with help from the country's central trade union congress, it was transformed into a more formal association. It has built craft and literacy centres for its members in which members are trained in various trades (ibid., 205). In Thailand, Chiangmai HomeNet began as a cooperative of homeworkers' groups. Its achievements include the establishment of a credit union and a cooperative (ibid, 196, 202).

Workers' Associations and the Union Movement

The growth of the informal sector has proved a serious challenge for labour movements in developing countries. On the one hand, feelings of solidarity and humanity make unions eager to help workers who, in general, are in an even more difficult situation than their own members. On the other hand, unions recognize that the growth of the informal sector reduces their bargaining power and threatens the rights and conditions of workers regularly employed in the formal sector. At a time when their own membership is declining, often severely, some unions fear that the added burdens posed by informal sector workers would simply be too great. As well, established unions often find it difficult to obtain financial support to defend informal sector workers' interests because of competition from non-governmental organizations (ILO, 1997:203). (This appears to be less of a problem for international unions, perhaps because as international organizations they are not in direct competition with the associations or the NGOs.)

Despite these obstacles, cooperation between the organized labour movement and informal workers' associations has been increasing. In some cases, a union will provide specific technical or political assistance to a workers' association. In Ghana, for example, the Industrial and Commercial Workers' Union (ICWU) has been training members of the Ghana Hairdressers' and Beauticians' Association in occupational health and safety (ILO, 1997:188); while in Brazil, the central trade union congress has lobbied for policies that would make it easier for small-scale producers, craftspeople, and other self-employed workers to pursue income-generating activities (ibid., 203).

In other cases, the association may form a special department (i.e., women's department) of a union, or its members may simply be invited to join the larger organization. In India, the now well-known Self-Employed Women's Association (SEWA) began as the women's wing of the Textile Labour Association before evolving into an independent union and forming alliances with international unions and federations (ibid., 204–5); while in Ghana, union constitutions have been revised to allow informal sector workers to join. Latin American unions appear particularly open to informal sector workers, in part because of legislation, in such countries as Brazil and Peru, allowing self-employed workers to form or join unions. The self-employed have assumed such importance in Brazil that the country's central trade union congress has established a separate branch specifically to address their concerns (ibid., 204).

An association strategy in between seeking specific assistance from trade unions and seeking to allow informal sector workers to join the unions is that of forming long-term alliances with them. We have already referred to the Indian organization SEWA, which has long enjoyed such alliances internationally with the IUF union and ICFTU confederation. In Caracas, Venezuela, the Coordinating Body of Informal Sector Retail Workers (CONIVE) has obtained legal advice and political support from two regional Latin American unions, the Latin American Central of Workers and the Latin American Federation of Retail Workers, in a bid to strengthen its bargaining position vis-à-vis the municipal authorities. With the help of its partners, CONIVE has sought to persuade the authorities to create a public market area in which small retail traders might operate, and to rescind a draft municipal order barring vendors from city streets (ILO, 1997:205–6).

In a few instances, informal associations have succeeded in bringing about change at the national political level. One such case involves PATAMBA, the Philippines' network of homeworkers' associations. Largely through PATAMBA's efforts, a National Steering Committee on Home Work was established in 1991. Gaining greater visibility through its participation in the Steering Committee, PATAMBA was later invited to take part in a National Tripartite Conference, which resulted in an Administrative Order providing significant improvements in homeworkers' legal status and working conditions, including the right to form or join associations of their own choosing (ILO, 1997:210).

ASSOCIATIONS OF MICRO-ENTREPRENEURS

Small-scale entrepreneurs, who are numerous throughout the developing world, face special difficulties. These typically include lack of marketable skills, lack of access to capital and credit, low levels of literacy, and lack of access to training and technology. These barriers tend to be even more formidable in the case of women, whose literacy levels are generally lower than those of men and who have less experience in the wider world (ILO, 1997:189). While institutions such as Bangladesh's Grameen Bank and Indonesia's Bank Rakyat have been successful at granting credit to micro-entrepreneurs, overall the demand for small-scale credit continues to outrun the supply (ibid., 190).

Like workers' associations, micro-entrepreneurs' associations may operate on a trade, neighbourhood, or area basis. And like the workers' associations, the micro-entrepreneurial ones may also link up with larger, more established employers' associations or trade bodies to obtain technical, legal, or lobbying assistance. Often, established employers' associations have supported the establishment of micro-entrepreneurs' associations. In a number of African countries, including Kenya, Nigeria, and

Uganda, the employers' associations provide active assistance to the informal associations, as by offering "Start your business" and "Improve your business" programs aimed at the informal sector (ILO, 1997:206–7).

A good example of a trade-based micro-entrepreneurs' association is the Panorama Rancho Estate Tricycle Operators and Drivers, Inc., or PARETODA, which has been operating in the Philippines since 1980. Eventually, PARETODA decided to join the Marikna Tricycle Operators' and Drivers' Association to benefit from the experience of the larger group's 60 other members. Thanks to the advice provided by more experienced members, local authorities granted PARETODA's request for a tricycle terminal (ILO, 1997:202, 207).

In Central America, with the decline in the state's role throughout most of the region, associations of micro-entrepreneurs have been playing an increasingly important role in economic renewal and the rebuilding of civil society after years of devastating wars. In 1992, associations of micro-entrepreneurs from seven Central American countries formed a Committee of Central American Micro-entrepreneurs (COCEMI), with an eye to coordinating efforts to upgrade the development of micro-enterprises and increasing affiliates' bargaining power at the country level (ILO, 1997:207). Through networking and lobbying, COCEMI promotes its affiliates' interests with national, regional, and international agencies. It also seeks to act as a conduit for technical and financial support to its national members' organizations (ibid., 208).

Elsewhere, informal sector associations are pooling their resources in an attempt to increase their productivity and bargaining power. In the African country of Benin, some 1600 micro-enterprises comprising a broad range of trades have established about 60 mutual savings and loan associations. Over time, the associations have had a high rate of recovery and good observance of repayment schedules. Recently they have begun to loan out their accumulated savings, thus further contributing to local economic development, and have also begun looking at ways to manage their assets jointly (ILO, 1997:207–9).

CONCLUSION

This chapter has examined some of the many effects economic globalization and regional economic integration have had on workers, their unions and informal organizations, and on national industrial relations systems. Among the most significant of these effects have been increased unemployment, decreased security of employment for those remaining employed, declining union membership rates, and decentralization of bargaining structures from national and industry to enterprise levels. The ability of national IR systems to regulate working conditions has generally been weakened, in large measure due to the growth of multinational enterprises, which ultimately are answerable to no national government at all and which have developed the ability to relocate production to more favourable environments on very short notice when national governments pursue policies that are not to their liking. In many developing countries, economic stabilization and restructuring programs introduced in the 1980s have led to a sharp decline in public sector employment and reduced real wages in the private sector. These developments, in turn, have forced many people into the informal sector, which as we have seen has grown markedly at the expense of the formal sector since the mid 1980s (see ILO, 1997:179).

Although there are many barriers to organization in the informal sectors, workers and micro-entrepreneurs in that sector have formed a wide variety of associations, some operating on a trade basis, others operating at the neighbourhood, regional, or even national level. In many cases, these informal associations have either received assistance from or formed alliances with more formal trade unions and employers' associations. In some cases, their members have even joined the larger organizations. Where they have operated, the informal associations have clearly benefitted their members. But the scope of informal organization, whether into workers' or micro-entrepreneurs' associations, remains relatively limited. All the available evidence suggests that informal sector workers and entrepreneurs seeking to improve their conditions through collective action of any kind will face an uphill fight for the foreseeable future.

Our world-wide review of IR systems and economic and working conditions suggests that in most of the developing world, workers face problems of a different order of magnitude than those generally faced in the developing world. In the latter, what we might refer to as industrial citizenship, including the right to join a union, bargain collectively, and if need be go on strike, remains restricted in many cases. This is certainly true in the developing world, as well. But there, workers also face restrictions on what we might call their economic citizenship, which can be defined as the ability, given a reasonable degree of effort, to hold paid employment in the formal labour force. For the most part, these restrictions are economic ones, resulting from a lack of sufficient economic opportunities in the formal economic sector. In some cases, such as the limitations put on women's labour force participation in certain countries, the restrictions are of a cultural nature. Whatever the cause, rural poverty levels of 30 to 80 percent throughout most of Africa and Latin America and much of Asia (see ILO, 1997:Table 6), together with the low labour force and formal sector participation rates to which we have already referred, attest to the developing world's "economic citizenship" crisis.

In closing, it seems appropriate to revisit the question of whether traditional IR terminology and mechanisms can usefully be applied to developing countries. We should admit from the outset that IR can't possibly be the same in the typical developing country as it is in Canada or the U.S. or a European country. To give just one example, the state's role is inevitably more limited (and also more ambiguous) in a country where a majority of workers are not employed in the formal sector. To many informal sector workers, state regulation, however well-intentioned, is more apt to be seen as harassment than as an attempt at protection. This said, the traditional IR institutions such as unions, employers' associations, and government agencies *do* operate, even in the developing world. The traditional institutions' enduring power is suggested by the fact that informal sector organizations such as workers' and micro-entrepreneurs' associations often seek to emulate them, and in some cases even to join them. Moreover, when a country's economic or political situation improves (as in the case of South Africa since the end of apartheid), there is a strengthening of the traditional institutions.[18]

Still, although there is much about employment relationships that traditional IR can explain, even in developing countries, there is also much that it cannot explain. For instance, in considering how workers' associations operate, we're apt to find that the neighbourhood or city is a more appropriate level of analysis than the workplace. And the tactics of sophisticated modern publicity campaigns aimed at bettering Third World employment conditions extend far beyond the picket line.

Clearly, full-fledged industrial citizenship remains the goal, for workers in the Third World as well as the First. In the former, however, most would probably agree that industrial citizenship means little in the absence of basic economic citizenship—the ability to earn a living in the formal labour force. It thus seems fair to say that economic citizenship is a necessary pre-condition of industrial citizenship. A logical corollary is that to understand the full range of employment relationships in developing countries, the industrial relationist must add to his traditional toolkit an understanding of economic, community, and regional development. Without these additional tools, his analysis will of necessity be limited to the more fortunate members of society, and will therefore be of little value from a practical perspective.

QUESTIONS FOR DISCUSSION

1) Have a chat with a classmate from a country other than your own. Compare his or her experiences with work and the IR system to yours. Pay particular attention to the role played by the labour movement in the two countries.

2) Distinguish between unfree, free, and partially free IR systems.

3) Distinguish between centralized and decentralized IR systems, and give at least two examples of each.

4) Within Canada, what's distinctive about Quebec's IR system? Do you think these distinctive traits will likely last very much longer?

5) How have the two free trade agreements affected the Canadian economy and IR system? Why has the impact been particularly great on low-wage industries?

6) How has globalization given more power to firms and managers?

7) Discuss the different ways in which employment has become more precarious in developed and developing countries.

8) Explain briefly why labour movements in centralized IR systems have generally fared better in recent years than those in decentralized systems.

9) Why is it now harder than in the past for national governments to introduce Keynesian economic policies that stimulate the economy and benefit workers and unions?

10) In what ways do you think informal workers' associations are an adequate substitute for trade unions? In what ways do they fall short? In your view, is it realistic to expect wide-scale mergers of the two in developing countries?

11) Are unions doing enough to build bridges with their counterparts in other countries? If you think they aren't, what else should they be doing?

12) Why must unions adopt different strategies to recruit workers from the service sector than they have generally used (and found successful) in recruiting workers from the manufacturing sector? If you were hired as an organizer for the Service Employees' International Union (which represents people such as janitors and other maintenance workers), what are some strategies you might use?

SUGGESTIONS FOR FURTHER READING

Adams, Roy. 1995. "Canadian Industrial Relations in Comparative Perspective." In M. Gunderson and A. Ponak (eds.), *Union-Management Relations in Canada* (3rd ed.). Don Mills, ON: Addison-Wesley. An excellent brief introduction to comparative IR, focussing mainly on systems in developed countries.

Ferner, Anthony, and Richard Hyman (eds.). 1992. *Industrial Relations in the New Europe*. Oxford: Blackwell. A thorough and thought-provoking collection of papers on IR systems in most European countries. On European countries, this book is far more detailed than the standard comparative IR text, Bamber and Lansbury (1993). It does not, however, cover any country outside of Europe, and thus may need to be supplemented either with Bamber and Lansbury or with one of the Asian books such as Frenkel (1993) or Verma, Kochan, and Lansbury (1995).

International Labour Office (ILO). 1997. *World Labour Report*, 1997-98. Geneva: ILO. Offers an extremely thorough (sometimes chilling) account of labour relations and working conditions around the world at the turn of the millennium. Contains a particularly thorough discussion of the new 'informal' sector. Extremely useful statistical tables.

Loxley, John. 1998. *Interdependence, Disequilibrium and Growth: Reflections on the Political Economy of North-South Relations at the Turn of the Century*. Ottawa: IDRC. Heavy going, but a most thoughtful and well-researched account of how globalization and structural adjustment programs have affected developing countries' economies. For an excellent brief treatment of globalization, see Giles (1996).

CHAPTER 14

KEY THEMES
AND ISSUES

Work-life balance? Well, maybe. This worker and mother is just one of the many Canadians facing increasing difficulties in meeting the combined demands of work and family responsibilities.

In this chapter, we step back from the examination of specific issues and topics that has dominated the previous chapters, with an eye to seeing where the Canadian IR system as a whole has been going, and where it may be headed in the years to come. The chapter focuses on five key themes that, in our view, raise critical issues of public labour policy. It features a look at these five key themes and at some important findings related to each, as well as a discussion of policy suggestions arising out of each theme. The chapter closes with a discussion of areas where further IR research appears most urgently needed.

This book has tried to provide an introductory survey of industrial relations that's both comprehensive and comprehensible. Along the way, we've examined such diverse topics as the Canadian economy's impact on management practice and the types of actions unions engage in, the ongoing crisis in the public sector, and such forms of industrial conflict as strikes and grievances.

In this chapter, the aim is to try to put the pieces together, and to take a broader look at the Canadian IR system and some of the directions in which it appears to be headed. We do this through an examination of five key themes that, at least to some extent, appear to cut across the specific treatment of various topics in the previous thirteen chapters and raise important issues for IR policy-makers.

In what follows, we start by looking at the themes themselves. You will note that the themes are often interrelated. For example, theme 4, the crisis in the public sector, may be linked directly to theme 5, the lack of safety in homes, communities, and workplaces. If you read the previous (international) chapter, you'll also recognize that many of the problems facing Canadian workers and their unions are pretty much the same as those facing workers and unions around the world.

KEY THEMES

The first of the five key themes (see Figure 14.1) is the impending demographic crisis resulting from the impending retirement of large numbers of workers. For years, economists and demographers have been warning of the problems that would result when large numbers of "Baby Boomers" started retiring. Now, it seems, the moment of truth may finally be at hand.

In the U.S., observers have warned that up to half of all workers in some occupations, including most notably nursing and elementary education, may retire over the next decade (Segal, 2001). Similar predictions have been made for Canada (see Schetagne, 2001). Shortages are likely to be even more severe in the public service and other parts of the public sector, where the work force is older than average and few retirees were replaced during the financial crisis of the 1990s (Dohm, 2000; Schetagne, 2001). Among the possible consequences could be major skills shortages as well as a leadership shortage in certain organizations and a strain on public services (Segal, 2001; Galt, 2000). In Canada, there is expected to be an "unprecedented crunch" on the pension and health-care systems (Sunter, 2001). The aging and

Figure 14.1

FIVE KEY THEMES

1) The impending demographic crisis.

2) Increasingly precarious nature of work.

3) Continuing lack of meaningful representation.

4) Continuing crisis in the public sector.

5) Threats to public health and safety in the workplace, community, and home.

retirement from the work force of large numbers of older Canadians is also expected to increase the considerable stress on families, who already suffer from governments' downloading of responsibility for health care, education, and other public goods on to them (Maxwell, 2001). In the labour market, impending retirements are expected to shift the balance of power back toward workers, after a generation in which power has been tilted strongly toward employers and managers. This should be particularly true for professionals and others with scarce skills, whom employers are making increasing efforts to accommodate, as by offering them flexible schedules and benefit packages or allowing them to work at home (Galt, 2000).

The second key theme has to do with the increasingly precarious nature of work in today's globalized and fiercely competitive economy—a fact that has important implications for all the actors in the IR system. Our examination of today's economy in Chapter 2 suggests that the changes that have taken place since the late 1980s have gone far beyond those normally associated with fluctuations of the business cycle. Quite simply, the world of work is a fundamentally different and far less secure place than it was 50 or even 20 years ago. Due largely to such developments as globalization, trade liberalization, and deindustrialization, unemployment remained as high during the 'boom' years of the late 1990s as it did during many previous recessions. Governments' growing preoccupation with deficits and the debt prevented the public sector from taking up the slack; indeed, the public sector experienced severe cuts in much of Canada. Even most who have jobs enjoy little real job security, and are often working far longer hours than workers of their parents' generation did. Management has responded to the fiercer competition it is facing by forcing workers to work longer and harder. In many firms, as we saw in Chapter 3, there appears to have been at least a partial reversion to the coercive drive approach prevailing before the First World War. The growing lack of job security is a key element of that approach, as are the low pay, minimal benefits, irregular hours, and enforced overtime found throughout much of the economy, but especially in the private service sector, which in recent years has been a major source of new Canadian jobs.

Since the terrorist attacks of September 11, 2001, employment has become even more precarious for Canadian workers. A sign of this has been an increase, during the fall of 2001, in part-time employment at the same time as full-time employment was declining. (See Chapter 2 for details.) Should the Canadian economy enter into a year-long recession in 2002, as many experts are now predicting, this trend would likely continue.

Related to the precarious nature of work is the continued, even growing lack of meaningful representation for many workers. Only about one-third of all Canadian non-farm workers are union members. Despite the Charter, many groups including domestics and, in some jurisdictions, professionals still don't even have the legal right to join a union. In the private service sector, while unions have made some gains in recent years, determined employer opposition continues to make it extremely difficult for unions to make appreciable headway. Elsewhere, the proliferation of self-employment, homeworking, and part-time, short-term and contractual work arrangements poses equally severe challenges for unions. In the public sector, membership rates have remained high, but the actual number of members has fallen in some jurisdictions, owing to continuing government cutbacks. Moreover, despite the generally improved economic climate of the past few years, many governments have continued to restrict public sector union members' bargaining rights—an issue important enough that it will be treated next as a separate theme.

Our fourth theme, the continuing crisis in the public sector, is related both to the previous theme and to the first one (the aging of the work force). For years, governments have forced public sector workers to do more with less, as they have placed a higher priority on deficit and debt reduction and on tax cuts than on maintaining adequate levels of public service. At times, as in the case of the E.coli outbreak in the drinking water of Walkerton, Ontario (see Mittelstaedt, 2001), the results have been tragic. The demographic situation will only aggravate the already severe public sector crunch. At a time when large numbers of public sector workers across Canada are reaching or nearing retirement age, the number of young people, from whom their replacements will be drawn, will continue to decline throughout the next decade (Auditor-General, 2000; Lowe, 2001). And as we noted in Chapter 9, in some parts of the public sector, most notably health care, Canadian governments face growing competition from the United States.

Despite this crisis in the area of public services, most Canadian governments have continued to place severe restrictions on public sector unions. The scope of public sector bargaining (see Fryer, 1995 and 2001) remains severely limited in most jurisdictions. And the strengthening economy has not stopped federal and provincial governments from using legislation to end public sector strikes. Between June 1998 and July 1999 alone, the two levels of government passed back-to-work legislation five times, while on several other occasions, the threat of such legislation induced public sector unions to call off their strikes (Lancaster House, 2001, 25:3/4). In some cases, as in that of Ontario's *Bill 13* (Back-to-School Law), passed in the spring of 2001 to end a school custodians' dispute, Canadian governments have defied international labour norms by unilaterally imposing contract terms in back-to-work legislation, without providing access to arbitration (ibid.). Similar action was taken during the summer of 2001 by the newly-elected B.C. Liberal government, which first used legislation to end its nurses' two-month overtime ban, and then passed further legislation imposing the terms of a new collective agreement (Lancaster House, 2001, 25:7/8), and which sought to restrict public school strikes by designating education as an essential service (ibid.). Where arbitration was already the dispute resolution method, as in the case of Ontario's health care sector, governments have moved to restrict arbitrators' freedom by insisting that awards take account of governments' "ability to pay" (Sack, 1998; Rose, 2000). Far from improving public sector union–management relationships, these heavy-handed actions by government have served only to aggravate what was already an extremely tense situation. The year 2001 saw a coast-to-coast wave of nurses' strikes as well as a series of lengthy transit strikes in Vancouver and several other western Canadian cities (Lancaster House, 2001, 25:7/8).

Our fifth and final theme, threats to health and safety in Canadian workplaces and communities, relates directly to the previous theme, since for the most part it is public sector workers who are responsible for the safety of Canada's workplaces and communities. This theme has been most apparent on Canada's airlines, where new security restrictions have been imposed in the wake of the September 11 attacks. Much of the new money in the December 2001 federal budget was directed at bolstering security on planes and at airports.

Serious as it is, the threat of terrorist attack is by no means the only potential risk to Canadians' health and safety. We've already spoken of the E.coli outbreak in Walkerton. In the wake of that tragedy, the Sierra Legal Defence Fund issued a report warning that without comprehensive, nation-wide action to protect drinking water, more such tragedies are a virtual certainty (see Mittelstaedt, 2001). In July 2001, people in the Ottawa area received an ironic if bitter reminder of the fragility of their water supply, when drinking fountains at an Environment Canada building in Hull, Quebec were found to contain up to five times the acceptable amount of lead (Bertrand and Petrou, 2001).

The situation with respect to the country's food supply is also far from reassuring. In 2001, two of Canada's four veterinary colleges had their international accreditation downgraded; these colleges were warned that they could lose their international accreditation altogether unless their decaying equipment and facilities are brought up to scratch (May 2001(a)). A loss of international accreditation would likely trigger a "brain drain" of veterinary students, professors, and researchers, which in turn could lead to threats to the country's domestic meat supply and meat exporting business, since Canada's major trading partners expect licensed veterinarians to be inspecting meat-packing plants and monitoring border crossings (ibid.). Veterinarians employed by the Canadian Food Inspection Agency (CFIA) have also complained that federal food inspections are "spotty at best" (May 2001(b)), while Health Canada drug evaluators have complained of being harassed to approve unsafe drugs for use in food animals (Bueckert, 2001). For its part, the Canadian Veterinary Association has warned that Canada is seriously lagging in research into animal diseases—an alarming finding at a time when nearly three-quarters of the diseases considered 'emerging' in humans have been found to come from animals (May 2001(c)). At the CFIA, relations between the agency and its vets have grown so bad that on December 17, 2001, vets in Quebec staged a wildcat strike to protest low wages, difficult working conditions (including shift work), and a lack of professional development opportunities (PIPSC, 2001).[1]

Health Canada, meanwhile, has been under fire for its delay in testing employees to find out which ones had been infected by a rare monkey virus (Sekeres and Edgar, 2001) and for failing to warn Canadians about the possible side effects of a once-common heartburn medication, which in March of 2000 led to the death of an Ontario teenager from cardiac arrest (Cryderman, 2001). The latter case, in particular, has led to concerns about the safety of the country's drug supply.[2]

KEY FINDINGS

The Demographic Crisis

The impending demographic crisis discussed earlier in this chapter and in Chapter 2 has already had significant effects on Canadian workplaces, particularly public sector workplaces. As more "Baby Boomers" retire, these effects are likely to become more serious.

Potential skill shortages have become a growing concern for both management and union officials, according to a Canada Labour and Business Centre Survey (CLBC, 2000). As noted earlier, these shortages could be particularly severe in areas such as nursing, where Canada faces stiff competition from the United States, or the federal public service, where the work force has long been even older than the national average (see Fryer, 2001). In the latter, as in many other organizations, loss of institutional knowledge and memory could prove a knotty problem, when the new wave of retirees is added to the large number of experienced workers forced out during the downsizing of the 1990s.

The stress on the public pension system is likely to be particularly severe, as a much smaller number of prime-age workers struggles to support a much larger number of retirees. In addition, health care and other public services are likely to be severely stretched, both because of increased demand for these services resulting from an aging population and because of a growing difficulty in attracting new recruits into nursing and other public sector professions.

Figure 14.2

SOME KEY FINDINGS

- Canada faces growing skills shortages and a public pension crunch due to a large number of impending retirements.

- Part-time employment has begun to increase again following the September 11 terrorist attacks.

- Many groups continue to be denied the right to join unions.

- For a majority of Canadian workers, union membership can now be obtained only through a vote.

- Heavy-handed government intervention, coupled with a growing demographic crisis, has aggravated already tense labour–management relations in the public sector.

- There is a growing threat to public health and safety in Canada's workplaces, homes, and communities.

Precarious Employment

Precarious employment was one of the themes discussed in our first edition. Regrettably, it remains a key theme today.

As we noted in Chapter 2, through the end of 2000, there had been a modest decline, over the past three to four years, in such indicators of precarious employment as self-employment and part-time employment as a percentage of total employment. But these improvements were quite modest, and far less than might have been expected, given the generally strong state of the economy. Overall, the situation for most Canadian workers didn't really change very much over that period. Most still enjoyed far less job security than did the vast majority of workers of their parents' generation. Relatively few Canadians could say with any certainty that they would still be in their present job a year later. And as before, relatively high unemployment levels by historical standards continued to exist side-by-side with large numbers of overtime hours, many of them unpaid.

Since the middle of 2001, and particularly since September 11, the situation has worsened significantly, as the Canadian economy has slid back toward recession. Large-scale layoffs have occurred or are occurring both in Nortel and other large high-tech firms and in public sector organizations, such as the government of British Columbia, which recently announced it would be cutting the size of its public service by roughly one-third. Aside from an increase in the general unemployment rate, a sign of the economy's worsening state is the increase in part-time, at the expense of full-time employment. While there will clearly continue to be many opportunities for most professionals and other highly skilled workers, the situation looks grim for those without specialized skills, who even prior to September 11 were starting to face increased unemployment (see Schetagne, 2001).

An unfortunate side effect of increased precariousness of employment has been a growth in the income and earnings gaps between the richest and poorest Canadians. Roy Adams (1997) has noted that in 1996, the poorest fifth of Canadian families received only 6.1 percent of the country's total income, the smallest share that segment of the population had received since the 1970s. In contrast, the richest fifth of families obtained 40.6 percent of the country's total income—its biggest share in more than two decades. Analyzing these findings, Adams warns that Canada is in danger of losing its compassion for the less fortunate and of becoming a nation made up largely of haves and have-nots.

Lack of Meaningful Representation

We noted in the previous (international) chapter that by international standards, union membership rates have held up relatively well in Canada. But this observation must be understood against a backdrop of steep decline in most other countries. Though admittedly not as bleak as in the U.S. (see Rose and Chaison, 2001), the prospects for Canadian union membership are far from promising.

To begin with, as we noted in Chapter 5, Canada's private sector union membership rates are declining. While public sector rates remain high, that sector's share of total employment seems likely to decline over time due to continuing government cutbacks and a growing ideological trend toward less government at all levels.

We also noted in earlier chapters that the existence or lack of facilitative labour legislation can be a critical factor in determining whether union membership increases or decreases. Over the past five years, the legal environment for union growth has certainly not improved and may indeed have deteriorated. As Rose and Chaison (2001) have noted, the decline of the NDP, which has generally passed legislation favourable to workers and unions when in power provincially, makes improvement of the legal environment problematic for the foreseeable future.

More than two decades after the freedom of association provisions of the Charter took effect, the members of many occupational groups continue to be denied the legal right to join a union. While the exclusion of management and confidential IR personnel may be justifiable, given policy-makers' desire to avoid creating conflict-of-interest situations, the same cannot be said of the exclusion of professionals, agricultural workers, and domestics, all of whom are denied unionization rights in a number of jurisdictions, as we noted in Chapter 8 (see also Peirce, 1989). Since provinces with restrictive exclusion policies generally have significantly lower membership rates than those with more liberal policies in this area (Chapter 8, Table 2), there is good reason to believe that these continuing exclusions may be one cause of lower membership rates.[3]

In other ways, the legislative environment has definitely worsened. In 1998, the Ontario government removed its labour board's ability to certify a union with less than majority support as a remedy for unfair employer labour practices (see Adams, 1998). Such a policy shift could well encourage employers to commit unfair labour practices against unions because it leaves the labour board without a meaningful or effective remedy, particularly in the case of unfair labour practices committed during organizing drives. Over the past five years, Ontario has also restricted its teachers' and nurses' rights considerably, both through the frequent use of back-to-work legislation to end disputes and by insisting that the government's "ability to pay" be considered in public sector interest arbitration awards. In British Columbia, the newly elected Liberal government not only restricted teachers' rights by defining education as an "essential service," but removed unions' ability to achieve certification on the basis of signed membership cards. Now, any union wishing to be certified must win an election, as was already the case in Alberta, Newfoundland, Nova Scotia, and Ontario. With this change in B.C.'s certification procedure, for the first time ever a majority of Canadian workers are subject to the vote procedure rather than the card count, which was long the norm in Canadian jurisdictions.

Crisis in the Public Sector

In the public sector, which was already in a state of crisis at the time our first edition was issued, massive cutbacks and continuing heavy-handed government intervention since then have served only to deepen the crisis.

In the federal public service, a number of studies, including the first Fyrer Committee report and the Public Policy Forum's *Levelling the Path*, have identified restrictive labour–management legislation as the source of continuing friction between the parties. The first Fryer report (Fryer, 2000) noted that the restrictive legislative framework had helped to destroy trust and respect between the parties. Similarly, *Levelling the Path* (PPF, 2000) has suggested that federal public service legislation provides little room for cooperation and thus sets the stage for a more antagonistic relationship. Suspension of bargaining and arbitration and the government's frequent imposition of back-to-work legislation have also been cited as causes of poor labour–management relations (Fryer, 2000). More recently, a major cause of friction was the government's offer of 2 or 2.5 percent wage increases, just months after MPs voted themselves a 20 percent pay increase and senior public service managers received a retroactive 8 percent increase (Naumetz, 2001).

The hostility of the labour–management relationship in the federal government is evidenced by recent developments such as the Quebec veterinarians' wildcat strike (discussed above) and the shifting of some occupational groups' union allegiances away from the traditional public service unions to more militant private sector unions. In 2001, for example, the Quebec-based Confédération des syndicats nationaux (CSN) won the right to represent correctional service officers previously represented by the Public Service Alliance. As well, the Canadian Auto Workers now represent certain groups of public service employees, while in 1999 the Teamsters Union narrowly missed becoming the veterinarians' bargaining agent. In a bid to improve morale and recognize superior performance, the government has come up with a number of ideas, among them that of rewarding superior performers with a "good quality tuque or scarf emblazoned with the department signifier" (Naumetz, 2001). However, such ideas have received a frosty reception from the public service unions, whose members, they suggest, would prefer to see more tangible signs of respect.

At the provincial level, years of pent-up inflation resulting from the pay freezes and rollbacks discussed earlier (see Chapter 9), combined with increased workloads and restrictive government policies, have led to a lethal situation, particularly in health care, where the demographic crunch is particularly severe and where provincial governments face serious competition both from each other and from the U.S. (Lancaster House, 2001, 25:7/8). (The Canadian Nurses' Association estimates that the current nationwide shortfall of 20 000 nurses will increase to 113 000 in the next decade—see ibid.). In both Nova Scotia and British Columbia, the situation deteriorated so badly that the nurses were forced to resign *en masse* to obtain (through final-offer arbitration in Nova Scotia) an offer they could live with (ibid.). While these provinces' nurses eventually received increases of 17 and 23.5 percent respectively, over a three-year period, concern has been expressed that other provinces may simply not be able to afford such large increases—a situation which in turn seems likely to lead either to further labour strife or a mass exodus of nurses from the poorer provinces, and ultimately to big interprovincial disparities in the quality of health care available (ibid.).

In public education, the demographic situation is not yet as serious as it is in health care. However, evidence from a recent U.S. study (Segal, 2001), which identifies elementary schoolteachers as the occupational group facing the largest number of retirements between 2003 and 2008, would appear to suggest that Canadian school systems, like hospitals, could soon be facing competition from their U.S. counterparts.

Threats to Public Health and Safety

In its December 2001 budget, the federal government placed heavy emphasis on increasing security on airplanes and, particularly, at airports. Among other things, screening procedures have been tightened at departure gates and air marshals placed on aircraft. However, longer-term threats to the country's food and water supply have remained largely unaddressed.

The inquiry into the Walkerton tragedy revealed that the Ontario government's cutbacks in the environment ministry may well have been at least partly responsible for the disaster. In the wake of that disaster, Ontario has tightened its drinking-water regulations substantially. However, other provinces, including Newfoundland, P.E.I., and B.C., have far weaker regulations, and even those provinces with relatively stringent regulations (Alberta, Ontario, and Quebec) fall far short of the standards in place in the U.S. (Mittelstaedt, 2001). Moreover, even if standards are improved, governments will still need to provide adequate staff to monitor and enforce those standards. So serious is the situation that the Sierra Legal Defence Fund (see Mittelstaedt, 2001) has warned that unless a comprehensive, nation-wide approach to the protection of drinking water is adopted, there will almost certainly be more Walkerton tragedies.

Canada could soon be facing an equally severe crisis with respect to its food supply, particularly its meat supply. It is particularly worrisome that although the country's meat inspection system is supposed to be audited every three years, no audit has been done since the Food Inspection Agency's creation in 1997 (May 2001(b)). Already there is a shortage of veterinarians (May 2001(b))—a shortage noted by the Auditor-General in his report for the year 2000. About 50 veterinary positions (or 10 percent of the agency's regular complement) have remained unfilled because of low pay, poor working conditions, and a lack of qualified graduates (May 2001(b)). The shortage will likely become more acute over the next few years due to the high average age of the vets, a third of whom will be eligible to retire within the next five years (PIPSC, 2001).

Further aggravating the situation is the potential loss of accreditation of two of the country's four veterinary colleges (May 2001(a)). And the lack of professional development opportunities and fractious labour–management relations at the food agency will do little to attract new recruits or, for that matter, to retain existing staff (see PIPSC, 2001). Already, Quebec veterinarians have complained that meat-packing plant inspection procedures are "spotty at best" (May 2001(b)). Even the food agency's regional director for Quebec has admitted that inspections are not being done as often as they should be (May 2001(b)). Other potential long-term threats to the meat supply are posed by a lack of basic research into animal diseases (May 2001(c)), staff shortages at the drug evaluation bureau of Health Canada,[4] and pressure on drug evaluators to approve potentially unsafe drugs for use in farm animals

(Bueckert, 2001), such as the drug carbadox, which has been found to leave carcinogenic residues in pork,[5] as well as the growing shortage of veterinarians.

There are also potential concerns about the country's drug supply. After the father of the teenage girl who died from taking the heartburn medication Prepulsid launched a class action lawsuit against Health Canada and the drug's manufacturer, it was revealed that the pharmaceutical companies routinely give money to Health Canada to oversee health studies (Cryderman, 2001). Moreover, Health Canada has no authority over the drug information distributed by pharmacists, nor is there any obligation for doctors to report adverse reactions—even deaths—resulting from particular drugs (Cryderman, 2001). As in the case of the country's drinking water, the lack of adequate regulations is of particular concern.

POLICY SUGGESTIONS AND PROPOSALS FOR ACTION

The following policy suggestions and proposals for action (see Figure 14.3 for a list of some of the most important ones) arise directly from the findings just discussed. While some of these proposals do seem to buck the current trend toward smaller government, it is important to note that recent economic and political developments have worked serious hardship on many Canadians in addition to leading to increased workplace conflict. It is also important to note that ideologically motivated cuts to government departments may already have contributed to death and illness (as in the case of Walkerton) and that further cuts could have a similar effect. Finally, it should be noted that a number of these proposals have already been put forward elsewhere and that most are of a fairly incremental nature.

With respect to the demographic crisis, there probably isn't a great deal that government or the other actors in the IR system can do, other than perhaps pay somewhat closer attention to demographic trends than they appear to have done so far. Two points *can* be made. At a time of growing skills shortages, recruitment and retention are obviously a priority for both private and public sector organizations. Providing employees with a reasonable degree of job security should help with both recruitment and retention. Few organizations wishing to attract and keep professionals

Figure 14.3

SOME KEY POLICY SUGGESTIONS AND ACTION PROPOSALS

- Introduce experience rating of EI premiums.
- Use tax incentives and legislation to reduce both overtime and regularly scheduled work hours.
- End exclusions from unionization rights of all groups other than management and confidential IR personnel.
- Implement the recommendations of the Fryer Committee and apply them to the broader public sector as a whole.
- Ensure that all public sector workers have access to meaningful dispute resolution systems.
- Establish a Royal Commission on public health and safety.

and others with scarce skills will be able to do so if the best they can offer them is a short-term contract, as has routinely been the case in the federal government (Auditor General, 2001).[6] As Jeffrey Pfeffer (1994) has noted, security of employment sends the signal that the organization is committed to its work force over the long term. Organizations seeking to prosper in an era of skill shortages need to ensure that they are sending that signal very clearly.

Growing skills shortages, together with the increasingly embattled position of Canada's public pension systems, make existing mandatory retirement policies look increasingly counterproductive. Such policies, in effect permitting employers to force employees to retire on reaching age 65, are now in place in Ontario and most other Canadian jurisdictions except Quebec and Manitoba (see Reid and Meltz, 2001:158). Many (including this author) would argue that such policies are discriminatory as such, and have no more place in a democratic society than policies that discriminate on the basis of race, gender, or religion. It should be noted that in a 1990 challenge to Ontario's mandatory retirement legislation, the Supreme Court of Canada agreed that the legislation violated the Charter since it constituted a form of age discrimination. However, the Court also said it was reasonable for the Ontario government to have passed the legislation because abolishing mandatory retirement could have far-reaching effects on the IR system (ibid.). Today, it would probably be truer to say that retaining mandatory retirement could have drastic effects on the IR (and public pension) system. Rather than forcing people to leave the work force (and thus start drawing on the public pension system), governments should be trying to think of strategies (such as phased retirement) to allow those who wish to keep on working to do so. A useful starting-point would be the abolition of all existing mandatory retirement legislation.

Turning to the economy, there are also limits to what governments, in particular, can do to increase job security. However, one measure the federal government might consider is fairly steep experience rating of EI premiums, which would mean that organizations laying off large numbers of workers would be forced to pay significantly higher premiums than other organizations. This in turn could help induce organizations to come up with more creative solutions to financial problems than wholesale layoffs.

In Chapter 2, we noted that many people are working far more hours than they would like to be, while others are working far fewer or in some cases none at all. Such a situation is bad for workers and their families, bad for the country and the economy as a whole, and not even very good for business in anything beyond the extremely short term. Government policy changes aimed at reducing the standard work week and reducing overtime are not a panacea, but could definitely help create and save jobs.

To begin with, governments could amend employment standards legislation to increase the premium that must be paid for overtime work (say, from the current 50 percent to 100 percent). Governments should also reduce the number of hours that must be worked before overtime must be paid—currently as high as 48 in some jurisdictions. In addition, all provinces should give workers the right to refuse over-time after putting in a standard week, a right currently available in only a few jurisdictions, and should set strict limits on the number of hours anyone can be made to work without a labour ministry permit.[7] Beyond that, employment standards legislation should be amended to allow anyone wishing to work shorter hours to do so at an equivalent reduction in pay (see Reid, 1997; Gunderson and Reid, 1998), and Canadian governments should start to follow the common European practice (see Peirce, 2000(b)) of granting tax concessions to firms that create or save jobs by reducing work hours.[8] The purpose of all these policy proposals is to provide employers with every possible incentive to hire additional workers to meet extra demand, rather than simply working existing staff longer and harder, as is now far too often the case.

As for access to meaningful representation, there are, once again, limits, particularly in such a harsh economic environment as the present one, to unions' ability to represent all those wishing such representation. The following handful of modest proposals may, however, be of some help. As we noted in the first edition, the outright exclusion of groups other than those whose *inclusion* would constitute a clear conflict of interest (i.e., management and confidential IR personnel) seems unconscionable. Apparently the Supreme Court of Canada agrees. In an 8–1 decision handed down in December of 2001, it struck down Ontario's longstanding exclusion of agricultural workers as a violation of the Charter's freedom of association provision. Particularly in the wake of this decision, the provinces should move quickly to end existing exclusions of agricultural workers, domestics, and professionals (see Chapter 8 for details as to the groups currently excluded). The exclusion of these and other groups from coverage under employment standards legislation should also be ended immediately.

Second, to facilitate the organization of homeworkers and other hard-to-organize workers, unions should be provided with their e-mail addresses and other necessary contact information to allow them to conduct organizing campaigns among such workers. The *Canada Labour Code* already includes a provision to this effect; now it is time for other jurisdictions to follow suit.

Third, the trend toward a mandatory certification vote is more than a little worrisome. Evidence from the U.S., where certification votes have long been required, suggests that where a vote is required, there is more opportunity for employers to influence the process, as by transferring or harassing union activists or by warning employees of the dangers of unionization. As a result, unions' success rate in certification drives is significantly lower where a vote is required (Weiler, 1983).

A cornerstone of Canadian IR policy has long been that the unionization decision should be the employees' alone to make. Opening the process to employer influence, as a vote seems inevitably to do, violates this important principle. In addition, the universal mandatory vote imposes a significant burden on already overtaxed labour boards. In our view, a vote is justified only where there is some evidence of tampering by one of the parties, or where a union is close enough to the 50 percent threshold that there is serious doubt as to whether the signed cards it has provided genuinely constitute majority support. Otherwise, certification through a count of signed membership cards should be the norm. Provinces now requiring a vote should amend their labour legislation to grant their labour boards discretion to certify unions on the basis of signed cards, as was the norm in Canada prior to the mid 1990s.

Fourth, and related to the certification issue, the "employer freedom to communicate" provisions now found in most jurisdictions seem to offer the potential of increased employer interference with unions. These provisions are of particular concern in the four jurisdictions that also require a vote for certification (Alberta, B.C., Nova Scotia, and Ontario) and in P.E.I., where communication around collective bargaining issues is specifically permitted. At a minimum, these provisions seem likely to increase union–management conflict in the workplace. In our view, they are inconsistent with the position, found in all Canadian labour relations acts known to the author, that employers should have no hand in the creation or operation of unions. For this reason if for no other, they should be abolished.

Fifth, all labour boards should have the power to certify a union with less than majority support where an unfair employer labour practice has clearly prevented employees' true wishes regarding unionization from becoming known. The 1998 change to the *Ontario Labour Relations Act* (see Adams, 1998) that removed this power from the labour board had the effect, at least in our opinion, of leaving that province's labour board without an effective remedy against unfair labour practices committed during certification drives. In our view, there was more than adequate protection for employers' interests in the old section 11(2) of the *OLRA*, which provided that a union would not be certified, even with majority support, when it had engaged in an unfair labour practice that had prevented employees' true wishes regarding certification from becoming known.

Finally, it is clear that unions themselves must broaden their focus if they are to survive in the current economic and political environment. In the previous chapter, we noted that increasingly in the developing world, the community rather than simply the workplace has become the focus for unionism and other types of collective worker action. Given many Canadian workers' lack of attachment to a particular job and workplace, the same could also be true in parts of Canada. Indeed, we would suggest that community unionism of the sort described by Carla Lipsig-Mumme (1995) may make a good deal of sense in some cases. A key focus of such unionization should be the development of new representative structures in which the union and community would share (Lipsig-Mumme, 1995:216). With such structures in place, workers who lost their jobs could continue to draw on the union for support, rather than being left totally isolated, as is now all too often the case. Moreover, as we also noted in the previous chapter, a community-based focus could increase organizing opportunities for private service sector workers and other hard-to-organize groups.

The ongoing crisis in the public sector has developed over many years and is the result of a variety of causes, including government cutbacks, a long-established pattern of adversarial industrial relations on the part of all parties, and government managers' lack of training in industrial relations, human resource management, and conflict resolution (see Fryer, 2000 and 2001). We believe that the recently released Fryer Report offers a good model for collaborative public sector labour relations. If implemented, it would lead to a public service dispute resolution system that, while recognizing the public interest, still manages to give the public service unions a chance to be heard. It would also lead to reduced designations and exclusions, an expanded scope of bargaining and consultation, a single redress process, and modernization and revamping of the *Public Service Staff Relations Act*.

The question now is whether the recommendations of the Fryer Report will be implemented. We believe they should be, because we believe that union–management tension will continue unless and until the public service unions are accepted as full partners in the government's day-to-day operations. However, despite the continuing high levels of labour–management conflict and growing recruitment and retention difficulties in the federal public service, it is still (as of late December 2001) not clear that the government possesses the political will to make more than cosmetic changes to its labour–management relations system.

We also believe that something like the Fryer model should be extended to the broader public sector, including health care and legislation, making due allowance for the different legislation governing different parts of the public sector. To a large extent, the problems found in the federal government labour–management relations system may be found throughout the public sector. The recent wave of strikes in health care and public transit is just one of the more dramatic manifestations of those problems.

A key issue at all levels is access to some kind of meaningful dispute resolution system. As we noted in Chapter 9, many different public sector groups do not enjoy the right to strike. It is imperative that groups which, for whatever reason, are unable to conduct meaningful strike action be given full access to binding arbitration. This includes both groups whose right to strike has been formally denied and groups that have had such a large proportion of their members designated as essential that strike action on their part is essentially futile. And if the arbitration process is to have any credibility with the parties, those chosen to arbitrate public sector disputes must be trained arbitrators and fully independent of the government. Equally important, governments must not attempt to influence arbitration outcomes by imposing "ability to pay" and other such criteria. Governments' failure to provide public sector workers with a meaningful dispute resolution system can only lead to further heightening of the already alarming levels of public sector labour–management conflict, and aggravation of the already serious recruitment and retention problems in many parts of the public sector.

As for health and safety, we noted earlier in the chapter that deep cuts at the Ontario environment ministry may have been one of the causes of the Walkerton tragedy. There is therefore good reason to be concerned that continuing public sector cutbacks could pose further threats to public health and safety. Of particular concern to us are the recently announced cuts in British Columbia's public service (B.C. Govt., 2001), which will result in a reduction of one-third of the public service over the next three years. The major purpose of these cuts appears to have been to finance the government's recently announced 25 percent across-the-board tax cuts (see ibid.). Unless the B.C. government started out seriously *overstaffed*, which no one has suggested was the case, it seems hard to believe that such deep cuts could not pose a serious threat to public health and safety.[9]

If legislatures can pass "balanced-budget" legislation, as a number have in recent years, then they should also be able to pass legislation requiring that services not be cut below a certain level. Canadian governments—federal and provincial alike—should also follow the lead of the French government (see Curry, 2001), which has made protection of the environment and the food supply priority areas.

Taken together, the various threats to public health and safety seem to us to have become so serious, and so varied, as to require concerted action. Now, while the memories of September 11 are still fresh, might be an appropriate time to strike a Royal Commission on Public Health and Safety. Such a commission should be charged with coming up with solutions that involve all stakeholders—employers, unions, community organizations, and individual citizens as well as governments. In coming up with solutions, the commission should think holistically, rather than isolating a particular aspect of the problem (airport security) as the government has tended to do in its responses to date.

Beyond that, the public sector unions will need to engage in intensive publicity campaigns to educate the public as to the very real threats to public health and safety posed by deep cuts in public sector cutbacks. As we noted in earlier chapters, many of those unions, including the Canadian Union of Public Employees (CUPE), the Public Service Alliance, and the Professional Institute of the Public Service of Canada, have already been engaging in these kinds of campaigns. Thus far, however, there seems to have been little attempt to link deep tax cuts to the threat to public safety—perhaps because the unions' members are among the beneficiaries of the tax cuts. If Canadian citizens are to be persuaded to pay for the continuing high levels of public service they have grown accustomed to, the next round of public sector union publicity campaigns will need to establish a clear link between excessive tax cuts and ongoing threats to public health and safety.

SUGGESTIONS FOR FURTHER RESEARCH

Both in this chapter and throughout the book as a whole, we have indicated various issues that seem to us in need of further research. The list below (see Figure 14.4), while by no means definitive, covers those areas where such research seems to us most urgent from a public policy perspective.

Given the prospect of skills shortages and of a growing drain on the pension system, governments and employers need to look for ways to help retain older workers and their institutional memory. Phased retirement and mentoring systems are two approaches that have already been tried. Research is needed to see how these

Figure 14.4

SOME KEY RESEARCH ISSUES

1) What are some ways to keep older workers with scarce skills on the job?

2) What are the main causes of the worldwide increase in precarious employment?

3) How can Canadian unions start focusing their efforts more at the community level?

4) How well have other countries maintained public sector workers' bargaining rights while proceeding with deficit and debt reduction?

5) What methods are other countries using to protect their food and water supplies and their environment?

and other possible approaches might work in practice.

The previous (comparative) chapter indicated that precarious employment has become a global problem. Given this fact, and given the huge impacts precarious employment has both on national economies and on individuals' quality of life, we believe that the problem needs to be tackled at the international level. In our view, an international body like the UN, in cooperation with international labour organizations such as the ILO, needs to examine in detail the causes for the recent increase in precarious employment. Then, on the basis of this examination, it needs to come up with concrete proposals for changes in the way economic and financial systems operate—changes that might reduce some of the most glaring economic disparities seen today, both within countries and between countries.

The comparative chapter also indicated that Canada has been far from alone in facing a crisis in its public sector. As Beaumont (1995:414) notes, the 1980s were a tough decade for the public sector in most advanced industrialized countries. The ILO study (1997) indicates that the 1990s were even tougher, not just in industrialized countries but particularly in developing ones, where structural adjustment programs imposed by international financial institutions led in many cases to deep cuts in public sector employment. More research is needed to determine whether other industrialized countries have been able to maintain public sector workers' basic bargaining rights better than Canada has in recent years, and, if so, by what means they have managed to ensure continuation of those rights.

With regard to representation, the comparative chapter indicated that unions in a number of countries have recently been taking more of a community-based approach to organizing. That chapter also looked at some of the growing number of cooperative ventures between unions in industrialized countries like Canada, and those in developing countries. Research is needed to determine to what extent a community-based focus might help Canadian unions expand, or at least hold their own in the face of an extremely adverse economic and political environment. The labour movement should also do research to determine what kinds of cooperative international ventures will best meet its members' needs, in addition to helping fellow union members in developing countries.

As for the issue of public health and safety, all of us have seen by now how security issues have been brought front and centre since the terrorist attacks of

September 11, 2001. A point we have tried to make throughout this chapter is that threats to public health and safety can come not just from knife-wielding terrorists on airplanes, but also from bacteria in our drinking water and diseases affecting our food supply. We also noted (see Curry, 2001) that France has made protection of its environment and food supply a priority. Research is needed to see how the French have done this, what the 'priority' designation means in practice, and what other advanced industrialized countries are doing to protect their food and water supplies and their environment.

The above list should be considered suggestive rather than definitive. No doubt many of you will by now have your own ideas as to where further research is most urgently needed. The one thing that can be said with certainty about the rapidly changing field of IR is that it offers almost limitless research opportunities for people of intelligence and imagination with an interest in public policy issues.

QUESTIONS FOR DISCUSSION

1) Do you agree with the author's choice of five key themes summarizing the main directions of Canadian IR today? If you do, which seem to you most important, and why? If you don't, what other themes would you prefer to see discussed?

2) Do you think Canadian union membership is likely to increase, decline, or stay about the same in the near future? What factors are most likely to lead it to increase or decrease, in your view?

3) Why is public health and safety such an important issue? What do *you* think governments, employers, unions, and ordinary citizens can do to make workplaces and communities safer?

4) Do you agree with the choice of issues for further research? If you don't, which issues seem to you most in need of research?

5) Overall, what would you say are some of the most important things you've learned from this book? If you plan to take further courses in this area, what would you like to learn from those courses?

SUGGESTION FOR FURTHER READING

Rose, Joseph, and Gary Chaison. 2001. "Unionism in Canada and the United States in the 21st Century: The Prospects for Revival." In *Relations Industrielles*, 56:1 (pp. 34–65). A very thorough examination of most of the key factors underlying potential union growth and decline in these two countries. The authors' prognosis for the labour movement is grim, particularly in the U.S.

ENDNOTES

Chapter 1

[1] One can learn a good deal about this insecurity by reading the so-called "GenX" fiction written by and (especially) aimed at people under 35. See, for example, Douglas Coupland's *Shampoo Planet*.

[2] This same definition has been usefully adopted by Adams (1993).

[3] On this point, see also Wood et al. (1975). For an even broader and more thought-provoking discussion of the ideas considered in this paragraph, see George Strauss, "Is IR Research Returning to Its Roots?" in *Perspectives on Work*, 3:1 (1999), pp. 59–60.

[4] For a useful discussion on the distinction between conflict over fundamental issues of principle and what might be described as "instrumental" conflict over issues like wages, see Kervin (1984).

[5] As is noted in more detail in Chapter 8 (labour law), the Supreme Court of Canada has recently come around to Beatty's point of view, at least with regard to Ontario's exclusion of agricultural workers.

[6] As we'll see in Chapter 8, Beatty's belief in the remedial powers of the Charter is shared by few other Canadian legal scholars or industrial relationists. However, the recent Supreme Court decision overturning Ontario's agricultural exclusion may perhaps win him some new allies.

[7] For a useful if brief discussion on Marxism and its application to industrial relations issues, see Godard (1994:36–45). I am indebted to Godard's discussion for much of the material in this paragraph.

[8] Much of the material in this paragraph has been drawn from Anderson et al. (1989).

[9] Readers should note that the term "political economy" is defined somewhat differently here than in Gunderson and Ponak (1995), who use the same term. Those authors don't have the equivalent of this book's reformist or Godard's liberal reformist perspective. Thus, Gunderson and Ponak's political economy perspective includes the work of many people whom Godard and the author would place in the reformist camp. The political economy perspective described in the first chapter of Gunderson, Ponak, and Taras (2001) is one of only two perspectives used there, and is in no way comparable to any of the five perspectives used in this book.

Chapter 2

[1] For example, the unemployment rate rose from 7.5% to 8.0% between November and December 2001 (Statistics Canada Daily, Jan. 29, 2001). Stat Canada's Jan. 11, 2002 analysis of its December 2001 Labour Force Survey indicated that part-time unemployment rose during the year 2001, while full-time employment fell.

[2] O'Hara (1993:37) estimates that "one fifth of Canada's student population is in school under duress." On page 38, he suggests that if involuntary university students were taken into account, the national unemployment rate would increase by 1 percent.

[3] An approach taken by some organizations is to have older workers mentor younger ones. In this capacity, they have the opportunity to use their hard-earned organizational knowledge.

[4] This discussion of women in the labour force is, of necessity, confined to women 25 and over since data for workers 15 to 24 aren't broken down by sex.

[5] In the federal public service, issues of this type make up a large share of unions' collective bargaining agendas.

[6] For a discussion from a slightly different perspective, see Godard (1994:422).

[7] This provision was in force in Ontario's labour relations act until the 1992 NDP government revisions.

[8] This may also be the case when work is done by outside contractors rather than by employees.

[9] In the federal public service, benefits like sick leave aren't provided for contracts of less than six months' duration.

[10] Such as the right to bargain collectively or to strike.

[11] EI regulations allow recipients to retain up to 25 percent of their benefits in earnings. Earnings above that threshold are deducted from the recipient's benefits.

[12] For an example of this kind of discussion, see the discussion of the "natural rate of unemployment" (NAIRU rate) in Reid and Meltz (2001:167–9).

[13] Here and elsewhere in the chapter, the term "unemployment rate" refers to the standard official measure labelled R4 by Statistics Canada, except as noted otherwise.

[14] The American epidemiologist Harvey Brenner has produced a sizeable body of work relating increases in national unemployment levels to increase in murder and other crimes, liver cirrhosis, and physical and mental hospitalization. For examples, see Brenner (1973) and Carrothers (1979:39). In addition, as Carrothers points out (1979:38), loss of employment, particularly over a long term, can lead to a serious lack of self-esteem both for the unemployed worker and for his or her immediate family and friends.

[15] B.C. has had double-digit unemployment in 9 of the past 20 years (see Table 2.4).

[16] During the 1982 to 1983 recession, the rate was 92 percent since at that time UI benefits were 60 percent of the normal wage.

Chapter 3

[1] The exclusion of management from IR textbooks and courses may, in part, have been a matter of academic turfsmanship, given that IR courses were frequently offered by economics departments and sometimes even combined with labour economics courses. (The Reynolds text cited earlier is designed for just such a split course.)

[2] The 2001 Ottawa-Hull "Yellow Pages" lists eight firms specializing in this area.

[3] In Canada, these trends appear to have been somewhat less pronounced. Godard (1994) does not offer evidence on productivity. However, his chart (p. 95) shows a significant reduction in strike intensity and in union membership rates, but not in the actual number of union members, during the decade. Of course, it may well be that welfare capitalism was less widely adopted in Canada than in the United States. Further research is needed in this area.

[4] Hunnicutt notes that New Deal era investigators looking into conditions in Southern textile plants in the early 1930s found widespread use of child labour and work weeks of 50 to 60 hours.

[5] Except as otherwise noted, this section is based entirely on the Kochan et al. (1984) article.

[6] For a useful if brief discussion of the now-famous Michelin Bill, see Anderson. (1989a: 221).

[7] The shrinking of IR departments, which as noted in the text tend to contain the group of managers most strongly committed to collective bargaining and union acceptance, may indirectly have had a similar effect.

[8] Two important issues arise, however, in connection with the recent survey data cited by such researchers as Thompson and Godard. First, are employers telling the truth? Many might consider it in their interest to profess a moderate attitude while behaving differently. Hence the weakness of questions addressing attitude. At a minimum, such questions would need to be supplemented by behavioural measures of various kinds. Second, are the employers surveyed by Thompson and Godard (and, in particular, responding to the surveys) representative of Canadian employers as a whole? The survey design described by Thompson suggests a strong "bias" in favour of large firms and firms in manufacturing industries, both of which might be expected to be less militantly opposed to unions than smaller firms and firms in service-related industries. We would also expect better-practice firms to be likelier to respond to such surveys than poorer-practice firms, since the latter would presumably be more apt to have "something to hide."

[9] This point is very much worth considering in connection with the 1985 breakaway of the Canadian Auto Workers from its parent American union. The breakaway is frequently ascribed to Canadian workers' greater militancy. We would argue that CAW leaders simply engaged in some quite rational calculation, saw that they could do far better by Canadian members in a separate Canadian environment, and acted accordingly. Whether Canadian workers are possessed of inherent traits making them "tougher" than their American counterparts seems quite beside the point.

[10] One important exception is the Maple Leaf Food Company agreement referred to in the first edition of this book (p. 139). In that case, United Food and Commercial Workers union members narrowly approved a deal that saw average wages reduced by more than 40%, after it became clear to them that the North American Free Trade Agreement had left Canadian pork producers unable to compete with lower-priced producers in the U.S. and Mexico. The Maple Leaf agreement, ratified in early 1998, doesn't appear to have been widely replicated elsewhere in the Canadian economy.

[11] Betcherman defines 'traditional' firms as those that have adopted fewer than four of the following innovations: formal communications or information-sharing systems, team-based work, formal training, employee involvement systems, and variable compensation.

Chapter 4

[1] As noted by Heron (1989:13), similar legislation was passed by the Canada West legislature in 1847.

[2] As noted by Morton and Copp (1980:34), the revised act excluded workers in positions involving public safety, such as gas and water and railway strikes. These workers still had no legal right to strike.

[3] Since the First World War, Berlin has been known as Kitchener.

[4] In fairness, Gompers' dislike of dual unions was not without cause. In 1885, according to Morton and Copp (1980:58), his own Cigar Markers Union had been undercut in a strike by the Knights, who had imposed their own rival union label.

[5] This contention seems logical enough, given that Canada was the last major western industrialized country to grant its workers collective bargaining rights.

[6] As Morton (1995:138) notes, the nickname is somewhat ironic, given that the plan was invented by none other than Canada's own Mackenzie King, during his stint as labour consultant to the Rockefellers.

[7] As Boivin (1982:437) notes, between 1915 and 1936, the Catholic unions accounted for only nine, or less than 2 percent, of the strikes officially called in Quebec.

[8] That is, 11 private sector jurisdictions. When the various public sector jurisdictions are taken into account, the number becomes several times that.

[9] In 1931 alone, according to White, there were more than 7000 deportations. Between 1903–1928, deportations had averaged slightly more than 1000 per year.

[10] Domestics and farm workers were excluded, as was management.

[11] On early postwar Atlantic labour law, see Forsey (1985). On Alberta's law, see Finkel (1986).

[12] I am indebted to Forrest (1997) for many of the ideas contained in this paragraph.

[13] See Morton and Copp (1989:233–234). In 1959, these disclosures would lead to the passage of the *Landrum-Griffin Act*, which imposed substantial restrictions on unions' internal operations with an eye to preventing further union racketeering.

[14] Through 1985 (Peirce, 1987:69), the Canada Labour Relations Board had accepted only 1 of 25 technological change applications brought before it under the federal legislation.

[15] On a similar note, see Crispo (1982).

[16] For much of this discussion, I'm indebted to Heron (1989:103–104).

[17] As readers will recall from the discussion of alternative measures of unemployment in Chapter 2, the numbers of workers and families affected by unemployment during any given year would have been far higher.

[18] The NDP did win one Ontario seat in the 2000 federal election, in a Windsor-area riding.

[19] This challenge appears even more daunting than before, now that the NDP has been crushed by the Liberals in B.C. and reduced to a minority government in its long-time stronghold, Saskatchewan.

Chapter 5

[1] In Canada, union density is normally defined as the percentage of paid non-agricultural workers belonging to unions. A rationale for excluding agricultural workers from the union density "denominator" is that such workers have often been excluded from unionization and in any case seldom join. However, as Murray (1995:162) points out, this rationale is not entirely consistent since members of other groups excluded from unionization rights, such as managers and confidential IR personnel, are counted as part of that denominator.

[2] Except as otherwise noted, the source for current union membership information in this section is Akyeampong (2001).

[3] Aggregate union membership rates used in this book are generally higher than the disaggregated rates drawn from Akyeampong's Labour Force survey data. In note 1 of his 1997 article, Akyeampong explains the difference as follows: "CALURA density rates in the construction industry in particular have traditionally been higher than those captured by household surveys like the Labour Force Survey, mainly because CALURA union membership includes both the unemployed and retired, and the household surveys do not." For this reason, provincial union density rates cited in Figure 5.2 appear to have fallen more sharply than they actually have, since the 1991 provincial union density data were drawn from CALURA, whereas the 2001 data were drawn from the Labour Force Survey. The overall situation regarding union membership data is far from satisfactory, but no better solution than using HRDC data for aggregate rates and Statistics Canada data for disaggregated rates seemed to be available at the time of writing.

[4] See note 2.

[5] For a more detailed look at legislative provisions and their effect on union growth, see Ng (1992) and Martinello (1996).

[6] The four NDP or PQ governments in provinces with above average density levels served for at least 10 years.

[7] The data contained in Table 5.2 do not provide anything approaching a complete breakdown by industry group; however, these were the only 2001 data available at the time of writing.

[8] In the United States, private sector labour legislation is under federal jurisdiction.

[9] In fairness, Meany's successors, Lane Kirkland and more recently John Sweeney, have given considerable attention to organizing (on Kirkland, see Winpisinger, 1989). However, by the 1980s, years of benign or not-so-benign neglect had left the American labour movement in such a weakened condition that many unions lacked the money and the people to mount effective organizing campaigns and instead made a conscious decision to devote their resources to protecting the interests of existing members (Chaison and Rose, 1991). For a more detailed discussion, see Lipsig-Mumme (1989).

[10] At least to a certain extent, Troy's arguments appear to have been accepted by Coates (1992).

[11] In Sweden, bargaining was conducted at the national level from the 1950s through the mid 1980s. After several years of shifting back and forth, bargaining was moved to the industry level for 1993 (Hammarstrom, 1993).

[12] For an interesting and useful discussion covering a number of the issues addressed in this section, see Chaison (1997).

[13] Specific tactics are more often planned by the local's negotiating committee. However, the negotiating committee must make sure it is in sync with the general membership's wishes, or it will have an extremely difficult time arriving at an agreement that the membership is willing to ratify.

[14] In the case of university professors, it should be noted that the profession's national organization, the Canadian Association of University Teachers, provides at least some of the same services that a labour federation would.

[15] Similar political functions are carried out by provincial labour federations in provincial capitals.

[16] Environmental issues, most of which involve multiple stakeholders, offer an excellent example of how the labour movement can put its specialized expertise (in this case, knowledge of negotiating strategy) to use in other public forums. In recent years, a special type of bargaining, known as multilateral negotiation, has evolved to address such environment-related issues as native land claims and cleanup of toxic waste sites.

[17] Rose (1995:21) cites one study that estimates that there were about 40 000 Canadian public sector union members in 1946. As Table 5.1 shows, this figure would have comprised less than 5 percent of all Canadian members at the time.

[18] Godard (1994:240) has noted that some local leaders have gone to the extent of offering door prizes or arranging social events after meetings in their bids to increase attendance. Elsewhere, this author has heard of unions that served wine and cheese at the meetings to try to get more members to turn out.

19 Inadequate child care is often cited in the literature as a factor explaining women's low attendance at union meetings and the low proportion of union officers who are women. Holding union meetings during working hours would appear to be an excellent solution, if this could be negotiated with the employer.

20 At least one union to which this author has belonged sent out monthly mailings soliciting members' opinions on a variety of issues. While it may be that the union would have achieved a higher response rate with e-mail than it did with its print questionnaires, the basic principle was a good one. Here again, with "hard copy" mailings as with meetings, there is all too frequently the problem of overload.

21 On the other hand, a close election may make an incumbent executive unduly conservative and fearful of pursuing new initiatives, particularly those involving cooperation with management. Such an executive may find it necessary to put up a show of toughness in a bid to shore up sagging support.

22 It is instructive to remember that a 1902 AFL convention saw a full 46 percent of the delegates voting in favour of a motion advocating socialism and cooperative industrial democracy, and that a decade later, a socialist candidate opposed Gompers for the federation presidency and won a full one-third of the vote. (Galenson and Smith, 1978:51).

23 See Lipsig-Mumme (1989) for a much more detailed discussion of these points from a strategic choice perspective.

Chapter 6

1 For a useful if brief discussion of the Webbs, see Craig and Solomon, (1996:76–80).

2 For a useful overview of the key issues here, see Verma (1995).

3 And for managers trained to distrust unions, as well; however, this is not the focus of the present chapter.

4 Anil Verma tends to fall into this camp, although less so in his 1995 and 2001 Gunderson and Ponak chapters than in many of his earlier works, such as the 1987 and 1989 articles cited in the reference list. With some reservations, Lemelin (1989) also takes this position.

5 It is generally accepted throughout the industrial relations literature that the union must be involved as a full partner in any joint cooperation schemes if the schemes are to succeed. For a classic and still very useful statement, see Kochan (1979, quoted in Downie, 1982). Another useful list can be found in Lemelin (1989).

6 In an eerie echo of the 1970s, the Public Service Alliance, in August 2001, withdrew from all consultative bodies as a protest against the federal government's failure to offer its members better contract terms. It rejoined those bodies once it had signed new collective agreements with the government.

7 In British Columbia, the Social Credit government in 1984 instituted the requirement of a certification vote (Craig and Solomon, 1993:145). That requirement was removed by an NDP government in 1992 (Craig and Solomon, 1993:215), but then reinstated by a new Liberal government elected in 2001.

8 This strike was described in detail in the first edition of this book at pp. 445–446.

9 In connection with this point, however, it must be noted that when your adversary is the government itself, only a secondary boycott is possible; no one can realistically boycott a government (other than, perhaps, by leaving the province or country in question).

[10] For an interesting and much more detailed discussion of the issues raised in this paragraph, see Godard (1994:210–221). An equally interesting discussion from a quite different perspective may be found in Reynolds (1982:492–498).

[11] These problems raise technical statistical issues that in this author's view are far too complex to be discussed in an introductory industrial relations textbook. Students with an extensive background in labour economics and statistics who wish to pursue these issues further will find useful discussions in Gunderson and Riddell (1993:388–397) and Gunderson and Hyatt (1995:322–324).

[12] In Canada, the impact of collective agreement coverage is a reasonably good approximation for a union wage impact, since there aren't many non-unionized workers covered by a collective agreement, except to some extent in Quebec (see Akyeampong, 2000).

[13] To Gunderson and Hyatt (2001:393), this finding is surprising. To us, it is far from surprising. Union membership rates are so much higher in the public than in the private sector that in Canada, in the former, unionized status is basically the norm. Moreover, as in the federal government, where excluded workers often receive the same salary and benefits as their unionized counterparts, it is often the case that the benefits of unionization in the public sector spill over into the non-unionized part of that sector.

[14] For a useful discussion around some of these points, see Godard (1994:217–219).

[15] For most of the material in this paragraph, I am indebted to Gunderson and Hyatt (1995:318–322) and to Gunderson's discussion in the previous (1989) edition of the book, pp. 353–356. Some use has also been made of Murray (1995:184–190).

[16] This author has observed this same attitude in his industrial relations students, many of whom have been local union activists.

Chapter 7

[1] It is not strictly accurate to say all workers are covered by EL. Certain groups are excluded in some jurisdictions. However, fewer workers and groups are excluded from EL coverage than from labour relations legislation coverage.

[2] For an interesting and very thoughtful critique of this aspect of collective bargaining, see Beatty (1983).

[3] On the extent of federal jurisdiction in labour relations and employment standards law, see HRDC, 2001 (b).

[4] In a survey of one of his introductory IR classes, the author found that 40 percent of the students had at one time or another been asked to include a photo on a job application form.

[5] The term "work standards" legislation has been used here to avoid possible confusion between "employment standards legislation" and "employment legislation," the term used to describe all the different types of legislation discussed in this chapter. It should be noted, however, that the term "employment standards" legislation is often used for this purpose. For example, the federal Human Resources Department uses it to describe the legislation outlined in Table 7.1.

[6] Except as otherwise noted, the source for all information in the work standards legislation section is HRDC, 2001 (a). Some reference has also been made to the revised (2000) Ontario *Employment Standards Act*.

[7] Adams' article, which first appeared in *Relations Industrielles*, 42, is quoted at length in LLCG (1991:980–992).

[8] For very senior people, especially those in a financial portfolio, contracts may even stipulate that employees cannot solicit the employer's customers for a given period after they have left the employer's service.

[9] *Baker v. Burns Foods Ltd.* (1977), 74 D.L.R. (3rd) 762 (Man. C.A., Matas J.A.) at 763–4, quoted in LLCG (1991:2-88 through 2-90).

[10] *Reber v. Lloyds Bank International Canada* (1984), 52 B.C. L.R. 90 (B.C.S.C., Mackoff J.) at 92–96, rev'd (1985), 7 C.E.E.L. 98 (B.C.C.A., Esson J.A.), quoted in LLCG (1991:2-90 through 2-92).

[11] As noted by McPhillips and England (1989:50), "salary" normally includes any fringe benefits the employee would have received had she or he remained on payroll.

[12] *Bardal v. The Globe & Mail Ltd.* (1960), 24 D.L.R. (2nd) 140 (Ont. H.C., McRuer C.J.H.C.) at 141–7, quoted in LLCG (1991:2-129 through 2-131).

[13] It should be noted that these findings do not please Eden, a critic of the whole notion of progressive discipline. For her detailed critique of this system of industrial justice, see (1992), "Progressive discipline: An oxymoron," *Relations Industrielles*, 47(3).

[14] Except for those below the minimum working age or over 65.

[15] Except as otherwise noted, all information on human rights legislative provisions has been drawn from this source.

[16] See the case of *Cashin vs. CBC*, (1986) 7 CHRR D/3203 [Nov. 25, 1985]. In this case, Roseanne Cashin, a CBC Radio reporter working in Newfoundland did not have her contract renewed after her husband, a well-known local union activist and political figure, was named to the board of Petro-Canada. CBC's position was that it would be perceived Ms. Cashin would lack objectivity in her reporting. However, the Human Rights Tribunal disagreed, and eventually, after a series of court cases, the Tribunal's decision was reinstated by the Federal Court of Appeal. For a brief discussion of this interesting case, see McPhillips (2001:226).

[17] (1986) 9 CEEL 135.

[18] *Alberta Human Rights Commission vs. Central Alberta Dairy Pool* (1990), 90 C.L.L.C. para. 17.025 (S.C.C.).

[19] *Hinds vs. Canada Employment and Immigration Commission* (1988), 10 CHRR 015683 (Can. Hum. Rights Tribunal).

[20] This amount may seem very small. However, under the federal act, the maximum amount an individual can receive in punitive damages was (and still is) $5000.

[21] See Beatty (1983) for a useful critique of traditional mandatory retirement policies and an elegant partial solution, which would impose mandatory retirement not at a given age, but after a given number of years of service.

[22] All the federal government agreements the author has worked with during his time at the Professional Institute contain specific prohibitions against sexual harassment, in addition to anti-discrimination clauses.

[23] Here, "fair representation" is based on a comparison reflecting the minority group's representation in either the Canadian work force as a whole or the segment of the Canadian work force from which the employer would logically hire new employees (i.e., the local labour pool).

[24] Implicitly, this language once again suggests the notion of the duty to accommodate.

[25] In this connection, I cannot help thinking of the gas station employee I once saw sitting on the top of one of the station's gas pumps, smoking.

[26] In Alberta and Prince Edward Island, such committees are set up at the discretion of the minister (McPhillips and England, 1995).

[27] Ontario's act was not the first providing for committees. In 1972 (Swinton, 1983), Saskatchewan's comprehensive *Occupational Health Act* provided for them. Earlier, a number of unions had obtained such committees through the collective bargaining process, and Canadian Labour Congress policy had stated that joint committees should be a cornerstone of occupational health and safety programs.

[28] Both must do so under the *Canada Code*.

[29] As various commentators note, it remains difficult to prove a relationship in the latter case. See, for example, CCH (1998c, 15, 406).

[30] The question here, of course, is the extent to which such an 'agreement' should be considered voluntary, particularly for relatively unskilled workers, immigrants, older women, people with disabilities, and other non-unionized workers with little labour market power. Where does persuasion end and duress begin in such cases?

[31] The workers' compensation board was renamed the Workplace Safety and Insurance Board, effective January 1, 1998.

[32] See Quebec's *Rioux* case and Ontario's *Vogue Shoes* case, discussed in Zwerling (1997:642–3 and 627–32), where two women were discharged solely on this basis. In connection with obesity cases, it would be interesting to see if (as one suspects) this basis for discrimination is used far more often against women than against men. If so, such discrimination might itself be a possible basis for Charter action.

Chapter 8

[1] In the Philippines, for example, as noted by Jimenez (1993:233), a major cause of increased strike activity during the 1960s was management's unwillingness to recognize unions or bargain with them.

[2] In Sweden (Hammarstrom, 1993), basic bargaining rights were achieved in 1906. In Denmark and in Australia, recognition came even earlier, in 1899 and 1904, respectively (Scheuer, 1992; Davis and Lansbury, 1993). In the United States, recognition came in 1935 (Carter, 1995).

[3] As Morton notes, railway workers and others in positions where public safety was involved were excluded from the amended act's protection. The exclusion thus set in motion the beginnings of the pattern of differential regulation of private and public sector workers still in effect in most of Canada today.

[4] The bill's official title is the *National Labor Relations Act*; however, it is usually referred to as the *Wagner Act* in honour of its main drafter, Senator Robert Wagner of New York.

[5] Since 1994, Ontario's provincial government employees have had the right to strike.

[6] On this point, see the *Lavigne* case, involving an Ontario community college instructor who did not like the fact that his union was using his dues for political causes with which he disagreed. The Supreme Court ruled in favour of the union, declaring that the union's freedom to spend dues for the collective good of the membership constituted a reasonable limitation on the Charter's freedom of association provision. For a more detailed discussion, see Swinton (1995:66–8).

7 Under the "laboratory of democracy" argument from political science implicitly advanced by Carter (1995:56), provinces or states are more likely to introduce legislative innovations than national governments because the risk in introducing the innovations at this lower level is far less. The "laboratory of democracy" argument also suggests that successful experiments will spread to other jurisdictions, as has indeed been the case in Canada. Some of Weiler's innovations, such as the use of grievance mediation in connection with expedited arbitration, have since spread to several other provinces.

8 Significantly, Saskatchewan, the one province that adopted a more or less 'pure' Wagner model, did not initially require grievance arbitration, changing its law to do so only in 1994.

9 The *OLRA's* provision refers only to employers.

10 In jurisdictions using a simple card count, employer interference would be less of an issue and the need for a quick vote less compelling.

11 In Ontario, the application must be made during the last three months of agreements of three years or less. For longer agreements, the application must be made during the last three months of the agreement's third and subsequent years (*OLRA*, section 63[2]).

12 This provision also applies to employers who might be trying to persuade employees not to join. One suspects, however, that it is aimed primarily at unions. Note that employer free speech provisions such as *OLRA*, sec. 70, would appear to conflict with this provision—unless one assumes that employers contact employees only at their homes after working hours.

13 Had Table 8.1 been prepared while Ontario's NDP government was still in power, that province would have had five liberal laws and one moderately liberal one. One of the Conservative government's first acts on taking over from the NDP in 1995 was to amend the labour relations act by restoring professional exclusions removed by the NDP and changing the certification procedure from a card count to a vote.

14 At least up until December 2001 and the Supreme Court ruling on Ontario's agricultural exclusion, discussed later in the section.

15 See Peirce (1989) for a more detailed discussion of the points raised in this paragraph.

16 Thompson (1982:385) suggested that the professional exclusions then in force in five jurisdictions were "clearly exceptional," and that those provinces would likely "join the national pattern" in time. Given that over the past 15 years, there has been no lasting change—Ontario dropped its professional exclusions in 1992 only to re-insert them in 1995—his forecast would seem to have been optimistic, to put it mildly.

17 See Beatty (1983) for an interesting and quite philosophical discussion of this exclusion, and of the philosophy behind Canadian exclusion policies more generally.

18 *Dunmore v. Attorney General of Ontario* (2001 SCC 94).

19 The language of the Supreme Court's ruling in the Ontario case (discussed later in the chapter) suggests that these narrower exclusions would probably survive a Charter challenge.

20 According to information contained in Akyeampong (2001), 61% of union members and a full two-thirds (67%) of employees live in provinces requiring a vote for union certification.

21 Quebec's anti-scab bill, discussed in the text above, was brought in following a picket-line incident that led to loss of life.

22 In this connection, the linguistic vagueness of many of the provisions is quite troubling. For example, what constitutes "undue" influence over employees? How can a labour board distinguish between reasonable and "undue" influence? And what constitutes a "fact or opinion reasonably held" under the B.C. legislation?

23 Several labour lawyers with whom the author has talked regarding this matter indicate that this is in fact the case. As well, the discussion in Godard (1994:296) strongly implies that this is the case, since the discussion does not mention any specific legislative provisions. For a more detailed discussion, see LLCG (1984:3–62 through 3–64).

24 See Boivin and Déom (1995) for a detailed account of how an industry goes about obtaining a decree.

25 Again, see Boivin and Déom (1995) for a more detailed look at construction bargaining arrangements.

26 In Ontario (*OLRA*, section 104[1–2]), these can go up to $2000 per day for an individual and $25 000 per day for a corporation or union.

27 As Godard notes (1994:297), in British Columbia, even this function has been assumed by the Labour Relations Board. It is not clear to this writer why more provinces haven't followed B.C.'s enlightened lead. Having all labour-related matters including picketing administered by a single tribunal would seem to be both more consistent and more efficient.

Chapter 9

1 As noted by Fryer (1995:355), in 1994 the Prince Edward Island government unilaterally rolled back public sector pay by 8.5 percent. Such a reduction amounts to roughly one month's pay per year, in a province where pay levels already lag behind those in most of the rest of Canada.

2 In principle, employees of government enterprises should be included in any count of public sector workers; however, the author has found it impossible to obtain accurate data as to the number of government enterprise employees in Canada. The number of public sector workers does not, therefore, include these employees.

3 In principle, the public sector also includes the employees of government enterprises such as the CBC and Ontario Hydro (through 2001). However, data on the number of government enterprise employees are not available, and therefore they have not been included for purposes of this discussion.

4 See Peirce (1989) for a more detailed discussion.

5 Rose (1995:21) notes that as of 1945, there were about 40 000 public sector union members, or roughly 5 percent of the country's total union membership. Almost certainly most would have been outside municipal workers, who faced less daunting legal obstacles to unionization partly because municipal workers have always been covered by general labour acts rather than by special, and generally more restrictive, public sector legislation. For a more detailed discussion of the evolution of municipal collective bargaining, see Graham (1995:181–183).

6 For a very thoughtful discussion of the NJC, see L.W.C.S. Barnes, *Consult and Advise: A History of the National Joint Council of the Public Service of Canada* (Kingston: Queen's IRC Press, 1975).

7 This structure has since been simplified considerably. The largest public service union, the Public Service Alliance of Canada (PSAC) now negotiates with the government at five bargaining tables.

8 In 1994, Ontario passed a new public service employment act granting its employees the right to strike (Fryer, 1995:346).

9 Between 1965 and 1974 (Ponak and Thompson, 1995:440), back-to-work legislation was invoked 12 times, or just slightly more than once a year. Six of the 12 back-to-work laws were in Quebec.

10 For a useful discussion of this change of attitude, see Godard (1994:262–263).

11 For as long as Bill 19 remained in effect. When an NDP government replaced Vander Zalm's Socreds in 1991, one of its first acts was to repeal this bill and the Compensation Stabilization program that had frozen public sector wages since 1982 (Craig and Solomon, 1996:365). The new government also did away with Bill 19's sweeping definition of essential services and replaced it with more limited essential services legislation roughly comparable to the Quebec legislation described earlier in the chapter (Craig and Solomon, 1996:235).

12 In other words, if federal government employees received a 1 percent wage increase, 1 percent of them would have to be laid off.

13 Throughout the Mulroney years, cabinet members, Commons committee heads, and Conservative MPs frequently attacked public servants and other public employees in the press. In a particularly notable attack, Commons Finance Committee chair Don Blenkarn said that after Ottawa voters turned out several Conservative MPs in favour of Liberals in the 1988 federal election, public servants should be prepared to take what was coming to them.

14 A 'socialist' feature of this legislation was that those earning less than $30 000 per year were exempted.

15 Initially, the Klein government sought to eliminate taxing authority for all boards. It backed down following a threatened constitutional challenge by the Catholic boards (Thomason, 1995:280).

16 In January 1999, the province's health care support employees were embroiled in a dispute with the hospital associations. After staging a one-day strike during the first week of January, CUPE (the union representing the health care workers) agreed to return to the bargaining table and not to stage any more strikes (CBC Radio News, January 10, 1999).

17 Fryer (2000:10) notes that the largest of these claims, by the Public Service Alliance, was for nearly $3.5 billion. This claim was settled after a Federal Court of Appeal decision favouring the union position. It should be noted that the pay equity issue remains a 'live' one for separate employers and agencies for whom no determination or settlement has been made.

18 In subsequent changes to the *PSSRA*, this number was reduced to 26 (Swimmer, 1995:390–391).

19 Whatever the merits of any Charter-based challenges to statutory designation of public sector bargaining agents, such designation appears to violate a key principle of Canadian labour legislation, namely that the employer should have no hand in the formation or operation of a union. Since government is ultimately the employer of all public sector workers, especially public servants, statutory designation of the bargaining agent amounts to its choosing which union will represent its workers. Somewhat similar provisions do exist in a few private sector labour acts; for example, Quebec's construction act (discussed in the previous chapter) specifies that construction workers must belong to one of five duly recognized associations.

20 The restriction on bargaining over pensions applies not just to federal and provincial government employees, but also to many municipal employees, teachers, and health care workers (Thompson and Ponak, 1995:431).

21 Among the most telling criticisms of "ability to pay" listed by Sack (1991) is the last of the seven he lists: that arbitrators are not in a position to measure public sector employers' ability to pay.

22 *CUPE vs.Ontario (Min. of Labour) (1999)*, 117 O.A.C. 340 (Div. Ct.).

23 As the Lancaster discussion of the case quoted here points out, Nova Scotia's registered

nurses were the most poorly paid in Canada prior to the award, a situation that was attracting recruiters from other provinces and the U.S. and had already induced some nurses to leave.

[24] For a fascinating if sometimes horrifying first-hand account of a controlled hospital strike in Vancouver, see Weiler (1980).

[25] As Craig and Solomon (1996:315–316) note, the government of Quebec has long refused to submit most disputes in the public and parapublic sectors to arbitration for just this reason.

[26] The committee's official name was the Advisory Committee on Labour Management Relations in the Federal Public Service. However, it was generally referred to as the Fryer Committee, and in the interest largely of economy, I have stuck to that tradition here.

[27] This tripartite body, modelled closely after a recommendation in the 1968 Woods Commission report, should not in any way be confused with the abortive Dispute Resolution proposed earlier by the Ontario government. As the Fyrer Committee notes (2001:32-37), such a commission should be chaired by an individual with a national reputation in public sector labour relations. He or she would be supported by union, management, and neutral members, all of whom would have significant experience in the field.

Chapter 10

[1] As Anderson (1989:212) notes, both must agree to the combination of certification units into a negotiation unit for a binding collective agreement to be signed.

[2] For a perceptive and thoughtful critique of the Ontario board's prevailing practice through the mid 1980s, see Forrest (1986), especially pages 846–847.

[3] Similarly, as Rogow notes, union leaders may favour centralized bargaining arrangements even at times when such arrangements are not in the union's economic interest, because of their philosophical belief that such arrangements can better promote worker solidarity than more "individualistic" decentralized ones.

[4] Through most of the postwar period, the "Big Four" tire manufacturers accounted for 85 percent of industry sales (Kochan, McKersie, and Cappelli, 1984:31).

[5] For a very useful overview of these developments, see Ferner and Hyman (1992b), especially pages xx–xxii.

[6] See Mishel (1986) for a useful discussion on the interaction between bargaining structure and economic conditions.

[7] It is not likely that centralized systems would have such an effect in bad times. In connection with this point, it should be noted that most of Tarantelli's data were compiled prior to the major recession of 1981–1983. At the same time, it should also be noted that inflation is generally of far less concern in bad times than in good.

[8] Centralized systems have also been associated with lower levels of unemployment (Tarantelli, 1986). For one thing, the social democratic governments under which such systems are adopted have tended to follow full-employment policies as a matter of principle. For another, the political bargaining in which these governments often engage with labour movements often leads to trade-offs, like the Swedish active labour market policy (Hammarstrom, 1993:200), which in turn have led to full employment guarantees in return for the unions' pledge to restrain wage demands and in some cases strike activity.

[9] A notable exception here was the Canada Post dispute in 1997, when, as we note in Chapter 12, management negotiator Jean Lafleur shoved union negotiator Phillipe Arbour to the floor as the latter attempted to enter a management hotel suite in Hull. The incident did little to improve the flow of negotiations or win public support for the corporation. It also led to Lafleur's immediate replacement as chief management negotiator.

10 As we noted in Chapter 9, intraorganizational bargaining tends to be particularly complex in the public sector, where organizations may receive funding from several different sources. An excellent example of intraorganizational conflict in practice appears in the "Bridgetown Manufacturing Company" case in Craig and Solomon (1996:501–505).

11 Godard's original wording is "strike" rather than work stoppage. However, management could presumably impose such costs through a lockout as well as a strike—hence the use of the broader term here.

12 The closest analogy the author can come up with (with apologies to readers who are not cooks) is that of preparing a cream or béchamel sauce. Such sauces seem to take an eternity to thicken, but then do so almost instantaneously. Also (another key element of the analogy), if it is not diligently attended to at the precise moment it is ready, the sauce will be ruined.

13 If one's business is export-oriented, this may entail monitoring ongoing political developments and trade policies in the countries to whom one is primarily interested in exporting.

14 Human Resources Development Canada puts out a number of publications listing various wage settlements, as do a number of provincial labour departments.

15 On at least two occasions known to the author, attendance was in excess of 50 percent of the organization's total membership, a particularly remarkable achievement given that on both those occasions, the meetings were held during the summer when a fair number of members were out of town.

16 Teams may wish to modify this rule in classroom simulations where peer evaluation is in effect, as it most often is, to prevent the chief negotiator from being at an unfair advantage when peer grades are being handed out. One way to do this is for the chief negotiator to assign all team members to speak on given issues or at certain times. Another is simply to ensure that all are given roles that give them plenty of useful work to do, and to ensure as well that each team member's contribution is duly noted in the introduction to any reports that are handed in to the instructor before or after the simulation.

17 Named for one Lemuel Boulware, vice-president of General Electric during the 1950s, who regularly took this approach to collective bargaining.

18 In connection with this general point, it may be relevant to note that Kervin (1989:203) suggests that negotiators are generally more tolerant of early hostile moves, which they view as "just part of the ritual" of negotiations, than of later threats, which are more likely to be regarded as exploitation or betrayals of trust.

19 Again, the Bridgetown case in Craig and Solomon (1996) offers an excellent illustration of this kind of behaviour.

20 Herein (in the author's view) lies the fallacy of compulsory conciliation.

21 As we noted in Chapter 9, these issues are typically treated as management rights rather than bargainable issues under most Canadian public sector bargaining legislation.

22 See P. Weiler (1980) for an extremely thoughtful and articulate exposition of this perspective from a Canadian point of view.

23 As well, violence and other forms of abuse, at home and on the job, are of growing concern to many unions, as well as government policy-makers. To help address these problems, recent agreements signed by the Canadian Auto Workers have included provisions making workplace advocates available to support women facing harassment on the job or abuse at home (Giles and Starkman, 1995:359).

24 It may be worth noting that in logging and in the garment industries, the two industries

that make the greatest use of piecework systems, most of the labour force is uneducated and many of the workers have few other options for gainful employment (Radforth, 1982; Grant, 1992:232–234). In the clothing industry in particular, extensive use has been made of immigrant women for whom the work is the "port of entry" into the Canadian labour market. These facts suggest that piecework systems would probably not be embraced voluntarily by the majority of workers.

[25] For a more detailed discussion of the evolution of shorter work hours, see Hunnicutt (1988) and Peirce (2000(b)).

[26] Anecdotal evidence from my students suggests that many workers dislike bumping provisions for essentially the same reason, because they mean that workers will not know for some time whether they have a job or what job they will be doing.

[27] More research is needed to determine why unions have not in fact raised technological change issues more frequently than they have.

[28] A good example would be the Swedish "active labour market system" whereby unions accepted management's right to hire and fire and to deploy new technology in return for income security and retraining rights. The system facilitated both occupational and geographic mobility (Kjellberg, 1992:96–97). For unfortunately brief discussions, see Kjellberg (1992) and Hammarstrom (1993).

[29] In practice, as the reader may already have guessed, there is often considerable overlap between these two factors. The ultimate source of the long-standing mistrust between management and the union may well be the declining long-term economic position of the firm or industry in question.

[30] For an extremely useful and much more detailed discussion of the points raised here, see Giles (1996).

Chapter 11

[1] News reports immediately after the end of these disputes suggested that this was the case in the aftermath of both the Canada Post strike and the earlier strike against United Parcel Service in the United States.

[2] The point that a strike or other crisis can serve as a catalyst for introducing such mechanisms is well made by Verma (1995). For a discussion of this point within the American setting, see Woodworth and Meek (1995).

[3] Such a refusal would be legal if the employee in question believed working conditions to be dangerous. See the employment law chapter for more detail on this point.

[4] The Ontario act contains one or two extremely minor differences in wording from the *Canada Code* definition.

[5] In the case of Ontario, seven days must have elapsed since the release of a conciliation board report or fourteen days since the Labour Minister's decision not to appoint such a board (the so-called 'No-Board' report). Under the *Canada Labour Code*, seven days must have passed in either case.

[6] More recent data do not distinguish between strikes and lockouts, and, therefore, a comparable breakdown is not available for the more recent period.

[7] For a brief discussion (probably quite adequate for the needs of most beginning students), see Gunderson, Hyatt, and Ponak (1995:374–375).

[8] An alternative, though basically similar, measure is the number of days lost per paid worker per year.

9 Data for 1997 are available in Figure 12.1 of the first edition (p. 438).

10 While the figure for Newfoundland looks low, it's significantly larger than that province's share of the Canadian population.

11 For a very useful discussion, see Kervin (1984).

12 On June 14, 2001, just as the Nova Scotia dispute was starting to heat up, the Home Excite News Service reported that about 3500 Ontario nurses per year are accepting jobs in these two countries.

13 For a fairly detailed overview, see Gunderson, Hyatt, and Ponak (1995:383–395).

14 The author does not agree with the rather dismissive attitude towards this perspective taken by Gunderson, Hyatt, and Ponak (1995:384). These writers state that while the asymmetric information perspective is appealing, it is not clear that the firm's private information "is so important in today's world of sophisticated information-processing. In addition, it is not clear why the parties do not agree to contractual arrangements whereby compensation depends on the true state of the firm, since that information is revealed over time." Such a statement seems naive in the extreme. Sophisticated computers or not, it is still possible to conceal information. As to why the parties do not agree to contractual arrangements of the sort just described, the reason should be self-evident. They do not agree to them because at least one of the parties (more likely management) believes it can get a better deal by concealing the true state of affairs than by being open. Nor is it necessarily self-evident that such information will be revealed over time (or at least in time to be of any benefit to the union). Had it not been in a fair number of employers' interest to conceal relevant information, unions would not have started calling strikes to obtain this information, and the asymmetric information perspective as such would never have been devised.

15 Throughout most of this paragraph, I am heavily indebted to the thoughtful discussion provided by Godard at pages 349 to 352.

16 For a useful and interesting discussion of the mediation process and the characteristics of good mediators, see Craig and Solomon (1996:300–306).

17 A few jurisdictions, mainly in the Atlantic region, do permit police to strike.

18 For an interesting discussion, see Ponak and Thompson (1989:395–396).

Chapter 12

1 At least one recent Canadian writer (Haiven, 1990) is critical of the ban on mid-term strikes.

2 The grievance process is often used for this purpose in the public service or other branches of the public sector, where (as noted in Chapter 9), the scope of bargainable issues is generally considerably restricted.

3 At the University of Ottawa (University of Ottawa, 1994), such grievances are initiated at step three of the grievance procedure. As well, the potentially greater seriousness of group grievances is reflected by the fact that they are initiated at step two of the procedure.

4 The case is *Re Denison Mines and U.S.W.A.*, 9 L.A.C. (3rd), 97–104. Individuals' names have been changed and deletions made to save space; otherwise the case is as originally published. Used by permission.

5 Not the grievor's real name. All names of individuals have been changed in this case.

6 This figure would almost certainly overrepresent the proportion of discharge and discipline-related grievances, given that unions send most discharge grievances through to arbitration.

[7] The majority of discharges under the category of union activity relate to illegal work stoppages. Others relate to refusals to cross picket lines, to union organizing, or to the conduct of union business.

[8] Sack also advises grievors to list their attempts to seek employment and the responses they have made, so they can prove to employers that they have made an honest attempt to mitigate (lessen) the damages resulting from the dismissal.

[9] See Sack (1994:141–142) for an interesting and somewhat more detailed discussion of the issues covered in this section.

[10] For a useful if brief review of these studies, see Thornicroft and Eden (1995:262–265 and 268–270).

[11] Such programs have now been established in four provinces: Newfoundland, Ontario, Alberta, and British Columbia. For a brief description, see Thornicroft and Eden (1995:264–265).

[12] For an original and thought-provoking critique of progressive discipline and the assumptions behind it, see Eden (1992).

[13] Interestingly, exactly the same proportion (12%) of those discharged for dishonesty were exonerated, a finding that suggests the arbitrators were not fully convinced the grievors hadn't committed the acts of which they were accused, since had the arbitrators been fully convinced, they presumably would have had no choice but to exonerate the grievors.

[14] Admittedly, Barnacle's sample of non-lawyer arbitrators was very small, since more than 80 percent of his arbitrators were lawyers.

[15] This list is an adaptation and expansion of one developed by Rose (1987).

[16] Counsel can, of course, be used to prepare the briefs, but this doesn't affect the length or cost of the hearing, though it does affect the cost of the process.

[17] As Craig and Solomon (1996:352) note, the oral decision takes effect immediately, but must be confirmed by a brief written decision as soon as possible (normally within 48 hours).

[18] Sometimes called something else, but the process is generally pretty much the same.

[19] Elliott and Goss (1994:18) estimate that grievance mediation costs are less than 15 percent those of arbitration.

[20] As Thornicroft and Eden (1995) note, there is little evidence available on private sector grievance mediation results in Canada.

[21] For more detailed results of grievance mediation in the American private sector, see Feuille (1992). Feuille's study also includes cost and time data.

[22] See Downie (1989) for a more detailed discussion of RBO and other related organizational development techniques.

[23] See Elliott and Goss (1994) for a detailed discussion of a broad range of these mechanisms.

[24] Again, this has often been the case with Canada Post. Stewart-Patterson (1987) indicates that during the 1980s, a sizeable portion of all grievances filed against the corporation had nothing to do with the collective agreement as such.

Chapter 13

[1] In some Asian countries, as noted in Table 7, female labour force participation hovers at or even below 10 percent.

2 The perceptive reader will recall that de-registration has sometimes been resorted to in Canada, as well, as in the case of the 1959 International Woodworkers of America strike in Newfoundland, which ended in Premier Joey Smallwood's decertifying the IWA. To be sure, de-registration has been rare in Canada, at least since the full legalization of private sector collective bargaining in 1944.

3 'Free' systems are also found in such highly-developed Pacific Rim countries as Australia, New Zealand, and Japan. Since the end of the apartheid era and the modernization of its labour relations regime, South Africa has also qualified as a 'free' system.

4 As Matsuda notes (201), the rest of the work force, many of whom are women, have traditionally earned far less, enjoyed much less job security, and been more apt to be involved in work-related accidents than the 'core' work force.

5 Lipsig-Mumme's apt term for the role played by the Japanese government is "statist entrepreneurism."

6 For a brief discussion of Tannenbaum, see Craig and Solomon (1993). A much more far-reaching discussion may be found in Larson and Nissen (1987).

7 See Adams (1995:510–511) for an interesting and (to this observer at least) somewhat horrifying view of working life in a Japanese firm providing the guarantee of lifetime employment.

8 As Déom and Boivin note (2001:508–9), these associations have established a central body, the Conseil du Patronat du Québec, to provide the province's employers with a united voice particularly in its dealings with the provincial government. No comparable body exists anywhere else in Canada (see Adams, 1995).

9 The ability of firms to use relocation threats as a bargaining tool has been recognized by industrial relationists for many years. This phenomenon is specifically discussed in the now-classic 1984 article by Thomas Kochan et al., "Strategic Choice and Industrial Relations Theory." What is new is the extent to which the threat of relocation, not just to another part of the country but to a different country, may now be a credible one.

10 The CCPA Monitor (Nov., 2001) offers a brief summary of this study. Its full text can be found at the CEPR Web site at www.cepr.org.

11 For an interesting discussion on issues around this point, see Adams (1995).

12 These figures are based on union density calculated as a percentage of the non-agricultural labour force. When union density is calculated as a percentage of wage and salary earners, we see some countries, such as Canada, Finland, and Sweden, whose density rates show a decline in Table 13.7, posting increases in their density rates. The reason for this is that these countries experienced increased unemployment between the two study periods and would presumably have had relatively fewer employed individuals (as a proportion of the working-age population) during the 1990s than they had had during the 1980s. Unfortunately, comparable two-period data for union density as a percentage of wage and salary earners were available for only a portion of the 64 countries listed in Table 13.7.

13 The removal of compulsory membership requirements may also help explain why union density rates dropped more sharply in Europe as a whole than one might otherwise have expected, given that continent's relatively strong support for unionism by world standards.

14 This may explain why Europe, which has many of the existing centralized IR systems, is spearheading the move toward shorter working hours.

15 The three countries that saw a decrease in company-level bargaining were all in Africa.

[16] As we noted in Chapter 8 (labour law), these groups include agricultural workers and homeworkers.

[17] As noted at p. 183 of the ILO study, a study carried out in Manila found that 4 percent of the city's informal sector units were less than a year old, and only 14 percent had lasted ten years or more.

[18] As noted in Table 13.7, South Africa's union density rates increased by more than 40 percent between 1985 and 1995.

Chapter 14

[1] According to the PIPSC news release, one-third of the agency's 500 veterinarians will be eligible to retire within the next five years.

[2] The victim's father, former Ontario MPP Terence Young, was so outraged by Health Canada's failure to warn Canadians of the potential side effects of a drug (Prepulsid) to which 38 deaths have been linked in the U.S. that he launched a $100 million class action lawsuit against the federal department and the drug's manufacturer. Young also said (Cryderman, 2001) that "Canadians would be safer without Health Canada."

[3] Just as this chapter was being completed, the Supreme Court of Canada ruled 8–1 that Ontario's exclusion of agricultural workers violates the Charter.

[4] As recently as July of 2001, the bureau had only 20 evaluators on staff, a number that even the bureau's head, Diane Kirkpatrick, admitted was inadequate (see Bueckert, 2001). Kirkpatrick has announced that the number of evaluators will be doubled (Bueckert, 2001); however, it is not clear that even this number will be adequate, or when the bureau will bring the 20 new evaluators on board.

[5] According to Bueckert (2001), Health Canada drug evaluators responsible for human health issues unanimously recommended that carbadox be banned but were overruled by bureau head Kirkpatrick, who requested additional information from the drug's manufacturers. Again, the fractious labour–management relations at the bureau, which as Bueckert has noted has been "wracked with conflict for years," will likely make it more difficult for the bureau to attract new employees or retain existing ones.

[6] The Auditor General noted in her report for 2001 that only about 10 percent of federal government employees are hired on indeterminate (i.e., permanent) contracts.

[7] In our view, the recent changes to Ontario's *Employment Standards Act* (discussed in Chapter 7) take the province in exactly the wrong direction. Though the prospect of stronger enforcement is welcome, eliminating the requirement of a labour ministry permit for extra-long hours and permitting employees to 'agree' to work far more than the standard number of hours in a week has the potential to work real hardship on workers, especially those with heavy family responsibilities.

[8] As noted in the first edition of this book, such provisions are already in place in Quebec.

[9] The Sierra Legal Defence Club report on water quality, discussed earlier, ranked B.C. among the lowest of the provinces. The report gave the province's water quality a grade of 'D,' with the comment: "Rich province, poor regulations." The report was issued while the previous NDP government was still in power. See Mittelstaedt (2001) and McAlastar (2001). After the B.C. government announced the cuts in mid-November 2001, B.C. Government and Service Employees Union president George Heyman warned that the cuts jeopardized children at risk and the safety of highways and drinking water. See B.C. Govt. (2001).

Canadian Sites

Human Resource Development Canada/Labour Canada Workplace Information Directorate

(http://labour.hrdc-drhc.gc.ca) One of the less user-friendly sites the author has experienced (about a '4.5' on a 5-point scale of difficulty). I have even seen seasoned reference librarians fail to access this site on occasion. But its vast wealth of information makes it worth the effort and the frustration. Here you can find information on subjects ranging from labour relations, employment standards, and health and safety legislation to work-family provisions in Canadian collective agreements, practical examples of labour–management cooperation, and trends in Canadian strike incidence. You can also find information on wage settlements in collective agreements and various other collective agreement provisions. If you are seeking information on legislation, it's important to remember, once you reach the Workplace Information Directorate home page, to click on the left-hand button marked "Strategic Policy and International Labour Affairs"—a choice which to say the least is not intuitively obvious. From there you can easily access the full gamut of Canadian labour law information. Unfortunately, a fair amount of information appears to be available only in PDF format, which not every home computer can read. Some documents must also be printed on 14" paper.

Note that while the site may not be user-friendly, WID staff definitely are. There's a button you need only click on to submit your request for information. On all occasions when I have done so, my query has been answered fully in less than 48 hours. Among the site's stronger features: its reprints of articles from *Workplace Gazette*, the excellent industrial relations quarterly published by the WID. For all its problems, and they are many, this is the single most important Web site for students of Canadian IR.

Statistics Canada

(www.statcan.ca) If what you're after is basic economic and employment-related data, this is an excellent and very user-friendly site. The home page gives you the choice of an alphabetical index or a subject-related index. From there, it's easy to obtain basic data on such subjects as the unemployment and inflation rates, the labour force, earnings, and the incidence of full-time and part-time work. You can also, without much difficulty, find information on employment by industry or occupation and comparative international data on strikes and lockouts.

If you're looking for more detailed information or for historical data, the site becomes more problematic. In recent years, StatCan has begun to operate on a "cost-recovery" basis, which means, in plainer English, that you have to pay for much of the data the agency has to offer. If you aren't careful, a search could end up costing you quite a bit of money. For historical data, you are best advised to start by consulting StatCan's collection of hard-copy publications.

All in all, this is a very good site (and a fine complement to the HRDC site listed previously) for beginning IR students. MBA students or others doing detailed research on a specific subject may find it less satisfactory.

Conference Board of Canada

(www.conferenceboard.ca) This non-profit organization centres its attention on economic analysis, public policy issues, and issues around organizational performance. Its Web site, which is reasonably if not totally user-friendly, offers buttons linking you to information on human resource management, leadership development, organizational excellence, education and lifelong learning, and management and e-business (among other things). The Conference Board frequently surveys both managers and union officials, and its Web site generally provides a pretty good sense of what these people expect the industrial relations outlook to be in at least the short term. Though not all IR students will find this site useful, those with an interest in human resource management and organizational performance certainly will. The site is also a good place to get a quick read on the economic outlook at both federal and provincial levels. MBA students, in particular, will find it worth bookmarking.

Canadian Policy Research Networks

(www.cprn.ca) Like the Conference Board, but to an even greater extent, CPRN is a generalist organization addressing a wide range of policy issues. These include health, governance, and the family in addition to issues around work and the workplace. CPRN's studies on work-related issues are always well-researched and balanced as between management and labour. Among the many first-rate studies available on its Web site are Graham Lowe's *Employer of Choice? Workplace Innovation in Government* and *What's a Good Job: The Importance of Employment Relationships*, by Lowe and Grant Schellenberg. CPRN is generous in allowing people to download complete documents from its Web site. The site's one drawback is that it isn't always easy to navigate, and some documents are available only in PDF format. Nonetheless, this is a good starting-point for anyone with an interest in public policy issues, particularly issues around public sector IR.

Union Sites

(Note: all are bilingual (French-English) unless otherwise indicated.)

Canadian Labour Congress

(www.clc-ctc.ca)   A straightforward and easy-to-use site focussing on national-level political issues affecting the labour movement: health care, unemployment insurance, the privatization of public services, free trade, and workplace discrimination. From the front page you can also access information about the CLC's upcoming convention and about the Congress' overall program.

Canadian Auto Workers

(www.caw.ca) This user-friendly site features a balanced mix of internal CAW business and discussion of broader political issues. Even as its members face devastating layoffs in the wake of widespread auto plant closures, the CAW remains interested in a full range of broader political and social issues, from the plight of the homeless in Toronto to the elimination of racism.

Canadian Union of Public Employees

(www.cupe.ca) In some ways, the CUPE site reminds me of the HRDC one listed previously. No union site I have seen is richer in information, but the site can also be difficult (at times maddeningly frustrating) to use. Not unexpectedly, given CUPE's membership, the site focuses heavily on public sector issues, particularly health care. But it also contains an eclectic range of information on subjects of potential interest to any unionist, from how to communicate to members to how to set up a Web site. There is even a songbook containing a couple dozen of the time-honoured union classics such as "Joe Hill" and "Solidarity Forever." The two major drawbacks are: a) the difficulty of knowing what material a non-CUPE member can access; b) the difficulty of reading sub-heads printed in a font normally reserved for ads in the back pages of the Saturday paper.

Communications, Energy & Paperworkers Union

(www.cep.ca) A balanced mix of internal business and regional and national news items of interest to members. A special feature of this site is its page devoted to the CEP's longstanding "Shorter Work Time Campaign." The home page contains a useful short statement of what the union is about overall. The site is generally though not invariably user-friendly.

La Confédération des syndicats nationaux

(www.csn.qc.ca) French only except for selected features ("Joining a Union"). An interesting contrast to most English-Canadian sites because of the international thrust of much of its news coverage. While the front page offers links to pages addressing internal union affairs, and while it contains news items about ongoing negotiations and developments in Quebec City and Ottawa, the extent of international news coverage is really quite striking. Recent news items included a call for Israel to end its occupation of Palestinian territory and features on Mexico and the Argentinian crisis.

Public Service Alliance of Canada

(www.psac.com) Somewhat more inward-looking than the private sector union sites surveyed above, the PSAC site focuses mainly on collective bargaining developments and other internal union business. The home page does contain a story on the UN Day for the Elimination of Racial Discrimination. An interesting special feature is the PSAC Youth Site, which among other things offers information on how young people can unionize their workplaces.

U.S. Sites

Bureau of Labor Statistics

(www.bls.gov) An extremely thorough listing of all kinds of labour- and employment-related information. Major topics are listed on the home page, with major subheadings. They include: inflation and consumer spending; wages; earnings and benefits; productivity; safety and health; international labour; occupations (occupational outlook); demographics; employment and unemployment; industries; business costs; and geography (covering state and municipal-level data). There's also a button devoted to publication and research papers, and even a kids' page listing career opportunities. In addition to the topical index found on the home page, an alphabetical index can easily be accessed, as well. Wage settlements arrived at through collective bargaining can be found under "wages." Very user-friendly. Students interested in U.S. labour information should start by consulting this site. Note that information on household income and income inequality should be obtained from the Census Department Web site, and information on minimum wages from the Department of Labor Web site, both listed below.

Department of Labor

(www.dol.gov) Major headings on the home page include laws and regulations; statistics; research and publications; and doing business with DOL. The minimum wage button takes you to a quite detailed and very interesting history of the development of minimum wage legislation in the U.S. There's also a detailed list of recent news stories related to labour and employment. Like the BLS site listed above, this one is quite user-friendly. However, some of its information duplicates that found on the BLS site. On the whole, this site is probably less useful than the BLS for users who don't live in the U.S.

Bureau of the Census

(www.census.gov) In addition to the topics listed above, contains information on employment-related subjects such as the labour force and working at home. However, many of the studies it lists are (as of early 2002) based on 1990 census data and hence seriously out of date. A supplementary survey from the 2000 census is fairly easily accessed and includes economic, social, and housing information; this may be of somewhat more interest. Not difficult to use but not super-easy either. The logic of the various topic headings isn't always readily apparent. Give it about a '3' on a 5-point user-friendliness scale. Consider this as a supplement to the two previous Web sites rather than as a primary source of information about the U.S. economy and labour scene.

AFL-CIO

(www.aflcio.org) As might be expected of a national-level labour federation, this site places primary emphasis on national political developments affecting working people. A "Bush Watch" chronicles and analyzes all major legislation introduced during the current president's administration. There are also front-page news stories on unemployment insurance, steelworkers' fight in behalf of retirees, the American labour movement's "No More Enrons" campaign, and the AFL-CIO's new "Agenda for America," a comprehensive political campaign aimed at mobilizing working families. The site's "Common Sense Economics" page features an "Executive Pay Watch" and stories about declining income equality, curbing corporate greed, and declining opportunities for young people in the new economy. The site is generally quite user-friendly.

CASE V.1

CBC Video Cases
SOME WORK AND SOME PLAY

High unemployment has become a virtual epidemic throughout the industrialized world. Even countries as prosperous as France and Germany have not been immune. Both have recently been suffering from double-digit unemployment which in turn has led to massive labour unrest.

One country which has proved an exception to the global pattern is the Netherlands. Lately it has become the envy of the rest of Europe with its 6.5 percent unemployment rate—about half that of most other European countries. Somehow, the Dutch seem to have managed to discover just about the right balance between work and play, while maintaining global competitiveness. As journalist Paul Workman suggests, the Netherlands is now "the closest thing Europe has to a tiger economy."

What makes the Dutch experience particularly remarkable is that fifteen years ago, the country's economy was in such bad shape that people used to refer to the "Dutch disease." Wages and unemployment were both high, and far too many people were on welfare.

How did the Netherlands turn things around? To start with, former Prime Minister Ruud Lubbers managed to induce the country's unions to accept a wage freeze and sign on to an agreement with business and government. In return for this, Dutch workers were given the shortest working hours in Europe. Initially, the experiment led to widespread public protest. Business leaders were skeptical as well. In time, however, most Dutch people, including business leaders, came to realize that shorter hours didn't have to mean reduced productivity. Quite the reverse.

Today, seeing that their wages and jobs are protected and that the country's economy is growing, unionized workers have become "amazingly cooperative" in accepting employers' demands for flexibility. The head of the country's metalworkers' union went so far as to encourage the country's only steel mill to modernize, even though the modernization would mean the loss of about 10 000 jobs. When asked how he could justify such a course of action to his members, the union leader pointed out that the mill was still running, unlike steel mills in neighbouring countries which had not gone in for modernization. Moreover, the remaining workers enjoy a 33-hour week and five weeks' annual vacation. Union-management cooperation has become such a way of life in the Netherlands that in 1996, the country didn't experience a single strike or lockout.

One key to the "Dutch miracle" is job-sharing. Another is extensive part-time work. For example, the metalworkers' union leader's wife, a social worker, works only part-time to allow herself more time with her children and more time to engage in her own pursuits, such as reading and study. She is one of a great many Dutch part-timers. In all, 33 percent of all Dutch workers are part-timers, compared with 19 percent of Canadian workers. But there's a big difference. In the Netherlands, unlike Canada, part-timers enjoy the same perks and benefits as their full-time counterparts, including pension rights.

Video Resource: "A Place That Works." From *The National*, March 26, 1997.

Far from interfering with the country's economic competitiveness, its family-friendly approach seems to have made the Netherlands even more competitive. As Paul Workman notes, it has become the seventh largest exporter in the world. Fully 45 percent of all companies starting a new business in Europe choose to locate in the Netherlands.

While there are concerns that even the robust Dutch economy may not be generating enough entry-level jobs for low-skilled workers, the country's political leaders appear confident the Netherlands can meet this challenge as it has met so many others in the recent past.

QUESTIONS

1) How did Prime Minister Lubbers set about curing the "Dutch disease"?
2) What role did the unions and unionized workers play in turning the "Dutch disease" into the "Dutch miracle"?
3) What advantages do you see to the Dutch approach to unemployment? What disadvantages?
4) Do you think the Dutch approach would work in Canada? Why or why not?

CASE V.2
CBC Video Cases
WAR OF WORDS*

In 1996, Ken King was brought in as the new publisher of the *Calgary Herald*. His mandate was to improve the paper's bottom line. With an eye to rebuilding business connections in an "optimistic, entrepreneurial" city, all of whose Members of Parliament were from the Reform Party, King moved the paper to the right. The rightward trend was accentuated after tycoon Conrad Black bought the paper in early 1997.

A key element of King's strategy was to forge "marketing agreements" between the *Herald* and its advertisers. While these partnerships did improve the *Herald's* bottom line, many journalists felt they distorted news coverage. For example, several questioned the repeated front-page coverage given to a *Herald*-supported production

Video Resource: "Strike," A segment of "War of Words." From *The National*, July 3, 2000.

*This case will be useful in connection with the discussion of the collective agreement, especially seniority clauses, contained in Chapter 10.

of *The Wizard of Oz*. There was also concern that paid advertising was sometimes made to look very much like editorial copy. In 1997, King himself left the *Herald*, but by then the new strategy was firmly in place.

On occasion, journalists were personally threatened or had their stories altered if they didn't toe the new corporate bottom line. For example, on one occasion sports reporter Mike Board wrote a negative story about the Calgary Flames, then a very weak National Hockey League team—but also a team with which the *Herald* had a marketing agreement. Board relates that: "I was called in and threatened with a variety of sanctions ranging from being fired to being taken off the [sports] beat." Eventually he was forced to apologize to Flames management for the negative coverage. With that incident, Board feels, the paper crossed the line between objective journalism and partisan advocacy for a local business.

On another occasion, two reporters filed a story about a court case just before deadline. The story was altered by editors and, in its published version, contained factual errors. So distorted was the new story that the defence attorney considered asking for a mistrial and the trial judge considered citing the paper for contempt.

Incidents such as these did little to foster harmonious relations between the journalists and the *Herald's* management. As the paper's profits increased, so did the tensions in its newsroom. In November 1998, the journalists formed a union. Six months later, they were out on strike—the first in the paper's history. Journalistic integrity was a key issue in the long and bitter dispute. So, too, was a seniority clause designed to protect senior journalists in the event of layoffs. In the words of Dan Gaynor, the publisher who replaced King, seniority clauses "protect the lazy." When told that the world-famous *New York Times* was among the papers whose agreements contain such seniority clauses, Gaynor replied that he didn't know much about what went on at the *Times*, but very possibly it could be an even better paper if it got rid of its seniority clause. Though the clause was similar to clauses in use at most North American newspapers, *Herald* management was adamant in insisting that it be removed.

Though the strikers mounted a strong publicity campaign and fought valiantly throughout the eight-month dispute, theirs was always an uphill battle in a city that has historically had little regard for unions. When the bitter dispute finally ended, it ended with the union's decertification.

QUESTIONS

1) Journalist Lisa Dempster, who was interviewed extensively in the report, insists that there must always be "an arm's-length relationship between the people who produce the news and those who market the paper." How can such an arm's-length relationship be maintained? Do you feel that marketing agreements such as those between the *Herald* and the Calgary Flames are compatible with that kind of arm's-length relationship?

2) Do you agree with Dan Gaynor that seniority clauses in newsrooms do little more than "protect the lazy"? What other purposes do you see such clauses as serving?

3) During the course of the report, Lisa Dempster also warned that the kind of problems then being faced by the *Herald* "could be coming soon to a paper near you." Has her prediction been borne out? Have you heard about similar problems affecting your local paper?

CASE
HS.1 Health and Safety Case
SPIELBERG AND CN RAILWAY COMPANY

A skilled machinist returns from vacation to find his shop in a state of total chaos. Because of the slippery condition of the floor around his wheel reprofiling machine, he slips and falls, injuring his finger. The next day he refuses to work until the situation is remedied. Should he be penalized for this action?

Parties: Spielberg / Canadian National (CN)

Forum: Canada Labour Relations Board

Jurisdiction: Canada

The worker was a machinist who had been employed by CN for about 10 years. He had an unblemished employment history with CN and his expertise had been recognized. His specialized job involved essentially the reconditioning of locomotive wheels that had worn out and had deteriorated over time. He was expected to be able to reprofile three or four pairs of wheels during a normal shift if the machine used for the purpose was in good working order.

The worker was also an active member of the workplace health and safety committee, responsible for questions on health and safety in the shop. He had submitted written reports on several occasions disclosing shortcomings in the shop facilities, particularly in the wheel reprofiling section where he worked. Before he went on vacation, he had reported the fact that the platform around the wheel reprofiling machine was slippery and had no guardrail, which posed a danger to health and safety. On his return from vacation, he found the shop in a state of total disorder. The reprofiling machine required repairs and the dangers and deficiencies he had reported in writing had not been remedied. The worker refused to work because of the slippery condition around the machine, which had caused him to slip and fall the day before, resulting in injury to his finger. He

Source: Adapted from Canadian Labour Relations Board Decision No. 757 Board File 950-99, 9/28/89, record #8994. © 1989, CCH Canadian Ltd. Reprinted from *Canadian Employment Safety & Health Guide* with permission. Some deletions have been made by the author for the purposes of this book and names have been changed.

requested that a Labour Canada officer be called to investigate the matter. The shop foreman refused and instead assigned the worker to perform other duties.

He later received a summons to a disciplinary hearing for alleged lack of productivity. The hearing led to the worker's being assessed 10 demerit points under the company's personnel management procedure known as the "Brown System" in disciplinary matters. Once an employee had accumulated a certain number of demerit points, he could be subject to dismissal.

The worker filed a complaint with Labour Canada alleging that his employer, in imposing the 10 demerit points against him, had contravened section 147(a) of the Canada Labour Code prohibiting any disciplinary or reprisal action against an employee who has exercised his rights under the Code or has sought the enforcement of any of the provisions of Part II of the Code. In this case, the complainant alleged that the disciplinary action taken by CN against him was the result of his insistence that safety standards should be complied with and of the fact that he had exercised his right to refuse unsafe work under Part II of the Code. The employer, in reply, essentially argued that the penalty imposed had no connection with the complainant's availing himself of the provisions of Part II of the Code.

QUESTIONS

1) Will the Board allow the machinist's penalty of 10 demerit points to stand? Why, or why not?

2) If you were the machinist's superior, how would you have handled this situation?

3) If you were senior management, in what light would you view the foreman's behaviour? How might you respond to the incident?

4) What might the machinist do, another time, to help ensure safe conditions without putting his own neck on the line to the same extent?

Human Rights Case
MITCHELL AND SUBWAY SANDWICHES

Can an employer legally discharge an employee for pregnancy or medical complications resulting from pregnancy?

Canadian

C. H. R. R.

Human Rights Reporter

British Columbia

Pregnancy

Indexed as: Mitchell v. Subway Sandwiches & Salads

Monica Mitchell, the complainant, filed a complaint (Exhibit 1) in which she alleged that Subway Sandwiches & Salads ("Subway"), the respondent, discriminated against her with respect to the terms and conditions of her employment and refused to continue to employ her because of her sex (pregnancy), contrary to what is now s. 13 of the *Human Rights Code*, R.S.B.C. 1986, c. 210 (as amended) (the "*Code*"). By letter dated March 20, 2000 (Exhibit 2), the Registrar of the Tribunal, in response to an application by counsel for the complainant, decided to add Sandra Stewart, also known as Sandra Olson, as a respondent to this complaint.

EVIDENCE

The complainant testified that she began working at Subway in April 1996. Her duties included making sandwiches, serving customers, dealing with the cash and cleaning the bathrooms. She worked the night shift from 7:00 p.m. to 2:00 a.m. with

---

Source: Adapted from (2001), 39 C.H.R.R. D/102, 2001 BCHRT 2. Some deletions have been made by the author for the purposes of this book and names have been changed.

N.B.: This case will be useful in connection with Chapter 7 (employment legislation).

a co-worker, Arnold Patton, who told her that her supervisor was Alice. The complainant understood that Ms. Stewart was the owner of Subway. The complainant testified that she had very little contact with Ms. Stewart, who rarely came in during the evening. The complainant had a three-month probationary period.

On July 22, 1996, the complainant saw Dr. Brown because she believed that she was pregnant. The pregnancy was confirmed the next day. The complainant testified that, when she informed her supervisor, Alice responded that she knew the complainant would not be able to continue to work throughout her pregnancy because she, Alice, had not been able to. Alice told the complainant that the best thing to do would be to lay her off when she had enough weeks to qualify for unemployment insurance.

The complainant testified that, in mid-August, she had another conversation with Alice, who told her that she had been informed by Ms. Stewart that the complainant could not be laid off simply because she was pregnant. The complainant's evidence was that Alice then gave her two choices: either quit her employment after giving one month's notice, or Subway would make it very difficult for the complainant to get another job in the future.

The complainant's mother, Dottie Mitchell, testified that she telephoned the Employment Standards Branch (ESB) after the complainant told her what Alice had said. Ms. Mitchell's evidence was that she was informed by ESB that an employer could not fire an employee simply because she became pregnant, and that the complainant should continue to work and to document anything of importance. Ms. Mitchell passed this information on to her daughter.

The complainant testified that Alice continued to approach her and ask her when she was going to give her notice. The complainant testified that she put Alice off by saying that she had no time to deal with it or that she had forgotten.

The complainant began to work some day shifts in mid-August. She understood that Alice continued to be her supervisor. The complainant said that she did not deal with Carla Ledbetter, another manager at Subway.

On August 25, the complainant was not feeling well. She went to Emergency at the West Coast General Hospital (the "Hospital") at 1:30 a.m., where she was examined and discharged. She was not scheduled to work that day.

The complainant worked an eight-hour shift on August 27.

The complainant testified that, on August 29, she saw Dr. Wilson because she was experiencing bad cramping and vaginal discharge. Dr. Wilson gave her an undated note to take two days off work. The complainant was scheduled to work the night shift that day. Her evidence was that she took the note to Alice and informed her that she would not be able to work that evening. According to the complainant, Alice refused to take the note and told the complainant that she "better come to work" and that if she did not show up she would not have a job because Alice wanted to spend time with her daughter and some of the other employees were sick.

The complainant's mother testified that she drove her daughter to Subway so that she could give Alice the note from Dr. Wilson. Ms. Mitchell said the complainant came out of Subway crying. The complainant testified that, when she and her mother got home, her mother telephoned Subway and asked to speak to the manager. The complainant testified that her mother told her that the manager said that, if the complainant did not come into work, there would be no job for her. The complainant stayed with her mother on August 29 and did not work her shift. She said that this was the first shift she missed because of her pregnancy.

The complainant testified that she was absent from work on August 29 and 30. Her evidence was that, on August 30, her grandfather had a heart attack and was admitted to the Hospital in the evening. She and her mother went out to look for the complainant's brother to take him to the Hospital. The complainant's evidence was that, because her brother was "hanging out" with his friends, she and her mother had to drive around Port Alberni to look for him. Her mother gave similar evidence.

The complainant testified that her co-worker, Arnold Patton, told her that an employee of the respondent saw her in uptown Port Alberni that night when she was out looking for her brother.

On the morning of August 31, the complainant, who continued to feel ill, again went to Emergency at the Hospital. She was seen by Dr. Richardson, who advised her to take another one to two days off work. The complainant testified that she did not take this note to Alice because two days earlier Alice had refused the note from Dr. Wilson.

The complainant returned to the Hospital on the morning of September 1 when she was diagnosed with a threatened miscarriage and was sent home with another note that she should take a few days off work. She was admitted to the Hospital that evening and suffered a miscarriage.

The complainant's mother testified that she telephoned Subway from the Hospital. She believed that she spoke to Ms. Stewart. Ms. Mitchell told the woman she spoke to that the complainant was in the Hospital having a miscarriage. According to Ms. Mitchell, the woman told her that she did not care, that the complainant was fired, and that she should not show up for work. Ms. Mitchell responded that the complainant could not be fired for being sick. The woman told Ms. Mitchell that someone had seen the complainant the evening of August 30.

On September 2, Ms. Mitchell told her daughter that she had been fired. The Record of Employment issued to the complainant on September 3 states that her employment was terminated because she "failed to show up for shifts."

The complainant testified that she did not receive any written or verbal reprimands from either Alice, Carla Ledbetter or Sandra Stewart.

Sandra Stewart testified that she has been the sole owner of Subway since 1995. She stated that Carla Ledbetter took over as manager from Alice on August 12 and that this was communicated to the employees by word of mouth. However, Alice did not leave Subway until September 24. Ms. Stewart left hiring and firing decisions to the manager.

Ms. Stewart testified that it was Ms. Ledbetter's decision to fire the complainant because of her missed shifts. Ms. Stewart did not know any of the details surrounding the missed shifts. She stated that she was informed that there were concerns about the complainant's performance but she had no first-hand knowledge about them. Ms. Stewart testified that she never spoke to the complainant's mother.

Carla Ledbetter testified that the complainant telephoned just before her shift to say that she could not work because her grandfather was in the Hospital and that she had to find her brother. Ms. Ledbetter's evidence was that she later learned that this explanation was not true because the complainant was seen in uptown Port Alberni. Ms. Ledbetter understood that Alice told the complainant that two hours' notice was required when she could not work.

Ms. Ledbetter testified that, after the complainant's mother informed Arnold Patton that the complainant could not work because she was in the Hospital having a miscarriage, she telephoned the Hospital to check on the accuracy of the information. According to Ms. Ledbetter, she was told that there was no one by the name of Monica Mitchell there. Because Ms. Ledbetter could not confirm that the complainant was in the Hospital, her employment was terminated.

ISSUE

The issue before me is whether the respondents refused to continue to employ the complainant because of her pregnancy, contrary to s. 13 of the *Code*.

DECISION

The complainant testified in a straightforward manner. There was no evidence to contradict her account of Alice's statement to her concerning her continuing to work during her pregnancy. Further, the evidence of the complainant's mother about her telephone call to ESB is consistent with the complainant's account of her conversation with Alice.

Ms. Ledbetter's evidence is that the decision was made to dismiss the complainant after she missed two shifts without providing adequate notice and for reasons which Ms. Ledbetter later determined to be untrue.

The complainant gave an account of her interaction with Alice on August 29 when she refused to accept Dr. Wilson's note and told the complainant that she "better come into work" or she would not have a job. I accept the complainant's testimony, which was not contradicted.

Ms. Ledbetter's evidence was that the complainant said that she could not come to work because her grandfather was in the Hospital and that Ms. Ledbetter later learned this was not true. This evidence is somewhat confusing because the complainant had a note from Dr. Wilson on August 29 that she was to take two days off work (Exhibit 4, tab 3). Therefore, on August 30, there would have been no reason for the complainant to say that the reason she could not come into work was because her grandfather had been hospitalized after a heart attack.

It seems to me more likely that the complainant's explanation on August 29 that she could not work because she was ill was doubted after someone from the respondent saw her in uptown Port Alberni on the night of August 30, when she was looking for her brother because their grandfather was in the Hospital. Her detailed account of the events that night, for example, her description of how her mother arranged pillows in the van so that the complainant would be comfortable, have satisfied me of the credibility of her evidence with respect to this incident.

Dr. Wilson's note refers simply to health reasons and makes no mention of the complainant's pregnancy. However, when her mother telephoned Subway on August 31, she advised them that the complainant could not work because she was having a miscarriage. While there is some confusion about whom the complainant's mother spoke to, Ms. Ledbetter's evidence makes it clear that she was aware of the content of the phone call.

Ms. Ledbetter's evidence was that she could not confirm this information when she telephoned the Hospital, and, as a result, the complainant's employment was terminated. Given the fact that the complainant was diagnosed as having a miscarriage on the morning of August 31, but was not admitted to the hospital until that evening, it appears that Ms. Ledbetter came to an incorrect conclusion about the veracity of the complainant's medical condition when she telephoned the Hospital and was informed that the complainant was not a patient there.

Discrimination on the basis of pregnancy constitutes discrimination on the basis of sex: *Brooks v. Canada Safeway* (1989), 10 C.H.R.R. D/6183 (S.C.C.). Adopting the reasoning that was applied in *Poirier v. British Columbia (Ministry of Municipal Affairs, Recreation and Housing)* (1997), 29 C.H.R.R. D/87 at D/91 (B.C.H.R.T.), I conclude that discrimination because of a miscarriage is a form of sex discrimination.

The respondents had an obligation to accommodate the complainant's pregnancy to the point of undue hardship. This legal obligation extends to accommodating a miscarriage, one of the possible outcomes of a pregnancy. It seems reasonable to me that such accommodation would require Subway to give the complainant both a reasonable opportunity to obtain and present medical confirmation of her miscarriage and also adequate time off to recover, if doing so would not amount to undue hardship.

Subway presented no evidence that accommodating the complainant would have amounted to undue hardship. Her position was not a skilled one that would have been difficult to fill. Indeed Ms. Ledbetter's evidence was that she returned to work to cover the complainant's absence. Ms. Ledbetter's unhappiness at having to return to work cannot be considered undue hardship.

QUESTIONS

1) What is the "duty to accommodate"? Why is it significant in this case?

2) Do you feel that the store management accommodated Ms. Mitchell to the point of "undue hardship"? Where would that point have come, in your view?

3) Had you been the adjudicator in this case, what would your decision have been, and why?

CASE
C.1

Certification Case
IBEW, LOCAL 529 AND MUDJATIK
MINING JOINT VENTURE

Should lead hands and foremen (first-line supervisors) be treated as members of management or regular workers for purposes of collective bargaining?

International Brotherhood of Electrical Workers, Local 529 and Mudjatik Thyssen Mining Joint Venture

Indexed as: Mudjatik Mining Joint Venture and I.B.E.W. Local 529

Saskatchewan Labour Relations Board, Gwen Gray, Chair, Bruce McDonald, Member and Leo Lancaster, Member.

May 9, 2000.

Source: Adapted from 65 C.L.R.B.R. (2nd 2000) at 204. Some deletions have been made by the author for the purposes of this book and names have been changed.

N.B.: This case will be very useful in connection with the discussion on exclusions in Ch. 8 (labour law).

DECISION OF THE BOARD:

BACKGROUND

International Brotherhood of Electrical Workers, Local 529 (the "union") applied to be certified for a bargaining unit composed of "all journeyman electricians, electrical apprentices, electrical workers and electrical foremen" employed by Mudjatik Thyssen Mining Joint Venture (the "Joint Venture") in Saskatchewan, north of the 51st parallel.

The Joint Venture filed a reply on June 23, 1999 and raised various issues relating to the union's application. Subsequently, an amended reply was filed by the Joint Venture on January 31, 2000. The parties to the Joint Venture are Thyssen Mining Construction of Canada Ltd. ("Thyssen") and Mudjatik Enterprises Inc. ("Mudjatik"). The Joint Venture denies that it is an electrical contractor as alleged in the union's application. It claims that there were approximately 30 employees employed by the Joint Venture at the time the application was filed.

On December 10, 1999, the union notified the Board and the Joint Venture that it sought to amend its application to include a claim for successorship and/or common unionized employer declarations pursuant to ss. 37 [am. 1994, c. 47, s. 19] and 37.3 [new SS. 1994, c. 47, s. 20] of the *Trade Union Act*, R.S.S. 1978, c. T-17 (the "Act") and s. 18 of the *Construction Industry Labour Relations Act*, 1992, S.S. 1992, c. C 29.11 (the "*CILRA 1992*"). In this regard the union was relying on a certification order dated August 29, 1975 for Thyssen.

At the hearing of this matter on February 1 and 2, 2000, the Joint Venture withdrew its amendment to the statement of employment dated July 21, 1999. The union agreed to permit the Joint Venture to amend its reply and the Joint Venture agreed to permit the union to amend its application. The parties dispute the status of Thomas Moore, Hiram Dant, and Michael Dawson.

FACTS

Thyssen is involved in the construction, maintenance and operation of mines. It is a subsidiary of Thyssen Schachtau GMBH of Germany. Thyssen was certified by the union on August 29, 1975 and was a party to collective agreements for the years 1976 and 1977. In 1980, it wrote to the union and advised that it would be represented in collective bargaining by the Saskatchewan Construction Labour Relations Council ("SCLRC"), which was then the designated representative employers' organization under the *Construction Industry Labour Relations Act*, SS. 1979, c. C-29.1 (the "*CILRA 1979*").

In 1984, SCLRC gave notice to the union to terminate the collective bargaining agreement then in effect on behalf of Thyssen and the other employers in the trade division.

In 1993, following the passage of the *CILRA 1992*, the union wrote Thyssen to engage it in collective bargaining under the framework established by the *CILRA 1992*. Thyssen responded to the correspondence by indicating that it was not a "unionized employer" and was not obligated to bargain with the union. Subsequently, the Construction Labour Relations Association of Saskatchewan Inc. ("CLR"), the designated representative employers' organization for the trade division, contacted Thyssen and advised it that it was subject to seven certification orders and was therefore a unionized employer within the meaning of the *CILRA 1992*. Various other pieces of correspondence were forwarded by the union to Thyssen after March 1993 but none of them received a response from Thyssen.

According to Mr. Samuel Slawson, former business manager for the union, during the period subsequent to the repeal of the *CILRA 1979* until March 1993, the union had contacted Thyssen on a regular basis to inquire as to whether or not it had need for electricians. Each time it was told that there was no current need for electricians. This period also coincided with the expansion of spin-off companies and the union suspected that Thyssen was hiring employees through a spin-off company called Thyssen Mine Development Corporation, a wholly owned subsidiary of Thyssen.

Mr. Charlie Miles, human resources coordinator for Thyssen, testified that Thyssen has no corporate records relating to its certification by the union or any other union and lacks any corporate knowledge of the events of the 1970s and 1980s pertaining to its collective bargaining obligations. Mr. Miles did not know the basis on which Thyssen asserted in March 1993 that it was not a unionized employer. The officer who made the assertion is no longer employed by Thyssen and was not called as a witness in these proceedings.

At the time of this application, Thyssen was working on three mining sites in northern Saskatchewan. On all three sites, it had entered into a joint venture agreement with Mudjatik, which is owned by Des Nedhe Development Inc., a corporation established by the English River First Nation. On all three joint ventures, Mudjatik represented and was agent for a variety of northern partners, including northern towns and northern First Nations.

The joint venture agreements contained the following common elements: (1) Thyssen acts as administrative manager of the joint venture; (2) Thyssen is responsible for appointing the project manager; (3) Thyssen hires, places and supervises all employees; (4) Thyssen and Mudjatik share responsibility for providing working capital, but Mudjatik is limited in its maximum exposure on each project; (5) Thyssen is paid a management fee based on revenues or profits; (6) Tron Power Inc., a corporation owned by the English River First Nation, coordinates the hiring and training of northern residents for the project, maintains a northern hiring pool and acts as northern liaison in return for a management fee. All revenues are shared on a 50/50 basis between Thyssen and Mudjatik.

Thyssen supplies all of the key personnel and, through them, the knowledge and skills to perform the work in question. Mudjatik provides some of the working capital and, through Tron Power Inc., access to northern resident employees. Thyssen prepared all of the tendering documents. The equipment used on the joint venture projects came from three sources: rental, project owner or Thyssen. Mr. Miles was unaware of any assets held in the name of the Joint Venture. The Joint Venture does not have an office but relies on the office space and staff of Thyssen. In addition, all salaried employees on the projects are paid by Thyssen and their salaries are billed back to the Joint Venture for reimbursement. Benefit plans for employees were maintained by Thyssen.

The joint venture arrangements between Thyssen and Mudjatik are required, in part, as a result of the surface leases negotiated between the province and the owners of the uranium mines, to ensure that northern residents benefit from the employment created by mine development and to ensure that northern communities and First Nations benefit from the same development. Mr. Miles indicated that Thyssen could not obtain work in the north without entering into a joint venture arrangement with northern companies.

In relation to the statement of employment, Mr. Miles testified that Hiram Dant is a long-term employee of Thyssen and acted as an electrical foreman at the McArthur River site. According to Mr. Miles, Mr. Michael Dawson is also a long-time employee of Thyssen and he worked as chief electrician at the McArthur River site. The documents indicate that Mr. Dawson and Mr. Dant recommend hiring, which is subject to approval by the project manager or the site superintendent. There is no evidence that either employee disciplined other employees. Both are hourly paid employees. They also have some input into the electrical quotes prepared by Thyssen.

Mr. Miles testified that Mr. Thomas Moore worked at the Cluff Lake site and was laid off for lack of work on May 7, 1999. He was subsequently rehired on June 21, 1999 at the McArthur River site. He was on lay-off for the period from May 7 to June 21, 1999.

RELEVANT STATUTORY PROVISIONS

The Board considered ss. 5(a), (b), (c), 37 and 37.3 of the Act and s. 18 of the *CILRA 1992*.

ARGUMENTS

The union also argued that Mr. Dawson and Mr. Dant should be included on the statement of employment as employees. The union noted that their duties are similar to electrical foremen and that they lack the power to hire and fire employees.

With respect to the successorship/common employer argument, the union argued that this case is a classic successorship with the assets, personnel and know-how transferred from the unionized employer, Thyssen, to the new employer, the Joint Venture.

The union also argued that s. 18 of the *CILRA 1992* applies to the factual situation. According to the union, the evidence demonstrates that Thyssen and the Joint Venture are associated or related businesses which are carried on under common control and direction. Thyssen controls all aspects of the work of the joint venture with Mudjatik adding working capital and labour force development. The work of the Joint Venture is indistinguishable from work formerly performed by Thyssen. Counsel argued that the extension of the union's certification order from Thyssen to the Joint Venture was not an unreasonable or unwarranted extension of collective bargaining rights. The union argued that the situation was similar to a traditional spin-off arrangement.

The union argued that the "abandonment" argument is not available to the employer as a matter of law under the Act or on the facts of this case. Counsel noted that, absent an allegation of fraud, the only provision permitting the rescission of a certification order is contained in s. 5(k) [am. S.S. 1983, c. 81, s. 4(1)], which permits employees to apply to rescind a certification order on an annual basis. The union argued that certification orders "belong" to the employees of an employer and that the Board should revise its previous decisions that permitted an employer to rescind a certification order based on the principle of abandonment. The union referred the Board to *Wappel Concrete & Construction Ltd. and I.U.O.E., Hoisting, Portable & Stationary Local 870*, [1984] April Sask. Labour Rep. 33 (File No. 302-83), which first dealt with the "abandonment" argument.

As a matter of fact, counsel argued that the abandonment principle does not apply because the Joint Venture has failed to demonstrate through its evidence that the union did intend to abandon its bargaining rights. The union noted that the Joint Venture did not establish that it hired any electricians in the period of the 1980s and early 1990s.

The union asked the Board to determine the successorship/related-employer issue first. If the certification order needed to be dealt with, the union requested that the Board reserve on the issue of ordering a vote, if a vote needed to be ordered.

Mr. Lear, counsel for Thyssen and the Joint Venture, argued that Mr. Moore was not an employee on the date the application for certification was filed.

The Joint Venture also maintains that Mr. Dant and Mr. Dawson are managerial employees and are excluded from the definition of "employee."

The Joint Venture disputes that there is any evidence that there has been a sale, lease, transfer or other disposition of Thyssen's business to the Joint Venture, as required to trigger the successorship provisions contained in s. 37 of the Act.

The Joint Venture also argued that the related-employer provisions set out in s. 37.3 of the Act and s. 18 of the *CILRA 1992* do not apply to the factual setting. Counsel argued that Mudjatik and Thyssen were totally separate entities with no overlapping ownership or interest outside of the contractual joint venture agreements. Mudjatik is not a "spin off" of Thyssen and should not be affected by the certification order binding Thyssen.

The Joint Venture also argued that the union abandoned its rights to be certified at Thyssen by its inactivity over a 14-year period, which corresponds to the period of time that Mr. Miles was employed by Thyssen.

ANALYSIS

Abandonment of Certification Order

In *Wappel Concrete & Construction Ltd.*, *supra*, the Board permitted an employer to rely on the doctrine of "abandonment" to effectively render a certification order void. The Board justified the application of the doctrine of "abandonment" in the following terms at p. 36:

> Underlying the doctrine of abandonment is the concern that a trade union, because of its inactivity, no longer represents employees in the bargaining unit.

And at p. 37:

> If a union seeks and acquires the right to act as exclusive bargaining agent for employees and then for an unreasonably long time ignores its responsibility to bargain in good faith for them it should lose its right to do so. Accordingly, any union that fails to actively carry out its duty to bargain collectively for the employees it represents, without a satisfactory explanation for its failure, will be found as a fact by this Board to have abandoned its bargaining rights. Although the Board will always be reluctant to infer that bargaining rights vested in a union have been abandoned, this case is one that is very clear.

In the *Wappel Concrete & Construction Ltd.* case, the certified trade union was certified with the employer in October 1959 and negotiated a one-year collective agreement. After that period, no further negotiations were entered into between the union and the employer and the union did not deal with any disputes or grievances of employees in the unit. The employer raised the abandonment defence in response to an application by the union filed in 1983 to bring the employer within the statutory provisions of the first *CILRA 1979*.

Subsequently, the defence of "abandonment" was relied on by the Board in *Morin and Aim Electric Ltd.*, [1985] Feb. Sask. Labour Rep. 27 (File No. 331-84), to carve out a portion of a certification order on whose behalf the certified trade union had not bargained and who in fact were represented by a different local of the same trade union on a voluntary recognition basis with the employer.

The Board has considered the abandonment argument on several occasions since the *Wappel* case, but the defence has not been accepted by the Board outside the two cases cited above. In *Gunnar Industries Ltd. and I.U.O.E., Local 870*, [1986] Sask. LRBR 749 (File No. 160-96), the Board rejected an abandonment argument in the following terms at p. 764:

In this case, the Union did contact the Employer and brought succeeding collective agreements to the attention of Mr. Kimery. They made a demand for the enforcement of the union security clause, they presented a notice to bargain, and they ultimately filed a grievance. It is true that these steps were taken at fairly lengthy intervals, and the Union did not seek the assistance of this Board in asserting their claims. At the same time, it must be remembered that the Union was making these efforts during a period when there was considerable confusion concerning industrial relations in the construction industry, and, in any case, they may not have known that there were employees falling under their jurisdiction at work for much of this time, given the flat denials of Mr. Kimery on this point. These circumstances fall far short of those in which a trade union might reasonably be regarded as having abandoned the bargaining rights granted in a certification Order.

The confusion concerning industrial relations in the construction industry related to the repeal of the *CILRA 1979* in 1983 by the passage of the *Construction Industry Labour Relations Repeal Act*, S.S. 1983-84, c. 2 (the *"Repeal Act"*), and the resulting debate over whether s. 4 of the *Repeal Act* continued in force the collective agreements negotiated under the terms of the *CILRA 1979*. This last issue was ultimately resolved by the Saskatchewan Court of Appeal in *U.A., Local 264 v. Metal Fabricating & Construction Ltd.* (1990), 84 Sask. R., 195, 69 D.L.R. (4th) 452 (C.A.); [leave to appeal to S.C.C. refused (1990), 93 Sask. r. 240*n*, 74 D.L.R. (4th) ix (note), 125 N.R. 240*n* (4 W.A.C. 240*n* (S.C.C.)]. The Court of Appeal interpreted s. 4 of the *Repeal Act* as continuing the pre-*Repeal Act* collective agreements in force until new collective agreements were concluded under the new system of collective bargaining. A description of the industry over the period from 1983 to 1990 is set out in *Dominion Co. and I.U.O.E., Local 870; PCL Industrial Constructors Ltd. and C.J.A., Local 1985,* [1994] 1st Quarter Sask. Labour Rep. 146 (File Nos. 158-93 and 176-93).

The Board had a further opportunity to examine the abandonment defence in *Marchuk Decorating Ltd. and P.A.T., Local 739,* [1998] Sask. LRBR 63 (File No. 009-97), where the Board held that an employer who represented to the certified union that it engaged no employees in the bargaining unit could not rely on the doctrine of abandonment to resist the enforcement of the existing certification order.

It would seem to the Board from a review of the cases referred to above that, before the principle of abandonment can be applied to the construction industry, the employer must establish that it employed tradespeople within the scope of the union's certification order during the period of the alleged abandonment. If there is no evidence that such tradespeople were employed by the employer during the alleged abandonment period, the principles set out in *Prince Albert Comprehensive High School Board, supra,* and *Vic West Steel Inc., supra,* would apply.

Secondly, it would seem to the Board that the employer must also explain how it came to employ tradespeople without reference to the hiring provisions contained in the relevant collective agreement. Once a collective agreement has been entered into between a union and an employer in the construction sector, the employer generally is obligated to obtain his employees from the union's hiring hall. Such agreements restrict the employer's ability to hire employees "off the street" except in unusual situations, such as an inability on the part of the union to provide sufficient employees. Where an employer is relying on the defence of abandonment, in our view, it must explain how it came to employ persons who are not members of the union. This may occur, for instance, if the certified union refused to provide members to the employer in response to the employer's request for tradespeople.

Third, in the context of the *CILRA 1992*, where negotiations and collective bargaining take place on a multi-employer basis through the designation of a representative employers' organization, it would be difficult for an individual employer to allege abandonment of bargaining rights where the certified trade union has negotiated or is attempting to negotiate a collective agreement with the representative employers' organization. Under the centralized system of bargaining, collective bargaining takes place at the level of the union and the representative employers' association. A unionized employer may have little direct contact with the certified union under this scheme. However, the ongoing collective bargaining between the union and the representative employers' organization is carried out with respect to the unionized employer and the employees covered by the union's certification order. An employer's lack of awareness of or involvement in the work of the representative employers' organization is not indicative of "abandonment" by the certified union.

Lastly, in most situations, employees in the bargaining unit who do not want to be represented further by the certified union have the ability to file to rescind the union's certification order on an annual basis. The Board should be reluctant, except in the most extreme cases, to find that a trade union has abandoned its representation certificate without testing the union's support through the vehicle of a rescission application and vote. This is the statutory mechanism established for continually checking employee support for a certified bargaining agent.

In the present case, the Joint Venture has not established that it did employ electricians during the period of the alleged "abandonment" by the union. In addition, it did not rebut the evidence of Mr. Slawson who testified that he regularly checked with the Joint Venture to see if it required tradespeople, and was consistently told "no." As a result, the Joint Venture has not established the first condition for claiming abandonment, *i.e.*, that the Joint Venture actually employed persons within the bargaining unit during the period in question.

Successorship

The union argued in this case that the Joint Venture is a successor employer to Thyssen Mining Construction of Canada Ltd. and is subject to the certification order and the collective agreement applicable to Thyssen Mining Construction of Canada Ltd. The union relies on s. 37 of the Act.

In *Cana Construction Co. and C.J.A., Locals 1805 & 1990* (1984), 9 CLRBR (NS) 175 at pp. 186-187, [1985] Feb. Sask. Labour Rep. 29 (File Nos. 199-84,

201-84 and 202-84), the Board set out the test for determining if an employer is a successor employer under s. 37 of the Act in the following terms:

> In order to determine whether there has been a sale, lease, transfer or other disposition of a business or part thereof, the Board will not be concerned with the technical legal form of the transaction but instead will look to see whether there is a discernable continuity in the business or part of the business formerly carried on by the predecessor employer and now being carried on by the successor employer. The *Trade Union Act* does not contain a statutory definition of "business" and the Board recognizes that it is not a precise legal concept but rather an economic activity which can be conducted through a variety of legal vehicles or arrangements. It has given the term "business" a meaning consistent with the comments of the Ontario Labour Relations Board in *Canadian Union of Public Employees v. Metropolitan Parking Inc.*, [1980] 1 Can LRBR 197 at 208:
>
> "A business is a combination of physical assets and human initiative. In a sense, it is more than the sum of its parts. It is a dynamic activity, a 'going concern,' something which is 'carried on.' A business is an organization about which one has sense of life, movement and vigour. It is for this reason that one can meaningfully ascribe organic qualities to it. However intangible this dynamic quality, it is what distinguishes a 'business' from an idle collection of assets. This notion is implicit in the remarks of Widjery, J. in Kenmir v. Frizzel et al., (1968) 1 All ER. 414...
>
> Widjery, J. took the same approach as that adopted by this Board, concentrating on substance rather than form, and stressing the importance of considering the transaction in its totality. The vital consideration for both Widjery, J. and the Board is whether the transferee has acquired from the transferrer a functional economic vehicle.
>
> In determining whether a 'business' has been transferred, the Board has frequently found it useful to consider whether the various elements of the predecessor's business can be traced into the hands of the alleged successor business; that is, whether there has been an apparent continuation of the business—albeit with a change in the nominal owner..."

In applying the test to a transfer in the construction industry, the Board commented as follows at p. 191 CLRBR, p. 41 Sask. Labour Rep.:

> In the Board's opinion, the "economic life" of a construction company may therefore depend upon the availability of a combination of component parts at a cost the market will bear and which include, among other things, the availability of skilled labour, managerial expertise, ownership of or access to necessary equipment, and (especially in the commercial, institutional and industrial sector) sufficient capital and financial stability.

In the present case, we find that the following factors apply:

(1) The Joint Venture has acquired all of its management expertise from Thyssen. Thyssen provides the Joint Venture with its key personnel in all areas of operation, from the tendering process, to the actual construction activities. Thyssen personnel completely manage the worksite.

(2) The business carried on by the Joint Venture is the same as was carried on by Thyssen prior to the creation of the Joint Venture. The Joint Venture is not engaged in a business operated by Thyssen prior to the creation of the Joint Venture.

(3) The Joint Venture operates with equipment from Thyssen and with the use of Thyssen's office facilities and support staff. Thyssen provides the benefit coverage to employees on the site.

(4) Practical operational control of the Joint Venture rests with Thyssen and depends on its expertise in mine construction.

(5) The remaining partners in the Joint Venture lack the mining construction expertise to obtain the work in question. Their partnership with Thyssen is essential to obtaining the work through the Joint Venture. The economic relationship between the partners is based on mutual gain, providing access for both to the work in question.

QUESTIONS

1) What is the *purpose* of the management exclusion contained in all Canadian labour relations legislation?

2) Why are exclusions such an important issue for unions individually, and for the labour movement as a whole? (Give at least two reasons).

3) What are some tests you might use to decide if a given employee should be considered a regular worker or a member of management?

4) Do you feel that Hiram Dant and Michael Dawson had more in common with the management community or with the electrician community?

5) Had you been the arbitrator in this case, what would your ruling have been, and why?

Certification Case
CUPE, LOCAL 79 AND CORPORATION OF THE CITY OF TORONTO

When a union is seeking to represent a bargaining unit containing large numbers of seasonal, part-time, and casual employees, who should be considered a bargaining-unit member for the purpose of determining whether the union has sufficient support to entitle it to a representation vote?

Canadian Union of Public Employees, Local 79 and The Corporation of the City of Toronto

Ontario Labour Relations Board, R. O. MacDowell, Chair; J. A. Rundle, Member; and H. Peacock, Member. July 3, 1996.

J. James Nyman, for union.

E. T. McDermott, for employer.

No. 2603–95–R.

R.O. MACDOWELL, CHAIR
(H. PEACOCK, MEMBER, CONCURRING)

This is an application for certification in which CUPE Local 79 seeks to represent a large group of City employees who are currently unrepresented. A significant number of those employees have sought membership in the union and have indicated in a secret ballot vote that they want the union to represent them. The question in this case is whether the union is entitled to certification as their bargaining agent—that is, whether the Board can give legal effect to the wishes of employees recorded in the representation vote.

The union and the City are no strangers to the collective-bargaining process. CUPE Local 79 already represents some 2800 "white-collar" employees in the so-called "inside workers' bargaining unit." CUPE Local 43 (a sister local) represents a

Source: Adapted from OLRB, No. 2603-95-R, in 32 CLRBR (2nd), 1996, pp. 1–49. Some deletions have been made by the author for the purposes of this book and names have been changed.

bargaining unit of 1800 "blue-collar" workers in the "outside workers' bargaining unit." Employees represented by the two CUPE locals work in proximity to the unrepresented workers affected by this application.

The two CUPE locals have been involved in collective bargaining with the City for decades. The issue in this case is whether another group of City employees is entitled to participate in that process.

The present application relates to a body of employees variously described as "part-time," "seasonal," or "casual," who work in the City's parks, community centres, and recreation programs. Their hours of work and work locations vary considerably, as does the actual work that they do. The number of casuals actively employed at any particular time also varies with the season and with the program mix offered by the City.

The parties are *agreed* that for the purposes of this certification application the unit of employees appropriate for collective bargaining should be described as follows:

> all casual employees employed by the corporation of the city of Toronto in the Recreation Division of the Department of Parks and Recreation, save and except supervisors, persons above the rank of supervisor, and persons for whom the applicant or any other trade union held bargaining rights as of October 10, 1995.

However, the parties are *not* agreed on the number of employees in this unit for the purposes of the application. In other words, the parties agree on the *description* of the bargaining unit, but they do not agree on its *composition*.

The term "casual employee" (or "recreation casual") is used by the City for payroll purposes to describe these casual workers in a general way, and distinguish them from the "regular" inside or outside workers who are already represented by CUPE. For convenience, we will use the same terminology in this decision. However, it is important to note that the term "casual employee" (as used by the City and applied to a particular individual) does not necessarily connote a continuing employment relationship with the City, either in a common-law contractual sense, or for the purpose of certification under the *Labour Relations Act*, 1995. That is one of the issues that divides the parties. Since these "recreation casuals" work intermittently, there is a dispute about just how many of them actually were "employees" at the time the certification application was filed.

Counsel for the City advised that, over the course of the year, the City hires as many as 2400–2500 of these "casual workers" who work for various lengths of time in the parks, playgrounds, and recreation centres scattered throughout the City. The peak program period is during the summer months when, we were told, the City needs roughly 1500 additional employees to work as lifeguards, supervise wading pools, organize sports activities, administer camp programs, and so on. Many of these individuals are students employed during their school vacation period, so when the summer is over, their jobs end and they go back to school. They may or may not return the following summer.

In the fall, the complement of casuals drops considerably. Counsel for the City advised that, for the autumn programs, between 700 and 900 individuals are engaged for activities as diverse as square dancing, piano lessons, or Red Cross certification. In the winter, *yet another group* of workers is engaged in respect of indoor programs or outdoor winter sports activities at the City's parks, ice rinks, and arenas.

We were told that only a small group of "recreation casuals" are working continuously — primarily because they have a skill (for example, piano training) that is in constant demand for particular programs or at a particular recreation centre. However, that core group comprises only 200 to 400 workers (the parties disagree about the numbers). The rest of the recreation casuals come and go in accordance with the City's needs. There is no necessary carry-over between, say, those casuals who act as lifeguards or supervise the wading pools in the summer, and the casuals who clean the ice rinks in the winter. The composition of the casual group is continuously changing.

The City says that up to 75 percent of the summer casuals are hired again in the following summer (the union disputes the percentage). But there is no legal commitment to do so. Nor is there any obligation on the casual to return if asked. In this sense, the casual workers' situation is quite different from someone with enforceable "recall rights" under a collective agreement.

...   .

By any measure, there is a substantial turnover of casual employees, since the number and composition of the casual group depends upon the seasons, the program mix that the City chooses to offer, and, of course, their own availability to return to a program that has been offered before. Indeed, it is interesting to note that even the City had difficulty identifying the precise number of casuals who had been employed over the past year. We were told that compiling a list of casuals was difficult because the work locations were geographically diverse and many of the payroll records were kept manually.

This application for certification was filed on October 10, 1995—that is precisely a month before Bill 7 came into effect. The material filed with the application therefore reflects the scheme of the Act that was in effect prior to November 10, 1995. However, because Bill 7 had certain retroactive features, it is agreed that the Board is obliged to apply the new Act to this application, even though it was filed "under the old system."

In support of this application for certification, the union has submitted 738 "membership" cards, and has estimated that, at the time the application was filed, the size of the bargaining unit was 840 persons. We were told that the union had been organizing for a number of months prior to the application, so its estimate is presumably based upon its contact with the various workplaces and its understanding of the ebb and flow of program activity. The union's estimate is generally consistent with the City's own estimate of the number of casuals *actively* working in the fall programs (see above).

In each case, the union card is signed by the individual worker concerned, is witnessed by another person, and indicates that the signer is applying for membership in the union. There is no real challenge to the form of this membership evidence either from the City or from any of the individuals who signed the cards. There is no reason to believe that the cards do not mean what they say: that the person signing the card wants to be represented by the trade union in a collective-bargaining relationship with the City.

The City has filed material in response to this application (which, as noted, was launched prior to the passage of Bill 7). The City's filing identified some 369 persons who were actively at work on Tuesday, October 10, 1995, the day on which the certification application was made.

The City has also filed a schedule of some 2455 other persons labelled "recreation casuals" who were not at work on the application date, but who had worked for the City at some point in the previous year. For the overwhelming majority of these individuals, the City has indicated that they were not scheduled to work on the application day, and that their expected date of return or recall was "unknown." The City's position is that all of these individuals (369 + 2045 = 2414) should be considered to be "employees in the bargaining unit" for the purposes of this certification application, *and further that if less than 40 percent of them have signed union membership cards, there can be no representation vote.*

It remains to be determined whether Bill 7 actually requires the kind of *pre-vote* arithmetic calculation proposed by the City, and, if it does, whether such calculation should be based upon the City's proposed list, material from the union, or some revised version of the City's list that emerges from inquiry or litigation. *The City asserts that an examination of this kind is required before any representation vote can be ordered.* The union's proposed interpretation of Bill 7 avoids this *pre-vote* exercise altogether—or, more accurately, shifts the focus to one of determining voter eligibility *after* the vote is ordered, rather than whether a vote should be taken at all. We shall have more to say about that later. At this point, it may be helpful to "do the arithmetic" in order to illustrate the dimensions of the problem.

For the 369 persons actively at work on October 10, 1995 (*i.e.*, literally "in" the proposed bargaining unit on the application date), the union has submitted 201 membership cards, which represents about 54 percent of the persons listed by the City as being at work on October 10. For the other 2045 persons not at work on October 10 (and for the most part not scheduled to return to work at any known date), the union has gathered a further 344 cards. Since the union's card-signing campaign took place in the weeks prior to the filing of the application for certification, it appears that by the time the application was filed, quite a number of the casuals who were working during the summer and had signed cards at that time, were no longer actively employed.

The union clearly has the support of the majority of the employees actively at work on October 10, 1995, and, therefore, unequivocally in the bargaining unit on the date the union applied for certification. Since the City says that there are around 900 individuals working in its fall programs, it is also clear that a significant proportion of them want to be represented by the union. However, if the bargaining unit actually contains 2400 to 2500 "employees" as the City claims, then the union's level of "card support" in that much larger group is only around 25 percent of this much larger number. And if the size of the bargaining unit is somewhere between 369 and 3000, it is currently impossible to determine the union's level of card support in percentage terms, without examining the actual situation of each person named on the employer's list to see whether such individual should be treated as an "employee" in the bargaining unit for the purposes of the certification process.

It is impossible to predict how long such analysis would take, particularly if the "facts" or their characterization are disputed, so that the Board would have to make specific determinations with respect to individual workers. But the union's estimate of "many months" is not at all unreasonable—especially if the test for inclusion in the bargaining unit for certification purposes ultimately turns on each individual's personal situation, his or her intention to return to work, or the likelihood that she or he will return to the program, position or location in which she or he had worked before. This could be a mammoth task, involving hundreds of individual inquiries, and by the time it was completed, the bargaining unit under review would likely have undergone significant change.

The nature of the inquiry urged upon us by the employer warrants some further elaboration, because it highlights what might be described as a "systemic concern" in the interpretation of Bill 7. The "process problem" raised by the City in this case is not at all unique. If the employer's interpretation of Bill 7 is right, quite a number of cases may require such pre-vote litigation to sort out the employee list. And that, in turn, may significantly impact on the way in which the Board handles certification applications under Bill 7. In other words, while the characteristics of this work group are a little unusual, the legal issue raised by the employer is extremely important for the way in which the certification process works generally—and ultimately whether the new system can actually deliver the five-day votes that are contemplated by the statute.

We should note that in this particular case, the union could not reasonably have known the precise number of "employees" in the bargaining unit, for, as we have already indicated, even the employer had some difficulty compiling a complete list. The union would have had some general information about the bargaining-unit size from its members in the field, from the casuals themselves and from an earlier application that was filed in the spring and later withdrawn. But the union would not know the precise number or identity of the employees in the bargaining unit in October, even where, as here, the bargaining-unit description was agreed upon. An agreement on the bargaining-unit *description* does not mean that there will be agreement on bargaining unit *composition*.

...   .

If uncertainty about the "employee list" is a basis for litigation, then there may be quite a lot of it. And if a "list dispute" of this kind can delay the "quick vote" contemplated by Bill 7, then there may be quite a few votes that are delayed—despite the terms of the statute.

...   .

On November 21, 1995, the Board (differently constituted) established a "voting constituency" for this application, based upon the agreed-upon bargaining-unit description. The Board also directed that a representation vote be taken, so that the "employees" affected by this application (whatever their number) could indicate, by secret ballot, whether or not they wanted to be represented by the union. In so doing, the Board took into account the material before it, its reading of what Bill 7 required, and the parties' agreement with respect to the bargaining-unit description. The Board was satisfied that the union's material demonstrated the requisite "appearance" of support required by section 8 of the Act, so that the union's right to certification depended on a test of employee wishes.

The City disagreed. The City took the position that no vote of employees *could* be taken, that no vote of employees should be taken, and further that if a vote were taken, the vote should not be counted and the wishes of employees should not be revealed.

The parties did not agree on the composition of the proposed bargaining unit, so they did not agree on the list of eligible voters in the voting constituency. The City maintained that there were 2500 to 3000 persons who were "employees" in the bargaining unit entitled to participate in the vote, and apparently sent letters to those individuals (or many of them) advising them of the vote and urging them to exercise their franchise. The union's view was that the votes consisted of the 800 or so employees actually at work in the City's fall programs when the application was filed.

To avoid delay, the union agreed that a vote could be taken using the City's expanded voters' list. But the union's agreement was made without prejudice to its position that the City's list grossly overstated the number of employees in the bargaining unit and thus the number of eligible voters.

The union's position was that the City's list contained the names of a large number of persons who were no longer "employees" on the City's payroll. In the union's view, the City had "loaded the list" with a huge number of names in order to precipitate "front end" litigation over the list, and derail the quick-vote procedure contemplated by Bill 7. The union points out that delaying the vote was in the employer's interest because in a bargaining unit like this one employee turnover would erode the union's base of support. And on a more general plane, if a union had to meet a test of correctness with respect to bargaining-unit size, it would significantly impede any union's ability to organize employees.

...   .

The representation vote in the instant case was taken on December 8, 1995. There were four separate polls in various parts of the city, with voting hours extending to 8 p.m. so that any individuals interested in the process would have an opportunity to exercise their franchise. Voters were invited to signify by secret ballot whether or not they wished to be represented by the trade union in a collective bargaining relationship with the City.

The turnout was quite low—only 342 persons. The union says that this low turnout reflects the casual workers' lack of actual attachment to the workplace, whatever their notional "employment status" might be, and points out that, in any case, everyone had an opportunity to vote, whether or not they chose to do so.

⋯   ⋯   ⋯

In the result, a significant majority of the ballots cast in the representation vote were cast in favour of the union. In other words, all of the arguably eligible voters were given an opportunity to cast ballots, the ballots were counted, and the union "won" the vote.

The union is content with that result. The City is not.

⋯   ⋯   ⋯

None of the employees (or potential employees) in the bargaining unit affected by this certification application has raised any challenge to the Board's decision to direct that a representation vote be taken to test their wishes. No employee has raised any question about the manner in which the vote was conducted. Nor does any employee or potential employee oppose the union's request that a certificate should issue based upon that representation vote. This case is a contest between the "institutional parties."

⋯   ⋯   ⋯

THE SCHEME OF THE ACT UNDER BILL 7

Bill 7 was introduced into the Legislature in October 1995 and became law about a month later on November 10, 1995. Much of the Bill was directed to repealing features of "Bill 40." But in addition, Bill 7 made a number of other changes, including a revised certification process.

The new scheme no longer permits certification based on membership cards alone. A representation vote has now become the exclusive method of testing employee wishes and is a requirement in every case.

However, in opting for "a vote in every case," the Legislature has not simply reverted to the former process for obtaining and conducting a representation vote. Instead, the Legislature has created an entirely new and quite different mechanism, relying on very quick five-day votes, to measure the employee wishes, while at the same time limiting the employer's opportunity to improperly interfere with the employees' freedom of choice.

The secret ballot replaces the signed membership card as the means of testing the employees' appetite for collective bargaining. But like the previous card-based model, the new system is designed to avoid a protracted "campaign" where the union and employer compete for the loyalties of employees. Because of the tight time-frames, there is less opportunity for behaviour that could attract unfair labour practice charges (quite a number of these are filed each year). The new system makes it very clear that time is of the essence: it is not just "a vote in every case;" the statute contemplates a *quick* vote in every case."

The five-day time-frame mentioned in the statute is the most critical characteristic of the new certification scheme. It not only defines the nature of the process, it also requires the Board to develop new administrative structures in order to meet the five-day target. Indeed, it is a target that we think the Board is required to meet if it can; moreover, it is a target that the Legislature must have intended that the Board *could meet* in most cases, applying the words of the new statutory scheme. The new certification process reflects a legislative trade-off: the elimination of the (relatively) *quick* card-counting model for certification, and the substitution of the *quick* vote model instead.

QUESTIONS

1) Why is the *City of Toronto* case potentially of great importance?

2) Whose arguments do you find more convincing: those of the employer or those of the union? Why?

3) What's the significance of "Bill 7," which has since been incorporated into the *Ontario Labour Relations Act*?

4) If you were the chair of the Ontario Labour Relations Board, would you allow the representation vote to stand? Why, or why not?

5) If you would not allow the representation vote to stand, how would you then proceed in this case?

6) There is considerable debate in the IR literature as to whether certification votes should be decided by a majority of bargaining unit members or a majority of those voting. Which do you think is the fairer standard, and why?

Unfair LabourPractice Case

CAW-CANADA AND MATRIX LOGISTICS

When a union activist is dismissed for smoking in the context of a recent union cer-tification campaign, how is a labour board likely to view that dismissal?

National Automobile, Aerospace, Transportation and General Workers' Union of Canada and Matrix Logistics Services Ltd.

Indexed as: Matrix Logistics Services Ltd. and CAW-Canada

Ontario Labour Relations Board

Laura Trachuk, Vice-Chair

May 1, 2001.

DECISION OF THE BOARD

This is an application under s. 96 [am. 1998, c. 8, s. 9; 2000, c. 38, s. 13] of the *Labour Relations Act*, 1995, S.O. 1995, c. 1, Sch. A (the "Act"). The applicant [National Automobile, Aerospace, Transportation and General Workers' Union of Canada (CAW-Canada)] (referred to as the "union") alleges that the responding party [Matrix Logistics Services Ltd.] (referred to as the "company") violated ss. 70, 72 and 76 of the Act when it terminated the employment of Joseph Conrad and Ian Fleming.

FACTS

The Board heard evidence from nine witnesses. Much of the evidence was contradictory and few of the witnesses were able to provide testimony which was

Source: Adapted from 71 C.L.R.B.R. (2nd 2000) at 210. Some deletions have been made by the author for the purposes of this book and names have been changed.

unaffected by self-interest. The Board has therefore based its decision on those facts which are not really in dispute or, where that is not possible, on the evidence which seems to be best supported by the undisputed facts or makes the most sense in the circumstances considering the balance of probabilities.

Background and History of Organizing Campaign

Matrix Logistics is a warehousing operation for drug store chains. It has a number of locations. The facts relevant to this application take place at the Mississauga warehouse. Both Mr. Conrad and Mr. Fleming were hired by the company in 1997. In the summer of 1999, Mr. Conrad and Mr. Fleming were given the newly created positions of "cleaners." The United Steelworkers of America ("USWA") commenced a union organizing campaign for the employees at the Mississauga location in 1999. Mr. Conrad was the key organizer. He was one of the initial contacts with the USWA, he collected cards on the day shift and amassed the cards that had been collected by employees on the other shifts to return to the USWA. Mr. Conrad's position with the USWA was well known.

In September 1999, the company replaced its management team at the Mississauga location. In early October 1999, with the USWA representation vote pending, the new management team held a meeting with employees. John Lindsay, the company vice-president, asked the employees to vote against the union and give the company six months to resolve any concerns they had. Mr. Conrad spoke at the meeting in favour of the USWA. Mr. Lindsay told the employees that if the company did not live up to its six-month commitment he was sure that Joseph Conrad would be back with another organizing drive and they could vote "yes" then. The USWA lost the vote on October 5, 1999. Mr. Conrad was one of the scrutineers.

In March 2000, six months after the vote, Mr. Conrad commenced a new organizing campaign as promised. The members of the former Retail Wholesale Department Store Union, which had been affiliated with the United Steelworkers of America in 1999, had become affiliated with the applicant. It was the applicant which commenced the campaign in 2000. Mr. Conrad advised some of the company's team leaders that the campaign would be starting. Leaflets were distributed on a few occasions in March and April 2000.

Around the time that the new campaign began. Mr. Conrad was asked to attend a meeting with Ted Steele, the company's director of human resources, and Fred Forsyth, the maintenance manager. They warned him to stop harassing employees about the union. Mr. Steele testified that his operations manager had told him that three employees had complained that Mr. Conrad had approached them about joining the union and that they felt harassed. Mr. Steele would not tell Mr. Conrad the names of the employees but said that next time, if it went further, he would. Mr. Conrad claimed that Mr. Steele said "next time, when I fire you, I will tell you their names." At the hearing neither Mr. Steele nor Mr. Forsyth could recall the names of the employees who had allegedly complained. Dave Martini, the union's business representative, sent Mr. Lindsay a letter protesting against the meeting and an alleged threat to fire Mr. Conrad. Counsel for the company subsequently sent a letter to Mr. Martini in which he denied the allegations in Mr. Martini's letter and in which he took the position that the union was barred from making an application for certification for a year, i.e., until October 2000, as a result of the unsuccessful campaign the year before. A lawyer representing the union warned that the union would respond to any perceived reprisals against Mr. Conrad and indicated that the union would apply for certification when it saw fit. The largest percentage of the total number of cards collected was collected in March. Fewer cards were collected in April, May and June. In April the company hired approximately 100 new part-time employees.

Approximately a month after Mr. Conrad's meeting with Mr. Steele and Mr. Forsyth, the day-shift operations manager, Hans Schreiber, also warned Mr. Conrad that he had received complaints that Mr. Conrad was harassing employees about the union. Mr. Conrad advised him that he was just telling the new employees that there was an organizing campaign in progress and that they could speak to him if they wanted information. Apparently there was some discussion between Mr. Conrad and Mr. Schreiber as to whether that could constitute harassment. Mr. Schreiber advised Mr. Steele about the conversation. Mr. Schreiber acknowledged in cross-examination that prior to his conversation with Mr. Conrad, Michael Jackson, the site manager, had advised him that Mr. Conrad had been spoken to about talking about the union on company time. Mr. Schreiber testified that he also advised his team leaders that Mr. Conrad had been spoken to on the matter.

Approximately one week later, the general manager of Matrix Logistics Canada, Hoyt Steed, also told Mr. Conrad to stop talking to employees about the union.

In June 2000, Mr. Conrad, pursuant to the company's "open door policy," complained to Mr. Steed that one of the team leaders, Daniel Matthews, had been rude in directing him to clean up a water spill. Two meetings were held to discuss the matter. At some point in the first meeting, according to Mr. Steed, Mr. Conrad said something like, "I would not refuse to clean up the spill because you would fire me" and Mr. Steed said, "Well there's a thought." Mr. Conrad was again advised to stop talking to employees. The issue of the union was also raised at both meetings. Mr. Conrad said Mr. Steed raised it. Mr. Steed said that he could not remember who raised it but that it always came up between him and Mr. Conrad. Mr. Steed testified that he was not aware that there was an organizing campaign at that time but that he was not sure that there was not. Mr. Steele said the union issue was raised by Mr. Conrad who claimed they were complaining about him talking to employees because of his union organizing activities. Mr. Steele said that it was acknowledged at the meeting that Mr. Conrad was the chief union organizer but that they denied that was why they were telling him to stop talking. Mr. Steele said they told him to stop talking to employees because it was disruptive. Mr. Steele said that at the end of the meeting Mr. Conrad was told to go do his job and not talk so much.

Mr. Steele testified that aside from a few days of pamphleting in March 2000 he had heard neither "hide nor hair" of the union when he terminated Mr. Conrad. He testified that the company knew Mr. Conrad was the chief organizer on the day shift. However, they were not aware of any involvement that Mr. Fleming had with the union. He claimed that if Mr. Fleming had any interest in the union it was because he was a "follower."

Mr. Conrad testified that he stayed involved with the campaign after he was terminated and that he kept in touch with the union's organizers. He was aware that the union stopped receiving membership cards after his termination. Counsel for the employer objected that this evidence was hearsay as Mr. Conrad was provided with the information by other union organizers.

Cleaners' Duties

The company claims that it terminated Mr. Conrad and Mr. Fleming not because of union activity but because they were taking cigarette breaks outside of one of the doors to its receiving docks. Employees are allowed to smoke outside if they are working. However, the company says that Mr. Conrad and Mr. Fleming had no work duties outside. The question of what the cleaners' duties were is therefore a significant factor in determining the *bona fides* of the terminations.

There were three full-time cleaners, Mr. Conrad, Mr. Fleming, and Sean O'Shea. There was also a part-time cleaner, Peter Guernsey, who was on light duties. The cleaners reported to Mr. Forsyth, the maintenance manager. Mr. Conrad and Mr. Fleming worked from 6:30 a.m. to 2:30 p.m. with one half-hour lunch and one 20-minute break. When they went out for lunch and breaks, they punched or scanned out. The cleaners' duties varied somewhat depending upon which warehouse they were working in, but essentially they involved driving around on vehicles called "double palette walkies," collecting cardboard and garbage and then putting cardboard in the cardboard compactor and garbage in the garbage compactor. They also did some cleaning and relieved the employee in the battery shop as needed.

The warehouse duties are divided into three contiguous areas, warehouse 10, warehouse 40/50, and warehouse 30. Until six to eight weeks prior to the termination, the three full-time warehouse employees would rotate into each area each week. However, six to eight weeks prior to the termination, Mr. O'Shea asked Mr. Conrad and Mr. Fleming if he could work exclusively in warehouse 30 because he was having health problems. They agreed to accommodate him. After that, Mr. O'Shea worked in warehouse 30, sometimes with Mr. Guernsey, who was on modified duties. Mr. Conrad and Mr. Fleming assisted them as needed. Mr. Conrad and Mr. Fleming rotated between warehouse 10 and warehouse 40/50. Mr. Forsyth testified that Mr. Conrad worked in warehouse 40/50 and Mr. Fleming worked in warehouse 10 and that that had been the situation since he started in February 2000. That was clearly not the case. Mr. Forsyth said the cleaners asked him if they could rotate and he said he would think about it. That was clearly not the case either. Mr. Forsyth never assigned them to any particular warehouse nor did he ever discuss a list of job duties with them.

Mr. Conrad and Mr. Fleming testified that the wind blew dust through a hole in the garbage compactor into the warehouse. The hole in the compactor was supposed to be covered by a steel plate but it was missing. Mr. Conrad and Mr. Fleming found that if they cut cardboard to fit the space and taped it on, it would stop the dust. However, the tape would not hold so it required daily repair. Mr. Fleming explained in cross-examination that there was a lip sticking out beneath the hole so the cardboard needed to be cut to fit. Mr. Fleming agreed the job could be done by one person but that it was easier with two because one could hold the cardboard up while it was cut and taped by the other. He testified that it was annoying to have to do this every day although it did provide an opportunity to have a cigarette. He said, however, that if it was not done, every time they dumped garbage in the compactor, dust blew back down the tunnel and in their faces. He said that he asked Mr. Forsyth for a mask because of the dust. He testified that cutting and putting on the cardboard took five to ten minutes. He also testified that since he became a cleaner he always went out to help "Randy." Randy was the driver for "UPAC," the company that collected the cardboard compactor. When the compactor was removed, a lot of cardboard pieces were left on the ground and had to be picked up. The company claimed that assisting Randy was exclusively the duty of the third cleaner, Sean O'Shea. However, all three of the cleaners testified that they all performed this task. Mr. Fleming said it took about ten minutes to pick up the cardboard.

Mr. Forsyth testified that he was aware of the hole in the compactor but that he never told Mr. Conrad and Mr. Fleming to cover it. He said that they had never filled out a maintenance requisition to have it repaired. However, he acknowledged that Mr. Conrad and Mr. Fleming had complained about dust and that Mr. Conrad had brought him to the compactor to show him how much dust there was. He said that he told Mr. Conrad it was not a perfectly sealed unit and that intake fans in the building caused negative air pressure which brought the dust in. He testified that he did not believe that covering the hole would stop the dust. He testified that he told them to use masks because of the dust and that he showed them where the masks were and they started using them. He also testified that Mr. Conrad came and asked for better dust masks and that he provided them.

Mr. Fleming also explained that there was a red light on the garbage compactor which would come on to indicate that it was full. However, it was possible to press another button to reset it. He testified that he would go outside to check the compactor when the red light came on before resetting it. Mr. Conrad explained that they went out to check the compactor to ensure that there was still play in the compactor arm so that it would not break. He testified that it had broken twice. Mr. Forsyth agreed that the compactor arm had broken.

Mr. Conrad testified that the cleaners also picked up garbage that fell on the ground outside when the garbage compactor was removed twice per week. This task sometimes involved a lot of sweeping. He also testified that they had to pick up cardboard that would slide underneath the compactor. Sometimes they shovelled snow and cleaned up around the shipping docks.

Mr. Fleming agreed in cross-examination that he went out door 11, which leads to the north receiving docks, three or four times per day. He said that that had been the case since they started the new conveyor system. He denied that he ever went out just to smoke a cigarette. He said that he always had some work to perform.

Mr. Conrad agreed in cross-examination that, except during the period in which he quit smoking, he more often than not lit up a cigarette when he went outside. He agreed that doing work outside provided an opportunity to smoke and that sometimes it provided an excuse to go outside and smoke. However, he said that he always performed some work that needed to be done when he went outside. He agreed that being able to smoke when he worked outside sometimes extended the period of time he stayed outside. He also agreed that it did not take two people to check the cardboard on the hole on the compactor.

Mr. Forsyth testified that the cleaners' duties had not changed since he started his position as maintenance manager in February 2000. His main concern from his arrival had been sorting out the material handling equipment and that he had not focused on the cleaners. Mr. Forsyth had no discussion with his predecessor, George Mitchell, about the cleaners or their duties. He testified in cross-examination that he accepted that the cleaners knew what they were doing and he did not feel it was necessary to review their duties with them. Nevertheless, Mr. Forsyth testified that the only cleaner who had a reason to go outside was Mr. O'Shea. Mr. O'Shea's only reason for going outside was to clean up the cardboard flaps that fall out when the UPAC driver took away the cardboard compactor. Mr. Forsyth testified that he told Mr. O'Shea that the person in warehouse 30 should go out and clean up the cardboard when the cardboard compactor was removed. He could not recall if Mr. Conrad or Mr. Fleming were there when he said that. He did recall that he did not say that no one else should go out to do that task. He acknowledged that Mr. Conrad and Mr. Fleming were to help Mr. O'Shea in warehouse 30 from time to time. During the period prior to the terminations, the UPAC driver was coming every day to remove the compactor. Mr. Forsyth testified that Mr. Conrad's only outside duty was to take out a garbage bin on the south side of the building (not outside door 11). It is not disputed that no one ever told Mr. Conrad and Mr. Fleming that they were not supposed to go outside.

Mr. Forsyth also agreed in cross-examination that he could not dispute that it was the cleaners' practice to cover the hole in the compactor with cardboard but he stated that no one told them to do it. Mr. Conrad said he had talked to Mr. Forsyth about the hole and that he had suggested covering it with cardboard.

On June 24, 2000, Mr. Forsyth held his first meeting with the cleaners on the day shift. As noted previously, he had never had a prior discussion with them about their duties. He had not assigned them their work or their work areas. At the meeting on June 24, 2000, Mr. Forsyth advised the cleaners that Jerry Flaherty was his assistant team leader. He also advised them that he was instituting a formalized break schedule, a copy of which he provided to them. He told them that they were taking too many unauthorized breaks and that a continuation of that behaviour could lead to discipline, including dismissal. There was no explanation at that time, or at the hearing, as to what he meant or what behaviour he was referring to, i.e., did he mean cleaners scanning out for more than one break? Did he mean going to the washroom too often? His agenda for that meeting says, "There has been many individuals taking more than one break and late lunch this is considered time theft and will not be tolerated anyone caught will be dismissed [*sic*]." Mr. Conrad denied that Mr. Forsyth said that at the meeting. Mr. Fleming could not recall but agreed it was possible it was said. Mr. O'Shea could not recall what was said was to happen, if the break schedule was not followed. Mr. Fleming testified that Mr. Forsyth said there had been complaints because they were in the lunchroom on breaks at different times than anyone else. However, the item is included on an agenda, which was identified by Mr. Forsyth and Mr. Flaherty and which was provided to the Board. The Board finds that unauthorized breaks were mentioned at the meeting. However, the agenda was never given to the cleaners. The cleaners were never given anything in writing except the break schedule. Nothing was posted. Many other things were also raised by Mr. Forsyth at the meeting. It appears that the break schedule was not popular and there was a lot of discussion about it because the cleaners thought it required them to take lunch too early.

In cross-examination, Mr. Forsyth testified that he understood that smoking was only permitted outside in designated areas and that the area outside door 11 was not a designated area. That view is not consistent with the company's policy, which permits smoking while working outside and is not restricted in any area. One would have expected that since Mr. Conrad and Mr. Fleming were terminated in Mr. Forsyth's presence for a violation of that policy he would have known about it. Mr. Forsyth's lack of knowledge on this point suggests that he and Mr. Steele never even discussed the theory upon which Mr. Conrad and Mr. Fleming were terminated. According to Mr. Forsyth, Mr. Conrad and Mr. Fleming should not have been smoking even if they were assisting Mr. O'Shea as it was not a designated area. He denied that if they were helping Mr. O'Shea it would have made a difference in whether they should be terminated because they were not "supposed to be there." He said that he considered it to be a firing offence for them to be outside their area and to be smoking outside the designated area. The company claims, however, that they were terminated for taking breaks outside.

Terminations

On July 12, 2000, Mr. Flaherty was walking by door 11. He saw Mr. Conrad and Mr. Fleming go out the door. He went and looked through the window and then immediately opened the door and told them to come back inside. They were outside for approximately one minute. Mr. Flaherty saw them standing at the bottom of the stairs from the door lighting up cigarettes. There was some dispute as to whether Mr. Fleming was actually lighting up; however, there was no dispute that he planned to do so. Mr. Conrad told Mr. Flaherty that they were going to check the cardboard that they placed over the hole in the garbage compactor to stop dust from blowing into the plant. Mr. Flaherty said something to the effect of "never mind the excuses and get back inside." They came back in. Mr. Flaherty testified that he then went to see Mr. Steele. As it was after 2:30, Mr. Steele said they would address it the next day. Mr. Steele said that he was considering suspending them at that point.

Mr. Fleming testified that around 1 to 1:30 on July 12, 2000, he and Mr. Conrad had just dumped some barrels into the compactor and were overwhelmed with dust. They had covered the hole in the garbage compactor with cardboard the day before so they went outside to check it. They just reached the bottom of the stairs when Mr. Flaherty came out. Mr. Conrad had a cigarette in his mouth. Mr. Fleming did not know whether he had had a chance to light it. Mr. Fleming was showing Mr. Conrad a $10 bill upon which, it appeared to him, an American flag was flying over the Parliament buildings. They were about to proceed to the compactor when Mr. Flaherty told them they should not be out there. They tried to tell him that they were going to look at the compactor but he said that he did not want to hear their excuses and he was not following them. Mr. Fleming then left while Mr. Conrad stayed behind and spoke to Mr. Flaherty. Mr. Fleming went to get more garbage bins. When he went to dump them into the compactor 20 minutes later, the dust was still blowing around. He there-fore grabbed some tape and cardboard and went outside to tape up the hole.

The evidence with respect to the next day, July 13, 2000, is rather confusing and contradictory. Mr. Steele testified that when he came to work that day, he found Mr. Forsyth and Tom Walker, the manager of loss prevention, reviewing a surveil-lance tape of door 11. Mr. Steele testified that they told him that both Mr. Conrad and Mr. Fleming had made several entrances and exits through that door that morn-ing. He also testified that he was told that Mr. Flaherty and Mr. Forsyth had seen *them* come in through door 11 at about 8:30. That appears to be the reason that they were reviewing the surveillance tapes. However the tapes show that Mr. Conrad and Mr. Fleming were *not* outside together that morning. The tape also shows no sign of Mr. Flaherty and Mr. Forsyth. Mr. Forsyth testified that he Mr. Flaherty decided to go down and look at door 11 on the morning of July 13th to see what number it was. When they got there they saw Mr. Conrad (and not Mr. Fleming) coming inside with a stick in his hand. Mr. Conrad apparently said "a good day for golfing" and walked by. They did not confront him or ask him what he had been doing. Instead, they decided to go and look at the tapes in the security office. The tapes they looked at showed the inside of door 11. There are cameras on the outside of the building as well. Mr. Forsyth testified that he wanted to see what the outside cameras showed but they were "broken or something." While Mr. Walker was getting ready to review the tapes, Mr. Steele came in. They told him they had seen Mr. Conrad coming in from outside. Mr. Steele testified that he did not stay at that point but arranged for a meeting to be held at 9:30. Mr. Forsyth said that they then viewed the tapes from the previous day and Mr. Conrad and Mr. Fleming came in and out so many times it was "ridiculous." (They came in and out three times.) He also said that they noticed that Mr. O'Shea had gone out the same door so they decided to bring all three of the cleaners in for an interview.

Mr. Steele's evidence was somewhat different. He said he reviewed at least some parts of the surveillance tapes of the inside of door 11 on the morning of July 13th prior to 11 a.m. He claimed that he reviewed the first exit on July 11th and possibly all of the exits on July 12th and the first one on July 13th. He testified that on the tape of July 12th they saw Mr. Fleming taking out a piece of plywood and then bringing the same piece back in. This appeared to be offered as support for his determination that something improper was going on. However, a close look at the tape shows that Mr. Fleming took out a piece of something that looks like cardboard and brought back a different shaped piece. Mr. Steele also testified that they were looking at the surveillance feed when they saw Mr. Conrad go out door 11 at 8:53. When he had not returned by 9:03, Mr. Steele ordered that the tape be pulled. No one went to see what Mr. Conrad was doing outside.

Mr. Conrad testified that he went outside on the morning of July 13, 2000, to see if there was enough play in the arm of the cardboard compactor. He said on Monday or Tuesday of that week the arm had become too tight and Mr. Forsyth had had to call UPAC to come and get the compactor right away. Mr. Conrad ascertained that there was enough room in the compactor arm and he came back inside. He went out again later and cleaned up with Mr. O'Shea and Mr. Walker when the UPAC driver came. He testified that later he covered the hole over the garbage compactor. On that occasion Mr. Fleming was with him. (That occasion must have been after the tape was removed as the tape does not show them going out together that morning.) On each occasion when Mr. Conrad went out, he lit a cigarette but he did not stay to finish it on the first occasion when he was checking the compactor arm.

Mr. Fleming testified that on the morning of July 13th at approximately 8 a.m. he was dumping cardboard when he heard a bang and thought it was Randy coming to take the cardboard compactor. He therefore went outside. When he went out he realized that Randy was not there and he came back inside. He testified that about 10:30 he went out with cardboard and tape to fix what he had done the day before to the hole in the compactor. He could not recall if Mr. Conrad was with him. He testified that the first time he went out he did not smoke but the second time he did.

Mr. Steele met with Mr. Forsyth at 11 a.m. on July 13th. He said they discussed the cleaners' duties. However, as noted above, it does not appear that the company's policy of permitting employees to smoke outside if they were working was discussed as Mr. Forsyth was unaware of that policy when he testified. Mr. Steele said that Mr. Forsyth advised him he had addressed the issue of "time theft" at the meeting of

June 24, 2000. He reviewed the break schedule and the record showing that the employees had swiped out for their scheduled breaks. He said that he decided that they were engaged in "time theft" and that they should be terminated.

Mr. Steele testified that he asked Mr. O'Shea to come to a meeting on July 13th as he had been seen exiting door 11 right before Mr. Conrad and Mr. Fleming. (In fact only Mr. Conrad went out after Mr. O'Shea.) The meeting took place prior to the meetings with Mr. Conrad and Mr. Fleming. Mr. Steele said he asked Mr. O'Shea what he was doing outside and he said that he went to meet the truck (the UPAC vehicle). He asked him if he saw Mr. Conrad and Mr. Fleming out there and he said that he had. He asked him what they were doing and he said "standing smoking cigarettes." However, the surveillance tapes show that only Mr. Conrad was outside with Mr. O'Shea on July 13th. Mr. O'Shea was not outside when Mr. Conrad and Mr. Fleming went out on July 12th. This fact throws both accounts of this conversation into doubt. Mr. Steele knew that as he had just seen Mr. O'Shea go outside on the surveillance tape before Mr. Conrad but not Mr. Fleming.

Mr. O'Shea testified that he was asked what he was doing outside that morning. In cross-examination he could not remember what date they had asked him about. He said he was asked if he saw Mr. Conrad and Mr. Fleming outside and he said that he had. Again this was not true, and Mr. Steele and Mr. Forsyth would have known it as they just reviewed the tape. Mr. O'Shea said he was asked what Mr. Conrad and Mr. Fleming were doing and he said smoking. He was asked whether they were working at the same time and he said no. He was asked if he had seen them smoking outside before and he said he had. At the hearing he said he also went out there three times per day to work and smoke. He said they were allowed to do this as they were cleaners. In the hearing he also said that he saw them go out three to five times per day but did not know how long they were out there. In cross-examination he acknowledged that he did not actually see them going out but he would see double palette walkies near door 11. He also testified that there were many of those walkies in the plant and they were all painted the same colour. Sometimes the ones he saw at door 11 would have red or yellow bins on the back which would mean they came from the warehouse 30 and he would assume those were Mr. Conrad's and Mr. Fleming's. Mr. O'Shea testified in cross-examination that he warned Mr. Conrad and Mr. Fleming separately in September 1999 that they were going to get caught going outside so frequently. They both denied receiving such a warning from him. Mr. O'Shea confirmed that he had seen Mr. Conrad and Mr. Fleming covering the hole on the garbage compactor with cardboard and tape. He testified that that job should only need to be done about once per week and should not take more than a minute but that they took 10 to 15 minutes. However, he acknowledged in cross-examination that he had never done it himself and was just guessing. He agreed that it was part of Mr. Conrad's and Mr. Fleming's job to come out to assist him when the cardboard compactor was taken away. Sometimes one would help and the other would smoke, sometimes they would both work and he would smoke.

Mr. Steele and Mr. Forsyth asked Mr. Conrad to meet with them with the intention of terminating him after they met with Mr. O'Shea. There was considerable disagreement as to what was said at this meeting. As the company relied upon the exchange at this meeting as evidence of Mr. Steele's good faith and Mr. Conrad's culpability, it will be set out in some detail. However, it is hard to find that any account is entirely accurate. Ultimately what took place was Mr. Steele asked Mr. Conrad what he was doing outside, Mr. Conrad told him, Mr. Steele said he did not believe him and fired him. It is not disputed that Mr. Steele had decided to fire Mr. Conrad before the interview. Nevertheless, Mr. Steele testified that he asked Mr. Conrad what he was doing outside on July 12th and he said he was going to cover the hole in the compactor because of the dust. Mr. Steele then said he asked how he was going to do that without tape or cardboard and that Mr. Conrad said "no comment." Mr. Conrad denies that. (If Mr. Conrad and Mr. Fleming went out on July 13th to tape up the compactor, it was after the surveillance tape had been removed so Mr. Steele would not know if they had cardboard and tape or not. The tape of July 12th does show them going out at one point with cardboard which apparently been [sic] out before they come back in.) Mr. Steele testified that he told Mr. Conrad that they had a large number of entrances and exits on tape and it was "time theft." He claims that Mr. Conrad said that if they had it on tape he would not comment. Mr. Steele said they then told him he was being fired for time theft, gave him a handwritten note to that effect, and walked him off the premises. It was acknowledged, however, that at some point Mr. Conrad said he had been cleaning up cardboard with Sean O'Shea but they told him the [UPAC] truck had left 35 minutes prior. (That did not make sense given what they had asked Mr. O'Shea. Furthermore, the tape for July 13, 2000, shows that Mr. O'Shea and Mr. Conrad were outside at the same time.) Mr. Steele said that he could not believe that Mr. Conrad was that stupid and that he had just given him cause to fire him. Mr. Conrad asked if he was supposed to get a warning and Mr. Steel said that Mr. Flaherty had given him a warning the day before. Mr. Conrad uttered a profanity and asked who Jerry Flaherty was. He said that he (Mr. Flaherty) might be Mr. Forsyth's assistant team leader but he was not his (team leader). He said that he had never seen a posting for that position. Mr. Steele said something like, "Thank you for saying that in front of us." At the time of this exchange Mr. Conrad already knew he was being fired. Apparently he made that comment about Mr. Flaherty as there had been no posting for his position according to the company's normal practice. Mr. Steele testified that he also told Mr. Conrad that Mr. Forsyth had warned him on June 24th about "time theft." Mr. Conrad denied that.

Mr. Forsyth testified in cross-examination that when Mr. Conrad was asked what he was doing outside, he described fixing the compactor arm and helping Mr. Fleming with the cardboard on the compactor and cleaning up the cardboard. Mr. Forsyth said they did not believe Mr. Conrad's explanation about the hole in the compactor. He said they did not believe his explanation about cleaning up after the cardboard compactor because the driver had left.

Mr. Steele and Mr. Forsyth then asked Mr. Fleming to come to a meeting. They had decided to terminate him before the meeting. Mr. Fleming did not know that Mr. Conrad had been fired. In examination-in-chief Mr. Steele claimed that he told Mr. Fleming that they had film evidence of him going out and taking breaks. Mr. Steele testified that he asked what they were doing and Mr. Fleming said "smoking." Mr. Fleming denied that. Mr. Steele said that he asked Mr. Fleming if he was begging to be caught and said, "I guess so." He asserted that Mr. Fleming said that if he had it to do over again he would not. Mr. Steele also said that he asked Mr. Fleming if he remembered Mr. Forsyth mentioning "time theft" at the meeting in June and that he remembered it was a serious issue. Mr. Steele told Mr. Fleming that he got himself caught up in a very unfortunate situation and that he could not treat him differently than any other individual in those circumstances so he was terminating him. Mr. Steele agreed that Mr. Fleming told him he was outside fixing the hole in the trash compactor. Mr. Steele also said, confusingly, that he did not discuss being outside on July 13th with Mr. Fleming. Mr. Steele said that was "moot" and they were only talking about July 12th. He said to Mr. Fleming, "I can't believe in your situation you would do this." (Mr. Steele was aware of some personal problems Mr. Fleming was having.) Mr. Steele acknowledged that he told Mr. Fleming that he was a good worker and that he had had high hopes for him and that he was caught up in a bad situation. He then offered to provide Mr. Fleming with an employment reference. Mr. Fleming called that evening to find out what kind of reference he would receive and Mr. Steele said that he would recommend him for employment.

Mr. Forsyth testified that they asked Mr. Fleming what he was doing outside and he said he was fixing the hole in the compactor. Mr. Forsyth said he asked him how he was going to do that without any tape. He also testified that Mr. Fleming said he went to see if the UPAC was there. Mr. Forsyth said they then asked him what he was really doing and he said "smoking." Mr. Forsyth then testified that they asked Mr. Fleming if he remembered what was said at the meeting (on June 24th) and he said he remembered being told about Mr. Flaherty and time theft and that if he had it to do over again he would not do it. Mr. Forsyth said Mr. Fleming was terminated because of time theft.

Mr. Fleming denied Mr. Steele's and Mr. Forsyth's account of the meeting. He testified that Mr. Steele asked him what he was doing outside and he said he was either helping Randy or taping up the garbage compactor. He believed that Mr. Steele was referring to the day the meeting was taking place, July 13th. He said that Mr. Steele did not believe he was outside doing what he claimed. He said that Mr. Steele asked him if he remembered Mr. Forsyth's warning about time theft at the meeting. He said he responded that he remembered the meeting but not what was said about time theft. Mr. Steele then said that "this is the part of the job I hate" and that it was one of the hardest decisions he had to make. Mr. Fleming testified that that is when he got nervous and asked if there was anything he could say to change Mr. Steele's mind. Mr. Steele said unfortunately Mr. Fleming was caught up in a bad situation and he could not "let go of one without the other." Mr. Steele then wrote his termination note and told him he was fired. Mr. Fleming said he called Mr. Steele later to find out what kind of reference he would give him. Mr. Steele said he was a good worker caught up in unfortunate circumstances and suggested he try "CFM" where they were hiring.

Again the Board does not find that any account of this meeting is very reliable. Mr. Fleming may well have acknowledged he was smoking but that was not an infraction of any rule or policy unless he was not working. It is clear he explained what tasks he was doing outside. Mr. Steele and Mr. Forsyth chose, or pretended, not to believe him for no apparent reason as neither had ever assigned duties to him or told him not to go outside.

Mr. Forsyth testified that when Mr. Conrad and Mr. Fleming said they were taping up the hole they were asked how they could do that without tape. In the hearing no one asked the witnesses if they actually had tape with them when they went outside. There did not appear to be any tape in their hands, but no one asked them if they had it somewhere else. The company did not rely in argument upon the apparent absence of tape as evidence of anything.

Mr. Steele testified that the only reason he terminated the two employees was because of their "theft of time." He claimed that he only considered Mr. Conrad's union involvement to the extent that it made him more cautious. He said that he considered suspending the two workers on July 12th for a "violation of policy" when they were "caught red-handed going out," but terminated them when he found it was a pattern. The Board queried Mr. Steele as to the policy to which he was referring. He said it was "going outside when they were supposed to be inside." Mr. Steele also testified that he believes Mr. Fleming to be a "follower" and that he would never have engaged in "time theft" on his own.

Mr. Steele testified that he went outside to look at the hole in the garbage compactor on July 12, 2000. There was no question that the hole was there and the Board was provided with a photograph of it. However, Mr. Steele claimed that he decided that it would not blow dust into the plant because of the "prevailing winds." However there is some question as to whether he did go out to look at the hole as there was no evidence that anyone told him on July 12th that that was the reason Mr. Conrad and Mr. Fleming gave for going outside that day. Mr. Steele testified in cross-examination that he had no idea how long the hole had been there nor whether it was usually covered with cardboard.

Mr. Conrad had no discipline on his file. The verbal warning he received in March 2000 was never recorded. Mr. Fleming also had no prior discipline on his file.

DECISION

The company argued that demonstrating that a union organizer was terminated for serious misconduct is an important indicator of a company's good faith. The other side of that coin, however, is that terminating a union organizer who has essentially no disciplinary record for a minor offence is an important indicator of a company's bad faith. In *Hallowell House Ltd. and S.E.I.U., Local 183*, [1980] 1 Can LRBR 499 at pp. 504-505, [1980] OLRB Rep. 35, para. 19, the Board made the following comments:

> Seldom will an employer admit that it has been motivated by anti-union animus in discharging an employee. The Board, therefore, is required to draw its own conclusion as to the employer's motivation and in doing so must draw inferences from the evidence. In discharging an employee, the Board looks for a reasonable explanation for discharge. If the employer provides little or no explanation for terminating an employee and there is concurrent evidence of union activity the Board may, depending on the circumstances, draw the inference that the employer had an anti-union animus and acted in violation of the Act. If the employer establishes good cause for discharge on the other hand, the Board will normally require more cogent evidence of union activity, the grievor's participation in the campaign and the employer's knowledge of it before being willing to draw an inference of anti-union motivation. The evaluation of the adequacy of the employer's reasons for discharge is not aimed at determining whether the employer had just cause for discharge but is rather a step in the more complex process of ascertaining the employer's motivation. While unfair discharge does not itself establish a violation of the Act, it may be evidence from which the Board will, in certain circumstances, draw an inference of anti-union animus.

In this case the company claimed that Mr. Conrad is guilty of "time theft." However, accusing Mr. Conrad of "theft" does not magnify what he did to a "serious industrial offence." At most he was guilty of wasting a few minutes in the same way that employees do every day in every workplace, in the same way that the two employees on the surveillance tape did when they stopped to chat for seven minutes. The Board did find that Mr. Forsyth warned the cleaners about "time theft" on June 24, 2000. However, there is no reason that the cleaners would have understood that to be a warning with respect to going outside to perform the tasks they had been performing regularly for a year. The evidence is that the cleaner's duties were assigned, or evolved, under George Mitchell, Mr. Forsyth's predecessor. There was no job description. When Mr. Forsyth started working in February 2000, he did not assign or change any duties. He held no meetings with the cleaners until June 24th. His evidence was that his focus was elsewhere. He did not even assign the cleaners to the areas in which they worked. The cleaners agreed to that themselves. Mr. Forsyth knew that he had never made either area or work assignments and he agreed that the cleaners knew their duties when he started his employment, so how could he be so certain that they had no duties outside? The answer is that he could not be certain. But he and Mr. Steele either refused to consider the possibility that Mr. Conrad and Mr. Fleming were telling the truth when they said they had duties outside, or they knew otherwise but chose to maintain that they had no such duties because they wanted to terminate Mr. Conrad. Yet the evidence demonstrated that Mr. Conrad and Mr. Fleming did have duties outside door 11. At the hearing, all three cleaners agreed that all three of them would help pick up when the UPAC driver came. All three agreed that Mr. Conrad and Mr. Fleming covered the hole in the garbage compactor. The evidence on the tape was that they did take cardboard out and bring back a different sized piece, consistent with the claim that they were covering the hole. Mr. Steele and Mr. Forsyth claim to have seen that on the tape. Mr. Forsyth agreed that they had complained to him about dust. There was no dispute that the arm on the compactor had broken twice, so trying to avoid that happening by checking the compactor was a good idea. No one claimed it was not.

Mr. Conrad and Mr. Fleming did go outside on a number of occasions on July 12th and 13th so the crucial factual question is whether they had work to do out there. The evidence with respect to July 11th is less reliable but the Board is prepared to assume they went out on a number of occasions that day as well. It is also undisputed that they often smoked cigarettes when they went out. However, it is the company's policy, well known to Mr. Steele, that employees are allowed to smoke if they are working outside. The company says that it terminated the employees because they had no work to do outside. However, the evidence disclosed that they did have work to do outside. The company ultimately argued that whatever tasks they were doing outside were not assigned to them or were excuses to go out and smoke. Certainly, Mr. Conrad and Mr. Fleming embraced opportunities to perform tasks outside. No doubt they were motivated to do so because they could smoke. However, it is hardly a termination offence for employees to do jobs they prefer or find to be easier rather than jobs they do not like or are more onerous when given the opportunity. The worst offence that Mr. Conrad and Mr. Fleming committed is that they both went out to check the hole in the compactor when one person could have done that.

QUESTIONS

1) What is your overall view of the way the company handled the union certification drive?

2) If you were a labour board chair, how would you respond to the evidence concerning Mr. Lindsay's speech of October 1999 on the subject of unionization at the company?

3) What is your view of the company's approach to health and safety issues, as illustrated in this case?

4) To the extent that the company had a significant problem with "time theft" caused by employees' smoking, how might it have addressed this problem, other than by dismissing certain employees?

5) Had you been the arbitrator or labour board chair in this case, what would your ruling have been, and why?

Arbitration Case
USWA, LOCAL 7884
AND FORDING COAL LTD.

Does an employer's prohibition of cellular phones in the workplace constitute an unreasonable infringement on employee's personal privacy?

Heard: November 5, 1997;

Decision rendered: January 21, 1998; British Columbia; D. L. Larson

Lynn Jenning, for the Union.

R. E. Lester, for the employer.

AWARD

The issue in this case is whether a rule established by the Company on September 11, 1996, that prohibits all employees from bringing personal cellular telephones into the workplace is valid.

The evidence relating to how the rule came about is not in dispute. Michael Wilson, superintendent, employee relations, testified that the matter did not arise out of any particular incident, but that it was generally based upon concerns relating to safety, productivity and efficiency. He testified that until the fall of 1996, cell phones were not a problem because they had not been a reliable means of communication in Elk Valley. However, when B.C. Tel established a new cell site and began to sell the service in the local mall, he concluded that it could become a problem and issued the policy.

When asked what was behind his safety concern, he replied that he became alive to the dangers of cell phones from news reports, combined with the fact that mining is inherently hazardous and that one must do everything possible to reduce the risk. He said that this mine encompasses a large geographic area with constant traffic on

Source: Adapted from 2–70 L.A.C. (4th 1998), pp. 33–43. Some deletions have been made by the author for the purposes of this book and names have been changed.

N.B. Instructors may find this case useful in connection with Chapter 7 on employment law.

the haulage roads. It is an open pit mine with huge equipment, including 170 and 240 ton Wabco trucks, on roads that can have a pitch of up to eight degrees and that must share the roads with a lot of other smaller vehicles.

As for productivity and efficiency, Mr. Wilson said that the mine is operating on very small margins, which requires maximum efficiency in order to remain profitable. He said that he could not even endorse the use of cell phones during breaks because that would be difficult to monitor and human nature being what it is, if employees were to have phones, they would use them during working time, particularly to take calls.

The Union conceded that there was good reason to be concerned with safety. Bill James, national representative, testified that they concurred that employees should not be permitted to use cell phones while operating heavy equipment or working in the plant because there are already a significant number of accidents. But he said that the Union considered that it would be appropriate that shop stewards and safety representatives be permitted to carry them. He said that would involve only 20 to 25 employees, equal to about 3 percent to 4 percent of the total workforce, depending upon the number of active stewards. Further, he said they would be distributed into all areas of the property over three shifts.

Currently employees have access to the Company hard-wire phone system by permission. If a foreman is not immediately accessible, the procedure is that the employee may request a truck driver to call the foreman on his two-way radio. The foreman will normally then come around some time later and if he thinks that it is important, will either take the employee to a telephone or arrange for someone else to do it.

It is not without significance that the employees of outside contractors who work on the property are permitted to use cell phones. Mr. Wilson explained that the Company tries not to interfere with the way they run their businesses. They usually have other customers who need to have access to them. On the other hand, he said that the allegations that Dan Wilcox, a management employee who works in the Purchasing Department, has been given permission to use a cell phone is incorrect and that what he has is a cordless phone that only works within a limited range from the base unit. Mr. Wilcox was not called as a witness and, since it involved a singular instance, even if true, I do not consider it to be sufficient to affect the integrity of the policy.

Sally Neal, who is classified as Pit Utility in the Mine Production Department, was a shop steward from 1994 to 1995. She is currently a safety representative for the Union. She testified that her job is located at the "spoils," which is where the large Wabco trucks dump overburden. The spoils tend to be a fair distance from the actual mine, but a "dump shack" has been set up by the Company to provide shelter. It has also been equipped with a two-way radio although Ms. Neal testified that the majority of the time it does not work. That was not disputed by the Company, which explained that the problem stems from the fact that the shack is on skids and is moved frequently.

She gave two examples of occasions when she was refused the use of Company phones in her capacity as a safety representative. She said that on December 18, 1996, she expressed concern to her foreman, Sam Golzo, that the shack had been placed on the opposite side of the road from the spoil. The problem was that it put her in a position of having to cross the road in the face of traffic. Her supervisor responded by giving her an alternate assignment of driving the buses that take employees to and from the mine. She said that she arrived at the mine at 1:30 p.m. during the lunch break. When Mr. Golzo came by she asked him if she could use the phone, to which he replied that he would have to ask Dave Downing, a control foreman. Over the radio, Mr. Downing asked if the call was for personal or union business. She said that when she told him that it was union related, he replied, "no," but he told her to take her lunch and wait for him. When he arrived at the dry, she said that she asked him why he did not permit her to use the phone during her lunch break. He explained that if she wanted to use the phone for union business she would have to book off work. But when she requested a union book off he refused it because there were too many off that day. She was then told to wait for Mr. Golzo to take her down to the buses. The result was that she ended up waiting a total of about 80 minutes including her lunch break, not being able to use the phone even though it was no more than 20 feet away.

The other example that she gave happened on July 6, 1997. On that day a rock went through the windshield of a front-end loader driven by Fred Arnold. When it was reported to her, she asked for permission to go and see it. When she got there she felt that it was a dangerous occurrence that required investigation. In the course of the investigation she asked for permission to use the phone to call Brad White at home in order to determine whether a screen guard might be the solution. Mr. Downing denied the request, stating that the investigation should be completed first, and that if she still felt that she would like to talk to Mr. White arrangements would be made. Based on that evidence, the Union took the position that a Company rule prohibiting all employees from possessing cellular phones on Company property is not reasonable in its application within the rule set out in *Re Lumber & Sawmill Workers' Union. Loc. 2537, and KVP Co.* (1965), 16 L.A.C. 73 (Robinson). While it conceded that there was a legitimate safety concern, specifically relating to employees using cell phones while working and operating machinery, it argued that the current rule is too broad and could not be supported by reference to any of the standard tests in the cases. Accordingly, it proposed that Union officials, including shop stewards and health and safety representatives, should be permitted to possess cellular telephones on Company property. Under the proposal, those officials would be entitled to use the phones in the following circumstances:

   (a) as of right, on their own time, without prior authorization;
   (b) as may be necessary on Company time, with authorization, which authorization would not be unreasonably withheld; and
   (c) as of right, during authorized leave for the purpose of conducting union business.

···   ···   ···

The Company takes quite a different position. On the authority of *Re British Columbia Railway Co. and C.U.T.E., Loc. 6* (1982), 8 L.A.C. (3d) 250 (Hope), Mr. Lester argues that the better view is now that an arbitration board does not have an inherent jurisdiction to determine whether a rule published by an employer is reasonable: *Bank of British Columbia v. Union of Bank Employees. Loc. 210* (1982), 133 D.L.R. (3d) 228 (S.C.), but can only monitor the application of the rule under its right to determine whether an employee has been disciplined for just and proper cause: *Re Religious Hospitallers of Hotel-Dieu of St. Joseph of the Diocese of London and Service Employees' Union. Loc. 210* (1983), 11 L.A.C. (3d) 1.51 (Saltman). As for the argument that the policy interferes with the administration of the Union, Mr. Lester says that, in point of fact, there is nothing in the policy that restricts the Union. He said that while the Union might like to be able to operate in a certain way, it has never had the right to use cell phones on Company property and that what it really wishes to do is enhance, facilitate, and improve the way that it carries out its functions. Since it is not a current right, he contends that the only way that it can be acquired by the Union is in the normal way, through collective bargaining.

··· ··· ···

Is the use of cell phones in the nature of a personal right similar to the right to privacy?

Ms. Jenning took up that point by arguing firstly, that for the Company to suggest that the use of cell phones by employees would be an enhancement of their existing rights should not be accepted. Secondly, she said that prior to the policy, employees had a right to bring cell phones to work just as they have a right to bring a lunch and that, instead of the Union seeking to obtain enhanced rights, it is the Company that seeks to limit individual employee rights.

There would appear to be some support in the collective agreement that safety representatives are distinguishable from shop stewards and that they could be enabled to use cellular telephones, based upon the fact that their investigative responsibilities are not constrained in the same manner as shop stewards. Without deciding the matter, under Article 7.02 a steward must obtain permission from his supervisor in order to take time off from work "to attempt to resolve a grievance," although that provision equally provides that the supervisor will not arbitrarily or unreasonably withhold permission. By contrast, no similar requirement is imposed on safety representatives under Article 8. Article 8.02 requires that the foreman and safety representative will determine whether an investigation of an accident is required and if they cannot agree, the matter may be referred under subsection (c) to a referee process. In the event of a complaint that a condition is unsafe or an unusual hazard exists, a safety representative may investigate under Article 8.07 on the condition that a complaint must first be made and the employee is not satisfied with the decision of his or her supervisor.

In those circumstances, one could conclude that the use of cellular telephones by safety representatives could be more easily accommodated because they are less regulated. A safety representative is entitled to initiate an investigation depending upon certain objective conditions, while a shop steward may be refused permission to take time off work by the subjective decision of a supervisor that there are overriding operational requirements.

However, while safety representatives and shop stewards have been given different degrees of independence, nowhere does the collective agreement purport to give either of them a right to use cell phones. Further, there is nothing in the investigative procedures contained in Articles 7 and 8 that would permit me to imply such a right. Accordingly, I have no jurisdiction to determine whether the current policy that prohibits all employees from bringing cellular phones to the workplace is reasonable. Even more, I have no jurisdiction to decide whether the proposal put by the Union is better; nor can I mandate an alternative.

The fact is that the rule is not arbitrary in the sense that it is based upon considerations of safety, a matter which is conceded by the Union. Indeed, it is difficult to see how cell phones could be made completely safe by virtue only of the employee being a shop steward or a safety representative. The concern expressed by Mr. Wilson was not that regulations could not be prescribed for when they could be used, as was proposed by the Union, but that these same employees will also be driving heavy equipment or operating plant machinery and that if they have them they will use them.

QUESTIONS

1) Why did management impose the ban on cellular phones in the first place? Do you think the ban was justified?

2) Is it reasonable for the union to argue that a ban on the use of cellular phones by union stewards and health and safety representatives constitutes interference with the union's workplace activities?

3) What would your decision have been had you been the arbitrator? Why?

4) Would the fact that outside contractors are allowed to use cellular phones, at least under certain conditions, affect your decision in this case?

5) The union has served notice that if this grievance is denied, it will challenge the ban as an unfair labour practice. Do you agree with this approach? If not, what alternative course might the union take?

ArbitrationCase
ONA, LOCAL 13 AND SUDBURY GENERAL HOSPITAL

Does the exclusion of management personnel from unionization rights under the labour relations act prevent individuals from simultaneously occupying a part-time management position and a position in a part-time bargaining unit?

Heard: November 25, 1997; Ontario; I. G. Thorne, S. Ursel, and Y. Campeau

Decision rendered: January 27, 1998

J. Janczur and others, for the union.

P. C. Hennessy and others, for the employer

AWARD

The Association has grieved that an individual holds positions at the Hospital as a part-time registered nurse and as a part-time employee in a position excluded from the bargaining unit, i.e., a management position. The Association contends that an individual cannot at the same time be a member of the bargaining unit and a member of management, and that the Hospital is in breach of the collective agreement in permitting this situation to come into being.

The parties proceeded on the basis of an agreed statement of facts, as follows:

1. Mary Carter is the trauma coordinator at Sudbury General Hospital. The position of trauma coordinator is a management position and is excluded from the bargaining unit.
2. Mary Carter commenced employment as trauma coordinator in 1991. When she commenced employment as trauma coordinator in 1991, the trauma coordinator position was a full-time position.
3. On July 2, 1996, Mary Carter was awarded a temporary part-time position in the Intensive Care Unit, which is a bargaining unit position.
4. On September 9, 1996, Mary Carter was awarded a regular part-time position in the Intensive Care Unit, a position which she continues to hold.

Source: Adapted from 70 L.A.C. (4th 1998), pp. 9–21. Some deletions have been made by the author for the purposes of this book and names have been changed.

5. Since commencing employment in the Intensive Care Unit, Mary Carter has continued as trauma coordinator on a part-time basis, a position that continues to be a management position.

Also in evidence were the postings for the temporary part-time position and for the regular part-time position mentioned in the above statement, together with a list of the applicants interviewed in connection with each posting, and a letter dated December 6, 1996, from the Association to the Hospital regarding this grievance.

We were advised that Ms. Carter had been notified of this hearing, but had chosen not to attend.

On September 10, 1996, the Association filed a grievance claiming a "violation of the collective agreement in the Employer's decision regarding the Trauma Director position" and asserting that the position should be within the bargaining unit. The remedy that the Association sought at the hearing was that Ms. Carter should be removed from the bargaining unit position in the Intensive Care Unit and that the position should then be posted in accordance with the collective agreement. In view of this change in the remedy requested, the Employer asked that the original grievance be withdrawn by the Association or dismissed by this board. The letter of December 6, 1996, referred to the change in the Association's stance. The letter referred to a grievance regarding the alleged impropriety of an incumbent holding a position in the ICU in the bargaining unit and the position of trauma director, a management position. The letter also purported to put the Hospital on notice "... that our position at arbitration will be that she should not have been awarded the bargaining unit ICU position."

···   ···   ···

The Hospital was of the view that nothing in the collective agreement prohibited one person from holding positions within and outside the bargaining unit and asked that the grievance be dismissed in any case.

Counsel for the Association elaborated on the Association's position that no one person could simultaneously hold a position in the bargaining unit and a management position. Such a situation was contrary to the scheme of the *Labour Relations Act*, 1995, S.O. 1995, c. 1, Sch. A, counsel argued, and assigning a bargaining unit position to a member of management was inconsistent with the collective agreement taken as a whole, since it existed to protect the rights and positions of members of the bargaining unit. What had occurred was also a specific violation of Article B-2 of the local agreement and of Article 10.11(a) of the central collective agreement. The former article restricted management from acting in a manner inconsistent with the collective agreement, while the latter prohibited nurses in supervisory positions excluded from the bargaining unit from performing duties normally performed by nurses in the bargaining unit, and its breach deprived other nurses of the right to claim positions available within the unit.

In counsel's submission this was more than a question of whether a member of management was doing bargaining unit work and was more fundamental: a member of management could not at the same time be in the bargaining unit. Membership in the bargaining unit of such a person would entitle her to attend meetings of the Association, to vote on Association matters, and to seek election to an office within the Association. Underlying the Association's position, counsel maintained, was the principle that it was persons who were excluded from the bargaining unit under the legislation, not positions. He illustrated this argument by reference to ss. 1(3), 15, 53, 70, and 114 of the *Labour Relations Act, 1995*, all of which were said to demonstrate the arm's-length nature of the relationship between employer and unions conceived by the legislation.

...   .

In the Hospital's submission, the Association was not able to show any violation of the collective agreement. Article B-1 restricted management from acting in a manner inconsistent with the provisions of the agreement, but the Association had not been able to show such an inconsistency, counsel maintained. The Association could show no breach of Article 10.11 since no evidence had been brought forward to show the impact of Ms. Carter having been awarded a bargaining-unit position and thus the tests set out in that article had not been met. In fact, counsel pointed out, Ms. Carter was the sole applicant for the temporary position so that no opportunity was lost to members of the bargaining unit; thereafter, in the Hospital's view, Ms. Carter was herself a member of the unit and entitled to the same consideration as any other member when she applied for the regular part-time position. Further, contrary to the Association's assertion, Article 19.04(b) of the central agreement appeared to contemplate what the Association said was prohibited: a member of the bargaining unit could be temporarily assigned to a higher classification not included in the bargaining unit.

...   .

Certain provisions of the collective agreement are relevant to the parties' submissions: In the local agreement:

Article A—Recognition

A-1 The Hospital recognizes the Association as the bargaining agent of all lay, part-time Registered and Graduate Nurses, employed by the Sudbury General Hospital of the Immaculate Heart of Mary at Sudbury, engaged in a nursing capacity, save and except Head Nurses, persons above the rank of Head Nurse, full-time employees, and persons specifically excluded by the decisions of the Ontario Labour Relations Board dated the 15th day of December 1970.

Article B—Management Rights

B-2 It is agreed that the Hospital may exercise any of the rights, powers and functions or authorities which the Hospital had prior to the signing of this Agreement, except those rights, powers, functions or authority which are abridged or modified by this Agreement, and these rights shall not be exercised in a manner inconsistent with the provisions of this Agreement.

In the Central agreement:

Article 10—Seniority

10.11(a) Nurses who are in supervisory positions excluded from the bargaining unit shall not perform duties normally performed by nurses in the bargaining unit which shall directly cause or result in the layoff, loss of seniority or service or reduction in benefits to nurses in the bargaining unit.

Article 19—Compensation

19.04(b) Where the Hospital temporarily assigns a Registered Staff Nurse to carry out the assigned responsibilities of a higher classification (whether or not such classification is included in the bargaining unit) for a period of one (1) full tour or more, at times when the incumbent in any such classification would otherwise be working, the nurse shall be paid a premium of one dollar and twenty cents ($1.20) per hour for such duty in addition to her or his regular salary. The Hospital agrees that it will not make work assignments which will violate the purpose and intent of this provision.

The contents of the sections of the *Labour Relations Act, 1995* referred to in argument can be summarized. Section 1(3)(b) provides that "… no person shall be deemed to be an employee … who, in the opinion of the Board, exercises managerial functions or is employed in a confidential capacity in matters relating to labour relations." Section 15 requires the Labour Relations Board not to certify a union "… if an employer … has participated in its formation or administration or has contributed financial or other support to it …." Similarly, section 53 deems an agreement between an employer and such an employer-influenced union not to be a collective agreement for the purposes of the Act. Section 70 prohibits an employer from participating in or interfering with the formation, selection or administration of a union. Section 114(2) assigns to the Labour Relations Board the determination of any question whether a person is an employee within the meaning of the Act.

The issue raised by the grievance appears to be a novel one, at least in the sense that there seem to be no reported awards dealing directly with it. While we heard no direct evidence on the point, it is reasonable to suppose that the sort of situation that might give rise to this issue is more likely to occur at the present time than might have been the case in the past. Budgetary pressures on hospitals have forced staff reductions and realignments of responsibilities. Lay-offs, bumping, or other circumstances may oblige employees to apply for positions involving a new mix of responsibilities. That seems to have been Ms. Carter's situation: her position outside the bargaining unit was reduced from a full-time to a part-time one and she applied for a vacancy in the part-time bargaining unit. Fortunately for her, she was able to obtain a temporary part-time position for which she was the only applicant. This may well have seemed a satisfactory situation for all concerned. In any event, no issue was made of Ms. Carter's status until after her later successful application for the regular part-time position. One way of looking at the present dispute is to consider, as the Hospital does, that at the time of her application for the latter position, Ms. Carter was a member of the bargaining unit with seniority. Another way of looking at it, as the Association does, is to take the view that by virtue of her holding a part-time management position, Ms. Carter was precluded from becoming a member of the bargaining unit and thus was not entitled to apply for the vacant position.

There is some support in the collective agreement for the view that individuals and not simply positions are excluded from the bargaining unit. Article A-1 in the local agreement does speak in terms of the exclusion of "… persons above the rank of Head Nurse … and persons specifically excluded by the decisions of the Ontario Labour Relations Board …." Beyond that, the Association cannot point to any specific provision that would preclude an individual from holding a part-time management position and a part-time bargaining unit position. Article 10.1 1(a) indicates a priority for nurses within the bargaining unit so far as the performance of duties normally performed by nurses is concerned, but it must be said that the article is directly applicable only in circumstances that have not been shown to be present here. On the other hand, the Hospital can point to Article 19.04(b) as an indication that the parties have not excluded the possibility that one individual may both be a member of the bargaining unit and a person assigned to act in a management position; again it must be said that the application of the article is restricted and could be viewed as an agreed exception to the principle of mutual exclusivity of management and bargaining-unit work—if such a principle exists.

This brings us to the Association's central contention: that the whole scheme and structure of the legislated labour relations regime supports its view that one person cannot be both in management and in the bargaining unit, and that this explains the lack of a clear reference to the point in the collective agreement.

···   ···   ···

12. The identification of management is fundamental to the scheme of collective bargaining, as set out in the Labour Relations Act. What is contemplated is an arm's-length relationship between the employees represented by a bargaining agent, on the one side, and the employer acting through management on the other side. The Act attempts to create a balance of power between these two sides by insulating one from the other. Employees, therefore, are protected from management interference and domination by the prohibitions against employer interference with trade union and employee rights.

   Management, by the same token, is protected by excluding from collective bargaining either persons exercising managerial functions, or persons employed in a confidential capacity in matters relating to labour relations. Collective bargaining rights, therefore, are not universal, but must be qualified by the need to preserve a countervailing force on the employer side.

It should be borne in mind that in this passage the Board was explaining why it was important to determine who was identified with management in ruling on an application for certification, a matter fundamental to the process of collective bargaining. The passage makes clear the Board's view of the need to create a balance of power and to protect each side from the sort of interference it describes. These concerns seem somewhat remote from the situation described to us in this case. It was suggested on behalf of the Association that if Ms. Carter were permitted to hold a position within the bargaining unit, she would be entitled to seek union office and otherwise participate in the affairs of the Association. We are uncertain whether that might be seen as management interference in the affairs of the Association or alternatively as a breach of duty by a member of management, but in any event there is no evidence that Ms. Carter has actually participated in union affairs in support of one interest or the other.

...   .

While none of the judicial and arbitral decisions before us directly considers the issue raised in this case, *Re Miller (supra)* does touch on one aspect of the problem. The decision of the Divisional Court examined an arbitration award that had determined that a newly created position of assistant manager was not within a bargaining unit stipulated to consist of "… all … employees save and except the Manager." In a judgment quashing the award the Court observed:

> There is nothing in the *Labour Relations Act* which provides that a voluntary collective agreement which covers persons other than employees as defined in the *Labour Relations Act* is invalid …

In this respect it is fair to say that the Court seemed to accept that it was open to the parties to extend the benefits of a collective agreement to individuals who might otherwise be deemed not to be members of the bargaining unit. That is consistent with our understanding of the capacity of the parties in this case to determine in their collective agreement whether one individual may simultaneously hold a part-time management position and a part-time bargaining unit position, or not.

We must say that any intention the parties may have had in this regard is unclear. It may be that their intent would become clear if there was evidence demonstrating some adverse effect on the interests of one party or the other. However, it is difficult to say that such an adverse effect has been demonstrated on the particular facts of this case. Ms. Carter, employed part-time in a management position, applied for a temporary part-time position within the bargaining unit. She was the only candidate and was appointed. It cannot be said that her appointment caused any loss to any member of the bargaining unit at that time. If other qualified applicants had come forward, the issue of Ms. Carter's right to apply for the position might properly have been raised. As matters stood, however, it does not appear that either party saw any impediment to her appointment. Rather than diminishing the bargaining unit, therefore, Ms. Carter's appointment made her a member of it. The situation was a little different when she applied for the regular part-time position since there were other applicants for that position from within the bargaining unit. However, by that time, it appears, Ms. Carter had been treated as a member of the bargaining unit for some time without objection.

...   .

The parties may wish to consider whether the issue raised by this grievance is one that should divide them. The drawing of a rigid line could work to the disadvantage of nurses both inside and outside the part-time bargaining unit who wished to pursue a job opportunity on the other side of the line. The parties may prefer to negotiate more precisely the extent to which a part-time employee may occupy a bargaining-unit position and one in a higher classification.

QUESTIONS

1) Given today's economic climate, what is the significance of this case?

2) Does the case provide you with what you consider adequate information concerning the nature of Ms. Carter's duties as trauma coordinator? If not, what additional information might be helpful?

3) Whose arguments do you find more convincing: the Hospital's or the Nurses' Association's?

4) If you were the arbitrator, what would your decision have been, and why?

5) What might the parties do to help prevent such cases from being taken to arbitration in the future?

Arbitration Case
DIVISION 4, RAILWAY EMPLOYEES DEPT. AFL-CIO AND CN RAILWAY COMPANY

What circumstances, if any, would justify an arbitrator's reinstating a man discharged for attacking a fellow employee with a knife?

In the Matter of an Arbitration between Canadian National Railway Company and Division No. 4, Railway Employees Department A.F. of L.—C.I.O. And in the Matter of the Grievance of A. McKay [The case was heard by a single arbitrator]; A hearing in this matter was held at Montreal on June 13, 1979.

AWARD

JOINT STATEMENT OF ISSUE

On October 6, 1978 Electrician A. McKay was working the 1600 to 2400 hours shift in the passenger car paint shop at Transcona Main Shops. At approximately 2115 hours an altercation occurred involving Mr. McKay and carman apprentice J. Jacot.

During the altercation Mr. McKay drew a utility knife from his tool pouch and Mr. Jacot was cut on the little finger of his left hand.

An investigation was conducted and the electrician was discharged for his part in the altercation.

The International Brotherhood of Electrical Workers appealed the company's decision requesting that Mr. McKay be reinstated in his former position and that the discipline assessed be similar to that assessed the other persons involved in the incident.

The company declined the appeal.

From the statement of all the employees concerned, it is clear that there was a fight between the grievor and another employee, and that as a result the other employee was injured (his hand was cut) by the grievor's utility knife. What is not clear is the degree of responsibility of the various persons involved.

Source: Adapted from Craig and Solomon (1993), pp. 588–589. Some deletions have been made by the author for the purposes of this book and names have been changed.

The grievor did participate in a fight and for that (except in clear cases of self-defence) some discipline would be warranted. He did, as well, draw from his pocket (and from the pouch protecting the blade) his utility knife. The use of any weapon, or the use of a tool as a weapon (even if the blade was very short) is obviously wrong, and for that too the grievor would be subject to discipline. I do not consider that the grievor was deliberately attacked by another employee or employees, so that he was in reasonable fear of serious injury. I do not consider, then, that there was that degree of justification that would excuse resort to such a weapon in the circumstances. Thus, for his participation in the fight, and especially for his use of a knife, I consider that the grievor would be liable to severe discipline.

It is necessary, however, in assessing the penalty imposed on the grievor to consider all the circumstances of this incident, as well as the grievor's disciplinary record. In this case the grievor, an electrician, had relatively short seniority, but had a clear disciplinary record and was regarded as a good employee. He was considered by his supervisor to be cooperative and of a good disposition. It appears that he immigrated to Canada from the Philippines a few years ago, and is of relatively slight build.

On the evening in question the grievor had been speaking to his wife on the telephone, mounted on a pillar just outside a foreman's office, with respect to their sick child. Several other employees, carmen and carman apprentices, were nearby, and one of them was anxious to use the telephone. The group considered that the grievor had been too long on the telephone and began to make noise, sing songs and, it seems, beat on a garbage can. While the evidence is conflicting on the point, it seems most likely that one of the employees, Mr. Jacot, actually threw a garbage can against the pillar on which the telephone was mounted. The grievor thought, perhaps not entirely without reason, that it was aimed at him, although I doubt that it really was.

Finally, the grievor hung up the telephone and some conversation took place between him and Mr. Jacot. Mr. Jacot, a carman apprentice, is a younger man than the grievor and is taller and heavier. The accounts of the matter differ, but it appears to me that the most probable account of what occurred is that Mr. Jacot taunted the grievor and invited him to fight. I have no doubt, from the material before me, that whatever the particular incidents may have been, Mr. Jacot was the overall aggressor, and that the grievor's conduct was provoked by the actions of the younger man and by the taunts of his companions. That the grievor was in fact frightened is, I think, the case, although obviously his reaction to the situation was an improper one.

As to the severity of the penalty imposed on the grievor, it is to be noted that there were six persons involved, to some extent, in the incident: the grievor on one hand and five other employees. Of those five, two would appear not to have been substantially implicated, and were not disciplined. Two others were assessed 10 and 20 demerits, respectively, for unnecessary harassment of a fellow employee. These penalties would appear to reflect the involvement of the employees concerned. The fifth member of the group that was harassing the grievor was Mr. Jacot, who was assessed 30 demerits and was suspended for 10 days. That is a substantial penalty and was, it would appear, merited. None of the penalties just described were appealed and they are not before me for determination.

QUESTIONS

1) What circumstances would justify the use of a knife in a fight?

2) If you were the arbitrator, what factors would you take into account in deciding what penalty to impose on Mr. McKay?

3) What would be your ruling in this case, and why?

CASE A.4

Arbitration Case
RWDSU, LOCAL 597 AND CITY CONSUMERS CO-OPERATIVE SOCIETY LTD.

Under what circumstances is a department store justified in dismissing an employee who fails to show up for a shift on very short notice?

Re City Consumers Co-Operative Society Ltd. and Retail, Wholesale and Department Store Union, Local 597

F. R. Woolridge, Q.C., L. McCormick, S. Marshall (Newfoundland)

June 15, 1982.

Source: Adapted from 6 L.A.C. (3rd 1982), pp. 74–79. Some deletions have been made by the author for the purposes of this book and names have been changed.

GRIEVANCE

The grievor claims her discharge for failure to work a scheduled shift was unjust.

FACTS

The facts are not in dispute.

The employer operates a large supermarket employing some 72 employees, including 21 cashiers, some part-time such as the grievor.

The store manager is Mr. McAulay, the assistant manager is Mr. Browne, and the head cashier, Ms. Lush, who is responsible for the shift scheduling of the part-time cashiers.

The grievor had been employed by the employer in September of 1981 and worked in the old store of the employer, where a notice was posted in the lunch-room that forbade shift changes among the cashiers because it was a frequent occurrence, and sometimes for seemingly frivolous reasons in the eyes of management, and it was difficult to find replacements due to an unwillingness on the part of some cashiers to cover for a shift of another, or to work overtime.

In the new year the employer moved operations to a new location on Topsail Rd. No such notice was posted there, and the rule was relaxed, but the employer requested that a reasonable period of notice be given before taking time off on a scheduled shift so that alternate arrangements to cover the shift could be made.

Some time in the month of February the grievor went to Ms. Lush and told of her plans to leave the province for two weeks to seek medical treatment. Absences of long duration such as this must be cleared with the manager, Mr. McAulay, to whom she was sent. McAulay was annoyed that the grievor was going in only two days' time, but because of the nature of the trip, and the fact that the grievor had travel plans already made, he agreed to the request, although he told her to give more notice in future.

The grievor was not told of any disciplinary consequences that would flow from any such future failure.

Commencing January 30, 1982, Mr. Browne, the assistant manager, had commenced keeping records of cashiers who failed to show up for scheduled shifts. These records were kept for two reasons. Overtime under this agreement is not compulsory, and the employer was having difficulty finding employees prepared to do overtime work, which, while not compulsory, must not be unreasonably refused. These records would show the occasions of failure to report, and the reasons why, so that they would provide a history of the cashiers' record and provide evidence in the event any disciplinary action was taken. Copies were given to the shop steward. One such record for employee Miller (exhibit Consent 3) will serve as an example. It reads as follows:

Department: Grocery
Sent to: Ann Miller
Date: Jan. 30/82
Message:
Jan. 6/82 Scheduled for work 5–9 but couldn't make it because she had company for supper.
Jan. 11 & 12/82 Late for work.
Jan.13/82 Couldn't make it from 1–5 or 6–9 because she had to take one of the boys out to the Dr.
Jan. 9/82 Asked to start work 1 instead of 1:30 but refused.
Jan. 18/82 Couldn't work today because she had to take one of the boys out to the Dr. Scheduled for 1–5.
Jan. 27/82 Scheduled for 1:30–5:30. Called 11 a.m. to say she wouldn't be in because of the snow.
Jan. 29/82 Scheduled for 9:30–1:30. Couldn't come because she never had any transportation.
Isaac Browne

On March 30, 1982, the grievor was scheduled to work the 1:30 p.m. to 5:30 p.m. shift for the next day. She went to Ms. Lush and asked permission to change that shift with one of the other cashiers because she had made a dental appointment for her children. Because such requests were again causing problems in scheduling, Ms. Lush had, some days or weeks before, gone to Mr. McAulay and suggested they revert to the old system of prohibiting such changes. McAulay had agreed. No notice had been posted but Ms. Lush feels that all the cashiers were notified. For that reason she told the grievor that there could be no change. The grievor then announced her intention to keep the dental appointment in any event and to miss the shift. She was not advised of the consequences of this action, because Ms. Lush was quite candid that she did not know what, if anything, the consequences would be.

Although Ms. Lush could not remember the incident, the grievor maintains that she called Ms. Lush at 12:15 p.m., March 31, 1982, one hour and 15 minutes before her shift was scheduled to start and confirmed that she would be absent. She failed to show up for the 1:30 p.m. shift, and another substitute cashier was found by 3:00 p.m.

At 3:00 p.m. or 3:30 p.m. on March 31, 1982, Ms. Lush notified Mr. Browne that the grievor had not come to work. At that point Mr. Browne decided to terminate the grievor, but in an effort to get her side of the story first, he telephoned her at home to see if she had an adequate explanation. When asked for an explanation the grievor pleaded the dental appointment had already been made. Mr. Browne suggested that was no excuse because she should make such arrangements on her own time since they were not the concern of the employer, and that such absences caused obvious scheduling difficulties. The grievor responded that regardless of these considerations she would do the same in the future if the occasion arose, and went on to complain about the poor management of the Co-op. Browne responded that if that was her attitude she need not bother to return to work. The grievor, then noticeably upset, thereupon announced her intention not to set foot in the store in future.

Shortly thereafter the grievor called both Ms. Lush and Mr. Browne, still obviously upset, and complained of her disappointment over how she had been treated by Browne. The grievor maintained that the employer was making a deliberate move to get rid of her, because other employees were getting away with the behaviour without penalty. Lush and McAulay backed Browne's decision and the grievor was discharged as of that date, and filed her grievance the next day.

CONSIDERATIONS

Was the grievor discharged for just cause?

By art. 25, the management's rights clause of this agreement, the employer has the unfettered right to "...plan, direct and control store operations...," which obviously includes scheduling, and each employee owes the employer the obligation to work when scheduled, and the cases are too numerous to mention that a failure to fulfil that obligation will provide just cause for the employer to discipline or discharge the employee in question.

The employer argued that not only was the grievor absent without permission, but compounded the problem by wilfully disobeying a legitimate direct order and displaying a defiant attitude when she announced her intention to repeat the offence in future, all of which amounted to insubordination properly grounding discharge.

It suggests she took no steps to find a replacement, and that given her attitude towards the job, particularly in the knowledge of the earlier warning in February, it would be pointless to reinstate her if she intends to disobey scheduling requirements.

The union does not condone this type of behaviour, but suggests the employer acted in a manner inconsistent with the way it treated other cashiers which amounted to discriminatory or arbitrary treatment of the grievor in a situation where it was never made clear to her that behaviour of this kind would suddenly lead to immediate discharge.

It points to exhibits Consents 4 to 9, which showed that since January 30, 1982, four cashiers have missed shifts ten times for reasons ranging from guests in to dinner to doctors' appointments for children and hospital visits, and says that in none of these cases was there ever imposed a more serious penalty than a reprimand memorandum placed in the employee's file. It therefore suggests that seeing this going on around her it was not unreasonable for the grievor to reach the conclusion that regardless of what the stated rule was with respect to shift changes or missing shifts, the employer would only respond to such behaviour with a reprimand memorandum, and she accordingly had no reasonable apprehension that discharge would result.

We feel there is some merit in this suggestion. On the occasion of the February incident, an absence of long duration rather than one shift was involved and the evidence is that she was warned not to give short notice for such required long absences again, and there has been no recurrence.

That type of absence required the permission of Mr. McAulay, and was treated quite differently from single shift absences or changes which were handled by Ms. Lush. Given the manner in which the employer elected to deal with such requests, it is not unreasonable for the grievor to conclude that an infraction of a single shift would be treated more leniently than for a long absence, and of course the best evidence available to the grievor as to how a single shift absence would be treated is how her fellow cashiers were treated when they committed the same offence.

The grievor had never been told such behaviour would lead to discharge—even Ms. Lush, her superior, was unaware of that. It would be wrong in principle to impose an unknown and unexpected penalty on an employee never made aware that a given infraction will reasonably attract that penalty, especially in a situation where an employer has acted in a manner to instill in the grievor's mind a belief that at most, she will receive a reprimand, and for these reasons we feel the penalty imposed was inappropriate.

Considerations of her insubordinate conduct are less easily resolved, since both before and after the scheduled shift the grievor made clear her fixed determination to disobey a legitimate direct order the employer had every right to make, and, moreover, made the quite unnecessary comment, even in the heat of the moment, that she fully intended to repeat the offence in the future.

QUESTIONS

1) What do you think of the department store's policy regarding shift changes? Does this kind of policy seem to you to be a good way to improve labour–management relations?

2) Does the grievor's attitude toward Mr. Browne and the company (as shown during Mr. Browne's call to her on March 31, 1982) justify her termination, in your view? Why, or why not?

3) If you were Mr. Browne, would you have conducted the March 31 interview with the grievor over the telephone? What might you have done differently this time?

4) Had you been a member of the store's management team, how would you have handled an employee exhibiting the kind of attendance record shown by the grievor?

5) Had you been the arbitrator, what would your decision have been in this case, and why?

Arbitration Case
HERE, LOCAL 75 AND
DELTA TORONTO EAST HOTEL

When an employee is discharged without the union representation provided for in his colllective agreement, will that discharge likely be sustained?

Re Delta Toronto East Hotel and Hotel Employees
Restaurant Employees Union, Local 75
[Indexed as: Delta Toronto East Hotel and H.E.R.E., Loc. 75 (Manners-Sutton) (Re)]
File No. Y-100782
Ontario
K.P. Swan
Heard: June 6, 2001
Decision rendered: June 8, 2001

AWARD

A hearing in this matter was held in Toronto on June 6, 2001, at which time the parties were agreed that the arbitrator had been properly appointed pursuant to the collective agreement, and that I had jurisdiction to hear and determine the matter at issue between them.

The matter is the grievance of Mr. James Manner-Sutton, #007/001/000, dated July 21, 2000. The grievance is to the effect that the termination of the grievor by letter dated July 20, 2000 was without just cause.

In addition to contesting the merits of the discharge, the Union also asserts that the circumstances in which the discharge was imposed constituted a breach of the collective agreement, specifically clause 12.6. That provision is as follows:

12.6 Suspension or dismissal:

(1999) in the event that the Employer is contemplating a suspension or dismissal, the Employer will ensure that the employee will be provided the opportunity to have the

---

Source: Adapted from 98 L.A.C. (4th 2001), pp. 31–40. Some deletions have been made by the author for the purposes of this book and names have been changed.

assistance of a Shop Steward. Should the employee not wish to have Union representation he/she will sign a waiver.

A claim by an employee that he/she has been unjustly suspended or discharged from his/her employment shall be treated as a grievance if a written statement of such grievance is lodged under step 1 of the grievance procedure within five (5) days of the beginning of the suspension or discharge.

Such special grievances may be settled by confirming the management's action in dismissing an employee, or by reinstating the employee or by any other arrangement which is just and equitable in the opinion of the conferring parties.

When an employee has been dismissed or if dismissal and resignation have been discussed, the Employer will inform the employee of his/her right to interview a shop steward for a reasonable period of time before leaving the premises.

The parties agreed that this issue should proceed as a preliminary matter, and they were essentially agreed on the facts on which the issue was to be determined. Those facts were placed before me by the opening statements of counsel and, there being no material dispute, the matter proceeded directly to argument.

It appears that, on July 19, 2000, the grievor was assigned to work as a Kitchen Guest-Contact employee. During the breakfast period, he was assigned to a food station where he prepared food items, including eggs, to the individual order of guests. A guest made a request of the grievor, and was sufficiently distressed by the grievor's response to fill out a comment card complaining about the incident.

It is not clear whether the Executive Chef, Mr. Charles Bernard, contacted the grievor during the course of that day to discuss the incident. Mr. Bernard would normally have done so had the comment card come to his attention, but he has no specific recollection of doing so that day. The grievor's evidence would be that no such contact occurred. In any case, it is clear that whatever contact might have occurred would only have been an informal request for further information, made in passing.

In any event, the issue came to the attention of Mr. Lester Brown, Director of Operations. The grievor has a significant disciplinary record of similar interpersonal difficulties with other employees, supervisors and guests. Mr. Brown concluded that the record, coupled with the customer complaint, would justify the grievor's termination, and he therefore had prepared the letter of termination dated July 20, 2000, for the signature of the Executive Chef.

On July 20, Ms. Mary Gorman, Director of People Resources, and the Executive Chef met in the Chef's office. The Chef then went to find the grievor to bring him back to meet with them both. The grievor's evidence would be that, on the way to the office, he asked the Chef what the meeting was about, and was told that he would find out when he got there. This exchange would apparently not be contradicted by any evidence from the Employer. Upon arrival at the meeting, the grievor was asked about the incident with the guest on the previous day, and offered some response. He was then informed that his employment was terminated, and the letter of termination, which had been at hand throughout the meeting, was given to him. At that point he asked something to the effect of "what about my union steward." Ms. Gorman asked if he would like a steward to be brought in, but the grievor responded in the negative. His testimony would be that it seemed to him to be too late, since he had already been terminated.

The Executive Chef then escorted the grievor outside the building, where the grievor stopped to smoke a cigarette. The Chef returned to the building, and brought the union steward to the grievor. The grievor then had the opportunity to discuss the matter with the union steward before he left, and the present grievance was filed. There is no dispute that the grievance was processed in the ordinary way through the grievance procedure, without any change in the Employer's position, and was properly referred to arbitration.

On this basis, the Union argues that the Employer was clearly in breach of the first paragraph of clause 12.6. This paragraph, in the Union's submission, requires that the Employer take steps to ensure that an employee is provided the opportunity to have "the assistance" of a shop steward, which is also referred to as "union representation" in the second sentence of the paragraph. The only way the Employer can escape that obligation is if the employee waives that right in writing, by signing a waiver of those rights.

While the Union acknowledges that the employee did have an opportunity to speak to the steward before leaving the premises, the Union argues that the circumstances of that interview might meet the requirements of the last paragraph of clause 12.6, but certainly cannot meet the requirements of the first paragraph. It is common ground between the parties that the first paragraph was added to the clause in the 1999 negotiations, the clause previously having consisted only of the last three paragraphs.

The Employer, on the other hand, argues that the purpose of the first paragraph is only to explain and augment the obligations of the Employer in respect of the last paragraph. It asserts that the Employer is required to ensure that employees are aware of the existence of the Union and the availability of shop stewards, but only for the purposes of the interview specified in the last paragraph, after termination and before leaving the premises. As to the requirement for a waiver, the Employer argues that this is merely to protect the Union against assertions of a failure of the duty of fair representation.

The Union relies on *Re Toronto (City) and C.U.P.E., Loc. 79* (1986), 24 L.A.C. (3d) 115 (T.A.B. Jolliffe); *Re Glengarry Memorial Hospital and C.U.P.E.* (1990), 11 L.A.C. (4th) 325 (Roach); and *Re Toronto (City) and C.U.P.E., Loc. 79 (Nzeakor)* (1995), 47 L.A.C. (4th) 197 (Charney). The last of these cases includes an extensive survey of the arbitral jurisprudence on the consequences of a failure by an employer to concede union representation rights in a disciplinary process. The Employer relies on the decision of the Ontario Divisional Court in *Cambridge Towel Corp. v. A.C.T.W.U.* (1988), 66 O.R. (2d) 793, and on three arbitration awards applying that decision.

In the *Cambridge Towel* case, the court quashed as patently unreasonable the award of an arbitrator which held that a failure to give three days' advance notice of a discharge to the union president, as required by the collective agreement, was a substantive right which could not be waived, and the breach of which resulted in the ensuing discipline being null and void.

The arbitrators in the three cases cited by the Employer all treat this decision as standing for the proposition that, in every case, an arbitrator should consider a purposive interpretation of the language of the collective agreement, to see what rights or protections are guaranteed to an employee, the extent to which those rights have been denied or withheld, the prejudice suffered by the employee by such a denial, and the appropriate remedy in all of the circumstances. With respect, I have no difficulty in accepting this as the correct way of interpreting any provision of a collective agreement, and in fashioning an appropriate remedy in all of the circumstances. Indeed, the arbitrators in the three cases cited by the Union appear to have taken a very similar approach.

Beginning with the purpose of the first paragraph of clause 12.6, despite the able submissions of counsel for the Employer, I am simply unable to accept that it has no other purpose than to provide structure for the rights specified in the last paragraph. Its placement at the beginning of the clause, separated from the last paragraph by two other paragraphs dealing with the grievance procedure, seems to me to highlight the obvious conclusion that the parties must have intended this to be an independent protection. It is also critical that the first paragraph speaks in a prospective mode, prescribing rights at a point when the Employer "is contemplating a suspension or dismissal." When contrasted with the language of the last paragraph, which applies when an employee "has been dismissed" or if dismissal or resignation "have been discussed," the only obvious conclusion is that the rights in the first paragraph must accrue before any disciplinary action has been taken which would involve either a suspension or a dismissal. There is no other rational interpretation of clause 12.6, read as a whole.

I note that other arbitrators have been able to infer the right to union representation from language which is not nearly as explicit as this, and have not hesitated to do so. In the two *Toronto (City)* cases cited by the Union, the language only defines the right as of "having ... a shop steward ... present at such meeting as an observer." Both arbitrators Jolliffe and Charney concluded, however, that this implied a right to union representation at that meeting. While the language before me does not expressly provide for a meeting or any other formality, it quite explicitly refers both to "assistance" and "representation," and sets the time for that to occur as when the Employer is still "contemplating" the discipline to be imposed.

The Employer asserts that the grievor suffered no prejudice. The Employer's assertion in this regard is unusual. It states that the decision to terminate the grievor's employment had already been taken by Mr. Brown, that neither of the two individuals who were present in the meeting with the grievor had any authority to alter that determination, that the person who had made the decision was not even there, and that therefore nothing that the grievor or a union representative could say on his behalf could possibly have done any good. If such an argument were accepted, the Employer could completely avoid the obligations it has taken on in the first paragraph of clause 12.6 in every case, simply by making its decision in advance of, or instead of, affording the employee the representation rights bargained for. For an employer to say that nothing said to it could possibly change its mind is simply to deny the right specified in the collective agreement. As a matter of the reasonable interpretation of the collective agreement, an employer cannot be permitted to assert that arguments which it has never provided the opportunity to be made would not have affected its decision.

All of the cases relied upon by the Employer are cases where the right bargained for was something far less than a right to union representation. Each of them involves an obligation to provide timely written notice of some kind, and in each case it has been concluded that the purpose of the clause is only to alert the union of the action taken, presumably to permit grievance rights to be pursued, and not provide for union representation prior to the disciplinary action being taken. The present is a very different case, as I have found above. The right bargained for by the Union is one which arbitrators have repeatedly found to be a substantive right, fraught with prejudice to the grievor if denied.

Once an employee has been terminated, there are significant disincentives to reversing that decision. There are issues of management solidarity, questions of managerial authority, and financial consequences which increase day by day as the employee remains away from work without pay. To deny the right of representation at the time that the parties have bargained for it means that it is denied forever. It is for that reason, in my judgment, that arbitrators have regularly treated denial of such a critical right as depriving the employer of the right to rely upon the disciplinary events to found any discipline. That is why arbitrators have typically found that a termination after such a denial is void from the outset, and cannot be cured by either the grievance procedure or, for that matter, even by a full adversarial hearing before an arbitrator.

QUESTIONS

1) Why is union representation of employees facing discharge or other severe disciplinary action extremely important?

2) In the employer's view, the grievor in this case effectively waived his right to union representation. Do you agree? Why, or why not?

3) Can you envisage circumstances that would justify the dismissal of an employee without union representation? What might those circumstances be?

4) How can the employer avoid having similar cases go to arbitration in the future?

5) Had you been the arbitrator in this case, what would your ruling have been, and why?

CASE A.6

Arbitration Case
OPSEU AND CANADIAN BLOOD SERVICES

At what point will the use of volunteers as drivers by a non-profit organization be considered to intrude on the union's rights under the collective agreement?

Re Canadian Blood Services and Ontario Public Service Employees' Union
[Indexed as: Canadian Blood Services and O.P.S.E.U. (Re)]
Ontario
P.A. Chapman, P. Munt-Madill and K. Butler-Malette
Decision rendered: January 9, 2001

AWARD

This dispute arises from a policy grievance filed by the union on August 11, 1999, alleging that the employer's use of volunteer drivers to transport blood donors is contrary to the collective agreement between the parties. The union seeks an order that the employer be required to use employee drivers in the bargaining unit to perform the disputed work.

At the hearing of this matter a number of witnesses testified, documents were entered into evidence, and both parties had an opportunity to make submissions

Source: Adapted from 94 L.A.C. (4th 2001), pp. 429–438. Some deletions have been made by the author for the purposes of this book and names have been changed.

concerning the facts, the language of the collective agreement, and the relevant law. Having had an opportunity to carefully consider the facts and the submissions of the parties, the following is our decision.

THE FACTS

Canadian Blood Services ("CBS") is the successor to the Canadian Red Cross in respect of blood services. This grievance relates to the operations of the CBS in the Ottawa region.

OPSEU represents various employees of the CBS including clinic assistants who conduct blood donor clinics, lab technicians who process blood, and drivers who drive equipment, blood products and personnel. The present complaint arises from the transportation department. OPSEU and CBS or its predecessor the Red Cross have had a fairly long bargaining history, although the collective agreement under which this grievance was filed was only recently signed.

The parties agree that prior to the negotiation of the current collective agreement the task of driving people who required transportation to donate blood at clinics or at the office of CBS, was assigned to volunteers, and not to employee drivers from within the bargaining unit. The Red Cross has a long history of volunteerism, which has been continued by the CBS, albeit with some changes.

Indeed, the employer argued that it was fundamental to both organizations that they deliver a range of services through the use of volunteers, including the actual donation of blood (and therefore the time of the volunteer donors) as well as assistance in the collection of blood. Volunteers have played a variety of roles in the latter respect, including recruiting donors by telephone, driving them to and from clinics, greeting donors at clinics, registering them, and assisting post-donation with refreshments. They also play an important role in the community in terms of recruiting blood donors, by speaking at service club functions, high schools and other public venues, and by organizing blood donor clinics, particularly in rural areas. Some duties have moved from volunteer to staff as the organization has evolved, including the telephone recruitment of donors, which used to be performed exclusively by volunteers but has recently been assigned mostly to paid staff.

The previous collective agreement included as Schedule B-7 a job description for drivers, parts of which are set out below:

II. Position Summary

Under the direction of the Transport Supervisor/Co-ordinator or delegate, the driver ... transports personnel, equipment, supplies, mail and blood, as directed.

III. Duties and Responsibilities

Collection
2. Transport staff, equipment and supplies to and from collection areas.

During the period the language on this position description was in effect, the Red Cross sought on a number of occasions to assign bargaining unit drivers to transport donors. Some drivers, supported by the union, objected to this assignment of work, on the basis that the transportation of donors did not form part of the job duties and responsibilities of the drivers. While the employer never conceded the union's position that the position description prohibited the assignment of such work to the drivers, it did withdraw its requests in the face of such objections.

In the most recent round of bargaining, the employer put forward a number of proposals, one of which was to amend the drivers' job description to add the transportation of donors. The union agreed to this proposal. There was no discussion in bargaining to suggest that this change would in any way curtail the previous practice with respect to the use of volunteers to driver donors. The employer's purpose in proposing the amendment to the job description, according to its testimony, was to permit it to assign drivers to transport donors when and if volunteers were unavailable. However, it is not clear that this rationale was specifically stated to the union in bargaining; it appears there was really no discussion about the reasons for the proposed change or its implications.

The relevant parts of the job description which forms Schedule B-7 to the new collective agreement now read as follows:

II. Position Summary

Under the direction of the *assigned supervisor*, the driver ... transports personnel, equipment, supplies, mail and blood *products*.

III. Duties and Responsibilities

Incumbent may be assigned to do some or all of the following responsibilities:

Collection

2. Transport staff, *donors, volunteers*, equipment and supplies to and from *clinics*. [Emphasis reflects new language and is present in the original document.]

Since the signing of the most recent collective agreement, the union has objected to the employer's continued use of volunteers to drive donors. It is the position of the union that when the driving of donors was not part of the duties and responsibilities on the drivers' job description, they ought not to do such work, but now that it has been included it is bargaining unit work which must be done by bargaining unit employees and cannot be performed by volunteers.

There was no significant dispute about the nature of the work in issue. The focus of the grievance is the operation of the "Life Bus" which picks up donors at various locations (usually companies which have agreed to permit their employers to attend at a clinic during a particular time period), delivers them to a clinic to give blood, and then returns them. Operation of the bus requires the holding of a special operator's licence, which the volunteer drivers have obtained.

The driving of donors is planned in advance, scheduled and then assigned to volunteer drivers. Volunteers are not assigned to replace employee drivers at the last minute: in fact the opposite is true, as the main concern of CBS in adding the driving of donors to the list of employee drivers' job responsibilities was to ensure that it would be able to assign employees to perform this work in the event that a volunteer was unavailable. Volunteer drivers operate the same vehicles that are regularly used by bargaining unit employees; they are simply booked out for use by that volunteer.

There has been no decline in the hours of drivers since the signing of the collective agreement; in fact, three part-time drivers have been hired since 1999, and overall hours have increased.

THE DECISION

The parties referred to a number of earlier arbitration decisions which have established a framework for the analysis of disputes over the assignment of duties alleged to be "bargaining unit work."

First, arbitrators have confirmed that employers generally reserve the right to assign work within their general discretion to manage the workplace, and that employees do not generally have a proprietary interest in a particular bundle of duties and responsibilities. Thus, the starting point where a dispute arises is not to require the employer to establish a contractual right to assign work to particular persons, but rather to look to the union to establish that an assignment is contrary to a provision of the collective agreement, express or implied (see the discussion at page 6 of *Re MacLeods Stores and C.A.SA.W., Loc. 6*, Hope, unreported decision dated October 2, 1985).

Clearly, the existence of language in the collective agreement which explicitly restricts the right of the employer to assign work performed by bargaining unit employees to those outside the unit is highly relevant to such a determination.

Even where such language exists, however, an arbitrator must establish the scope of the protection, and whether disputed work falls within the definition of "bargaining unit work," in order to determine whether a particular assignment is contrary to the agreement (see for example *Re Hotel Dieu Hospital and Service Employees Union, Loc. 210*, Rayner, unreported decision dated January 5, 1995).

Where there is no express provision limiting the assignment of bargaining unit work, an arbitrator must nonetheless look to other provisions of the agreement, including the scope and recognition clauses, job classification language, and job descriptions where they form part of the agreement, to consider whether there is any implied restriction (see the discussion in *Re Orenda Ltd. and I.A.M., Lodge 1922* (1972), 1 L.A.C. (2d) 72 (Lysk) at pages 74 to 75).

And finally, it is generally accepted that the assignment of work must be in good faith, and may be subject to arbitral review if an improper purpose, such as the deliberate erosion of the bargaining unit or an attempt to undermine the collective agreement, is established (see for example *Hotel Dieu, supra*, at page 8).

In the present case the union can point to no specific provision in the collective agreement which limits the right of management to assign work normally performed by bargaining unit members to others, including volunteers. Instead, it relies more generally on the collective agreement, including the scope and recognition clause contained in Article 2, the language concerning position descriptions in Article 31, and, most importantly, the job description for the driver position, which as noted above forms Schedule B-7 to the Collective Agreement.

Taken as a whole, the union submits, these provisions clearly restrict the performance of those duties which appear on the job description to employee drivers within the bargaining unit. In support of this argument, the union relies upon an unreported decision which is discussed in *Re Orenda, supra*, at page 75, in which Arbitrator Shime, in adjudicating a dispute between the same parties, concluded that "the specific consideration given to the job classifications, occupational groups and job descriptions can only reflect an intent that the work falling within the purview of those considerations is to be performed by employees in the bargaining unit and not assigned to persons outside the bargaining unit."

There is no question that the job description for the drivers, and the other language in the collective agreement which relates to job classifications, is relevant to assessing whether or not there is any implied restriction on the employer's ability to assign work outside of the bargaining unit. The relevant position description language is reviewed above; the parties also made reference to the following provisions of the collective agreement:

Article 2–Recognition

2.01 The Employer recognizes the Union as the exclusive bargaining agent of all non-professional employees (support staff) of the Canadian Blood Services working at or out of the Toronto, London, Hamilton and Ottawa Blood Services Centres, together with all employees hired to work in or out of specific locations outside the boundaries of the aforementioned Blood Services Centres as set out in the Certificate issues by the Labour Relations Board of Ontario dated the 8th day of August, 1994 employed as Clinic Assistants, Clerical Staff, Transport Staff, Laboratory Helpers, Data Entry Clerks and Utility Persons, Telerecruiters save and except Co-ordinators, Supervisors, Assistant Supervisors, Administrative Assistants performing supervisory functions or involved in confidential matters related to labour relations and persons employed above these ranks.

Article 31—Position Description

31.01 All employees are entitled to have in their possession, a copy of their current Position Description. It is understood that position descriptions as appended to this contract are current as of the date of signing of this agreement ...

31.02 The Position Description shall accurately reflect only those duties which are applicable to all members of that position.

31.03 Any employee who is not required by her Centre's administration to perform all of the standard duties of her Position Description shall receive no reduction in her weekly rate of pay.

31.04 An employee cannot be required to perform duties which are not contained in his position description.

31.05 Supervisors will not customarily perform the duties of the bargaining unit employee.

31.06 a) If the Employer creates a new Position Description it shall establish the job description and wage rate and give written notice to the Union of the new wage rate.

   b) If the Union objects within thirty (30) days of receipt of the written notice from the Employer of the wage rate, such objection shall become the basis of a meeting between a representative of the Union and a representative of the Employer. Should such meeting result in a revision to the wages, the wage rate shall be retroactive to the date of implementation of the new Position Description, unless otherwise mutually agreed.

   c) Failing resolution of the objections, the matter shall be determined by arbitration.

Not having the whole of the Shime award to review, I cannot compare the language contained in that agreement to that contained in the collective agreement negotiated by the instant parties, and I do not know how explicit the job descriptions were, although they are described in the decision as "elaborate." In this case, though, we are not satisfied that either the job description(s) *or* the collective agreement language taken as a whole establish any clear restriction on the employer's ability to continue to assign the driving work in issue to volunteers.

It is interesting that the job descriptions all contain the following introductory language: "incumbent *may* be assigned to do *some* or *all* of the following responsibilities" (emphasis added). This general statement seems to mitigate against a claim that all of the duties listed are necessarily the exclusive responsibility of the drivers, at least vis-à-vis other employees who may be assigned the same duties, and arguably at least with respect to volunteers as well.

The position description language in the agreement itself also fails to establish any clear restriction on the assignment of work to volunteers. As reviewed above, Article 31 requires that employees be provided with a copy of their current job description and establishes a process for the negotiation of wage rates for new positions, neither of which provision limits the employer in its assignment of work. Both 31.02 and 31.03, like the job descriptions, specifically contemplate employees not performing all of the duties of their position as set out on the position descriptions. And the limits which are contained in the Article are significant only because they highlight the absence of any further restriction relating to bargaining unit work: Article 31.04 provides that employees cannot be required to perform duties which are not contained in their position descriptions, but does not address the converse problem, where duties referenced on the description are *not* assigned; and Article 31.05 specifically limits the assignment of bargaining unit work outside of the unit in one very specific situation, preventing supervisors from customarily performing the duties of a bargaining unit employee. The failure to include any similar prohibition with respect to volunteers is particularly significant in an organization where volunteers play such a critical role, in many cases working side-by-side with paid staff.

One issue which is unclear from our review of the two *Orenda* decisions, and about which the parties disagree, is the role which past practice might play in assessing the significance of any implied restrictions on the assignment of bargaining unit work asserted to exist in a collective agreement. Both decisions consider the relevance of a past practice of performance of bargaining unit work by a foreman, and appear to suggest that where such a practice is established the assignment may be justified, so long as it is relatively consistent with past practice (*Re Orenda, supra*, at page 76). In the present case, of course, past practice supports entirely the employer's assignment of donor driving to volunteers, as employees have never been assigned this task regularly, and have in fact refused to perform it even occasionally when requested to do so by the employer. The union asserts that past practice has no relevance in the present case, given the changes in the job description language negotiated in the last agreement. Certainly that would be the case were the issue before me the ability of the employer to assign donor driving to employee drivers, as it is undisputed that both parties understood that by the change this would now be permitted, despite the union's earlier objections. It is not at all clear, though, that the changes which were negotiated related to the drivers' present claim to *exclusive* entitlement to the work—certainly the negotiating history evidence which was called establishes that, at a minimum, there was no discussion of this issue, and no statement by either party that the change would have the effect claimed by the union.

One way in which past practice may be relevant is in determining whether the work of driving donors can be properly considered the exclusive work of the bargaining unit, or whether it was "shared work." In the *Hotel Dieu* case, *supra*, the arbitrator permitted the assignment of various tasks to volunteers at a hospital despite explicit language in the collective agreement which limited the employer's ability to assign "duties or work within the bargaining unit" to persons excluded from the unit. The grievance was dismissed "on the ground that the work was shared, prior to the use of volunteers among three groups (employees in two separate bargaining units as well as co-op students outside any unit) and was, therefore, not the exclusive work of the bargaining unit" (at page 8). Again, the evidence here establishes clearly the practice of the employer in assigning this work to volunteers, as well as the employer's desire that the work be "shared" with employees in the bargaining unit to the extent at least that employee drivers might be assigned to do the work as required.

The union's argument in the present case, given the clear practice of having volunteers drive donors to and from clinics in the past, really rests entirely on the change in the language of the driver job description in the last round of collective bargaining, which is reviewed above. It claims that the addition of the references to the driving of donors results in an exclusive assignment of that work to employee drivers, and prohibits the employer from continuing to use volunteers in that capacity. This argument is not supported by the negotiating history evidence which was called, as noted above, and having carefully examined the language in question we are unable to conclude that such a significant change constitutes a reasonable interpretation of the language on its face. The better interpretation, in our view, is that the addition of the terms "donors" and "volunteers" operates only to more clearly *permit* the employer to assign the transportation of such persons to employee drivers, rather than to *require* that such work be performed by bargaining unit personnel.

The union argues that to permit the employer to continue to use volunteers in these circumstances will erode the union's bargaining rights. Certainly there has been no loss of work arising from the continued assignment of volunteer drivers: the employer's assertion that driver hours have actually risen since the change was not challenged; and as drivers were not previously doing this work there can have been no loss of particular assignments. In fact, to interpret the change in the language of the position description as requiring the assignment of donor driving to employees in the bargaining unit would result in an accretion of work to the bargaining unit, which would be an unusual outcome and one not consistent with the claim that an erosion is threatened.

However, the union further asserts that a decision supporting the employer's assignment with respect to the driving work would permit (and possibly encourage) the employer to assign other bargaining unit work to volunteers, resulting in a clear threat to the integrity of the bargaining unit. There is no merit to this suggestion: nothing in this decision either invites or permits the employer to assign work which has been performed by bargaining unit members in the past to persons outside of the unit, volunteers or otherwise; and there is no basis on the present facts to impute such a goal to the employer.

In any event, the final test to be considered in assessing whether a work assignment made by an employer is appropriate is whether or not it was made in good faith, and central to that assessment is the question of whether or not the assignment was made in order to erode the integrity of the bargaining unit. As the employer's actions in seeking to maintain the existing allocation of the driving work do not have such an effect, there can be no basis to question its motives or allege bad faith in the present case. But were the employer in the future to consider a wholesale transfer of work to volunteers, as the union speculated in its final argument, we have no doubt that the issue of good faith would be engaged.

QUESTIONS

1) Why is the use of volunteers by non-profit organizations becoming an increasingly contentious issue, for unions and for the non-profit organizations themselves?

2) Do you believe, on the evidence presented in the case, that the blood service was barred from using volunteers as drivers?

3) Do you think that the continued use of volunteers as drivers poses a threat to the union or its members in this case?

4) Could the union and the Canadian Blood Services have worked out a resolution to this admittedly difficult issue, do you think? What might that resolution have been?

5) Had you been the arbitrator in this case, what would your ruling have been, and why?

REFERENCES

ABELLA, Irving. (1975). "Oshawa, 1937." In *On strike: Six key labour struggles in Canada 1919–1949*. Toronto: Lorimer. Reprinted in L. S. MacDowell and I. Radforth (Eds.). (1991). *Canadian working class history*. Toronto: Canadian Scholars' Press.

ADAMS, George. (2001). *Canadian labour law*. 2nd edition. Aurora, ON: Canada Law Book. Some use has also been made of the 1st (1998) edition of the same book.

_____. (1978). *Grievance arbitration of discharge cases*. Kingston: Queen's Univ. Industrial Relations Centre.

ADAMS, Roy. (1997, Dec. 30). "Income gap threatens core Canadian values. In *Hamilton Spectator*, p. D3.

_____. (1995a). "Canadian industrial relations in comparative perspective." In M. Gunderson and A. Ponak (Eds.), *Union-management relations in Canada* (3rd ed.). Don Mills, ON: Addison-Wesley. Some use has also been made of Adams' comparative chapter in the 2nd edition (1989) of the same book.

_____. (1995b). *Industrial relations under liberal democracy: North America in comparative perspective*. Columbia, SC: Univ. of South Carolina Press.

_____. (1993). "'All aspects of people at work': Unity and division in the study of labour and management." In R. Adams and N. Meltz (Eds.), *Industrial relations: Its nature, scope, and pedagogy*. Metuchen, NJ: Scarecrow Press.

_____ (ed.). (1991). *Comparative industrial relations: Contemporary research and theory*. London: Harper Collins Academic.

_____. (1987). "Employment standards in Ontario: An industrial relations systems analysis." *Relations Industrielles*, 42. Reprinted in LLCG. (1991). *Labour law: Cases, materials and commentary* (5th ed.). Kingston: Queen's IRC Press.

_____. (1985). "Should works councils be used as industrial relations policy?" *Monthly Labor Review*, 108:7 (July).

ADELL, Bernard. (1988a). "Law and industrial relations: The state of the art in common law Canada." In G. Hébert, H. Jain, and N. Meltz (Eds.), *The state of the art in industrial relations*. Kingston and Toronto: Queen's Univ. Industrial Relations Centre and the Univ. of Toronto Centre for Industrial Relations.

_____. (1988b). "Introduction." In *Labour law under the Charter: Proceedings of a conference sponsored by Industrial Relations Centre/School of Industrial Relations and Faculty of Law, Queen's University*. Kingston: Queen's Law Journal and Industrial Relations Centre.

AKYEAMPONG, Ernest. (2001, autumn). "Fact-sheet on unionization." In Statistics Canada, *Perspectives on labour and income*, 13:3, pp. 46–52.

_____. (1999, autumn). "Unionization—an update. " In Statistics Canada, *Perspectives on labour and income*, 11:3, pp. 45–65.

_____. (1997, winter). "A statistical portrait of the trade union movement." In Statistics Canada, *Perspectives on labour and income*, 9:4.

ALLIANCE (Newsletter of the Public Service Alliance of Canada). Various articles, 1999 through 2001, connected with Goose Bay Canadian Forces Base and National Gallery of Canada strikes.

ANDERSON, John. (1989a). "The strategic management of industrial relations." In *Union-management relations in Canada* (3rd ed.).

_____. (1989b). "The structure of collective bargaining." In *Union-management relations in Canada* (2nd ed.). Use has also been made of Anderson's bargaining structure chapter in the 1st edition (1982) of the same book.

_____. (1979). "Local union democracy: In search of criteria." *Relations Industrielles*, 34.

ANDERSON, John, and Morley Gunderson. (1982). "The Canadian industrial relations system." In *Union-management relations in Canada* (1st ed.).

ANDERSON, John, Morley Gunderson, and Allen Ponak. (1989). "Frameworks for the study of industrial relations." In *Union-management relations in Canada* (2nd ed.).

ARNOPOULOS, Sheila. (1974). Various *Montreal Star* articles, reprinted as "Immigrants and women: Sweatshops of the 1970s." In I. Abella and D. Millar (Eds.), (1978). *The Canadian worker in the twentieth century*. Toronto: Oxford Univ. Press.

ARTHURS, Harry. (1988). "The right to golf." In *Labour law under the Charter*.

ARTHURS, Harry, Donald Carter, Judy Fudge, Harry Glassbeek, and Gilles Trudeau. (1988). *Labour law and industrial relations in Canada*. Toronto: Butterworths. Some use has also been made of the 1993 edition of this same book.

ASH, Philip. (1967). "Measurement of industrial relations activities." *Journal of Applied Psychology*, 51:5. Reprinted in A. Nash and J. Miner (Eds.). (1973). *Personnel and labour relations: An evolutionary approach*. New York: MacMillan.

ASHENFELTER, Orley, and John Pencavel. (1969). "American trade union growth." *Quarterly Journal of Economics*, 83.

AUBRY, Jack. (1998, July 30). "Windfall 'a long time coming' for underpaid workers." *Ottawa Citizen*, p. A-1.

AUDITOR-GENERAL. (2000 and 2001). *Report of the Auditor-General of Canada*. Ottawa: Office of the Auditor-General.

B.C. Government. 2001. "B.C. government to shed 11,500 jobs, deepest public cuts in Canadian history." Unsigned Canadian Press story, Nov. 20, 2001.

BLS (Bureau of Labour Statistics, 2001). Information on U. S. union membership drawn from BLS Web site in December 2001. (For more detailed information about the site, please see the Annotated List of Web sites.)

BAIN, George, and Farouk Elsheikh. (1976). "Trade union growth in Canada: A comment." *Relations Industrielles*, 31.

BAKER, William. (1983). "The miners and the mediator: The 1906 Lethbridge strike and Mackenzie King." *Labour/Le travailleur*, 11 (spring). Reprinted in *Canadian working class history*.

BALDERSTON, C. C. (1933). "Recent trends in personnel management." *Management Review*, 22:9. Reprinted in *Personnel and labour relations*.

BALES, Kevin. (2001, Nov.). "Slave owners making $12 billion a year from trafficking." In *CCPA Monitor*, 8:6.

BAMBER, Greg, and Russell Lansbury. (1993). *International and comparative industrial relations* (2nd ed.). London and New York: Routledge.

BAMBER, Greg, and Gillian Whitehouse. (1993). "Appendix: Employment, economics, and industrial relations: comparative statistics." In *International and comparative industrial relations* (2nd ed.).

BAMBERGER, P., and L. Donahue (1999). "Employee discharge and reinstatement: Moral hazards and the mixed consequences of last chance agreements." In *Industrial and Labor Relations Review*, 53, pp. 1–20.

BARBASH, Jack. (1988). "The new industrial relations in the U.S.: Phase 2." *Relations Industrielles*, 43.

_____. (1984). *The elements of industrial relations*. Madison: Univ. of Wisconsin Press.

BARNACLE, Peter. (1991). *Arbitration of discharge grievances in Ontario: Outcomes and reinstatement experiences*. Kingston: Queen's IRC Research and Current Issues Series #62.

BEAN, Ron. (1994). *Comparative industrial relations: An introduction to cross-national perspectives* (2nd ed.). London: Routledge.

BEATTY, David. (1987). *Putting the 'Charter' to work: Designing a constitutional labour code*. Montreal: McGill-Queen's.

_____. (1983). "Ideology, politics, and unionism." In K. Swan and K. Swinton (Eds.), *Studies in labour law*. Toronto: Butterworths.

BEATTY, David, and Steve Kennett. (1988). "Striking back: Fighting words, social protest and political participation in free and democratic societies." In *Labour law under the Charter*.

BEAUMONT, P. B. (1995). "Canadian public sector industrial relations in a wider setting." In G. Swimmer and M. Thompson (Eds.), *Public sector collective bargaining in Canada*. Kingston: Queen's IRC Press.

BEMMELS, Brian. (1998). "Gender effects in discharge arbitration." *Industrial and Labour Relations Review*, 42:1.

"BENEFITS given to same-sex spouses." (1998, February 7). *Toronto Sun*, p. 20.

BENG, Chew Song, and Rosalind Chew. (1995). "The development of industrial relations strategy in Singapore." In A. Verma et al. (Eds.), *Employment Relations in the Growing Asian Economies*. London and New York: Routledge.

BERCUSON, David, and David Bright (Eds.). (1994). *Canadian labour history: Selected readings*. Toronto: Copp Clark Longman.

BERGMAN, Paul. (1988). *Relations by objectives: The Ontario experience*. Kingston: Queen's IRC Research and Current Issues Series #55.

BERNARD, Robert, D. Cosgrave, and J. Welsh (1998). *Chips and Pop: Decoding the Nexus Generation*. Toronto: DFait.

BERRIDGE, John. (1995). "The United Kingdom." In Ingrid Brunstein (Ed.), *Human resource management in Western Europe*. Berlin and New York: de Gruyter.

BERTRAND, Jean-Francois, and Michael Petrou. (2001, July 22). "Environment building has toxic water in pipes." In *Ottawa Citizen*.

BETCHERMAN, Gordon. (1999). "Workplace change in Canada: The broad context." In A. Verma and R. Chaykowski (Eds.), *Contract and commitment: Employment relations in the new economy*. Kingston: Queen's IRC Press.

BETCHERMAN, Gordon, and Kathryn McMullen. (1986). *Working with technology: A survey of automation in Canada*. Ottawa: Economic Council of Canada.

BETCHERMAN, Gordon, Kathryn McMullen, Christina Caron, and Norm Leckie. (1994).

The Canadian workplace in transition. Kingston: Queen's IRC Press.

BETTER Times. (1997) and (1998). Various issues.

BLAND, Susan. (1983). "Henrietta the homemaker, and Rosie the riveter." *Women's Study Journal, Atlantis*. Reprinted in *Canadian working class history*.

BLEASDALE, Ruth. (1981). "Class conflict on the canals of Upper Canada in the 1840s." *Labour/Le travailleur*, 7 (spring). Reprinted in *Canadian working class history*.

BLOCK, Richard. (1993). *Unionization, collective bargaining and legal institutions in the United States and Canada*. Kingston: Queen's Univ. IRC Press.

BOWLBY, Geoff. (2001, Jan.). "The labour market: Year end review." In Statistics Canada, *Perspectives on labour and income*, 13:1.

BRAVERMAN, Harry. (1974). *Labor and monopoly capital*. New York: Monthly Review Press.

BRENNER, Harvey. (1973). *Mental illness and the economy*. Cambridge: Harvard Univ. Press.

BRETT, Jeanne, and Stephen Goldberg. (1983). "Grievance mediation in the coal industry: A field experiment." *Industrial and Labor Relations Review*, 37.

_____. (1979). "Wildcat strikes in bituminous coal mining." *Industrial and Labor Relations Review*, 32.

BRONFENBRENNER, Kate. (1992). "Seeds of resurgence: Successful union organizing strategies." Paper presented at 1992 Annual Meeting of the American Sociological Association.

BROWN, Andrew, and Stephen Frenkel. (1993). "Union unevenness and insecurity in Thailand." In S. Frenkel (Ed.), *Organized Labor in the Asia-Pacific Region*. Ithaca, NY: ILR Press.

BROWN, H. F. (1934–1935). "Industrial relations activities survive a critical test." *Personnel Journal*, 13. Reprinted in *Personnel and labour relations*.

BROWN, Lorne. (1970). "Unemployment relief camps in Saskatchewan, 1922–1936." In *Saskatchewan history*. Saskatoon: Saskatchewan Archives Board. Reprinted in *Canadian working class history*.

BRUCE, Peter. (1990). "The processing of unfair labour practice cases in the U.S. and Ontario." *Relations Industrielles*, 45.

_____. (1989). "Political parties and labor legislation in Canada and the U.S." *Industrial Relations*, 28 (spring).

BRUNSTEIN, Ingrid. (Ed.). (1995). *Human resource management in Western Europe*. Berlin and New York: de Gruyter.

BRYCE, George, and Pran Manga. (1985). "The effectiveness of health and safety committees." *Relations Industrielles*, 40:2.

BUECKERT, Dennis (2001, July 9). "Some scientists at Health Canada say they are being harassed." Canadian Press.

BULLEN, John. (1986). "Hidden workers: Child labour and the family economy in late nineteenth-century urban Ontario." *Labour/Le Travail*, 18 (fall). Reprinted in *Canadian working class history*.

BUTTON, Tony. (1990). *The Canadian railway office of arbitration alternative*. Kingston: Queen's IRC School of Industrial Relations Research Essay #29.

CCH. (1998a, May). Information on employment standards legislation. In *Employment standards*. Don Mills, ON: Author.

_____. (1998b, May). "Human rights legislation." In *Employment standards*. Don Mills, ON: Author.

_____. (1998c, May). "Health and safety legislation" (including workers' compensation). In *Employment standards*.

_____. (1998d, May). "Labour relations legislation. " In *Employment standards*.

CLBC (Canadian Labour and Business Centre, 2000). "Viewpoints 2000." Ottawa: CLBC.

CNW (Canada NewsWire, 2001, May 23). "Georgetti announces resolution of SEIU-CAW dispute."

CAMERON, Dan. (2001, September). "The crisis in public-sector bargaining in Saskatchewan." In Policy Options, pp. 28–32.

CANADA Labour Views. (1997). Article from January 24 on Ontario Labour Relations Board certification of a union at a Wal-Mart department store. Article from November 17 on changes to workers' compensation legislation in Ontario.

CANADIAN Auto Workers (CAW). (nd). "CAW statement on the reorganization of work."

CANADIAN Labour Congress (CLC). (1997). *Women's work: A report*. Ottawa: Author.

CANADIAN Labour Market and Productivity Centre (CLMPC). (1997). *Changing times, new ways of working: Alternative working arrangements and changes in working time*. Ottawa: Author.

CANADIAN Paperworkers' Union (CPU). (1990). "The team concept and the restructuring of the workplace." *CPU Journal*, 10:2.

CANADIAN Union of Public Employees (CUPE). (nd). List of courses prepared by and available from the union's education department.

CANSIM. (1998). Statistics Canada, CANSIM, Matrix 3472 (employment by industry). Ottawa: Statistics Canada.

CARDIN, Jean-Real. (1967). Canadian labour relations in an era of technological change. Economic Council of Canada Special Study #6. Ottawa: Supply and Services.

CARPENTER, C. U. (1903, April). "The working of a labor department in industrial establishments." *Engineering Magazine*, 25:1. Reprinted in *Personnel and labour relations*.

CARROTHERS, A. W. J., E. E. Palmer, and W. B. Rayner. (1986). *Collective bargaining law in Canada*. 2nd edition. Toronto: Butterworths.

CARROTHERS, Arthur W. J. (Chair). (1979). *Report of the commission of inquiry into redundancies and lay-offs*. Ottawa: Supply and Services (Labour Canada). This report contains a discussion of Harvey Brenner's "social pathology" statistics relating unemployment to physical and mental illness and crime.

CARTER, Donald. (1997). "The duty to accommodate: Its growing impact on the grievance arbitration process. " *Relations Industrielles*, 52.

_____. (1995). "Collective bargaining legislation." In *Union-management relations in Canada* (3rd ed.). Use has also been made of Carter's labour law chapters in the 1st (1982) and 2nd (1989) editions of the same book.

CASSELMAN, Karen. (1998, December 21). Labour relations officer, grievances and arbitration section, Canada Post. Telephone interview.

CAVALLUZZO, Paul. (1988). "Freedom of association—Its effect upon collective bargaining and trade unions." In *Labour law under the Charter*.

CHAISON, Gary. (1996). *Union mergers in hard times: The view from five countries.* London and Ithaca: ILR Press.

_____. (1982). "Unions: Growth, structure, and internal dynamics." In *Union-management relations in Canada* (1st ed.). Use has also been made of the union structure chapter by Gary Chaison and Joseph Rose in the 2nd (1989) edition of the same book.

CHAISON, Gary, and Joseph Rose. (1991). "The macrodeterminants of union growth and decline." In G. Strauss, D. Gallagher, and J. Fiorito (Eds.), *The state of the unions.* Madison: IRRA Press.

_____. "Turnover among the presidents of Canadian national unions." *Industrial Relations*, 16.

CHAYKOWSKI, Richard. (1995). "The structure and process of collective bargaining." In *Union-management relations in Canada* (3rd ed.).

CHAYKOWSKI, Richard, and Anil Verma. (1992). "Canadian industrial relations in transition." In R. Chaykowski and A. Verma (Eds.), *Industrial relations in Canadian industry*. Toronto: Dryden.

CHRISTIE, Innis. (1980). *Employment law in Canada*. Toronto: Butterworths.

CLARKE, Oliver. (1993). "Conclusions." In *International and comparative industrial relations* (2nd ed.).

CLEGG, Hugh. (1976). *Trade unionism under collective bargaining: A theory based upon comparisons of six countries.* Oxford: Blackwell.

COATES, Mary Lou. (1992). "Is there a future for the Canadian labour movement?" Kingston: Queen's IRC Current Issues Series.

_____. (1991). "Work and family issues: Beyond 'swapping the mopping and sharing the caring.'" Kingston: Queen's IRC Press Current Issues Series.

COHEN, Marjorie. (1987). *Free trade and the future of women's work.* Toronto: Garamond/CCPA.

COLLECTIVE Bargaining Review (CBR). (1996) and (1997). Various issues. Ottawa: HRDC.

COMMONS, John et al. (1918). *History of labor in the United States.* New York: Macmillan.

_____. (1909, November). "American shoemakers: 1648–1895." *Quarterly Journal of Economics*, 24.

COMMUNICATIONS Workers of Canada (CWC). (1992). Organization chart outlining the union's main activities.

COWDRICK, Edward. (1934–1935). "Collective bargaining in 1934." *Personnel Journal*, 13:5. Reprinted in *Personnel and labour relations*.

CRAIG, Alton. (1967). "A model for the analysis of industrial relations systems." Paper presented to the Annual Meeting of the Canadian Political Science Association held in Ottawa.

CRAIG, Alton, and Norman Solomon. (1996). *The system of industrial relations in Canada* (5th ed.). Scarborough, ON: Prentice-Hall. Some use has also been made of the 1st (1983) and 4th (1993) editions of the same book.

CRAIN, Marion. (1994). "Gender and union organizing." *Industrial and Labor Relations Review*, 47:2.

CRISPO, John. (1982). "The future of Canadian industrial relations." In *Union-management relations in Canada* (1st ed.).

CRYDERMAN, Kelly. (2001, July 11). "Canadians would be safer without Health Canada." In *Ottawa Citizen*.

CUNNINGHAM, J. B., and T. H. White (Eds.). (1984). *Quality of working life: contemporary cases*. Ottawa: Supply and Services (Labour Canada publication).

CURRENT Scene: The current industrial relations scene in Canada. (1991). Kingston: Queen's University Industrial Relations Centre.

CURRY, Bill. (2001, Oct. 2). "French minister checks out Canada's public service." In *Hill Times*.

CURTIS, C. H. (1966). *The development and enforcement of the collective agreement*. Kingston: Queen's Industrial Relations Centre.

DASTMALCHIAN, Ali, and Ignace Ng. (1990). "Industrial relations climate and grievance outcomes." *Relations Industrielles*, 45.

DAVIS, Edward, and Russell Lansbury. (1993). "Industrial relations in Australia." In *International and comparative industrial relations* (2nd ed.).

DEERY, Stephen, and Richard Mitchell (Eds.). (1993). *Labour law and industrial relations in Asia*. Melbourne: Longman.

DÉOM, Esther, and Jean Boivin (2001). "Union-management relations in Quebec." In *Union-Management Relations in Canada*, 4th edition. Use has also been made of the Quebec chapters written first by Boivin, then by Boivin and Déom, in the first three editions of this book (1982, 1989, and 1995).

DEUTSCH, Arnold. (1979). *The human resources revolution: Communicate or litigate*. New York: McGraw-Hill.

DIEBEL, Linda. (2001, Nov.). "Mexican women sewing Canadian lingerie exploited, underpaid." In *CCPA Monitor*, 8:6.

DIGBY, C., and W. Craig Riddell. (1986). "Occupational health and safety in Canada." In W. Craig Riddell (Ed.), *Canadian labour relations*. Toronto: Univ. of Toronto Press.

DITCHBURN, Jennifer. (1998, June 23). "Ottawa dropping court fight over same-sex benefits." *London Free Press*, p. A-10.

DOHM, Arlene. (2000). "Gauging the effects of retiring baby-boomers." In *Monthly Labor Review*, July, 2000, pp. 17–25.

DONNER, Arthur (Chair). (1994). *Report of the advisory group on overtime and hours of work*. Ottawa: Supply and Services.

DOWNIE, Bryan. (1992). "Industrial relations in elementary and secondary education: A system transformed?" In *Industrial relations in Canadian industry*.

_____. (1989). "Union-management co-operation in the 1980s and beyond." In *Union-management relations in Canada* (2nd ed.). Some use has also been made of the same author's chapter on the same subject in the 1st (1982) edition of the same book.

_____. (1985). Statements in human resource management class, Master of Industrial Relations program, Queen's University, winter term.

_____. (1984). Remarks on the negotiation process in the negotiation and conflict resolution course in the School of Business, Queen's University, fall term.

DOWNIE, Bryan, and Mary Lou Coates. (1993). *The changing face of industrial relations and human resource management*. Kingston: Queen's IRC Current Issues Series.

DRACHE, Daniel. (1984). "The formation and fragmentation of the Canadian working class: 1820–1920." *Studies in Political Economy*, 15 (fall). Reprinted in *Canadian labour history*.

DRACHE, Daniel, and Harry Glassbeek. (1992). *The changing workplace: Reshaping Canada's industrial relations system*. Toronto: Lorimer.

DUBIN, R. (1959). "Constructive elements of industrial conflict." In A. Kornhauser et al. (Eds.), *Industrial conflict*. New York:

McGraw-Hill. Reprinted in *Labour law*, (5th ed.).

DULLES, Foster R., and M. Dubofsy. (1984). *Labour in America: A history* (4th ed.) Arlington Heights, IL: Harlan Davidson.

DUNLOP, John. (1958). *Industrial relations systems*. Carbondale, IL: Southern Illinois Press.

DUNNETTE, Marvin. (1971). "Research needs of the future in industrial and organizational psychology." Paper presented at 1971 American Psychological Association meetings, Washington, D. C. Reprinted in *Personnel and labour relations*.

DUNNETTE, Marvin, and Bernard Bass. (1963). "Behavioral scientists and personnel management." *Industrial Relations*, 2 (May). Reprinted in *Personnel and labour relations*.

DUXBURY, L., L. Dyke, and N. Lam. (1999). *Building a world-class workforce: Career development in the federal public service*. Ottawa: Treasury Board of Canada Secretariat.

DUXBURY, L., C. Higgins, C. Lee, and S. Mills. (1991). "Balancing work and family: A study of the federal public sector." Ottawa: no publisher.

EASTMAN, Byron. (1983). "Canadian union growth." *Relations Industrielles*, 33.

EATON, J. K. (1975). "The growth of the Canadian labour movement." *Labour Gazette*, 75.

ECONOMIC Council of Canada (ECC). (1987). *Innovation and jobs in Canada*. Ottawa: Supply and Services.

ECONOMIC Council of Newfoundland and Labrador (ECNL). (1989). "Equity capital and economic development in Newfoundland and Labrador." Ottawa: Economic Council of Canada Local Development Paper #8.

ECONOMIST (The Economist). (2001). "A global game of dominoes." Unsigned article from the August 2001 edition appearing on the *Economist's* Web site, August 23, 2001.

EDEN, Genevieve. (1993). "Industrial discipline in the Canadian federal jurisdiction." *Relations Industrielles*, 48:1.

_____. (1992). "Progressive discipline: An oxymoron." *Relations Industrielles*, 47:3.

EHRENBERG, Ronald, and R. Smith. (1985). *Modern labor economics*. Glenview, IL: Scott-Foresman.

ELLIOTT, David, and Joanne Goss. (1994). *Grievance mediation: How and why it works*. Aurora, ON: Canada Law Book.

ENGLAND, Geoffrey. (1988). "Some thoughts on constitutionalising the right to strike." In *Labour law under the Charter*.

_____. (1987). "Part-time, casual, and other atypical workers: A legal view." Kingston: Queen's Univ. Industrial Relations Centre, Research and Current Issues Series Paper #48.

ENGLISH, Michele (Manager, Nfld. Workers' Compensation Board). (1995) and (1996). Personal conversations and presentations to various industrial relations classes at Memorial University.

EPSTEIN, Abraham. (1932). "Employees' welfare: An autopsy." *American Mercury*, 25:99 (March). Reprinted in *Personnel and labour relations*.

ERSKINE, Lillian, and Trevor Cleveland. (1917). "New men for old." *Everybody's*, 36 (April). Reprinted in *Personnel and labour relations*.

EVENSON, Brad. (1998, July 30). "Equal pay for women is still decades away." *Ottawa Citizen*, p. A-3.

FASHOYIN, Tayo. (1991). "Recent trends in industrial relations theory and research in developing countries." In R. Adams (Ed.), *Comparative industrial relations: Contemporary research and theory*. London: Harper Collins Academic.

FAWCETT, Blair. (1998). "Selected provisions in major collective agreements: Wage incentive plans, 1988 to 1998." *Workplace Gazette*, fall.

"FEDERATION to end role as central labour group." (1997, August 22). *The Globe & Mail*, p. A-8.

FERGUSON, G. V. (1935). "An Alberta prophet (1935 model.)" *Canadian Forum*, April. Reprinted in J. L. Granatstein and P. Stevens (Eds.) (1972). *Forum*. Toronto: Univ. of Toronto Press.

FERNER, Anthony, and Richard Hyman. (1992a). "Industrial relations in the new Europe: Seventeen types of ambiguity." Introduction to A. Ferner and R. Hyman (Eds.), *Industrial relations in the new Europe*. Oxford: Blackwell.

_____. (1992b). "Italy: Between political exchange and micro-corporatism." In A. Ferner and R. Hyman (Eds.), *Industrial relations in the new Europe*. Oxford: Blackwell.

FEUILLE, Peter. (1999). "Grievance mediation." In A. E. Eaton and J. H. Keefe (Eds.), *Employment dispute resolution and worker rights*. Champaign, IL: IRRA Series.

_____. (1992). "Why does grievance mediation resolve grievances?" *Negotiation Journal*, 8:2 (April).

FINKEL, Alvin. (1986). "The cold war, Alberta labour and the Social Credit regime." *Labour/Le Travail*, 21 (spring, 1988). Reprinted in *Canadian working class history*.

FISCHER, Frank. (1968). "The personnel function in tomorrow's company." *Personnel*, 45:1 (January-February). Reprinted in *Personnel and labour relations*.

FISHER, E. G., and Brian Williams. (1989). "Negotiating the union-management agreement." In *Union-management relations in Canada* (2nd ed.). Some use has also been made of Williams' negotiation chapter in the 1st (1982) edition of the same book.

FISHER, E. G., and S. Kushner. (1986). "Alberta's construction labour relations during the recent downturn." *Relations Industrielles*, 41:4.

FISHER, Robert, and William Ury. (1983). *Getting to yes: Negotiating agreement without giving in*. New York: Penguin.

FISHER, Sandra, and Jon Peirce. (1995). "Labour education in Newfoundland." *Workers' Education*, 10 (October).

FITCH, John. (1917). "Making the boss efficient." *Survey*, 38 (June 2). Reprinted in *Personnel and labour relations*.

FLANDERS, Alan. (1970). "Collective bargaining: A theoretical analysis." In A. Flanders (Ed.), *Management and unions*. London: Faber and Faber. Excerpt reprinted in LLCG. (1991). *Labour law: Cases, materials and commentary* (5th ed.). Kingston: Queen's IRC Press.

FOISY, C. (1998). "Is arbitration too slow and legalistic?" In M. Hughes and A. Ponak (Eds.), *Conference Proceedings of the 16th Annual University of Calgary Labour Arbitration Conference*. Calgary: Industrial Relations Research Group and University of Calgary.

FOOT, David. (1997, October 14). "Youth unemployment: A 'bust' priority." *The Globe & Mail*, p. A-23.

FORREST, Anne. (1997). "Securing the male breadwinner." *Relations Industrielles*, 52:1.

_____. (1989). "The rise and fall of national bargaining in the Canadian meat-packing industry." *Relations Industrielles*, 44:2.

_____. (1986). "Bargaining units and bargaining power." *Relations Industrielles*, 41:4.

FORSEY, Eugene. (1985). "Labour and the Constitution in Atlantic Canada." In E. Forsey (Ed.), *Perspectives on the Atlantic Canada labour movement and the working class experience*. Sackville, NB: Mount Allison University Centre for Canadian Studies.

_____. (1982). *Trade unions in Canada, 1812–1902*. Toronto: Univ. of Toronto Press.

FRANK, David. (1983). "The trial of J. B. McLachlan." In *Historical papers* (pp. 208–225). Reprinted in D. Frank and G. Kealey (Eds.). (1995). *Labour and working-class history in Atlantic Canada*. St. John's: Institute of Social and Economic Research.

FREEMAN, Richard. (1989). "On the divergence in unionism among developed countries." Washington: National Bureau of Economic Research Working Paper #2817.

FREEMAN, Richard, and James Medoff. (1984). *What do unions do?* New York: Basic Books.

_____. (1979). "The two faces of unionism." *The Public Interest*, 57.

FRENKEL, Stephen. (1993). *Organized labor in the Asia-Pacific region: A comparative study of trade unionism in nine countries.* Ithaca, NY: ILR Press.

————. (1993a). "Australian trade unionism and the new social structure of accumulation." In *Organized labor in the Asia-Pacific Region.*

FRIEDMAN, Milton. (1962). *Capitalism and choice.* Chicago: Chicago Univ. Press. Excerpt reprinted in *Labour law.*

FRYER, John. (1995). "Provincial public sector labour relations." In *Public sector collective bargaining in Canada.*

FRYER, John (chair, 2001). *Working together in the public interest.* Final Report of the Advisory Committee on Labour Management Relations in the Federal Public Service. Ottawa: Treasury Board of Canada Secretariat.

————. (chair, 2000). *Identifying the Issues.* First Report of the Advisory Committee on Labour Management Relations in the Federal Public Service. Ottawa: Treasury Board of Canada Secretariat.

FUDGE, Judy. (1988). "Labour, the new Constitution, and old style liberalism." In *Labour law under the Charter.*

FUERSTENBERG, Friederich. (1993). "Industrial relations in Germany." In *International and comparative industrial relations* (2nd ed.).

GALENSON, Walter, and R. S. Smith. (1978). "The United States." In J. Dunlop and W. Galenson (Eds.), *Labor in the twentieth century.* New York: Academic.

GALLAGHER, Daniel, and Kurt Wetzel. (1980). "Centralized multi-employer negotiations in public education: An examination of the Saskatchewan experience in the public sector." *Journal of Collective Negotiations in the Public Sector,* 9:4.

GALT, Virginia. (2000, Nov. 3). "War for talent being waged on all fronts." In *The Globe & Mail,* p. B-12.

————. (1994, June 6). "Reinventing the labour movement." *The Globe & Mail.*

GANDZ, Jeffrey. (1979). "Grievance initiation and resolution: A test of the behavioural theory." *Relations Industrielles,* 34.

GANDZ, Jeffrey, and J. D. Whitehead. (1989). "Grievances and their resolution." In *Union-management relations in Canada* (2nd ed.). Some use has also been made of Gandz's grievance chapter in the 1st (1982) edition of the same book.

GANNON, Marvin. (1972). "Entrepreneurship and labor relations at the Ford Motor Company." *Marquette Business Review* (summer). Reprinted in *Personnel and labour relations.*

GEORGE, Claude. (1968). *The history of management thought.* Englewood Cliffs: Prentice-Hall.

GÉRIN-LAJOIE, Jean. (1993). "Quelques contrastes entre les secteurs privé et public au Québec." In *The Industrial Relations System: Proceedings of the 29th Annual Conference of the Canadian Industrial Relations Association.* Charlottetown, P. E. I., Canada.

GILES, Anthony. (1996). "Globalization and industrial relations." In *The globalization of the economy and the worker: Selected papers presented at the 32nd Annual Canadian Industrial Relations Conference.* Montreal, QC, Canada.

GILES, Anthony, and Akivah Starkman. (2001). "The collective agreement." *Union-management relations in Canada* (4th ed.) Use has also been made of the same authors' collective agreement chapter in the 3rd edition of the same book, and of the chapter by Giles and Hem Jaim in the same book's 2nd edition.

GLADSTONE, Alan. (1980). "Trade unions, growth and development." In *Labour and Society,* 5:1, pp. 49–68.

GLASSBEEK, Harry, and S. Rowland. (1979). "Are injuring and killing at work crimes?" *Osgoode Hall Law Journal,* 17, pp. 506–594.

GODARD, John. (2001). "Beyond the high-performance paradigm? An analysis in variation in Canadian managerial perceptions of reform programme effectiveness." In *British Journal of Industrial Relations,* 39:1, pp. 25–52.

_____. (1995). "Labour and employee relations in the Canadian private sector: Report to participants in the LERS Survey." University of Manitoba Faculty of Management. Working paper.

_____. (1994). *Industrial relations: The economy and society.* Toronto: McGraw-Hill Ryerson. See also the 2nd edition of this book (Toronto: Captus, 2000).

_____. (1991). "The progressive HRM paradigm: A theoretical and empirical re-examination." *Relations Industrielles,* 46.

GODARD, John, and Thomas Kochan. (1982). "Canadian management under collective bargaining." In *Union-management relations in Canada* (1st ed.).

GOETSCHY, Janine, and Annette Jobert. (1993). "Industrial relations in France." In *International and comparative industrial relations* (2nd ed.).

GOLD, Alan. (1993, May). Conversation with the author in Montreal.

GOLDBERG, Stephen. (1989). "Grievance mediation: A successful alternative to labor arbitration." *Negotiation Journal,* 5.

GOLDBLATT, H. (1974). *Justice denied.* Toronto: Labour Council of Metropolitan Toronto.

GORDON, Sandra (2001, June 26). "Canadian businesses fall short in training." In *Ottawa Citizen,* p. C-2.

GOSPEL, Howard, and C. Littler. (1982). *Managerial strategies and industrial relations.* London: Heineman.

GOULDEN, Joseph. (1972). *Meany.* New York: Atheneum.

GRAHAM, Katherine. (1995). "Collective bargaining in the municipal sector." In *Public sector collective bargaining in Canada.*

GRANT, Michel. (2000). "Quebec." In M. Thompson et al. (Eds.), *Regional Differences in Industrial Relations.* No place of publication given: Canadian Industrial Relations Association.

_____. (1992). "Industrial relations in the clothing industry: Lessons for survival." In *Industrial relations in Canadian industry.*

GUNDERSON, Morley. (1986). "Alternative methods for dealing with permanent layoffs and plant closings." In W. C. Riddell (Ed.), *Adapting to change: Labour market adjustment in Canada.* Toronto: Univ. of Toronto Press. Reprinted in *Labour law.*

GUNDERSON, Morley, and Allen Ponak. (1995). "Industrial relations." In *Union-management relations in Canada* (3rd ed.).

GUNDERSON, Morley, and Frank Reid. (1998). "Worksharing and working time issues in Canada." Montreal: Institute for Research in Public Policy.

_____. (1995). "Public sector strikes in Canada." In *Public sector collective bargaining in Canada.*

GUNDERSON, Morley, and Douglas Hyatt. (2001) "Union impact on compensation, productivity, and management of the organization." In *Union-management relations in Canada* (4th ed.) use has also been made of the same authors' chapter on the same topic from the 3rd (1995) edition of the book, and of Gunderson's chapter in the 2nd (1989) edition of the same book.

GUNDERSON, Morley, Douglas Hyatt, and Allen Ponak. (2001). "Strikes and dispute resolution." In *Union-management relations in Canada* (4th ed.). Use has also been made of the same authors' strike chapter from the 3rd (1995) edition of the same book, and of the strike chapter by John Anderson and Morley Gunderson from this book's 1st (1982) edition.

GUNDERSON, Morley, Douglas Hyatt, and Craig Riddell (1999). *Pay differences between the government and private sectors.* Ottawa: Canadian Policy Research Networks.

GUNDERSON, Morley, John Kervin, and Frank Reid. (1989). "The effect of labour relations legislation on strike incidence." *Canadian Journal of Economics,* 22.

GUNDERSON, Morley, L. Myszynski, and J. Keck. (1990). *Women and labour market poverty.* Ottawa: Advisory Council on Status of Women. In *Labour law.*

GUNDERSON, Morley, and W. C. Riddell. (1993). *Labour market economics: Theory, evidence and policy in Canada* (3rd ed.). Toronto: McGraw-Hill Ryerson.

HRDC (Human Resources Development Canada, 2001(a)). Employment standards legislation in Canada. Found on the HRDC website at http://labour.hrdc-drhc.gc.ca/psait/spila/lmnec_eslc/index/cfm/doc/english.

HRDC (Human Resources Development Canada, 2001(b)). Industrial relations legislation in Canada. Found on the HRDC website at http://labour.hrdc drhc.gc.ca/psait_spila/lmric_irlc/index/cfm/doc/english.

HRDC (Human Resources Development Canada, 1999, May 10). "Statistical analysis: Occupational injuries and fatalities, Canada." Ottawa: HRDC.

HRDC (Human Resources Development Canada). (1998). Selected work stoppage data from the Work Stoppage Bureau, Workplace Information Directorate.

HRDC (Human Resources Development Canada). (1994). Federal preventive mediation program description.

HAIVEN, Larry. (1995). "Industrial relations in health care: Regulation, conflict and transition to the 'wellness model'." In *Public sector collective bargaining in Canada*.

_____. (1990). "Hegemony and the workplace: The role of arbitration." In L. Haiven, S. McBride, and J. Shields (Eds.), *Regulating labour*. Toronto: Garamond.

HAIVEN, Larry, Stephen McBride, and John Shields. (1990). "The state, neo-conservatism, and industrial relations." In *Regulating labour*.

HALPERN, Norman. (1984). "Sociotechnical systems design: The Shell Sarnia experience." In J. B. Cunningham and T. H. White (Eds.), *Quality of working life: contemporary cases*. Ottawa: Supply and Services (Labour Canada publication).

HAMMARSTROM, Olle. (1993). "Industrial relations in Sweden." In *International and comparative industrial relations* (2nd ed.).

HANNIGAN, John. (1986). "Laboured relations: Reporting industrial relations news in Canada." Toronto: Univ. of Toronto Centre for Industrial Relations.

HAWORTH, Nigel. (1993). "Unions in crisis: Deregulation and reform of the Asian union movement." In *Organized labor in the Asia-Pacific region*.

HAYDEN, Anders. (1998a, April). "35-Hour week shakes Europe." In *Ontario New Democrat*, p. 11.

_____. (1998b). *Europe's new movement for work time reduction*. Toronto: 32 Hours.

HEBDON, Robert. (1992). "Ontario's no-strike laws: A test of the safety valve hypothesis." In *Proceedings of the 28th Annual Conference of the Canadian Industrial Relations Association*.

HÉBERT, Gérard. (1995). "Public sector collective bargaining in Quebec." In *Public sector collective bargaining in Canada*.

HENEMAN, Herbert. (1969). "Toward a general conceptual system of industrial relations: How do we get there?" In Gerald Somers (Ed.), *Essays in industrial relations theory*. Ames, IA: Iowa State Univ. Press.

_____. (1960, July). "Manpower management: New wrapping on old merchandise." In Univ. of Minnesota Industrial Relations Center "Special Release" 2. Reprinted in *Personnel and labour relations*.

HERON, Craig. (1996). *The Canadian labour movement: A short history*. Toronto: Lorimer. Considerable use has also been made of the 1989 edition of the same book.

_____. (1984). "Labourism and the Canadian Working Class." *Labour/Le Travail*, 13 (spring). Reprinted in *Canadian labour history*.

HERTZ, Noreena. (2001, Nov.). "As governments abandon public sphere, corporations take over." In *CCPA Monitor*, 8:6.

HÉTHY, Lajos. (1991). "Industrial relations in Eastern Europe: Recent development and trends." In *Comparative industrial relations*.

HOLMAN, Worthington. (1904). "A 5000 brain-power organization." *System*, 4:2 (August). Reprinted in *Personnel and labour relations*.

HOME EXCITE (various dates in 2001). Various articles on Nova Scotia health care and other public sector strikes, drawn from the Home Excite Web site.

HUNNICUTT, Benjamin. (1988). *Work without end: Abandoning shorter hours for the right to work*. Philadelphia: Temple Univ. Press.

HUNT, Gerald. (1997). "Sexual orientation and the Canadian labour movement." In *Relations Industrielles*, 52:4.

HYMAN, Richard. (1983). "A critical view of industrial democracy systems." In *Essays in collective bargaining and industrial democracy*. Toronto: CCH Canadian. Excerpt reprinted in *Labour law*.

_____. (1975). *Industrial relations: A Marxist introduction*. London: MacMillan.

ILO (International Labour Office, 1997). *World Labour Report*, 1997–8. Geneva: ILO.

ICHNIOWSKI, Casey. (1986). "The effects of grievance activity on productivity." *Industrial and Labor Relations Review*, 40.

ISMI, Asad. (2001, Nov.). "Report says EDC is putting people and the environment at risk." In *CCPA Monitor*, 8:6.

JACKSON, Andrew (Chief Economist, CLC). (1997). Presentation at "32 Hours" conference, Toronto, November 22.

JACKSON, Edward T. (1998). "Worker ownership and community economic development." Paper presented to CLC conference on Jobs and the Economy, Ottawa, February.

_____. (1997). "ETIs: A tool for responsible pension fund investment." *Making Waves*, 8:2.

JACKSON, Edward T., and François Lamontagne. (1995). "Adding value: The economic and social impacts of labour-sponsored venture capital corporations on their investee firms." Ottawa: CLMPC.

JACKSON, Edward T, and Jon Peirce. (1990). "Mobilizing capital for regional development." Ottawa: Economic Council of Canada Local Development Paper #21.

JACKSON, Richard. (2001). "Collective bargaining legislation." In *Union-management relations in Canada*, 4th edition.

_____. (1995). "Police and firefighter labour relations in Canada." In *Public sector collective bargaining in Canada*.

JACOBI, Otlo, Berndt Keller, and Werner Muller-Jentsch. (1992). "Germany: codetermining the future." In *Industrial relations in the new Europe*.

JENSON, Jane, and Rianne Mahon. (1993). "North American labour: Divergent trajectories." In J. Jenson and R. Mahon (Eds.), *The challenge of restructuring: North American labour movements respond*. Philadelphia: Temple Univ. Press.

JIMENEZ, Ramon. (1993). "The Philippines." In *Labour Law and Industrial Relations in Asia*.

JOHNSTON, T. L. (1962). *Collective bargaining in Sweden*. London: Allen and Unwin.

JOYCE, George (Conciliator, Nfld. Ministry of Labour). (1996). Statements made to various industrial relations classes at Memorial University concerning the Ministry's preventive mediation program.

KASSALOW, Everett. (1963). "Unions in the new and developing countries." In E. Kassalow (Ed.), *National labor movements in the postwar world*. Chicago: Northwestern Univ. Press.

KEALEY, Gregory. (1985). "The Canadian working-class: Past, present and future." In *Perspectives on the Atlantic Canada labour movement and the working class experience*.

_____. (1984). "1919: The Canadian labour revolt." *Labour/Le Travail*, 13 (spring). Reprinted in *Canadian labour history*.

KEALEY, Gregory, and Bryan Palmer. (1982). *Dreaming of what might be: The Knights of Labour in Ontario, 1880–1900*. Cambridge: Cambridge Univ. Press.

_____. (1981). "Bonds of unity: The Knights of Labor in Ontario." *Histoire Sociale/Social History*. Reprinted in *Canadian working class history*.

KELLER, Berndt. (1991). "The role of the state as corporate actor in industrial relations systems." In *Comparative industrial relations*.

KERVIN, John. (1989). "The science of bargaining." In A. Sethi (Ed.), *Collective bargaining in Canada*. Scarborough: Nelson.

_____. (1988). "Sociology, psychology and industrial relations." In *The state of the art in industrial relations*.

_____. (1984). "Strikes: Toward a typology of causes." In *Proceedings of 21st Annual Meeting of Canadian Industrial Relations Association*. Guelph, Ontario, Canada.

KILPATRICK, Ken. (1998, March 9) "Maple Leaf vote 'won on fear.'" *Toronto Star*, p. B1.

KING, Carlyle. (1944). "The CCF sweeps Saskatchewan." *Canadian Forum*, July. Reprinted in *Forum*.

KJELLBERG, Anders. (1992). "Sweden: Can the model survive?" In *Industrial relations in the new Europe*.

KOCHAN, Thomas. (1980). *Collective bargaining and industrial relations*. Homewood, IL: Irwin.

KOCHAN, Thomas, and Paul Barrocci. (1985). *Human resource management and industrial relations: Text, readings, and cases*. Boston: Little Brown.

KOCHAN, Thomas, and Paul Osterman. (1994). *The mutual gains enterprise: Forging a winning partnership among labor, management, and government*. Boston: Harvard Business School Press.

KOCHAN, Thomas, Robert McKersie, and Peter Cappelli. (1984). "Strategic choice and industrial relations theory." *Industrial Relations*, 23:1.

KUMAR, Pradeep. (1993). *From uniformity to divergence: Industrial relations in Canada and the United States*. Kingston: Queen's IRC Press.

KUMAR, Pradeep, Gregor Murray, and Sylvain Schetagne. (1998). "Adapting to change: Union priorities in the 1990s." *Workplace Gazette*, fall.

KUMAR, Pradeep, and Noah Meltz. (1992). "Industrial relations in the Canadian automobile industry." In *Industrial relations in Canadian industry*.

KUNDE, Diana. (1998, October 10). "Skilful salary negotiation can pay off for job seekers." *Ottawa Citizen*, p. K-5.

KURUVILLA, Sarosh, and Ponniah Arudsorthy. (1995). "Economic development strategy, government labour policy and firm-level industrial relations practices in Malaysia." In *Employment relations in the growing Asian economies*.

KUWAHARA, Yasuo. (1993). "Industrial relations in Japan." In *International and comparative industrial relations* (2nd ed.).

LABERGE, Roy. (1976). *The labour beat: An introduction to unions*. Ottawa: Media Algonquin.

LABOUR Law Casebook Group (LLCG). (1991). *Labour law: Cases, materials and commentary* (5th ed.). Kingston: Queen's IRC Press. Use has also been made of the draft 4th edition (1984) of the same book.

LABOUR *law under the Charter: Proceedings of a conference*. (1988). Kingston: Queen's Law Journal and Industrial Relations Centre.

LACEY, Robert. (1986). *Ford: The men and the machine*. Toronto: McClelland & Stewart.

LAFFER, Kingsley. (1974). "Is industrial relations an academic discipline?" *Journal of Industrial Relations*, 16 (March).

LAKEY, Jack. (1998, May 14). "Winery boycotted for backing Tories." *Toronto Star*, p. B-1.

LAM, Helen, and Yonatan Reshef. (2000). "Are quality improvement and downsizing compatible? A human resources perspective." In *Workplace Gazette*, 3:3, pp. 85–93.

LANCASTER HOUSE. (2001). Various issues of Lancaster House's *Collective Agreement Reporter*, containing analyses of changing labour legislation.

LARSON, Simeon, and Bruce Nissen (Eds.). (1987). *Theories of the labor movement*. Detroit: Wayne State Univ. Press.

LAWSON, Chris (Communications Specialist, CUPW). (1998). Personal interview. September 8.

LAXER, James. (1986). *Leap of faith: Free trade and the future of Canada*. Edmonton: Hurtig.

LEAP, T. L., and D. W. Grigsby. (1986). "A conceptualization of collective bargaining power." *Industrial and Labor Relations Review*, 39.

LEGGETT, Chris. (1993). "Singapore." In *Labour law and industrial relations in Asia.*

LEMELIN, Maurice. (1989). "Quality of working life and collective bargaining: Can they co-exist?" In A. Sethi (Ed.), *Collective bargaining in Canada.* Scarborough: Nelson.

LEWICKI, Roy, David Saunders, and John Minton. (1997). *Essentials of negotiation.* Chicago and Toronto: Irwin.

LEWIN, David. (1999). "Theoretical and empirical research on the grievance process and arbitration: A critical review." In *Employment dispute resolution and worker rights.*

LEWIS, Gregg. (1986). *Union relative wage effects: A survey.* Chicago: Univ. of Chicago Press.

LIPSIG-MUMME, Carla. (2001). "Trade unions and labour relations systems in comparative perspective." In *Union-management relations in Canada,* 4th edition.

_____. (1995). "Labour strategies in the new social order: A political economy perspective." In *Union-management relations in Canada* (3rd ed.).

_____. (1989). "Canadian and American unions respond to economic crisis." *Journal of Industrial Relations,* 31.

LIPTON, Charles. (c. 1973 [1967]). *The trade union movement of Canada, 1827–1959.* Toronto: NC Press.

LOGAN, Harold. (1948). *Trade unions in Canada.* Toronto: Macmillan.

LONG, Richard. (1992, July). Conversation with the author in Toronto.

LORWIN, Val. (1954). *The French labor movement.* Cambridge: Harvard Univ. Press.

LOW, Stephen. (1963). "The role of trade-unions in the newly independent countries of Africa." In *National labor movements in the postwar world.*

LOWE, Graham. (2001, May 16). "Job quality: The key to attracting, developing and retaining workers of all ages." Keynote address to the IMPA-CANADA National Training Conference, Fredericton, N.B. Ottawa: Canadian Policy Research Networks.

_____. (2001a). *Employer of choice? Workplace innovation in government: A synthesis report.* Ottawa: Canadian Policy Research Networks.

_____. (1980). *Bank unionization in Canada: A preliminary analysis.* Toronto: Univ. of Toronto Centre for Industrial Relations.

LOWE, Mick (2001, Apr. 3). "Solidarity? Whatever..." In *Straight Goods.*

LOXLEY, John. (1998). *Interdependence, disequilibrium and growth: Reflections on the political economy of north-south relations at the turn of the century.* Ottawa: IDRC.

LUCE, Sally. (2000). "Public service demographics and the employees of the next generation." Ottawa: Public Service Commission.

MacDONALD, Robert. (1967). "Collective bargaining in the postwar period." *Industrial and Labor Relations Review,* 20:4 (July). Reprinted in *Personnel and labour relations.*

MacDOWELL, Laurel Sefton. (1982). "The 1943 steel strike against wartime wage controls." *Labour/Le Travailleur,* 10.

_____. (1978). "The formation of the Canadian industrial relations system during World War II." *Labour/Le Travailleur,* 3. Reprinted in *Canadian working class history.*

MACLEOD, Leslie. (2000). *Ontario Management Board Secretariat Final Report on the Grievance Administration Project.* Toronto: Management Board Secretariat.

MAKI, Dennis. (1982). "Political parties and trade union growth." *Relations Industrielles,* 37.

MALLES, Paul. (1976). *Canadian labour standards in law, agreement, and practice.* Ottawa: Supply and Services.

MANLEY, John. (1986). "Communists and autoworkers: The struggle for industrial unionism in the Canadian automobile industry, 1925–1936." *Labour/Le Travail,* 17 (spring). Reprinted in *Canadian working class history.*

MANUSPHAIBOOL, Supachia. (1993). "Thailand." In *Labour law and industrial relations in Asia*.

MARSDEN, Richard. (2001). "Labour history and the development of modern capitalism." In *Union-management relations in Canada*, 4th edition.

MARSHALL, Katherine. (2001, spring). "Part-time by choice." In *Perspectives on work and income*, pp. 20–27. Ottawa: Statistics Canada.

MARSHALL, Stan (Research Officer, CUPE). (1998). Telephone interview, September 9.

MARTINELLO, Felice. (1996). "Correlates of certification application success in British Columbia, Saskatchewan, and Manitoba." *Relations Industrielles*, 51.

MATHEWSON, Stanley. (1931–1932). "A survey of personnel management in 195 concerns." *Personnel Journal*, 10:4. Reprinted in *Personnel and labour relations*.

MATSUDA, Yasuhiko. (1993). "Japan." In *Labour law and industrial relations in Asia*.

MAXWELL, Judith (2001). "Rethinking institutions for work in the new economy." Presentation to Canadian Industrial Relations Association, Quebec City, May 27, 2001.

MAY, Kathryn. (2001a, July 13). "Vet colleges face loss of international accreditation." In *Ottawa Citizen*.

_____. (2001b, July 13). "Federal food inspections 'Spotty at best.'" In *National Post*.

_____. (2001c, July 23). "Canada lagging in animal disease research, vets say." In *National Post*.

_____. (1998, July 30). "Two hundred thousand share in landmark award." *Ottawa Citizen*, p. A-1.

McALASTAR, Trish (2001, Jan. 18). "Making the grade." In *The Globe & Mail*.

McCALLUM, Margaret. (1986). "Keeping women in their place: The minimum wage in Canada, 1910–1925." *Labour/le Travail*. Reprinted in *Canadian working class history*.

McCAMBLY, James. (1990, August 21). "Why Canadian labor needs to stay politically neutral." *The Globe & Mail*, p. A-15. Reprinted in A. Craig and N. Solomon. *The system of industrial relations in Canada* (4th ed.).

McCORMACK, Ross. (1975). "The industrial workers of the world in Western Canada, 1905–1914." *Historical Papers*. Reprinted in *Canadian working class history*.

McINTOSH, Robert. (1987). "The boys in the Nova Scotia coal mines, 1873–1923." *Acadiensis*, 16:2 (spring). Reprinted in *Labour and working-class history in Atlantic Canada*.

McKAY, Ian. (1991). "None but skilled workmen." From *The craft transformed*. Reprinted in *Canadian working class history*.

_____. (1983). "Strikes in the Maritimes: 1901–1914." *Acadiensis*, 13:1 (fall). Reprinted in *Canadian labour history*.

McKINLEY, Patrick. (1997, August 22). "Labour group to fold." *Winnipeg Free Press*, p. B-1.

McPHILLIPS, David. (2001). "Employment legislation." In *Union-management relations in Canada* (4th ed.). Some use has also been made of the employment legislation chapter by McPhillips and Geoffrey England in the 2nd (1989) and 3rd (1995) editions of the same book.

MELTZ, Noah. (1989a). "Industrial relations: Balancing efficiency and equity." In J. Barbash and K. Barbash (Eds.), *Theories and concepts in comparative industrial relations*. Columbia, SC: Univ. of South Carolina Press.

_____. (1989b). "Interstate versus interprovincial differences in union density." *Industrial Relations*, 28.

_____. (1985). "Labor movements in Canada and the United States." In Thomas Kochan (Ed.), *Challenges and choices facing American labor*. Cambridge: MIT Press.

MILLS, D. Quinn. (1989). *Labor-management relations* (4th ed.). New York: McGraw-Hill.

MINNEHAN, Robert, and W. S. Paine. (1982). "Bottom lines: Assessing the economic and legal consequences of burnout." In W. S. Paine (Ed.), *Job stress and burnout:*

Research, theory, and intervention perspectives. Beverly Hills: Sage.

MISHEL, Lawrence. (1986). "The structural determinants of union bargaining power." *Industrial and Labor Relations Review*, 40:1.

MITCHELL, Nancy. (1996). "Coming to a national park in your area: ETOs." *Alliance*, summer.

MITTELSTAEDT, Martin (2001, Jan. 18). "Walkerton disasters foreseen across Canada." In *The Globe & Mail.*

MOOGK, Peter. (1976). "In the darkness of a basement: Craftsmen's associations in early French Canada." *Canadian Historical Review*, 58. Reprinted in *Canadian working class history.*

MORTON, Desmond. (1995). "The history of the Canadian labour movement." In *Union-management relations in Canada* (3rd ed.). Use has also been made of Morton's labour history chapter in the 1st and 2nd (1982 and 1989) editions of the same book.

MORTON, Desmond, and Terry Copp. (1980). *Working people.* Toronto: Deneau & Greenberg. Some, although less, use has also been made of Morton's 1984 and 1990 editions of the same book.

MOUAT, Jeremy. (1990). "The genesis of Western exceptionalism: British Columbia's hard-rock miners, 1895–1903." *Canadian Historical Review*, 71. Reprinted in *Canadian working class history.*

MUIR, J. Douglas. (1971). "Decentralized bargaining: Its problems and direction in the public education systems of Ontario and the Western provinces." *Relations Industrielles*, 26.

MURDOCK, Rebecca. (1997). "Organizing the service sector: The fight for 40 at Starbucks." *Canadian Dimension*, 31:6 (November).

MURRAY, Gregor. (2001). "Unions: Membership, structure, actions and challenges. " In *Union-management relations in Canada* (4th ed.). Some use has also been made of Murray's chapter on unions in the 3rd (1995) edition of the same book.

MURRAY, Thomas. (1971, March). "It's hell in personnel." Reprinted in *Personnel and labour relations.*

NAUMETZ, Tim. (2001, Aug. 8). "PS hopes to boost morale with free tuques." In *Ottawa Citizen.*

NELSON, Joyce. (1998). "The art of the deal." *Canadian Forum*, April.

NG, Ignace. (1992). "The probability of union membership in the private sector." *Relations Industrielles*, 47.

NG, Ignace, and Ali Dastmalchian. (1989). "Determinants of grievance outcomes: A case study." *Industrial and Labor Relations Review*, 42:3.

NIVEN, M. M. (1967). *Personnel management, 1913–63: The growth of personnel management and the development of the institute.* London: Institute of Personnel Management.

NOLAN, Dennis, and Roger Abrams. (1997). "Trends in private sector grievance arbitration." In J. Stern and J. Najita (Eds.), *Labor arbitration under fire.* Ithaca and London: Cornell Univ. ILR Press.

NYLAND, Chris. (1989). *Reduced worktime and the management of production.* Cambridge: Cambridge Univ. Press.

OPSEU (Ontario Public Service Employees' Union, 2000a, Oct. 3). "Mine mill remains determined to resist concessions." From OPSEU Cambrian College Local 655 Web site.

OPSEU (2000b, Sept. 27). Resolution passed by Sudbury Regional Council. From OPSEU Cambrian College Local 655 Web site.

O'HARA, Bruce. (1993). *Working harder isn't working.* Vancouver: New Star.

ONTARIO FEDERATION OF LABOUR (OFL). (1994). *Annual program report.* Toronto: Author.

OSTERMAN, Paul. (1988). *Employment futures: Reorganization, dislocation, and public policy.* New York: Oxford University Press.

OSTRY, Sylvia, and Mahmood Zaidi. (1979). *Labour economics in Canada* (3rd ed.). Toronto: MacMillan.

OWEN, John. (1989). *Reduced working hours: Cure for unemployment or economic burden?* Baltimore and London: Johns Hopkins Univ. Press.

OWEN, William. (1940–1941). "Decentralize personnel work." *Personnel Journal*, 19. Reprinted in *Personnel and labour relations: An evolutionary approach.*

PIPSC (Professional Institute of the Public Service of Canada, 2001, Dec. 17). "Canadian food inspection veterinarians walk off the job." PIPSC press release.

PPF (Public Policy Forum, 2000). *Levelling the path: Perspectives on labour management relations in the federal public service.* Ottawa: Public Policy Forum.

PSAC (Public Service Alliance of Canada). Various articles drawn from PSAC Web site, www.psac.com, 1999 through 2001, on National Gallery of Canada and CFB Goose Bay strikes. For more detail on the PSAC Web site, please see the Annotated List of Web Sites.

PSES (Public Service Employee Survey, 1999). *Turning Results Into Action.* Ottawa: Treasury Board of Canada Secretariat.

PSSRB (Public Service Staff Relations Board, 2001). *Union of Canadian Correctional Officers–CSN (Applicant) and Treasury Board (Correctional Service Canada) (Employer) and Public Service Alliance of Canada (Intervenor).* 2001 PSSRB 25, File 142-2-356. Before J.W. Potter, Deputy Chairperson.

PSSRB (Public Service Staff Relations Board, 2000). *Union of Canadian Correctional Officers–CSN (Applicant) and Treasury Board (Correctional Service Canada) (Employer) and Public Service Alliance of Canada (Intervenor).* 2000 PSSRB 106, File 142-02-356; 150-02-49. Before Yvon Tarte, Chairperson.

PACHOLIK, Barb. (1998, April 3). "Ruling confirms gays entitled to same benefits as heterosexuals." *Saskatoon Star-Phoenix*, p. A-3.

PALMER, Bryan. (1986). "Listening to history rather than historians: Reflections on working-class history." *Studies in Political Economy*, 20 (summer). Reprinted in *Canadian labour history.*

PANITCH, Leo, and Donald Swartz. (1988). *The assault on trade union freedoms: From coercion to consent revisited.* Toronto: Garamond.

PARK, Young-bum, and M. B. Lee. (1995). "Economic development, globalization, and practices in industrial relations and human resource management in Korea." In *Employment relations in the growing Asian economies.*

PATTERSON, John. (1901, January). "Altruism and sympathy as factors in works administration." *Engineering Magazine*, 20. Reprinted in *Personnel and labour relations.*

PEACH, David, and David Kuechle. (1975). *The practice of industrial relations.* Toronto and New York: McGraw-Hill Ryerson.

PEIRCE, Jon. (2000). *Canadian Industrial Relations*, 1st edition. Scarborough: Prentice-Hall.

_____. (2000a). "The case for a shorter work week." Ottawa: Carleton Centre for the Study of Training, Investment and Economic Restructuring.

_____. (1998a, May 14). "Plenty of militancy left in Canadian unions." *Toronto Star*, p. A-14.

_____. (1998b, March 20). "Jobless rate still far too high." *Toronto Star*.

_____. (1996). "The sad saga of the late and little-lamented Newfoundland 'white paper' provisions on labour relations." In *Proceedings of the 1995 Canadian Industrial Relations conference.* Montreal, QC, Canada.

_____. (1995). "George Meany and the decline of the American labour movement." St. John's: Memorial Univ. School of Business, working paper.

_____. (1993). "An end to American exceptionalism?" In *The Industrial Relations System: Proceedings of the 29th Conference of the Canadian Industrial Relations Association.* Charlottetown, P. E. I.

_____. (1989). "Exclusions from collective bargaining legislation in Canada."

Unpublished Master of Industrial Relations essay. Kingston: Queen's Univ. Industrial Relations Centre.

_____. (1987). "Collective bargaining over technological change in Canada: A quantitative and historical analysis." Ottawa: Economic Council of Canada Discussion Paper #338.

PELLEGRINI, Claudio. (1993). "Industrial relations in Italy." In *International and comparative industrial relations* (2nd ed.).

PERLMAN, Selig. (1966(1929)). *A theory of the labor movement*. New York: Kelley.

PFEFFER, Jeffrey. (1994). *Competitive advantage through people: Unleashing the power of the work force*. Boston: Harvard Business School Press.

PICARD, Laurent (Chair). (1967). *Report of the inquiry commission on the St. Lawrence ports*. Ottawa: Department of Labour.

PONAK, Allen, and Corliss Olson. (1992). "Time delays in grievance arbitration." *Relations Industrielles*, 47.

PONAK, Allen, and Mark Thompson. (2001). "Public sector collective bargaining." In *Union-management relations in Canada* (3rd ed.). Use has also been made of the same chapter in the first three editions of this book (1982, 1989, 1995), written by one or both of the same authors in each case.

PONAK, Allen, and Morley Gunderson. (1995). "Future directions for Canadian industrial relations." In *Union-management relations in Canada* (3rd ed.).

POSNER, R. (1977). *Economic analysis of the law* (2nd ed.). Toronto: Little Brown. Excerpts reprinted in *Labour law*.

PRICE, Robert. (1991). "The comparative analysis of union growth." In *Comparative industrial relations*.

PUBLIC Service Alliance of Canada (PSAC). (1998). Various information leaflets and notices to members (mainly, though not entirely, on the issue of pay equity).

RADFORTH, Ian. (1991). Statements made during various labour history classes, Univ. of Toronto, fall semester.

_____. (1982). "Woodworkers and the mechanization of the pulpwood logging industry of Northern Ontario: 1950–1970." *Historical Papers/Communications historiques*. Reprinted in *Canadian labour history*.

RANDAZZO, Daniel. (1995). *The 1995 annotated Ontario labour relations act*. Scarborough, ON: Carswell.

RAVENHORST, A. M. (1990). "Industrial relations in Korea: The backdrop to the current drama." *Comparative Labor Law Journal*, 11:3. Quoted in Park Young-ki. (1993). "South Korea." In *Labour law and industrial relations in Asia*.

REID, Frank. (2001, Nov. 1). Talk on HRDC's short-term compensation policy (worksharing) at Canadian Institute conference.

_____. (1997). Presentation at "32 Hours" conference, November 22. Toronto, ON, Canada.

_____. (1982). "Wage-and-price controls in Canada." In *Union-management relations in Canada* (3rd ed.).

REID, Frank, and Noah Meltz. (2001). "Social, political, and economic environments." In *Union-management relations in Canada* (4th ed.). Use has also been made of the same authors' chapter on the economy from the same book's 3rd (1995) edition, and from its 2nd (1989) edition, cited in the text as Meltz and Reid (1989).

REITSMA, Stephen. (1993). "The Canadian corporate response to globalization." Ottawa: Conference Board of Canada Report #106-93.

RENAUD, Stephane. (1997). "Unions and wages in Canada." In *Selected Papers from the 33rd Annual Canadian Industrial Relations Conference*. Quebec City: CIRA.

REUTHER, Victor. (1976). *The brothers Reuther and the story of the UAW*. Boston: Houghton Mifflin.

REYNOLDS, David. (1995). "The right to strike in the public sector: A comparative analysis of Canada, Germany, Japan, and Sweden." Unpublished paper: St. John's, Nfld.

REYNOLDS, Lloyd. (1982). *Labor economics and labor relations* (8th ed.). Englewood Cliffs: Prentice-Hall.

RICHARD, K. Peter (Commissioner). (1997). *The Westray story: A predictable path to disaster*. Province of Nova Scotia (no place of publication given).

RICHARDSON, J. Albert. (1985). "The role of organized labour in today's Atlantic Canada." In *Perspectives on the Atlantic Canada labour movement and the working class experience.*

ROBB, Roberta. (1987). "Equal pay for work of equal value: Issues and policies." In *Canadian Public Policy*, 13. Reprinted in *Labour law.*

ROBERTS, Wayne, and John Bullen. (1985). "A heritage of hope and struggle: Workers, unions, and politics in Canada, 1930–1982." In M. Cross and G. Kealey (Eds.), *Modern Canada 1930s–1980s*. Toronto: McClelland & Stewart. Reprinted in *Canadian labour history.*

ROBINSON, Archie. (1981). *George Meany and his times: A biography*. New York: Simon and Schuster.

ROBINSON, Ian. (1994). "NAFTA, social unionism, and labour movement power in Canada and the United States." *Relations Industrielles*, 49:4 (fall).

_____. (1990). *Organizing labour: Exploring Canada-U. S. union density divergence in the post-war period*. New Haven: Yale University Ph. D. dissertation.

ROGOW, Robert. (1989a). "The structure of collective bargaining." In *Collective bargaining in Canada.*

_____. (1989b). "Collective bargaining law." In *Collective bargaining in Canada.*

ROSE, Joseph. (2000). "The ghost of interest arbitration." In *Canadian Labour and Employment Law Journal*, 8, pp. 253–289.

_____. (1995). "The evolution of public sector unionism." In *Public sector collective bargaining in Canada.*

_____. (1992). "Industrial relations in the construction industry in the 1980s." In *Industrial relations in Canadian industry.*

_____. (1991). "The emergence of expedited arbitration." *Labour Arbitration Yearbook, I.*

_____. (1987). "Innovative grievance arbitration systems." Hamilton: McMaster Univ. Faculty of Business Research.

_____. (1986a). "Legislative support for multi-employer bargaining: The Canadian experience." *Industrial and Labor Relations Review*, 40:1.

_____. (1986b). "Statutory expedited grievance arbitration: The case of Ontario." *Arbitration Journal*, 41.

_____. (1982). "Construction labour relations." In *Union-management relations in Canada* (1st ed.).

ROSE, Joseph, and Gary Chaison. (2001). "Unionism in Canada and the United States in the 21st century: The prospects for renewal." In *Relations Industrielles*, 56:1, pp. 34–65.

_____. (1990). "New measures of union organizing effectiveness." In *Industrial Relations*, 29.

SCSJ (Sudbury Coalition for Social Justice, 2001, Feb. 16). "Injunction decision reflects bias towards Falconbridge-Noranda." From SCSJ Web site.

_____. (2000, Oct. 11). "An injury to one is an injury to all." From SCSJ Web site.

SACK, Jeffrey. (1998). "Ability to pay and the appointment of arbitrators: Back to the future." In *Labour Arbitration Yearbook*. Toronto: Lancaster House, pp. 393–407.

_____. (1994). *Winning cases at grievance arbitration*. Toronto: Lancaster House.

_____. (1991). "The ability to pay in the public sector: A critical appraisal." In *Labour Arbitration Yearbook*, Vol. 2, pp. 277–298.

SANDERSON, John. (1976). *Labour arbitrations and all that*. Toronto: Richard de Boo.

SASS, Bob. (1993). "The work environment board and the limits of social democracy in Canada." *International Journal of Health Services*, 23.

_____. (1989). "The art of collective bargaining." In *Collective bargaining in Canada.*

SAUVÉ, Robert. (1971). "La négociation collective sectorielle." *Relations Industrielles*, 26:1.

SCHELLING, Thomas. (1957). "Bargaining, communication, and limited war." *Journal of Conflict Resolution*, 1:1.

SCHETAGNE, Sylvain. (2001). *Building bridges across generations: A response to the aging workforce.* Ottawa: Canadian Council on Social Development.

SCHEUER, Steen. (1992). "Denmark." In A. Ferner and R. Hyman (Eds.), *Industrial relations in the new Europe.* Oxford: Blackwell.

SCOTT, F. R. (1945). "Ode to a politician." Reprinted in M. Wilson (Ed.). (1969). *Poets between the wars.* Toronto: McClelland & Stewart.

_____. (1932). "Communists, senators, and all that." *Canadian Forum*, January. Reprinted in *Forum*.

SEEGER, Pete. (1972). *The Incompleat Folksinger.* Lincoln: Univ. of Nebraska Press.

SEGAL. (2001, Feb.). "Segal special report: The aging of Aquarius: The baby boom generation matures." No place of publication given.

SEKERES, Matthew, and Patti Edgar. (2001, July 25). "Monkey virus tests 3 weeks late." In *Ottawa Citizen*.

SETHI, Amarjit (Ed.). (1989). *Collective bargaining in Canada.* Scarborough, ON: Nelson.

SEXTON, Jean. (1987). "First contract administration in Canada." In *Proceedings of the spring, 1987 meeting of the IRRA.* Boston, Massachusetts, America. Reprinted from *Labour Law Journal* (August).

SHELLENBARGER, Sue. (1998, October 7). "Time off is workers' answer to stress." *Ottawa Citizen*, p. G-32. (Reprinted from *Wall Street Journal*).

_____. (1997, December 22). "The worst work-family train wrecks of 1997." *The Globe & Mail*, p. B-11.

SHERIDAN, M., D. Sunter, and B. Diverty. (1996). "The changing workweek: Trends in weekly hours of work." *Canadian Economic Observer.* Ottawa: Statistics Canada Cat. 11-010-XPB (September).

SHIELDS, John. (1990). "Building a new hegemony in British Columbia." In L. Haiven,

S. McBride, and J. Shields (Eds.), *Regulating labour.* Toronto: Garamond.

SHIELDS, Margo. (2000, spring). "Long working hours and health." In Statistics Canada, *Perspectives on labour and income*, pp. 49–56.

SHIPPING Federation of Canada. (1972). Brief on job security submitted to Judge Alan Gold (arbitrator for the Port of Montreal).

SIMS, Andrew (Chair). (c. 1996 [1995]). *Canada Labour Code, part I, seeking a balance.* Ottawa: Minister of Public Works and Government Services.

SINGH, R. (1976). "Systems theory in the study of industrial relations: Time for reappraisal?" *Industrial Relations Journal*, 7 (fall).

SKRATEK, S. (1993). "Grievance mediation: How to make the process work for you." In *Labor Law Journal*, 44, pp. 507–511.

SLICHTER, Sumner. (1929). "The current labor policies of American industry." *Quarterly Journal of Economics*, 43 (May). Reprinted in *Personnel and labour relations*.

SMITH, Anthony. (1993). "Canadian industrial relations in transition." *Relations Industrielles*, 48.

SMITH, Jennifer, and Susan Snyder. (1998). *Facing the challenge: Recruiting the next generation of Canadians to the public service.* Ottawa: Public Policy Forum/Public Service Commission.

SNYDER, Ronald. (1995). *The annotated Canada labour code.* Scarborough: Carswell.

SOKOLIK, Stanley. (1969). "Reorganize the personnel department?" *California Management Review*, 11:3 (spring). Reprinted in *Personnel and labour relations*.

SOLOMON, N., P. Andiappan, and D. Shand. (1986). "Canadian union presidents: An empirical study." *Relations Industrielles*, 41.

SOMMER, Neal, and Stewart Saxe. (2001). *Understanding the Labour Relations Act.* 2nd edition. Aurora, ON: Canada Law Book Co.

STAT CAN (1998). "Labour force update." Statistics Canada, Cat. No. 71-005-XPB, winter. Ottawa: Author.

_____. (1997). "Labour force update: Youths and the labour market." Statistics Canada, Cat. No. 71-005-XPB, spring. Ottawa: Author.

STEED, Judy. (1994, January 9). "Algoma's man of steel." *Ottawa Citizen*. Reprinted in *The system of industrial relations in Canada* (4th ed.).

STERN, R. N., and J. C. Anderson. (1978). "Canadian strike activity: Union centralization and national diversity." In J. Stern (Ed.), *Proceedings of the 30th Annual Meeting of the Industrial Relations Research Association*. Madison: IRRA.

STEWART-PATTERSON, David. (1987). *Post-mortem: Why Canada's mail won't move*. Toronto: MacMillan.

STOREY, Robert. (1983). "Unionization versus corporate welfare: The Dofasco way." *Labour/Le Travailleur* (fall).

STRAUSS, George. (1999). "Is IR research returning to its roots?" In *Perspectives on Work*, 3:1 (1999), pp. 59–60.

_____. (1991). "Union democracy." In G. Strauss et al. (Eds.), *The state of the unions*. Madison: IRRA Press.

SUMMERS, Clyde. (1991). "Unions without majorities: The potential of the NLRA." In *Proceedings of the 43rd Annual Meeting of the Industrial Relations Research Association*. Madison: IRRA.

SUNTER, Deborah (2001, spring). "Demography and the labour market." In Statistics Canada, *Perspectives on labour and income*, pp. 28–39.

SUSSMAN, Deborah. (2000, autumn). "Unemployment Kaleidoscope." In Statistics Canada, *Perspectives on Labour and Income*, 13:1 12:3, pp. 9-15.

SWIMMER, Gene (ed., 2000). *Public sector labour relations in an era of restraint and restructuring*. Toronto: Oxford Univ. Press.

_____. (1995). "Collective bargaining in the federal public service of Canada: The last twenty years." In *Public sector collective bargaining in Canada*.

SWIMMER, Gene, and Mark Thompson. (1995). "Collective bargaining in the public sector: An introduction." In *Public sector collective bargaining in Canada*.

SWINTON, Katherine. (1995). "The Charter of Rights and public sector labour relations." In *Public sector collective bargaining in Canada*.

_____. (1983). "Enforcement of occupational health and safety: The role of the internal responsibility system." In *Studies in labour law*. Reprinted in *Labour law*.

SWINTON, Katherine, and Kenneth Swan. (1983). "The interaction between human rights legislation and labour law." In *Studies in labour law*. Reprinted in *Labour law*.

TARANTELLI, Ezio. (1986). "The regulation of inflation and unemployment." *Industrial Relations*, 25:1.

TASK Force on Microelectronics. (1982). *In the chips: Opportunities, people, partnership*. Ottawa: Supply and Services.

TEPLITSKY, Martin. (1992). *Making a deal*. Toronto: Lancaster House.

TERKEL, Studs. (c1975 [1972]). *Working*. New York: Avon.

"32 Hours" (1998). Budgetary Submission. From 32 Hours Web site.

THOMASON, T., H. Zwerling, and P. Chandra. (1992). "Labour relations in the Canadian textile industry." In *Industrial relations in Canadian industry*.

THOMASON, Terry. (1995). "Labour relations in primary and secondary education." In *Public sector collective bargaining in Canada*.

THOMPSON, Mark. (1995a). "The management of industrial relations." In *Union-management relations in Canada* (3rd ed.). Some use has also been made of his chapter on management in the 4th (2001) edition of the same book.

_____. (1995b). "The industrial relations effects of privatization: Evidence from Canada." In *Public sector collective bargaining in Canada*.

_____. (1982). "Collective bargaining by professionals." In *Union-management relations in Canada* (1st ed.).

THOMPSON, Mark, and Allen Ponak. (1992). "Restraint, privatization, and industrial relations in the public sector in the 1980s." In *Industrial relations in Canadian industry*.

THOMPSON, Mark, and Gene Swimmer. (1995). "The future of public sector industrial relations." In *Public sector collective bargaining in Canada*.

THORNICROFT, Kenneth, and Genevieve Eden. (1995). "Grievances and their resolution." In *Union-management relations in Canada* (3rd ed.). Some use has also been made of Thornicroft's chapter on the same subject in the 4th (2001) edition of the same book.

TIME ALMANAC (2002). Boston: Family Education Company, 2001.

TROFIMENKOFF, Susan. (1977). "102 muffled voices: Canada's industrial women in the 1880s." *Women's Study Journal, Atlantis*. Reprinted in *Canadian working class history*.

TROTTA, Maurice. (1976). *Handling grievances: A guide for management and labor*. Washington: Bureau of National Affairs.

TROY, Leo. (1992). "Convergence in international unionism et cetera: The case of Canada and the U.S.A." *British Journal of Industrial Relations*, 30.

UNDERHILL, Frank. (1932). "The cooperative commonwealth federation." *Canadian Forum*, August. Reprinted in *Forum*.

UNITED Steelworkers of America (USWA). (1991). *Empowering workers in the global economy, a labour agenda for the 1990s*. Papers prepared for a conference in Toronto, October 1991.

UNIVERSITY of Ottawa. (1994). Collective agreement between Univ. of Ottawa and Association of Part-Time Professors, Univ. of Ottawa.

VERMA, Anil. (1995). "Employee involvement in the workplace." In *Union-management relations in Canada* (3rd ed.).

_____. (1992). Statement made in Ph. D. seminar in advanced industrial relations topics. University of Toronto Centre for Industrial Relations, winter term.

VERMA, Anil, and Richard Chaykowski. (1999a). "Employment and employment relations at the crossroads." In *Contract and Commitment*.

_____. (1999b). "Business strategies and employment relations." In *Contract and Commitment*.

VERMA, Anil, and Daphne Taras (2001). "Employee involvement in the workplace." In *Union-management relations in Canada*, 4th edition.

VERMA, Anil, and Joseph Weiler. (1992). "Industrial relations in the Canadian telephone industry." In *Industrial relations in Canadian industry*.

VERMA, Anil, and Peter Warrian. (1992). "Industrial relations in the Canadian steel industry." In *Industrial relations in Canadian industry*.

VERMA, Anil, T. Kochan, and R. Lansbury (Eds.). (1995). *Employment relations in the growing Asian economies*. London: Routledge.

WID (WORKPLACE Information Directorate), Human Resources Development Canada. (1998). Data on strikes obtained from Work Stoppage Bureau.

_____. (1997). *Directory of labour organizations in Canada*. Ottawa: HRDC. Use was also made of the 1993 and 1996 editions of the same book.

WAGAR, Terry. (1996). *Employee involvement, strategic management and human resources: Exploring the linkages*. Kingston: Queen's IRC Press.

_____. (1994). *Human resource management practices and organizational effectiveness: Evidence from Atlantic Canada*. Kingston: Queen's IRC Press.

_____. (1994b). "The effects of lawyers on non-discipline/discharge arbitration cases." In *Journal of Labor Research*, 15, pp. 283–293.

WALTON, Richard, and Robert McKersie. (1991). *A behavioral theory of labor negotiations: An analysis of a social interaction system* (2nd ed.). Ithaca: ILR Press.

_____. (1963). *A behavioral theory of negotiations*. New York: McGraw-Hill.

WARD, Bob. (1974). *Harvest of concern.* Toronto: Ontario Federation of Labour. Reprinted in *The Canadian worker in the twentieth century.*

WARRIAN, Peter. (1996). *Hard bargain: Transforming public sector labour-management relations.* Toronto: McGilligan.

WEBB, Sidney and Beatrice Webb. (c. 1920 [1897]). *Industrial democracy.* New York: Longmans.

WEILER, Joseph. (1984). "Grievance arbitration: The new wave." In J. Weiler and P. Gall (Eds.), *The labour code of British Columbia in the 1980s.* Calgary and Vancouver: Carswell.

WEILER, Paul. (1983a) "Promises to keep." *Harvard Law Review,* 96:8 (June).

_____. (1983b). "Protecting the worker from disability: Challenges for the eighties." *Report to Ontario Ministry of Labour.* Reprinted in *Labour law.*

_____. (1980). *Reconcilable differences: New directions in Canadian labour law.* Toronto: Carswell.

WEINER, Nan. (1995). "Workplace equity." In *Public sector collective bargaining in Canada.*

WELLS, Don. (1993). "Are strong unions compatible with the new model of human resource management?" *Relations Industrielles,* 48.

WHITE, J. F. (1932). "Deportations." *Canadian Forum,* July. Reprinted in *Forum.*

WHITE, Julie. (1997a). *Changing times: Shorter hours of work in the Communications, Energy and Paperworkers' Union.* Ottawa: CEP.

_____. (1997b). Conversation with the author concerning the CEP's educational activities around work hours, December.

WHITE, Robert. (1995). "Workers' education builds strong rights." *Workers' Education,* 10 (October).

WINPISINGER, William. (1989). "A machinist and a left-of-center progressive." In P. Quaglieri (Ed.), *America's labor leaders.* Lexington, MA: Lexington Books.

WOOD, S. J. et al. (1975). "The 'industrial relations system' concept as a basis for theory in industrial relations." *British Journal of Industrial Relations,* 3 (November).

WOODWORTH, Warner, and Christopher Meek. (1995). *Creating labor-management partnerships.* Reading and Don Mills: Addison-Wesley.

WORTHY, James. (1948). "Changing concepts of the personnel function." *Personnel,* 25:3 (November). Reprinted in *Personnel and labour relations.*

YODER, Dale. (1962). *Personnel management and industrial relations* (5th ed.). Englewood Cliffs: Prentice-Hall.

YOUNG-KI, Park. (1993). "South Korea." In *Labour law and industrial relations in Asia.*

ZUSSMAN, David, and Jak Jabes. (1989). *The vertical solitude: Managing in the public sector.* Halifax: Institute for Research on Public Policy.

ZWERLING, Harris. (1997). "Obesity as a covered disability under employment discrimination law: An analysis of Canadian approaches." *Relations Industrielles,* 52:3.

PHOTO CREDITS

GLOSSARY OF INDUSTRIAL RELATIONS TERMS[1]

Accreditation:* The process used to certify an organization of employers as the bargaining agent for a unit of employers.

All-Canadian Congress of Labour (ACCL): Early twentieth century labour federation and rival to the Trades and Labour Congress (see **CLC** below). Unlike the TLC, the ACCL organized workers on an industry-wide rather than craft basis. It lasted from 1927 to 1940.

American Federation of Labor (AFL): U.S.-based labour federation and forerunner of the current AFL-CIO.

Arbitration: The process through which a neutral party, or a panel containing representatives of both parties to the dispute but chaired by a neutral party, hears both sides of the dispute and issues an award. It is important to distinguish between *interest arbitration*, where the terms of a collective agreement are established, and *grievance* or *rights arbitration*, where disputes over the interpretation of the agreement are settled. Interest arbitration is further divided into *conventional arbitration*, where the arbitrator is free to fashion an award based on any aspect of the parties' submissions, and *final offer arbitration*, where he or she must choose one party's submission or the other. Finally, it is also important to distinguish between *compulsory* or *binding arbitration*, which is required by law in the case of disputes affecting certain groups (such as police and firefighters) that are not permitted to strike, and *voluntary arbitration*, which the parties to a dispute may agree to in the absence of any statutory requirement.

Asymmetry of information: In collective bargaining disputes, a situation that exists when one party (normally the company) has significantly more information about the firm's true financial situation than the other. In such cases, a union may sometimes be forced to call a strike to determine whether or not the company is telling the truth when it says it cannot afford to meet the union's demands.

Bargaining agent:* The organization that is the exclusive representative of a group of workers or employers [but normally workers] in the process of collective bargaining.

---

[1] Many of these terms are taken from Labour Canada, *Glossary of Industrial Relations Terms* (Ottawa: Supply and Services Canada, 1984). Such terms are marked with an asterisk. The Labour Canada definitions may have been shortened or altered to update the current factual situation. In a few cases, minor editorial and grammatical changes have also been made, or additions made in bracketed insertions. Otherwise, the definitions should be considered as having been taken verbatim from the Labour Canada glossary.

Bargaining unit:* A group of employees in a firm, plant, or industry that has been certified by a labour relations board as appropriate to be represented by a union for purposes of collective bargaining.

Berlin Convention: Crucial convention of the Trades and Labour Congress held in 1902 in Berlin (now Kitchener), Ontario. This convention set the Canadian labour movement firmly on a moderate and international path. Notably, it banned **dual unionism** (defined below), stipulating that no national union would be recognized by the TLC when an international union existed.

Boycott:* An organized refusal on the part of employees and their unions to deal with an employer, with the objective of winning concessions. *Primary boycotts* usually take the form of putting pressure on consumers not to buy the goods of an employer directly involved in a dispute. *Secondary boycotts* are those in which pressure is exerted on employers not directly involved in a dispute, e.g., workers of Company A refuse to buy or handle goods of Company B, which is engaged in a labour dispute.

Bumping:* Exercise of seniority rights by [more senior] workers to displace less senior ones when business conditions require layoffs or the discontinuance of departments.

Business agent:* A full-time officer of a local union who handles grievances, helps enforce agreements, and performs other tasks in the day-to-day operation of the union.

Call-back pay:* Compensation, often at higher wage rates, for workers called back on the job after completing their regular shift.

Canadian Auto Workers (CAW): Industrial union representing Canadian workers in the auto industry; in a celebrated split it broke away from its parent, the American-based United Auto Workers, in 1985. The CAW's official name is now the National Automobile, Aerospace and Agricultural Implement Workers' Union of Canada.

Canadian Congress of Labour (CCL): Mid-twentieth century labour federation and rival to the Trades and Labour Congress from 1940 to 1956, when it merged with the TLC. Like its predecessor, the **ACCL** (see above), the CCL organized workers on an industry-wide rather than craft basis and placed considerable emphasis on political action.

Canadian Labour Congress (CLC):* Canada's national labour body, formed in 1956 from the merger of the Trades and Labour Congress and the Canadian Congress of Labour.

Centrale de l'enseignement du Québec (CEQ): Former confessional federation representing both teachers and support staff in Quebec's education system.

Centrale des syndicats démocratiques (CSD):* A federation of Quebec unions founded in 1972 by unions that broke away from the Confédération des syndicats nationaux (CSN).

Certification:* Official designation by a labour relations board or similar government agency of a union as sole and exclusive bargaining agent, following proof of majority support among employees in a bargaining unit.

Checkoff:* A clause in a collective agreement authorizing an employer to deduct union dues and, sometimes, other assessments, and transmit these funds to the union.

Chilling effect: Where conventional interest arbitration is the normal dispute resolution system, this refers to the parties' unwillingness to make concessions at the bargaining table, in the belief that the arbitrator will choose a middle position and relieve them of the responsibility of making choices that may be unpalatable from an internal political perspective.

Closed shop:* A provision in a collective agreement whereby all employees in a bargaining unit must be union members in good standing before being hired.

Coercive drive: A management approach most common in the 19th century, which sought to 'motivate' employees primarily through fear and intimidation, in the interest of extracting the maximum possible amount of work out of them.

COLA clause:* Literally, a cost of living adjustment. A clause built into a collective agreement that links wage or salary increases to changes in the cost of living during the life of the contract.

Communications, Energy and Paperworkers Union (CEP): National union formed as a result of the merger of unions in the communications, energy, and pulp and paper industries.

Compressed work week: A form of alternative work arrangement that allows employees periodic days off in return for working slightly longer hours on other days. Under one common form of compressed work week, employees work about 45–50 minutes longer per day and receive a day off every two weeks.

Concession bargaining: This refers to situations in which the union is forced to agree to a wage freeze, wage reduction, or reduction in existing benefit levels in order to come to a new collective agreement.

Conciliation:* A process that attempts to resolve labour disputes by compromise or voluntary agreement. The conciliator is often a government official. Conciliation is a prerequisite to legal strike/lockout action in almost all Canadian jurisdictions. [Note that conciliation has been replaced by mediation in some jurisdictions, and that the two processes have generally become quite similar in recent years.]

Confédération des travailleurs catholique du Canada (CTCC): Catholic confessional union federation launched in Quebec in 1921. Later in the twentieth century the CTCC would sever its ties with the Catholic Church and reform itself as the **Confédération des syndicats nationaux** (see below).

Confederation of National Trade Unions (CNTU): A Quebec-based central labour body that had its origin in the confessional unions of the early 1900s. In Quebec, this federation is known as the **Confédération des syndicats nationaux (CSN)**.

Congress of Industrial Organization (CIO): First American industrial union federation, formed shortly after the passage of the *Wagner Act* by John L. Lewis and others who had broken with the AFL. In 1955, the two federations reunited.

Contingent work: Work done by individuals who enjoy little or no job security because they are employed on a temporary, part-time, or contractual basis and can generally be laid off on little or no notice.

Contracting-out:* The use by employers of workers outside their own work force to perform tasks previously performed by the employers' own employees.

Co-Operative Commonwealth Federation (CCF): Social democratic party and forerunner to the New Democratic Party, launched in the early 1930s in Calgary and Regina.

Craft union:* A union that limits its members to a particular craft (i.e., bricklayers).

Decertification:* The procedure for removing a union's official recognition as exclusive bargaining representative.

Demand-deficient unemployment: An overall lack of jobs, especially at provincial or national levels.

Direct union wage impact: The premium a worker receives for union membership.

Discouraged workers: Unemployed workers who have given up looking for work because they believe no work is available for them.

Distributive bargaining: Adversarial bargaining, in which one party's gain is normally the other's loss.

District labour councils: Bodies designed to advance the labour movement's interests at local and municipal levels.

Dual unionism: Competition between two or more unions to represent workers in the same sector.

Employee Assistance Program (EAP): Counselling services, often established through collective bargaining, which typically offer employees assistance on a broad range of issues, from alcohol- and drug-related problems to marital and financial ones.

Expedited arbitration: This applies to any grievance arbitration system that has introduced procedures or mechanisms to speed up the process of resolving the grievance. Among the most common procedures in expedited systems are the use of a single arbitrator rather than a three-person panel, and (in private industry) the use of a standing arbitrator or umpire who can hear several cases in a day, instead of just one as in the case of ad hoc arbitrators.

Fact-finding: A dispute resolution system whereby the investigator (fact-finder) does a thorough investigation of the facts of the situation and issues a report. In Canada, this form of dispute resolution has most commonly been used in the public sector.

Final offer arbitration (FOA), also known as **final offer selection (FOS):** A form of interest arbitration where the neutral must choose one party's submission or the other. It may be carried out on a total-package or issue-by-issue basis.

Flexible work week (flextime):* A system that provides workers with some freedom in deciding when they start and finish work, subject to the requirement that they be present during certain 'core' hours and fulfill a certain minimum attendance requirement each day.

Fragmented union structure: A union structure marked by a large number of small unions.

Frictional unemployment:* Unemployment due to time lost in changing jobs rather than a lack of job opportunities.

Fringe benefits:* Non-wage benefits such as paid vacations, pensions, health and welfare provisions, life insurance, etc., the cost of which is borne in whole or in part by the employer. Such benefits have accounted for an increasing part of worker income and labour costs in recent years.

Gainsharing plans: Plans whereby the benefits of increased productivity and improved labour–management cooperation are shared between firms and their employees.

Grievance: Officially, an allegation by either party that the other has violated the collective agreement in some way. *Individual* grievances involve the application of the agreement to one member. *Group* grievances result from a combination of several similar individual grievances seeking a common redress. A *policy* grievance involves a question of the agreement's general application or interpretation.

Grievance mediation: A grievance settlement mechanism whereby a third-party neutral (sometimes from the provincial or federal labour ministry) seeks to help the parties resolve the dispute in question themselves rather than sending the dispute through to arbitration. Often grievance mediation is used in conjunction with systems of **expedited arbitration** (see above).

Independent union (or Independent local):* A union that is not affiliated with and remains independent of any labour federation.

Indirect union wage impact: The effect unions have on the wages of non-unionized workers. There are two major types, operating in totally opposite directions: a) the *crowding impact*, a reduction that occurs when workers laid off in the unionized sector because unionized wages have made firms uncompetitive spill over into the non-unionized sector, eventually depressing wage levels there as well; b) the *threat effect*, which occurs when firms increase workers' wages to prevent them from joining unions, or to keep them from quitting and joining a unionized firm.

Industrial relations system (Dunlop): An "analytical subsystem of an industrial society" governing individuals' workplace behaviour. An IR system comprises certain actors, certain contexts, a body or web of rules governing the actors' workplace behaviour, and a common ideology binding the system together.

Industrial union: A union organized on the basis of product, normally at a plant-wide or industry-wide level, in contrast to a craft union that is organized along the basis of particular skill lines. Industrial unions have normally made more of an effort than craft unions to organize semi-skilled and unskilled workers, and have tended to seek to achieve their objectives through political action as well as through economic means such as strikes.

Industrial Workers of the World (IWW): Radical, western-based union of the early twentieth century.

Integrative bargaining: Bargaining of a problem-solving nature, in which both sides may come out ahead.

International union: As normally used in Canada, this term refers to unions headquartered in the United States but which also have Canadian members.

Involuntary part-time work: Part-time work performed by employees who would rather be working full-time.

Jurisdiction (union):* The area of jobs, skills, occupations and industries within which a union organizes and engages in collective bargaining. *Jurisdictional disputes* refer to conflicts between two or more unions over the right of their membership to perform certain types of work.

Knights of Labor: First American labour federation, founded in Philadelphia in 1869. The Knights practised social unionism and organized on a industrial and geographic rather than a craft basis.

Labour force: This comprises all persons 15 and over who are either employed or are unemployed but actively seeking employment.

Layoff:* Separation from employment as a result of a lack of work.

Local union:* The unit of labour organization formed in a particular locality, through which members participate directly in the affairs of their organization.

Lockout: The suspension of work by an employer or refusal by an employer to allow employees to enter the work premises. Normally lockouts occur during collective bargaining disputes. They may be thought of as employer strikes.

Maintenance of membership provision:* A form of union security provision in a collective agreement stating that no worker need join the union as a condition of employment, but that all workers who voluntarily join must maintain their membership for the duration of the agreement.

Management rights provision: Provision in a collective agreement either laying out specific aspects of the employer's operations not subject to collective bargaining (e.g., hiring or manufacturing), or stating that all matters not specifically included in the collective agreement will not be considered subject to collective bargaining or any other form of discussion with the union.

Mandatory retirement: Compelling employees to retire upon reaching a certain age (normally 65). It is legal in most Canadian jurisdictions because all but a few apply the anti-discrimination provisions of their human rights acts only to workers aged 64 and under.

Mediation: A process, which may be used either during interest or rights disputes, whereby the third-party neutral actively engages the parties with a view to getting them to reach a voluntary agreement. Traditionally, mediation was more interventionist than **conciliation** (see above); however, in recent years the distinction between the two has tended to become blurred, except insofar as the term 'conciliation' is applied only to interest disputes.

Med-Arb (officially, Mediation-Arbitration): A dispute resolution system where the third-party neutral first attempts to bring the parties to a voluntary agreement through mediation, but if that fails, will impose a settlement.

Modified union shop provision:* A type of union security provision which stipulates that non-union members already employed need not join the union, but all new employees must join, and those already members must remain in the union.

Moonlighting: A situation where an individual holds more than one paid job at the same time.

Narcotic effect: Under systems where bargaining disputes are resolved through conventional interest arbitration, this refers to situations where the parties become so dependent on the arbitrator to make their decisions for them that they lose the ability to fashion their own agreements.

National Labor Relations Act (**NLRA**): More commonly known as the *Wagner Act*, this legislation, passed in 1935 as part of U.S. President Franklin D. Roosevelt's "New Deal," was the first American law to grant workers the right to bargain collectively and to strike.

National union: As normally used in Canada, a union whose headquarters and all of whose members are in Canada.

One Big Union (OBU): Short-lived western-based socialist industrial union launched in 1918.

Open shop:* An enterprise in which union membership is not required as a condition of securing or retaining employment.

Paternalistic management: In pre-industrial society, when most of those in employee status worked for friends or relatives, a system of management operating on the basis of personal supervision, often by an owner-manager working alongside his or her employees.

Pattern bargaining: Industry-wide bargaining arrangements whereby the agreement worked out between the union and the first company (often known as the 'target' company) is adopted by all other companies in the industry.

Picketing:* Demonstrating near the employer's place of business by union members (pickets) to publicize the existence of a labour dispute, persuade workers to join a strike or join the union, or to discourage customers from buying or using the employer's goods or services, etc.

Preventive mediation: Voluntary third-party assistance, normally applied outside of the collective bargaining process and aimed at improving the parties' communication and overall relationship with an eye to reducing grievance levels. Preventive mediation programs are now being offered by the federal and almost all provincial labour ministries.

Principled bargaining: Related to **integrative bargaining** (see above), this type of bargaining emphasizes the separation of issues from personalities, a focus on the parties' underlying interests, and the invention of win-win options. It is sometimes known as *interest-based bargaining*.

Probationary period: An initial trial period during which the employer decides if it wishes to retain the employee in question indefinitely, and during which the employee may be dismissed far more easily than after he or she attains indefinite status.

Progressive discipline: A system of discipline whereby the penalties are increased for each succeeding offence and the employee is made aware of the possibility of further penalties, up to and including discharge, should he or she repeat the offence in question. Except in the case of extremely serious offences such as theft, fraud, or assault, arbitrators normally expect employers to have carried out progressive discipline before discharging an employee and will usually overturn dismissals where progressive discipline has not been carried out.

Progressive human resource management: An umbrella term that refers to a broad range of human resource strategies and policies aimed at motivating employees positively, rather than negatively, through fear, as in the case of the **coercive drive** approach to management (see above). The overall aim of progressive HRM is to increase workers' loyalty to the organization and improve their productivity. Typically progressive HRM strategies include paying generous benefits. In some cases, they may entail a fundamental reorganization of work, delayering of management hierarchies, etc.

Quality of Working Life (QWL):* A process designed to assist employers, unions, and employees in implementing joint problem-solving approaches within organizations in the interests of improved labour–management relations, organization effectiveness, and employee work satisfaction.

Quebec Federation of Labour (QFL): Quebec provincial wing of the Canadian Labour Congress. Because of Quebec's distinctive political situation, the QFL has more power than other provincial federations affiliated to the CLC.

Rand Formula: Union security provision, originally worked out as part of a settlement of a strike at the Ford Motor Company, whereby no worker is required to join the union but all must pay it an amount equal to the union's regular dues as a condition of employment.

Rank-and-file:* Individual union members who have no special status either as officers or shop stewards.

Residual management rights doctrine: The view, held by most arbitrators, that any rights not specifically laid out in the collective agreement are to be considered management rights.

Right-to-work states: Under the *Taft-Hartley Amendments* to the *Wagner Act*, states which have passed legislation banning union security provisions. Most such states are in the southern or midwestern U.S.

Scientific management (also known as **Taylorism**): A system of management launched by F.W. Taylor whereby tasks were broken down into their smallest possible components and quotas set on the basis of elaborate time-motion studies.

Seniority: An employee's standing in the organization, based on length of continuous employment. There are two main types of seniority provision in collective agreements. *Benefit status* provisions are used to determine a worker's entitlement to accrued benefits such as vacation time, pensions, and severance pay. *Competitive status* provisions are used to determine a worker's status relative to other workers in situations involving layoff, promotion, transfer, choice of shifts, and the like.

Social unionism: This type of unionism, the type most often practised in Canada, believes that unions should seek to improve workers' well-being as a whole, outside the workplace as well as within it. It therefore relies on political action as well as collective bargaining to achieve its objectives.

Strategic choice framework (or **theory**): A 3-level IR theory developed in the U.S. by Thomas Kochan and his associates that stresses the linkages between a firm's IR and HR policies and strategies and its overall competitive strategies.

Strike: A concerted (i.e., planned) activity involving a collective refusal to work.

Strikebreakers:* Persons who continue to work during a strike or who accept employment to replace striking workers. Also known as scabs.

Structural unemployment: A situation in which there is a mismatch of available jobs and skills, or in which unemployed workers live in different locations from those where jobs are available.

Taft-Hartley Act: Legislation, passed in the U.S. in 1947 as a series of amendments to the *Wagner Act*, which severely limited the powers of the American labour movement. The most significant feature was the "right-to-work" provision, which allowed states to outlaw union security provisions, in effect setting themselves up as union-free zones.

Tripartism:* Consultation between representatives of labour, management, and government on matters of mutual interest. [In Europe, where it plays a more prominent role than it does in North America, it may well involve formal negotiations over major social and economic policies.]

Two-tier wage systems: Systems whereby newly hired employees receive significantly lower wages than existing employees.

Unfair labour practice:* A practice on the part of either union or management that violates provisions of federal or provincial labour law.

Union acceptance: A management approach to unions that accepts unionization as inevitable and focuses on obtaining the best possible agreement through collective bargaining.

Union avoidance: A management approach to unions that seeks to prevent the formation of unions in the workplace.

Union density: The percentage of organizable workers belonging to unions. In Canada, this term has normally referred to the percentage of non-farm workers belonging to unions.

Union raiding:* An attempt by one union to induce members of another union to defect and join its ranks.

Union replacement (or **removal**): A management approach that seeks to rid the organization of existing unions.

Union security clauses:* Provisions in collective agreements designed to protect the institutional authority and ensure the financial stability of the union.

Union shop:* A workplace where every worker covered by the collective agreement must become and remain a member of the union. New workers need not be union members to be hired, but they must join after a certain number of days.

Union steward:* Union member ordinarily elected to represent workers in a particular shop or department.

United Food and Commerical Workers (UFCW): International union representing large numbers of Canadian workers employed in retail businesses.

Welfare capitalist management: A system of management, most common between the two world wars, in which companies sought to cement employees' loyalty and remain union-free by providing a broad range of benefits and establishing in-house consultation systems. A forerunner of **progressive human resource management** (see above).

Wildcat strike: A work stoppage carried out during the life of the collective agreement, and normally without the union's authorization. For this reason, wildcats are illegal—and are also normally very short.

Work rules: Collective agreement provisions regulating the actual production process and other on-the-job conditions of work. Examples include the minimum number of workers required to do any given job, and restrictions on the performance of production work by supervisory personnel.

Work sharing: Plan by which working time is generally reduced to prevent layoffs. Under the federal government's Work Sharing Program, in effect since 1982, employees work a four-day week and receive Employment Insurance (EI) benefits for the day they don't work. At current EI benefit levels, this means employees receive 91% of their regular wages for a four-day week.

Work to rule:* A practice where workers obey to the letter all laws and rules pertaining to their work, thus effecting a slowdown. The practice may also involve a refusal to perform duties that, though related, are not explicitly included in the job description (e.g., teachers may refuse to coach after-school sports).

Workers' compensation:* Compensation payable by employers collectively and on a no-fault basis for injuries sustained by employees in the course of their employment. Each province has an act governing the compensation of injured workers.

Workers' Unity League (WUL): Communist labour federation formed in 1930 and devoted to "militant industrial unionism and socialist revolution."

INDEX